# THE ROUTLEDGE COMPANION TO QUALITATIVE RESEARCH IN ORGANIZATION STUDIES

This comprehensive book collects contributions from leading international scholars to highlight the diverse qualitative approaches available to organizational researchers, each grounded in its own philosophy. The editors provide a cutting edge, globally oriented resource on the state of qualitative research methodologies, helping readers to grasp the theories, practices, and future of the field.

Beginning with an overview of qualitative methodologies, the book examines ways in which research employing these techniques is conducted in a variety of disciplines, including entrepreneurship, innovation, strategy, information systems, and organizational behavior. It offers timely updates on how traditions like case studies, ethnographies, historical methods, narrative approaches, and critical research are practiced today and how emerging trends, including increasing legitimacy and feminization, are impacting the domain. The final chapters provide templates for engaging with the future as well as essays that critically assess how qualitative inquiry has evolved within organization studies. Readers will become acquainted with contemporary tools for conducting qualitative studies, learning to appreciate the emerging domains of qualitative inquiry within a dynamic and complex organizational world.

Doctoral students and early-career researchers in organizational studies, especially those engaged with general management, organizational behavior, human resource management, innovation, entrepreneurship, and strategy, will benefit from reading this relevant and inclusive handbook.

**Raza Mir** is the Seymour Hyman Professor of Management at William Paterson University, USA. He is also the co-editor of *The Routledge Companion to Philosophy in Organization Studies*, published in 2015.

**Sanjay Jain** is Assistant Professor of Management at the Nazarian College of Business at California State University – Northridge, USA.

For Farah, Safdar and Sahir – for whom words finally fail.

For Ami & Roshan – the nectar and light of my life!

# THE ROUTLEDGE COMPANION TO QUALITATIVE RESEARCH IN ORGANIZATION STUDIES

*Edited by*
*Raza Mir and Sanjay Jain*

NEW YORK AND LONDON

First published 2018
by Routledge
605 Third Avenue, New York, NY 10017
4 Park Square, Milton Park, Abingdon, Oxon OX14 4RN

First issued in paperback 2022

*Routledge is an imprint of the Taylor & Francis Group, an informa business*

© 2018 Taylor & Francis

Typeset in Bembo
by Wearset Ltd, Boldon, Tyne and Wear

*Library of Congress Cataloging in Publication Data*
Names: Mir, Raza A., editor. | Jain, Sanjay, 1965 October 2– editor.
Title: The Routledge companion to qualitative research in organization studies /
edited by Raza Mir & Sanjay Jain.
Description: 1 Edition. | New York : Routledge, [2017]
Identifiers: LCCN 2017016296 | ISBN 9781138921948 (hbk) |
ISBN 9781315686103 (ebk)
Subjects: LCSH: Organization–Research. | Qualitative research.
Classification: LCC HD30.4 .R686 2017 | DDC 302.3/50721–dc23
LC record available at https://lccn.loc.gov/2017016296

ISBN 13: 978-1-03-247664-3 (pbk)
ISBN 13: 978-1-138-92194-8 (hbk)

DOI: 10.4324/9781315686103

# CONTENTS

# Contents

# FIGURES

# TABLES

# CONTRIBUTORS

**Chahrazad Abdallah** is Associate Professor at the Université du Québec à Montréal (UQAM), Canada. She holds a Ph.D. in Management from HEC Montréal, Canada. Her research focuses on strategy and creativity as ambiguous discursive practices in pluralistic organizations. She also has a strong interest in qualitative research methods and more specifically ethnography. Her work was published in the *Journal of Management Studies*, the *Journal of Organizational Change Management*, and the *SAGE Handbook of Qualitative Business and Management Research Methods*.

**Shaz Ansari** is a Professor of Strategy at Judge Business School, University of Cambridge and Visiting Faculty at Rotterdam School of Management, Erasmus University. He holds a Ph.D. from the University of Cambridge. He serves on the editorial boards of *Academy of Management Review*, *Organization Science*, *Journal of Management Studies*, and *Organization Studies*, and is a member of the Erasmus Research Institute of Management (ERIM). His research interests include institutional processes and diffusion of practices; social movements, social and environmental issues in management, technological, management, and disruptive innovations; reputation management, and bottom-of-the-pyramid strategies. He has published in several leading academic journals including *Academy of Management Journal*, *Academy of Management Review*, *Strategic Management Journal*, *Organization Science*, *Journal of Management Studies*, *Research Policy*, *Industrial and Corporate Change*, *Strategic Organization*, and *Organization Studies*.

**Ted Baker** is George F. Farris Professor of Entrepreneurship at Rutgers Business School and a Senior Fellow of the Bertha Centre for Social Innovation and Entrepreneurship at the University of Cape Town Graduate School of Business. He received his Ph.D. in Sociology from the University of North Carolina at Chapel Hill. His work explores the processes through which entrepreneurship sometimes allows people to pursue their goals and become who they want to be despite common problems of resource constraint and adversity.

**Hans Berends** is Professor of Innovation and Organization at the Knowledge, Information, and Innovation (KIN) Research Group, at Vrije Universiteit Amsterdam. His research interests concern processes and practices of innovation within and across organizational boundaries. His current research focuses on organizing processes for digital innovation. He teaches qualitative and process research methods at various levels.

**Derron G. Bishop** is an Assistant Professor in the Department of Business Administration at the University of Delaware's Lerner College of Business. He received his Ph.D. in Business Administration from Penn State University and holds degrees from Brigham Young University (M.B.A., B.A. in Communication) and Utah State University (M.S. in Instructional Design). His qualitative research delves into the processes, boons, and burdens surrounding morally distinct individuals in the context of corporate ethics and compliance programs, scandal, executive succession, and threats to organizational values. Most recently, his research has uncovered processes connecting specific values content (self-transcendence), positive moral emotions, and collective voice.

**Catherine Cassell** is Professor of Organisational Psychology and Dean at Birmingham Business School, University of Birmingham, UK. She has a longstanding interest in the use of qualitative methods in management and organizational research. Together with Gillian Symon she has published four books with Sage on the topic, the most recent being *Qualitative Organisational Research: Core Methods and Current Challenges*. She is also the author of *Conducting Research Interviews for Business and Management Students*, published by Sage in 2015 and together with Ann Cunliffe and Gina Grandy, editor of the forthcoming *Sage Handbook of Qualitative Methods in Business and Management Research*.

**Katherine Chen** is Associate Professor in the Department of Sociology at The City College of New York and the Graduate Center, CUNY. Using organizational ethnography, she researched how the Burning Man organization combined collectivist-democratic and bureaucratic practices to address common challenges such as recruiting and retaining members and coordinating with multiple parties; she published an award-winning book, *Enabling Creative Chaos: The Organization Behind the Burning Man Event*. Her articles on prosumption, storytelling, and creativity have been published in *American Behavioral Scientist*, *Nonprofit and Voluntary Sector Quarterly*, *Qualitative Sociology*, *The Sociological Quarterly*, and other journals.

**Elena Dalpiaz** is Assistant Professor of Strategy at the Imperial College Business School, Imperial College London, South Kensington Campus, London, UK. Her research examines how meaning making within organizations affects strategy processes, organizational change, and new venture creation. In particular, she is interested in understanding how strategy makers and organizational members use institutional logics, organizational narratives, business templates, and taken-for-granted socio-cultural understandings to shape strategic and organizational change and start new ventures.

**Stephanie Decker** is Professor of Organization Studies and History at Aston Business School in Birmingham, UK, and co-editor of *Business History*. Her research combines approaches from organization studies and history, and focuses on the history of business in Africa, the uses of the past by organizations, and historical methodology for social sciences. Her work has been published in a range of journals, including *Academy of Management Review*, *Journal of Management Studies*, *Organization*, *Business History Review*, and *Business History*.

**Deborah Dougherty** received her Ph.D. from MIT, and was a faculty member at Wharton, McGill, and Rutgers, and is now Distinguished Visiting Professor at NC State. She researches organizing for sustained product innovation and complex, science-based innovation. She taught innovation management at the B.S., M.B.A., and Ph.D. levels along with many other courses. She chaired the Technology and Innovation Management Division at AOM (1998–2003), and served as senior editor for *Organization Science* and on five other journal editorial boards. She recently completed a book entitled *Taking Advantage of Emergence: Productively Innovating in Complex Innovation Systems* (2016).

**Kathleen M. Eisenhardt** is the S.W. Ascherman M.D. Professor at Stanford University and Co-director of the Stanford Technology Ventures Program. Her recent book (with Don Sull) is *Simple Rules: How to Thrive in a Complex World*, which explores how simple rules tame complexity in a variety of contexts. Her research emphasizes the strategy and organization of technology-based companies in high-velocity markets. She is currently working on theory-building research in nascent ecosystems, venture boards, and strategy in two-sided markets. She is also working on developing a richer understanding of theory building from multiple cases and its ties to complementary methods.

**Ingrid Erickson** is Assistant Professor at the School of Information Studies at Syracuse University. She received her Ph.D. from the Center for Work, Technology, and Organization in the Department of Management Science and Engineering at Stanford University. Her research centers on the way that mobile devices and ubiquitous digital infrastructures are influencing how we work and communicate with one another, navigate and inhabit spaces, and engage in new types of sociotechnical practices.

**Anne-Laure Fayard** is Associate Professor of Management in the Department of Technology Management and Innovation at NYU Tandon School of Engineering, and is affiliated with the Department of Management and Organizations at NYU Stern Business School. Her research interests involve communication, collaboration, culture, and space, with a focus on interactions, particularly those between people and technology. Her work has been published in several leading journals such as *Administrative Science Quarterly, Information System Research, Organization Science*, and *Organization Studies*. She is also the author, with Anca Metiu, of *The Power of Writing in Organizations*. Prior to joining NYU Tandon, Anne-Laure was a faculty member at INSEAD in Singapore and France. She holds a Ph.D. in Cognitive Science from the Ecole des Hautes-Etudes en Sciences Sociales (Paris), an M.Phil. in Cognitive Science from Ecole Polytechnique (Paris), and an M.Phil. in History and Philosophy of Science from La Sorbonne (Paris).

**Andrew E.F. Fultz** is a Ph.D. student at Rutgers Business School. His research interests revolve around commercial and social entrepreneurship, specifically focusing on the mechanisms leading to operational sustainability and effectiveness, along with the mechanisms that lead to expansion and enhancement of the impact made by these entrepreneurs. His current research focuses on entrepreneurial bricolage and the micro-foundations of dynamic capabilities in young firms.

**Raghu Garud** is Alvin H. Clemens Professor of Management and Organization and the Research Director of the Farrell Center for Corporate Innovation and Entrepreneurship, Pennsylvania State University. Raghu's research explores the emergence of novelty and its adoption. Specifically, he is interested in understanding how new ideas emerge, are valued, and become institutionalized. Raghu is currently working on *Managing in the Age of Disruptions*.

**Dennis A. (Denny) Gioia** is the Robert and Judith Klein Professor of Management in the Smeal College of Business at the Pennsylvania State University. He holds degrees in both Engineering Science and Management from Florida State University. In former lives, he worked as an engineer for Boeing Aerospace at Cape Kennedy in 1969–1970 on the build and launch teams for the Apollo 11, 12, and 13 missions to the moon and for Ford Motor Company as corporate recall coordinator in the 1970s. In his academic life, his research and writing interests focus on the ways in which organizational identity, image, learning, and knowledge are involved in sensemaking, sensegiving and organizational change. His work spans the spectrum from the philosophical, theoretical, and empirical to the methodological, educational, and practical, and has appeared in many of the top journals in management, as well as in numerous book chapters and proceedings. He is a Fellow of the Academy of Management.

**Melissa E. Graebner** is Associate Professor of Management at the University of Texas at Austin. She received her Ph.D. in Management Science and Engineering from Stanford University. Her research has been published in the *Academy of Management Journal*, *Administrative Science Quarterly*, *Strategic Management Journal*, and *Strategic Organization*. Her research interests include strategy in entrepreneurial ventures, post-merger integration, trust in interorganizational relationships, and qualitative research methods. She has received research awards from the *Academy of Management Journal and Strategic Organization*.

**Nina Granqvist** is Assistant Professor of Management at Aalto University School of Business. Her research focuses on exploring the emergence of novelty in fields and market categories. Her studies draw on multiple theoretical frameworks, including institutional work, temporality, market categorization, practices, language, and affect. Empirically, she conducts qualitative grounded analyses of extensive data sets on emerging technologies, food trends, and creative industries, to name a few. Her research has been published in the leading journals, including *Academy of Management Journal*, *Organization Science*, *Journal of Management Studies*, and *Organization Studies*.

**Thomas Greckhamer** is Catherine M. Rucks Professor of Management at Louisiana State University. He earned his Ph.D. in Management from the University of Florida. His research interests are at the intersection of organization studies, strategic management, and research methods, focusing on empirical applications of as well as theoretical and methodological contributions to set theoretic and qualitative approaches. His work has been published in the *Strategic Management Journal*, *Organization Studies*, *Organization Science*, *Organizational Research Methods*, *Qualitative Inquiry*, and *Qualitative Research*, among others. He currently serves as Associate Editor for *Organizational Research Methods*.

**Suho Han** is a Ph.D. candidate in strategic management at the McCombs School of Business, University of Texas at Austin. His research interests include examining longitudinal processes associated with new venture growth and the case method. He is particularly interested in how the interactions among actors vital to new ventures (e.g., founders, early-stage investors, and advisers) influence processes related to entrepreneurial resource acquisition and trust in new ventures. His dissertation examines the behaviors and decision processes of angel investor groups through a multiple-case study, focusing on how they overcome uncertainty during investment decision making and how these organizations evolve. He holds a B.S. and M.A. in Economics from the University of Washington and Indiana University, respectively.

**Sanjay Jain** will be joining the Nazarian College of Business at California State University – Northridge, as an Assistant Professor of Management, in the fall of 2017. He received his Ph.D. in Management from New York University. His research interests include technology evolution, industry emergence, market construction, qualitative methods, and innovation processes in emerging economies. His research has been published in the *Academy of Management Journal*, *Research Policy*, *Organization Studies*, *Strategic Entrepreneurship Journal*, *Industrial and Corporate Change*, and *Asia-Pacific Journal of Management*. He has received research awards from the Western Academy of Management and the Entrepreneurship Division of the Academy of Management.

**Aparna Joshi** is the Arnold Family Professor of Management at the Smeal College of Business, Penn State University. She received her Ph.D. from the SMLR, Rutgers University. Her research interests include gender inequality, diversity, status, and expertise recognition in teams. Her current research involves combining qualitative and quantitative methods to unpack gender inequality in organizations. She is also collaborating on a number of grounded theory projects to understand the experiences of disabled workers across various organizational contexts.

**Galina Kallio** is a researcher at Aalto University School of Business, Department of Management Studies. Her research focuses on the emergence of new economic practices at grassroots. She draws on practice theories and brings forth an interdisciplinary perspective, combining anthropological and sociological approaches, to explore the concepts of value, exchange, temporality, and work. Empirically, she draws on extensive qualitative data sets to study the rise of food movements, alternative ways of organizing, and practices of sharing and exchange.

**Farzad Rafi Khan** graduated with a Ph.D. in Strategy and Organization from McGill University, Canada in 2005. He is currently an Associate Professor at the College of Industrial Management, King Fahd University of Petroleum and Minerals, Saudi Arabia. His research interests center on exploring state capitalism and imperialism, impacts of organizations on society, critical approaches to management, and Islamic business ethics. He has published in various academic journals including *Human Relations*, *Journal of Business Ethics*, *Organization*, and *Organization Studies*.

**Glen E. Kreiner** is Professor of Management and the John and Becky Surma Dean's Research Fellow at Penn State University's Smeal College of Business. He has published his research in a wide variety of top management journals (including *AMR*, *AMJ*, *JAP*, and *Organization Science*). His research areas include professional identity, dirty work/stigma, work–family interface, cognitive disabilities at work, and organization identity. He is also engaging in projects dealing with mindfulness at work, stigmatized managers, ethics officers, health coaches, "transient" or "nomadic" professionals, identity threats, and workers on the autism spectrum. He has published conceptual, quantitative, and qualitative work, with a special emphasis on using grounded theory. He teaches resident M.B.A., executive M.B.A., online M.B.A., and Ph.D. courses on topics such as teams, leadership, organizational behavior, and qualitative research methods.

**Ann Langley** is Professor of Management at HEC Montréal, Canada and holder of the Chair in Strategic Management in Pluralistic Settings. Her research focuses on strategic change, inter-professional collaboration, and the practice of strategy in complex organizations. She is particularly interested in process-oriented methodology. In 2013, she was co-guest editor with Clive Smallman, Haridimos Tsoukas, and Andrew Van de Ven, of a Special Research Forum of *Academy of Management Journal* on Process Studies of Change in Organizations and Management. She is also co-editor of the journal *Strategic Organization*, and co-editor with Haridimos Tsoukas, of a book series, *Perspectives on Process Organization Studies*, published with Oxford University

Press. She is Adjunct Professor at the Université de Montréal and by the University of Gothenburg.

**Paul M. Leonardi** is the Duca Family Professor of Technology Management at the University of California, Santa Barbara. His research and teaching focus on helping companies to create and share knowledge more effectively. He is interested in how implementing new technologies and harnessing the power of informal social networks can help companies take advantage of their knowledge assets to create innovative products and services.

**Peng Liu** is Assistant Professor of Information Systems and Decision Sciences at Steven G. Mihaylo College of Business and Economics, California State University, Fullerton. He received his Ph.D. from Eli Broad College of Business at Michigan State University. His research interests include organizational routines and capabilities, and business value of IT. He has published research articles in journals such as *Journal of Management Studies* and *Information Systems Management*.

**Saku Mantere** is Associate Professor of Strategy and Organization at the Desautels Faculty of Management at McGill University. His research focuses on strategic organizations, on questions such as what it is that makes organizations strategic, and how strategic management affects organizations. He is particularly interested in strategic change, middle-management agency, and strategy discourse, as well as in more general methodological issues in management studies, such as the practice of qualitative research and researcher reasoning in theorizing about organizations.

**Anca Metiu** is a Professor of Management at ESSEC Business School. She earned her Ph.D. from the Wharton School of the University of Pennsylvania, and her M.B.A. from the University of Illinois at Urbana-Champaign. Her research examines collaboration, innovation, and communication processes in collocated and distributed teams. Some of her current research projects examine the role of play in high-tech organizations, the process of knowledge transfer in a development context, and the gender dynamics in the open source software community. Her research has been published in *Administrative Science Quarterly*, *Organization Science*, and *Organization Studies*. Her co-authored book *The Power of Writing and Organizational Communication: From Letters to Online Interactions* appeared in 2012. She is an editorial board member at *Organization Science* and *Organization Studies*.

**Alexandra Michel** is faculty at the University of Pennsylvania's Graduate School of Education. She received her Ph.D. from the Wharton School, University of Pennsylvania. Before returning to Penn, she taught at the Marshall School of Business, University of Southern California. Prior to her graduate studies, she worked at Goldman Sachs, New York City, first as a banker in mergers and acquisitions and then with the Chief of Staff. Her ongoing ethnographic research tracks investment bankers for more than 15 years, analyzing how innovations in knowledge work practices shape and are shaped by new forms of human functioning. Her research is featured in over 40 international TV, radio, and press outlets.

**Raza Mir** is Professor of Management at William Paterson University. His research mainly concerns global capitalism, multinational corporations, and issues relating to power and resistance in organizations. Raza is working on a forthcoming book titled *Multinational Corporations: A Critical Essay*. He is the co-editor of the *Routledge Companion to Philosophy in Organization*

*Studies* (2016). He is also interested in Urdu literature, and is the author of *The Taste of Words: An Introduction to Urdu Poetry* (2014). He recently served as the Chair of the Critical Management Studies Division of the Academy of Management.

**Jinia Mukerjee** is Assistant Professor in Management at Montpellier Business School, France. She holds a Ph.D. in Management Science from SKEMA Business School, and a Doctorate in Science from Aix Graduate School of Management, Aix-Marseille Université, France. In her research, she examines how work is carried out in innovative organizations, predominantly using ethnographic methods. More particularly, she strives to understand the role of play in group work processes, and how groups' collective identity influences work practices and organizing. Jinia has previously worked as a clinical psychologist. Passionate about writing in general, she also writes short stories and poems.

**Cristina Neesham** (B.A.*Buch* Ph.D.*Melb*) is a social philosopher and business ethicist based at Swinburne Business School, Melbourne, Australia. Cristina's research interests focus on using philosophical methods to inform the strategic management of systemic problems in organizations and their environments and to design ethical capability building projects for industry, government, and professional practice. Cristina's work has been published in leading academic journals and book series in the fields of business and professional ethics, and social philosophy of management and organization. She is section editor of the *Springer Handbook of Philosophy of Management*, and editorial board member of *Philosophy of Management* and the *Journal of Philosophical Economics*.

**Andrew J. Nelson** is Associate Professor of Management at the University of Oregon, where he also serves as Associate Vice President for Entrepreneurship and Innovation. He received his Ph.D. in Management Science and Engineering from Stanford University. Andrew's research leverages both qualitative and quantitative data to explore the emergence, development, and commercialization of new technologies and technology-based fields, offering special attention to the role of occupational, organizational and entrepreneurial influences. His ongoing research projects focus on contexts ranging from digital music, to green (sustainable) chemistry, to biotechnology.

**Heli Nissilä** is a researcher at Aalto University School of Business, Department of Management Studies. Her work concerns nascent sustainable fields and markets, in particular the collective enactment of legitimacy at the intersection of different communities. She draws from extensive qualitative data sets and addresses this topic from different perspectives, such as temporality and the legitimation of new fields, how positive visions and expectations are crafted for rising fields or the role of "collective spaces of enactment," like technology conferences or demonstration projects, in field emergence.

**Timothy E. Ott** is a Ph.D. candidate in the Stanford Technology Ventures Program at Stanford University, and will be joining the University of North Carolina as an Assistant Professor in 2017. His research centers on the role of cognition in strategic decision making within organizations. He is particularly interested in exploring cognition in entrepreneurial firms and nascent markets. He connects research on top management teams, entrepreneurial firms, strategic decision making, and firm capabilities. Tim's dissertation uses a combination of multiple-case study and simulation methods to study the process of how executives handle interdependence among decisions to form holistic strategies in novel settings.

**Pinar Ozcan** is Associate Professor of Strategic Management at Warwick Business School. She specializes in strategy, entrepreneurship, and the emergence of new markets. Primarily using single, comparative and multiple cases, her research aims to contribute to our understanding of the emergence and evolution of markets from the perspective of entrepreneurs, their strategies and interactions with the environment (e.g., partners, competitors, and key institutions such as government and regulators).

**Brian T. Pentland** is the Main Street Capital Partners Intellectual Capital Endowed Professor in the Broad College of Business at Michigan State University. His creative work has appeared in *Academy of Management Review, Accounting, Organizations and Society, Administrative Science Quarterly, JAIS, Journal of Management Studies, Management Science, MIS Quarterly, Organization Science, Organization Studies*, on YouTube, and elsewhere. He received his Ph.D. in Management from the Massachusetts Institute of Technology in 1991 and S.B. in Mechanical Engineering from the Massachusetts Institute of Technology in 1981.

**E. Erin Powell** is Assistant Professor of Management at Clemson University. She received her Ph.D. in Technology Management from North Carolina State University. Erin's research focuses on founder identity, heterogeneity of motivations among entrepreneurs, and resourcefulness in entrepreneurship. Her work has been published in the *Academy of Management Journal* and other outlets.

**Davide Ravasi** is Professor of Strategic and Entrepreneurial Management at the Cass Business School, City University London, and Visiting Professor at the Aalto School of Business, Helsinki. His research examines interrelations between organizational identity and culture, and strategy in times of change, and how visuality and materiality influence sensemaking. He is interested more generally in cultural processes influencing how new objects and new practices come to be, and whether and how they are adopted by individuals and organizations. His work has appeared in *Administrative Science Quarterly, Academy of Management Journal, Organization Science* and *Journal of Management Studies*, among others.

**Violina Rindova** is the Captain Henry W. Simonsen Chair in Strategic Entrepreneurship and the Research Director of the Lloyd Greif Center for Entrepreneurial Studies at the Marshall School of Business, University of Southern California. She teaches and studies strategic innovation – how firms create value, intangible assets, and new market opportunities through unconventional strategies across a variety of industry contexts. Her work has been published in the premier management journals and has received multiple grants and awards, including the "Thought Leadership" award from the Entrepreneurship Division of the Academy of Management (2009), and the award for outstanding scholarly contribution from *Strategic Organization* (2012).

**Srinivas Sridharan** is Associate Professor of Marketing, and Associate Dean, Grant Development at the Monash Business School, Monash University, Australia. His research examines market behavior in impoverished settlements in large cities of developing countries. He has published findings on consumer issues and entrepreneurial models in subsistence, and written about implications for business and marketing strategy and public policy. He uses quantitative as well as qualitative approaches to data collection and analysis, and in a current project, is using participatory action research methods. Current projects examine: transformative, growth-oriented subsistence entrepreneurs in India; smallholder farmer market behaviors in Zimbabwe and Uganda; and community-driven, market-oriented water and sanitation management approaches in Pacific Island countries.

**Philipp Tuertscher** is Associate Professor of Technology and Innovation and member of the KIN Research Group at the VU Amsterdam. Philipp's research explores organizational mechanisms and social practices for collaborative innovation in a variety of settings. Besides studying collaborative communities such as Linux, Wikipedia, and Threadless, Philipp has been studying innovation processes in large-scale scientific collaborations at CERN. His work has appeared in the *Academy of Management Annals*, *Information Systems Research*, *Organization Science*, and *Organization Studies*.

**Cathy Urquhart** is Professor of Digital and Sustainable Enterprise at MMU Business School. She is an editorial board member for the *Information Systems Journal* and *Information Technology and Development*. She has published in many top journals such as the *Journal of the Association of Information Systems*, the *European Journal of Information Systems*, the *Journal of Information Technology*, *Information Systems Journal*, and others. Her research interests include the use of digital innovation for societal good, and also grounded theory. Her 2013 book on grounded theory, published by Sage, is called *Grounded Theory for Qualitative Research: A Practical Guide*. Her website can be found at: www.business.mmu.ac.uk/our-staff/modb/profile/index.php?profile_id=899 and her email address is c.urquhart@mmu.ac.uk

**Emmanuelle Vaast** is Associate Professor of Information Systems at the Desautels Faculty of Management of McGill University, Montreal, Canada. Her research examines how social practices emerge and change with new technologies and how these new practices are associated with organizational and change dynamics. Emmanuelle has been fascinated by the new practices and social and societal changes associated with social media such as blogs and microblogs. Because of this interest, she has begun to explore the opportunities and challenges of combining qualitative and quantitative analysis of electronically collected data.

**Marleen van der Haar** works as Senior Researcher at Het PON, an institute for research and consultancy on social issues in Tilburg, the Netherlands. She is an Affiliated Researcher at the Institute for Management Research, Radboud University Nijmegen. Trained as a cultural anthropologist, she received her Ph.D. in 2007 from Utrecht University. Between 2008 and 2016 she was Post-doctoral Researcher and Lecturer at VU University Amsterdam and Radboud University Nijmegen. Her work on framing, and category making in particular, in the context of gender and ethnicity has been published, among others, in *Politics and Gender* (2016), *Journal of Race, Ethnicity, and Politics* (2016), *Women's Studies International Forum* (2013), *Politics, Groups, and Identities* (2013), and *Journal for International Relations and Development* (2013).

**R. Daniel Wadhwani** is Associate Professor of Management and Fletcher Jones Chair in Entrepreneurship at University of the Pacific. He also holds appointments in the Department of Management, Politics, and Philosophy at Copenhagen Business School and the Department of Economics at Kyoto University. A historian by training, he uses historical sources, methods, and reasoning to examine the foundations of entrepreneurial action and the origins and evolution of organizations and markets. He is the co-editor of *Organizations in Time: History, Theory, Methods* (2014), which examines the epistemic, theoretical and methodological opportunities and challenges of integrating historical research and reasoning into management and organizational research.

**Rene Wiedner** is an Assistant Professor at Warwick Business School, University of Warwick and an Associate Fellow at St Edmund's College, University of Cambridge. He received his Ph.D. in Management Studies from the Judge Business School, University of Cambridge. His research focuses on change and innovation in the public sector and creative industries. He is currently conducting a global study on vinyl record manufacturing in the digital age.

**Tammar B. Zilber** is Associate Professor of Organization Theory at the Jerusalem School of Business, The Hebrew University, Israel. Her research focuses on the dynamics of meaning and action in institutional processes. Focusing on the micro-foundations of institutions, she examines the role of discursive acts (like narrating) in constructing institutional realities; the institutional work involved in creating and maintaining fields, given field multiplicity; spatial and emotional mediations of institutional dynamics; the interrelations between institutional logics and institutional work; and the translation of institutions over time and across social spheres. In her research, she uses qualitative methods, and she has written about narrative research, field level ethnography, and the analysis of context.

# 1

# EMBRACING A CONSTRUCTED BOUNDARY

## Mapping Qualitative Research in Organizational Studies

*Raza Mir and Sanjay Jain*

Imagine, if you will, Charles Darwin sitting at a desk in Cambridge in December 1836. Having returned from his voyage on the HMS *Beagle*, he was busy cataloging his notes and his species collections, and developing a theory of natural selection. His work ran afoul of religious and scientific authority, but Darwin remained undeterred. Two decades of analysis and exploration would eventually lead to the 1859 publication of his magnum opus, *On the Origin of Species*, which would revolutionize our thinking about the transformation of lifeforms over time, and give rise to a new understanding of evolutionary biology that endures till today.

As Darwin's work was creating a sensation in the world of the natural sciences, an unknown political theorist named Karl Marx was poring through the records at assorted libraries in London and Manchester, pulling up details about worker compensation in emerging industries, and theorizing ways in which a new regime called capitalism was emerging from the ruins of feudal relations of production. Capitalism was premised on the ways in which money would be transformed into capital, and Marx audaciously predicted that it would become the dominant techno-economic paradigm of the late nineteenth and the twentieth century. The publication of his *Das Kapital* in 1867 gave us the concept of labor theory of value, which was to transform the way we looked at economics and social justice.

Likewise, Sigmund Freud, a practicing doctor, was systematizing his patient research in the field of psychology and developing a theory of the unconscious. He worked with individual cases, but believed that he had hit upon certain elements of the basic human condition. Based on his findings, Freud began to develop generalized therapeutic techniques, which he collectively termed "psychoanalysis." This included the use of free association, the recasting of sexuality as a phenomenon that emerged in infancy, and the act of defining new constructs such as the Oedipus complex. His work, which was formalized in 1899 through his book *The Interpretation of Dreams*, forever changed the way we understood human neuroses, and endures as an important psychotherapeutic regimen till today.

It might have surprised these eminent thinkers to know that by the standards of the academic nomenclature of the twenty-first century, their work could be considered *qualitative research*. Much like Molière's bourgeois gentleman who, when told about the distinction between prose and poetry, exclaimed "par ma foi, il y a plus de quarante ans que je dis de la prose, sans que j'en susse rien" (Good lord, for over 40 years I have been speaking prose and I did not know it), Darwin, Marx and Freud may have exclaimed, "Good lord, for over forty years (give or take), we have been conducting qualitative research and we did not know it!"

We present the above set of examples to highlight that the boundary between qualitative and quantitative research is a spurious construct, that good theory-building or theory-confirming research charts a continuous arc, and to break that continuity into a binary taxonomy is an act of social construction that is neither helpful nor productive. Qualitative researchers continuously deploy numerical data in their analysis, just as quantitative researchers utilize constructs derived from non-numerical analysis in their work. The "statistical turn" in social sciences, as developed by the logical empiricists of the Vienna Circle in the early twentieth century, privileged statistical analysis over observational data, creating a schism between *verstehen* (the interpretive understanding of phenomena) and *erklären* (the search for a causal explanation for things), that doomed many of the social sciences, including the emerging field of management studies, into a series of paradigm wars. For the longest time, qualitative approaches were deemed nothing more than "storytelling," unworthy of rigorous empirical scrutiny. Of course the landscape was dynamic, and slowly began to change. In many social sciences, qualitative research is back with a bang, demanding its share at the table of legitimacy.

Spurious though the qualitative/quantitative divide may be, we inherit a theoretical and methodological landscape where this binary is an accepted feature of our professional nomenclature. For the moment perhaps, it is necessary to engage in an act of *strategic essentialism*, or to embrace the category in order to transcend it. To that extent, this volume is presented as a way to clarify the multiplicity of research traditions that populate the qualitative end of the spectrum. It is accepted shorthand in our field that qualitative research works best in the theory-building realm, while quantitative research is better suited for theory confirmation. Qualitative research is more associated with the philosophical traditions of induction, while quantitative research is often deductive, moving from the general to the specific. More controversially, qualitative research seeks to associate itself with an interpretive epistemology, while quantitative studies are more associated with a positivist or functionalist paradigm. As many chapters in this volume show, these binaries are subject to vigorous contestation; there are positivist qualitative researchers and inductive statisticians galore. But the orthodoxies of our field have moved us in the direction of water-tight compartments, where a mutual suspicion characterizes the interaction between the two camps.

Another attendant side effect of this binary has been the relative *feminization* of qualitative research. There is an unspoken machismo associated with quantitative research, whereby qualitative methods are often consigned to the periphery of academic research. The metaphor that occurs to us is one of an army on the march, where quantitative researchers arrogate to themselves the role of soldiers, while qualitative researchers function as cooks, serving the army.

But times change, and metaphors can be re-appropriated. An army after all, marches on its stomach. And over time, especially in the past decade, qualitative research has begun to see a flowering. Dissertations that exclusively use qualitative methods are grudgingly being passed by Ph.D. committees. Influential journals are beginning to add qualitative experts to editorial boards. And of course, books like the one in your hand (or on your screen) are being commissioned by academic presses. The qualitative turn, it appears, has well and truly reached the reluctant shores of management theory.

To re-appropriate the metaphor of cooking and qualitative research further, let us visualize it as a succession of tasks. Well before the cooking process begins, ingredients have to be assembled and prepped. This may include clarifying the philosophical conundrums associated with inquiry, finding appropriate sites, negotiating access and developing a contingent roadmap of data collection. Fires have to be lit and temperatures managed. This includes the actual act of fieldwork, be it participant observation, interviewing, and transcribing, or the cataloging of secondary data. Diverse cooking techniques (think ethnography, grounded theory, process analysis, case studies, or qualitative comparative analysis) transform ingredients in different ways. A good dish needs to be simmered, stewed, and spiced to be deemed ready. That of course constitutes data analysis, be it through concept cards, linguistic analysis, content analysis performed either through tabulation or through computer programs, the extraction of recurring themes, or the emergence of "theory" from "story." Finally, a dish must be plated and presented to look appetizing and inviting. This final act involves the transformation of the research into journal articles, books, or book chapters that are deemed publish-worthy by one's peers. Researchers often talk of methodological toolkits that help them in their research. We could instead talk pots and pans, stoves and ovens. To that end, the diverse approaches to qualitative research are discussed at great length in this book. The mosaic of techniques, experiences, foundations, and traditions that this book represents will hopefully appeal to a variety of readers, for which we have our esteemed contributors to thank.

## Motivations

In 2000, as newly minted assistant professors in organizational studies, we were invited to conduct a Professional Development Workshop by the Research Methods Division of the Academy of Management (AOM). Needless to say, we were not the experts here; our job was to curate a workshop where well-recognized scholars would help new faculty and doctoral students negotiate the terrain of qualitative research. As an aside, this particular workshop then constituted one of only two sessions devoted to qualitative research in the entire research methods division, an exemplar of the dominance of quantitative research in the corridors of the AOM. We put the workshop together, without knowing what to expect. Imagine our astonishment when the hall that was allotted to us quickly filled to capacity with a bunch of participants, whose age indicated that many of them were new doctoral students. The atmosphere in the workshop was electric. Participants engaged with the experts, spoke among themselves, developed networks, and stayed in touch with each other and with the presenters. It was clear that we had hit upon a lack in the AOM meetings.

Over time of course, the terrain has changed. Many more sessions are now devoted to qualitative research, papers using qualitative techniques have been presented routinely at the conference in a variety of divisions, and the space for discussing qualitative research has increased considerably. However, energized by our first experience, we have conducted this workshop continuously over the past nearly two decades. The experts have changed and varied; we have used ethnographers and case study experts, Marxists and functionalists, people who work with traditional firms and those who use social media and visual technologies. The participant base has shifted a bit too, with some more senior scholars in attendance as well. Each time, the feedback we have received from the participants has been similar, though certain shifts have been apparent over time. We may briefly catalogue our initial experiences and our *current experiences* as follows:

1   New scholars were very interested in qualitative techniques, but had very little idea how to go about putting projects together. *A similar confusion remains, though it has been much alleviated by the variety of research that has been produced and consumed.*

2   The general perception was that dissertations based solely on qualitative methodologies would not find favor with committees, and even if passed, would constitute the "kiss of

death" in the job market for freshly minted Ph.D.s. *This perception has unfortunately withstood the test of time, to an extent that we are reluctantly forced to accept it as a truism. The job market for new researchers is fickle, and often, the use of cutting-edge statistical methods is seen by recruiters as a sign of interesting and promising research, while interesting qualitative research sometimes gets shorter shrift. Top schools are sometimes an exception to this rule, though even that is subject to scrutiny.*

3    The best possible course for a dissertation was seen as a mixed-method approach, involving a quantitative component that augmented some qualitative work. Perhaps a few interviews could lead to a questionnaire, or an analysis of documents such as annual reports of companies could yield to constructs that could be studies through computational analysis of databases. This led to a distressing lack of understanding about how qualitative research gets conducted. *Some clarity appears to have emerged about how the philosophy of science and its attendant metaphors impact the actual doing of research, but it is still slow and unclear. It is our experience that good research involves a process whereby the questions determine the choice of method, but insecurity in younger scholars often leads them in a direction where a dissertation is presented as a "report of effort" rather than an act of inquiry. To that end, the "mixed-methods" approach still rears its head, despite our words of caution.*

4    Qualitative research was seen as too time-consuming and resource-intensive, and not suitable for people seeking swift completion of dissertations, or on the tenure clock. Ethnographies were especially considered avoidable. *A greater number of younger researchers seem ready to commit to the longue durée of some qualitative projects. Also, quality ethnographic work has been published in management journals, demystifying the process somewhat. Other longer projects have included textual analysis of large quantities of written data, longitudinal analysis of single cases, and multi-case approaches.*

5    Despite the odds, most participants felt that qualitative research was more interesting to read and more inspirational as a technique to follow. *Happily, this feeling has endured, though the self-selection of participants of course makes us suspect that this does not reflect the way in which qualitative research is viewed in management academia as a whole.*

6    Participants were often concerned with issues that were more affiliated with quantitative techniques (such as reliability and validity), which tended to put them on the defensive when they attempted to explain their research to their peers and to anonymous reviewers of journals. *This condition persists, and the main value added by the experts in workshop panels was to explain ways in which they got their work published in mainstream journals despite facing similar obstacles. It does remain a problem in the peer-review process, which is an action item for those of us who are on journal editorial boards; we need to choose reviewers who are conversant with the methodology deployed by submitters in their papers.*

We could go on, but perhaps the overall understanding of the problems faced by interested researchers has been made clear. Qualitative research is seen as hard labor, relatively unrewarded, high risk, and uncertain, but simultaneously as satisfying, creative, and stimulating. To that extent, we felt motivated to continue with the workshop, and over time, developed the idea of formalizing our insights in the form of this book.

Of late, the terrain of publication has also shifted, making room for qualitative research. Not only do we see a greater number of papers in prestigious journals that use qualitative techniques, there have been many good books published on qualitative research. These include edited anthologies such as ours, books written by single authors, books that seek to explicate one particular technique (such as content analysis or ethnography), and collections of published articles on qualitative research. We see our book as joining the chaotic discussion, as just another rainbow that is formed by the emerging waterfall that is qualitative research in organizational studies. We have curated this book with an eye to diversity of approaches. In effect, it is a printed version of "Ask the Experts." The authors that have contributed to this volume represent veritable experts in the sub-field that they have addressed, but they most certainly do not share any paradigmatic singularity. To that extent, each chapter is designed to be consumed on a stand-alone basis, though some thematic congruity has emerged, as we discuss later in the introduction. The chapters here include personal reflections, analyses of specific projects, explications of particular techniques, discussion of unique forms of data analysis, and occasional critiques of the field from a variety of subaltern perspectives. One thing that characterizes all chapters however, is *currency*. The chapters in this book are located in the here and now, and focus on doing qualitative research in the twenty-first century. They update methodologies, connect our field to other social sciences and technological traditions, and offer ways forward for a methodological terrain that is in danger of being hijacked by tired templates and recycled insights. Our hope is that the book will emerge as a contingent sourcebook for qualitative methodologies in organization studies, which will primarily serve graduate students and newly minted faculty but will also acquaint seasoned scholars with methodologies and approaches with which they are only peripherally acquainted.

## The Underpinnings of Qualitative Research

While an explicit discussion of the philosophical foundations of qualitative research is performed very well in one of the chapters in this book, we would like to make a few observations about certain concepts that animate discussions of qualitative research, and research in general.

It is by now an accepted truism that the clarification of *ontological* and *epistemological* assumptions is very important in qualitative research. Ontological and epistemological positions tend to be correlated; to that extent, when an approach is classified as being positivist, realist, critical-realist or constructivist, we are in essence referring to closely banded ontological and epistemological assumptions. Positivists (and to some extent realists) may be visualized as holding a flashlight in a dark room. They illuminate different aspects of existing reality, while throwing others into the shadows. Enough flashlights, and the entire room becomes visible and mappable. Constructivists, on the other hand, see reality as a lump of clay that the researcher then fashions into a shape, and the reader interprets. Both the researcher and the reader engage in independent acts of creation, producing constructs that derive their legitimacy through construction (return on equity is accepted as a measure of firm performance because enough management academics agree that it is; to an environmental activist, it may be a pointless artifact, and to a labor organizer, it may even be a symbol of poor performance).

Researchers must also analyze the much used but rarely understood concept of *methodology*. The term *methodology* is much broader than mere *method*. A method is a tool or a technique that is used in the process of inquiry. However, methodology needs to be used specifically as a way to express an "intricate set of ontological and epistemological assumptions that a researcher brings to his or her work" (Prasad, 1997: 2). Methodological approaches are closely associated therefore with ontological and epistemological positions, as well as ways in which researchers plan to bring *rigor* to theory research, and the analytical approaches they bring to bear in the analysis of their data. It is here that qualitative researchers need to develop their own standards of what constitutes rigorous research in specific methodological traditions.

At this stage, however, a few clarifications are important. Often, the research traditions of our field succumb to the temptation to evaluate qualitative research according to templates that have been developed for large sample research. It is tiresome for qualitative researchers to encounter queries about reliability and validity from journal reviewers. Ethnographers are tripped up about issues of "generalizability," while issues of "falsifiability" are directed against hermeneuticians. One political question that continues to animate research in the social sciences relates not to higher-order constructs like "wisdom," "knowledge," or even "information," but that lowly term "data." What constitutes data in social environments where the signal-to-noise ratio is way lower than in the neater laboratories that cause us to (misinformedly) envy our counterparts in the natural sciences? We may have finally declared an uneasy truce in the methodology wars between the qualitative and quantitative approaches. But debates about the legitimacy of what constitutes "data" have continued to rage in a variety of spheres. Often, the interlocutors of a new approach are those who constitute the canonical tradition from which the new technique emerges. For example, to stay within qualitative research, consider the emergence of the technique of ethnomethodology in sociology (it has since migrated to a variety of social sciences, including management studies). Traditional sociologists initially derided ethnomethodologists for their needless focus on the quotidian. What could be learned from watching people go about their work, with no triggering events? However, the latter painstakingly staked out a claim that the most commonplace and regular social activities were worthy of being considered research data since they provided links to the organization of society (Garfinkel, 1967). Eventually, management researchers like Henry Mintzberg used ethnomethodological approaches to develop definitions of management that enriched our field.

Equally important, we must consider the issue of axiology, or ethics. Qualitative researchers must necessarily hold themselves to higher ethical standards than quantitative researchers, for the simple reason that they are dealing with human respondents, who engage with them in an atmosphere of trust and mutual sharing. Issues of gaining access, transparency of objectives and ways in which research findings will be shared with informants constitute an important element of ethics. Of course, the issue of ethics carries its own set of ambivalences. Some of the best research has been carried out surreptitiously. For example, Upton Sinclair, the muckraking journalist, conducted a stealthy study of the conditions under which laborers worked in the meat-packing industry in the United States at the turn of the twentieth century. Had he not done so, there would not have been the public furor that his findings created (interestingly presented not as a scholarly or journalistic piece, but as fiction in his 1906 novel *The Jungle*) that eventually led to the Pure Food and Drug Act and the Meat Inspection Act (Barkan, 1985).

On the other hand, many researchers who imbed themselves in organizations with the tacit approval of top management provide pointlessly hagiographic accounts of organizations, which are later shown to be corrupt (Rishi and Singh, 2011). Indeed, the issue of ethics is fraught, but it is extremely important for researchers to be cognizant of the ethical implications of their research. Management researchers have been insufficiently criticized for carrying the water for capitalists at the expense of labor, the environment, and disadvantaged stakeholders. For example, the construct of corporate social responsibility has often been misused to advocate for lesser oversight of corporations by society, and this construct is unreflectively peddled by organizational theorists as some sort of overarching legitimizer for an organization's relentless pursuit of value, at the expense of other marginalized social actors (Marens, 2010).

In short, qualitative research must submit itself to a higher standard of rigor and ethics in order to gain acceptance from its counterparts. This is especially true in a discursive terrain where quantitative and statistical approaches are given the imprimatur of authority, and have less to prove than qualitative techniques. However, qualitative researchers must simultaneously free themselves from the burden of having to subject their methodologies or their analytic approaches to modes of judgment derived principally from statistical analysis. It is time to produce our own internal parameters of what constitutes good research, but at the same time, throw away the yokes of reliability, validity, sample size, and a simplistic understanding of the falsifiable and the tautological.

## Theories

When we embarked upon the task of putting this book together, we were determined not to give our contributors too much direction, choosing instead to let them work on areas of their expertise, and letting them guide us toward a structure. As editors, we visualized our role as minimal, legislating on nothing more than word limits, syntax, and an occasional interjection. As the chapters emerged, we were able to place them into five loosely connected sub-groups, which we titled Theories, Traditions, Contexts, Journeys, and Frontiers and Reflections.

In the "Theories" section, we have four chapters that do not reflect explicitly on any particular methodologies of research, but rather focus on issues of philosophical import or socio-historical context. This section comprises four chapters that theorize philosophical traditions, critical approaches, feminist interpretivism, and a critique of organizational imperialism from an Islamic perspective.

Cristina Neesham begins by discussing the philosophical foundations of qualitative research. She concludes that "qualitative organizational researchers need to reflect more deeply on the ways in which they use philosophy and theory to formulate and support their empirical research questions," an idea that resonates deeply with us as editors. She reflects on the challenges posed by researchers through the multiplicity of paradigms. How can interpretive scholars coexist with positivists? What do critical scholars have to teach functionalists? How can postcolonial approaches square off against approaches that use Western templates of epistemology as default referents? Neesham ends with a call for reflective research, where philosophical differences are simultaneously acknowledged and valued by their practitioners.

Examining the critical strands of social theory as they manifest themselves in organizational qualitative research, Thomas Greckhamer observes that "critical qualitative inquiry holds great potential and promise for organization studies because it offers the constructive potential to contribute to developing the lines of thought that are needed to identify and overcome oppressive organizational structures." Greckhamer provides a taxonomy of research traditions that refuse to take the socio-organizational status quo as a sedimented given, discussing critical feminism that challenges male referents in research, critical race theory that prevents whiteness from becoming a benign referent identity, critical discourse analysis that seeks to undercover regimes of power in organizational communication, critical ethnography that problematizes the quotidian ways in which oppressive hierarchies are institutionally enacted, and critical action research that seeks to provide context to the subaltern subjectivities of the organizational arena.

Elaborating further on the feminist tradition from an interpretive perspective, Marleen van der Haar focuses on ways in which qualitative research can be used to question the default assumptions of patriarchy that are built into positivistic research traditions. Her work takes her in a more poststructuralist direction, seeing "woman" more as an analytical category than a fixed identity. Her chapter incorporates auto-ethnographic elements, showing the ways in which postmodern and interpretive approaches intersect, especially in the arena of category making. One important takeaway from her work is that of *Critical Frame Analysis*, a technique that has been used by feminists and other interpretive scholars to study meaning making.

Farzad Rafi Khan firmly locates his identity position as a Muslim on the wrong end of the imperialism divide. In his withering critique, "the powerful insights of qualitative research are like a towering giant whose feet are firmly planted in mid-air." Khan wonders whether it is his destiny to remain "the other" in this debate about what constitutes a valid subject for critique. In an era marked by Islamophobia in the public sphere, Khan firmly and insistently goes back to the philosophical traditions of Islam, and examines ways in which it has had a history of informing inquiry in the past, and a potential to do more of it in the future, despite the constant attempts by imperialists to interrupt that exchange.

The purpose of the chapters in this section is to ask for a greater level of transparency on the part of qualitative researchers in examining the philosophical assumptions that underpin their research. Whether we like it or not, each one of us is a philosopher, going about our life and research with a fundamental set of assumptions. Making them clear will help readers understand where we are coming from, and in turn whether to accept or challenge our findings. Additionally, issues of power and privilege implicate us axiologically; we researchers are ethically implicated in what we may mistakenly present as denatured and distant research. We are activists, whether we like it or not. The positions we take determine the direction of the world of organizations.

## Traditions

Qualitative researchers in organization studies have deployed a repertoire of techniques to gather and analyze data and communicate findings and insights pertaining to organizations. In the section titled "Traditions," we present eight chapters that provide an updated understanding of these techniques, including the multi-case approach, the single-case tradition, historical analysis, narrative analysis, ethnographic techniques, and strategies pertaining to writing and communication.

The first two chapters in this section cover case-based analysis. Kathleen Eisenhardt and Timothy Ott discuss the use of multiple sites to build theory. They make a strong case for rigor, which

> does not rest on superficial criteria like precise writing format, following the self-proclaimed "rules" of an analytic approach, or even extensive details about the research journey. Rather, rigor depends upon … strong emergent theory, well-grounded in accurate data, research design that reveals the focal phenomenon, and intriguing research and related insights.

Eisenhardt and Ott critique "deductive researchers who misunderstand core features of the method such as theoretical sampling and replication logic," and offer ways by which multi-sited case studies can expose different facets of a theoretical problem, and provide greater explanatory power to qualitative inquiry.

Pinar Ozcan, Suho Han, and Melissa Graebner go in a complementary direction, examining ways in which single-case studies can be used "to study complex and rare organizational processes in detail as well as longitudinally." They review 38 single-case studies published in management journals, and examine motivations for using single cases (often over long periods of time) as issues of access, data collection, and data analysis. They conclude their chapter with a variety of useful suggestions on how single-case studies can be written up and presented.

Daniel Wadhwani and Stephanie Decker provide a powerful and passionate endorsement for historical research. They argue that "historical epistemology and methodological practices are better understood as a form of situated scholarly inquiry in which the researcher interprets or analyzes the past from a position in the present through a process of abductive reasoning." Some of the facets of historical analysis they discuss include the treatment of evidence, the establishment of explanations, the attempt at understanding, and the foundations for evaluative conclusions. Wadhwani and Decker conclude by considering the implications for the role of historical discourse within management and organization studies more broadly.

Tammar Zilber advocates a narrative approach, which moves research beyond a rational model into the disorganized world of social action. As she suggests, social action is a messy business, and so theoretical insights based on a "strong" narrative approach tend to offer a complex understanding of organizational processes, one that is fraught with conflicts, power relations, collective rather than individualistic explanations, unintended consequences and local circumstances.

Zilber discusses a variety of narrative approaches such as biographies, interview-based studies, composite narratives, and "small stories" that explicitly analyze ways in which reality is constructed.

Anne-Laure Fayard observes that the work of ethnography should be seen as an act of *bricolage*, defined as constructing structures from available materials in haphazard manners rather than conforming to set plans. She advocates that

> rather than quibble over methods and tools to determine if they belong or are aligned with conventional ethnography, however, it is more fruitful to think of all methods as complementary to and supportive of enacting the ethnographic stance understood as improvisational and experimental.

She also discusses the role played by newer ethnographic approaches including video ethnography, team-based ethnography, and virtual ethnography, which are themselves a response to the reality that "the phenomena studied by ethnographers become more global and distributed and thus less 'visible' to the traditional lone observer, and as technology becomes as ubiquitous for those we study as for us."

Alexandra Michel suggests that while organizational ethnography, like its counterpart versions in cultural ethnography, involves immersion, it needs to free itself from the ontological assumption of what constitutes the "field" in which the researcher is expected to operate. Network ethnographies, multi-sited fieldwork, semiotic analysis, all have a role to play in organizational analysis. Michel examines the twin epistemological commitments of ethnography, studying contextual variance, and self-transformation through immersion, in organizational contexts. She argues that organizational ethnographers have a unique opportunity to invigorate the entire methodological tradition. In order to do so, they need to analyze the "types of innovations [that] are necessary for organizational ethnography in response to a changing ethnographic object, while observing shared theoretical commitments."

Chahrazad Abdallah advocates using nonfiction as a template to inform qualitative research in the organizational realm. As she suggests,

> using creative nonfiction writing techniques can inspire us to develop some of these multiple narrative forms and by the same token, to reinvent the writing of organizations. Focusing on writing more vivid ethnography that not only provides strong theoretical argumentative constructions but also engaging, appealing and compelling depictions of the "lives of others."

Abdallah sees research as an interpretive, critical, gendered, pragmatic and ethical endeavor, and sees writing not only as a mere act of evocative communication, but as something more productive, "a unique way of knowing, a method of inquiry conveying experiential and sensible knowledge."

Jinia Mukerjee and Anca Metiu provide a comparison between ethnography and journalism. They suggest that "ethnographic reports of work can benefit from following several specific journalism practices." These include emotional aspects of work, detailed description, the use of visual data, backstories, narrative style, authorial and subject-centered voices, sensitivity to context and heterogeneity, and collaborative teamwork. Long-form journalism, especially as conducted by sensitive and situated journalists, carries the cadence of an ethnographic account, and has the ability to be evocative and persuasive, and ethnographers could learn from journalists to incorporate some of those elements into their craft.

Different as these chapters are, they share a fierce commitment to originality in perspective. The collective contention is that the act of qualitative research involves multiple acts of production, right from the time of gaining access to the time of presenting research as written work. They offer key practical suggestions on how to conduct research in a variety of traditions and contexts, and also engage in reflection about how each tradition can move into the twenty-first century. They remind us that the traditions of qualitative research remain but a work in progress, and the innovative approaches of today stand a good chance of becoming the traditions of tomorrow, and that an unreflective obeisance to current traditions merely dooms us to mediocrity. Also, they underscore the fact that good qualitative research is hard work. It develops and demands its own standards of rigor, which is consistent with the theoretical and methodological traditions to which it adheres.

## Contexts

In examining some of the contexts – both traditional and more contemporary – in which qualitative studies have made their mark, we were struck by the diversity of methodological traditions (even within the qualitative realm) that have been deployed to study specific phenomena. For example, Davide Ravasi, Violina Rindova, and Elena Dalpiaz indicate how the study of organizational culture has historically involved quantitative methods, ethnographies, and semiotic analysis. To this, they bring their own unique brew (dare we say toolkit) to analyzing the cultural toolkits (Swidler, 1986) of organizations – this, in turn, being an artifact of the way in which we now conceptualize these entities. Theorizing and methodology coevolve – a recurring insight within this volume.

Raghu Garud, Hans Berends, and Philipp Tuertscher further highlight the diversity of qualitative methodologies that have been employed within the domain of innovation studies. These include both variance-based traditions (as epitomized by the Eisenhardt and Gioia approaches) and process-oriented methodologies, each with their own epistemology, ontology, and axiology. A particularly insightful distinction that they develop involves understanding "process as experienced" versus "process as observed" that resonates with the distinction between "emic" and "etic" approaches to understanding organizational phenomena. These distinctions themselves need to be understood not as dualities, but as points on a larger spectrum that afford the possibility of multiple hybrid qualitative approaches to understanding innovation as a phenomenon.

Ted Baker, Erin Powell, and Andrew Fultz comprehensively map the impact that qualitative studies have had on the field of entrepreneurship. In doing so, they make a compelling case for how the outputs of well-crafted work in this arena are, by their very nature, likely to be subjective and idiosyncratic. From their perspective, this should not be a cause for panic. Worse yet, this should not lead to methodological conservatism, a scenario in which only a few well-known approaches (and only certain types of evidence) are considered acceptable. Rather, adopting a "big tent" approach that embraces both the diversity of, and the messiness inherent in doing qualitative research is likely to provide a wider pool of useful insights that further enhance the intellectual foundations of the domain.

In addition to the domains of organizational culture, innovation, and entrepreneurship – which, at this stage, are fairly well established areas within the field – the chapters in this section examine how qualitative scholarship is shaping some of the nascent domains of inquiry within organization studies. Qualitative approaches have long been recognized to be particularly well suited for exploring emergent phenomena. Here, they typically play a constitutive role, helping establish the conceptual language, trajectory of inquiry, and associated guideposts that guide subsequent investigation. Moreover, scholars working in the space often provide "emergent" methodologies – i.e., tools and techniques of inquiry that, while drawing inspiration from the larger qualitative toolkit, are both situated within and well suited for examining the particular phenomena of interest.

Here, we showcase a few such "emergent" methodologies, each associated with an exciting and significant nascent domain of inquiry. The chapters by Paul Leonardi and Ingrid Erickson provide key methodological guidelines for the study of materiality that are particularly pertinent in the context of the ongoing digitalization of our organizations and society. Srinivas Sridharan takes us on an entirely different journey as he reflects on the unique challenges associated with conducting research in subsistence environments – scenarios that reflect the living conditions of the majority of humanity. And finally Nina Granqvist, Galina Kallio, and Heli Nissilä proffer a set of practices relevant to studying the construction of new industries and markets – arenas of activity that are likely to have a profound impact on our future. Taken together, these lines of inquiry highlight how qualitative methodologies are uniquely positioned to address the "grand challenges" that we now face (see also Eisenhardt, Graebner, and Sonenshein, 2016).

More significantly, these chapters suggest that distinct domains of inquiry likely require their own unique "tools of the trade" that build on the larger toolkit that qualitative researchers have developed and honed over the years. Put differently, they indicate how our theoretical understandings and methodological approaches to studying/understanding phenomena are inextricably interlinked. An alternate interpretation would indicate that, even operating within the qualitative realm, there are potentially different ways to "peel the potato," each leading to its own unique assemblage of insights that then vie with one another in the marketplace for ideas. From our vantage point, this further underscores the pressing need to avoid "standardization" of this form of research, even as it imposes the costs associated with customization – costs that can and should be cheerfully borne through an appreciative nod to the nuance, care, and integrity taken to conduct such work.

## Journeys

After having seasoned exponents of the craft specify evolution in methodologies and their application in diverse contexts, we turn to exploring specific paths that researchers have traversed in crafting their qualitative studies. In turning the spotlight on the process of studying process, our intent is to "pry open the black box" (Rosenberg, 1982) and reveal glimpses of how such work is done – i.e., identify relevant trade-offs, specify creative resolutions, foreshadow challenges, etc. – through the experiences of those actively involved in this domain. The narratives presented here are often deeply personal (for which we are grateful to the authors for sharing them) but in all cases reflect the care and meticulousness with which these journeys have been navigated. In keeping with our cooking metaphor, they are also inherently messy in situ and often idiosyncratic in their flavoring and seasoning, but deeply satisfying to anyone who subscribes to the notion that variety is the spice of life!

Glen Kreiner, Derron Bishop, and Aparna Joshi provide an illuminating account of the worldviews of quantitative and qualitative researchers and offer suggestions on how interested scholars can make forays "to the other side" (i.e., the world of qualitative insight). They eloquently reveal some of the fundamental differences in philosophy and practice between these two approaches of inquiry – barriers that, with fortitude and an appreciative mindset, can be converted into bridges. Moreover, they reaffirm important milestones that make for a pleasurable and productive (qualitative) journey, reflect on key attributes of travelers on this path, and provide invaluable preparatory tips to those willing to go on this trip.

Rene Wiedner and Shaz Ansari build on this platform by providing a refreshing take on perhaps the most perplexing facet of the qualitative researcher's voyage: the research design. They make a compelling case for embracing what they term an "emergent" research design – one that advocates for gradual immersion in the field, requires a yen for awareness and the willingness to remain open, acknowledges messiness, and above all values transparency. In doing so, they demystify the tired reference to "the iterative process of data collection and analysis" that most qualitative studies allude to. Their confessional tales provide a fascinating insider view of the complexity, ambiguity, messiness, blind alleys, elements of surprise, and slivers of insight (which gradually cohere into findings) that are inherent in the journey of a qualitative researcher – one that makes their work invariably idiosyncratic but also consistently compelling. Overall, they offer a gripping ringside account of the processes by which qualitative research actually (and typically) gets done.

The chapters by Katherine Chen and Saku Mantere separately dwell on critical challenges that qualitative researchers face once they are further along in their voyage. Chen provides a number of useful tips that enable the transition from the voluminous data that such scholars usually generate to tangible outputs (books, articles, etc.) into which such effort needs eventually to translate. She clearly conveys the vital significance of the social dimension of the research process and the need to leverage the benefits that accrue from such interactions – a facet that often gets submerged when researchers immerse themselves deeply in the field. Mantere, in his piece, adroitly puts his finger on an important milestone that voyagers on this journey need to cross – making a theoretical contribution. He succinctly articulates the underlying trade-offs that this involves – in terms of balancing data, argument, and extant discourse – and how quality scholarship simultaneously addresses this triad. Crucial to this endeavor is making a creative leap – one that makes qualitative research as much an artistic endeavor as a scientific one.

Finally, as part of the closing link to the research cycle, Andrew Nelson offers a package of prescriptions aimed at making the outputs of our scholarly endeavors more cumulative and (presumably) impactful. Drawing on the example of the open source software movement, he makes a strong case for establishing institutional structures and mechanisms that enable qualitative scholars to make their data and analysis more readily transparent to others within the community. This would likely have a number of positive impacts: enable researchers to more precisely trace the logic underlying the leap from data to insight, demystify the perceived fragility of qualitative research ("it's just a bunch of stories"), serve as a useful pedagogical tool, and more generally enhance cumulativeness of our research findings in a particular domain. In taking this long view, Nelson reminds us that constructing a big tent for qualitative research in organization studies will likely require ongoing self-reflection that translates into research practices that robustly and thoughtfully address the careful scrutiny of insiders and outsiders.

The journeys described in this section (and elsewhere in the volume) highlight the myriad trajectories that scholars traverse in the qualitative pursuit of answers to their research questions. As depicted, these paths are inherently messy, non-linear, co-evolutionary, socially mediated, and incomplete (i.e., permanently in beta) – i.e., they are quite the contrast from the orderly and systematic journey portrayed within accounts of "objective" scientific inquiry. At one level, this is only to be expected given the wide range of ontologies, epistemologies and axiologies – or simply put, different underlying assumptions or points of view – that these researchers bring to the table while conducting their inquiry. However, the apparent idiosyncrasies in these paths, rather than be viewed with undue suspicion, should be embraced for the generativity that they likely bring to future research quests. In providing intimate details on the performative aspects of qualitative research, our intent is not just to spotlight the passion and perseverance that drives such inquiry but also to suggest that there are new paths waiting to be discovered and articulated, ones that will keep our qualitative traditions modern.

## Frontiers and Reflections

We close the book with a set of chapters that collectively, look to the future ahead and to paths traversed as a means to offering us another perspective on the current state of qualitative research in organization studies. Even as the world we live in affords us various new opportunities to explore the nature of organizations and organizing, it also presents a time for us to reflect on how our methods and methodologies can appropriately address new realities. To illustrate: in a world increasingly deluged by "big" data, what role do nuance and careful interpretation – the calling cards of a qualitative researcher – play? Are her/his tools and temperament adequate and relevant to the changing demands of academic inquiry? Taken further, even as qualitative studies gets more of a voice in the mainstream organizations discourse, has its ongoing institutionalization marginalized certain approaches and narrowed modes of inquiry? And what overarching mechanisms can be put into place to avoid these tendencies from taking hold? The contributors to this section elucidate a wide-ranging set of views on these issues, providing provisional templates for engaging with the future as well as critically assessing the paths that have been forged by qualitative inquiry – rich forage for conversations that will certainly be continued!

The frontiers explored in this volume traverse novel forms of data as well as original analytic approaches. Catherine Cassell outlines the many opportunities, as well as challenges, of employing visual data in qualitative studies of organizing. On this front, the ubiquity of technology to capture the human experience – as manifest in the smartphones and other recording devices of today – has opened up abundant opportunities to create multimedia-savvy research designs that can fundamentally transform the richness of our theorizing (see also Fayard in this volume). Emmanuelle Vaast and Cathy Urquhart tap into a second domain – social media data – that is likely to become a staple of many qualitative investigations going forward (see also the chapter by Erickson for more work on this front). Here, it is highly likely that researchers will need to proactively craft entirely new tools and techniques that enable us to more effectively – and in a more integrated manner – capture the increasingly digital/virtual fabric and vibe of our organizations and society. Finally, Brian Pentland and Peng Liu articulate an original approach to studying a venerable concept: the organizational routine. These forays represent just a sampling of the myriad directions in which organization studies – and by association, the qualitative methodologies to study them – are transforming. However, they underscore how the emergence of new/untapped forms of data and the quest for a deeper exposition of extant concepts can spur innovation in qualitative research techniques. More generally, they call attention to an underlying theme of this volume – the vibrant, evolving, *living* nature of qualitative methodologies.

To conclude, we have three pioneers and highly respected exponents of qualitative research in organization studies provide their thoughts on the state of this field. Deborah Dougherty, in her inimitable style, makes a compelling case for the need to migrate away from the prevalent "confirmation" narrative that currently pervades the field, to one that she terms the "discovery" narrative – i.e., one that relies on abductive reasoning, explains learning events, and addresses grand challenges. In providing a new frame to the evaluation of our endeavors, she emphasizes how context and contingency – reflected in the key insights that we obtain during our research journey – need to be afforded center-stage in our narratives. This, in turn, will require changes in mindsets – or at the very minimum, an openness to alternate approaches – on the part of the scholarly community, be they playing the role of reviewers, editors, or authors. Denny Gioia, on the other hand, provides us with a perceptive, personal account of how the present has come to be – i.e., the long, difficult road that his work – and more generally, qualitative research – has had to traverse in order to gain a semblance of legitimacy in a world largely populated by deductively and quantitatively oriented scholars. His chronicle commends the progress that has been made by the community on this front. In doing so, it both evokes inspiration as well as serves as a prototype for future similar journeys that will hopefully open up new vistas – and ensure the variety and vitality – for this form of inquiry.

While Dougherty attends to imagining new futures and Gioia traverses the hard-fought past, Ann Langley's perspective is firmly rooted in the present and the pragmatic – a "must-read" guide for anyone toiling away on their qualitative projects and engulfed with feelings that they are not making headway. Her essay highlights a number of "traps" into which scholars can readily fall while doing such work, and then provides sage advice on how one can avoid/address these. In doing so, she distils the essence of what makes a qualitative study feel like fine wine – deep data, inspired coupling between data and theory that culminates in a creative leap, and a stirring story to tie it all together. In many ways her essay is also a savory reminder of what makes this kind of research distinctive, compelling, and impactful. From our perspective, such a return to roots is a particularly apt way in which to close this volume and launch into our own journeys!

## Conclusion: Resisting Institutional Pulls

Taken as a coherent whole, the chapters in this book, besides constituting a powerful case for qualitative research, provide a vivid portrayal of the paths traversed, the state of the art, as well as possible futures for this form of inquiry. They serve to remind us of the power and the allure of a well-woven "story" – one that simultaneously serves as the basis of provisional theorizing and is strongly embedded in persuasive data and evidence. A key theme that we have sought to highlight in this volume is the sheer diversity of qualitative approaches available to the researcher, each grounded in their own underlying philosophy. Given this, we believe that members of the community – in their various roles and capacities – need to acknowledge and nurture the diversity of the biosphere, so to speak (see also van Maanen, 1995), rather than submit the domain to being pigeonholed – dare we say stereotyped – into a much narrower conception of this "alternate" approach.

Another key – and definitely intriguing – theme emerging from this volume is the inherently dynamic nature of qualitative methodologies themselves. This is reflected in a number of the chapters across the book that provide timely and relevant "updates" on how different traditions – be they case studies, ethnographies, historical methods, or narratives – are being practiced by their exponents in the twenty-first century. At the surface level, we have attempted to provide a guide to the "state of the art" of qualitative inquiry into organizational phenomena. At a deeper level, however, we hope to have sensitized the reader to the (potential) affordances that taking a dynamic view of our tools of inquiry provides – one that requires creativity and perseverance but also ensures that these methods remain relevant and alive!

Finally, the handbook also attempts to chart some of the emerging directions and domains for qualitative studies of organizations and organizing. This has been a long-standing strength of this methodological tradition, given that it lends itself well when adopting an exploratory mindset to understanding emergent phenomena. In addition to highlighting ongoing and nascent investigations on such trends as the digitization of organizations/society, crafting markets for underserved communities and the emergence of new industrial sectors, the chapters also underscore the coupling that exists between phenomena and method – further contributing to the dynamic perspective on methodology that we alluded to earlier. Along these lines, living in an era in which we are constantly deluged with data (of all varieties!) is likely to require innovative recombination of our existing tools – one that potentially involves (re)constructing existing boundaries with the quantitative world – as a means to crafting new ways of sensemaking and sensegiving of our brave new world of organizing as well as more generally, maintaining relevance and sanity!

While non-linear, somewhat messy, and reliant on creative leaps – i.e., as much of an art as a science – the hallmark of the qualitative perspective has always been that, when well done, it produces interesting research that reflects an inclusive approach. There has been much prior conversation on the "interesting" part, and therefore, we end this introduction with a plea for greater levels of "inclusiveness" – an inclusiveness that incorporates heterogeneities of perspective and context, and engages with difference in a spirit of democratic equality.

In this spirit of inclusiveness, it is perhaps very important to acknowledge some of the shortcomings of bad qualitative research as well. From untheorized data to cherry-picked quotes, and from undeveloped theoretical frameworks to grossly generalized findings, there have been several submissions to journals and edited volumes that purport to do qualitative research, and only give it a bad name. In some cases, qualitative research ends up becoming the last refuge of the mathphobic doctoral student, who views it a place of refuge from the demands of statistical analysis rather than an interesting point from which they can conduct original research. Likewise, while journal editorial boards are often heavier on the quantitative side, the tendency of poor qualitative researchers to blame rejected pieces on "gatekeeping by the statistics mafia" should be greeted with a healthy dose of skepticism (though it does happen). In the end, the best we can hope for is that the burgeoning and emerging community of qualitative researchers in management academia will hopefully emerge into an organic structure of apprenticeship, which will ensure that interesting and persuasive qualitative research continues to get published and gain influence.

While we are loath to offer a manifesto for qualitative research going forward (recognizing as we do its heterogeneity and the specificity of its multiple traditions), we would like to end with three important suggestions that affect all qualitative research.

The first is that those of us devoted to qualitative research must resist thinking, speaking, and evaluating that research using quantitative thinking. We must act to educate journal editors, gatekeepers of conferences, and blind reviewers of our own submissions that the standards by which qualitative research is deemed good or bad cannot be derived from criteria that are themselves beholden to large sample data analysis.

Second, while ethical considerations are paramount in qualitative research, we need to debunk the narrow understanding of ethics as "following rules." Ethics is not just about protection of the individual subject of our research, but represents a broader concern, imbued in traditions of resistance and emancipation. Ethics implies ensuring that our work is not deployed to protect the powerful at the expense of the oppressed, or to naturalize power relations as normal or normative. Sometimes, resistance is the most ethical option, both for us as researchers, and for the subjects we study.

Finally, and in the same spirit, we need to be aware of the institutional pulls that our research will be subject to, and also be ready to resist them. It can be argued that in a world characterized by the dominance of neoliberal economic policies, officialized organizational (including qualitative) research has developed an "institutional" character. An institution may be defined broadly as a social pattern that owes its survival to it being constantly practiced, and accepted as important and useful. While it initially emerges out of need, and out of the prodding of those who exercise power, an institution eventually acquires a legitimacy of its own, emerging as a social "truth." In fact, once a practice or a set of practices is ordained as an institution, it acquires the status of a self-fulfilling prophesy, generating its own logic as it proceeds. Anyone who opposes the internal logic of an institution risks illegitimacy among the community of practitioners that become a part of the institution. Over time, the success of certain forms of qualitative research (at the expense of others) can be attributed in part to this institutional character. Some of the artifacts of the institutionalization of mainstream qualitative research include:

- a system of hierarchy of research outlets, where researchers are only rewarded for publishing in certain kinds of journals, and other forms of research are cast onto the periphery;
- professional societies (e.g., AOM) that facilitate the creation of a network of actors, where regimes of research can be enforced. This in turn privileges research conducted from certain geographical spaces and institutional affiliations;
- the emergence of sets of formal and informal rules regarding researcher behavior, ownership of ideas and citation criteria;
- a prescribed agenda for sharing research ideas characterized by the belief that "underperforming" organizations would benefit by emulating the "successful" organizations in their midst, thus joining the list of "winners" in the era of globalization;
- the isomorphic pulls within specific sub-segments (e.g., strategy) towards the use of similar variables, what constitutes an appropriate research question, and what analytic techniques are *de rigeur*;
- the injunction that institutions remain "apolitical," and the subsequent casting of even fundamental ethical issues as "political" and therefore beyond the pale of analysis or comment.

We have tried to assert in this introduction that as qualitative researchers, or as researchers in general, we should not feel obligated to submit willy-nilly to these institutional pulls. Indeed, the coercive powers of such institutional norms are often exaggerated, as are the rewards of mimetic compromise. Good research will win out. It may initially seem as if we are tilting at windmills, but over time, the research that stands out is that which begins from a place of authenticity, and adheres to principles that the purveyors of research value above careerist expediency and paradigmatic compromise. Good research resists the siren call of institutionalization. It challenges the "common sense" assumptions of the field and brings them into the realm of the questionable. It seeks to theorize the untheorizable, and anthropologize the dominant. To use the language of organizations, good, transparent and effective research must necessarily go beyond the institutional pulls of the dominant paradigms of the field – even those that it creates! Put simply – the revolution is ongoing!

# References

Barkan, I.D. (1985). Industry invites regulation: the passage of the Pure Food and Drug Act of 1906. *American Journal of Public Health*, *75*(1), 18–26.

Eisenhardt, K.M., Graebner, M.E., and Sonenshein, S. (2016). Grand challenges and inductive methods: rigor without rigor mortis. *Academy of Management Journal*, *59*(4), 1113–1123.

Garfinkel, H. (1967). *Studies in Ethnomethodology*. Englewood Cliffs, NJ: Prentice-Hall.

Marens, R. (2010). Destroying the village to save it: corporate social responsibility, labour relations, and the rise and fall of American hegemony. *Organization*, *17*(6), 743–766.

Prasad, P. (1997). Systems of meaning: ethnography as a methodology for the study of information technologies. In Lee, A. and Degross, J. (eds.), *Qualitative Methods and Information Research*, Boston, MA: Kluwer, 1–33.

Rishi, M., and Singh, A. (2011). Corporate governance and international best practices: the case of Satyam. *Journal of Services Research*, *11*(1), 121–132.

Rosenberg, N. (1982). *Inside the Black Box: Technology and Economics*. Cambridge: Cambridge University Press.

Swidler, A. (1986). Culture in action: symbols and strategies. *American Sociological Review*, *51*(2), 273–286.

Van Maanen, J. (1995). Style as theory. *Organization Science*, *6*(1): 133–143.

# PART I

# Theories

# 2

# PHILOSOPHICAL FOUNDATIONS OF QUALITATIVE ORGANIZATIONAL RESEARCH

*Cristina Neesham*

## The Nature of Qualitative Research: Reflexivity and Philosophy

Qualitative social research has traditionally been distinguished from its quantitative counterpart by its commitment to asking 'why', 'what' and 'how' questions about social phenomena – rather than 'how much' and 'to what extent' questions. Its vocation is therefore to discover or interpret the substance of social life rather than measure any particular dimensions of it (Denzin and Lincoln 1998, 2011; Spencer *et al.* 2014). In this process, the researcher as subject of knowledge and valuation engages in illuminating not only the reality they are studying but also themselves in relation to that reality and their participation in it. As Leavy (2014: 1) put it, 'qualitative research is an engaged way of building knowledge about the social world and human experience, and qualitative researchers are enmeshed in their projects'. Thus, qualitative research is not just a complement set to answer questions that quantitative research cannot address, but represents a distinct body of research practices, with its own rigours and standards (Denzin and Lincoln 2011). One such distinctive characteristic of qualitative research is its propensity for reflecting on its own practice and on the relationship between researcher and researched. Within this relational process, qualitative inquiry is, by its very nature, bound to delve more deeply into foundational, philosophical questions.

Although explicit reflection on one's own philosophical assumptions is a matter of crucial importance for both quantitative and qualitative research, thus suggesting that the distinction between the two approaches may have been overplayed, it has been recognized as a prominent feature of the latter, based on an understanding of social phenomena as open to complex, unpredictable change and influence from the researcher's gaze as creative of worlds rather than merely recording external stimuli (Morgan and Smircich 1980: 498):

> Quantitative techniques may have an important but only partial role to play in the analysis and understanding of the process of social change … The requirement for effective research in these situations is clear: scientists can no longer remain as external observers, measuring what they see; they must move to investigate from within the subject of study and employ research techniques appropriate to that task.

Qualitative research is therefore at home in the social sciences, expanding the breadth and depth of the research effort to more appropriate levels.

Just as for quantitative research, the philosophical foundations of qualitative research refer to certain assumptions that its various paradigms and approaches have to rely on, by logical necessity, in explaining and justifying themselves – in terms of their various interpretations of the nature of the phenomena under study; the role and status of the researcher; the nature of the relationship between researcher, other human beings and (non-human) phenomena; and the defining features of the research process as a relation between theory and practice. As a social process of inquiry for the purposes of advancing knowledge, research is inescapably grounded in the researcher's worldview (Geertz 1989). Therefore, its philosophical propositions, as answers to first-order questions, are omnipresent, whether acknowledged or not. Even a researcher who dismisses the need for philosophical reflection on the basis that their job is to respond to the question 'What is happening out there?' by simply reporting what they observe takes the implicit stance that one can know reality *as it is*, without mediation – thus plunging into one of the most controversial ideas in the history of philosophy.

At the heart of any 'why' question in qualitative inquiry there is a philosophical axiom – that is, a proposition believed to be self-evident or to require no demonstration, which logically establishes the truth of all other valid inferences made in the research process. This axiom is of philosophical interest in that it ultimately relates to a first-order, all-encompassing, universal question of the kind: what is the nature of reality? of human knowledge? of value? of purposeful human action? But what an empirical researcher is prepared to take for granted can cause headaches for generations of philosophers. Reflecting philosophically on our research axioms enables us to maintain our intellectual acuity under the pressure of the most numbing analgesics.

One such analgesic dwells in the separation of organizational research from primary social research domains such as sociology, psychology, anthropology, economics and political science. Our focus on organizational research here does not seek to tear it away from its humanist roots in order to justify instrumentalist objectives as points of distinction. On the contrary, it is meant to illuminate how specific concerns of organizational research are related to and embedded in the broader concerns of primary social inquiry. Hence, the purpose of this chapter is to explore the types of philosophical questions addressed in the assumptions adopted by various streams of qualitative organizational research; discuss the various paradigms, conceived as sets of philosophical assumptions, their influence on the study of organizations, and approaches to paradigm classification most popularly adopted in this field; and evaluate the challenges and opportunities experienced by qualitative researchers in advancing humanist (rather than instrumentalist) knowledge of organizations in theoretically sound and practically meaningful ways.

## Philosophical Spheres in Qualitative Organizational Research

Traditionally, philosophical assumptions in qualitative social research have been grouped into three main categories – labelled as pertaining to ontology (as philosophy of existence and reality), epistemology (as philosophy of knowledge), and axiology (as philosophy of value). Due to our focus on the study of organizations, our discussion of philosophical foundations of qualitative inquiry has five important points of departure from similar explorations of qualitative social research in general. First, we emphasize the particular relevance of ontological assumptions of *becoming* and not only of *being*, about processes and not only about states – by illustrating the role of process philosophy in enriching the theoretical perspectives of organizational research. Second, we nuance the objectivist–subjectivist distinction employed in classifying organizational ontologies and epistemologies (see Burrell and Morgan 1979) by appealing to fallibilism as a meta-critique of knowledge claims, and thus opening the possibility for more refined perspectives on 'constructs of dubious ontological status' typically produced in organizational research, such as 'structure, culture, leadership' (Powell 2001: 213) and even organization itself. Third, we distinguish between axiology (as the domain of meta-ethics and theory of value) and its applications, in the form of ethics and politics of value – and we take a closer look at the role of ethical and political questions in informing various research paradigms in the study of organizations. Fourth, we distinguish between the concept of 'methodology' in philosophy (as reflection on the practice of philosophy itself) and the role of philosophical assumptions (usually belonging to one of the other philosophical categories – such as ontology, epistemology or ethics) in legitimating the methodology of empirical organizational research. Finally, we add to the discussion the rather neglected philosophical area of praxeology, as foundational reflection on the nature of purposeful human action, hence of both research practice and organizational action as particular cases of it. Praxeological assumptions are particularly important in organizational research because they provide the logic underpinning the relationships among modalities of existence, possibility and value, and they indicate how these modalities should be articulated and integrated in legitimizing the research project. Hence, we will discuss questions pertaining to four philosophical spheres – namely, the ontological, epistemological, axiological and praxeological – and relate them to issues of research practice that are specific to organizational inquiry.

## *The Ontological Sphere*

Ontology is the domain of philosophy that deals with questions about *being* and *becoming*. The nature of reality – that is, of what exists, in whatever form or process, whether independently or in some relation to us (and to other 'things' that exist) – is its concern. Hence, most statements in ontology are 'is' statements. In other words, the language of ontology relies on modalities of existence.

Organizational qualitative research practice shares with the wider domain of social research in general the preoccupation for cogently explaining the nature and status of various phenomena under study, especially in relationship with the nature and status of the inquirer (Delanty 2005; Denzin and Lincoln 2011; Rosenberg 2008). Hence, some social research theorists have found it difficult to separate between ontological and epistemological questions in this domain (see Burrell and Morgan 1979). It does, however, also raise specific questions about the organization, our central object of inquiry. Such questions could be: what kind of 'thing/it' is an organization? what kind of reality is it an example of? what kind of 'things'/reality/realities exist in, and in relation with, an organization? and, what is the nature of (organizational) reality for an organizational researcher? Does the fact that we tend to approximate definitions of organizations by metaphors (see Morgan 1997) indicate an ontological complexity we are not quite prepared for?

As an alternative to analogical-metaphorical thinking, some organization theorists have taken an active interest in process metaphysics (see Whitehead 1929/1967; Bergson 1946; Rescher 1996) in order to better explain how organizational phenomena, never static, morph and de-morph continuously in successions of emergent events rather than designed structures. This increasingly influential body of work has played a crucial role in contemporary developments in the study of identity (Schultz 2012), materiality (Carlile *et al.* 2013), sensemaking (Hernes and Maitlis 2010) and change (Langley *et al.* 2013) in organizations.

## *The Epistemological Sphere*

Epistemology's representative action verbs are: *knowing; believing* and *doubting; verifying* and *falsifying*. Most generally, this sphere deals with how we human beings acquire and develop knowledge about reality. The language of epistemology is therefore dominated by 'can' propositions – or, otherwise put, the modality of possibility.

The qualitative organizational researcher shares with the social researcher in other fields a concern for the quality of evidence and its role in establishing trustworthy belief, in developing sound criteria for such trustworthiness (Denzin and Lincoln 2011). Furthermore, they both ask: do we access the 'reality' under study *as it is*, or are there angles, filters, biases and limits in our attempts to understand it?

More specifically, however, the organizational researcher is interested in understanding the nature of the knowledge involved in the particular ways in which organizational phenomena can be known. Reflection on foundational epistemological commitments is essential to good research practice, helping the researcher understand and cope with the realization that making such commitments is unavoidable, while any particular commitment is contestable (Johnson and Cassell 2001). The objective–subjective dichotomy most often used in encapsulating the range of researchers' views of the nature of the knowledge they produce, namely, as truth available out there, independently of the enquirer, versus as a reciprocal construction of belief in the interaction between researcher and researched, can be both transcended and relativized by considerations of fallibilism, whereby the possibility of not knowing (or failing to know) the truth of any epistemological premise is never completely removed, in any process of inquiry, however coherent (Gettier 1963). It is philosophical reflection that enables us to ask critical questions such as (Powell 2001: 213):

> Which theories of truth … do organizational researchers explicitly or tacitly accept? What kinds of propositions … dominate organizational discourse? What foundations … do organizational researchers use to justify knowledge claims? In what sense do organizational researchers regard their claims as true and warranted?

In doing so, qualitative research paves the way for suitably comprehensive reflection on social phenomena for quantitative analysis as well.

## *The Axiological Sphere*

By definition, axiology deals with *value* and (particularly relevant for organizational research) *valuing*. Its propositions are mainly modals of obligation and normativity – that is, they are 'should' propositions. Their subject is the nature of value and valuing processes. It has been said that, in social research, axiological assumptions refer to the values of the researcher and how they influence the research process (Spencer *et al.* 2014), but studying organizations adds new layers of complexity to axiological questions, which require deeper levels of reflection on the challenges posed by organizations and their management practices, as symbolic realities (Kostera 2012; McKinlay *et al.* 2012), to the researcher–researched relationship.

In this chapter, we will set aside primary axiological questions, such as *what is the nature of value?*, and explore instead two of its discrete applications, in the form of *ethics* (which deals with values of the Good), and *political philosophy of value* (which deals with values related to the Powerful, or Power). Questions of *ethics* in qualitative organizational research are, fundamentally, concerned with reasons why the research is considered worthwhile, with its ultimate purpose. Here one can identify, across the field, a wide range of answers, from those anchoring the Good in meeting the needs of organizations and management practitioners (Argyris 1964, 1993; Herzberg *et al.* 1959; McGregor 1960) to those that go beyond organizational rationale and give primacy to improvements in the human condition – be it in the well-being of individuals, groups, communities or society more generally (Dierksmeier 2016; Melé 2016). Whether instrumentalist or humanist, or enacting combinations in between, organizational researchers will adopt an ethical stance, be it explicit or tacit.

In the realm of normativity there are also *political* questions to be addressed, such as: what is the role of the researcher? should research inquiry convert into, or be driven by, a political agenda? and, if so, what should this agenda be set to achieve? In this context, the *politics* of research calls for *ethical* justifications of its own (Rosenberg 2008). The reflective researcher will not only be interested in understanding who benefits from their research, or whose interests are well represented and whose are ignored or undermined, but will also be prepared to question the political and ethical legitimacy of a variety of qualitative research approaches, including their preferred stance: on what *ethical* basis should the premises of the research project's *political* agenda, or their political implications, be accepted? Increasingly, organizational theorists have grown to acknowledge that all research has political implications – even when no political goals are explicitly adopted. The usual effect of the latter is one of adding epistemic legitimacy and support to the social and political status quo (Dehler and Welsh 2016; Klikauer 2014). It is therefore not surprising that a counterbalancing research agenda, aimed at voice-giving and emancipation of the subordinate, the disadvantaged, the vulnerable and the oppressed, has not only to be explicit but also to challenge the very possibility of value neutrality in organizational research generally, irrespective of theoretical-philosophical persuasion.

## The Praxeological Sphere

Understood as the philosophical domain studying purposeful human action (Alexandre and Gasparski 2000; Kotarbinski 1965), praxeology can be defined in terms of *choosing, (en)acting, applying, practising* and *performing*. Therefore, we argue, it is to this heading that our theoretical discussions of methodology in organizational research should be more appropriately subsumed, given that insights into the philosophy of designing purposeful human action have a central role in the conceptualization of research methodology applications as both structured and agentic practice. In support of this suggestion, we note that methodologically reflective questions (that is, meta-questions) about research design are often similar, in essence, to praxeological questions, understood in a broad (non-economistic) sense. Keen to address the confusion, often encountered in the literature, between philosophical and derived (second-order, empirical domain-generated) questions in research methodology, Delanty (2005), for example, clearly distinguishes between philosophy and methodology in social research.

Appeal to praxeology enables us to discuss in a more systematic fashion important debates in organizational theory around the *performativity* and *anti-performativity* of particular kinds of research practices and critiques (Delbridge 2014; Fleming and Banerjee 2016; Schaefer and Wickert 2016). Moreover, for organizational research, Bourdieu's social praxeology (Bourdieu 1977, 1990) is particularly relevant, as it explores the possibilities of research as action upon and produced by organizations as symbolically mediated entities (Everett 2002).

## Research Paradigms in Organization Studies: Exogenous Influences and Endogenous Issues

Inspired by epistemologies of the natural sciences, social research has a long tradition of grouping its practices into *paradigms*. According to Kuhn (1962/2012), a scientific paradigm is an exemplary way of practising research generally accepted by a community of researchers, in a given period. A paradigm is informed by a particular worldview and, related to it, a particular perspective on the purpose, nature, structure and standards of the research process. Its most fundamental assumptions about the research world – including multiple and nuanced relations between researcher and researched – are philosophical, most usually pertaining to the four spheres previously discussed. It is a well-established convention in philosophical explorations of qualitative social research to outline and structure the evolution of theoretical thinking in the field in terms of a (more or less) historical sequence of paradigms (see Creswell 2014; Crotty 1998; Delanty 2005; Denzin and Lincoln 1998; Guba and Lincoln 1994; Ormston *et al.* 2013; Prasad and Prasad 2002; Trigg 2001).

For the purposes of a summarized discussion, four of the broadest, most distinctive paradigms have been selected here: namely (post-)positivism, social constructionism, critical inquiry and pragmatism. In focusing on the first three, we are guided by Habermas's (1971/2015) analysis of knowledge as related to human interests. Accordingly, the connection between empirical and analytical research approaches and technical interests is represented by (post-)positivism; historical and hermeneutic knowledge directed by practical interests is discussed under social constructionism; while critical inquiry reflects critically oriented (and, one may say, subversive) knowledge driven by emancipatory interests. We add pragmatism as one of the most influential paradigms of social research since Habermas's categorization was published. We will explore the key features of each of the four paradigms in turn below, also with reference to sub-paradigms that have proven relevant in the study of organizations.

## Post-Positivism

Following anti-positivist critiques in both natural and social sciences, post-positivism amends and improves, philosophically and methodologically, on a position that remains, in essence, ontologically realist and epistemologically objectivist. While confidence in absolute, universal, complete and non-interventionist knowledge may have waned under the influence of Heisenberg's indeterminacy principle (Lindley 2008), Popper's (1964) falsificationist criteria (Popper 2005) and Gettier's (1963) fallibilist argument (Powell 2001), in post-positivism the researcher's orientation for methodological development is still guided by the goal of apprehending reality (believed as identifiable, in significant ways, as independent of our consciousness) through as little intrusion and influence as possible. Truth is still to be discovered rather than constructed, with testability, replication and predictability remaining central concerns for the research project – although, unlike in classical positivism, the ultimate goal is now probability rather than certainty. For the post-positivist researcher, the world, regarded as a collection of objects, can be known, albeit partially, with satisfactory approximation to its objective state, using methods based on rigorously assessed evidence. Unified and unifying standards of evidence assessment continue to represent the progressive ideal of the disciplined researcher, who should perfect their instruments to reduce impact of their own intervention and bias, and to exclude value judgements.

An incursion into the evolution of organizational qualitative research literature suggests that, to start with, post-positivism is not meant to be the natural ground for qualitative research anyway, as the latter has historically distinguished itself and gained independent legitimacy by promoting interpretive methods that break away from foundational realism and objectivism. Yet editors of major organizational research journals continue to report that a significant amount of qualitative post-positivist research is consistently being submitted and published in the field (see Rynes and Gephart 2004; Skinner *et al.* 2000). They also signal combinations of qualitative and quantitative methods, and draw our attention to potential pitfalls created by using research standards and criteria unreflectively. Although it may appear easier to invest in confidence in our epistemic proximity to reality, as it seems to reduce the need for scrutinizing discrepancies between the world and our mental models, potential limitations and distortions induced by the research process may eventually compromise the value of the research endeavour.

We note that, in the positivist tradition of organization studies, qualitative research is treated as complementary to its quantitative counterpart, in recognition of the fact that the two streams specialize in addressing different types of research questions. Anti-positivist critiques have played an important role in qualitative research, gaining both theoretical and empirical ground in more recent times. For example, a topic such as human needs in organizations, once dominated by positivism and quantitative methods (see the industrial psychology movement directed by the works of Herzberg, McGregor, McClelland and others), have more recently been rejuvenated through qualitative methods driven by interpretive and critical perspectives (Contu *et al.* 2010; Hancock 1999; Townley 1995).

## Social Constructionism

Made explicit in Berger and Luckmann's book *The Social Construction of Reality* (1966), the notion of social constructionism opposes the key ontological and epistemological tenets of positivism and post-positivism by arguing that social reality is not populated by objects but created by subjects through their experiences and relationships. Social context dependent, reality can consist of multiple realities. This is because knowledge is mediated by meaning creation – a process characterized not by discovery but by social interaction and negotiation. There is no knowledge until the data is interpreted – and interpretation is a matter of intersubjective construction, not objective emergence.

The relativism introduced in social research by social constructionist positions, primarily through the privileging of qualitative approaches (Czarniawska 2003; Holstein and Miller 2006), has led to a proliferation of varieties of social constructionism, identified by some theorists as historical-genealogical, discursive, narrative, interpretive, claim-making and contextual (see Holstein and Gubrium 2013), or as symbolic interactionism, phenomenology, ethnomethodology and hermeneutics (Spencer *et al.* 2014). In this context, organizational research has proven a fertile ground for the application of social constructionism. Some theorists have even argued that the whole domain of administrative science, for example, can only produce subjective, socially constructed truth. As the dominant medium of social knowledge is language, organizational researchers necessarily produce language that is ambiguous, metaphorical, performative. As such, language structures and shapes the knowledge it identifies and communicates (Astley 1985). With the 'linguistic turn' as the clearest and strongest feature of anti-positivism (Rorty 1992), the Enlightenment's ideal of transparent and exact scientific language as a neutral vehicle for universal knowledge is dealt a lethal blow.

Most streams of social constructionism theorized by philosophers of the social sciences have had their schools of thought and seminal effects on qualitative organizational research. We will expand on two of the most representative sub-genres of social constructionism here – namely, phenomenology, and historical-genealogical studies – in each case emphasizing research challenges that are specific to the study of organizations.

The *phenomenological approach* has its origins in the philosophy of Edmund Husserl (1931), whose core tenet is that our experiences are the source of all our knowledge of reality. Thus, the phenomena we can and should study are not events as they occur in the world but our experiences of those events. The outcomes of research are not neutral accounts of independent objects of inquiry but explicitly acknowledge characteristics of experiencing subjects (including the researcher), of the ways they make sense of the world through their experiences. For phenomenologist social researchers (see Sanders 1982), there is no social reality other than that created by people's perceptions, moulded by their social context. As Husserl (1931) explains, the centrepiece of phenomenological research is intentional analysis, which focuses on *intentionality* as the relationship between the external source of the subject's experience and its effects on the subject's consciousness. This approach is further developed by Heidegger (1988) into hermeneutics, an interpretive philosophical method coherent with the ontological and epistemological tenets of phenomenology.

Husserl's and Heidegger's ideas have been summarized and applied for the purposes of qualitative research in the social sciences by Moustakas (1994), who describes as specific to phenomenological research those methodologies anchored in ethnography, grounded theory, hermeneutics, empirical phenomenological study and heuristic research. Empirical phenomenological research, in particular, relies on the analysis of subjective accounts of events, provided by individuals who are interviewed and/or observed in a privileged position of experiencing those events. In the study of organizations, Sanders (1982) outlines a phenomenological research model for the discipline of management, stating its main contribution to the field in terms of a significant enhancement of the researcher's ability to delve into the deeper structures of phenomena, in ways that would not be available to the established scientific-normative paradigms. However, as Gill (2014) remarks, very few organizational studies have actually applied Sanders's model. Other sources of reference have been Giorgi (2010) and Smith (2004) in psychology, van Maanen (1989) in education, and Benner and Wrubel (1989) in nursing. Gill (2014) suggests that there are at least two directions available for organizational research to advance knowledge using phenomenological methodologies. The first is to refer to the philosophical work of Merleau-Ponty (1964), by paying attention to the relationship between conscience and body, their role in shaping experiences – and thus making embodied experiences the focus of research into organizational phenomena. The second makes appeal to Schütz's sociology (1967), in particular his idea of intersubjectivity. Schütz's work has already generated important streams in the organizational studies field, such as sensemaking research (see Weick 1995), but its potential for studying various types of organizations as intersubjectively generated social worlds is much wider.

The *historical-genealogical approach*, largely represented by the philosophical and methodological ideas of Michel Foucault (*Discipline and Punish* 1977/1979, *The History of Sexuality* 1980–1990, *The Care of the Self* 1986), has exercised for decades a significant influence on qualitative organizational research. As explained by Miller (2013), Foucault's work guides our understanding of how discursive constructions of human beings into subjects (as subjected objects of power) occur in organizations. The socially created subjects of reality are disciplined into being through techniques of surveillance, understood as hierarchical observation, and normalizing judgement, that is the evaluation of individuals by reference to a given standard of normality. Thus, socially institutionalized power produces both ontologically (i.e., forms and structures of 'reality') and epistemologically (i.e., 'objects and rituals of truth') (Foucault 1979: 194). Like prisons, hospitals, schools and universities, organizations of all kinds apprehend individuals as docile bodies disciplined through discourse. But it is the organization's dominant discourse that defines normality, not autonomous voices of individuals – thus sentencing the silenced alternatives to powerlessness, vulnerability and disadvantage. The extraordinary self-reproducing power of this dominant discourse resides in its ability to incorporate into its self-established structures concern for the needs of individuals and for their agency, transforming them into voluntary instruments of their own alignment with their organizationally defined identity – and, therefore, instruments of the organization's control over them.

Using a Foucauldian lens, Fairhurst and Putnam (2004) identify three ways in which the relationship between discourse and organization can be interpreted – namely, as an 'object', as a condition of 'becoming', or as 'grounded in action' (Fairhurst and Putnam 2004: 10). They advocate for all three perspectives to be engaged in the research design, so that richer data can be secured. This does not require making the three orientations theoretically compatible but holding them in tension with each other, in order to illuminate the relative, contextual nature of the findings produced by each approach. In another application of social constructionism, this time to studies of strategic management practices in organizations, Samra-Fredericks (2008) shows how Foucault's views of subject-constitutive discourse contribute to 'researching the every-day fine grained constitution of phenomena' (Samra-Fredericks 2008: 140). Similar studies of discourse-constructed organizational processes have been undertaken in entrepreneurship (e.g., Downing 2005).

The combination of a radical subjectivism with the analysis of institutionalized systems of definition and control of the subject (Baudrillard 1988), and with a social theorizing of the human condition as ontologically and epistemologically contingent (Arendt 1958; Lyotard 1984; Heller and Feher 1989) has led to *postmodernism*, a paradigm of social and organizational research increasingly recognized as distinct. Postmodern thinking, characterized by an extensive relativization of knowledge foundations (Lyotard 1984) and a cultural turn (Rowlinson and Hassard 2014), has challenged the study of organizations to pursue innovative directions, such as the de-differentiation of phenomena and the blurring of boundaries between agency and structure (Clegg 1990), experimentation with post-bureaucratic organizational forms (Parker 1992), the replacement of explanations based on institutional logics with a deeper understanding of 'signifying acts originating in imagination', such as 'social practices and rituals' (Komporozos-Athanasiou and Fotaki 2015: 334), and emotional empathy and aesthetic appreciation of abuses of power, with a view to increasing individuals' resistance to autonomy-suppressing organizing (Hayes *et al.* 2016).

Both Foucauldian constructionism and postmodernism have been accused of ultra-relativist ontologies and nihilist epistemologies that have led to paralysing despair in ethics, politics and praxis. Understanding agency as de-centred from the individual and, instead, diffuse across complex social relationships is seen as severely impairing individuals' capacity to induce social change (see Michael 1996; Newton 1998). This view of subjectification as implying loss of agency and power to effect social change has, however, been questioned by Caldwell (2007), who in response argues that, to move organizational research forward, 'a synthetic and practice-oriented concept of agency would have to mediate between classical ideas of intentional action, autonomy and choice and ideals of embodied agency as always changing and always open to reinvention' (Caldwell 2007: 789).

To help overcome some of the limitations of current social constructionist research in organizations, Hosking (2011) proposes a new type of constructionism, namely, relational constructionism, which is arguably more appropriate for organizational research. Here the hard, essentialist self-other distinction is replaced by a soft, diffuse relation which assumes that persons and worlds emerge through dialogical processes. The most significant implication of this approach is that it affirms 'dialogical practices as ways of relating that can enable and support multiple local forms of life rather than imposing one dominant rationality on others' (Hosking 2011: 47). Hosking's proposal can be better understood in the context of responses to postmodernism from critical inquiry (in particular Habermasian theory of communicative action, 1984, 1985) and pragmatism (see Rorty 1992).

## *Critical Inquiry*

Following the ontological and epistemological implications of social constructionism away from the (post-)positivist agenda and into a focus on ethical and political implications for qualitative research, we use the umbrella term 'critical inquiry' to label a wide spectrum of philosophical-theoretical perspectives where the values of the researcher are made explicit and called to legitimize the research process itself as a factor of both knowledge production and social change. Central to this movement is the intellectual tradition instigated by the Frankfurt School, with the works of Horkheimer (1947/1974), Adorno (1966/2008), Marcuse (1964), and later Habermas (1971/2015, 1984, 1985) and Honneth (1991). Taking distance from previous aspirations (in both positivism and some forms of social constructionism) for research to be descriptive, explanatory and value neutral, critical theorists insist that values and value judgements are inescapable and that, consequently, research is a political act. Noting that claims of value neutrality at best unwittingly reinforce the status quo and at worst are used to fix the existing social order rather than explore alternatives, critical theorists advocate for social research linked to 'a progressive political agenda', which reveals 'inequalities and injustice' (Baert 2005) and takes normative positions conducive to significant social change.

Critical theory shares with the wider social constructionist and interpretivist movements the notion that social reality, shaped by economic and political forces into social structures, can only be known (inter-)subjectively. It is the emphasis on the role of values, as socially and historically constituted and mediated by power relations, that clearly distinguishes critical research programmes from descriptive social constructionism. Inspired by active care for human suffering, critical inquiry is attracted to contexts of disadvantage and discrimination – seeking to reveal silenced voices, emancipate oppressed social categories, and challenge the existing social order. Influenced by Marxist analysis and critique of ideology, the work of critical theorists illustrates how 'we can discover our real interests and the interests of those who encourage ideological delusion even when they themselves do not realize what their interests are' (Rosenberg 2008: 131). Rosenberg suggests that, while the application of Marxian theory to socio-economic exploitation enacted in employment relations may have failed in practice, its fundamentals of ideology critique can still be fruitfully engaged in examining gender, race or sexual orientation. For us, this explains why and how critical theory has proven to be a fertile ground for the emergence of a range of emancipatory social research perspectives and programmes, such as feminism, critical race theory, queer theory and postcolonialism.

In organizational research, critical theory has informed not only labour process theory, as the expression of a traditional Marxist interest in the political economy of labour–capital relations, but also many other spheres of social discrimination and inequality. As Alvesson and Deetz (2006: 259) point out:

> the central goal of critical theory in organizational studies has been to create societies and work places which are free from domination, where all members have an equal opportunity to contribute to the production of systems that meet human needs and lead to the progressive development of all.

In doing so, critical management research has been established as an increasingly strong area of critique of not only traditional positivist and interpretivist paradigms but also of early Marxism, in particular its monistic materialism (Baert 2005). For example, Wray-Bliss (2002) undertakes a critical analysis of British labour process research and shows how, despite an emancipatory agenda, it appropriates worker subjectivity and, in particular, the voices of women and other marginalized groups.

According to Adler *et al.* (2007) and Thompson (2009), it is the task of critical management studies to revitalize labour process theory through an agenda of changing management practices by continuously questioning the political economy of the employment relationship in capitalism and thus seeking to transform it from within. More broadly, critical management research is defined as an anti-performative endeavour focusing on reflexivity, denaturalization of entrenched social practices and relations, deconstruction of ideology, and humanization of management practices in general (Fournier and Grey 2000). For this purpose, Mir and Mir (2002) apply Wright-Mills's concept of sociological imagination to organizational practice, define the concept of organizational imagination, and argue for an active role of the researcher in questioning and transforming social institutions to benefit the powerless. Inspired by this idea, we can further suggest that the research imagination has developed new sub-paradigms of emancipatory studies of organization. For example, Benschop and Verloo (2016) note that feminist approaches to organization studies (as outlined by Calás and Smircich 1996/2006) have cross-fertilized with postcolonialist perspectives (see Prasad 2003; Westwood and Jack 2007; Westwood *et al.* 2014), leading to postcolonial feminism as a productive direction of organizational research (see Özka-zanç-Pan 2015). Despite its seminal influence, critical management and organization research has also received its own, endogenous, critique. Fletcher and Seldon (2016), for instance, have recently evaluated and classified critical approaches to entrepreneurship, distinguishing between consensus and dissensus approaches – that is, those engaging in critique *for* entrepreneurship as a practice that requires reflection and improvement, and those adopting a critique *of* entrepreneurship as a fundamentally problematic practice.

To summarize, in reaction to (post-)positivism, interpretive paradigms such as social constructionism and critical theory (together with related emancipatory approaches) have earned the status of legitimate research projects in their own right, with philosophical-theoretical foundations just as rigorous as the positivist (Denzin and Lincoln 2011). However, while some organizational theorists (see Prasad and Prasad 2002) take a conciliatory position which does not seek to displace (post-)positivism but achieve comparable legitimacy for interpretivist perspectives, critical theorists have consistently and fundamentally questioned the legitimacy of positivism (Fournier and Grey 2000). This line of thought has also led to interventionist research in organizations (see Baard 2010), which seeks not only to critique the foundations of the social systems and structures observed but also to change them through the research process.

## *Pragmatism*

Originally informed by American pragmatist philosophy, in particular James (1907), Dewey (1929/1984), Peirce (1934) and Rorty (1992), the pragmatist perspective in social research proposes that we should abandon any aspiration to forms of knowledge that transcend contextual (historical and cultural) boundaries and that truth itself is, can and should be defined in terms of successful consequences, depending on the values and interests embedded in the research endeavour as a social project (Baert 2005). Rorty (1992) agrees with Kuhn (1962/2012) that there is no universal and perennial criterion of scientific success and that such criteria are culturally determined through conventions of the scientific community of each era. But pragmatists do not only criticize (post-)positivism for its naturalist and mimetic fixations – that is, its 'spectator theory of knowledge', as Dewey (1929/1984: 19) puts it. They identify deeply seated deterministic tendencies in interpretivist and critical post-Marxist approaches as well. Both the American New Left, represented by Wright-Mills, for example, and the cultural Left of European source, derived from the works of Foucault (1979, 1986) and Derrida (1967) – the former for preserving residues of Marxist historical determinism, and the latter for inducing a new form of determinism through its self-referential discourse – are found unable to construct solutions and achieve political impact (Rorty 1992).

As Habermas (1971/2015) suggests, at the intersection of pragmatism and critical theory, research (and especially social research) is a form of social action reflecting the cognitive interests and needs of a particular society's research community. Hence, there is no essence that can be attributed to scientific inquiry as such, and knowledge develops through non-representational dialogue between historically and culturally situated researchers (Rorty 1992). At first sight, pragmatist epistemology may not appear different from its social constructionist and critical inquiry counterparts in any significant way. However, a clear point of departure from all pre-ceding paradigms is its interpretation of the role of values in the research project. Taking the view that axiological assumptions precede ontological and epistemological propositions leads pragmatists to locate paradigmatic tensions in the *purpose* of research rather than its methods (Baert 2005). Accordingly, pragmatist thinking does not reject (post-)positivist methods if they are justified by acknowledged goals of prediction and control, and it accepts the legitimacy of social constructivist methods when the explicit aim of the research is interpretation. For this reason, pragmatism has proven one of the most tolerant perspectives with regard to multi-paradigm research, especially qualitative social research.

Pragmatism's flexibility is primarily due to its emphasis on questioning the classical dichoto-mies dividing the preceding paradigms, and on seeking to close the gaps. As summarized by Wicks and Freeman (1998), with respect to the objective–subjective distinction, pragmatists acknowledge that there is reality outside the subject but no such thing as objective access to it. Accordingly, facts and interpretations are inseparable, and all scientific discourse is just another narrative, with its own language game rules. But this is not a completely relativistic, anything-goes kind of game – for, if we regard research activity as directed by the need to solve practical problems rather than by a contemplative desire to describe the world to ourselves, then we are able to apply a consistent, intersubjectively determined, criterion for relevant knowledge. Con-textually defined and constrained, this criterion is also liberating, in that it enables us to select from multiple paradigms valuable elements of research method and practice without being side-lined in irrelevant (in pragmatist parlance, useless) disputes.

In the context of organizational research, pragmatism can lead us to seek knowledge that is 'useful in the sense of helping people to better cope with the world or to create better organiza-tions' (Wicks and Freeman 1998: 129). In this endeavour, epistemology and normative ethics of research go hand in hand. Multiple interpretations are not all indifferent or equal but evaluated according to their relevance for given purposes established through social practice. Furthermore, pragmatism helps us distance ourselves more easily from our deeply ingrained conceptual frameworks – thus opening up new opportunities for avoiding undesirable self-fulfilling prophecies in socio-economic behaviour (for example), and for imagining and enacting altern-ative behaviours.

Given that many of the constituent terms of qualitative empirical studies of organization cannot be observed or measured, pragmatism may provide a legitimate and sufficiently effective alternative to truth-testing theories (McKelvey 2009). But, far from being anti-theory, prag-matism emphasizes the need for researchers to strengthen the connection between theory and practice, in a praxeological approach that improves theory by elevating its relevance require-ments. This approach is particularly important for organizational management scholarship, as it provides a more effective balance between flexible choice of multiple research methods and unifying research standards (Wicks and Freeman 1998). Encouraged by the integrating effects of pragmatist applications in organizational research, some organizational theorists explicitly use pragmatism to justify the use of multiple paradigms and thus put an end to 'the paradigm wars'

(Goles and Hirschheim 2000: 260). It has been found that paradigm pluralism has had a beneficial, albeit indirect, effect on the advancement of qualitative organizational research – for, in increasing the variety of research methods applied, it has enriched the potential for novel, valuable organization and management ideas to emerge (Goles and Hirschheim 2000).

However, philosophical pragmatism has also had its fair share of criticism, on at least two accounts. First, due to its reliance on practical usefulness in epistemic evaluations, it has been accused of sliding into instrumentalist fallacies (Baert 2005), whereby emphasis on usefulness can lead to valuing means over ends, and to perverse effects such as having the intrinsic values of humanism succumb to technocratic priorities. We should also note that narrower views of what constitutes the practically relevant for a particular research community at a particular point in time may blind or bias thinkers against ideas ahead of their time. As history of humankind shows, great ideas may often prove to be out of sync with their time, so to speak, and only a disinterested, contemplative curiosity may be able to maintain a record of them, making it possible for their usefulness to be discovered much later, in unpredictable ways.

Second, pragmatism has been appraised by some philosophers as lacking in political sensitivity. While acknowledging that particular values and interests shape the research programme of a particular community, it does not appear to be further refined to identify and question whose values and interests are actually being served – as a community experiencing a homogeneous or harmonious unity in this respect is difficult to imagine and even more difficult to obtain in practice. Due to an all-inclusiveness that encourages equality while glossing over power asymmetries that are pervasive in social settings (Hogan 2016), pragmatist research has been found wanting in the very humanism it professes, and thus yielding consequences that support the status quo. Noted in philosophy and social theory, these difficulties remain unresolved for organizational and management research as well – where they are particularly important, given the lack of humanism and the hegemonic influence of social-conservative ideologies still manifest in the study of organizations.

## A Dilemma: Paradigmatic Thinking, or First-order Philosophical Reflection?

Having explored several influential paradigms in qualitative organizational research, it is time we question the very idea of relying on already theorized paradigms as a substitute for independent philosophical reflection on our own research practice. Perhaps the qualitative organizational researcher, true to the fundamental role of reflexivity in their work, should beware of the stereotyping and reductionism that may result from adopting paradigmatic sets of philosophical assumptions based on historical-authoritative rather than self-reflective criteria. While some logical limitations can be identified in particular contexts, for most combinatorial associations or exclusions a significant exception can be expected. For example, it has often been assumed that a (post-)positivist ontology can hardly provide logical support for a social constructionist epistemology. However, precisely in organizational research, Borges *et al.* (2016) show that the two assumptions can function productively together, if understood in dialectical relation.

A return to individual philosophical premises and to personalized, independently achieved foundational coherence in one's qualitative research programme is even more important in organization studies, where not only single paradigms but entire paradigm taxonomies have routinely been adopted as proxies for philosophical-theoretical documentation and justification of empirical studies. One such example is Burrell and Morgan's (1979) general classification of paradigms of social research, along two axes (namely, objectivity–subjectivity; and regulation–radical change), into four categories: functionalism, interpretive paradigm, radical humanism and radical structuralism. Out of the two axes, only one (objective versus subjective) pertains to philosophy as such – and it conflates ontology and epistemology without much explanation.

The other (regulation versus radical change) belongs to the narrower, applied domain of social order theory. A nuanced evaluation of the benefits and limits of Burrell and Morgan's taxonomy is offered by Scherer and Patzer (2008).

One of the most widely applied paradigm classifications in organizational research, often used in field mapping exercises (see, for example, Grant and Perren 2002, or Goles and Hirschheim 2000), Burrell and Morgan's (1979) taxonomy has produced innovative contributions to management and organization theory in the context of encouraging multi-paradigm supported theory building and empirical research (see Gioia and Pitre 1990; Hassard 1991). However, it has also led to reductionist thinking, particularly in empirical studies. To address this problem, Deetz (1996) proposes that we should seek a deeper understanding of normative, interpretive, critical and dialogical studies in terms of the nature of their discourse.

We note that, when paradigm classifications are applied uncritically, no further opportunity is taken to deepen reflection on the diversity and nuances of the philosophical assumptions involved. In fact, what are discussed are not individual philosophical assumptions but broad paradigmatic labels that facilitate grouping theories and (rather forcibly) articulating them with particular sets of generalizations.

To overcome this difficulty, when exploring philosophical approaches relevant to specific directions and subfields, some organizational researchers have referred back to the basics of philosophical assumptions rather than uncritically adopting popular paradigm classifications. A good example of this approach is Poole *et al.*'s (2000) own typology for research approaches in organizational change. Also, in an effort to address themselves in a relevant way to management practitioner-researchers, Gill and Johnson (2010) start from individual philosophical assumptions to illustrate the building blocks of the research process and the implications of adopting different assumptions. In this manner, they outline the discrete philosophical foundations of grounded theory, methodological monism, nomothetic and ideographic methods, and key philosophical debates and disputes in interpretive analysis. Similarly, a good discussion of philosophical (especially praxeological) premises in qualitative organizational leadership research is provided by Klenke (2014).

## The Future of Qualitative Organizational Research: Challenges and Opportunities

Qualitative organizational research shares with other social science fields several concerns, such as: balancing the need to maintain explanatory power with sensitivity to an increasing diversity and complexity of social phenomena; articulating recognizable standards for qualitative research (despite the open plurality of methodological possibilities); and establishing areas of commensurability across different qualitative approaches (Spencer *et al.* 2014). Most of these challenges are related to ontological and epistemological assumptions. But there are also axiological (mainly, ethical) and praxeological challenges that are specific to the study of organizations, at least when considering its past and present. Therefore, a key question that must be raised at this point is: what should be the *purpose* of qualitative organizational research as *purposeful* human action? Or, to put it in political terms, how should qualitative organizational research be legitimized as social (and not just intellectual) practice?

Given the long history of instrumentalist research in the organization and management fields, which has led to uncritical performativity (Fournier and Grey 2000; Wickert and Schaefer 2015), emphasis on the values of *humanism* and *responsibility* as intrinsic to any qualitative inquiry becomes paramount. In embracing humanism, however, qualitative organizational research should be responsive to less dominant voices and contribute to their empowerment. As a whole field, it should take on, for instance, the challenge of postcolonial critique and be more open to non-Western philosophical assumptions and research methodologies. An interesting example of such an endeavour is the application of Eastern philosophy to research in strategy and management undertaken by Li (2012), who discusses Eastern philosophy by taking an alternative approach to the very basic understanding of what constitutes a philosophical assumption. This approach, in turn, leads to innovative insights into how qualitative research could be conducted differently in the fields of strategy and management.

In conclusion, qualitative organizational researchers need to reflect more deeply on the ways in which they use philosophy and theory to formulate and support their empirical research questions – so that they seek to contribute to knowledge more meaningfully, through problematization and challenging foundational assumptions rather than through literature gap spotting practices that reinforce established theoretical views (Alvesson and Sandberg 2011). In advancing research open to humanist priorities and self-knowledge, qualitative organization and management scholarship should aspire to the epistemic standards and ethical values of a political philosophy of human action.

# References

Adler, P.S., Forbes, L.C. and Willmott, H. (2007) '3 critical management studies', *The Academy of Management Annals*, 1(1): 119–179.

Adorno, T.W. (1966/2008) *Lectures on Negative Dialectics*, trans. R. Livingstone, Cambridge: Polity Press.

Alexandre, V. and Gasparski, W.W. (eds) (2000) *The Roots of Praxiology: French Action Theory from Bourdeau and Espinas to Present Days*, vol. 7, New Brunswick NJ and London: Transaction.

Alvesson, M. and Deetz, S. (2006) 'Critical theory and postmodernism approaches to organizational studies', in S.R. Clegg, C. Hardy, T.B. Lawrence and W.R. Nord (eds) *The Sage Handbook of Organization Studies*, 2nd edn, London: Sage, pp. 255–283.

Alvesson, M. and Sandberg, J. (2011) 'Generating research questions through problematization', *Academy of Management Review*, 36(2): 247–271.

Arendt, H. (1958) *The Human Condition*, Chicago IL: University of Chicago Press.

Argyris, C. (1964) *Integrating the Individual and the Organization*, New York: John Wiley.

Argyris, C. (1993) *Knowledge of Action*, San Francisco CA: Jossey-Bass.

Astley, W.G. (1985) 'Administrative science as socially constructed truth', *Administrative Science Quarterly*, 30(4): 497–513.

Baard, V. (2010) 'A critical review of interventionist research', *Qualitative Research in Accounting and Management*, 7(1): 13–45.

Baert, P. (2005) *Philosophy of the Social Sciences: Towards Pragmatism*, Cambridge: Polity Press.

Baudrillard, J. (1988) *Selected Writings*, ed. M. Poster, Stanford CA: Stanford University Press.

Benner, P. and Wrubel, J. (1989) *The Primacy of Caring: Stress and Coping in Health and Illness*, Menlo Park CA: Addison-Wesley.

Benschop, Y. and Verloo, M. (2016) 'Feminist organization theories: islands of treasure', in R. Mir, H. Willmott and M. Greenwood (eds) *The Routledge Companion to Philosophy in Organization Studies*, London: Routledge, pp. 100–112.

Bergson, H. (1946) *The Creative Mind: An Introduction to Metaphysics*, trans. M.L. Andison, New York: Citadel.

Borges, A.F., de Brito, M.J., Brito, V.D.G.P. and Enoque, A.G. (2016) 'Contributions to a dialogue between critical realism and social constructionism in organization studies', *Cadernos EBAPE*, 14(2): 391–405.

Bourdieu, P. (1977) *Outline of a Theory of Practice*, Cambridge: Cambridge University Press.

Bourdieu, P. (1990) *The Logic of Practice*, Cambridge: Polity Press.

Burrell, G. and Morgan, G. (1979) *Social Paradigms and Organizational Analysis: Elements of the Sociology of Corporate Life*, London: Heinemann Educational.

Calás, M. and Smircich, L. (1996/2006) 'From the "woman's point of view": feminist approaches to organization studies', in S. Clegg, C. Hardy and W. Nord (eds), *Handbook of Organization Studies*, London: Sage, pp. 218–257.

Caldwell, R. (2007) 'Agency and change: re-evaluating Foucault's legacy', *Organization*, 14(6): 769–791.

Carlile, P.R., Nicolini, D., Langley, A. and Tsoukas, H. (eds) (2013) *How Matter Matters: Objects, Artifacts, and Materiality in Organization Studies*, Oxford: Oxford University Press.

Clegg, S. (1990) *Modern Organizations: Organization Studies in the Postmodern World*, London: Sage.

Contu, A., Driver, M. and Jones, C. (2010) 'Editorial: Jacques Lacan with organization studies', *Organization*, 17(3): 307–315.

Creswell, J.W. (2014) *Qualitative, Quantitative, and Mixed Methods Approaches*, 4th edn, London: Sage.

Crotty, M. (1998) *The Foundations of Social Research: Meaning and Perspective in the Research Process*, St. Leonards, Australia: Allen and Unwin, pp. 1–17.

Czarniawska, B. (2003) 'Social constructionism and organization studies', in R.I. Westwood and S. Clegg (eds) *Debating Organization: Point-counterpoint in Organization Studies*, Malden MA: Blackwell Publishing, pp. 128–139.

Deetz, S. (1996) 'Crossroads-describing differences in approaches to organization science: rethinking Burrell and Morgan and their legacy', *Organization Science*, 7(2): 191–207.

Dehler, G.E. and Welsh, M.A. (2016) 'Galumphing and critical management studies', in C. Grey, I. Huault, V. Perret and L. Taskin (eds) *Critical Management Studies: Global Voices, Local Accents*, London: Routledge, pp. 206–226.

Delanty, G. (2005) *Social Science: Philosophical and Methodological Foundations*, 2nd edn, New York: Open University Press.

Delbridge, R. (2014) 'Promising futures: CMS, post disciplinarity, and the new public social science', *Journal of Management Studies*, 51(1): 95–117.

Denzin, N.K. and Lincoln, Y.S. (1998) *The Landscape of Qualitative Research*, vol. 1, London: Sage.

Denzin, N.K. and Lincoln, Y.S. (2011) *The Sage Handbook of Qualitative Research*, London: Sage.

Derrida, J. (1967) *De la grammatologie*, Paris: Minuit.

Dewey, J. (1984) *The Quest for Certainty* [1929], in *The Later Works, 1925–1953*, Carbondale IL: Southern Illinois University Press.

Dierksmeier, C. (2016) *Reframing Economic Ethics: The Philosophical Foundations of Humanistic Management*, Dordrecht: Springer.

Downing, S. (2005) 'The social construction of entrepreneurship: narrative and dramatic processes in the coproduction of organizations and identities', *Entrepreneurship Theory and Practice*, 29(2): 185–204.

Everett, J. (2002) 'Organizational research and the praxeology of Pierre Bourdieu', *Organizational Research Methods*, 5(1): 56–80.

Fairhurst, G.T. and Putnam, L. (2004) 'Organizations as discursive constructions', *Communication Theory*, 14(1): 5–26.

Fleming, P. and Banerjee, S.B. (2016) 'When performativity fails: implications for critical management studies', *Human Relations*, 69(2): 257–276.

Fletcher, D. and Seldon, P. (2016) 'A critical review of critical perspectives in entrepreneurship research', in H. Landstrom, A. Parhankangas, A. Fayolle and P. Riot (eds) *Challenging Entrepreneurship Research*, London: Routledge, pp. 131–154.

Foucault, M. (1979) *Discipline and Punish: The Birth of the Prison*, trans. A. Sheridan, New York: Vintage Books.

Foucault, M. (1984) *The History of Sexuality: An Introduction*, trans. R. Hurley, London: Penguin Books.

Foucault, M. (1986) *The Care of the Self: The History of Sexuality*, vol. 3, New York: Pantheon.

Fournier, V. and Grey, C. (2000) 'At the critical moment: conditions and prospects for critical management studies', *Human Relations*, 53(1): 7–32.

Geertz, C. (1989) 'Anti anti-relativism', in M. Krausz (ed.) *Relativism: Interpretation and Confrontation*, Notre Dame IN: Notre Dame University Press, pp. 51–72.

Gettier, E.L. (1963) 'Is justified true belief knowledge?', *Analysis*, 23(6): 121–123.

Gill, J. and Johnson, P. (2010) 'The role of theory in management research', in J. Gill and P. Johnson (eds) *Research Methods for Managers*, 4th edn, Los Angeles CA: Sage, pp. 38–68.

Gill, M.J. (2014) 'The possibilities of phenomenology for organizational research', *Organizational Research Methods*, 17(2): 118–137.

Gioia, D. and Pitre, E. (1990) 'Multiparadigm perspectives on theory building', *Academy of Management Review*, 15(4): 584–602.

Giorgi, A. (2010) 'Phenomenology and the practice of science', *Existential Analysis*, 21(1): 3–22.

Goles, T. and Hirschheim, R. (2000) 'The paradigm is dead, the paradigm is dead … long live the paradigm: the legacy of Burrell and Morgan', *Omega*, 28(3): 249–268.

Grant, P. and Perren, L. (2002) 'Small business and entrepreneurial research meta-theories, paradigms and prejudices', *International Small Business Journal*, 20(2): 185–211.

Guba, E. and Lincoln, Y.S. (1994) 'Competing paradigms in qualitative research', in N.K. Denzin and Y.S. Lincoln (eds) *Handbook of Qualitative Research*, Thousand Oaks CA: Sage, pp. 105–117.

Habermas, J. (1971/2015) *Knowledge and Human Interests*, New York: John Wiley and Sons.

Habermas, J. (1984) *The Theory of Communicative Action*, vol. 1, Boston MA: Beacon Press.

Habermas, J. (1985) *The Theory of Communicative Action*, vol. 2, Boston MA: Beacon Press.

Hancock, J. (1999) 'Baudrillard and the metaphysics of motivation: a reappraisal of corporate culturalism in the light of the work and ideas of Jean Baudrillard', *Journal of Management Studies*, 36(2): 155–175.

Hassard, J. (1991) 'Multiple paradigms and organizational analysis: a case study', *Organization Studies*, 12(2): 275–299.

Hayes, L., Hopkinson, C. and Taylor, A.G. (2016) 'Problematising qualitative research in organisations: three voices, three subjectivities, three struggles', *Qualitative Research in Organizations and Management: An International Journal*, 11(2): 127–146.

Heidegger, M. (1988) *The Basic Problems of Phenomenology*, trans. A. Hofstadter, Bloomington IN: Indiana University Press.

Heller, A. and Feher, F. (1989) *The Postmodern Political Condition*, Cambridge: Polity Press.

Hernes, T. and Maitlis, S. (2010) *Process, Sensemaking, and Organizing*, vol. 1, Oxford: Oxford University Press.

Herzberg, F., Mausner, B. and Snyderman, B. (1959) *The Motivation to Work*, New York: John Wiley.

Hogan, B. (2016) 'Pragmatism, power, and the situation of democracy', *Journal of Speculative Philosophy*, 30(1): 64–74.

Holstein, J.A. and Gubrium, J.F. (eds) (2013) *Handbook of Constructionist Research*, 2nd edn, New York and London: Guilford Press.

Holstein, J.A. and Miller, G. (eds) (2006) *Reconsidering Social Constructionism: Debates in Social Problems Theory*, New Brunswick NJ: Transaction.

Honneth, A. (1991) *The Critique of Power: Reflective Stages in a Critical Social Theory*, trans. K. Baynes, Cambridge MA: MIT Press.

Horkheimer, M. (1974) *Eclipse of Reason*, New York: Continuum.

Hosking, D.M. (2011) 'Telling tales of relations: appreciating relational constructionism', *Organization Studies*, 32(1): 47–65.

Husserl, E. (1931) *Ideas: General Introduction to Pure Phenomenology*, trans. W.R.B. Gibson, New York: Macmillan.

James, W. (1907) *Pragmatism: A New Name for Some Old Ways of Thinking*, New York: Longmans.

Johnson, P. and Cassell, C. (2001) 'Epistemology and work psychology: new agendas', *Journal of Occupational and Organizational Psychology*, 74(2): 125–143.

Klenke, K. (2014) 'Sculpting the contours of the qualitative landscape of leadership research', in D. Day (ed.) *The Oxford Handbook of Leadership and Organizations*, Oxford: Oxford University Press, pp. 118–145.

Klikauer, T. (2014) *Seven Moralities of Human Resource Management*, London: Palgrave Macmillan.

Komporozos-Athanasiou, A. and Fotaki, M. (2015) 'A theory of imagination for organization studies using the work of Cornelius Castoriadis', *Organization Studies*, 36(3): 321–342.

Kostera, M. (2012) *Organizations and Archetypes*, Cheltenham, UK: Edward Elgar.

Kotarbinski, T. (1965) *Praxiology*, New York: Pergamon Press.

Kuhn, T.S. (1962/2012) *The Structure of Scientific Revolutions*, Chicago IL: University of Chicago Press.

Langley, A., Smallman, C., Tsoukas, H. and Van de Ven, A.H. (2013) 'Process studies of change in organization and management: unveiling temporality, activity, and flow', *Academy of Management Journal*, 56(1): 1–13.

Leavy, P. (2014) 'Introduction', in P. Leavy (ed.) *The Oxford Handbook of Qualitative Research*, Oxford: Oxford University Press, pp. 1–13.

Li, P.P. (2012) 'Toward research-practice balancing in management: the yin-yang method for open-ended and open-minded research', in C.L. Wang, D.J. Ketchen and D.D. Bergh (eds) *Research Methodology in Strategy and Management*, vol. 8, Bingley: Emerald, pp. 91–141.

Lindley, D. (2008) *Uncertainty: Einstein, Heisenberg, Bohr, and the Struggle for the Soul of Science*, New York: Anchor Books.

Lyotard, J.F. (1984) *The Postmodern Condition: A Report on Knowledge*, vol. 10, Minneapolis MN: University of Minnesota Press.

McClelland, D.C. (1975) *Power: The Inner Experience*, Oxford: Irvington Press.

McGregor, D. (1960) *The Human Side of Enterprise*, New York: McGraw-Hill.

McKelvey, B. (2009) 'From fields to science: can organization studies make the transition?', in R.I. Westwood and S. Clegg (eds) *Debating Organization: Point-counterpoint in Organization Studies*, Malden: Blackwell Publishing, pp. 47–72.

McKinlay, A., Carter, C. and Pezet, E. (2012) 'Governmentality, power and organization', *Management and Organizational History*, 7(1): 3–15.

Marcuse, H. (1964) *One Dimensional Man*, London: Routledge and Kegan Paul.

Melé, D. (2016) 'Understanding humanistic management', *Humanistic Management Journal*, DOI 10.1007/s41463-016-0011-5.

Merleau-Ponty, M. (1964) *The Primacy of Perception*, ed. James Edie, Evanston IL: Northwestern University Press.

Michael, M. (1996) *Constructing Identities: The Social, the Nonhuman and Change*, Thousand Oaks CA: Sage.

Miller, L. (2013) 'Foucauldian constructionism', in J.A. Holstein and J.F. Gubrium (eds) *Handbook of Constructionist Research*, 2nd edn, New York and London: Guilford Press, pp. 251–274.

Mir, R. and Mir, A. (2002) 'The organizational imagination: from paradigm wars to praxis', *Organizational Research Methods*, 5(1): 105–125.

Morgan, G. (1997) *Images of Organization*, Thousand Oaks CA: Sage.

Morgan, G. and Smircich, L. (1980) 'The case for qualitative research', *Academy of Management Review*, 5(4): 491–500.

Moustakas, C. (1994) *Phenomenological Research Methods*, Thousand Oaks CA: Sage.

Newton, T.J. (1998) 'Theorizing subjectivity in organizations: the failure of Foucauldian Studies?', *Organization Studies*, 19(3): 415–447.

Ormston, R., Spencer, L., Barnard, M. and Snape, D. (2013) 'The foundations of qualitative research', in J. Ritchie, J. Lewis, C. McNaughton Nichols and R. Ormston, *Qualitative Research Practice: A Guide for Social Science Students and Researchers*, London: Sage, pp. 1–26.

Özkazanç-Pan, B. (2015) 'Postcolonial feminist contributions to cross-cultural management', in N. Holden, S. Michailova and S. Tietze (eds) *The Routledge Companion to Cross-Cultural Management*, London: Routledge, pp. 371–379.

Parker, M. (1992) 'Post-modern organizations or postmodern organization theory?', *Organization Studies*, 13(1): 1–17.

Peirce, C.S. (1934) 'Pragmatism and pragmaticism', in *Collected Papers*, vol. 5, ed. C. Hartshorne and P. Weiss, Cambridge MA: Harvard University Press.

Poole, M.S., Van de Ven, A.H., Dooley, K. and Holmes, M.E. (2000) *Organizational Change and Innovation Processes: Theory and Methods for Research*, New York: Oxford University Press.

Popper, K. (2005) *The Logic of Scientific Discovery*, London: Routledge.

Powell, T.C. (2001) 'Fallibilism and organizational research: the third epistemology', *Journal of Management Research*, 1(4): 201–219.

Prasad, A. (2003) *Postcolonial Theory and Organizational Analysis: A Critical Engagement*, New York: Palgrave Macmillan.

Prasad, A. and Prasad, P. (2002) 'The coming of age of interpretive organizational research', *Organizational Research Methods*, 5(1): 4–11.

Rescher, N. (1996) *Process Metaphysics: An Introduction to Process Philosophy*, Albany NY: State University of New York Press.

Rorty, R. (ed.) (1992) *The Linguistic Turn: Essays in Philosophical Method*, Chicago IL: University of Chicago Press.

Rosenberg, A. (2008) *Philosophy of Social Science*, 3rd edn, Boulder CO: Westview.

Rowlinson, M. and Hassard, J. (2014) 'History and the cultural turn in organization studies', in M. Bucheli and R.D. Wadwhani (eds) *Organizations in Time: History, Theory, Methods*, Oxford: Oxford University Press, pp. 147–168.

Rynes, S. and Gephart Jr, R.P. (2004) 'From the editors: qualitative research and the "Academy of Management Journal"', *Academy of Management Journal*, 47(4): 454–462.

Samra-Fredericks, D. (2008) 'Social constructionism in management and organization studies', in J.A. Holstein and J.F. Gubrium (eds) *Handbook of Constructionist Research*, 2nd edn, New York and London: Guilford Press, pp. 129–152.

Sanders, P. (1982) 'Phenomenology: a new way of viewing organizational research', *Academy of Management Review*, 7(3): 353–360.

Schaefer, S.M. and Wickert, C. (2016) 'On the potential of progressive performativity: definitional purity, re-engagement and empirical points of departure', *Human Relations*, 69(2): 215–224.

Scherer, A.G. and Patzer, M. (2008) 'Paradigms', in S. Clegg and J.R. Bailey (eds) *International Encyclopedia of Organization Studies*, Thousand Oaks CA: Sage, pp. 1218–1222.

Schultz, M. (ed.) (2012) *Constructing Identity in and around Organizations*, Oxford: Oxford University Press.

Schütz, A. (1967) *The Phenomenology of the Social World*, Evanston IL: Northwestern University Press.

Skinner, D., Tagg, C. and Holloway, J. (2000) 'Managers and research: the pros and cons of qualitative approaches', *Management Learning*, 31(2): 163–179.

Smith, J.A. (2004) 'Reflecting on the development of interpretative phenomenological analysis and its contribution to qualitative research in psychology', *Qualitative Research in Psychology*, 1(1): 39–54.

Spencer, R., Pryce, J.M. and Walsh, J. (2014) 'Philosophical approaches to qualitative research', in P. Leavy (ed.) *The Oxford Handbook of Qualitative Research*, Oxford: Oxford University Press, pp. 81–98.

Thompson, P. (2009) 'Labour process theory and critical management studies', in M. Alvesson, T. Bridgman and H. Willmott (eds), *The Oxford Handbook of Critical Management Studies*, Oxford: Oxford University Press, pp. 100–122.

Townley, B. (1995) '"Know thyself": self-awareness, self-formation and managing', *Organization*, 2(2): 271–289.

Trigg, R. (2001) *Understanding Social Science*, 2nd edn, Oxford: Blackwell.

Van Maanen, M. (1989) 'Pedagogical text as method: phenomenological research as writing', *Saybrook Review*, 7(2): 23–45.

Weick, K.E. (1995) *Sensemaking in Organizations*, Thousand Oaks CA: Sage.

Westwood, R.I. and Jack, G. (2007) 'Manifesto for a postcolonial international business and management studies: a provocation', *Critical Perspectives on International Business*, 3(3): 246–265.

Westwood, R., Jack, G., Khan, F. and Frenkel, M. (eds) (2014) *Core-Periphery Relations and Organization Studies*, London: Palgrave Macmillan.

Whitehead, A.N. (1967) *The Aims of Education and Other Essays*, New York: Simon & Schuster.

Wickert, C. and Schaefer, S.M. (2015) 'Towards a progressive understanding of performativity in critical management studies', *Human Relations*, 68(1): 107–130.

Wicks, A.C. and Freeman, R.E. (1998) 'Organization studies and the new pragmatism: positivism, anti-positivism, and the search for ethics', *Organization Science*, 9(2): 123–140.

Wray-Bliss, E. (2002) 'Interpretation-appropriation: (making) an example of labor process theory', *Organizational Research Methods*, 5(1): 81–104.

# 3

# CRITICAL APPROACHES TO QUALITATIVE RESEARCH

*Thomas Greckhamer*

The major assumptions and basic sets of beliefs about the world held by researchers shapes the social and organizational research they conduct (Burrell and Morgan, 1979; Guba, 1990; Morgan and Smircich, 1980). Accordingly, our understanding of organizations is enriched by applying various theoretical lenses that build on different assumptions in order to uncover different dimensions of organizational life and of organizations' impact on their members as well as their environment (Morgan, 1986). Critical approaches are a vital aspect of this variety of theoretical lenses because they focus on a key dimension of organizations that has been uncritically accepted by mainstream organization studies: that over the course of human history organizations have served as instruments of social domination and that they are shaped by "asymmetrical power relations that result in the majority working in the interests of the few" (Morgan, 1986: 275). From a critical theory perspective, the various functional organization theories that paired with positivist methodologies, constitute mainstream organization studies, have uncritically accepted and even obscured this fundamental divergence of interests that shapes organizations and that results from and reproduces the structure of contemporary capitalism; this uncritical acceptance of the status quo has resulted in mainstream theories' failure to theorize and address fundamental social problems emanating from it (Adler, 2009; Adler and Jermier, 2005; Benson, 1977).

Critical approaches to organization studies, also referred to as radical organization theory or critical management studies, analyze organizational phenomena through the lenses of conflict, power, and domination in order to unveil how organizations are shaped by and intertwined with the structure of contemporary capitalism (Adler et al., 2007; Alvesson, 1985; Alvesson and Deetz, 2000; Burrell, 1979; Prasad, 2005). Thereby, they complement mainstream organization studies by challenging basic assumptions underlying organization theories as well as the ends served by theories and empirical research, and by offering alternative theories built on exposing and challenging asymmetries of power underlying the nature of organizational life through research that openly communicates its values and ideological commitments to further the interests of stakeholders other than the managerial and owner classes (Alvesson, 1985; Burrell, 1979; Mir and Mir, 2002; Smircich and Calás, 1995).

While some of the aims of critical research may be pursued either by qualitative or by quantitative approaches, the dominance of qualitative critical research stems from the possibilities of integrating assumptions and insights from critical theory into the research process and from the incompatibility of key assumptions of critical theory with assumptions of positivism infused into quantitative research (Alvesson and Ashcraft, 2009). In this chapter, I outline how qualitative approaches to organization studies inspired by critical theory enrich our understanding of organizations. To do so, I begin by describing the defining characteristics of critical inquiry; I then illustrate the potential of critical approaches to provide vital alternative and complementary theoretical insights to mainstream theories in different subfields of organization studies, before highlighting a selection of valuable critical approaches for organization studies.

## The Foundations of Critical Inquiry

Critical inquiry, one of the key paradigms currently operating in the social sciences (Guba and Lincoln, 1994; Lincoln and Guba, 2000), denotes a distinct way of analyzing social relations. In a narrow sense, the term critical theory is usually associated with the Frankfurt School of Social Theory,[1] which in turn has been heavily influenced by the work of Karl Marx and has loosely been defined as a school of Western Marxism (Held, 1980; Therborn, 1970). More broadly, the term critical social theory refers to a diverse but interrelated range of traditions focused on cultural critique of contemporary capitalist societies that have mingled the seminal thought of the Frankfurt School with related authors and lines of thought, including poststructuralism[2] (Agger, 1991, 1998).

The different strands of critical theory offer counterpoints to dominant functionalist positivist theories of social science generally and of organizations specifically. They share a commitment to critiquing and transforming dominant views of how organizations should be managed and studied as well as an overarching key set of tenets that informs these efforts to critique and transform (Agger, 1991, 1998; Alvesson, 1985; Burrell, 1979; Horkheimer, 1937; Jermier, 1998; Scherer, 2009). First, they start from the premise that capitalist societies are shaped by a concentration of power in the hands of relatively small elites and large corporations that benefit from a systematic exploitation of a disenfranchised majority of society as well as of the natural environment. Second, they assume that domination is structural and that people's lives are continuously shaped by larger social institutions, hence social scientists must analyze any social phenomenon in a wider social context. Third, they hold that realities and structures of oppression and domination are socially constructed and that they become seemingly unchangeable by creating a false consciousness that obscures the socially constructed nature of reality through ideology, hegemony, and/or one-dimensional thinking. Fourth, they assert that mainstream positivist functionalist social science research contributes to developing and sustaining this false consciousness by accepting, portraying, and legitimizing the status quo as both inevitable and rational. Fifth, while mainstream theory and research is portrayed as value neutral and as oblivious to its own investment in the status quo, critical theory openly declares its ideological commitments to disrupt social reproduction and to elucidate societies' systems of oppression, exploitation, and domination that are obscured by ideology. Sixth, the objective of critical inquiry is to change fundamental oppressive structures in society and to emancipate all people from oppression by producing knowledge that can provide the basis for political and social action aimed at transforming the social world in line with its ideological commitments; to accomplish this objective, researchers should not take any aspects of social and organizational realities for granted as neutral expressions of their proper functioning.

The pursuit of emancipatory knowledge of critical inquiry implies three fundamental and interrelated elements (Fournier and Grey, 2000): a focus on reflexivity and on the transparency of ideological commitments; a focus on disrupting false consciousness by denaturalizing aspects of social reality; and a focus on disrupting social reproduction through a stance of progressive performativity.

## *Reflexivity and Openly Ideological Science*

Starting from the premise that any social theory or research is undergirded and shaped by political-ideological interests, from its very inception critical theory has emphasized the need for reflexivity as a foundational element (Horkheimer, 1937). Critical approaches assume that reflexivity is crucial because researchers' subjectivity and interests are always imprinted on the knowledge they produce, independent of whether this was the researchers' intention (Harding, 1987, 2004). Because of this imprinting, from the vantage point of critical theory research is a social practice that needs to be accountable (Steffy and Grimes, 1986) because all theories, systems of knowledge, and facts are embedded in and reflect particular and relativistic world-views. Reflexivity is needed to give account of and to understand how knowledge is influenced by researchers' subjective experiences and their positions within particular socio-historical, economic, moral, and political systems. This includes reflexivity of individual and collective or even civilizational assumptions of how researchers think or what they consider to be "the world" or "reality" through established categories or concepts (Scheurich and Young, 1997). It further includes exploring how science and research agendas are controlled by disciplines and public institutions (Harding, 2004).

The seeming avoidance of values, which is a defining characteristic of traditional positivist theories, is considered problematic because it is "the strongest value commitment of all" (Agger, 1991: 111) and because claims of value neutrality impair critical examinations of the shaping influence of values and interests, thus making theories and frameworks susceptible to being shaped by and complicit with economic and political projects of dominant groups (Harding, 2004). For critical theory, then, knowledge that acknowledges its underlying value commitments and partiality is both less distorted and its distortions are more visible and thereby revisable compared to knowledge that discounts its partiality (Kincheloe and McLaren, 2000). Attuning researchers to the assumptions that underlie their empirical research through reflexivity is the foundation to challenge knowledge produced by traditional perspectives by exposing their exclusions and dominant assumptions and to pursue research with emancipatory objectives. It also is considered to be critical theory's key methodological contribution to the social sciences (Agger, 1991) that in recent years has gained increasing attention also in organization studies (e.g., Alvesson et al., 2008; Johnson and Duberley, 2003).

## *Denaturalization and False Consciousness*

The second foundational element of critical theory is rooted in the observation that different forms of oppression can be sustained when individuals develop a so-called false consciousness that leads them to accept socially constructed realities as seemingly "unchangeable," "objective," or "naturalized." In order to reach its emancipatory interest to promote democratic transformation of social structures to the benefit of society broadly as opposed to the benefit of a small elite, critical theory emphasizes the importance of relieving individuals of this false consciousness by "denaturalizing" social reality (Agger, 1998; Alvesson, 1985; Jermier, 1985).

Denaturalization involves reverting processes of social construction also referred to as alienation and reification. Alienation is the "process by which man forgets that the world he lives in has been produced by himself" (Berger and Pullberg, 1965: 200). This in turn enables the reification or naturalization[3] of key aspects of socially constructed realities, including prevalent forms and structures of social domination; this means they become apprehended "as if they were something else than human products – such as facts of nature, results of cosmic laws, or manifestations of divine will" (Berger and Luckmann, 1967: 89). To revert processes of alienation and reification, critical theory focuses on elucidating how characteristics of these realities become naturalized as fixed and external objects by concealing their systematic (i.e., ideological) distortions and the process of their construction (Deetz, 1992). Moreover, critical theory's ideological critique recognizes that just as "objective social reality exists not by chance, but as the product of human action, so it is not transformed by chance" (Freire, 2000: 51). Accordingly, it aims to produce emancipatory knowledge to inform political and social action for human liberation and social justice (Alvesson, 1985; Freire, 2000; Held, 1980) through conscientization, i.e., a process that enables people to have a deeper awareness of the socio-cultural reality that shapes their lives as a precondition for developing the capacity to transform this reality (Freire, 1970).

## *Subverting Social Reproduction through Progressive Performativity*

Critical theory's third foundational element is its declared aim to subvert social reproduction (Horkheimer, 1937; Therborn, 1970). According to critical theory, this contrasts the non-critical traditional theoretical frameworks' (and their positivist approaches') "performative intent," i.e., that they have effectively become subservient to capitalist ideology and that therefore their purpose (even if inadvertently) is to serve the interests of dominant groups by subordinating knowledge and truth to efficiency (Agger, 1991; Alvesson, 1985; Alvesson and Deetz, 2000). For organization studies, this means that theory and research are unquestionably directed towards increasing organizational performance (Fournier and Grey, 2000).

Critical theory aims to break with this performative intent in order to disrupt the status quo and to facilitate emancipation from structures of oppression. As such, it is anti-performative in that it is interested in "performativity only in that it seeks to uncover what is being done in its name" (Fournier and Grey, 2000: 17). While critical theory from its very inception has emphasized critique for the purpose of change (Horkheimer, 1937), some later work in this tradition has been criticized for not moving beyond a stance of "anti-performativity," which showcases the shortcomings of contemporary capitalism but otherwise does not work towards actively transforming it (Therborn, 1970). Noting that this is too limited in that it falls short of the emancipatory objective of critical approaches to affect social change, recent authors have emphasized the need to more fully harness the performative potential of critical theory and inquiry. The notion of critical performativity emphasizes the potential for research to engage with specific organization theories to open up new ways of understanding and engaging with organizational phenomena in ways that affect managerial discourse and practice through active and subversive interventions (Alvesson and Spicer, 2012; Spicer et al., 2009).

## Critical Inquiry as Counterpoint to Mainstream Organization Studies

In this section, I draw on selected examples from the literature to demonstrate that and how qualitative critical inquiry can provide much needed alternatives and counterpoints to mainstream research on key themes in the different domains of organization studies. These examples do not constitute an extensive review of the literature but rather are intended to illustrate how qualitative inquiry, building on the key tenets of critical approaches discussed above (i.e., reflexivity, denaturalization, and progressive performativity), enables researchers to advance alternative insights on major topics of study in all areas of organization studies research. Collectively these examples also illustrate the rich diversity of critical inquiry approaches.

I begin with strategic management, which has come to take a central role in organization studies as well as in contemporary capitalism (Grandy and Mills, 2004; Greckhamer, 2010). In its mainstream, strategy research has largely revolved around explaining why some firms are more successful than others and how firms can attain competitive advantages underlying this success (Bowman et al., 2002). However, starting with Shrivastava's (1986) seminal challenge of the ideological foundations of strategic management, a stream of critical approaches has pinpointed the void of reflexivity and critical self-appraisal of motivations and core assumptions that underlie the mainstream theories of strategic management (e.g., Levy et al., 2003; Whipp, 1999). In short, critical approaches aim to unmask power relations in the social realities produced and reproduced through strategic management, by converting "strategy" from a descriptive label connoting a domain of researchable objects such as strategies, markets, competencies, opportunities, top management teams, etc., to discourses that constitute the objects, social realities, and institutions that researchers are urged to study and managers are urged to act upon (Clegg et al., 2006; Ezzamel and Willmott, 2004, 2008).

A selection of diverse examples serves to illustrate that critical inquiry enables much needed alternative insights to what strategy is, how it shapes organizational realities, and what from a critical theory position it could and should be. For example, several studies by Vaara and colleagues show how critical discourse analysis enables alternative insights regarding core strategy topics such as mergers and acquisitions. Specifically, in one study these authors problematize how mergers and acquisitions are justified and legitimized through public media discourse (Vaara and Tienari, 2002), whereas in another study they explore how mergers and acquisitions are used to legitimize the global restructuring of industries (Vaara et al., 2006). In yet another critical discourse analysis study, Vaara and colleagues (Vaara et al., 2010) explore the power effects of strategic plans as a specific discursive genre.

Along similar lines, Greckhamer (2010) uses a critical discourse analysis approach to denaturalize the fundamentally ideological functions of strategic management theory by showing how Michael Porter's work expanded strategic management discourse to envelop economic development, the discursive mechanisms by which this expansion was accomplished, and how these mechanisms were normalized. Ezzamel and Willmott (2008) focus on how discursive practices emerge and are promoted as well as justified, by studying how strategy activity is articulated, mobilized, and enacted; in doing so, their study provides a possible account of how the discursive practices they studied emerged and were promoted and justified. A different line of critical inquiry has explored issues related to strategy and actors' identities. For example, building on the notion that discourse distributes power and privileges among actors by constructing subject positions (Hardy and Phillips, 2004), research has explored the dynamics of identity construction through strategy discourse and practice (Laine et al., 2016), as well as how strategy discourse impairs versus enables participation in strategy practice (Mantere and Vaara, 2008).

To give an example that showcases the political–ideological nature of data sources frequently used in mainstream strategy research, the critical hermeneutic study by Prasad and Mir (2002) explores the ideological content and character of CEOs' letters to shareholders of U.S. oil companies in their respective historical context. Along different lines, Levy and Egan (2003) demonstrate the value of critical neo-Gramscian theory to analyze corporate political strategies and how a Gramscian approach can enrich theorizing about institutions by providing a theory for analyzing structure–agency relationships. To give a final example, the work by Jermier (1985) implies how critical approaches question ownership structures, which are a key taken-for-granted domain of mainstream strategy research.

The literature has also established the potential of critical inquiry to complement mainstream research on entrepreneurship. An influential mainstream definition has conceptualized "the field of entrepreneurship as the scholarly examination of how, by whom, and with what effects opportunities to create future goods and services are discovered, evaluated, and exploited"

(Shane and Venkataraman, 2000: 219). Critical scholars, on the other hand, note that the presence of entrepreneurship has come to be attributed to success whereas its absence has come to be attributed to failure (Armstrong, 2005). More generally, critical scholars conceptualize entrepreneurship, both as an academic field of study and an interrelated area of public policy, as a political-ideological project that aims to reproduce conservative social, political, and economic assumptions and behaviors as well as to shape public policy and public discourse (Armstrong, 2005; Tedmanson et al., 2012).

For example, Ogbor (2000) provides an ideological critique of key theoretical constructs associated with entrepreneurship and argues that they are inadequate tools for analyzing the diverse range of possibilities and constraints for new business creation because the very concept of entrepreneurship is discriminatory, infused with gender and racial biases, and ideologically controlled. Similarly, based on a critical feminist approach, Ahl and Marlow (2012) argue that entrepreneurship discourse is persistently marked by a hidden gender bias that is not consistent with the idea that entrepreneurial success is determined by personal effort, concluding that critical research is needed to shed light on who can be recognized as an entrepreneur and what it entails to be an entrepreneur. Likewise building on a critical feminist perspective, Calás et al. (2009) seek to reframe theory and research on entrepreneurship from an emphasis on positive economic activity to create wealth to entrepreneurship as activities for social change, which places emphasis on the interests served through entrepreneurship and thereby includes the possibility of a variety of outcomes.

Not unlike research on strategic management and entrepreneurship, research in organizational behavior remains strongly dominated by functionalist positivist theories (primarily from social and applied psychology) paired with an emphasis on a certain kind of rigor that aims to secure the objectivity of the conduct and outcome of research (Alvesson and Deetz, 2000).[4] Jackson and Carter (2000) note that the primary implicit or explicit purpose of traditional organizational behavior theory and research is "providing techniques for manipulating organizational behavior" (p. 5) whereas "the purposes that organizations serve, and thus the purposes to be served by manipulation of organizational behavior, are treated as obvious, and beyond question" (p. 6). Here again, a few examples demonstrate how critical inquiry provides much needed alternative theoretical and empirical insights on main organizational behavior topics, including (but not limited to) leadership, teams, motivation, diversity, and identity.

To begin with, work by Adler (2007) showcases how a critical approach building on labor process theory can inform central research themes in organizational behavior such as teams and motivation. For example, it illustrates that theories and empirical research on motivation may need to be expanded towards collectivist sources of motivation in organizations that aim to increase the effectiveness of their labor process by redesigning jobs towards mobilizing and holding responsible collectives of workers. He also suggests that beyond studying the functionalist aspects of teams to improve organizational performance, research should study teams as tools of normative and coercive control as well as the various tensions resulting from this control. To give an example for the potential of critical approaches to leadership studies, Zoller and Fairhurst (2007) highlight how a critical approach to leadership can provide the basis for theorizing agency in organizations that has implications for our understanding of how organizational members may mobilize resistance against organizational policies, how they influence organizational change, and what attributions they hold of leadership. Alvesson and Spicer (2012) complement these insights on leadership by highlighting the need for critical studies that develop strong critiques of leadership ideology as a general source of domination while at the same time developing the potential for progressive performativity on leadership that appreciates potential situations in which leadership in local organizations may be needed.

Another example is a stream of critical research on organizational diversity that provides a much needed counterpoint to mainstream organizational behavior research on this topic by emphasizing three fundamental issues (Zanoni et al., 2010: 13–14): that identities are socially constructed and that critical inquiry is needed to denaturalize how processes of social identity construction in organizations are shaped by "the vantage point of a dominant identity of white, heterosexual, western, middle/upper class, abled men" (p. 13); the need to study how organizational and societal contexts shape identities and therefore the meaning of diversity; and the need to theorize that and how power relations result in de facto structurally unequal access to and distribution of resources between socio-demographic groups. In this line of research, Zanoni's (2011) study of diversity in an automobile company illustrates that conceptualizing diversity as an intersection of sets of socio-demographic identities inscribed within class relations is a viable tool for understanding how inequality in contemporary organizations is produced and sustained by exploiting distinct socio-demographic identities in the organizations' labor force that reflect unequal potential to produce economic value.

The domain of international organization studies, which broadly encompasses comparative and cross-cultural management, the national business systems approach, comparative institutionalist perspectives, and intersections of all of these with the broader literature on international business and this literature's focus on multinational corporations, has been the most resistant to the evolution of a critical perspective (Jack et al., 2009: 871). Although functionalist positivist theories and empirical approaches dominate this domain, critical scholars have demonstrated the potential of critical inquiry also for this domain of organization studies.

To give a specific example, focusing on one of the core phenomena of international organization studies, i.e., multinational corporations (MNCs) and their operations, Levy (2008) shows the importance of critical analyses to understand how MNCs and their operations perpetuate social inequality and oppression in an international context through a combination of market and political power. In this vein, Hodge and Coronado's (2006) critical discourse analysis illustrates the increasing influence of the ideologies and practices of MNCs on the agendas of national governments. To give another example, Greckhamer and Cilesiz (2012) illustrate the potential of critical approaches to provide alternative paths to study phenomena related to "emerging economies," an important area of research at the nexus of international and strategic management research.

A vital strand of critical organization studies in the international domain builds on a postcolonial perspective, which emphasizes that international business research exhibits continuities with the colonial project (Jack and Westwood, 2006). Scholars following in this tradition point to the dearth of non-Western organizational knowledge, to misguided applications of Western theories and knowledge in non-Western study contexts, and to oversimplified representations of "the Other" in Western management discourses (Frenkel, 2008: 925). Özkazanç-Pan (2008) further highlights that a postcolonial perspective can provide analytic lenses that illuminate how mainstream international management "knowledge" materially impacts the non-West; she also proposes a research agenda that disrupts the hegemony of a Eurocentric epistemology that from a postcolonial perspective is even embedded in critical approaches.

## Critical Inquiry Approaches

In the previous section I have illustrated that critical inquiry enables researchers to pursue much needed alternatives and counterpoints to the bulk of functionalist positivist approaches in organization studies. To realize this potential, organizational scholars can draw on a diverse range of established critical qualitative approaches. In this section, I briefly discuss a selection of well-established critical approaches and for each of these approaches I refer to key literature to provide interested readers with entry points for further reading.

Overall, the different approaches to critical qualitative inquiry build on the central tenets of critical inquiry discussed above. Accordingly, they share the commitment to transformative research that exposes and critiques different forms of oppression, inequality, and discrimination in social life; connect meanings to broader socio-historical contexts and to structures of social power and control; aim for theory building that both respects as well as confronts and challenges taken-for-granted interpretations of individual's daily lived experiences; and aim to speak with rather than to or for marginalized groups (Lather, 2003). Some of these approaches, including critical feminism and critical race theory that I discuss below, are dedicated specifically to shed light on and overcome the oppression and domination of particular groups of people.

## Critical Feminism

Feminist theory and research overall "is old enough to have a history complete with its own set of labels" (Tong, 1998: 1) and as such is a contested field in its own right (St. Pierre, 2000). The range of feminist theories share the core claim that "women's interests have been unjustly subordinated to those of men" (Martin, 1990). Accordingly, the different feminist approaches on a general level are all critical and political in that they critique the status quo of the social, economic, cultural, and institutional positions of women in society and their resulting experiences; however, the degree of critique and the nature of politics assumed and focused on vary across approaches (Calás and Smircich, 1996). Within the family of feminist approaches, critical feminism assumes that all knowledge, social institutions, and structures have a long history of being gendered and shaped by male dominance, resulting in women being historically disadvantaged; critical feminism's key ideological commitment is to overcome this form of gender domination, which includes the aim to bring the feminist perspective to bear on broader social problems (Calás and Smircich, 1996, 2014).

More specifically, a critical feminist approach subsumes three central commitments aimed at reshaping the status quo of ideological and institutional structures. First, it makes gender and gender relations a key substantive focus of analysis; second, it explicitly embraces the political aim to promote equality between women and men; and third it aims to describe the world in correspondence with women's experiences and to identify the fundamental social transformations of the status quo that are necessary for full gender equality (Rhode, 1989). Arguing that conventional epistemological positions are androcentric (male-dominated) and exclude researchers from gaining certain knowledge that corresponds with women's experiences, critical feminist scholars emphasize the need for epistemological in addition to methodological considerations (Harding, 1987). Harding (2004) further notes that, from the point of view of critical feminism, women are only an example of a marginalized and/or oppressed group and therefore other oppressed groups could benefit from appropriating its epistemological and methodological positions.

## Critical Race Theory

Another critical approach committed specifically to overcome the oppression and domination of a particular group of people is critical race theory; this critical interpretative framework is promising for organization studies because the field so far has largely neglected and marginalized race as an analytical category (Holvino, 2010; Nkomo, 1992). Acknowledging the importance of class-based and gender-based theoretical approaches of critical and feminist research, critical race theory emphasizes that they are insufficient to explore issues of racial domination (Ladson-Billings and Tate, 1995). Critical race theory's overarching objective is to transform ingrained relationships among race, racism, and power that position people of color as inferior (Delgado and Stefancic, 2001; Scheurich and Young, 1997; Tate, 1997). To do so and to enable analyses of racism as a system of oppression, it aims to shed light on the ways race and racism are deeply embedded within contemporary (U.S.) society (Parker and Lynn, 2002).

Critical race theory is built upon several key assumptions (Tate, 1997). First, it assumes that racism is deeply engrained in legal, cultural, and psychological aspects of U.S. society. Second, it notes that arguments such as neutrality, objectivity, color-blindness, and meritocracy are frequently used as camouflages for the self-interest of powerful entities of society. Third, it emphasizes the need to analyze how people are "raced," i.e., how individuals' experiences are shaped by the socially constructed realities of race and race relations. Fourth, it challenges ahistorical positions regarding race and race relations and embeds research on individuals' experiences related to race in an examination of contextual and historical factors.

Furthermore, critical race theory aims to unpack different layers and kinds of racism. Specifically, Scheurich and Young (1997) argue that different forms of racism impact the epistemologies underlying our research. They also outline the different kinds of racism: overt and covert racism at the individual level that may bias individuals' thinking but may be covered up with socially accepted reasons; institutional racism embedded in organizations' standard operating procedures or in society at large (also referred to as societal racism), and civilizational racism that is engrained in broad civilizational assumptions that are vital to how a civilization's members construct their world and their experience in it but that they are not typically conscious about.

Critical race theory also entails the notion of intersectionality first introduced by Crenshaw (1989). Arguing that race and gender are not mutually exclusive but rather interrelated categories of experience and analysis in that they represent interrelated systems of domination and oppression, Crenshaw (1989: 140) emphasizes that research should focus on these intersections because "the intersectional experience is greater than the sum of racism and sexism." Intersectionality is vital for organization studies because the importance of intersections such as those among race, class, and gender, for organizational life have so far not been widely acknowledged in the field (Holvino, 2010; Nkomo, 1992). Concluding their review of feminist theories, Calás and Smircich (1996: 236) note the importance of the intersections among critical approaches by emphasizing that "it's not only about 'gender' any more, as both women and men, from both First and Third Worlds, employed and unemployed, with and without families, struggle with inequality, injustice, inequity and intolerance."

## *Critical Discourse Analysis*

Critical discourse analysis is a vital critical inquiry approach that provides the theoretical and methodological tools to analyze the constitutive role of language in constructing social reality. In short, discourses can be defined as structured collections of meaningful texts that construct social reality (Burman and Parker, 1993; Phillips et al., 2004). Critical discourse analysis is the systematic study of the texts that constitute a discourse in order to understand its role in the construction of inequality, dominance, and oppression in social reality with the purpose of challenging and transforming social reality in these regards (Fairclough, 1993; Luke, 1996; Van Dijk, 1993). In doing so, it focuses on links between language and power and assumes that ideologies and power structures shape the representation of "knowledge" or "facts" about "reality" from the perspective of a particular interest (Fairclough, 1985; Luke, 1996).

Not all discourse analysis is critical, and critical discourse analysis differs from other forms of discourse analysis by embracing the basic tenets of critical theory and by taking an explicit socio-political stance that represents its principles, value commitments, and objectives (Van Dijk, 1993). From this openly ideological position, it aims to analyze the hidden ideologies and technologies of control concealed in a body of text that guide thought and action to the exclusion of other possibilities by defining particular meanings associated with sets of concepts, objects, and subject positions, thereby shaping power relations that characterize social settings and influencing what can be said and by whom (Hardy and Phillips, 2004). Discourse analyses of this kind provide "the means to highlight the possibility that things could be or could have been different" (Iedema, 2011: 1172) and thereby facilitate the exploration of a range of key themes of critical research (Fairclough, 1985, 1993; Iedema and Wodak, 1999). For example, they enable the investigation of systematic relationships between discourses and wider social and cultural structures and processes, particularly how discourses construct and reproduce power relations; how discourses construct the rationalities or logics underlying organizations and institutions, as well as how these logics, and the organizations and institutions they support, become taken-for-granted; and how understanding gained through discourse analysis can serve as a resource to challenge and disrupt structures of power, dominant ideological positions, and the social relations and organizational practices that constitute organizations.

## Critical Ethnography

Another vital critical qualitative approach to study organizational realities is critical ethnography. Overall, critical ethnography is "conventional ethnography with a political purpose" (Thomas, 1993: 4) that "begins with an ethical responsibility to address processes of unfairness or injustice within a particular lived domain" (Madison, 2005: 5). Put differently, critical ethnography draws on conventional ethnographic data collection methods for the empirical investigation of everyday cultural experiences using participant observation; however, it is concerned with asking fundamentally different questions and pursuing fundamentally different objectives than classical ethnography. Specifically, whereas ethnography in an interpretivist tradition considers cultural contexts and lifeworlds as descriptive objects and aims to provide an interpretative description of them, critical ethnographers conceptualize these cultures and lifeworlds as ideological productions and reproductions that they aim to disrupt through openly ideological alternative accounts (Koro-Ljungberg and Greckhamer, 2005).

The overarching purpose of critical ethnography is to account for the dialectical relationship between social structural constraints of human agency and its relative autonomy with the emancipatory objective of freeing individuals from sources of domination and oppression (Anderson, 1989). While interpretivist ethnography readily concedes that ordinary action observed in a social situation must be understood in its social context, Forester (1992) notes that critical ethnography starts from the premise that "the very context itself is not given but made, inherited and appropriated in subtle political ways" (p. 47) and that it "aims to explore the continuing performance and practical accomplishment of relations of power" (p. 62). Thereby, critical ethnography enables researchers to emphasize different concerns related to various disenfranchised groups as well as to focus on intersectionality, i.e., on how current social relations are (re)produced by intersections of social dimensions including class, gender, and race (Anderson, 1989; Foley, 2002).

## *Critical Action Research*

Action research is an approach that represents a confluence of research, consulting, social action, and reflection (Wolfram Cox, 2012), and it has long been recognized that this approach has potential for critical inquiry (Johansson and Lindhult, 2008).[5] From its very origins, action research was conceptualized as an approach towards social research that tackles the challenge of combining the two emphases of generating theory and of changing a social system through researchers' actions on or in this system (Lewin, 1946; Rapoport, 1970; Susman and Evered, 1978). Its advocates maintain that it has unique and desirable characteristics, both as a research method and as a social intervention technique, and some authors use the term participatory action research to signify research in which researchers become full collaborators with members of organizations to study and transform those organizations (Greenwood et al., 1993). However, pure consulting and/or advocacy projects and projects that do not make theoretical and/or empirical contributions to the social sciences by definition are not action research (Bradbury Huang, 2010).

Critical action research projects aim at the emancipation of underprivileged groups by helping members of these groups to develop a critical and reflective understanding of dominant ideologies and coercive structures that shape their lifeworlds (Johansson and Lindhult, 2008; Kemmis, 2001). A key influence in this regard has been the seminal work of Paulo Freire (1970, 2000), which does not consider critical scholars' responsibility to transform the social settings they study; it rather emphasizes the importance of denaturalizing taken-for-granted assumptions through conscientization of individuals in the respective setting so that these individuals are empowered to transform the setting on their own accord.

## Conclusion

As noted in the introduction, over the course of human history organizations have served as instruments of social domination and they have been marked by asymmetrical power relations (Morgan, 1986). Critical qualitative inquiry holds great potential and promise for organization studies because it offers the constructive potential to contribute to developing the lines of thought that are needed to identify and overcome oppressive organizational structures (Alvesson, 1985). Indeed, critical scholars have argued that the grave and sustained man-made (and therefore unnecessary) suffering in our contemporary world makes it an ethical responsibility for organizational scholars to contribute to a critical organization science that illuminates organizational and institutional structures of exploitation and oppression and that combines theory with revolutionary action to contribute towards the emancipation of those suffering from these structures (Adler and Jermier, 2005; Frost, 1980).

Theory and research informed by critical inquiry's openly political and ideological approaches are shaped by a strong normative component not only to study how social realities are but also to theorize and research how from their standpoint they ideally could and should be, as well as how they could be transformed towards this ideal (Jermier, 1998). Like any theoretical approach to organizations, critical inquiry is guided by particular assumptions and as such only enables a partial understanding of organizational phenomena. However, by taking into account the political and ideological aspects of organizations neglected by positivist and functionalist organization studies (Alvesson, 1985; Benson, 1977; Frost, 1980; Jermier, 1985), it allows researchers to connect socio-historic context, structure, and individual lived experiences in ways that can inform intellectual and political transformations of how we study and understand organizational phenomena (Mir and Mir, 2002).

# Notes

1 This school took its name from the Institut für Sozialforschung (Institute for Social Research) that was set up in Frankfurt am Main in 1923 and includes the work of a group of scholars who were associated with it before they had to leave Germany due to the Nazi Regime's rise to power.

2 Poststructuralism encompasses the work of a diverse group of (French) theorists, whose work collectively represents a *movement of thought* embodying different forms of critical practice (Agger, 1991; Poster, 1989). Both critical inquiry and poststructuralism are effectively critiques of dominant (positivist) approaches to "scientific" knowledge production and they are "both alike and different" (Alvesson and Deetz, 2006: 272), with each in its own way "interrogating taken-for-granted assumptions about the ways in which people write and read science" (Agger, 1991: 106). In this chapter I use the terms critical theory and critical inquiry as heavily influenced by but not strictly limited to the denotation of the Frankfurt School of Critical Theory.

3 Naturalization refers to reification that mystifies social reality as a given or "natural" condition (Shrivastava, 1986; Fournier and Grey, 2000).

4 While not providing any examples below, I note that mainstream human resource management suffers from similar theoretical and practical limitations in that it takes for granted the basic economic and political structures of contemporary organizations and omits a concern for how political-economic structures impact organizations and individuals' work places in them (Nord, 1974).

5 The basic stance of action research that the raison d'être of social sciences is to contribute to the solution of social problems is reflected in Kurt Lewin's remark that "research that produces nothing but books will not suffice" (1946: 35); this stance makes action research an apparent fit for critical inquiry. However, action research is not necessarily critical but rather may also be positivist or interpretivist (Johansson and Lindhult, 2008; Kemmis, 2001).

# References

Adler, P. 2007. The future of critical management studies: A paleo-marxist critique of labour process theory. *Organization Studies*, 28, 1313–1345.

Adler, P. 2009. Marx and organization studies today. In: Adler, P. (ed.) *The Oxford Handbook of Sociology and Organization Studies: Classical Foundations*, Oxford: Oxford University Press, pp. 62–91.

Adler, P. and Jermier, J. 2005. Developing a field with more soul: Standpoint theory and public policy research for management scholars. *Academy of Management Journal*, 48, 941–944.

Adler, P., Forbes, L. and Willmott, H. 2007. Critical management studies. *The Academy of Management Annals*, 1, 119–179.

Agger, B. 1991. Critical theory, poststructuralism, postmodernism: Their sociological relevance. *Annual Review of Sociology*, 17, 105–131.

Agger, B. 1998. *Critical Social Theories: An Introduction*, Boulder, CO: Westview Press.

Ahl, H. and Marlow, S. 2012. Exploring the dynamics of gender, feminism and entrepreneurship: Advancing debate to escape a dead end? *Organization*, 19, 543–562.

Alvesson, M. 1985. A critical framework for organizational analysis. *Organization Studies*, 6, 117–138.

Alvesson, M. and Ashcraft, K. 2009. Critical methodology in management and organizations research. In: Buchanan, D. and Bryman, A. (eds.) *The SAGE Handbook of Organizational Research Methods*, London: Sage, pp. 61–77.

Alvesson, M. and Deetz, S. 2000. *Doing Critical Management Research*, London: Sage.

Alvesson, M. and Deetz, S. 2006. Critical theory and postmodernism approaches to organizational studies. In: Clegg, S., Hardy, C., Lawrence, T. and Nord, W. (eds.) *The Sage Handbook of Organization Studies*, Thousand Oaks, CA: Sage, pp. 255–283.

Alvesson, M. and Spicer, A. 2012. Critical leadership studies: The case for critical performativity. *Human Relations*, 65, 367–390.

Alvesson, M., Hardy, C. and Harley, B. 2008. Reflecting on reflexivity: Reflexive textual practices in organization and management theory. *Journal of Management Studies*, 45, 480–501.

Anderson, G. 1989. Critical ethnography in education: Origins, current status, and new directions. *Review of Educational Research*, 59, 249–270.

Armstrong, P. 2005. *Critique of Entrepreneurship*, New York: Palgrave Macmillan.

Benson, J.K. 1977. Organizations: A dialectical view. *Administrative Science Quarterly*, 22, 1–21.

Berger, P. and Luckmann, T. 1967. *The Social Construction of Reality: A Treatise in the Sociology of Knowledge*, New York: Doubleday & Company.

Berger, P. and Pullberg, S. 1965. Reification and the sociological critique of consciousness. *History and Theory*, 4, 196–211.

Bowman, E., Singh, H. and Thomas, H. 2002. The domain of strategic management: History and evolution. *In:* Pettigrew, A., Thomas, H. and Whittington, R. (eds.) *Handbook of Strategy and Management*, London: Sage, pp. 31–52.

Burman, E. and Parker, I. 1993. Introduction – discourse analysis: The turn to the text. *In:* Burman, E. and Parker, I. (eds.) *Discourse Analytic Research: Repertoires and Readings of Texts in Action*, London: Routledge, pp. 1–13.

Burrell, G. 1979. Radical organization theory. *In:* Dunkerley, D. and Salaman, G. (eds.) *International Yearbook of Organization Studies*, London: Routledge, pp. 90–107.

Burrell, G. and Morgan, G. 1979. *Sociological Paradigms and Organizational Analysis*, London: Heinemann.

Calás, M. and Smircich, L. 1996. From "the woman's point of view": Feminist approaches to organization studies. *In:* Clegg, S., Hardy, C. and Nord, W. (eds.) *The Sage Handbook of Organization Studies*, London: Sage, pp. 218–257.

Calás, M. and Smircich, L. 2014. Engendering the organizational: Feminist theorizing and organization studies. *In:* Adler, P., Du Gay, P, Morgan, G. and Reed, M. (eds.) *The Oxford Handbook of Sociology, Social Theory, and Organization Studies*, Oxford: Oxford University Press, pp. 605–659.

Calás, M., Smircich, L. and Bourne, K. 2009. Extending the boundaries: Reframing "entrepreneurship as social change" through feminist perspectives. *Academy of Management Review*, 34, 552–569.

Clegg, S., Courpasson, D. and Phillips, N. 2006. *Power and Organizations*, London: Sage.

Crenshaw, K. 1989. Demarginalizing the intersection of race and sex: A black feminist critique of antidiscrimination doctrine, feminist theory and antiracist politics. *University of Chicago Legal Forum*, 140, 139–167.

Deetz, S. 1992. *Democracy in an Age of Corporate Colonization*, Albany, NY: State University of New York Press.

Delgado, R. and Stefancic, J. 2001. *Critical Race Theory: An Introduction*, New York: New York University Press.

Ezzamel, M. and Willmott, H. 2004. Rethinking strategy: Contemporary perspectives and debates. *European Management Review*, 1, 43–48.

Ezzamel, M. and Willmott, H. 2008. Strategy as discourse in a global retailer: A supplement to rationalist interpretive accounts. *Organization Studies*, 29, 191–217.

Fairclough, N. 1985. Critical and descriptive goals in discourse analysis. *Journal of Pragmatics*, 9, 739–763.

Fairclough, N. 1993. Critical discourse analysis and the marketization of public discourse: The universities. *Discourse & Society*, 4, 133–168.

Foley, D. 2002. Critical ethnography: The reflexive turn. *International Journal of Qualitative Studies in Education*, 15, 469–490.

Forester, J. 1992. Critical ethnography: On fieldwork in a Habermasian way. *In:* Alvesson, M. and Willmott, H. (eds.) *Critical Management Studies*, London: Sage, pp. 46–65.

Fournier, V. and Grey, C. 2000. At the critical moment: Conditions and prospects for critical management studies. *Human Relations*, 53, 7–32.

Freire, P. 1970. Cultural action and conscientization. *Harvard Educational Review*, 40, 452–477.

Freire, P. 2000. *Pedagogy of the Oppressed*, New York: Continuum.

Frenkel, M. 2008. The multinational corporation as a third space: Rethinking international management discourse on knowledge transfer through Homi Bhabha. *Academy of Management Review*, 33, 924–942.

Frost, P. 1980. Toward a radical framework for practicing organization science. *Academy of Management Review*, 5, 501–507.

Grandy, G. and Mills, A. 2004. Strategy as simulacra? A radical and reflexive look at the discipline and practice of strategy. *Journal of Management Studies*, 41, 1153–1170.

Greckhamer, T. 2010. The stretch of strategic management discourse: A critical analysis. *Organization Studies*, 31, 841–871.

Greckhamer, T. and Cilesiz, S. 2012. Critical and poststructural approaches to strategy research: Theoretical and methodological suggestions. *In:* Wang, C., Ketchen, D. and Bergh, D. (eds.) *West Meets East: Building Methodological Bridges*, Bingley: Emerald, pp. 3–38.

Greenwood, D., Whyte, W. and Harkavy, I. 1993. Participatory action research as a process and as a goal. *Human Relations*, 46, 175–192.

Guba, E. (ed.) 1990. *The Paradigm Dialog*, Newbury Park, CA: Sage.

Guba, E. and Lincoln, Y. 1994. Competing paradigms in qualitative research. *In:* Denzin, N. and Lincoln, Y. (eds.) *Handbook of Qualitative Research*, Thousand Oaks, CA: Sage, pp. 105–117.

Harding, S. 1987. The method question. *Hypatia*, 2, 19–35.

Harding, S. 2004. A socially relevant philosophy of science? Resources from standpoint theory's controversiality. *Hypatia*, 19, 25–47.

Hardy, C. and Phillips, N. 2004. Discourse and power. *In:* Grant, D., Hardy, C., Oswick, C. and Putnam, L. (eds.) *The Sage Handbook of Organizational Discourse*, London: Sage, pp. 299–317.

Held, D. 1980. *Introduction to Critical Theory: Horkheimer to Habermas*, Berkeley and Los Angeles, CA: University of California Press.

Hodge, B. and Coronado, G. 2006. Mexico Inc.? Discourse analysis and the triumph of managerialism. *Organization*, 13, 529–547.

Holvino, E. 2010. Intersections: The simultaneity of race, gender and class in organization studies. *Gender, Work, and Organization*, 17, 248–277.

Horkheimer, M. 1937. Traditionelle und kritische Theorie. *Zeitschrift für Sozialforschung*, 6, 245–294.

Huang, B.H. 2010. What is good action research? *Action Research*, 8, 93–109.

Iedema, R. 2011. Discourse studies in the 21st century: A response to Mats Alvesson and Dan Kärreman's "decolonializing discourse." *Human Relations*, 64, 1163–1176.

Iedema, R. and Wodak, R. 1999. Introduction: Organizational discourses and practices. *Discourse & Society*, 10, 5–19.

Jack, G. and Westwood, R. 2006. Postcolonialism and the politics of qualitative research in international business. *Management International Review*, 46, 481–501.

Jack, G., Calas, M., Nkomo, S. and Peltonen, T. 2009. Critique and international management: An uneasy relationship? *Academy of Management Review*, 33, 870–884.

Jackson, N. and Carter, P. 2000. *Rethinking Organizational Behavior*, Harlow, Essex: Pearson Education.

Jermier, J. 1985. "When the sleeper wakes": A short story extending themes in radical organization theory. *Journal of Management*, 11, 67–80.

Jermier, J. 1998. Introduction: Critical perspectives on organizational control. *Administrative Science Quarterly*, 43, 235–256.

Johansson, A. and Lindhult, E. 2008. Critical versus pragmatic scientific orientation in action research. *Action Research*, 6, 95–115.

Johnson, P. and Duberley, J. 2003. Reflexivity in management research. *Journal of Management Studies*, 40, 1279–1303.

Kemmis, S. 2001. Exploring the relevance of critical theory for action research: Emancipatory action research in the footsteps of Jürgen Habermas. *In:* Reason, P. and Bradbury, H. (eds.) *Handbook of Action Research: Participative Inquiry and Practice*, London: Sage, pp. 91–102.

Kincheloe, J. and McLaren, P. 2000. Rethinking critical theory and qualitative research. *In:* Denzin, N. and Lincoln, Y. (eds.) *Handbook of Qualitative Research*, Thousand Oaks, CA: Sage, pp. 279–313.

Koro-Ljungberg, M. and Greckhamer, T. 2005. Strategic turns labeled ethnography: From description to openly ideological production of cultures. *Qualitative Research*, 5, 285–306.

Ladson-Billings, G. and Tate, W. 1995. Toward a critical race theory of education. *Teachers College Record*, 97, 47–68.

Laine, P.-M., Meriläinen, S., Tienerai, J. and Vaara, E. 2016. Mastery, submission, and subversion: On the performative construction of strategist identity. *Organization*, 23, 505–524.

Lather, P. 2003. Critical inquiry in qualitative research: Feminist and poststructural perspectives: Science "after truth." *In:* deMarrais, K. and Lapan, S. (eds.) *Foundations for Research: Methods of Inquiry in Education and the Social Sciences*, New York: Routledge, pp. 203–216.

Levy, D. 2008. Political contestation in global production networks. *Academy of Management Review*, 33, 943–963.

Levy, D. and Egan, D. 2003. A neo-gramscian approach to corporate political strategy: Conflict and accommodation in the climate change negotiations. *Journal of Management Studies*, 40, 804–829.

Levy, D., Alvesson, M. and Willmott, H. 2003. Critical approaches to strategic management. *In:* Alvesson, M. and Willmott, H. (eds.) *Studying Management Critically*, 2nd ed., Newbury Park, CA: Sage, pp. 92–110.

Lewin, K. 1946. Action research and minority problems. *Journal of Social Issues*, 2, 34–46.

Lincoln, Y. and Guba, E. 2000. Paradigmatic controversies, contradictions, and emerging confluences. *In:* Denzin, N. and Lincoln, Y. (eds.) *The Handbook of Qualitative Research*, Thousand Oaks, CA: Sage, pp. 163–188.

Luke, A. 1996. Text and discourse in education: An introduction to critical discourse analysis. *Review of Research in Education*, 21, 3–48.

Madison, D. 2005. *Critical Ethnography: Method, Ethics, and Performance*, Thousand Oaks, CA: Sage.

Mantere, S. and Vaara, E. 2008. On the problem of participation in strategy: A critical discursive perspective. *Organization Science*, 19, 341–358.

Martin, J. 1990. Deconstructing organizational taboos: The suppression of gender conflict in organizations. *Organization Science*, 1, 339–359.

Mir, R. and Mir, A. 2002. The organizational imagination: From paradigm wars to praxis. *Organizational Research Methods*, 5, 105–125.

Morgan, G. 1986. *Images of Organization*, Thousand Oaks, CA: Sage.

Morgan, G. and Smircich, L. 1980. The case for qualitative research. *Academy of Management Review*, 5, 491–500.

Nkomo, S. 1992. The emperor has no clothes: Rewriting "race in organizations." *Academy of Management Review*, 17, 487–513.

Nord, W. 1974. The failure of current applied behavioral science: A Marxian perspective. *The Journal of Applied Behavioral Science*, 10, 557–578.

Ogbor, J. 2000. Mythicizing and reification in entrepreneurial discourse: Ideology-critique of entrepreneurial studies. *Journal of Management Studies*, 37, 605–635.

Özkazanç-Pan, B. 2008. International management research meets the "rest of the world." *Academy of Management Review*, 33, 964–974.

Parker, L. and Lynn, M. 2002. What's race got to do with it? Critical race theory's conflicts with and connections to qualitative research methodology and epistemology. *Qualitative Inquiry*, 8, 7–22.

Phillips, N., Lawrence, T. and Hardy, C. 2004. Discourse and institutions. *Academy of Management Review*, 29, 635–652.

Poster, M. 1989. *Critical Theory and Poststructuralism*, Ithaca, NY: Cornell University Press.

Prasad, A. and Mir, R. 2002. Digging deep for meaning: A critical hermeneutic analysis of CEO letters to shareholders in the oil industry. *Journal of Business Communication*, 39, 92–116.

Prasad, P. 2005. *Crafting Qualitative Research: Working in the Postpositivist Traditions*, Armonk, NY: M.E. Sharpe.

Rapoport, R. 1970. Three dilemmas in action research. *Human Relations*, 23, 499–513.

Rhode, D. 1989. Feminist critical theories. *Stanford Law Review*, 42, 617–638.

Scherer, A. 2009. Critical theory and its contribution to critical management studies. *In*: Alvesson, M., Bridgman, T. and Willmott, H. (eds.) *The Oxford Handbook of Critical Management Studies*, Oxford: Oxford University Press, pp. 29–51.

Scheurich, J. and Young, M. 1997. Coloring epistemologies: Are our research epistemologies racially biased? *Educational Researcher*, 26, 4–16.

Shane, S. and Venkataraman, S. 2000. The promise of entrepreneurship as a field of research. *Academy of Management Review*, 25, 217–226.

Shrivastava, P. 1986. Is strategic management ideological? *Journal of Management*, 12, 363–377.

Smircich, L. and Calás, M. 1995. Introduction. *In*: Smircich, L. and Calás, M. (eds.) *Critical Perspectives on Organization and Management Theory*, Aldershot: Dartmouth Publishing, pp. xiii–xxviii.

Spicer, A., Alvesson, M. and Kärreman, D. 2009. Critical performativity: The unfinished business of critical management studies. *Human Relations*, 62, 537–560.

St. Pierre, E. 2000. Poststructural feminism in education: An overview. *International Journal of Qualitative Studies in Education*, 13, 477–515.

Steffy, B. and Grimes, A. 1986. A critical theory of organization science. *Academy of Management Review*, 11, 322–336.

Susman, G. and Evered, R. 1978. An assessment of the scientific merits of action research. *Administrative Science Quarterly*, 23, 582–603.

Tate, W. 1997. Critical race theory and education: History, theory, and implications. *Review of Research in Education*, 22, 195–247.

Tedmanson, D., Verduyn, K., Essers, C. and Gartner, W. 2012. Critical perspectives in entrepreneurship research. *Organization*, 19, 531–541.

Therborn, G. 1970. The Frankfurt School. *The New Left Review*, 63, 65–96.

Thomas, J. 1993. *Doing Critical Ethnography*, Newbury Park, CA: Sage.

Tong, R. 1998. *Feminist Thought: A More Comprehensive Introduction*, Boulder, CO: Westview Press.

Vaara, E. and Tienari, J. 2002. Justification, legitimization and naturalization of mergers and acquisitions: A critical discourse analysis of media texts. *Organization*, 9, 275–304.

Vaara, E., Sorsa, V. and Pälli, P. 2010. On the force potential of strategy texts: A critical discourse analysis of a strategic plan and its power effects in a city organization. *Organization*, 17, 685–702.

Vaara, E., Tienari, J. and Laurila, J. 2006. Pulp and paper fiction: On the discursive legitimation of global industrial restructuring. *Organization Studies*, 27, 789–810.

Van Dijk, T. 1993. Principles of critical discourse analysis. *Discourse & Society*, 4, 249–283.

Whipp, R. 1999. Creative deconstruction: Strategy and organizations. *In:* Clegg, S., Hardy, C. and Nord, W. (eds.) *Managing Organizations: Current Issues*, London: Sage, pp. 11–25.

Wolfram Cox, J. 2012. Action research. *In:* Symon, G. and Cassell, C. (eds.) *Qualitative Organizational Research*, London: Sage, pp. 371–388.

Zanoni, P. 2011. Diversity in the lean automobile factory: Doing class through gender, disability and age. *Organization*, 18, 105–127.

Zanoni, P., Janssens, M., Benschopp, Y. and Nkomo, S. 2010. Unpacking diversity, grasping inequality: Rethinking difference through critical perspectives. *Organization*, 17, 9–29.

Zoller, H. and Fairhurst, G. 2007. Resistance leadership: The overlooked potential in critical organization and leadership studies. *Human Relations*, 60, 1331–1360.

# 4

# DOING FEMINIST RESEARCH QUALITATIVELY

## A Review of What *Interpretive* Feminist Research Means Today

*Marleen van der Haar*

## Introduction

Most of the empirical work done by feminist scholars in the social sciences can be labelled as qualitative. Some argue that qualitative methods are the "most appropriate for understanding women's experiences" (Silverman 2001: 220). The argument here is that as a critique to non-feminist research, which often was and is quantitative, feminist research needs to use qualitative methods "to protest against the status quo" (Reinharz 1993: 69). Others seem to not reflect on the matter and take for granted that the two go together. For example, the editors of a 2015 thematic issue on gender in management research in the leading *Academy of Management Journal* (AOM) write, after introducing the first three papers, "that this issue *also* includes two quantitative reviews" (Joshi, Neely, Emrich, Griffiths and George 2015: 1463; my italics). Without marking the type of research of the earlier studies in the thematic issue, this way of phrasing suggests that qualitative research is the default option when working from a feminist perspective. The above suggests that a handbook on qualitative research would not be complete without a chapter on the feminist approach.

Nonetheless, there is a large body of literature about feminist research practice and there exist many chapters presenting an overview of the diversity of feminist qualitative research (see for example Hesse Biber 2012; Olesen 2005; Spierings 2016; Prasad 2005). This chapter will single out one approach, nested in or at least related to the postmodern strand of feminism (Verloo and Lombardo 2007). More concretely, we focus on the relations between the interpretive approach and postmodern feminist work and assess if the two might develop into *interpretive* feminist work. The adjective interpretive here is deliberatively preferred over the classification of qualitative research to emphasize the post-positivist starting point and to avoid that this particular research approach is being evaluated by criteria designed for positivist research (Yanow and Schwartz-Shea 2006), which is usually rejected by feminist scholars. Also, this term has the potential to take us out of the impasse created by the juxtapositioning of quantitative versus qualitative research perspectives based on positivist and interpretive epistemological assumptions (Cole and Stewart 2012: 369, following Ann Lin's argument for the use of multiple methods), something that often happens in methods discussions.

The starting point for this chapter on what could be called *interpretive* feminist research has been some reflections from my own journey as a researcher, having worked in the field of organization studies, public administration and political science. Trained as a cultural anthropologist, an ethnographic approach has become my standard mode in designing and conducting projects and studies. Observations and interviewing here are the main research methods. In this discipline, meaning making and identity are central research themes to understand how groups give meaning to the world they live in and how shared meanings give a sense of belonging and identity. During my Ph.D. period I got acquainted with discursive analysis from a critical stance, which enabled me to analyze power relations, dominant voice, in- and exclusion. Here, text analysis, most often of all sorts of documents but also of the transcription of interaction data (for example, meetings between a social worker and a client; see van der Haar 2007), is the central research method. As a result, my work took on a more explicit focus on language and interaction. Including a feminist approach in my work is fairly recent and has been influenced mostly by critical scholars from the field of gender and politics. Thinking about this chapter and reading literature about feminist research for it made me realize how very close the critical stance in the ethnographic work from an anthropological perspective and the discursive work in critical policy studies is to postmodern feminism (on the overlap between interpretive work and feminist research, see also Yanow and Schwartz-Shea 2006: 211).[1]

A second observation based on personal experience in the academic world is that whereas a critical, interpretive perspective already may raise eyebrows from some colleagues in the social sciences, writing explicitly from a feminist stance or even merely speaking about gender can count on skepticism from students and colleagues to selection committees for jobs and research funding. As academic feminism has been built upon criticism about androcentric and positivist research (Spierings 2016), resistance often comes from scholars working with mainstream paradigms (Benschop and Verloo 2016: 107). Despite many successes of feminist research, Benschop and Verloo (2016), for example, point out that feminist insights are not discussed or even silenced in mainstream theories of organizations and management. They call for an integration agenda to improve the impact of feminist insights in mainstream theory building. A recent study of academic curricula of various disciplines in the Netherlands shows that gender still is not a structural issue in academic education; even when gender issues are dealt with, they are not automatically discussed from a theoretical or analytical perspective on power and social relations (Roggeband, Bonjour and Mügge 2016). Nevertheless, the Oxford University Press study book on *Business Research Methods* for business and management students, for instance, weaves in the feminist perspective quite extensively at several moments in its qualitative research section (Bryman and Bell 2015). Interestingly, the book devotes a page to feminist critique on structured interviewing in the quantitative section as well (Bryman and Bell 2015: 235).

The need to build bridges across disciplines and paradigms and the need to get the feminist approach more widely integrated makes me decide to strategically focus this chapter not too much on discussing conflicting ideas and standpoints (for a discussion on this issue see, for example, Benschop and Verloo 2016). As a consequence, I will mainly explore issues related to the interpretive feminist approach. The particular focus of the chapter is a result of the auto-ethnographic elements mentioned above (see the work of Davis and Nencel (2011) and Reger (2014) for examples of the use of auto-ethnography as a feminist method). Besides, it is also partly inspired by the input I received from colleagues; almost exclusively so-called white women in their thirties – like myself – working in the field of political science, business administration, sociology and cultural anthropology in the Netherlands and Belgium who answered my question to email me literature that inspired them when they wrote from a feminist perspective.[2]

After a brief overview of the three major strands in feminism, I turn to the interpretive approach in more detail. After having explained the commonalities between a feminist and an interpretive approach, I elaborate on discursive analysis. I present Critical Frame Analysis as an example of a bridging methodology. Then, I will discuss a particular research focus, namely category making. I end the chapter with a reflection on what the interpretive feminist research brings to the knowledge production on framing and its implications for understanding inequalities.

## Three Feminist Strands

There is a huge diversity under the umbrella of the feminist approach. In this section I will briefly sketch out three major strands. Before doing so, I first present Clare Chambers's (2013) to-the-point definition of feminism. According to her, feminism is the refusal of patriarchy (2013). She further explains this by introducing three theses that all forms of feminism share, and which I find useful when I teach my students in the introductory course on gender, power and politics. First, she argues, gender is a significant social cleavage, which, second, is not normatively neutral but unequal, placing women in the disadvantaged and men in the advantaged group, and third, the patriarchal gender division is considered normatively wrong and needs political action to change the situation (2013). As to the latter, Chambers (2013: 10) emphasizes that feminism is "inherently a reforming or revolutionary movement." As to how feminist critique is expressed may depend on the degree to which one associates as activist or academic feminist. Prasad (2005: 159) in this context argues that most feminists weave political agendas into academic work. Moreover, what kind of change is aimed at depends among others on "what is considered to be the problem" (after Bacchi 1999). Chambers's description of feminism above translates to a (qualitative) feminist research agenda of problematizing "women's diverse situations as well as the gendered institutions and material and historical structures that frames those" (Olesen 2005: 236).

Because the description of feminism is explicitly normative, namely rejecting male domination and aiming at gender equality, I distinguish strands of feminism based on the different representations of gender and gender equality (Verloo and Lombardo 2007). Within academic feminism, three major epistemological strands are usually distinguished: liberal, radical and postmodern feminism (Verloo and Lombardo 2007). I discuss the three stances from a political science perspective, which means that I explain for each tradition their vision and the accompanying political strategy to come to a situation of gender equality. This exercise is by no means intended to draw clear-cut boundaries, but meant to provide a sketchy overview of the diversity of visions on what is considered the problem with gender.

Liberal feminists usually assume that the world is gender neutral and that equality will be achieved when there are equal opportunities (Verloo and Lombardo 2007: 23). Here, gender equality is considered to be a problem of achieving sameness (Verloo and Lombardo 2007: 23). Liberal feminists focus on individual women and men, and gender equality in the context of individual agency and choice (Benschop and Verloo 2016: 101–102). In their review of the impact of the feminist approach in organization studies, Benschop and Verloo argue that in this particular strand, one seems to be satisfied once "women are also included in the myth that 'everyone can make it to the top'" (Benschop and Verloo 2016: 103).

Radical (and cultural) feminists depart from the idea of difference between women and men, and problematize the unquestioned male norm women (and men) must adhere to (Verloo and Lombardo 2007: 23). Moreover, women's difference is often qualified as inferior to men. Politically, women in this tradition would have to be compensated for the unequal situation via positive action. Whereas liberal or equality feminists are usually looking for reform within the present system, radical feminists are critical towards present social systems (Holmes 2007: 77).

In postmodern feminism the whole gendered world is problematized. Criticism about oppressive social systems is expressed with a plea for transformation. Gender mainstreaming, in which the gendered norms of what is male or female are continuously questioned, is seen as the answer to move beyond the shortcomings of the equality and difference approaches (Verloo and Lombardo 2007: 24).

Just as much as feminist research criticizes the androcentric and positivist perspective in other research, and feminism meets resistance from other more mainstream paradigms, feminism is also being criticized from within. Holmes even claims that "feminism has always been a debate" (2007: 78). A central debate is about equality and difference, as discussed above. The problem with acknowledging that women are different from men is the tendency to homogenize women (I will pick up this issue later in the section on category making) and neglect particular experiences as a result of social positionings of women (Holmes 2007: 78) This debate is often discussed along the lines of race/ethnicity. This is so because in large parts of the world race/ethnicity is a social category on the basis of which historically major and enduring cleavages and inequalities have been (re)produced (Verloo 2006). Black feminists calling attention to the specific disadvantaged situation of women of color has become emblematic for this debate. To discuss their specific experiences with inequality, Crenshaw (1991) coined the term intersectionality to point to the intersecting of social categories such as gender, class, race/ethnicity and sexuality in the context of oppression. According to McCall (2005: 1771) intersectionality is the most important theoretical contribution of the field. It is used both as a normative theoretical argument and an approach to do research on the interaction of categories of difference (Hancock 2007: 63).

I briefly highlight two more major aspects of the ongoing debate on the extent to which feminism is inclusive or is biased as a result of the politics of knowledge production (Benschop and Verloo 2016: 108). First, Third World feminism or postcolonial feminism critiques the ethnocentric (Western or Eurocentric) and homogenized conception of feminism and patriarchy (Mohanty in Dhamoon 2013). Second, recent antiracist feminist scholars who study processes of othering and its impact in the context of a post-September 11, 2001 world critique the replication of exclusion and superiority in academic (feminist) work (Dhamoon 2013; see for example, Razack 2004 on social and political responses to violence against women in Muslim communities in Norway).

## The Common Ground in Feminist and Interpretive Approaches to Research

I now turn to the methodological aspects of feminism. Based on ontological and epistemological grounds, Prasad (2005: 173) argues that feminists "almost uniformly reject … a positivist scientific procedure."[3] Their focus on understanding "*subjective* lifeworlds" from a perspective of inequality and implications of power (differences), and contextualizing these makes a contrast to the positivist (cl)aims of objectivity and universality (Prasad 2005; Hesse-Biber and Leavy 2007). In the same vein, feminist scholars employ reflexivity with regard to their own "social location" and conceptual frameworks and – as we are our own "instrument" – work with that in every phase of the research, from research design to writing up the study (based on Sandra Harding in Hesse-Biber and Leavy 2007: 16–17). Here, Harding emphasizes that what is regarded as a problem by researchers is in itself often colored by the researcher's social location. Harding (2004: 31–32) sums up four key elements of feminist standpoint theory. First, it intends to "map the practices of power" in order to understand how "oppressive social relations" are constructed and reproduced (something she describes as "studying up"). Second, she argues, it shows from this different perspective "how hierarchical structure works." Third, because oppressed groups may very well believe the dominant "distorted representations of social relations" themselves, studying their lifeworlds alone may not enable mapping the practices of power. And, fourth, feminist standpoint theory projects are oriented towards groups, not individuals, and aim to raise group consciousness (Harding 2004).

The feminist standpoint theory perspective relates very well to the starting points of interpretive work (Yanow and Schwartz-Shea 2006: 211). Both share a phenomenological starting point in the sense that both perspectives intend to understand social reality from the perspective of the actor in a specific situation (Benschop and Verloo 2016). Based on this perspective, feminist standpoint theory argues that women's experiences need to be studied by applying methods that do not depart from and therefore replicate the androcentric bias (Brouns 1995a). Furthermore, both perspectives recognize that the researcher herself is also part of social reality and for that matter a reflection on one's own position has to be taken into account in the way data are collected and analyzed (Yanow and Schwartz-Shea 2006: 211). Further, the *social* construction of reality (the title of Berger and Luckmann's famous 1966 book; Yanow 2006: 14; her italics) then emphasizes that meaning making is shared; through so-called intersubjectivity collective social reality can be studied. Accordingly, feminist methods and interpretive methods share (1) a conversational style of interviewing, (2) writing in which the reflective researcher is present and (3) a refusal to treat research data as objective and universal (Yanow and Schwartz-Shea 2006: 211).

The ontological heart of the interpretive approach is social constructivism, a post-positivist tradition that starts from the idea that we as (groups of) individuals in interaction construct meanings that may determine how we think and act. That is, language is seen as a model of and a model for the world (Yanow 2003). This implies that framing may pre-structure action (Yanow 2003). In this vein, the example about the use of language in the AOM-journal from the introductory paragraph illustrates how wording frames our world. For researchers, after analyzing the meaning making, this observation then opens up the possibility to explore the implications of this particular framing (Yanow 2006). In feminist work, these implications are studied in the context of power, often about in- and exclusion and inequality in all sorts of social issues. The constructivist concept of gender, which can be defined as "the socially produced differences between being feminine and being masculine" (Holmes 2007: 2), has become the central concept along which these social issues are analyzed. A central assumption in feminist research is that gender is a "significant social cleavage" (Chambers 2013: 15) that enables and constrains the way both men and women live their lives. It not only impacts on individual lives, identities and how people live together, but institutions are gendered too (Brouns 1995b). As to the latter, this means that gender relations are reproduced in how we organize our societies (Brouns 1995b).

Meaning making from the ontological position that we socially construct our lifeworld is best studied via ethnographic research methods such as participant observation and in-depth interviewing, but also discourse analysis of texts enables the analysis of subjective experiences (Prasad 2005; Yanow 2006). The analysis of research data through the interpretive lens typically focuses on the implications of particular framings. From a critical perspective as well as a standpoint theory perspective, these analyses often discuss implications in the context of power; what is the impact of dominant frames on in- and exclusion?

In the next two sections I discuss how, from an interpretive feminist approach, meaning making can be studied via discursive analysis of texts. First, I will present a methodological tool, Critical Frame Analysis. In the second section, I elaborate on categories as a research focus in discursive analysis.

## Bridging Methodology: Critical Frame Analysis

An example of how to study meaning making via discursive analysis of texts is Critical Frame Analysis (CFA) (Verloo 2005, 2007). Verloo's work builds on Bacchi's (1999) feminist approach to policy analysis in which problem representation is key, Schön and Rein's (1994) work on framing in the context of policy controversies, and Benford and Snow's (2000) contribution of strategic framing to social movement theory. In all three of these approaches the focus is on frames and framing in order to understand the way issues are represented in and through language. Verloo (2005) combines these insights to address the multiple interpretations in policy making and to deconstruct which frames are dominant and which frames get excluded. Her main contribution to these policy framing studies is that she developed a systematic how-to tool that enables comparative work. Yet, in this context I want to highlight the potential of CFA as a bridging methodology. Before doing so, I first go into more details about the methodological tool.

Verloo (2005, 2007) developed Critical Frame Analysis to be able to study the diversity of gender and gender equality frames in a large number of European gender equality policy documents. On the basis of this approach she could show that different and sometimes competing interpretations of gender equality affect the way gender equality policies are framed (Verloo and Lombardo 2007: 43). The central concept of a policy frame has been defined by Verloo as "an organising principle that transforms fragmentary or incidental information into a structured and meaningful problem, in which a solution is implicitly or explicitly included" (Verloo and Lombardo 2007: 33). CFA intends to reveal explicit and implicit representations that socio-political actors offer about policy problems and solutions in policy documents (Verloo and Lombardo 2007: 31). The central elements in the methodological tool are sensitizing questions for diagnosis (what is considered to be the problem?), prognosis (what to do?) and call for action (who should do that?). The "critical" in CFA indicates a specific interest in deconstructing power dynamics. In that context, who gets voice, which "voice" (or perspective) gets included and which voices are left out are inherently part of the analysis (Verloo and Lombardo 2007). Accordingly, one can show the implications of the particular ways in which a social issue is framed. Bacchi in this context emphasizes that these "interpretations are interventions" (1999: 1–2). Practically, a so-called super text template serves as a tool to structure and facilitate comparative work, for instance between European countries, type of texts (such as laws, policy plans, civil society documents), policy domains, discursive strategies or naming and labelling (category making).

This kind of frame analysis is an attempt to compare cases without losing sight of the specificities of each case. Because of the emphasis on situatedness and contextualization in the interpretation of data, most qualitative and interpretive work is based on single-case studies. Verloo's challenge here was – and in that sense CFA is a bridging methodology – to develop an instrument open enough to enable an inductive perspective, but at the same time providing a structure that enables the inclusion of more cases and the possibility to do comparative work. Moreover, this methodology is not designed to serve feminist studies per se. In a recent reflection on the use of CFA van der Haar and Verloo (2016) write that gender and intersectionality can be added to the power dimension in the sensitizing questions. This new methodology therefore shows the possibility of connecting the feminist perspective to other disciplinary fields and paradigms. This is also important in the context of the lack of crossovers, especially into mainstream research (Benschop and Verloo 2016).

## Crossover between Literature: The Case of Category Making

Part of the ongoing equality or sameness and difference debate in the feminist research is the theoretical discussion about category making, which is not exclusive to the feminist approach. For example, categories based on social groups, their usage and their implications for in- and exclusion also play an important role in critical or interpretive research on policy making and the state (Hancock 2007; Stone 1988; Yanow 2003). In these studies, categories are taken to be an important device in meaning making. Drawing on a social constructivist starting point, both the work on category making in feminist research and critical policy research emphasize the social constructiveness of categories in use, and show the essentializing or reifying effect of naming and labelling (for example, Crenshaw 1991; Meadow 2010; Verloo 2006; Yanow, van der Haar and Völke 2016). Moreover, they draw attention to the implications for (reinforcing) stigmatization, marginalization and exclusion.

One example of a study based on a crossover between literatures from different disciplines is Meadow's (2010) study of legal gender categories. Here, Meadow combines critical literature on category making in the context of the state and state institutions, as well as queer theory (in which the binary classification of gender as identity is rejected; Holmes 2007) on legal categories, with a feminist sociologist perspective. This theoretical embedding is used to study how the literal gender order is constructed and how institutions gender individuals (Meadow 2010). Her discursive analysis is based on 38 U.S. court cases from the time span 1966–2007, which are analyzed from an inductive grounded theory approach based on Strauss and Corbin (Meadow 2010). Meadow studied cases in which transgender and transsexual litigants asked for a reclassification of their legal gender and shows how gender categories and gender logics are institutionalized. This subject is as insightful as it is because gender reclassification requests create a "category crisis" (Garber in Meadow 2010: 815) at these institutional sites. The study reveals that the gender order that the involved judges (re)produce is primarily based on the heterosexual conjugal family. Meadow explains that judges, in their assessment of whether to label an individual as a woman or a man, draw on body logics and hetero-logics, which she critiques as privileging particular social roles of men and women. She concludes that current legal constructs of gender cannot keep up with the demands for gender fluidity (2010: 832).

Like the interpretive work on, for example, Dutch state-defined categories to distinguish the (non-)migrant background inhabitants of the Netherlands (Yanow, van der Haar and Völke 2016), Meadow's (2010) study shows how categories are expressions of dominant meanings that are institutionalized. At the same time, they also enable reflection on what is considered "normal" and what is considered problematic. As both studies show how gender/sexuality and race/ethnicity work as organizing structures of society (Hancock 2007), the focus of the analysis always includes the implications of the use of categories in institutionalized settings on inclusion and exclusion. It would be worthwhile for critical scholars with a focus on language to take notice of the similar patterns found in these different fields. That is, here, the feminist approach – both in terms of approach and research subject – is of interest for a broader community of scholars.

## Conclusion

This chapter, for which I used auto-ethnographic elements from my own academic journey, shows how a postmodern feminist perspective relates to interpretive work. Starting from a social constructivist perspective, the two share a similar interest in studying meaning making in the context of who has the power to define. As a result, taking a critical perspective, both also study the implications of these power relations. For that matter, the knowledge production on framing and its implications for understanding inequalities could benefit from this *interpretive* feminist approach.

Benschop and Verloo (2016: 108) argue that the impact of feminist theorizing of power, inequalities, justice and equal opportunities is influenced by the disciplinary fragmentation within social sciences and epistemological compartmentalization following the boundaries between the different feminist strands and propose to overcome this by creating dialogue and collaboration. In this chapter I have tried to give two possible subjects for dialogue and collaboration in the context of discursive analysis: the methodological tool of Critical Frame Analysis and the focus on category making. Both of them have the potential to connect the feminist perspective to other disciplinary fields and paradigms.

## Notes

1 Note that as a result of this personal journey perspective, the literature I discuss here is selective and does not do justice to the richness of the field.
2 I thank Rosalind Cavaghan, Eline Severs, Laura Visser, Laura Berger, Niels Spierings, Liza Mügge and Saskia Bonjour for sharing their thoughts and literature lists with me.
3 Whereas earlier methodological discussions among feminists were about the need to use specific feminist methods to capture women's experiences and to escape the androcentric bias, currently some feminist scholars argue that it is not so much the methods themselves but how methods are applied and interpreted that holds an androcentric bias (Spierings 2016).

## References

Bacchi, Carol. 1999. Introduction: Taking problems apart. In: Bacchi, Carol, *Women, Policy and Politics: The Construction of Policy Problems*. London: Sage, 1–13.
Benford, Robert D. and David A. Snow. 2000. Framing processes and social movements: An overview and assessment. *Annual Review of Sociology*, 26: 611–639.
Benschop, Yvonne and Mieke Verloo 2016. Feminist organization theories: Islands of treasure. In: Mir, Raza, Hugh Wilmott and Michelle Greenwood (eds) *The Routledge Companion to Philosophy in Organization Studies*. London/New York: Routledge, 100–112.
Brouns, Margo. 1995a. Feminisme en wetenschap. In: Brouns, Margo, Marianne Grünell and Mieke Verloo (eds) *Vrouwenstudies in de jaren negentig. Een kennismaking vanuit verschillende disciplines*. Bussum: Coutinho, 11–28.
Brouns, Margo. 1995b. Kernconcepten en debatten. In: Brouns, Margo, Marianne Grünell and Mieke Verloo (eds) *Vrouwenstudies in de jaren negentig. Een kennismaking vanuit verschillende disciplines*. Bussum: Coutinho, 29–52.
Bryman, Alan and Emma Bell. 2015. *Business Research Methods*. Oxford: Oxford University Press.
Chambers, Clare. 2013. Feminism. In: Freeden, Michael and Marc Stears (eds) *The Oxford Handbook of Political Ideologies*. DOI: 10.1093/oxfordhb/9780199585977.013.0010.
Cole, Elizabeth R. and Abigail J. Stewart. 2012. Narratives and numbers: Feminist multiple methods research. In: Hesse Biber, Sharlene Nagy (ed.) *The Handbook of Feminist Research: Theory and Praxis*. Los Angeles, CA/London/New Delhi: Sage, 368–378.
Crenshaw, Kimberley. 1991. Mapping the margins: Intersectionality, identity politics, and violence against women of color. *Stanford Law Review*, 43(6): 1241–1299.
Davis, Kathy and Lorraine Nencel. 2011. Border skirmishes and the question of belonging: An autoethnographic account of everyday exclusion in multicultural society. *Ethnicities*, 11(4): 467–488.
Dhamoon, Rita Kaur. 2013. Feminisms. In: Waylen, Georgina, Karen Celis, Johanna Kantola and S. Laurel Weldon, (eds) *The Oxford Handbook of Gender and Politics*. DOI: 10.1093/oxfordhb/9780199751457.013.0003.
Hancock, Ange-Marie. 2007. When multiplication doesn't equal quick addition: Examining intersectionality as a research paradigm. *Perspectives on Politics*, 5(1): 63–79.
Harding, Sandra. 2004. A socially relevant philosophy of science? Resources from standpoint theory's controversiality. *Hypatia*, 19(1): 25–47.

Hesse Biber, Sharlene Nagy (ed.). 2012. *The Handbook of Feminist Research: Theory and Praxis*. Los Angeles, CA/London/New Delhi: Sage.

Hesse-Biber, Sharlene Nagy and Patricia Lina Leavy. 2007. *Feminist Research Practice*. Thousand Oaks, CA/London/New Delhi: Sage.

Holmes, Mary. 2007. *What Is Gender? Sociological Approaches*. London: Sage.

Joshi, Aparna, Brett Neely, Cynthia Emrich, Dorothy Griffiths and Gerry George. 2015. Gender research in AMJ: An overview of five decades of empirical research and calls to action. *Academy of Management Journal*, 58(5): 1459–1475.

McCall, Lesley. 2005. The complexity of intersectionality. *Signs*, 30(3): 1771–1800.

Meadow, Tey. 2010. A rose is a rose: On producing legal gender classifications. *Gender and Society*, 24: 814–837.

Olesen, Virginie. 2005. Early millennial feminist qualitative research: Challenges and contours. In: Denzin, Norman K. and Yvonna S. Lincoln, *The Sage Handbook of Qualitative Research*. Thousand Oaks, CA/London/New Delhi: Sage, 235–278.

Prasad, Pushkala. 2005. *Crafting Qualitative Research: Working in the Postpositivist Traditions*. Armonk, NY/London: M.E. Sharpe.

Razack, Sherene H. 2004. Imperilled Muslim men, dangerous Muslim men and civilized Europeans: Legal and social responses to forced marriages. *Feminist Legal Studies*, 12: 129–174.

Reger, Jo. 2014. The story of a slutwalk: Sexuality, race and generational division in contemporary feminist activism. *Journal of Contemporary Ethnography*, 44(1): 84–112.

Reinharz, Shulamit. 1993. Neglected voices and excessive demands in feminist research. *Qualitative Sociology*, 16(1): 69–76.

Roggeband, Conny, Saskia Bonjour and Liza Mügge. 2016. Gender in het curriculum: marginaal of integraal? *Tijdschrift voor Genderstudies*, 19(2): 127–140.

Schön, Donald and Martin Rein. 1994. *Frame Reflection: Toward the Resolution of Intractable Policy Controversies*. New York: Basic Books.

Silverman, David. 2001. *Interpreting Qualitative Data: Methods for Analysing Talk, Text and Interaction*. London/Thousand Oaks, CA: Sage.

Spierings, Niels. 2016. Introduction: Gender and comparative methods. *Politics & Gender*, 12(3). https://doi.org/10.1017/S1743923X16000350.

Stone, D. 1988. *Policy Paradox and Political Reason*. Boston, MA: Little, Brown.

van der Haar, Marleen. 2007. *Ma(r)king Differences in Dutch Social Work: Professional Discourse and Ways of Relating to Clients in Context*. Dissertation. Amsterdam: Dutch University Press.

van der Haar, Marleen and Mieke Verloo. 2016. Starting a conversation about critical frame analysis: Reflections on dealing with methodology in feminist research. *Politics & Gender*, 12(3). https://doi.org/10.1017/S1743923X16000386.

Verloo, Mieke. 2005. Mainstreaming gender equality in Europe: A critical frame analysis approach. *Greek Review of Social Research*, 117 B: 11–34.

Verloo, Mieke. 2006. Multiple inequalities, intersectionality and the European Union. *European Journal of Women's Studies*, 13(3): 211–228.

Verloo, Mieke (ed.). 2007. *Multiple Meanings of Gender Equality: A Critical Frame Analysis of Gender Policies in Europe*. Budapest/New York: CEU Press.

Verloo, Mieke and Emanuela Lombardo. 2007. Contested gender equality and policy variety in Europe: Introducing a critical frame analysis approach. In Verloo, Mieke (ed.) *Multiple Meanings of Gender Equality: A Critical Frame Analysis of Gender Policies in Europe*. Budapest/New York: CEU Press, 21–49.

Yanow, Dvora. 2003. *Constructing "Race" and "Ethnicity" in America: Category-Making in Public Policy and Administration*. Armonk, NY: M.E. Sharpe.

Yanow, Dvora. 2006. Thinking interpretively: Philosophical presuppositions and the human sciences. In: Yanow, Dvora and Peregrine Schwartz-Shea (eds) *Interpretation and Method: Empirical Research Methods and the Interpretive Turn*. Armonk, NY/London: M.E. Sharpe, 5–26.

Yanow, Dvora and Peregrine Schwartz-Shea (eds). 2006. *Interpretation and Method: Empirical Research Methods and the Interpretive Turn*. Armonk, NY/London: M.E. Sharpe.

Yanow, Dvora, Marleen van der Haar and Karlijn Völke. 2016. Troubled taxonomies and the calculating state: Everyday categorizing and "race-ethnicity" – the Netherlands case. *Journal of Race, Ethnicity, and Politics*, 1: 187–226.

# 5

# QUALITATIVE MANAGEMENT RESEARCH IN THE SHADOW OF IMPERIALISM

## Some Elementary Remarks on Its Othering Processes from a Muslim Perspective

*Farzad Rafi Khan*

## Introduction

Scholars have noted the absence of non-Western voices in management scholarship (Calás and Smircich 1999). They graciously extended an invitation to scholars from the Global South to participate in the conversations on management from their own authentic worldviews and distinctive epistemic resources. Almost a decade and a half later Mir and Mir (2013) pointed out that apart from a smattering of articles (e.g. Khan and Koshul 2011) appearing almost exclusively in a few scant special issues (e.g. Jack *et al.* 2011; Alcadipani *et al.* 2012), non-Western voices have yet to make any noticeable mark in management and organization studies (MOS) including in its register of qualitative research. Western epistemic conventions dominate the field and their non-Western counterparts remain marginalized or othered. Why is that the case?

In this chapter I wish to address this question, drawing from my own experiences as an academic from and situated in the Global South trying to publish qualitative management research from a non-Western perspective. In my case that perspective is orthodox Islam. It is a tradition that, while containing variegated and contested understandings within it, nonetheless holds Islam to be a universal divinely revealed religion with traditionally trained scholars called *'ulema* (the equivalent of Rabbis in orthodox Judaism) as the most authoritative interpreters of this dispensation.

I would like to share with you how in this struggle of raising my own voice emerging from the epistemic resources of orthodox Islam I have experienced the processes of othering circulating in qualitative management research, even though ironically neither I nor anyone else for that matter is an other. As the great postcolonial theorist Robert Young (2012) points out, there is no 'Other'. After all, whoever falls in that category is a flesh and blood human being, not some alien species. There are, however, as Young goes on to note, othering processes which take that human being and unjustifiably alienate or marginalize her. That is, make her othered. What are the othering processes at work in qualitative management research that perpetuate its Eurocentric character? And what do these othering processes mean for qualitative management researchers who are othered, who have to digest it in their everyday existence? This essay is hopefully a first stab at addressing these questions. Taking my cue from the burgeoning work on reflexivity (Alvesson *et al.* 2008; Gilmore and Kenny 2015) and auto-ethnography (Bartunek 2006; Learmonth 2007; Van Buskirk and London 2008; Prasad 2014) in MOS, I wish to reflect upon the othering processes that I have been confronting as a follower of orthodox Islam who is engaging with the tribe of Western management qualitative researchers and their totemic knowledge rituals and claims.

Let me be clear at this juncture. I am not providing *the* authoritative experience of Muslims practising qualitative management research with the othering processes they have encountered when plying their craft. I am simply presenting here the othering processes that I have been facing as an orthodox Muslim engaging with qualitative research in the MOS field situated in the West. These are based on my own two decades of experience as an orthodox Muslim in the MOS academic community. I do hope that what I share will resonate with my qualitative research colleagues who also feel having been othered. However, that is for them to decide. At this point my intent is in raising the level of debate on othering processes in qualitative management research that putatively showcases itself to oppose them rather than settling the issues arising from them.

In what follows, I shall narrate the challenges and issues that I face as a Muslim qualitative management researcher who strives to be a practising orthodox Muslim. I conceptualize these challenges as belonging to two realms: ideational and material. Ideational problems refer to those challenges and issues that spring from qualitative research management knowledge as currently constituted either based on realist or constructivist epistemologies. In the second category lie those concerns that stem from the material historical events and social practices that have come to shape the wider cultural formation of the West in which the qualitative management research tribe is embedded. For example, the material event of belligerent military action carried out by certain Western powers (e.g. the United States and Britain) against Muslim states (e.g. Iraq, Afghanistan, Yemen, Somalia, Pakistan, and the list is likely to be extended under the Trump presidency) might create a culture of hostility or demagoguery against a Muslim and all that the Muslim represents, thus, forming a formidable challenge to her. In such a charged context, space in management studies may not be given where the Muslim's views can be expressed, or if expressed, would be read with such prejudice as to be derisively dismissed a priori on the conviction that the 'barbaric' other is bestial and, thus, simply incapable of any worthy idea.

The two above-mentioned categories are being treated here, for analytical purposes, as separate. However, it should be pointed out that the issues and challenges found under one category may shade into or overlap into those found in the other category. Moreover, these issues and challenges being quite numerous, cannot all be discussed here. Instead, I will focus on the most important challenges facing me in each of the two realms, beginning with the ideational.

## The White Scholar's Burden

One major culprit generating othering in qualitative management research is the sheer weight of Eurocentrism in the field where for much of its theoretical concerns the othered was considered irrelevant and given no space to represent herself (Calás and Smircich 1999). One continuing reality of Eurocentrism is that the othered who can represent themselves from their own epistemic resources just do not exist. They have to be represented by us (the privileged West-based scholars of course in our own epistemic fashions).

This Eurocentric presupposition (i.e. there is no other who exists who is fully acquainted with our cosmology but yet believes in a different one which he can use to communicate and dialogue with us) is so widely albeit implicitly held that we find many passages which echo it, even in otherwise sensitive and thoughtful works such as the piece by Calás and Smircich (1999). For example, calling for the need to have a more inclusive conversation, they write:

> Thus, if *we* are to really engage in a global conversation, postcolonial theories are an excellent place for *us* to start learning how to write *in* theoretical voices that allow spaces for 'the other' to 'speak back'.
>
> *(1999: 662–663; my emphasis)*

The above passage takes the concerned presupposition as its unstated, taken-for-granted context. That is, it has been written as if the othered with her own worldviews does not exist and, therefore, since there is no othered to represent herself, the burden of representation, as the passage states, is on *us*, and *we* must learn how to write in a way that carries the other's speech *back* to *us*. In other words, Calás and Smircich's (1999) message of the need to learn how to represent the other, is based on the said taken-for-granted presupposition. The othered, one of whom is perhaps this author, who can write back to the management tribe, to slightly paraphrase the Sudanese political scientist El-Affendi (1991), the thoughts of her (othered) universe in the language of our (the West's) town, is simply not there. Therefore, it is up to *us* (Western qualitative research management academics) to learn writing in new ways, so that the othered speech can be recovered and voiced.

Thanks to this presupposition blinder, a discourse that I call 'A White Scholar's Burden', is produced. It mirrors closely its colonial predecessor. The natives have to be assisted and it is up to us to do the needful. The tacit assumption in all this is that either the natives do not exist or are incapable of conversing with *us*. Either way this native, and I trust others in a similar situation, will not feel flattered.

The foregoing basically explicated the somewhat ubiquitous presupposition that has thus far blinded the qualitative research management tribe to the possibility of the other producing scholarship in her own worldview. As long as this blinder exists, there appears in effect to be no space available for me and I trust other non-Western minorities to participate on our own terms. The hand wringing by the establishment for more Third World content is simply a message of the white scholar's burden, a self-invitation to themselves to speak on behalf of the othered, as my above commentary on Calás and Smircich suggests, not an invitation for the othered to speak. Thus, the othered does not speak. For me and for many of my similarly positioned Muslim colleagues with whom I have discussed this issue, this is indeed the message. Thus, we shelve our worldviews, adopt the accepted worldviews of the qualitative management tribe and pen our tales based on them. No wonder a dean in one of the universities where I worked in Muslim South Asia, cognizant of this reality, gave my colleagues and me the helpful advice to avoid using local data and the local epistemic resources of Islam for our research. Ethnocentrism and its variant Eurocentrism continue unabated. The qualitative management research tribe keeps on worrying about them, ironically not seeing, thanks to the blinder, that the manner in which they bemoan the situation helps in reproducing it.

Hopefully, this essay, by making us aware of such a presupposition blinder, will help the qualitative research management tribe in the task of removing it, thereby creating a more receptive atmosphere for the othered to speak back. However, the need to overcome this presupposition blinder is just one of many challenges and issues that confront me as the Muslim othered.

## Knowledge in Mid-air

While the white scholar's burden is an external impediment for us to go beyond the gates guarding 'proper' qualitative research scholarship, the other ideational barrier is that the epistemic resources in qualitative research considered acceptable in the positivists to the constructivist factions are not satisfying to ground any claims on reality. Much ink has been spilled in the paradigm wars with no clear victor emerging from the positivist or the constructivist camps. The conclusion is that the paradigm debate is irresolvable because the axioms on which they are based are incommensurable (Alvesson *et al.* 2008). There are no common terms of engagement between the two tribal camps. I beg to differ.

As an outsider and to use a Sufi metaphor, qualitative researchers appear to be searching outside on the road where there is a streetlight for a key that has been lost inside the house. No wonder the search is not getting anywhere. Discovery often first entails searching for other lights (knowledge) rather than just using the ones available. There is a light available to the academy not being used that for a Muslim makes the incommensurability thesis a non-issue. That light is logic, naïve and crude though it may sound to Westernized ears.

A Muslim aware of his knowledge tradition is sensitized to the presence of logic. Al-Ghazali, the eleventh-century Muslim theologian par excellence, used it to devastating effect to protect orthodox Islamic creedal formulations from the onslaught of neo-Platonic thought (Al-Ghazali CE 1100). The constructivists will be rolling up their eyes at this naïve and medieval suggestion. I suggest they roll up their sleeves and open up an elementary book on logic (e.g. Copi and Cohen 2008). Logic is simply rules of reasoning and has little to say about validating knowledge claims on empirical reality. To say that leprechauns exist is as logical as to say that I am writing this paper. Logic helps us with assessing the coherence of an argument (e.g. a square is a circle or proposition *p* is also simultaneously −*p* (not *p*) are meaningless statements), not so much with testing its truth claims. No logician will say that Russell's formulation that 'Golden mountains are golden' proves the existence of golden mountains because it is logical.

As classical Muslim scholars recognized, human beings, no matter from what belief structure, rely on logic (rules of reasoning in the strict sense of the contradiction *p* and the negation of *p* simultaneously holding is meaningless) in formulating their positions. When I apply this insight to the paradigm wars, the whole affair loses much significance. Allow me to explain.

When a postmodern says that meaning is slippery I do not think that she is simultaneously holding that meaning is not slippery. Clearly, there is an authorial intent and a desire to communicate a message with a meaning that may or may not get through as intended to the recipient. I doubt any postmodern author wishes to affirm and negate each and everything she says at the instantaneous point of enunciation. To accept such universal possibilism where even contradictions (e.g. proposition *p* and its negation −*p*) simultaneously hold implodes meaning. Conversation ends. When I can say that you have passed could also mean at the same time you have failed, what do the terms 'pass' and 'fail' then denote? If black is simultaneously white, as in the example used by Rumi's father, then what is black and what is white (Lewis 2000)?

This is also Chomsky's point in that logic is extremely useful in detecting incoherence, as in his classic formation 'Colourless green ideas sleep furiously' (Chomsky 2002: 15) where grammatically correct sentences such as this one turn out to be incoherent and do not contain any meaning. Just as Chomsky (2002) shows that syntax is independent from meaning, so too is our ability to see fundamental incoherence reached independently of any paradigm we may hold. One may be a theist or an atheist and still agree that the statement that it is raining and not raining makes no sense. Logic transcends paradigms or is found in all of them, including postmodernism, notwithstanding the bizarre and embarrassing appropriation of the particle–wave duality debate in physics to make the contrary point (Sokal and Bricmont 1998). I have not yet come across any physics paper or physicist that makes the incoherent claim that light while a wave is simultaneously also not a wave.

From this it follows that the paradigms are not incommensurable in that they share logic between them and logic can be used to at least assess the coherence of their positions. Al-Ghazali did this brilliantly. His major beef with major philosophers in his time period was their lack of reflexivity in applying to themselves the same rigorous logical reasoning by which they judged others and found them wanting. When Al-Ghazali (CE 1095) did so, especially in his profound tract *Tahâfut al-falâsifa* (The Incoherence of the Philosophers), he demonstrated that the major, often Greek in provenance, philosophical systems of thought in vogue among the intellectual class in his day ended up making claims that contradicted their own epistemic standards. They were found to be self-referentially incoherent, much like the claim that all truth is relative or we do not believe in dogma which itself is a dogmatic statement.

Qualitative management research, either in the constructivist or positivist camp, I feel, is not that far from the unreflexive philosophers of Al-Ghazali's days who studiously avoid applying on themselves their own epistemic standards they use for judging opposing philosophical schools, particularly those outside the current Western epistemic canon. When I carry out, albeit in quite a superficial fashion, the Al-Ghazalian task of checking for coherence in qualitative management research, I too find the results not very satisfying from an epistemic perspective. Constructivists implode on themselves. If all truths are mere conventions and socially constructed, then what about this statement? As a Muslim, a constructivist epistemology is incoherent at the most primitive and basic levels of rules of reasoning and that is perhaps why Berger and Luckmann (1967) studiously avoided applying their own standard to their own theory.

Similarly, when I subject the positivist camp to a coherence test, the results are equally unsatisfying. Most of the positivists are rooted in natural scientific materialism, sharing with it its ontological presupposition that reality is simply a brute fact (Bunge 1998). It just exists and there is no purpose or reason behind its existence. Hence a brute fact. If I take this brute fact argument to its logical conclusion, as Stephen Parrish (1997) has done, we again reach an incoherent end. If the universe exists purely on chance (i.e. as a brute fact) then so would everything in it exist on chance. Human beings would also exist by chance, their cognitions also would be arbitrary or exist by chance and their resultant thoughts are therefore also arbitrary, which means that brute fact theory is also purely arbitrary as it is a result of human cognition. If so, then there is no basis why we should place any value on it as being true as it claims to be an outcome of pure chance. Brute fact theory, which undergirds the positivist paradigm, undermines all knowledge (as all knowledge is coming from chance-like arbitrary processes) and thus it refutes itself. So much for population ecology!

When I teach doctoral students in the Muslim Global South, there is quite a bit of awkwardness when we realize that to us the powerful insights of qualitative research are like a towering giant whose feet are firmly planted in mid-air. At best they are convenient fictions. This realization does not really excite much enthusiasm and thus reduces in us the desire to engage with qualitative management research, thereby strengthening the othering. It also makes us wonder if there is any point to us participating in this knowledge enterprise, apart from quelling the sharp prods emanating from the dull compulsions of economic living, to use a phrase of Marx.

## Homogenous Pluralism

Related to the paradigm wars, is the agreement in qualitative management research that the wars suggest the fact of pluralism in management studies (Pfeffer 1993; Van Maanen 1995), especially the corpus of works in it based on qualitative research. This pluralism appears quite homogenous when I reflect upon it, from my vantage point of orthodox Islam.

Admittedly, there appears to be considerable diversity of *beliefs* in the management academy that make up the bulk of its scholarship, what with all the *isms*, such as feminism, Marxism, poststructuralism and managerialism, to name a few. However, if one digs deeper, one finds them all to be permutations of a singular noetic structure based on material atheism defined here as rejection of belief in a conscious, sacred and immutable transcendental reality which is unseen yet impacts the seen world.

Knowledge stems only from the human being and there are no other sources of knowledge (e.g. Revelation). This is to say then that, to use the Qur'anic metaphor of a tree, the *isms* are simply the many twigs or branches belonging to a single tree (worldview) rooted in material atheism, which is *believed* to be True and Correct and, therefore, serves as the unquestioned, accepted default generative noetic structure from which all worldviews are constructed. Thus, for an orthodox Muslim, and, I trust, for others ascribing to a worldview rooted in a conscious sacred, there appears to be no or at least substantive diversity or pluralism as all the *isms* appear to be reflections of only one worldview: material atheism. Sure there are articles from Judeo-Christian scriptures (e.g. Pava 1998) or Buddhist perspectives (e.g. Kernochan *et al.* 2007), but these are so few as to be effectively non-existent.

Of course, one could object to the lumping of so many diverse positions ranging from positivist to constructivist perspectives into one worldview. Nonetheless it is a view that is prescribed by contemporary Muslim theologians and scholars writing on these matters, such as the American Iranian philosopher and theologian Syed Hossein Nasr (1990), who see the wider Western social scientific academy as being atheistic. And what one is concerned with here is mapping and documenting *a* Muslim perception and not so much with the validity of the latter or what it *ought* to be.

Continuing, then, with this perception, the position of having a noetic structure in the sacred is the norm for human history, and it is the mainstream perspectives with their denial of a conscious unseen that appear to be quite unique and an anomaly. As Nasr (1990: 98) writes:

> As long as man has lived on earth, he has buried his dead and believed in the afterlife and the world of the Spirit. During the 'hundreds of thousands' of years of human life on earth, he has been traditional in outlook and has not 'evolved' as far as his relations with God and nature, seen as the creation and theophany of God, are concerned. Compared to this long history … the period of the domination of modernism stretching from the Renaissance in Western Europe in the 15th century to the present day appears as no more than a blinking of an eye. Yet it is during this fleeting moment that we live; hence the apparent dominance of the power of modernism before which so many Muslims retreat in helplessness, or which they join with that superficial sense of happiness that often accompanies the seductions of the world.

Given this perception of Western scientific knowledge rooted in the *belief* in material atheism, unconnected to the sacred, individuals in my position find themselves, like Prophet Abraham (peace be upon him), faced with the question of how to engage with a dominant culture which is antithetical to one's beliefs. This Abrahamic question raises many concerns. These are quite succinctly articulated by the Sudanese political philosopher El-Affendi (1991: 88):

> We are all being overtaken by, absorbed into, this expanding universe, the center of which lies beyond our control … Our decision is: we want to be effective, to influence

our world, to change it. And to live in it, to participate in its affairs. But we also do not want to be someone else to do this.

But to what extent is one 'allowed' to be oneself and participate in the dominant culture of our time … in this age of pluralism (or polytheism, to use Weber's characterization), where everyone is free to worship the god of his choice, and no one is entitled to ask which is the True God. We Abrahamites want to turn our face away from this multiplicity of gods who may all be false gods, but can certainly not all be true. But what are we doing in the pantheon, then? How can we preach our one True God at the festival that is content to celebrate polytheism? Well, by doing just that: preaching, making our stance perfectly clear. Our problem with 'pluralism', though, is that its tolerance comes to an end when its basis is questioned. You are all right around the place if you are a polytheist with a different god. But if you reject all gods and want out, then you have a problem.

A Muslim researcher, as the above quote aptly conveys, is riddled with doubts when reading the academy's celebration of pluralism. This is especially the case when one is cognizant of its convenient and self-referentially incoherent understanding of pluralism where there is almost no space for those who wish 'to ask which is the True God'. Moreover, someone in my situation has to deal with the question of why would the secular priesthood of the qualitative research management academy 'tolerate' a speech rooted in the unseen sacred whose very presence directly or implicitly challenges or *problematizes* the unquestionable, above reproach, basis (i.e. material atheism) on which the 'diverse' idols in its temple are constructed. As El-Affendi says:

> Is there a choice between perpetual marginalization outside the traditions of Western scholarship and virtual absorption within them? Could we make our voice heard within this towering hall, and if we did, will it die within the noise because it would not be different, or would it only be a minor note within an imposing symphony the conductor of which lies beyond our reach?
>
> *(1991: 84)*

Hence material atheism on which much of qualitative management research is predicated is a profoundly othering process. The prospects it generates for researchers like me are either banishment (i.e. 'perpetual marginalization') outside the Western MOS academy if we wish to work with theistic perspectives that are belligerently rejected by reviewers who helpfully advise me to submit my works to journals in theology or virtual absorption within it by letting go of such perspectives and prostrating to the epistemic Gods currently holding sway there. If these are apparently the two unsavoury prospects that confront an orthodox Muslim and, I would trust, othered researchers whose worldviews have not been mainstreamed, why bother writing from our own sacred epistemic resources? Easier is it not to be an Uncle Tom (accept and work with the established master Western epistemic conventions) and earn our wages (publications)?

## The Imperial Problem

In terms of othering processes stemming from historical and material social practices, the most difficult in this category, and perhaps the most formidable of all, is the legacy of a string of material events known as Western imperialism, arguably beginning from at least the time of Columbus's 'discovery' and sadly continuing today with the current acts of Western aggression in Iraq being one of its many presently ongoing manifestations. This imperialism not only physically assaulted and othered human beings particularly in the Third World but it also engaged in a material production of texts and practices that demonized them as well. This demonization was required so that tremendous violence could be carried out against the othered, for what one was then expurgating was not one's fellow human beings, but some sub-human species, which by being made sub-human or 'savage' had, as Bauman (2000) says, its moral demands cancelled and, thus, could be treated with an attitude of ethical indifference. An attitude extremely serviceable to Empire as it is quite congenial to the use of force because the pain and suffering inflicted on the othered is a matter of pure irrelevance to it and, thus, would pose no serious moral problems that might otherwise dampen the enthusiasm for efficiently carrying out the good work of Empire.

A result of this demonization or polemics of Empire has been that a wall of prejudice has been created which has seeped deeply into Western consciousness, forming a generative base from which spring a stream of ongoing texts and (mis)understandings of the othered that are produced by and in turn reproduce this wall. This wall is a major problem for an orthodox Muslim. I have called it the imperial problem as it arises significantly from the imperial encounter with the othered.

The imperial problem is one that practically almost all members of the othered would experience. Western civilization in modern times, more than any other civilization, has had, it could be argued, the somewhat unique distinction of waging, ostensibly often in the name of self-defence, war on and demonizing, at one time or another, almost the rest of humanity, ranging from the Indian 'savages' of North America to the 'gooks' of Vietnam (Chomsky 1993) and now the 'sand-niggers' of Iraq (Gordon and Trainor 2007). Though what will follow would be an exposition of the imperial problem from the perspective of an orthodox Muslim, many of the issues and concerns discussed here would resonate with non-Muslim othered as well given, as stated above, the shared nature of this problem.

The imperial problem is particularly acute in the case of Islam in the West, even before the terrorist attacks of 9/11. Five years before 9/11 Nasr (1996: 551) was saying:

> the only political unity observed in the West these days appears in its hatred of Islam, as shown in the case of Bosnia and Chechnya, where one has observed, with very few exceptions, the uniformity of silence, indifference, and inaction by various voices in the West in the face of the worst kind of human atrocities.

The seeds of this hatred can be traced, at least to the time of the first crusades, where polemical tracts against Muslims as 'heathens' began to be produced (Asad 1982). However, in spite of this enmity, the West respected Islam and its civilization and society, borrowing heavily its science and philosophy, art and architecture, literature and mystical symbols, as well as some of its major institutions, such as colleges of education (Makdisi 1981). There are many reasons for this respect, the most primary being that the West and the Islamic World had an affinity in that they shared the principle of a belief in the sacred, and were more or less on equal footing in terms of military and political prowess, which made it difficult for the West to view Islam as an insignificant other.

The pivotal event that began the end of the respect of Islam in the West, according to Norman Daniel's (1997) authoritative study on the genealogy of erroneous Western myths about Islam and its practitioners, was the reconquest of the Iberian Peninsula completed in 1492. The reconquest signified the end of eight centuries of Muslim civilization in Spain in particular and in Europe in general. What came next was the Spanish Inquisition with its mass slaughter campaigns that effectively exterminated and expelled the indigenous Jewish and Muslim populations. During the reconquest, much was added to the polemics against Islam. Distortions done at that time have persisted till today and form much of what is currently (mis)understood in the West to be Islam (Daniel 1997). However, it was in the next two centuries, what is hailed as the flowering of the Renaissance period, that the open hatred of Islam, the kind we witness in the contemporary era, took hold of the Western imagination. In the words of Nasr (1996: 553):

> This was the period of humanism in the nonreligious sense of the term – anthromor-phism, opposition to the certitude brought about by faith, individualism based upon rebellion against all higher authority, and also Eurocentrism, all of which have characterized the Western worldview ever since. These ideas stood not only against the West's religious heritage, but even more so against Islam, which has always opposed severely any titanic and Promethean view of humanity and has emphasized man's humble state before the grandeur and majesty of the Divine.

Since then much has been spewing forth from this hatred of Islam that has reinforced and further intensified it. Of course, a few Muslim extremists have worsened the situation, especially in the post-9/11 era, by resorting to senseless terrorism, thus providing further grist for the mills of demonizing Islam. The net result is what has above been called the imperial problem. The centuries of misrepresenting Islam has sunk deep into Western consciousness, forming a generative base from which spring an ongoing stream of such texts and (mis)understandings of the other that are produced by and in turn further deepen this base. From Disney cartoons such as *Aladdin*, where the villains are shown with distinctively Arab characteristics and the Islamic penal punishments are mocked, to everyday headlines like 'The Red Menace is Gone. But Here's Islam' (Sciolino 1996) appearing in the agenda-setting media, one hears a consistent drumbeat of anti-Islam polemics, with the recent Republican primaries of 2016 and the soon to be inaugurated Trump administration marching to that beat.

This drumbeat reductively shrinks Islam to 'brutality, fanaticism, hatred and disorder' (Ahmed 1988: 1). To an orthodox Muslim negotiating herself in the Western management academy, this reductive view of Islam, the imperial problem, produces great consternation of a kind that would be felt by an African-American speaking about the contributions of Black African civilizations in an all-white assembly in Alabama prior to the civil rights reforms of the 1960s. To paraphrase Said (1997: xxi), one experiences feelings of guilt and being constantly on trial, which is perhaps precisely the feelings one is meant to have in the overall hostile atmosphere.

From the relentless insistence of the mass media, where a Muslim's faith, culture and people are seen as a source of threat and where the Muslim is deterministically associated with violence, to the 'playful' banter of colleagues that assign 'terrorist' attributes to you, it is not difficult to imagine, with slight empathy, how all this would make a Muslim qualitative management researcher constantly feel uncomfortable. I remember having a conversation as a doctoral student in a common student office with two other fellow students, one from Iran and the other from Turkey. In the conversation, we were discussing movies and one of us just said 'That movie bombed'. Just then a white North American colleague of ours popped his head in and said 'Why is it that with you guys we only hear about bombs'. This was his attempt at a joke. We laughed it off but the insult and the hurt remained.

Being the butt of such jokes, with their imperial problem provenance, makes us the othered again ask the question whether it is worthwhile expending efforts in engaging with the qualitative management tribe in othered vocabularies (e.g. orthodox Islam) given that the imperial problem may make it incapable for them to listen. One can and many do give up and the imperial problem thus succeeds in othering us.

If one decides to make such efforts then one still ends up courting other dangers. One runs the risk of providing privileged insider information that otherwise would not be accessible to the West, which can then be used by powerful institutions there to further undermine the othered. The Foucauldian 'Knowledge is Power' problematic is quite real, especially in the context of Islam. In the words of El-Affendi (1991: 84–85):

> Firstly, there is no secret that Western scholarship in the fields of Orientalism and 'area studies' has not shied away from acting as the handmaiden of imperialist designs of control and hegemony over the people they 'studied'. Western scholars, journalists, politicians, and 'diplomats' form closely knit mutually dependent communities that hang together abroad and interact frequently at home (as advisers, sources, etc.), with constant personnel movements across the boundary lines. It is not inconceivable, therefore, that my contribution to Western scholarship in this specific area could end up strengthening the instruments of control and manipulation deployed by Western imperialist interests bent on containing the Islamic revival I so much cherish and hope to advance.

What is to be done is not so clear cut. However, the above 'Knowledge is Power' problematic seems to be the least of a Muslim's worries in the present scenario of Islam–West relations. Muslims are eager to dialogue because not only is it strongly encouraged in their tradition, but also because they are of the opinion that the more the world accurately knows about Islam, the better, as they view ignorance to be the major handicap preventing the West from dealing peacefully with Islam on its own terms.

## Conclusion

Why do I care what a Muslim has to say about the state of qualitative management research and its othering processes? Substitute for Muslim the following: Jew, Black, Gay or Woman. Now ask if you are still comfortable in posing that question. Even if Muslims end up reconfirming your understanding about qualitative management research, that piece of information is still worthy to know that others who do not share your worldviews end up with the same conclusions. And when they do not on some issues, as I hope I have done here, you have learned something different.

In this chapter, I have refracted qualitative management research through the filter of being an orthodox Muslim qualitative management researcher. This familiar terrain I hope no longer looks the same. Paradigm wars and the philosophical debates ironically show the absence of philosophy in qualitative management research education. Incommensurability, as I see it, can be easily bridged between the positivist and constructivist camps in that both share and accept logic and thus there is terms of engagement between them. However, when we apply this common standard, we find that epistemologically the camps cease to exist in any convincing fashion. Moreover, the camps are not all that different when viewed from a theistic perspective, such as that of Islam. There are variations on the singular theme of material atheism and that seems to be the only epistemic game in town. Thus, pluralism vanishes from this perspective. When this absence is combined with the palpable presence of the belligerent history of the West and the rest, there appears to be a lack of space available to publish content using othered worldviews, protests to the contrary notwithstanding. In fact, these protests couched as a white man's burden of the established scholars taking on the responsibility of inscribing the othered, exacerbate the situation further. They prevent the realization that the othered do exist and are capable of conversing using their own worldviews.

This flow of history and ideas makes swimming against its currents a treacherous affair and many an othered scholar stops the struggle and drifts onto familiar mainstream research channels. No point taking arms against a sea of troubles, especially when the penalties to deviate are menacing, from economic impoverishment to social stigmatization. Herein may lie some additional clues, taken from an untried source (i.e. the Muslim othered), as to why the field continues to remain embarrassingly Eurocentric.

In spite of all these challenges, nonparticipation in qualitative MOS is not an option. For sure, not to wade in (i.e. to stay away from the Western dominated qualitative management tribe), would save one from having to suffer the insolence of the gods of highly privileged Western epistemologies where you can only be allowed admission if you prostrate to one of them and denounce all current heresies, particularly essentialism and theism. However, it would effectively preclude one from making acquaintances and later friendships with other members in the qualitative management research tribe. It is these friendships that can sire the creation of networks that would collaborate to open up the margins, for not just orthodox Muslims but different othered scholars, to visibility in the academy. This visibility would help make the qualitative management research tribe aware of the existence of the othered comfortable in her own worldviews, thus reversing the presupposition blinder, mentioned earlier, where it was presupposed away that the othered could possibly exist. Now that the othered with the visibility brought by the formation of scholarly networks would be in sight, qualitative management research may give serious consideration to othered perspectives, which would hopefully make it easier to legitimately pursue and publish insightful and edifying research, enriching qualitative management research.

Whether such networks of friendship would be formed, given the othering processes identified here, is for history to determine. The odds are slim. Being that as it may, one must engage. For the othered like me there is not much to go on at this point except a bias for hope and solidarity. However, let us not forget Roger Bacon. He, and that too in the supposedly 'dark' middle ages, wore an Islamic dress (turban and all) at Oxford and lectured about learning from Islam (Nasr 1996) – a public position that he would perhaps be hard pressed to make in these 'postmodern' times thanks to the imperial problem that has gone on steroids after 9/11. Surely then there must be a few Bacons out there in the qualitative management research community. Time for you to step up as well and let us do research relating to one another on the magnificent precept laid out by the great Jalaluddin Rumi: 'You and I have to live as if you and I never heard of a you and an I'.

# References

Ahmed, A.S. (1988) *Discovering Islam: Making Sense of Muslim History and Society*, London; Routledge & Kegan Paul.

Alcadipani, R., Khan, F.R., Gantman, E. and Nkomo, S. (2012) 'Southern voices in management and organization knowledge', *Organization*, 9: 131–143.

Al-Ghazali, A.H. (CE 1095) *Tahâfut al-falâsifa*, trans. M.E. Marmura (2000) *The Incoherence of the Philosophers: A Parallel English-Arabic Text*, Provo, UT: Brigham Young University Press.

Al-Ghazali, A.H. (CE 1100) *Munqidh Min Al-'dal'al*, trans. R.J. McCarthy (1980) *Freedom and Fulfillment: An Annotated Translation of Al-Ghazali's Munqidh min al-Dalal and Other Relevant Works of Al-Ghazali*, Boston, MA: Twayne.

Alvesson, M., Hardy, C. and Harley, B. (2008) 'Reflecting on reflexivity: Reflexive textual practices in organization and management theory', *Journal of Management Studies*, 45: 480–501.

Asad, M. (1982) *Islam at the Cross Roads*, Gibraltar: Dar Al Andalus.

Bartunek, J.M. (2006) 'The Christmas gift: A story of dialectics', *Organization Studies*, 27: 1875–1894.

Bauman, Z. (2000). *Modernity and the Holocaust*, Ithaca, NY: Cornell University Press.

Berger, P.L. and Luckmann, T. (1967) *The Social Construction of Reality: A Treatise in the Sociology of Knowledge*, London: Penguin Press.

Bunge, M.A. (1998) *Philosophy of Science*, New Brunswick, NJ: Transaction.

Calás, M.B. and Smircich, L. (1999) 'Past postmodernism? Reflections and tentative directions', *Academy of Management Review*, 24: 649–671.

Chomsky, N. (1993) *Year 501: The Conquest Continues*, Boston, MA: South End Press.

Chomsky, N. (2002) *Syntactic Structures*, New York: Mouton de Gruyter.

Copi, I.M. and Cohen, C. (2008) *Introduction to Logic*, Upper Saddle River, NJ: Pearson/Prentice Hall.

Daniel, N. (1997) *Islam and the West: The Making of an Image*, Oxford: Oneworld.

El-Affendi, A. (1991) 'Studying my movement: Social science without cynicism', *International Journal of Middle East Studies*, 23: 83–94.

Gilmore, S. and Kenny, K. (2015) 'Work-worlds colliding: Self-reflexivity, power and emotion in organizational ethnography', *Human Relations*, 68: 55–78.

Gordon, M.R. and Trainor, B.E. (2007) *Cobra II: The Inside Story of the Invasion and Occupation of Iraq*, New York: Vintage Books.

Jack, G., Westwood, R., Srinivas, N. and Sardar, Z. (2011) 'Deepening, broadening and re-asserting a postcolonial interrogative space in organization studies', *Organization*, 18: 275–302.

Kernochan, R.A., McCormick, D.W. and White, J.A. (2007) 'Spirituality and the management teacher: Reflections of three Buddhists on compassion, mindfulness, and selflessness in the classroom', *Journal of Management Inquiry*, 16: 61–75.

Khan, F.R. and Koshul, B.B. (2011) 'Lenin in Allah's court: Iqbal's critique of Western capitalism and the opening up of the postcolonial imagination in critical management studies', *Organization*, 18: 303–322.

Learmonth, M. (2007) 'Critical management education in action: Personal tales of management unlearning', *Academy of Management Learning and Education*, 6: 109–113.

Lewis, F. (2000) *Rumi: Past and Present, East and West: The Life, Teaching and Poetry of Jalâl al-din Rumi*, Oxford; Boston, MA: Oneworld.

Makdisi, G. (1981) *The Rise of Colleges: Institutions of Learning in Islam and the West*, Edinburgh: Edinburgh University Press.

Mir, R. and Mir, A. (2013) 'The colony writes back: Organization as an early champion of non-Western organizational theory', *Organization*, 20: 91–101.

Nasr, S.H. (1990) *Traditional Islam in the Modern World*, London: Kegan Paul International.

Nasr, S.H. (1996) 'Islam and the West: Yesterday and today', *American Journal of Islamic Social Sciences*, 13: 551–562.

Parrish, S.E. (1997) *God and Necessity: A Defense of Classical Theism*, Lanham, MD: University Press of America.

Pava, M.L. (1998) 'The substance of Jewish business ethics', *Journal of Business Ethics*, 17: 603–617.

Pfeffer, J. (1993) 'Barriers to the advance of organizational science: Paradigm development as a dependent variable', *Academy of Management Review*, 18: 599–620.

Prasad, A. (2014) 'You can't go home again: And other psychoanalytic lessons from crossing a neo-colonial border', *Human Relations*, 67: 233–257.

Russell, B. (2004) *Mysticism and Logic*, Mineola, NY: Dover Publications.

Said, E.W. (1997) *Covering Islam: How the Media and the Experts Determine How We See the Rest of the World*, New York: Vintage Books.

Sciolino, E. (1996) 'The red menace is gone. But here's Islam', *New York Times*, 21 January, p. 1.

Sokal, A.D. and Bricmont, J. (1998) *Fashionable Nonsense: Postmodern Intellectuals' Abuse of Science*, New York: Picador USA.

Van Buskirk, W. and London, M. (2008) 'Inviting the muse into the classroom: Poetic license in management education', *Journal of Management Education*, 32: 294–315.

Van Maanen, J. (1995) 'Style as theory', *Organization Science*, 6: 133–143.

Young, R.J.C. (2012). 'Postcolonial remains', *New Literary History*, 34: 19–42.

# PART II

# Traditions

# 6

# RIGOR IN THEORY BUILDING FROM MULTIPLE CASES

*Kathleen M. Eisenhardt and Timothy E. Ott*

## Introduction

Theory building from multiple cases is a research strategy that has played a significant role in fields such as strategy, organization theory, entrepreneurship, and organizational behavior over the past 80 years, ranging from classic studies like Whyte's study of street corner society (1943) and Chandler's (1962) exploration of corporate organizational structure to contemporary work. Research using this method is disproportionately recognized by awards such as the *Academy of Management Journal*'s annual best paper prize (Gersick 1988; Gilbert 2005; Ferlie et al. 2005; Graebner 2009), is often highly cited (Baker and Nelson 2005; Eisenhardt 1989b; Harris and Sutton 1986), and is seen as generating some of the "most interesting" published research (Bartunek et al. 2006).

Yet while theory building from multiple cases is an important research strategy, there is confusion around how to judge whether a particular study is rigorous. Some of this confusion comes from deductive researchers who misunderstand core features of the method such as theoretical sampling and replication logic. Other confusion stems from imposing criteria that may be only superficially relevant to rigor or particularly ill-fitting for multiple cases (Bansal and Corley 2012). In this chapter, we explore what theory building from multiple cases is, its evolution as a research method, criteria by which its rigor can be accurately judged, and false criteria that may be unhelpful or even flawed. We also comment on the current and future states of theory building from multiple cases.

## What Is Theory Building from Multiple Cases?

Theory building from multiple cases is a research strategy that combines a grounded theory-building process with case study research design and analytic logic. By a *case study*, we simply mean a stand-alone, thick description of specific instantiations of a given phenomenon which is usually crafted from multiple data sources (Yin 2013). Case studies may rely on historical data such as Hargadon and Douglas's (2001) account of Thomas Edison's venture into electric lighting, ethnographic observations such as Kaplan's (2008) study of strategy making in the telecommunications industry, or a mix of data sources such as Garg and Eisenhardt's (in press) examination of strategic decision making by boards of directors in entrepreneurial firms that blends interviews, observations, and survey data. Regardless of the specifics, the hallmark of a case is deep immersion in a phenomenon, often with embedded (i.e., nested) levels of analysis (Eisenhardt 1989a). By *grounded theory building*, we mean the process of inducting theory from emergent patterns within data (Glaser and Strauss 1967). In theory building from multiple cases, the cases are the empirical evidence from which researchers induct theoretical constructs and relationships among them, and support them with underlying theoretical logic (Eisenhardt et al. 2016). The aim of this research strategy is to build strong new or elaborated theory.

Theory building from multiple cases has a long history within the social sciences. An early example is Whyte's (1943) famous ethnography that compares Italian street gangs in Boston. Another early example in economic history is Chandler's (1962) classic study of the emergence of the multi-divisional form in several iconic corporations including DuPont and General Motors. The method, however, became more explicit and codified with the publication of two books. The first explicates grounded theory building (Glaser and Strauss 1967) by defining the core research process, and explaining key concepts like theoretical sampling and theoretical saturation. The second expands understanding of cases (Yin 2013) by similarly defining the process of conducting case study research and central concepts like replication logic and embedded design. Together, these works helped to launch the take-off of this research strategy in the 1980s. Throughout the 1980s and 1990s, theory building from multiple cases became increasingly popular and accepted in mainstream journals. While more rigorous than in the past, multi-case theory building at this time was more relaxed than it is today. As an illustration, Eisenhardt's (1989b) study of fast strategic decision making in six entrepreneurial firms was motivated by observing that the research question of how to make a fast strategic choice effectively addressed an intriguing and relevant topic. Indeed, simply having a "cool" research question was enough for most reviewers. No explicit propositions were required. The emergent theory was often more cross-sectional than processual and took a positivist stance. In fact, research using theory building from multiple cases at this time often emphasized the close tie of many elements of the research process to traditional deductive research (albeit while indicating differences such as theoretical sampling) (Eisenhardt 1989a). The intent was to accelerate mainstream acceptance by creating a clearly articulated bridge to the dominant approach of deductive theory-testing research.

By the early 2000s, the editorial process in the major journals had shifted toward demanding that the research question be well-positioned in extant research streams (not just be "cool"), formal propositions be articulated, and emergent theory be processual by illuminating a sequence or flow of events over time (Eisenhardt and Graebner 2007). Theory building from multiple cases became more accurately understood as relevant to philosophically diverse scholars who are nonetheless interested in a systematic research strategy to build theory from data. Thus, theory building from multiple cases is used across a variety of types of qualitative research including interpretivist research with its focus on in-person lived experience and ethnographic work emphasizing rich observation of culture (Kaplan 2008).

More broadly, theory building from multiple cases complements other theory-building approaches such as formal modeling, computational simulation, and arm-chair theorizing. Often (although not always), the research seeks to explain variation in processes or outcomes, and to provide insight into managerial implications. As an example, the research from Stanford Technology Ventures Program (our research and teaching center) has developed normative insights into how entrepreneurs and executives alike succeed (or not) in high-velocity environments such as through fast decision making (Eisenhardt 1989b), effective negotiation of venture acquisitions (Graebner 2009), building high-performing alliance portfolios (Ozcan and Eisenhardt 2009), and successful venture capital fundraising (Hallen and Eisenhardt 2012). Such insights are driven by a multiple-case research theory-building strategy that often can provide better grounding, more variation in the data, and greater generalizability than single-case research. It would have been difficult, if not impossible, to have obtained these insights with other methods.

Our specific focus here is theory building from multiple cases, typically between two and 12. Single-case research has the advantage of enabling the study of a unique or extreme situation that may not be accessible through other methods (e.g. Tripsas 2009). By contrast, multiple-case research has the advantage of making it more likely that the resulting theory will be accurate, generalizable and parsimonious (Eisenhardt 1991; Eisenhardt and Graebner 2007).

*Theoretical sampling* is at the heart of theory building from multiple cases (Eisenhardt 1989a). Theoretical sampling involves selection of cases based on their likelihood of illuminating the focal phenomenon, and seeks theoretical generalizability (Glaser and Strauss 1967). It contrasts with random sampling which centers on drawing observations from a population and seeks generalizing to the population. Theoretical sampling enables the researcher to hone in on the phenomenon, create opportunities for comparison across cases, and adjust the data collection to take advantage of new insights and unexpected opportunities.

*Replication logic* is also central to theory building from multiple cases. Replication logic means that each case stands on its own as an individual unit of analysis, much like individual laboratory experiments. Thus, the researcher uses each case to replicate the insights from some other cases, contrast with some cases, and elaborate the emergent theory to fit the case (Yin 2013). Frequently, researchers also use an embedded design in which there are multiple units of analysis. For example, Smith (2014) explores how the top management teams of six strategic business units within a single Fortune 500 firm balance exploration and exploitation across multiple decisions within each firm. The emergent theory fits each of the cases. Similarly, Hallen and Eisenhardt (2012) use an embedded design to study how entrepreneurs strategically form ties with venture capitalists by inducting their emergent theory using data about the tie formation process in nine Internet security ventures and over multiple rounds of financing within each venture.

An important point is that theory building from multiple cases effectively complements other research approaches. The method can yield propositions that can be formally tested using econometric methods. For example, Hallen's (2008) work on initial tie formation of entrepreneurial firms was informed by his earlier multiple-case theory-building study of how entrepreneurs gain investments (Hallen and Eisenhardt 2012) (despite the deductive paper's making it through the publication cycle first!) Theory building from multiple cases can also be useful for developing the "simple" baseline theory that can seed simulation research. For example, Brown and Eisenhardt's (1997) work led to insights about simple rules that Davis et al. (2009) extended by using simulation methods to conduct computational experiments that could not have been undertaken in the "real world." Theory building from multiple cases can also complement formal modeling by providing high-level initial insights that mathematical models can more precisely unpack. For example, Helfat and Eisenhardt (2004) describe the intertemporal economies of scope employed by a major Fortune 500 firm. Building on an earlier "theory building from multiple cases" study (Galunic and Eisenhardt 2001), the authors describe how product-market responsibilities were routinely reallocated among business units within this firm. They found that the firm created value through resource relatedness by redeploying resources between business units ("intertemporal economies of scope") during this reallocation. Sakhartov and Folta (2014) then used a formal model to extend the prior work by unpacking the contingencies surrounding resource redeployment to sharpen how synergistic resources created value.

## Rigor in Theory Building from Multiple Cases

Four major criteria shape the rigor of research that uses theory building from multiple cases. As described below, rigor is best assessed by the strength of the emergent theory, quality of the grounding of that theory in the data, precision of the research design, and whether the research question is intriguing and appropriate for the method (see Table 6.1).

### *Strong Emergent Theory*

First and foremost, rigorous theory building from multiple cases rests on whether the emergent theory is accurate, internally coherent, and parsimonious – i.e., strong theory. As noted above, the aim of theory building from multiple cases is the development of strong (and novel) theory. So, the emergent theory must be more than engaging stories and detailed diagrams. Rather, like all strong theory, it requires well-defined constructs, clear relationships among those constructs, and compelling underlying logic that supports these relationships. Moreover, the process of grounded theory building makes strong theory more likely to emerge. That is, the researcher repeatedly iterates between the data and emergent theory, and later with the extant literature, until a theory (i.e., constructs, relationships, and logic) that closely fits the cases emerges.

An excellent example of strong emergent theory occurs in the Heinze and Weber (2016) study of how intrapreneurs effectively used political tactics to assimilate "integrative medicine" – i.e., the combination of Eastern and Western medical practices – into their large healthcare organizations. In describing their process theory for intrapreneurial political action, the authors carefully define each of their emergent constructs (e.g., jurisdiction over resources), and indicate how each construct was measured (e.g., multiple examples of each construct's measures). They then go on to indicate how the different constructs temporally and logically relate to one another (e.g., concurrent v. sequential). The authors also provide the underlying logical arguments for *why* the constructs are related in the way they propose (e.g., successful actors gain jurisdiction over resources and leverage their status prior to engaging in other tactics because these former tactics create a protective environment).

In addition, strong theory requires addressing alternative explanations and specifying boundary conditions. Alternative explanations increase confidence in the validity of the theory while boundary conditions specify the scope of the theory and determine its generalizability. Pache and Santos (2013) provide a helpful illustration in their study of blending institutional logics in French social service enterprises. The authors build an emergent theory regarding the effectiveness of "selective coupling" of elements from alternative institutional logics. Yet they also thoughtfully address alternative explanations for success such as founding period and organizational size, and identify the boundary conditions for their theory such as situations with institutional competition.

Finally, strong theory is parsimonious – i.e., as simple as possible while still including the core insights of the theory that contribute to the accuracy of the theory. Multiple-case research is particularly useful in this regard because the juxtaposition of multiple cases is likely to increase creative insight while the iterative comparison and contrast among cases and with the extant literature help researchers to abstract from the specifics of any individual case, develop an accurate theory, and avoid the trap of building an overly complex theory that fits every small detail of an idiosyncratic case. So while an advantage of theory building from cases is the use of detailed and fine-grained data, it also helps to enable the emergence of a strong theory on which core theoretical elements occur at an appropriate level of abstraction. By contrast, complex "spaghetti" diagrams and convoluted arguments are rarely the elements of strong theory.

Table 6.1 Rigor in Theory Building from Multiple Cases

| Criteria for Rigor | Definition | Research Steps | Traps |
|---|---|---|---|
| Strong emergent theory | Accurate, internally coherent, and parsimonious emergent theory. | • Define each construct sharply.<br>• Indicate how each construct is measured.<br>• Specify relationships between constructs.<br>• Provide underlying arguments for why the constructs are related in the proposed way.<br>• Repeatedly iterate between data and emergent theory, and later with the extant literature, to abstract up from specific cases to more accurate and parsimonious theory.<br>• Address alternative explanations. | • Avoid complex "spaghetti" diagrams and fitting theory to every detail of cases.<br>• Avoid vague definitions and inaccurate construct measures. |
| Compelling evidence | Grounding of each construct for each case with well-measured and appropriate data. | • Collect data from multiple types of sources and informants – e.g., interviews, observation, press releases, and social media.<br>• Match data sources with the research question and design.<br>• Present data to ensure readers can confirm the systematic grounding of emergent constructs and theory in the data – e.g., use of construct tables, process diagrams, temporal bracketing, and timelines are often effective. | • Avoid partial or no grounding of constructs in data for each case.<br>• Avoid building theory from pre-conceived notions rather than data.<br>• Avoid force-fitting data into inappropriate writing templates like data structures. |
| Theoretical sampling and research design | Selection of cases to yield data about the focal phenomenon while controlling unwanted variation and creating generalizability. | • Choose cases in which the focal phenomenon is apparent and in the foreground while simultaneously placing in the background and even controlling for unnecessary or unhelpful variation.<br>• Choose a research design that matches the research question – e.g., polar types, racing, or antecedent matching – either explaining variation or creating variation that improves generalizability. | • Avoid random sampling if possible. |
| Intriguing research question | Unanswered and wide-open question, given high bar for insight and originality. Often "how" questions about process. | • Read the current literature precisely to understand its major gaps, conflicts, or unrealistic assumptions.<br>• Emphasize process phenomena, especially complex, equifinal or configurational ones. | • Avoid incremental questions.<br>• Avoid "how much" questions – e.g., effect size is of interest. |

## Compelling Evidence

Rigorous theory building from multiple cases also rests on grounding emergent constructs in compelling and convincing data. The first step in achieving this grounding is the researchers' immersion in rich data about the focal phenomenon, typically by collecting extensive data from multiple types of sources and informants. Unlike traditional deductive research, theory building from multiple cases rarely involves easily measured, objective constructs like size and age (Powell and Baker 2014; Rogers et al. 2016). This puts a premium on triangulation of multiple types of data from multiple sources to increase confidence that the constructs are accurately captured (Jick 1979). A combination of qualitative and quantitative data can be particularly useful in helping the researcher to maintain some distance from their own preconceptions and biases. In addition, while interviews and observation are common sources of the detailed case chronologies that undergird theory building from multiple cases, it is also useful to complement these data types with other data sources such as archival data, surveys, and real-time information. Press releases are a classic source, but with the explosion of social media – blogs, Facebook, Twitter, and YouTube to name a few – the researcher can also gather data that were generated in real time (Toubiana and Zietsma in press).

A second important step in providing compelling evidence is matching data sources with the research question and design of the study. Some research questions are effectively addressed through interviews, but others are better addressed with observational data, deep historical dives, or other approaches. For instance, Garg and Eisenhardt (in press) studied how entrepreneurial CEOs effectively manage strategic decision making with their boards. The authors relied on multiple waves of interviews with key informants such as CEOs, venture executives and board members. Yet given the focus on board-level interaction, the authors also collected extensive observational data on the board meetings themselves. Observing actual board meetings enabled the researchers to more accurately ground their emergent process theory constructs in the most relevant data. This approach got to the heart of the research question by ensuring data from highly relevant interactions among CEOs and board members as they debated strategic direction.

Perhaps most importantly, grounding constructs in a compelling way within the data requires researchers to convey this grounding to the reader. This means providing the relevant data to readers in a way that they can clearly see the tie between the emergent constructs and theory with the actual data that grounds them. Although a "data structure" table has become a popular way to tie constructs to measures (or alternatively, tie codes to themes), it does not actually reveal the data (Gioia et al. 2013). So while useful as an organizing device, it does not address whether the data are compelling. A "data and themes" table links examples of data to a particular theme or construct. But while these tables may work well for single-case researchers who then also use a rich textual narrative to reveal the focal case (Gioia et al. 2013), they rarely work well for multiple-case researchers. The reason is that these tables do not clearly tie the data grounding each construct to each case. Further, there is typically insufficient space in journal articles to provide a detailed narrative for each case in a multiple case as is likely when reporting single-case research.

Instead, an often more relevant approach for theory building from multiple cases is creating separate "construct tables" for each focal construct that summarize the evidence supporting that construct on a case-by-case basis. For instance, Battilana and Dorado (2010) study the efficacy of two microfinance ventures trying to alleviate poverty in Bolivia. The authors use separate tables for each case that track a variety of data (e.g., number of branches, return on equity) over time to ground the key construct of "operational evolution" for readers. They later use other tables with mostly qualitative data from both firms to compare the core processes of hiring and socialization. This enables the authors to highlight the similarities and differences between the two ventures, and permits the reader to see clearly which data underlie the emergent theory. Using a similar approach, Davis and Eisenhardt (2011) also use construct tables to report the evidence for each of their emergent constructs by case. More broadly, researchers may find other reporting techniques like process diagrams, temporal bracketing, and timelines (Langley 1999) to also be useful for conveying the grounding of emergent theory in the data. Regardless of the presentation approach, our key point is that rigorous research using theory building from multiple cases requires grounding the emergent theoretical constructs in compelling and convincing data that is made clearly available to readers. This practice helps to ensure both that emergent theory is accurate and true to the empirical context, and that its constructs are measurable and thus that the theory is testable.

## Theoretical Sampling and Research Design

Rigorous theory building from multiple cases also depends on effective theoretical sampling and research design. As per above, theoretical sampling involves the selection of cases to improve the likelihood of strong theory. It typically involves choosing cases in which the focal phenomenon is apparent and in the foreground while simultaneously placing in the background and even controlling for unnecessary or unhelpful variation. Our point is that the research design (and its related use of theoretical sampling) is essential for rigorous theory building from multiple cases. There are several common and effective theoretical sampling designs.

When the research question focuses on explaining variation, a "*polar types*" research design can be effective. In theoretical sampling for polar types, the researcher chooses cases at extremes (e.g., very high and very low performing) in order to sharpen the contrast between patterns in the data. This type of sampling makes it easier for the researcher to observe patterns in the constructs, relationships, and the logic of the phenomenon of interest. For example, Martin and Eisenhardt (2010) use a polar-types design in their study of how executives successfully create cross-business-unit collaborations in multi-business organizations. They studied six software firms. Within each firm, the authors worked with corporate executives to select two recent collaborations for the study – one high performing and one low performing. This approach made the organizational differences among the collaborations more apparent while also controlling for the individuals involved. That is, the two collaborations within each firm involved mostly the same people and yet produced widely differing outcomes. It thereby yielded an emergent theory for how multi-business firms effectively "rewire" the collaborative connections among their businesses.

While "polar types" can be an effective design, it is not always possible to know a priori where the variance (if any) will occur or the research question may focus on similarities rather than differences. Here an effective approach can be choosing cases which are likely to reveal the focal phenomenon and to manage the variation across cases. That is, the researcher chooses cases in a way that will ensure, remove, and/or control variance. An example is the study by Garg and Eisenhardt (in press) of how CEOs effectively (and ineffectively) engage in strategic decision making with their boards. The authors purposely chose ventures in which the CEO was a first-time CEO in order to increase the probability that they would observe a range of CEO behaviors – some effective and some not. In addition, they chose ventures that had raised at least a Series B round of venture capital such that they were likely to be sufficiently mature to be engaging in strategy making. They also selected ventures in the information technology sector to both study a sector where strategy making would be frequent as well as to control for sector variance across the cases. In other words, the authors selected cases with an understanding of where there was likely to be variation and where there was not.

Another approach to improving the likelihood of variance across cases is to use a "*racing*" design in which the actors within the focal cases begin some process at the same time and then "race" to a "finish line." This research design is meant to reveal the processes by which emergence winners, also-rans, and losers emerge, and thus improve the empirical base for inducting a variance theory about processes (e.g., McDonald and Eisenhardt 2017). An illustration is the study by Ozcan and Eisenhardt (2009) of the formation of alliance portfolios by new entrant-publishers in the nascent mobile gaming industry. The study illustrates how entrepreneurial firms with similar starting positions nonetheless progressed along different paths chosen by their entrepreneurs. At the end of the study, there were clear winners and losers. Similarly, Hannah and Eisenhardt (2016) studied the "race" to superior performance by five U.S. residential solar ventures that began in the same year. At the end of the "race," one firm dominated the industry while another had failed.

While some research questions center on variance, other research questions are focused on similarity. In this situation, researchers again choose research designs and cases based on their likelihood of revealing the focal phenomenon. Here, however, theoretical generalizability is particularly important. This calls for sampling the phenomenon in a variety of settings. An example of this research design is Bingham and Eisenhardt's (2011) study of what entrepreneurs learn from their ventures' experiences in successive entries into new countries. For this paper, they selected six firms that were able to internationalize effectively, but purposely also chose ventures from culturally distinct home countries (i.e., Singapore, the United States, and Finland) to improve the likely generalizability of their emergent theory beyond a single country.

Overall, theoretical sampling and research design importantly influence the rigor of research that uses theory building from multiple cases. The above is not an exhaustive typology of research designs but rather is suggestive of possibilities that are likely to lead to more rigorous research because researchers are exploring cases that are more likely to illustrate the focal phenomenon while also control for unwanted variation and enhance theoretical generalizability.

## *Intriguing Research Question*

A final aspect of rigor in research that uses theory building from multiple cases is an intriguing research question that both fits the method and produces insightful theory. A key challenge in using theory building from multiple cases is the high bar for insight and originality in the publication process. The first step in clearing this bar is to understand the relevant extant literature thoroughly such that researchers select intriguing and wide-open questions that fit the method. A major way to find these questions is to begin by reading the literature precisely.

For instance, Davis and Eisenhardt (2011) were interested in R&D innovation collaboration between major firms. At first glance, there is much prior research in this area (e.g., Anand and Khanna 2000). However, a precise reading of that research reveals that it is focused principally on structural antecedents to collaborations such as prior collaborations together and whether the focal firms have dedicated alliance functions, are roughly the same size, and have similar country backgrounds. Yet this extant research often neglects the actual collaboration processes and a rich conception of their outcomes. This led to the specification of the study's research question: How do firms effectively collaborate in R&D collaborations?

Similarly, Graebner (2009) began her study of venture acquisitions with a thorough reading of the mergers and acquisitions (M&A) literature. She found that the existing literature emphasized the buyer's perspective, and implicitly assumed that the seller was unimportant. From that understanding of the extant literature, she studied 12 ventures in three sectors (in each sector, three firms were acquired and a fourth could have been acquired but declined). This led Graebner to a series of theory-building papers in which she explicated the role of the seller in the acquisition process – i.e., decision to sell (Grabner and Eisenhardt 2004), negotiation between the buyer and seller (Graebner 2009), and integration of the selling firm by the buyer (Graebner 2004). Theory building from multiple cases was particularly appropriate here because existing theory taking the seller's perspective simply did not exist, despite the fact that sellers were often extremely important in the acquisition process and often determined whether an acquisition occurred at all. Instead, the buyer point of view dominated the extant research.

A precise reading of the literature can also reveal intriguing research questions that are driven by conflict within the literature or other problematic features such as unrealistic assumptions. Here, research questions tend to be more tightly scoped in the existing theory, and theory building from multiple cases can provide researchers with the rich data needed to untangle complex processes that may have led to the limitations of prior work. For example, Ozcan and Eisenhardt (2009) explored how firms originate high-performing portfolios of ties with other firms. Prior work had identified alliance portfolios as theoretically important to firm performance but offered only descriptive accounts of a deterministic evolution of portfolios as a function of firm status and resources. Thus, this work did not account for either the origin of portfolios or the role of strategic action. The authors used theory building from multiple cases to study how six rival entrepreneurial ventures strategically created their alliances portfolios over time, and inducted an emergent theoretical framework that described the process and added to the theoretical understanding of the origin of alliance portfolios and network evolution.

More broadly, theory building from multiple cases is well-suited to process studies and related "how" research questions. Here, processes unfold over time, longitudinal data are a must-have and mechanisms that compose the processes may only be observable through the rich and fine-grained data. Moreover, this research method is especially powerful when the processes are complex, equifinal, or involve configurations. For example Hallen and Eisenhardt (2012) used this research strategy to uncover equifinal processes – i.e., entrepreneurs can build ties to venture capitalists through either existing ties or a set of four sequential and overlapping behavioral activities. Similarly, Pache and Santos (2013) used theory building from multiple cases to study how hybrid logics were created at French social enterprises by merging practices from social welfare and commercial logics. They too found equifinal processes. Configurations are also relevant. For example, Battilana and Dorado (2010) used theory building from multiple cases to study how microfinance ventures in Bolivia attempted to alleviate poverty. The authors developed detailed cases around two hybrid ventures, and were able to track the evolution of organizational practices and identity at each. Through these rich data, they identified the complex configurational relationships among hiring, training, incentives, and promotion that led to one venture becoming more self-sustaining than the other and thus better able to fulfill its mission to alleviate poverty.

In contrast, theory building from multiple cases is less useful for other research questions or agendas. In particular, other methods are often more applicable when the question is embedded in well-developed theory or the researchers are interested in putting additional variables and interaction effects into the analysis. Theory building from multiple cases also has little to offer when the interest is in effect sizes or the size and directionality of interactions. In general, these are more "how much" questions as opposed to "how" questions for which regression-based analysis of large data sets tends to be more informative. Finally, there is often confusion between a variance v. process study that arises because two meanings of "process" exist in the literature. Processes can mean behavioral activities like hiring, decision making, and forming alliances.

This is our meaning and as such can be studied in terms of variance (differences) among processes or similarities. Process can also refer to a focus of similarities which is not our meaning here.

Overall, our point is that the rigor of theory building from multiple cases is influenced by whether the focal research question is both intriguing and well-suited to the method such as addressing a process or "how" question. When this occurs, the result is more likely to be novel and insightful emergent theory.

## What Is Not Rigor?

Thus far, we have argued that the rigor of theory-building research using multiple cases depends upon the strength of the emergent theory, the degree to which that theory is grounded in the data in compelling fashion, the quality of the research design, and whether the research question and thus resulting theory are intriguing, novel, and insightful. That said, readers and reviewers sometimes impose less relevant criteria including narrow standards for writing formats, rigid rules for data and data analysis notably around grounded theory building, and excessive requests for reporting the details of the research journey.

One example is requiring a precise writing format like data structures which suggests rigor but does not necessarily create rigor. Rather, the more important criteria revolve around whether the authors have convincingly conveyed the data that underlie their theory, regardless of whether they use a "standard" format. Similarly, disallowing quantitative data per se is also unhelpful as such data can offer useful triangulation and insight into qualitative evidence. As long as the researcher justifies why the data relate to understanding and describing the focal phenomenon, the use of unusual data types including quantitative data is reasonable. A rigid set of rules for what constitutes grounded theory building (e.g., such as a precise number of observations needed for theoretical saturation or insistence on an interpretivist lens) (Suddaby 2006) is also false rigor. Instead, grounded theory building is a "big tent" of varied approaches that centers on constant comparison between data and emergent theory (Walsh et al. 2015).

A final example of false rigor is requiring researchers to give a very lengthy discussion of their research journey. While this may be interesting, it may also take up precious journal space which is typically in very short supply, especially for multiple-case studies that are often particularly affected by page limits. To be clear, transparency in how the researcher conducted the study is useful, particularly regarding choices that may materially affect research outcomes. However, the quality of the theory, its grounding in compelling data, a valid research design, and the novelty and relevance of the research question are more closely associated with rigor as per above. Moreover, it is likely to be impossible to accurately convey the research journey as it often involves unexpected bolts of insight and serendipity that are difficult to convey (Klag and Langley 2013). Including details of the research process that would not change the interpretation of the data may also distract readers from the features of the research process that are critical to understand. An excellent example of balance between transparency and "oversharing" is how Graebner (2009) describes her study of trust in negotiations between buyers and entrepreneurs in venture acquisitions. In her methods section, she informs readers that informants were not explicitly asked about trust in the interviews since that was not the original focus of her study. This was important for readers to know because the informants' spontaneously speaking about trust revealed that it was a major factor in their decision making, as opposed to a response to or attempt to please the interviewer. In contrast, other details of the research journey that were not materially relevant, such as themes found in some but not all cases, were left out of the methods description.

## Boundary Conditions and Future Directions

A critical question is whether our four criteria for rigorous theory building from multiple cases (i.e., strong theory, compelling evidence, theoretical sampling and research design, and intriguing research question) extend across the varieties of qualitative research. In our view, the answer is "yes" – if the researchers' aim is theory building and their approach uses multiple cases. So, for example, some ethnographic research seeks to build theory using multiple cases (Seidel and O'Mahony 2014). Here, we think that our criteria fit well although there may be further insistence by reviewers and others to maintain proper data collection that is consistent with the norms of ethnography such as the "right way" to perform observation. But if the intent of the ethnography is a classic pure description of a particular culture, then our criteria are less relevant since strong emergent theory that generalizes is not the aim. Similarly, interpretivist research that seeks to build theory from multiple cases fit our criteria, but again reviewers and others may impose additional criteria that are associated with the interpretivist philosophical stance of obtaining data from the perspective of the lived experiences of the informants.

In contrast, single-case research that seeks to build theory is more distinctive. While it should fit the criteria of strong theory, compelling evidence, and an intriguing question, theoretical sampling and especially research design are likely to be less elaborate and germane. Moreover, the approach to writing is likely to be different. Single-case research is often written effectively by developing the case narrative and then the emergent theory (Gioia et al. 2013). But this writing approach is usually too long for multiple-case research that must fit into the page limits of most journal publications. So multiple-case research is often written best by intertwining the emergent theory with examples of supporting case evidence.

Finally, theory building from multiple-case research is an evolving research strategy. Going forward, we expect greater codification of the different types of research designs that go beyond polar types, racing, and other designs that we described here. The selection of cases remains an art but will likely become more of a "science." This will enhance rigor. We also expect that more researchers will conduct multi-method work that combines theory building from multiple cases with other methods like econometric analysis, QCA, computational simulation, and formal models. This trend is already beginning. We expect that this trend will improve rigor by sharpening the contrast between methods and thus improve researchers' approach to rigor. Greater use of digital sources of data is likely in the future (and indeed is already happening) and will bring to the foreground greater use of quantitative data for theory-building research. That said, these data do not change the basic criteria of rigorous research, in our view. Perhaps the most important future development will be greater understanding of the fundamental criteria of rigorous research, and the corresponding avoidance of false rigor that imposes arbitrary or even damaging rigidity on researchers.

## Conclusion

We began by noting the significant role of theory building from multiple-case study research within a variety of fields of inquiry. Rigorous research within this method is, of course, of prime importance. Yet, there has been confusion from a variety of perspectives about how to judge the rigor of research that uses this method. We have attempted to make the case that rigor does not rest on superficial criteria like precise writing format, following the self-proclaimed "rules" of an analytic approach, or even extensive details about the research journey. Rather, rigor depends upon many of the same criteria that characterize most, if not all, rigorous research. That is, rigor rests on a few core criteria – strong emergent theory, well-grounded in accurate data, a research design that sharply reveals the focal phenomenon, and an intriguing research question and emergent theory. The aim is the *best* possible research, not research that fits into a narrowly defined box.

# References

Anand, B.N. and Khanna, T., 2000. Do firms learn to create value? The case of alliances. *Strategic Management Journal*, 21(3), pp. 295–315.

Baker, T. and Nelson, R.E., 2005. Creating something from nothing: Resource construction through entrepreneurial bricolage. *Administrative Science Quarterly*, 50(3), pp. 329–366.

Bansal, P.T. and Corley, K., 2012. Publishing in AMJ – Part 7: What's different about qualitative research? *Academy of Management Journal*, 55(3), pp. 509–513.

Bartunek, J.M., Rynes, S.L., and Duane Ireland, R., 2006. What makes management research interesting, and why does it matter? *Academy of Management Journal*, 49(1), pp. 9–15.

Battilana, J. and Dorado, S., 2010. Building sustainable hybrid organizations: The case of commercial microfinance organizations. *Academy of Management Journal*, 53(6), pp. 1419–1440.

Bingham, C.B. and Eisenhardt, K.M., 2011. Rational heuristics: The "simple rules" that strategists learn from process experience. *Strategic Management Journal*, 32(13), pp. 1437–1464.

Brown, S.L. and Eisenhardt, K.M., 1997. The art of continuous change: Linking complexity theory and time-paced evolution in relentlessly shifting organizations. *Administrative Science Quarterly*, 42(1), pp. 1–34.

Chandler, A.D., 1962. *Strategy and Structure: Chapters in the History of the Industrial Enterprise*. Cambridge, MA: MIT Press.

Davis, J.P. and Eisenhardt, K.M., 2011. Rotating leadership and collaborative innovation: Recombination processes in symbiotic relationships. *Administrative Science Quarterly*, 56(2), pp. 159–201.

Davis, J.P., Eisenhardt, K.M., and Bingham, C.B., 2009. Optimal structure, market dynamism, and the strategy of simple rules. *Administrative Science Quarterly*, 54(3), pp. 413–452.

Eisenhardt, K.M., 1989a. Building theories from case study research. *Academy of Management Review*, 14(4), pp. 532–550.

Eisenhardt, K.M., 1989b. Making fast strategic decisions in high-velocity environments. *Academy of Management Journal*, 32(3), pp. 543–576.

Eisenhardt, K.M., 1991. Better stories and better constructs: The case for rigor and comparative logic. *Academy of Management Review*, 16(3), pp. 620–627.

Eisenhardt, K.M. and Graebner, M.E., 2007. Theory building from cases: Opportunities and challenges. *Academy of Management Journal*, 50(1), pp. 25–32.

Eisenhardt, K.M., Graebner, M.E., and Sonenshein, S., 2016. From the editors: Grand challenges and inductive methods: Rigor without rigor mortis. *Academy of Management Journal*, 59(4), pp. 1113–1123.

Ferlie, E., Fitzgerald, L., Wood, M., and Hawkins, C., 2005. The nonspread of innovations: The mediating role of professionals. *Academy of Management Journal*, 48(1), pp. 117–134.

Galunic, D.C. and Eisenhardt, K.M., 2001. Architectural innovation and modular corporate forms. *Academy of Management Journal*, 44(6), pp. 1229–1249.

Garg, S. and Eisenhardt, K.M., in press. Unpacking the CEO-board relationship in entrepreneurial firms. *Academy of Management Journal*.

Gersick, C.J.G., 1988. Time and transition in work teams: Toward a new model of group development. *Academy of Management Journal*, 31(1), pp. 9–41.

Gilbert, C.G., 2005. Unbundling the structure of inertia: Resource versus routine rigidity. *Academy of Management Journal*, 48(5), pp. 741–763.

Gioia, D.A., Corley, K.G. and Hamilton, A.L., 2013. Seeking qualitative rigor in inductive research: Notes on the Gioia methodology. *Organizational Research Methods*, 16(1), pp. 15–31.

Glaser, B.G. and Strauss, A.L., 1967. *The Discovery of Grounded Theory: Strategies for Qualitative Research*. New Brunswick, NJ: Transaction.

Graebner, M.E., 2004. Momentum and serendipity: How acquired leaders create value in the integration of technology firms. *Strategic Management Journal*, 25(8–9), pp. 751–777.

Graebner, M.E., 2009. Caveat venditor: Trust asymmetries in acquisitions of entrepreneurial firms. *Academy of Management Journal*, 52(3), pp. 435–472.

Graebner, M.E. and Eisenhardt, K.M., 2004. The seller's side of the story: Acquisition as courtship and governance as syndicate in entrepreneurial firms. *Administrative Science Quarterly*, 49(3), pp. 366–403.

Hallen, B.L., 2008. The causes and consequences of the initial network positions of new organizations: From whom do entrepreneurs receive investments? *Administrative Science Quarterly*, 53(4), pp. 685–718.

Hallen, B.L. and Eisenhardt, K.M., 2012. Catalyzing strategies and efficient tie formation: How entrepreneurial firms obtain investment ties. *Academy of Management Journal*, 55(1), pp. 35–70.

Hannah, D. and Eisenhardt, K.M., 2016. How firms navigate cooperation and competition in nascent ecosystems, working paper, University of Texas at Austin.

Hargadon, A.B. and Douglas, Y., 2001. When innovations meet institutions: Edison and the design of the electric light. *Administrative Science Quarterly*, 46(3), pp. 476–501.

Harris, S.G. and Sutton, R.I., 1986. Functions of parting ceremonies in dying organizations. *Academy of Management Journal*, 29(1), pp. 5–30.

Heinze, K.L. and Weber, K., 2016. Toward organizational pluralism: Institutional intrapreneurship in integrative medicine. *Organization Science*, 27(1), pp. 151–172.

Helfat, C.E. and Eisenhardt, K.M., 2004. Inter-temporal economies of scope, organizational modularity, and the dynamics of diversification. *Strategic Management Journal*, 25(13), pp. 1217–1232.

Jick, T.D., 1979. Mixing qualitative and quantitative methods: Triangulation in action. *Administrative Science Quarterly*, 24, pp. 602–611.

Kaplan, S., 2008. Cognition, capabilities, and incentives: Assessing firm response to the fiber-optic revolution. *Academy of Management Journal*, 51(4), pp. 672–695.

Klag, M. and Langley, A., 2013. Approaching the conceptual leap in qualitative research. *International Journal of Management Reviews*, 15(2), pp. 149–166.

Langley, A., 1999. Strategies for theorizing from process data. *Academy of Management Review*, 24(4), pp. 691–710.

McDonald, R. and Eisenhardt, K., 2017. Parallel play: Start-ups, nascent markets, and the search for a viable business model, working paper, Harvard Business School.

Martin, J. and Eisenhardt, K., 2010. Rewiring: Cross-business-unit collaborations and firm performance in multi-business organizations. *Academy of Management Journal*, 53(2), pp. 265–301.

Ozcan, P. and Eisenhardt, K.M., 2009. Origin of alliance portfolios: Entrepreneurs, network strategies, and firm performance. *Academy of Management Journal*, 52(2), pp. 246–279.

Pache, A.C. and Santos, F., 2013. Inside the hybrid organization: Selective coupling as a response to competing institutional logics. *Academy of Management Journal*, 56(4), pp. 972–1001.

Powell, E. and Baker, T., 2014. It's what you make of it: Founder identity and enacting strategic responses to adversity. *Academy of Management Journal*, 57(5), pp. 1406–1433.

Rogers, K., Toubiana, M., and DeCelles, K., 2016. Drawing fine lines behind bars: Pushing the boundaries of researcher neutrality in unconventional contexts. In K.D. Elsbach and R.M. Kramer, eds. *Handbook of Qualitative Organizational Research: Innovative Pathways and Methods*. New York: Routledge, pp. 66–76.

Sakhartov, A.V. and Folta, T.B., 2014. Resource relatedness, redeployability, and firm value. *Strategic Management Journal*, 35(12), pp. 1781–1797.

Seidel, V.P. and O'Mahony, S., 2014. Managing the repertoire: Stories, metaphors, prototypes, and concept coherence in product innovation. *Organization Science*, 25(3), pp. 691–712.

Smith, W.K., 2014. Dynamic decision making: A model of senior leaders managing strategic paradoxes. *Academy of Management Journal*, 57(6), pp. 1592–1623.

Suddaby, R., 2006. From the editors: What grounded theory is not. *Academy of Management Journal*, 49(4), pp. 633–642.

Toubiana, M. and Zietsma, C., in press. The message on the wall? Emotions, social media, and the dynamics of institutional complexity. *Academy of Management Journal*.

Tripsas, M., 2009. Technology, identity, and inertia through the lens of "The Digital Photography Company." *Organization Science*, 20, pp. 440–461.

Walsh, I., Holton, J., Bailyn, L., Fernandez, W., Levina, N., and Glaser, B., 2015. Rejoinder: Moving the management field forward. *Organizational Research Methods*, 18(4), pp. 620–628.

Whyte, W.F., 1943. *Street Corner Society: The Social Structure of an Italian Slum*. Chicago, IL: University of Chicago Press.

Yin, R.K., 2013. *Case Study Research: Design and Methods*, ed. L. Bickman and D.J. Rog. Thousand Oaks, CA: Sage.

# 7

# SINGLE CASES

## The What, Why, and How

*Pinar Ozcan, Suho Han, and Melissa E. Graebner*

Single cases have been an important methodology used by scholars to advance the field of management. Scholars have used single cases to examine a variety of complex organizational processes from corporate venturing (Burgelman, 1983) to organizational identity (Dutton and Dukerich, 1991), change (Huy, 2002), and sensemaking (Weick, 1993). Single cases have also been used at the industry level to trace the emergence of new markets (Ozcan and Santos, 2015). Despite the novel and rich theoretical insights produced from single cases, this methodology can be one of the most intimidating and challenging for organizational scholars (Yin, 2014). Researchers without proper training or familiarity in single-case research may see this methodology as one to avoid, rather than one to exploit. Moreover, other than Yin (2014), there is limited work on how to conduct rigorous and systematic single-case research in the management field. Hence, our motivation for this chapter is to provide scholars with a roadmap in conducting rigorous single-case research by highlighting the specific choices available to scholars when using single cases, the trade-offs to these choices, and strategies available to researchers in mitigating some of the challenges associated with single-case research.

To inform our roadmap in conducting single-case research, we systematically reviewed 38 single-case studies published in four top management journals[1] across various management topics (organizational behavior, strategy, organizational theory) and over time, which helps capture changes in how the methodology may have evolved. Specifically, our review includes five seminal articles published before 2000, three articles published during 2000 to 2005, 14 articles published during 2006 to 2010, and 16 articles published during 2011 to 2016. We were deliberate in selecting more studies from the last five years to capture the latest in how researchers are conducting single-case research. To place these 38 studies into context, a search of single or comparative case studies (i.e., two cases), or articles emphasizing the use of single cases as a methodology, yielded 104 articles during this same time period. Further, several special issues have showcased single-case studies examining a variety of theoretical perspectives such as institutional theory (Suddaby et al., 2010), culture in organizations (Weber and Dacin, 2011), and organizational processes related to change (Langley et al., 2013).

In the remainder of this chapter, we start by providing insight into the motivations for using single cases followed by choices regarding study design. Next, we cover topics related to field access, data collection, and analysis, and conclude our chapter by discussing ways to present single-case findings.

## Motivation: Why Single Cases?

Single cases are advantageous for four main reasons. First, researchers can gain an in-depth understanding of complex organizational phenomena from a variety of perspectives over time. Second, single cases allow researchers to take advantage of unusual access to a phenomenon that may not be easily observable to outsiders. Third, the case may be an instantiation of a rare phenomenon or process for which multiple-cases may not exist and the study of one case is enough to produce new theory. Therefore, the rationale for single-case research should be to satisfy one of three conditions: (1) the case is an unusual phenomenon; (2) the case has not been accessible to researchers before; or (3) the case can be observed longitudinally. Corresponding to Yin's (2014) rationales for conducting single-case research, these are similar to choosing a case that is "extreme" (i.e., unusual), "revelatory," or "longitudinal." Dutton and Dukerich's (1991) study on the Port Authority of New York and New Jersey, Weick's (1993) seminal study on the Mann Gulch fire disaster of 1949, and Tripsas and Gavetti's (2000) investigation of the Polaroid Corporation are prominent examples of single-case studies in management. First, these studies examined extreme cases of a particular phenomenon. The Port Authority was an unusual case of an organization responding to a highly visible and salient issue (homelessness), the Mann Gulch fire was an extreme case of organizational disintegration, while Polaroid was an unusual example of organizational inertia. Second, these cases were studied in detail over time from multiple perspectives and data sources that included several interviews and rich archival data.

A fourth reason for using single cases is to examine a phenomenon at a fine-grained level of detail that cannot be achieved through multiple cases or other methods such as large sample statistical studies. For instance, single cases are ideal for investigating complex social processes. In fact, the majority of the articles we reviewed have a strong link to organizational process research (Langley, 1999; Langley et al., 2013; Van de Ven, 1992), which largely focuses on questions examining "how and why things emerge, develop, grow, or terminate over time" (Langley et al., 2013: 1). The studies in our review emphasized four theoretical processes: (1) evolutionary change processes, i.e., the unfolding of a variety of phenomena such as how corporate venturing processes (e.g., Burgelman, 1983) or alliance negotiations (e.g., Ariño and Ring, 2010) unfold, how organizational identity changes after a merger (e.g., Clark et al., 2010), or how strategy is formulated in adhocracy (e.g., Mintzberg and McHugh, 1985); (2) organizational response to external events, i.e., behaviors within organizations subsequent to specific changes in the environment such as the Port Authority of New York and New Jersey's response to rising homelessness (Dutton and Dukerich, 1991), or a team of firefighters reacting to an unpredictable wildfire (e.g., Weick, 1993), or organizational change initiatives as a result of increased industry competition (e.g., Thomas et al., 2011); (3) work processes, i.e., daily interactions between individuals in organizations such as brainstorming (Sutton and Hargadon, 1996), the incorporation of a new technology (e.g., Bailey et al., 2011; Mazmanian, 2013), or achieving workplace inequality (e.g., Chan and Anteby, 2016); and finally (4) institutional field level change, i.e., the impact of interactions between individuals and organizations on a particular institutional field, such as the influence of dominant actors on new market emergence (e.g., Ozcan and Santos, 2015), regulatory change by entrepreneurs (e.g., Gurses and Ozcan, 2015), or the micro-processes among diverse actors to change an institution dominated by organized crime (e.g., Vaccaro and Palazzo, 2015). As apparent from above, the majority of these studies used the organizational level as the primary unit of analysis for the processes they studied while some used the interorganizational or institutional field level.

Relatedly, single cases allow researchers to study a complex process over a very long period of time that would not be practical through multiple cases. Tripsas and Gavetti's (2000) study on Polaroid is an exemplary longitudinal single case. The authors gained access to extensive archival data (public data and company archives) and conducted interviews with several informants throughout the firm's history. This resulted in a detailed historical examination of Polaroid from its founding in 1937 to its attempts at adapting to digital imaging technology in the late 1990s. The authors used this longitudinal case to ultimately develop theory on the interplay between a firm's capabilities, managerial beliefs, and organizational adaptation to radical technologies. At the industry level, the Ozcan and Santos (2015) single-case study on mobile payments examined the longitudinal and complex process of market emergence, considering factors related to various industry players and their interaction both at global and local levels to develop theory on why market emergence at the convergence of different industries may get delayed.

Overall, single cases provide several advantages. They allow researchers to examine a previously unobservable or rare instantiation of a particular phenomenon longitudinally and at a fine-grained level of detail, which would not be feasible using multiple cases. Given these advantages, researchers should strive to select a case that fits one of three rationales of being extreme, revelatory, or longitudinal. In the next section, we discuss ways to design a single-case study, with a particular emphasis on trade-offs related to using different single-case study designs.

## Study Design

Once the researcher has selected a case that is either extreme, revelatory, or longitudinal, another choice for researchers is to consider whether to use an embedded versus holistic case design. An embedded case design involves examining subunits (e.g., individuals, project teams) within a larger case (e.g., department, project, company). This design choice offers two main benefits (Yin, 2014). First, researchers can examine a specific phenomenon more systematically and in more detail, leveraging the replication logic that is typical of multiple cases (Eisenhardt and Graebner, 2007; Eisenhardt and Ott, this volume). Second, embedded cases can help alert researchers to potential changes in the research focus as case analysis proceeds. This can be particularly useful in alerting the researcher to different theories or literature that fits with the emerging findings, ultimately saving researchers time and energy while leading to theory that is more grounded in the data.

Among the single-case studies we examined, some studies clearly used logical subunits within their single case as part of the research design, while others were less explicit in using embedded cases but collected data from different levels of analysis within the case (e.g., Beck and Plowman, 2014; Hardy and Maguire, 2010; Vuori and Huy, 2016). For the studies using some form of embedded cases, researchers identified and used a variety of sub-cases. When the single case was at the organizational level, work teams, corporate venture projects, or functional departments were used as embedded cases (e.g., Bailey et al., 2011; Burgelman, 1983; Dutton and Dukerich, 1991; Galunic and Eisenhardt, 2001; McPherson and Sauder, 2013). For instance, in their study of organizational adaptation at Omni Corporation, Galunic and Eisenhardt (2001) embedded their single case with business units within Omni, which allowed a replication logic. If the single case was a phenomenon involving multiple organizations such as a merger or alliance, researchers used the involved organizations as embedded cases (e.g., Ariño and Ring, 2010; Clark et al., 2010; Denis et al., 2011; Hoffman, 2007). Further, researchers used embedded cases at the country level if their case was the emergence of a global market (e.g., Ozcan and Santos, 2015).

The decision to use embedded cases largely depends on the nature of the case and the research question. If multiple subunits exist within the case and examining these units provides additional insight into the phenomenon of interest, then embedded cases can be advantageous.

However, if the research question examines a holistic organizational level process where sub-units do not add theoretical insight, or if the case doesn't have clear subunits, then a holistic case design may be more appropriate. When choosing a holistic case design, researchers should be aware of certain risks such as the analysis remaining too abstract with less specific measures or a limited ability in noticing changes to the research focus. To mitigate these risks, researchers can collect data from different levels of analysis within their case (e.g., lower-level employees to upper management), which can result in more fine-grained insights into the phenomenon. For example, Vuori and Huy's (2016) study examining Nokia did not utilize embedded cases but collected data from several informants across the firm's hierarchy including individuals from top management, middle management, and engineers. The data from these informants, coupled with extensive archival data, led to a rich framework regarding the role of shared emotions on innovation. In other words, despite the case being largely holistic in nature, the use of data from several sources and hierarchies within the firm mitigated the risks associated with holistic cases.

As a final note on study design, we find that while the advantages of a single-case design and of multiple cases are more established, less has been said about comparative cases. Comparative cases are "at the sweet spot" between single- and multiple-case studies. The use of two cases can be advantageous as replicating the findings from one case with the other can lead to more robust and generalizable theory without too much compromise on the richness of their data. Comparative case designs have been used extensively within management (e.g., Gurses and Ozcan, 2015; Kellogg, 2011; Noda and Bower, 1996; Rindova and Kotha, 2001). They can be useful either due to the contrast between the chosen cases (e.g., Battilana and Dorado, 2010; Gurses and Ozcan, 2015; Kellogg, 2011) or due to their similarity (e.g., Heinze and Weber, 2015). For instance, Gurses and Ozcan (2015) used a wide range of archival data including interview transcripts from the 1940s to 1980s in order to compare and contrast how providers of two distinct technologies (over the air and cable TV) fought to establish pay TV services in the United States. Their comparison of one failed initiative (over the air pay TV) with a successful one (cable pay TV) led to robust results in how, in their endeavor to establish new products and services, entrepreneurs can mitigate resistance from industry incumbents through a set of framing and collective action strategies. On the other hand, the Heinze and Weber (2015) study used two integrative medicine (IM) programs inside large healthcare organizations to reinforce findings about how institutional intrapreneurs work to initiate logic change in highly institutionalized organizations. Regardless of whether the comparative case design is used to emphasize similarity or contrast, the selection of the two cases is an important choice for researchers. For instance, if the research setting is in a specific industry like in the studies above, the two cases should be similar on several dimensions (e.g., time period, size, product offering, etc.) to rule out alternative explanations and to focus on the main processes of interest.

Overall, the decision to use embedded cases within a single case, a holistic single case, or comparative cases largely depends on the case itself (e.g., the presence of logical sub-units) and the research question (e.g., a holistic organizational level process). The use of embedded cases is generally more advantageous since the phenomenon can be examined in more detail and changes in research focus may be more apparent. However, holistic cases can also be approached systematically by collecting data from lower levels of analysis. Finally, comparative case designs allow direct replication of findings and potentially stronger theory. Based on the nature of a case and research focus, researchers should consider these trade-offs when considering which design is most appropriate for their study.

## Field Access

Once a study design is chosen, another challenge is obtaining field access for data collection. Within our review, 22 articles used observations as one component of data collection, but only eight of these explicitly gave information regarding authors' field access. The commonality across these eight articles is that field access was obtained mainly by the authors' personal ties such as previous or current employment within the case setting, a research relationship, or a simply personal relationship. When the researcher does not have any personal ties to key informants for the study, there are still ways to gain access. In our experience, industry conferences where key informants for the study are likely to be present are great ways to meet in person and introduce one's research in order to gain access after the conference. In addition, we have found short introductory emails to key informants an effective way to approach them. The email should provide clear links to the researcher and to the study (we recommend putting up a simple website describing the research before approaching potential informants). It should briefly describe the benefits of participation (including a report or presentation made available to the informants) and ensure anonymity both for the informants and their company, if appropriate. We also recommend not asking for more than 20–30 minutes of the informants' time for the start as a 45- or 60-minute conversation can seem very long for busy managers. Finally, suggesting a specific time to speak (i.e., "how is next Monday morning 10 am?") rather than asking when they are available is an effective way to help potential informants commit to participating in the study.

During interviews with initial informants, it is important to ask the informants for introductions to their colleagues or other individuals who are knowledgeable or close to the phenomenon. This "snowballing" technique helps researchers leverage their initial contact to provide legitimacy to their follow-up introductions. Also, researchers should make sure to ask their informants if they'd be open to being contacted for follow-up questions. This helps to set expectations for future contact which can help to maintain field access as the case study proceeds and for potential future research.

## Data Collection

Single-case research typically requires a large amount of data since the justification of using one case is often unusual access to a level of granular detail not permitted by multiple cases. Researchers can generally collect three types of qualitative data: (1) interviews, (2) archival data, and (3) observations. While interviews with key informants are an efficient means "to gather rich, empirical data" (Eisenhardt and Graebner, 2007: 28) that capture both real-time and retrospective processes of interest, archival data can provide researchers with familiarity into the case and also serve to triangulate findings. Finally, observations allow researchers to observe their case directly in real time. In the following sections, we provide in-depth analysis on these three data sources by examining the patterns of data collection, the choices available in collecting the data, and the strategies available to researchers in mitigating potential risks associated with data collection.

### *Interviews*

Interviews are one of the most important sources of data for case research (Yin, 2014) and should always be included if the opportunity exists. Depending on the research question of the single case, interviews can be more or less critical. For instance, Chan and Anteby's (2016) case study within the Transportation Security Administration (TSA) in a large urban airport focused on examining employees' experiences with task segregation, thus interviews asking employees about how they performed tasks were the most appropriate means for data collection as opposed to other data sources.

The choice of how many interviews to conduct for a single case depends on the availability of other data sources (e.g., archives). In our review, we observed that those single-case studies with only a few or no interviews (e.g., Ariño and Ring, 2010; Hampel and Tracey, 2016; Maguire and Hardy, 2013; Rojas, 2010; Weick, 1993) typically had access to substantial archival data. For instance, Weick's (1993) case study on the Mann Gulch fire did not have any surviving informants yet he had access to Norman Maclean's detailed novel (Maclean, 1972) examining the incident. Similarly, Ariño and Ring's (2010) study examining an alliance negotiation had only three interviews, yet the authors had access to 150 pages of written communications surrounding the negotiations.

Conducting longitudinal interviews is highly beneficial for examining how complex processes unfold over time within one's case study. Conducting interviews with informants at two or more points in time is not always easy as individuals may move position or it may be difficult for the researcher to convince them to speak for a second or third time. However, given the advantages particularly for process studies, researchers should attempt to conduct longitudinal interviews if the opportunity exists. When using longitudinal interviews in a study, we recommend providing clear information in the methods section about which specific informants were interviewed, how many times, and how much time passed in between as interviewing only some informants multiple times or with different time gaps may lead to biases in the data.

If conducting longitudinal interviews are not an option, authors can still trace the unfolding of a phenomenon longitudinally by conducting interviews with informants close to the phenomenon and in real time. For example, Dutton and Dukerich's (1991) study on the New York Port Authority and the growing issue of homelessness used 25 interviews. Even though these interviews were not longitudinal, data were collected as the homeless issue was still an ongoing concern for the Port Authority and with informants directly involved with the issue. Similarly, other studies without longitudinal interviews collected data on their cases as they unfolded in real time such as during an organizational change (Crossan and Berdrow, 2003; Plowman et al., 2007; Sonenshein, 2010; Thomas et al., 2011), alliance negotiation (Ariño and Ring, 2010) or merger (Denis et al., 2011), or simply to observe organizational rituals (Dacin et al., 2010) or daily work (Bailey et al., 2011).

One difference in conducting interviews for single-case studies is greater customization of interview questions. Compared to multiple-case research, where similar questions must be asked across cases to examine similarities or differences of a phenomenon, interview questions for single cases can be customized for different informants, which can be especially useful to obtain data on a phenomenon at different points in time and across informants. The data can be triangulated among informants in same time periods or with other data (e.g., archival data).

For conducting interviews within the single (as well as the multiple-case) design, we recommend the semi-structured interview format. A semi-structured interview implies that there are specific topics that the interviewer wants to cover in the interview but also gives the power to the interviewer to ask further questions in order to explore the views expressed by the participants (Bryman and Bell, 2015). In a semi-structured interview, the order of the questions is varied according to the flow of each interview (Bryman and Bell, 2015). To avoid informant bias, researchers can use multiple informants who are knowledgeable on the phenomenon within the single case (Miller et al., 1997), attempt to conduct interviews as the phenomenon unfolds or has recently just occurred (Huber, 1985), and use interview techniques (e.g., "courtroom" questioning, event tracking, nondirective questioning) that are known to yield accurate information from informants (Eisenhardt, 1989).

If speaking in person or over the phone is not possible, email interviews may also be used by researchers. The disadvantage of this method is that it is time consuming because there is a time lag with sending the questions and getting the answers back and so forth (Cassell and Symon, 1994). Also, the interviewer cannot dig deeper into interesting topics that may emerge during an actual interview. On the other hand, this time delay can be advantageous as it gives both the interviewer and interviewee time to reflect on their responses (Cassell and Symon, 1994).

Finally, in order to get the most out of an interview, we recommend audio recording the interview upon getting the informant's consent. In addition, it is very important to take notes during the interview as audio files can be corrupted or difficult to transcribe due to noise. The researcher's notes are also very useful for reconstructing the interview afterwards. Our experience suggests that if the researcher types up the interview notes before going to sleep that evening, they can reproduce most of the interview content based on the notes, using the audio file to fill in the blanks.

## Observations

Observations are another important source of data in single-case research since they allow researchers to observe complex social and behavioral processes unfolding in real time. The choice of observational setting depends on the study's research question. Our review reveals three common settings for conducting observations for single cases: (1) meetings, (2) work interactions, and (3) conventions or conferences. While studies examining processes associated with daily work typically focused on meetings and interactions among employees (Bailey et al., 2011; McPherson and Sauder, 2013; Sonenshein, 2010; Sutton and Hargadon, 1996; Thomas et al., 2011), researchers of strategy as practice typically observed meetings among senior managers, executives, or board members (Beck and Plowman, 2014; Clark et al., 2010; Crossan and Berdrow, 2003; Denis et al., 2011; MacKay and Chia, 2013). Lastly, observations of conventions or conferences were typically used in studies examining interactions across organizations (e.g., Gioia et al., 2010; Hardy and McGuire, 2010; Ozcan and Santos, 2015). For instance, in their study of the emergence of the global mobile payment market, observations at mobile and banking conferences worldwide were a key source to Ozcan and Santos (2015) in increasing the accuracy of their data about local and global interaction between the involved players.

## Archival Data

In addition to interviews and observations, archival data is another significant source of data for single cases. Archival data is particularly useful to familiarize researchers with their case or to gain additional insights. Great examples are the Sonenshein (2010) study that used 115 documents of archival data to construct a "running history" of the change process within a single retail site of a Fortune 500 retail firm undergoing strategic change. Similarly, McPherson and Sauder's (2013) study on a drug court utilized academic studies and reports to better understand how drug courts function. In addition, archival data can also help triangulate data from interviews or observations (Bailey et al., 2011; Burgelman, 1983; Vuori and Huy, 2016).

Archival data can also be used as the main source of data for analyzing a case, particularly for historical cases on which the researcher can find large amounts of archival data (e.g., books, press articles, magazines, academic articles) and where interviewing informants knowledgeable about the case may not be an option (e.g., Hampel and Tracey, 2016; Maguire and Hardy, 2013;

Mintzberg and McHugh, 1985; Rojas, 2010; Weick, 1993). In addition, it is important that the theoretical focus of the case involves examining the use of text. For example, the Maguire and Hardy (2013) study of how meanings around risk are constructed in the chemical industry in Canada appropriately used archival data on discourse, which existed in abundance for the case, as the main data source given the theoretical focus on discourse and meaning making.

Archival data can also be a great source of second-hand quotes by individuals associated with the case from interviews, speeches, or even emails. This is particularly important for historical cases where informants are no longer alive (e.g., Hampel and Tracey, 2016; Rojas, 2010; Weick, 1993). If gaining access to correspondence between individuals (e.g., emails) is not an option, researchers can look for interviews in books about the case (Weick, 1993), press articles that included interviews (e.g., Danneels, 2011), video interviews (e.g., Vaccaro and Palazzo, 2015), interviews conducted for an earlier research project (MacLean and Behnam, 2010), or relevant speeches that have been recorded or transcribed (Dutton and Dukerich, 1991). Finally, blogs, twitter feeds, and social media posts can also be a great source of second-hand quotes from individuals. We recommend researchers to familiarize themselves with these new channels of communication both for contacting and collecting data from individuals.

In collecting and later analyzing large chunks of archival data, software tools such as NVivo can be quite helpful in marking specific themes within text and doing advanced searches to explore possible relationships between the themes. NVivo can manage different data formats including multimedia-based data (videos) and allow researchers to transfer their archival data as a single project file, which makes co-analyzing data much easier. In our experience, NVivo is quite a useful tool. However, it has shortcomings such as taking a long time to import large data sets and errors occurring during the transfer of files between Mac and PC computers.

## Data Analysis

There are two main analytical strategies available to single-case researchers for data analysis. One is to create in-depth case histories, which is a straightforward way to organize a large amount of data in a descriptive fashion (Eisenhardt, 1989). Researchers can add data to a running description of their case, helping to increase familiarity with the case as data collection and analysis proceeds. Also, the emerging case history may help researchers notice gaps in data collection or potential changes in research focus. Examples of case histories include: Mintzberg and McHugh's (1985) detailed case study on the National Film Board of Canada, which identified and tracked how strategies emerged over six distinct periods from 1939 to 1975. Tripsas and Gavetti's (2000) study on Polaroid, which examined the evolution of the firm's capabilities and managerial beliefs in a detailed case narrative starting with the early founding of the firm and then examining the firm in ten-year increments from 1980 to 1998. Hoffmann's (2007) study on alliance portfolios focused on analyzing the sequence of events underlying the development of alliance portfolios in two business units within Siemens. Similarly, in a study on how meanings are negotiated by senior and middle managers during organizational change, Thomas et al.'s (2011) data analysis involved extracting quotes related to two key meanings in a chronological order and then tracing how negotiations over these meanings unfolded over time.

Another method is to categorize data from lower to higher levels of abstraction (Gioia et al., 2013). This method generally involves a "first-order analysis" where researchers develop a list of categories based on terms or phrases used by informants, a "second-order analysis" where researchers seek to examine potential relationships among these categories by grouping the first-order categories into a smaller number of categories and finally combining the second-order themes into higher-order theoretical dimensions. For instance, in Dacin et al.'s (2010) study on dining rituals at Cambridge, the authors first coded their interviews for words or phrases regarding the social processes within dining rituals. Then, the authors collapsed these codes into higher-level categories, which were then further collapsed into common theoretical dimensions that helped to provide a framework regarding Cambridge dining micro-rituals.

In our opinion, the case history approach to data analysis is very useful for the researcher to develop a deep understanding of the case, to fill in the gaps in the story, and to write a thorough paper. The case histories are also great for "seeing" potential future papers from the data and can be used to write them. However, as researchers typically cannot attach entire case histories to their paper during the review process, this approach makes the data less transparent to the reviewers. On the other hand, the "Gioia method" of data categorization allows the researcher to show more of the data analysis process in the final paper in the form of figures and tables, but may not allow the researcher to form as great an understanding of the data compared to building a case history from scratch. One strategy would be to combine these two analytical methods. A simplified version of the case history can be included in the paper, thus providing researchers with familiarity of the case and showing readers a timeline of key events with theoretical relevance, along with how the data were grouped into aggregate categories. Also, researchers can show where certain higher-order themes were more or less prevalent throughout their case history.

Once an inductive model has been developed through one of these two approaches, researchers can utilize certain strategies to check the model's validity. In their study examining the role of shared emotions among middle and top managers in Nokia's downfall, Vuori and Huy (2016) presented their initial findings to 23 informants across the firm and sent four-page summaries of the key findings to 331 top and middle managers who worked for Nokia during their study period, asking for feedback. The general feedback was that their model accurately described what unfolded in Nokia and several middle managers provided additional examples regarding shared emotions. Also, during the review process, the authors conducted follow-up interviews with informants to confirm the findings from prior interviews. Through this entire process, the authors had confirmation that their model was indeed accurate and inductively derived from the data. Similarly, McPherson and Sauder's (2013) study on how individuals manage different institutional logics in their day-to-day work lives in a drug court presented findings to drug court personnel and met with the full court to discuss findings and observations. Thus if possible, we recommend presenting the key findings of the study to a variety of informants who can confirm, disconfirm, or suggest improvements to the model, which is considerably easier to accomplish in single-case studies set in one organization compared to multiple-case studies involving multiple organizations.

## Presentation of the Data

The presentation of the data is critical for managing the review process. Particularly when the single case is longitudinal, the researcher is left with the choice of whether or not to present it chronologically. The chronological presentation allows the readers to follow it like a story that unfolds over time. However, as authors using this approach, we have sometimes been criticized by reviewers that the theoretical framework was too "buried" inside the story, undermining the theoretical rigor of the case. Another option is to build the story around theoretical constructs, which has the disadvantage of breaking the flow of the story. In our opinion, a good approach is to maintain the case chronology as much as possible but to put theoretical signposts within the story, which can then be integrated into a theoretical framework in the discussion section as well as in the figures. Good examples of this can be found in Gurses and Ozcan's comparative case study on the emergence of pay TV (2015) and in Hampel and Tracey's single case on destigmatization at Thomas Cook travel agency in Victorian Britain (2016).

Another key strategy to show reviewers the richness of the data and the rigor of the analysis is the effective use of tables and figures. If the findings are distinct from one another and low in number, dedicating a table to each finding to present the strength of evidence may be a good idea. For instance, in their examination of how radical change occurs in a church over time, Plowman et al. (2007) provide separate tables for the two main findings related to the initial changing organizational conditions that are the source of change and the subsequent actions that amplify change. Otherwise, a more extensive "main table" such as in Sutton and Hargadon (1996) may work better. In their main table, they present six consequences of brainstorming within IDEO with the corresponding level of support from each data source ranging from "sporadic," "moderate," to "strong" evidence. This provides readers with an overview of how the findings were triangulated among different types of data. Another strategy, which is well suited for data that include events and longitudinal processes, is to present the data through temporal brackets identified through theoretical constructs (Langley, 1999). Mintzberg and McHugh's (1985) study on strategy formation is a prominent example using temporal bracketing. The authors use several graphs and timelines to show different phases in each of their identified strategies over the period of their case. Similarly, the Ozcan and Gurses (2016) study on the categorization of dietary supplements divides the single case into two phases, the movement of dietary supplements to a different category, followed by the creation of an entirely new category, which is supported by timelines and figures. Finally, when using the "Gioia method," it is important to include a figure that clearly lays out how the data were categorized from first-order to higher-order aggregate dimensions. Clark et al.'s (2010) study on organizational identity change during a merger of two hospitals does this effectively through figures showing first-order concepts, second-order themes, and the resultant theoretical dimensions, as well as tables with representative quotes for first-order concepts.

## Conclusion

The future of single-case methods in management is promising. For instance, single-case research is heavily used in strategy within the growing strategy-as-practice perspective (e.g., Jarzabkowski and Kaplan, 2015; Jarzabkowski and Spee, 2009; Kaplan, 2008; Vaara and Whittington, 2012), which is concerned "with the doing of strategy" (Jarzabkowski and Spee, 2009: 69), i.e., the actors, their tools, and actions that shape strategy. Single-case research is an important methodology for researchers in this stream, as it allows researchers to go deep within organizations to examine interactions among actors and the specific tools involved in strategy making. More broadly, single-case research can also help tackle "grand challenges," i.e., societal problems that require extensive collaboration and coordination among actors and technologies such as global hunger, poverty, or disease (Eisenhardt et al., 2016), by examining the processes through which actors address and attempt to resolve these complex social problems. For instance, a case study of a community in which homelessness has been eliminated would be a worthwhile endeavor even as an extreme case.

In terms of how single-case research is conducted, future research may incorporate new types of data such as video ethnography techniques and social media (e.g., blogs, Twitter) to supplement traditional interview and observational data. Video ethnography can provide real-time data on the interactions between individuals, while social media archives can give researchers insight into evolutionary changes related to executive and firm-level decisions as well as interactions between individuals regarding a phenomenon.

Table 7.1 Summary of Single-Case Studies Reviewed for This Chapter

| Study | Research Question | Empirical Setting | Level of Analysis | Rationale for Setting | Micro-process | Theoretical Focus | Primary Data Collection |
|---|---|---|---|---|---|---|---|
| Burgelman (1983) | What is the process of internal corporate venturing? | The new venture division within a large diversified firm | Organization | Extreme case | Strategy as practice | Evolutionary change process | Real time |
| Mintzberg and McHugh (1985) | How is strategy formulated in adhocracy? | The National Film Board of Canada | Organization | Extreme case | Strategy as practice | Evolutionary change process | Retrospective |
| Dutton and Dukerich (1991) | How are organizations and their environments interrelated over time? | Port Authority of NY/NJ | Organization | Extreme case | Daily work | Organizational response to external event | Real time |
| Weick (1993) | Why do organizations unravel and how can they be made more resilient? | Mann Gulch fire disaster | Organization | Extreme case/ Access to historical data | Daily work/Strategy as practice | Organizational response to external event | Retrospective |
| Sutton and Hargadon (1996) | How is brainstorming used in organizations? | IDEO | Organization | Extreme case | Daily work | Work processes | Real time |
| Tripsas and Gavetti (2000) | How does managerial cognition influence the evolution of capabilities and thus contribute to organizational inertia? | Polaroid Corporation | Organization | Extreme case/ Access to historical data | Strategy as practice | Evolutionary change process | Retrospective |
| Marginson (2002) | How do management control systems affect managers' strategic activities? | UK telecommunications firm | Organization | Extreme case | Strategy as practice | Evolutionary change process | Real time |

| Crossan and Berdrow (2003) | How does organizational learning explain the phenomenon of strategic renewal? | Canada Post Corporation (CPC) | Organization | Extreme case/Field access | Strategy as practice | Evolutionary change process | Real time |
| Hoffmann (2007) | What determines the configuration and evolution of the alliance portfolio? | Siemens | Organization | Extreme case/Data availability/Field access | Strategy as practice | Evolutionary change process | Retrospective |
| Plowman et al. (2007) | How do nonlinear dynamics work in organizations undergoing change? | A church that created a homeless ministry | Organization | Emergent patterns/ Extreme case | Daily work | Evolutionary change process | Real time |
| Danneels (2007) | What is the process of technological competence leveraging? | A new technology developed within a chemical instrument firm | Organization | Extreme case | N/A – Strategy content | Evolutionary change process | Retrospective |
| Rojas (2010) | How does power influence institutional change? | 1968 Third World Strike at San Francisco State College | Organization | Extreme case/ Access to historical data | Interactions between individuals | Organizational response to external event/ Evolutionary change process | Retrospective |
| Ariño and Ring (2010) | How do perceptions of fairness influence alliance negotiations? | Alliance between a Spanish distributor of medical equipment and Argentinian manufacturer of chemicals | Inter-organizational | Extreme case | Interactions between individuals and organizations | Evolutionary change process | Real time |

continued

Table 7.1 Continued

| Study | Research Question | Empirical Setting | Level of Analysis | Rationale for Setting | Micro-process | Theoretical Focus | Primary Data Collection |
|---|---|---|---|---|---|---|---|
| Gutierrez et al. (2010) | How do individuals retain identification with an institution while dis-identifying with organizational aspects? | Voice of the Faith (a lay organization of Catholics, organized in response to Catholic Church's sex scandal in Boston) | Organization | Extreme case | Interactions between individuals | Organizational response to external event/ Evolutionary change process | Real time |
| Danneels (2011) | Why are some firms able to renew themselves when environmental changes threaten their viability? | Smith Corona | Organization | Extreme case | N/A – Strategy content | Evolutionary change process | Retrospective |
| MacLean and Behnam (2010) | How do organizational members respond to decoupling within organizations? | A large mutual life insurance company | Organization | Extreme case | Daily work | Evolutionary change process | Retrospective |
| Tilcsik (2010) | How does the process preceding decoupling unfold inside organizations? | Post–Communist government agency | Organization | Extreme case/ Long-term access | Daily work | Evolutionary change process | Real time |
| Clark et al. (2010) | How does organizational identity change during major organizational transformations? | The merger of two healthcare organizations | Inter-organizational | Extreme case | Strategy as practice/ Interactions between individuals and organizations | Evolutionary change process | Real time |

| Study | Research question | Empirical context | Level of analysis | Sampling strategy | Data focus | Process focus | Temporal orientation |
|---|---|---|---|---|---|---|---|
| Gioia et al. (2010) | What are the processes involved in organizational identity formation? | Founding of a college within a state-university system | Organization | Extreme case | Interactions between individuals and organizations | Evolutionary change process | Retrospective |
| Hardy and McGuire (2010) | How do new narratives emerge from discursive processes? | The UN conference that resulted in the Stockholm Convention on Persistent Organic Pollutants | Institutional field | Extreme case/Data documentation | Interactions between individuals and organizations | Institutional field level change | Real time |
| Sonenshein (2010) | How do employees respond to managers' meaning making regarding organizational change? | A single retail site within a Fortune 500 retail company undergoing a strategic change | Organization | Extreme case/Field access | Daily work | Evolutionary change process | Real time |
| Dacin et al. (2010) | What is the process through which institutions are maintained? | The dining hall at the University of Cambridge | Organization | Extreme case | Daily work/Interactions between individuals | Work processes | Real time |
| Thomas et al. (2011) | How are meanings negotiated by senior and middle managers during organizational change? | One cultural change workshop held within a telecommunications company in the UK | Organization | Extreme case | Daily work/Interactions between individuals | Organizational response to external event | Real time |
| Tracey et al. (2011) | What kinds of institutional work are required when institutional entrepreneurs create new organizational forms? | Social enterprise focusing on providing employment for the homeless | Organization | Extreme case | Daily work/Interactions between individuals | Evolutionary change process | Retrospective |

*continued*

Table 7.1 Continued

| Study | Research Question | Empirical Setting | Level of Analysis | Rationale for Setting | Micro-process | Theoretical Focus | Primary Data Collection |
|---|---|---|---|---|---|---|---|
| Bailey et al. (2011) | How does the use of digital technologies during work affect the coupling between employees and objects? | US automobile manufacturer | Organization | Extreme case | Daily work | Work processes | Real time |
| Wasserman and Frenkel (2011) | What is the role of organizational aesthetics (OA) in identity regulation? | Israeli Ministry of Foreign Affairs | Organization | Extreme case | Daily work/ Interactions between individuals | Work processes | Real time |
| Denis et al. (2011) | What is the process behind escalating indecisions? | Large university hospital in Quebec | Organization | Emerging patterns | Strategy as practice | Evolutionary change process | Real time |
| Maguire and Hardy (2013) | What are the organizational processes through which products and technologies become risky? | Chemical risk assessment in Canada | Institutional field | Extreme case/Field access | N/A – Meaning making through textual analysis | Evolutionary change process | Retrospective |
| McPherson and Sauder (2013) | How do actors manage institutional logics in their day-to-day organizational activities? | A drug court | Organization | Extreme case | Daily work/ Interactions between individuals | Work processes | Real time |

| | Research question | Case | Level of analysis | Case selection | Focus | Level of change | Temporal |
|---|---|---|---|---|---|---|---|
| Wijk et al. (2013) | How does collaborative work between activists and field incumbents emerge and affect the organizational field under challenge? | Outbound Tour Operators Association in the Netherlands | Institutional field | Extreme case | Interactions between individuals across organizations | Institutional field level change | Real time |
| MacKay and Chia (2013) | How do actions interact with chance environmental circumstances in affecting organizations? | Canadian automotive firm | Organization | Emergent patterns/ Extreme case | Strategy as practice | Evolutionary change process | Real time |
| Mazmanian (2013) | How do individuals differently use a new technology within a firm? | A mid-sized footwear and apparel company | Organization | Extreme case | Daily work/ Interactions between individuals | Work processes | Real time |
| Beck and Plowman (2014) | How does interorganizational collaboration occur? | Columbia shuttle disaster | Inter-organizational | Extreme case | Daily work/ Interactions between individuals | Evolutionary change process | Real time |
| Brown et al. (2015) | What role does human capital play during strategic change? | Non-profit hospital in the U.S. | Organization | Extreme case | Strategy as practice | Organizational response to external event/ Evolutionary change process | Retrospective |
| Vaccaro and Palazzo (2015) | How can institutional change succeed in environments dominated by organized crime? | Anti-Mafia organization in Sicily, Italy | Organization | Extreme case/Field access | Interactions between individuals across organizations | Institutional field level change | Real time |

*continued*

Table 7.1 Continued

| Study | Research Question | Empirical Setting | Level of Analysis | Rationale for Setting | Micro-process | Theoretical Focus | Primary Data Collection |
|---|---|---|---|---|---|---|---|
| Hampel and Tracey (2016) | How does an organization remove stigma and become legitimate? | Cook's travel agency – Victorian Britain | Organization | Extreme case | Interaction between organization and external audience | Evolutionary change process | Retrospective |
| Vuori and Huy (2016) | How do emotions and bounded rationality influence the innovation process? | Nokia | Organization | Extreme case | Strategy as practice | Evolutionary change process | Retrospective |
| Chan and Anteby (2016) | How does task segregation lead to workplace inequality in job quality? | TSA | Organization | Example of an "intensity case" – phenomenon is present but not present in an unusual manner | Daily work | Work processes | Real time |

Single-case research can also be used to expand management theory on a global scale. Recent calls have been made for management researchers to investigate neglected national and cultural contexts, such as the African continent (George et al., 2016) or to integrate emergent theories from Asia with existing management theories (Barkema et al., 2015). Single cases can enable researchers to develop a particularly detailed and nuanced view of organizations and phenomena embedded within these national contexts, which can both influence existing theories and lead to the development of new theories.

Overall, we highly recommend single-case studies as a way to study complex and rare organizational processes in detail as well as longitudinally. High-quality single-case research can produce rich theory on organizational phenomena. It can also provide a great basis for writing teaching cases afterwards. As laid out in the chapter, there are many trade-offs that researchers face in terms of study design, data collection, analysis, and presentation of single-case research. When possible, we suggest making the approach more systematic through an embedded case design, data collection at different levels of analysis, and by emphasizing the theoretical model in the presentation through clear constructs and signposts to help researchers in the review process. Also, researchers may want to consider comparative cases to improve generalizability if feasible.

In closing, we hope that the roadmap we provided in this chapter will encourage and inspire many researchers in their pursuit of both interesting and systematic single-case studies.

## Note

1 *Academy of Management Journal, Administrative Science Quarterly, Organization Science,* and *Strategic Management Journal.*

## References

Ariño, A. and Ring, P. S. (2010). The role of fairness in alliance formation. *Strategic Management Journal, 31*(10), 1054–1087.

Bailey, D. E., Leonardi, P. M., and Barley, S. R. (2011). The lure of the virtual. *Organization Science, 23*(5), 1485–1504.

Barkema, H. G., Chen, X.-P., George, G., Luo, Y., and Tsui, A. S. (2015). West meets East: New concepts and theories. *Academy of Management Journal, 58*(2), 460–479.

Battilana, J. and Dorado, S. (2010). Building sustainable hybrid organizations: The case of commercial microfinance organizations. *Academy of Management Journal, 53*(6), 1419–1440.

Beck, T. E. and Plowman, D. A. (2014). Temporary, emergent interorganizational collaboration in unexpected circumstances: A study of the Columbia space shuttle response effort. *Organization Science, 25*(4), 1234–1252.

Brown, J. A., Gianiodis, P. T., and Santoro, M. D. (2015). Following doctors' orders: Organizational change as a response to human capital bargaining power. *Organization Science, 26*(5), 1284–1300.

Bryman, A. and Bell, E. (2015). *Business Research Methods* (4th ed.). Oxford: Oxford University Press.

Burgelman, R. A. (1983). A process model of internal corporate venturing in the diversified major firm. *Administrative Science Quarterly, 28*(2), 223–244.

Cassell, C. and Symon, G. (1994). *Qualitative Methods in Organizational Research: A Practical Guide.* Thousand Oaks, CA: Sage.

Chan, C. K. and Anteby, M. (2016). Task segregation as a mechanism for within-job inequality. *Administrative Science Quarterly, 61*(2), 184–216.

Clark, S. M., Gioia, D. A., Ketchen, D. J., and Thomas, J. B. (2010). Transitional identity as a facilitator of organizational identity change during a merger. *Administrative Science Quarterly, 55*(3), 397–438.

Crossan, M. M. and Berdrow, I. (2003). Organizational learning and strategic renewal. *Strategic Management Journal, 24*(11), 1087–1105.

Dacin, M. T., Munir, K., and Tracey, P. (2010). Formal dining at Cambridge colleges: Linking ritual performance and institutional maintenance. *Academy of Management Journal, 53*(6), 1393–1418.

Denis, J.-L., Dompierre, G., Langley, A., and Rouleau, L. (2011). Escalating indecision: Between reification and strategic ambiguity. *Organization Science*, 22(1), 225–244.

Danneels, E. (2007). The process of technological competence leveraging. *Strategic Management Journal*, 28(5), 511–533.

Danneels, E. (2011). Trying to become a different type of company: Dynamic capability at Smith Corona. *Strategic Management Journal*, 32(1), 1–31.

Dutton, J. E. and Dukerich, J. M. (1991). Keeping an eye on the mirror: Image and identity in organizational adaptation. *Academy of Management Journal*, 34(3), 517–554.

Eisenhardt, K. M. (1989). Building theories from case study research. *Academy of Management Review*, 14(4), 532–550.

Eisenhardt, K. M. and Graebner, M. E. (2007). Theory building from cases: Opportunities and challenges. *Academy of Management Journal*, 50(1), 25–32.

Eisenhardt, K. M., Graebner, M. E., and Sonenshein, S. (2016). Grand challenges and inductive methods: Rigor without rigor mortis. *Academy of Management Journal*, 59(4), 1113–1123.

Galunic, D. C. and Eisenhardt, K. M. (2001). Architectural innovation and modular corporate forms. *Academy of Management Journal*, 44(6), 1229–1249.

George, G., Corbishley, C., Khayesi, J. N. O., Haas, M. R., and Tihanyi, L. (2016). Bringing Africa in: Promising directions for management research. *Academy of Management Journal*, 59(2), 377–393.

Gioia, D. A., Corley, K. G., and Hamilton, A. L. (2013). Seeking qualitative rigor in inductive research notes on the Gioia methodology. *Organizational Research Methods*, 16(1), 15–31.

Gioia, D. A., Price, K. N., Hamilton, A. L., and Thomas, J. B. (2010). Forging an identity: An insider-outsider study of processes involved in the formation of organizational identity. *Administrative Science Quarterly*, 55(1), 1–46.

Gurses, K. and Ozcan, P. (2015). Entrepreneurship in regulated markets: Framing contests and collective action to introduce pay TV in the U.S. *Academy of Management Journal*, 58(6), 1709–1739.

Gutierrez, B., Howard-Grenville, J., and Scully, M. A. (2010). The faithful rise up: Split identification and an unlikely change effort. *Academy of Management Journal*, 53(4), 673–699.

Hampel, C. E. and Tracey, P. (2016). How organizations move from stigma to legitimacy: The case of Cook's travel agency in Victorian Britain. *Academy of Management Journal*. doi: 10.5465/amj.2015.0365.

Hardy, C. and Maguire, S. (2010). Discourse, field-configuring events, and change in organizations and institutional fields: Narratives of DDT and the Stockholm Convention. *Academy of Management Journal*, 53(6), 1365–1392.

Heinze, K. L. and Weber, K. (2015). Toward organizational pluralism: Institutional intrapreneurship in integrative medicine. *Organization Science*, 27(1), 157–172.

Hoffmann, W. H. (2007). Strategies for managing a portfolio of alliances. *Strategic Management Journal*, 28(8), 827–856.

Huber, G. P. (1985). Temporal stability and response-order biases in participant descriptions of organizational decisions. *Academy of Management Journal*, 28(4), 943–950.

Huy, Q. N. (2002). Emotional balancing of organizational continuity and radical change: The contribution of middle managers. *Administrative Science Quarterly*, 47(1), 31–69.

Jarzabkowski, P. and Kaplan, S. (2015). Strategy tools-in-use: A framework for understanding "technologies of rationality" in practice. *Strategic Management Journal*, 36(4), 537–558.

Jarzabkowski, P. and Spee, A. P. (2009). Strategy-as-practice: A review and future directions for the field. *International Journal of Management Reviews*, 11(1), 69–95.

Kaplan, S. (2008). Framing contests: Strategy making under uncertainty. *Organization Science*, 19(5), 729–752.

Kellogg, K. C. (2011). Making the cut: Using status-based countertactics to block social movement implementation and microinstitutional change in surgery. *Organization Science*, 23(6), 1546–1570.

Langley, A. (1999). Strategies for theorizing from process data. *Academy of Management Review*, 24(4), 691–710.

Langley, A., Smallman, C., Tsoukas, H., and Van de Ven, A. H. (2013). Process studies of change in organization and management: Unveiling temporality, activity, and flow. *Academy of Management Journal*, 56(1), 1–13.

MacKay, R. B. and Chia, R. (2013). Choice, chance, and unintended consequences in strategic change: A process understanding of the rise and fall of NorthCo Automotive. *Academy of Management Journal*, 56(1), 208–230.

Maclean, N. (1972). *Young Men and Fire*. Chicago, IL: University of Chicago Press.

MacLean, T. L. and Behnam, M. (2010). The dangers of decoupling: The relationship between compliance programs, legitimacy perceptions, and institutionalized misconduct. *Academy of Management Journal*, *53*(6), 1499–1520.

McPherson, C. M. and Sauder, M. (2013). Logics in action: Managing institutional complexity in a drug court. *Administrative Science Quarterly*, *58*(2), 165–196.

Maguire, S. and Hardy, C. (2013). Organizing processes and the construction of risk: A discursive approach. *Academy of Management Journal*, *56*(1), 231–255.

Marginson, D. E. W. (2002). Management control systems and their effects on strategy formation at middle-management levels: Evidence from a U.K. organization. *Strategic Management Journal*, *23*(11), 1019–1031.

Mazmanian, M. (2013). Avoiding the trap of constant connectivity: When congruent frames allow for heterogeneous practices. *Academy of Management Journal*, *56*(5), 1225–1250.

Miller, C. C., Cardinal, L. B., and Glick, W. H. (1997). Retrospective reports in organizational research: A reexamination of recent evidence. *Academy of Management Journal*, *40*(1), 189–204.

Mintzberg, H. and McHugh, A. (1985). Strategy formation in an adhocracy. *Administrative Science Quarterly*, *30*(2), 160–197.

Noda, T. and Bower, J. L. (1996). Strategy making as iterated processes of resource allocation. *Strategic Management Journal*, *17*(S1), 159–192.

Ozcan, P. and Gurses, K. (2016). Playing cat and mouse: Contests over regulatory categorization of dietary supplements in the U.S. (Manuscript under review).

Ozcan, P. and Santos, F. M. (2015). The market that never was: Turf wars and failed alliances in mobile payments. *Strategic Management Journal*, *36*(10), 1486–1512.

Plowman, D. A., Baker, L. T., Beck, T. E., Kulkarni, M., Solansky, S. T., and Travis, D. V. (2007). Radical change accidentally: The emergence and amplification of small change. *Academy of Management Journal*, *50*(3), 515–543.

Rindova, V. P. and Kotha, S. (2001). Continuous "morphing": Competing through dynamic capabilities, form, and function. *Academy of Management Journal*, *44*(6), 1263–1280.

Rojas, F. (2010). Power through institutional work: Acquiring academic authority in the 1968 Third World Strike. *Academy of Management Journal*, *53*(6), 1263–1280.

Sonenshein, S. (2010). We're changing – or are we? Untangling the role of progressive, regressive, and stability narratives during strategic change implementation. *Academy of Management Journal*, *53*(3), 477–512.

Suddaby, R., Elsbach, K. D., Greenwood, R., Meyer, J. W., and Zilber, T. B. (2010). Organizations and their institutional environments – bringing meaning, values, and culture back in: Introduction to the special research forum. *Academy of Management Journal*, *53*(6), 1234–1240.

Sutton, R. I. and Hargadon, A. (1996). Brainstorming groups in context: Effectiveness in a product design firm. *Administrative Science Quarterly*, *41*(4), 685–718.

Thomas, R., Sargent, L. D., and Hardy, C. (2011). Managing organizational change: Negotiating meaning and power-resistance relations. *Organization Science*, *22*(1), 22–41.

Tilcsik, A. (2010). From ritual to reality: Demography, ideology, and decoupling in a post-communist government agency. *Academy of Management Journal*, *53*(6), 1474–1498.

Tracey, P., Phillips, N., and Jarvis, O. (2011). Bridging institutional entrepreneurship and the creation of new organizational forms: A multilevel model. *Organization Science*, *22*(1), 60–80.

Tripsas, M. and Gavetti, G. (2000). Capabilities, cognition, and inertia: Evidence from digital imaging. *Strategic Management Journal*, *21*(10–11), 1147–1161.

Vaara, E. and Whittington, R. (2012). Strategy-as-practice: Taking social practices seriously. *Academy of Management Annals*, *6*(1), 285–336.

Vaccaro, A. and Palazzo, G. (2015). Values against violence: Institutional change in societies dominated by organized crime. *Academy of Management Journal*, *58*(4), 1075–1101.

Van de Ven, A. H. (1992). Suggestions for studying strategy process: A research note. *Strategic Management Journal*, *13*(S1), 169–188.

Vuori, T. O. and Huy, Q. N. (2016). Distributed attention and shared emotions in the innovation process: How Nokia lost the smartphone battle. *Administrative Science Quarterly*, *61*(1), 9–51.

Wasserman, V. and Frenkel, M. (2011). Organizational aesthetics: Caught between identity regulation and culture jamming. *Organization Science*, *22*(2), 503–521.

Weber, K. and Dacin, M. T. (2011). The cultural construction of organizational life: Introduction to the special issue. *Organization Science*, *22*(2), 287–298.

Weick, K. E. (1993). The collapse of sensemaking in organizations: The Mann Gulch disaster. *Administrative Science Quarterly*, *38*(4), 628–652.

Wijk, J. van, Stam, W., Elfring, T., Zietsma, C., and Hond, F. den. (2013). Activists and incumbents structuring change: The interplay of agency, culture, and networks in field evolution. *Academy of Management Journal*, *56*(2), 358–386.

Yin, R. K. (2014). *Case Study Research: Design and Methods* (5th ed.). Thousand Oaks, CA: Sage.

# 8

# CLIO'S TOOLKIT

## The Practice of Historical Methods in Organization Studies

*R. Daniel Wadhwani and Stephanie Decker*

### Introduction

Historical research and reasoning are now flourishing in management and organization studies. The contention that history provides a unique scholarly perspective on organizations and organizing was made as early as the 1990s by Zald (1993) and Kieser (1994), but a clearly identifiable "historical turn" has taken place only in the last decade as a wave of publications have cumulatively elaborated on the nature of history and its value in organizational research (Maclean et al., 2016; Rowlinson et al., 2014; Wadhwani and Bucheli, 2014). The intellectual movement has spilled into the related fields of strategy (Ingram et al., 2012; Vaara and Lamberg, 2016), entrepreneurship (Lippmann and Aldrich, 2016; Wadhwani and Jones, 2014), international business (Jones and Khanna, 2006), human resources (Bruce and Nyland, 2011; Hassard, 2012), and business and society (Stutz and Sachs, 2017).

Despite this significant progress, historical research methods and practices remain comparatively underdeveloped and under-articulated in management and organizational scholarship. The wave of scholarship at the intersection of history and organization studies over the last decade has proceeded in large part through conceptual analysis and synthesis of the relationship between the fields of history and organization studies (Godfrey et al., 2016). With notable exceptions (Decker, 2013; Kipping et al., 2014; Yates, 2014), considerably less attention has been devoted to the grounded practices of historical inquiry and interpretation, and the problem-solving processes that confront researchers as they articulate questions, critique evidence, develop interpretations, and arrive at evaluative conclusions.

As a default, historical methods often continue to be inaccurately presented as a form of inductive theory building from cases (Eisenhardt, 1989; Glaser and Strauss, 1967; Miles and Huberman, 1994), an approach that typically removes the position and perspective of the researcher as an integral part of the knowledge claims produced and the methods used (Mantere and Ketokivi, 2013). But historical epistemology and methods more typically acknowledge that historical perspective shapes historical knowledge claims, and employs methodological practices designed to deal with evidence, explanation, understanding, and evaluation reflexively (Kipping et al., 2014). In contrast to other traditions of qualitative social science research methods that do reflect on the role of the researcher in the research process (Hatch and Yanow, 2003), it is the position of the historical researcher in time that has methodological and at times theoretical implications (Wadhwani and Bucheli, 2014).

In this chapter we present a view of historical methods that foregrounds the position and perspective of the researcher in the historical research process. Such an approach emphasizes that historical research involves interpreting or analyzing the past from a position in the present through a process of reflexive, abductive reasoning, rather than through procedural, inductive methods. The title of the chapter refers to Clio, the muse of history in classical Greek mythology, and what we contend to be the practice-based, tool-creating nature of historical research processes, as a researcher grapples with examining, explaining, and evaluating events and actions that lie in the past. In practice, historical research does not involve a procedural, step-by-step approach to interpretation and analysis aimed at deriving objective concepts and categories. Rather, it involves a series of methodological problems and solutions encountered by a situated historical researcher producing interpretations about events and actions in the past that is attentive to analyzing and interpreting empirical puzzles or phenomena in light of previous and extant explanations.

Such an approach necessarily begins by examining the question of the researcher's stance in the present in relationship to the production of historical knowledge about the past. As we highlight in the next section, it is by addressing the situated stance of the researcher that historical practices and methods differ from conventional case study methods. Building on the situated nature of historical researchers, we then explain the practices involved in the research process, including the production of evidence, the development of explanations, the attempt at understanding, and the evaluation of findings. We conclude by discussing how such a practice-based view of historical methods sheds light on the broader dialogue on historical approaches to management and organization studies.

## The Situated Nature of the Historical Researcher

Reflecting on the situated nature of the historical researcher is important to understanding historical methods in practice, and to delineating the fundamental difference between historical research and traditional case study methodology in management and organizational research (Eisenhardt, 1989; Yin, 2009). As Mantere and Ketokivi (2013) have pointed out, within organization science "methodological texts are written as if the reader were a rational actor who is able to overcome cognitive limitations through rigorous application of scientific reasoning principles." The researcher's stance and cognitive perspective on the subject are designed to be excluded from the analysis or interpretation through "computational" processes (Mantere and Ketokivi, 2013) that allow for key constructs to emerge "inductively" from the case evidence.

In contrast, in historical reasoning the temporally situated perspective of the researcher – in which a scholar in the present develops interpretations about events and actions in the past – is inseparable from the historical knowledge claims developed (Danto, 1965; Gadamer, 1975). Unlike in cross-sectional and even conventional longitudinal case study research, historical claims involve assigning significance to actions or events in light of their consequences, a process that requires a retrospective point of view (Wadhwani and Bucheli, 2014). For instance, the introduction of the assembly line in automobile manufacturing in the 1910s can be analyzed historically in the context of the subsequent organizational, economic, social, and cultural consequences of the development of the mass market for cars over the course of the twentieth century. Such knowledge claims could not be proffered by a contemporary researcher studying Ford's assembly line in December 1913, nor by a conventional longitudinal study by researchers that tracked its development in subsequent months and years, for the consequences took decades to unfold and had repercussions that contemporary researchers could not have anticipated. Historical knowledge claims interpreting and analyzing the consequences of the assembly line for the organization of cities, the development of car culture, and for its environmental repercussions can only be made once we take into account the temporal point of view of the researcher in the present looking back.

The situated stance of the historical researcher looking back is essential to the kinds of unique knowledge claims history allows scholars to make. The retrospective nature of historical inquiry, for instance, offers the opportunity to make claims about processes that take a long time to unfold, or social structures – such as institutions – that may be best observed in long historical view (Braudel, 1958). It allows scholars to consider contingencies, conjunctures, and events that shape the development of organizations and industries over time (Sewell, 2005). And it allows scholars to analyze and excavate patterns in meaning (Gadamer, 1975) and power (Foucault, 1991) that are rooted in the deep past and difficult to grasp when looking at the present.

Because the situated perspective of historical research is integral to the character of historical knowledge claims, historical research practices cannot be reduced to computational methods (Mantere and Ketokivi, 2013) designed to objectively remove the researcher from the interpretation (Miles and Huberman, 1994). Rather, the position of the researcher vis-à-vis the subject points to a need for reflective and critical examination of how one's perspective in the present shapes the process through which knowledge claims are made, including how evidence is identified and interpreted as fact, explanations are derived, understanding is sought, and evaluations are made. Indeed, because historical inquiry arises in the present it suggests that the character of this reflexive process is ultimately formed through a dialogue of past and present, in which the preconceptions we hold in the present are challenged and revised through historical inquiry that confront us with surprising evidence and interpretations about the past. The essence of the reflexive historical process, therefore, is hermeneutical in that historical inquiry involves a dialogue between present and past in which research and reasoning renders new insights or challenges to what we previously thought we understood (Gadamer, 1975; Ricoeur, 2004).

The situated nature of historical knowledge claims also points to their abductive, rather than inductive, character (Mantere and Ketokivi, 2013). Peirce (1878) distinguished between induction, which he defined as "reasoning from particulars to the general law," and abduction, which he defined as reasoning "from effect to cause." Also known as "inference to the best explanation," abductive reasoning involves considering alternative theoretical and conceptual explanations in light of evidence or observations, and arriving at the best explanation or best guess among many from the point of view of an epistemic community (Niiniluoto, 1999). Thus, abduction involves not only "discovery" of new explanations (Alvesson and Karreman, 2007) but also confirmatory claims about the best or most truthful explanation (Niiniluoto, 1999). Historical research and reasoning typically follow abductive interpretive processes in that they examine empirical puzzles or phenomena and consider new explanations or understandings that explain the puzzle or phenomenon in a way that challenges the pre-conceived constructs and explanations we hold. In this sense, historical reasoning inherently involves comparing multiple explanations of actions and events in the past, typically proceeding by challenging existing or taken-for-granted explanations by offering new ones, rather than a purely inductive process by which explanations emerge from evidence separate from an existing explanation or theory that already claims to account for it.

Historical reasoning, in practice, is thus an inherently revisionist process, in which the researcher confronts an existing explanation and proffers an alternative one in light of a particular empirical puzzle or phenomenon. Conceptual or theoretical advancement, in this sense, proceeds not by identifying and filling "gaps" in theory but by challenging, revising, and replacing previous explanations or constructs within the historiography (i.e., the previous historical writing and explanation on the subject). Revisionism – a constant re-seeing or re-interpretation of the past – is hence an integral part of historical methods and practices, and integrally linked to the situated nature of the historical researcher constantly reconsidering the relevance of the past from the perspective of the evolving present (Ricoeur, 2004).

The reflexive, abductive, and revisionist nature of historical inquiry has implications for the methodological practices of how evidence is established as fact, how explanations are constructed, how understanding is sought, and how evaluations are determined. We turn to those processes in the next section.

## Elements of Historical Practice

How does the situated perspective and reflexive, abductive process of historical reasoning shape research practices? Following Leblebici (2014), we use Runciman's (1983) description of methodology as involving four aspects of the research process: *reportage*, or how research aims to accurately report the "facts" of social action from evidence; *explanation*, how it systematically accounts for cause and effect; *understanding*, how – if at all – it recounts the experience of human actors themselves; and *evaluation*, the basis on which resulting claims are judged.[1] Though there can of course be considerable variation in these practices within disciplines, the more functionally oriented social sciences *tend to* accomplish these methodological tasks by systematically collecting data based on observations (reportage), in order to test causal hypotheses rooted in theory (explanation), using assumptions about how humans act in relatively functionally consistent ways (understanding) in order to make judgments on the behavior, event, or action (evaluation).

Table 8.1 summarizes our account of how these research processes are handled in historical practice. In the sections that follow, we explain how each of these practices grow out of the situated perspective involved in historical research, and provide explanations that describe and justify the methodological practice. In outlining these practices, we do not contend that all historians share a set of standardized assumptions and techniques for addressing the methodological elements of the research process. There is considerable methodological heterogeneity and diversity within history (De Jong et al., 2015; Decker et al., 2015), as there is within most vibrant scholarly disciplines. More importantly, as we explain above, historical practice has evolved and

*Table 8.1* Elements of Historical Research Practice

| Element | Practices |
| --- | --- |
| Reportage | Source criticism |
| | Triangulation |
| Explanation | Periodization |
| | Narrative construction |
| Understanding | Hermeneutics |
| | Critical hermeneutics |
| | Foucauldian analysis |
| Evaluation | Theory |
| | Understanding |
| | Power |

continues to evolve as historical researchers encounter the challenges and problems of exploring particular research subjects and domains. Instead, our goal is to point to a *range* of methodological practices that have developed within history to deal with the issues of reportage, explanation, understanding, and evaluation in recounting human action from the past and to emphasize the value of such practices in organizational research today.

It is important to acknowledge and name these practices explicitly because many of them are otherwise not widely recognized in social science methodology due to the writing conventions of historical scholarship and because establishing an explicit methodological language is crucial to both interdisciplinary dialogue and to advancing historical research in management and organization studies (Decker, 2013; Kipping et al., 2014; Rowlinson et al., 2014; Yates, 2014).

We begin by discussing historical methods of *reportage* in reconstructing facts and actions from primary sources. Next we discuss the contextualization of historical events in time and place as a way to offer an *explanation* for causality, as opposed to the more reductive and parsimonious view of causality valued in many of the other social sciences. Third, we point to the historical tradition's emphasis on reconstructing the subjective experience and cognition of actors as essential to historical *understanding*. Finally, we show how this historical perspective or hindsight is critical to the ways in which historical scholarship provides an *evaluation* of actions and developments in the past.

## Reportage through Reconstruction from Primary Sources

The historical tradition's particular concern with source analysis grows out of the fact that the phenomena being studied are not directly observed, and the traces it leaves are subject to selection, distortion, and de-contextualization with time (Howell and Prevenier, 2001; Kipping et al., 2014; Lipartito, 2014). The problems of evaluating sources and using them to reconstruct events and actions (i.e., the facts of an historical account) have formed one set of important methodological issues in historical research. Thus, in contemporary historical terminology, primary sources are treated differently from data in that they represent only traces from the past rather than direct observations of it (Lipartito, 2014; Rowlinson et al., 2014).

Reconstruction refers to the historical practice of reporting events and actions by identifying archives and sources (Decker, 2013). The selection of a source from an archive makes the source a piece of evidence. The evidence is then interpreted to establish historical facts. Factuality depends on source criticism, ideally triangulated between different sources, archives, and accounts.

Kipping et al. (2014) describe three aspects of *source criticism*: validity, credibility, and transparency. *Validity* refers to the authenticity and provenance of a source. It includes consideration of not only whether the source is genuine or not, but also evaluation of why and how a particular trace may have survived and what it tells us about what other sources did not. Thus, assessing validity involves considering the institutional setting in which a source is found, and the organizational structure of record keeping, the power relationships, and the institutional structures that have led to the existence or lack of existence of a documentary record (Lipartito, 2014; Schwarzkopf, 2013). As Decker (2013) points out, for example, organizational histories are fundamentally shaped by whether or not archives are kept and made available, and what kinds of histories we can and cannot tell as a result.

Assessing source *credibility* pertains to determining the relative "primacy" of a source in addressing the research question at hand. While in most social sciences, primary data is synonymous with facts or evidence, in historical research the relationship between primary sources and "facts" refers to its relative proximity to the event being studied and to acknowledgement that the event itself is never directly observed by the researcher. Contrary to the popular view of what makes a source primary, it is immaterial whether a source has been published or not; the defining feature is its closeness in time and space to the event, phenomena, or puzzle being examined. Classic primary sources are unique archival documents, as well as in some cases contemporary media reporting. Secondary sources are accounts based on primary sources. Also the definition of a primary source depends on the research subject. For example, history textbooks for schools are tertiary sources relative to the historical events they recount (as they themselves are based on secondary academic accounts), but they are primary sources if the research question is how history was taught at a specific point in time (Lipartito, 2014; Rowlinson et al., 2014).

Historical practice also values source *transparency*. Unlike in qualitative and even some forms of quantitative evidence, historical research standards require that the specific instances of actors, actions, and language conveyed in a historical account should be traceable to specific documentary sources, and verifiable by other researchers. Anonymization, except in exceptional cases, is considered invalid for several reasons. First, because historical research is based on specific empirical puzzles or phenomena, other scholarly readers expect and evaluate research based on the thoroughness with which extant documents on the empirical subject have been consulted. Second, source transparency emerged as an important aspect of the study of history, which conceived of itself initially as an empirical science distinct from rhetorical and popular uses of history, with its blurred lines between history-as-nonfiction and history-as-myth.

Historical researchers often rely on multiple sources to establish a pattern of facts related to the research question, a process sometimes referred to as *triangulation* (Kipping et al., 2014). Within management and organization studies, triangulation often refers to using multiple types of data in order to converge on an "objective account" of what happened. While this is one way in which triangulation is used in historical practice, it also serves other, often more important purposes in the establishment of patterns of facts. For instance, triangulation is typically used because no single source can provide an adequately complete account of the actors, actions, and events involved in addressing an empirical question. Hence triangulation is employed as a way to establish a plausible pattern of facts that can address the research question as a whole. Just as importantly, triangulation in history is used to identify and understand *divergent* accounts of an event. Using multiple sources to study a labor strike or a shift in human resource policy from the perspective of workers and community members as well as from management's perspective (Hassard, 2012), for instance, is not designed to establish convergence on what happened but rather to identify divergent perspectives and to explore how they mattered. Source criticism and triangulation, therefore, serve the crucial purpose of allowing the situated historical researcher to critically reconstruct facts from traces that have survived through time.

## Explanation through Contextualization

Contextualization plays a central role in historical methodology because it is through the placement of reconstructed events and actions in temporal context that they are given sense and significance (Kipping et al., 2014; Wadhwani, 2016). Historical practice emphasizes contextualization of sources in time and place as a way of deriving the relation between an event or phenomenon and what happened before and after it (Danto, 1965). In short, contextualization is the most basic way in which historical research establishes explanation, or causation, in the Runciman (1983) sense. This may come as a surprise to many social scientists, who often see context as "background" and hence a given condition. But, in historical practice, contexts are interpreted conditions that place an event or action into a causal or semantic relationship in time. It is by recounting linked and related developments that preceded and came after a focal event in the flow of time that the event's complex and contingent causes, significance, and consequences are established (Sewell, 2005). Hence the way in which different historians contextualize the same events or processes are subject to scholarly debate and often have theoretical implications.

Contextualization in time is established through the practices of *periodization* and *narrative construction*. *Periodization* is the process through which events or actions are organized into coherent periods, eras, or epochs (Rowlinson et al., 2014). Periods are determined iteratively, as the researcher moves between research questions, the historiography, and the sources (Kipping et al., 2014; Lipartito, 2014). A research question focused on the origins of the Hawthorne Studies (Hassard, 2012), for instance, would have a different periodization than a research question that considered the rise of big business in the 19th and early 20th centuries (Chandler, 1977). In the process, a researcher may challenge the periodization used by other scholars in order to consider the event or development from an alternative perspective. Lamoreaux et al. (2003), for instance, challenge Chandler's (1977) interpretation of the rise of big business by adopting a longer perspective that incorporates the eventual decline of the advantages of corporate scale in the late twentieth century.

Periodization matters for explanation because variations in how historical studies organize time allow the researcher to entertain different types of causal explanations. Periods that are short in duration and focus on events, for instance, typically assign agency to human actors and consider action at the individual, or sometimes group, level (Levi, 2012). Periodizations of longer duration, in contrast, allow historical researchers to consider structural factors shaping action. Studies of societal institutions and institutionalization, for instance, typically take at least a multi-decade duration in periodization to identify patterns of persistence and change (Baumol, 1990). Historians even consider periodization at geological time scales, in considering how geography shapes society and history (Braudel, 1958).

Particular studies may also combine or layer periodizations in order to identify complex causes and consequences of an event not only in the actions immediately preceding and coming after it, but also in its confluence with slowly unfolding social, political, and intellectual developments forming over decades, and even processes at work over centuries – what the historian Ferdinand Braudel called the "multiplicity of time" (Braudel, 1958). In this regard, the interpretation of complex periodizations accounts in part for why historical methods are particularly good for multi-layered and complex understandings of causality (Ingram et al., 2012; Sewell, 2005).

*Narrative construction* typically works in conjunction with periodization to establish causal explanation in historical practice. Like periodization, narrative organizes evidence in ways that assign causes and consequences to events and actions through their organization in time (Danto, 1965; Ricoeur, 1984; White, 1975). Historical research typically uses narrative in different ways than it is employed in the social sciences (Rowlinson et al., 2014). As Gaddis (2002, 62) points out, whereas many social scientists "tend to embed narratives within generalizations," historians often "embed our generalizations within our narratives." In other words, while social scientists often provide a story to illustrate a generalization, the results of the analysis are not presented as a narrative. Historical narratives, in contrast, synthesize and represent the past, combining at minimum the description of the results with its analysis, and often a discussion of method may be inserted at specific points where the underlying evidence is more difficult to interpret. What is explained is the evidence, not the event as such (Megill, 2007, 128–131, 246 FN115). To explain the evidence, historical narrative proposes sequence, causality, or indeed interdependency and contingency. This means that the elements that constitute the interpretation through narrative can be separated from the underlying evidence, which can be interpersonally verified.

Though sometimes seen by other social scientists simply as a series of facts or events that "chronicle" developments, historical narratives are better understood as complex representations (Ankersmit), maps (Gaddis), or models of social action in time related to a research question or problem under consideration. In other words, historical narratives seek to provide a coherent and selective representation of the past, rather than a pure chronicle of all events and actions related to the topic (Danto, 1965; White, 1975). In this sense, historical narratives, unlike chronicles, are not simply arrangements of evidence but rather involve first the selection of relevant actors, actions, and events based on the judgments of the historical researcher, and second pulls these elements together in a plot that creates distinctly multi-causal and interdependent explanations. The goal of such a synthesis is to provide a more complete or alternative explanation to the ones offered by existing accounts. The resulting narrative "fits" together developments in a temporal order that accounts for phenomena under consideration and competes with alternative existing narrative accounts in explaining the historical phenomenon (Ricoeur, 1984). These competing historical narratives constitute the historiography of the field – the range of competing accounts. The value of the creation of new historical narratives, in this sense, is akin to the creation of new and alternative explanations of a phenomenon that once seemed familiar and explained by extant theory. In this sense it is through the construction of new narratives that historical reasoning engages in abduction and the establishment of revisionist explanations.

Given the limitations on sources and the creation of new data, how and why do new historical narratives develop? New narratives are possible for a number of reasons. Occasionally, the discovery of new or unused sources makes alternative historical accounts possible. More commonly, however, new historical narratives develop precisely because interpretations are open to new perspectives and developments that lead researchers to reconsider the narrative elements that matter and the temporal order that holds the narrative together. In other words, changes in historical perspective may lead to the creation of new narratives that emphasize actors, actions, and events that were once considered marginal or that reconfigure a temporal ordering that was once taken for granted.

The rise of developing countries and postcolonial movements, for instance, has played an important role in reshaping the once Eurocentric interpretations of world history (Appleby et al., 1995). This has had more wide-ranging methodological implications in terms of addressing how power relations are inscribed in the archives (Stoler, 2009). Within business history, the re-emergence of small entrepreneurial firms and the limited competitiveness of large, industrial enterprise in the late twentieth century have led historians to reconsider the Chandlerian narrative synthesis of the rise of big business (Lamoreaux et al., 2003). For instance, Sabel and Zeitlin (1997) explicitly acknowledge the importance of alternative narrative representation as a foundation for their challenge to the Chandlerian synthesis. In organizational history, reinterpretations of the role of the Hawthorne Studies, or the legacy of Mayo or Weber present revisionist narratives of commonly held beliefs (Bruce and Nyland, 2011; Hassard, 2012; O'Connor, 1999).

## Understanding Actors through Hermeneutic Interpretation

A significant tradition in historical thought has contended that explanations of action (i.e., causality alone) are insufficient in historical methods, and that "historical science" required *understanding* evidence from the point of view and experience of actors as a basis for comprehending their actions (Collingwood, 1946; Dilthey, 2002 [1910]). This claim was based on both the idea that one needed to understand the perspective of actors in order to identify motives and causation, but also because understanding their experiences was an aim of social science in itself. Although strains of social and economic history have sometimes downplayed this methodological task, assuming instead that actions could be explained through universal behavioral principles (Hempel, 1942), the methodological requirement within most branches of mainstream history has in fact been to emphasize more heavily the importance of reconstructing the subjective basis of experience. In the second half of the twentieth century, this methodological concern evolved in ways that emphasized that historians' attempts to understand their subject's perspective should not come at the cost of denying one's identity as a present-day researcher with present-day concerns (Danto, 1965; Gadamer, 1975). In this sense, historical methodology has become more sensitive to the historical researcher's own position and perspective in time, as a product of the present.

Historical practice related to the task of understanding the subjects of research has in large part been shaped by hermeneutic thought (Gadamer, 1975). A body of theory and philosophy related to how meaning arises from texts, hermeneutics emphasizes the value of empathetic interpretation that seeks to understand a text from the point of view of the author producing the text (Stutz and Sachs, 2017). In particular, hermeneutics emphasizes the process of interpreting a text by placing it within the broader contexts in which it was produced in order to understand authorial intent. Interpretation proceeds through the "hermeneutic circle" in which the researcher moves back and forth between text and context until a stable meaning is derived. Strictly speaking, hermeneutic philosophy sometimes posits that an interpreter in the present cannot fully understand the perspective and meanings ascribed by actors in the past because of the fundamentally situated character of both the researcher and the subject, but in the process of seeking to understand a historical actor or text the interpreter may converge around a common "horizon" that casts light back on the present (Gadamer, 1975). Such hermeneutic interpretation is increasingly common in much of the historical research in organization studies (Kipping et al., 2014; Stutz and Sachs, 2017). For instance, it has been used to examine the perspective of oil industry executives during the oil crisis of the 1970s (Prasad and Mir, 2002) and to understand the changing ways in which art market actors valued modern Indian art in the late twentieth century (Khaire and Wadhwani, 2010).

A related methodological practice is that of microhistory (Levi, 2012), today perhaps better known as ethnographic history (Rowlinson et al., 2014), which explains the relationship between the retrospective knowledge of the researcher and the cognition of the historical actors best. Ginzburg (2012) for instance, described his approach with reference to the ethnographic categories of *emic* and *etic*: The first describes an attempt to access the perspective of those experiencing historical events, and is in essence a way to reconstruct the cognition of historical actors by understanding their context (Levi, 2012, 122). This approach does not deny the unique and present-centered position of the researcher, who represents the *etic* perspective by bringing in theoretical concerns and analytical tools that determine the shape of the narrative. Thus the strength of any historical narrative relies on its ability to balance the *etic* perspective, which through retrospective knowledge determines the periodization and plot, with an *emic* approach that seeks to reconstruct the cognition of historical actors by placing them in their proper space and time. Hence, historical work of that sort seeks balance between the past and the present – between the historian's representation and the reality of the past (Gaddis, 2002, 123; Rahikainen and Fellman, 2012, 33–34; Trouillot, 1995). Steedman (2002, 69), for example, refers to the past as something "which does not now exist, but which once did actually happen; which cannot be retrieved, but which may be represented."

Related work has also explored the role of language in shaping meaning and the role of power within discourses of meaning. Hermeneutic concerns over the role of meaning brought considerable attention to how language and discourse comes to structure meaning and interpretation. Thus, the hermeneutic philosophical basis of historical practices directed at achieving understanding laid the foundations for the "linguistic turn" in historical research. Influenced by the work of Foucault, historical research has also become more attuned to analyzing how power is established through discourse and meaning (Foucault, 1991). Thus, historical practices shaped by hermeneutics have taken a critical approach to meaning in the last few decades. This has prompted important work in organizational history, such as Carter et al. (2002) and Rowlinson and Hassard (1993).

## Evaluation through Hindsight

The previous sections explained that when engaging in the research tasks of reportage, explanation, and understanding, historical practice involves grappling with the opportunities and challenges presented by the historical researchers' own position in the future looking back. Hindsight also provides the perch from which historical researchers judge the "lessons" or conclusions of their histories for their audiences in the present. But the form and content of the lessons or conclusions may be shaped by a variety of different evaluative motives.

Within organization studies, where "theory building" is valued as paramount, much of the focus in recent years has been on the usefulness of *history to theory* (Kipping and Üsdiken, 2014). And, in fact, the hindsight that historical perspective provides is especially useful for several kinds of theory building. History, for instance, has long been recognized as uniquely suited for examining organizational and social processes (Langley, 1999; Maclean et al., 2016; Pettigrew, 1992), such as institutionalization (Suddaby et al., 2014) and organizational learning (Fear, 2014). In part that is because history provides the longer perspectives, accounts for the complex causal patterns, and incorporates the contingent events that short-term process research has difficulty studying. History is also increasingly recognized as a way to study the discursive and rhetorical construction of organizations and markets, as actors "use" history toward organizational ends (Hargadon and Douglas, 2001; Schultz and Hernes, 2013; Suddaby et al., 2010). And, historical evaluation and methods are also promising as a means of evaluating normative theoretical claims, such as those related to corporate social responsibility and the role of business in society (Stutz and Sachs, 2017).

Considerably less well recognized within organization studies are the other (non-theory oriented) kinds of evaluative claims that historical research can make using hindsight. One such set of claims pertains to the use of historical inquiry to deepen *understanding* of situations or conditions in the present (Gadamer, 1975). The basic premise of this evaluative orientation is that to better recognize where we are and where we could go, we have to understand where we have been. Rather than focusing on the construction and evaluation of theoretical claims, such an approach uses historical narrative of the origins and evolution of phenomena in order to deepen understanding of them in the present. Gompers (1994), for instance, examines the origins of venture capital as a way to understand the character of entrepreneurial finance in modern America, and McKenna (2006) examines the history of management consulting to better understand how it came to play such an important role in modern business enterprise. While historical narratives oriented toward deepening understanding of major conditions or problems that confront organizations are undervalued in organization studies, the evaluative orientation toward deepening understanding of a condition or problem in the present is very common in other fields, including in mainstream history.

History can also be used to *critique* sources of power in the present. An evaluative orientation toward critique typically focuses on examining the origins of power that are so deeply rooted in knowledge and discourse that they are imperceptible to everyday actors in the present. It is only by examining the origins and development of these discourses of power and patterns of disempowerment, and by comparing them to previous ways of asserting power and order that we can begin to identify and critique it. Foucault (1991) for instance, develops a "genealogical approach" to studying the origins of such forms of taken-for-granted power. While such a critical approach to history remains rare within organization studies, it has flourished around a few topics, such as those related to the developed history of human resources and management (Braverman, 1974; Bruce and Nyland, 2011; Hassard, 2012; O'Connor, 1999).

## Conclusion: History beyond Theory

Historical research introduces unique epistemological and methodological sensibilities into the practice of qualitative research in organization studies. In this chapter we focused in particular on the situated nature of the historical researcher in time, and the important methodological and intellectual implications of the retrospective nature of historical research design. In summary, historical research is reflexive, in that good historical practice is about a dialogue between the past and the present; abductive, as researchers iteratively seek out best explanations for empirical phenomena by drawing on or developing theory; and revisionist, in that historical knowledge advances through the evaluation of competing narratives about the past by a community of researchers. We unpacked this by focusing on Runciman's description of methodology as addressing the following issues: reportage, explanation, understanding, and evaluation. In historical practice, reportage is developed through source criticism and triangulation; explanation is based on contextualization using tools such as periodization and narrative construction; and understanding is developed through hermeneutical and Foucauldian analysis. Finally, evaluation does not always lead to theorization in the sense of organizational theory, but can focus on understanding unique events within their historical context and through the experience of historical actors, or in terms of power dynamics. For historians, theory also encompasses the explanation of unique events which may not be fully, or even not at all, generalizable to a broader category.

We focused on research practices because we believe they are crucial for unlocking the potential of using historical methods to develop organization theory. If history is to actually contribute to theory, it has to be practiced. To engage in the abductive reasoning processes that history requires, organization scholars will need to *apply* historical methods to empirical puzzles and phenomena in which alternative narratives are considered and existing understandings overturned. Revisioning the past, as we have claimed, is essential to historical research processes, but it is also important to seeing theory anew, and why historical revisionism is in fact inherently a theory-building process.

But the chapter has also argued that much of the value of the historic turn lies beyond the "synthesis of history and theory" that has received much attention in recent years. Historical discourse plays a broader role in any community, whether it is a nation state, an ethnic group, or a professional association. Generating theoretical knowledge from history is only one of its discursive roles, aimed at considering and revising the epistemic constructs that are used in the community. Equally important, and much less appreciated, are the other two roles that this paper suggests represent important paths forward for the role of history in qualitative organizational research. The first of these is to generate understanding for the community: where it and its objects of analysis came from. The other is to generate critique, particularly of the sources of power, in order to consider the community and its received constructs in ways that allow for the possibility of change. History has the potential to play these roles in management and organizational research, and the turn toward history remains as much promise as reality, until organization scholars embrace these other forms of historical knowledge, as much as they have embraced its value for understanding theory. We believe for this to be realized, greater attention needs to be paid to Clio's toolkit, by which we mean the array of historical research practices that offer methodological and theoretical opportunities to organizational research into the past.

## Acknowledgments

We thank Matthias Kipping for his contributions to an earlier version of this paper. We also thank Raza Mir and Sanjay Jain for their helpful comments and their patience as editors.

## Note

1 Runciman uses the term "description" rather than "understanding" to refer to the scholarly process of recounting the subjective experience of the actors being studied, but here we use "understanding" both because it is clearer and because others have also more often used the term. For a recent discussion of Runciman that influenced our own choice in using him to describe methodology, see Leblebici (2014).

## References

Alvesson, M. and Karreman, D. (2007). Constructing Mystery: Empirical Matters in Theory Development. *Academy of Management Review*, 32, 1265–1281.

Appleby, J., Hunt, L., and Jacob, M. (1995). *Telling the Truth about History*. New York: Norton and Company.

Baumol, W. J. (1990). Entrepreneurship: Productive, Unproductive, and Destructive. *Journal of Political Economy*, 98, 893–921.

Braudel, F. (1958). *Histoire et sciences sociales: la longue durée*. Paper presented at the Annales. Histoire, Sciences Sociales.

Braverman, H. (1974). *Labor and Monopoly Capital: The Degradation of Work in the Twentieth Century*. New York: NYU Press.

Bruce, K. and Nyland, C. (2011). Elton Mayo and the Deification of Human Relations. *Organization Studies*, 32, 383–405.

Carter, C., McKinlay, A., and Rowlinson, M. (2002). Introduction: Foucault, Management, and History. *Organization*, 9, 515–526.

Chandler, A. D. (1977). *The Visible Hand: The Managerial Revolution in American Business*. Cambridge, MA: The Belknap Press of Harvard University Press.

Collingwood, R. G. (1946). *The Idea of History*. Oxford: Clarendon Press.

Danto, A. C. (1965). *Analytical Philosophy of History*. Cambridge: Cambridge University Press.

De Jong, A., Higgins, D., and van Driel, H. (2015). Towards a New Business History? *Business History*, 2015, 5–29.

Decker, S. (2013). The Silence of the Archives: Business History, Post-Colonialism and Archival Ethnography. *Management and Organizational History*, 8, 155–173.

Decker, S., Kipping, M., and Wadhwani, R. D. (2015). New Business Histories! Plurality in Business History Research Methods. *Business History*, 57, 30–40.

Dilthey, W. (2002 [1910]). *Selected Works. Vol. III: The Formation of the Historical World in the Human Sciences (Edited with an introduction by Rudolf A. Makkreel and Frithjof Rodi)*. Princeton, NJ: Princeton University Press.

Eisenhardt, K. M. (1989). Building Theories from Case Study Research. *Academy of Management Review*, 14, 532–550.

Fear, J. (2014). Mining the Past: Historicizing Organizational Learning and Change. In M. Bucheli and D. Wadhwani (eds.), *Organizations in Time*. Oxford: Oxford University Press, 169–191.

Foucault, M. (1991). *Discipline and Punish: The Birth of a Prison*. London: Penguin.

Gadamer, H. G. (1975). *Truth and Method*. New York: Seabury Press.

Gaddis, J. L. (2002). *The Landscape of History: How Historians Map the Past.* New York: Oxford University Press.

Ginzburg, C. (2012). Our Words, and Theirs: A Reflection on the Historian's Craft, Today. In S. Fellman and M. Rahikainen (eds.), *Historical Knowledge: In Quest of Theory, Method and Evidence.* Newcastle upon Tyne: Cambridge Scholars Publishing, 97–120.

Glaser, B. G. and Strauss, A. L. (1967). *The Discovery of Grounded Theory: Strategies for Qualitative Research.* Chicago, IL: Aldine.

Godfrey, P. C., Hassard, J., O'Connor, E. S., Rowlinson, M., and Ruef, M. (2016). What Is Organizational History? Toward a Creative Synthesis of History and Organization Studies. *Academy of Management Review*, 41, 590–608.

Gompers, P. (1994). The Rise and Fall of Venture Capital. *Business and Economic History*, 23, 1–26.

Hargadon, A. B. and Douglas, Y. (2001). When Innovations Meet Institutions: Edison and the Design of the Electric Light. *Administrative Science Quarterly*, 46, 476–501.

Hassard, J. (2012). Rethinking the Hawthorne Studies: The Western Electric Research in Its Social, Political and Historical Context. *Human Relations*, 65, 1431–1461.

Hatch, M. J. and Yanow, D. (2003). Organization Theory as an Interpretive Science. In C. Knudsen and H. Tsoukas (eds.), *The Oxford Handbook of Organization Theory.* New York: Oxford University Press, 63–87.

Hempel, C. (1942). The Function of General Laws in History. *Journal of Philosophy*, 39, 35–48.

Howell, M. and Prevenier, W. (2001). *From Reliable Sources: An Introduction to Historical Methods.* Ithaca, NY and London: Cornell University Press.

Ingram, P., Rao, H. and Silverman, B. S. (2012). History in Strategy Research: What, Why, and How? In S. J. Kahl, B. S. Silverman and M. A. Cusumano (eds.), *History and Strategy.* Bingley, UK: Emerald, 241–273.

Jones, G. and Khanna, T. (2006). Bringing History (Back) into International Business. *Journal of International Business Studies*, 37, 453–468.

Khaire, M. and Wadhwani, R. D. (2010). Changing Landscapes: The Construction of Meaning and Value in a New Market Category – Modern Indian Art. *Academy of Management Journal*, 53, 1281–1304.

Kieser, A. (1994). Why Organization Theory Needs Historical Analyses – And How This Should Be Performed. *Organization Science*, 5, 608–620.

Kipping, M. and Üsdiken, B. (2014). History in Organization and Management Theory: More Than Meets the Eye. *Academy of Management Annals*, 8, 535–588.

Kipping, M., Wadhwani, R. D., and Bucheli, M. (2014). Analyzing and Interpreting Historical Sources: A Basic Methodology. In M. Bucheli and R. D. Wadhwani (eds.), *Organizations in Time: History, Theory, Methods.* Oxford: Oxford University Press, 305–329.

Lamoreaux, N. R., Raff, D. M. G., and Temin, P. (2003). Beyond Markets and Hierarchies: Toward a New Synthesis of American Business History. *American Historical Review*, 108, 404–433.

Langley, A. (1999). Strategies for theorizing from process data. *Academy of Management Review*, 24, 691–710.

Leblebici, H. (2014). History and Organization Theory: Potential for a Transdisciplinary Convergence. In M. Bucheli and D. R. Wadhwani (eds.), *Organizations in Time: Theory, History, Methods.* New York: Oxford University Press, 56–99.

Levi, G. (2012). Microhistory and the Recovery of Complexity. In S. Fellman and M. Rahikainen (eds.), *Historical Knowledge: In Quest of Theory, Method and Evidence.* Newcastle upon Tyne: Cambridge Scholars Publishing, 121–132.

Lipartito, K. J. (2014). Historical Sources and Data. In M. Bucheli and R. D. Wadhwani (eds.), *Organizations in Time: History, Theory, Methods.* Oxford: Oxford University Press, 284–304.

Lippmann, S. and Aldrich, H. (2016). A Rolling Stone Gathers Momentum: Generational Units, Collective Memory, and Entrepreneurship. *Academy of Management Review*, 51, 658–675.

McKenna, C. D. (2006). *The World's Newest Profession: Management Consulting in the Twentieth Century.* Cambridge: Cambridge University Press.

Maclean, M., Harvey, C., and Clegg, S. (2016). Conceptualizing Historical Organization Studies. *Academy of Management Review*, amr. 2014.0133.

Mantere, S. and Ketokivi, M. (2013). Reasoning in Organization Science. *Academy of Management Review*, 38, 70–89.

Megill, A. (2007). *Historical Knowledge, Historical Error: A Contemporary Guide to Practice.* Chicago, IL and London: University of Chicago Press.

Miles, M. and Huberman, M. (1994). *Qualitative Data Analysis: An Expanded Sourcebook*. Thousand Oaks, CA: Sage.

Niiniluoto, I. (1999). Defending Abduction. *Philosophy of Science*, 66, S436–S451.

O'Connor, E. (1999). The Politics of Management Thought: A Case Study of the Harvard Business School and the Human Relations School. *Academy of Management Review*, 24, 117–131.

Peirce, C. (1878). Deduction, Induction, and Hypothesis. *Popular Science Monthly*, 13, 470–482.

Pettigrew, A. (1992). The Character and Significance of Strategy Process Research. *Strategic Management Journal*, 13, 5–16.

Prasad, A. and Mir, R. (2002). Digging Deep for Meaning: A Critical Hermeneutic Analysis of CEO Letters to Shareholders in the Oil Industry. *Journal of Business Communications*, 39, 92–116.

Rahikainen, M. and Fellman, S. (2012). On Historical Writing and Evidence. In S. Fellman and M. Rahikainen (eds.), *Historical Knowledge: In Quest of Theory, Method and Evidence*. Newcastle upon Tyne: Cambridge Scholars Publishing, 5–44.

Ricoeur, P. (1984). *Time and Narrative*. Chicago, IL: University of Chicago Press.

Ricoeur, P. (2004). *Memory, History, Forgetting*. Chicago, IL: University of Chicago Press.

Rowlinson, M. and Hassard, J. (1993). The Invention of Corporate Culture: A History of the Histories of Cadbury. *Human Relations*, 46, 299–326.

Rowlinson, M., Hassard, J., and Decker, S. (2014). Research Strategies for Organizational History: A Dialogue between Historical Theory and Organization Theory. *Academy of Management Review*, 39, 250–274.

Runciman, W. (1983). *A Treatise on Social Theory*. Cambridge: Cambridge University Press.

Sabel, C. F. and Zeitlin, J. (eds.) (1997). *World of Possibilities: Flexibility and Mass Production in Western Industrialization*. Cambridge and New York: Cambridge University Press.

Schultz, M. and Hernes, T. (2013). A Temporal Perspective on Organizational Identity. *Organization Science*, 24, 1–21.

Schwarzkopf, S. (2013). Why Business Historians Need a Constructive Theory of the Archive. *Business Archives*, 105, 1–9.

Sewell, W. H. (2005). *Logics of History: Social Theory and Social Transformation*. Chicago, IL: University of Chicago Press.

Steedman, C. (2002). *Dust: The Archive and Cultural History*. New Brunswick, NJ: Rutgers University Press.

Stoler, A. L. (2009). *Along the Archival Grain: Epistemic Anxieties and Colonial Common Sense*. Princeton, NJ: Princeton University Press.

Stutz, C. and Sachs, S. (2017). Facing the Normative Challenge: The Potential of Reflexive Historical Research. *Business and Society*.

Suddaby, R., Foster, W. M. and Mills, A. J. (2014). Historical Institutionalism. In M. Bucheli and R. D. Wadhwani (eds.), *Organizations in Time: History, Theory, Methods*. Oxford: Oxford University Press, 100–123.

Suddaby, R., Foster, W. M., and Quinn Trank, C. (2010). Rhetorical History as a Source of Competitive Advantage. *Advances in Strategic Management*, 27, 147–173.

Trouillot, M.-R. (1995). *Silencing the Past: Power and the Production of History*. Boston, MA: Beacon Press.

Vaara, E. and Lamberg, J.-A. (2016). Taking Historical Embeddedness Seriously: Three Historical Approaches to Advance Strategy Process and Practice Research. *Academy of Management Review*, 41, 633–657.

Wadhwani, R. D. (2016). Entrepreneurship in Historical Context: Using History to Develop Theory and Understand Process. In F. Welter and W. B. Gartner (eds.), *A Research Agenda for Entrepreneurship and Context*. Cheltenham, UK: Edward Elgar, 65–78.

Wadhwani, R. D. and Bucheli, M. (2014). The Future of the Past in Management and Organizational Studies. In M. Bucheli and R. D. Wadhwani (eds.), *Organizations in Time: History, Theory, Methods*. New York: Oxford University Press, 3–30.

Wadhwani, R. D. and Jones, G. (2014). Schumpeter's Plea: Historical Reasoning in Entrepreneurship Theory and Research. In M. Bucheli and R. D. Wadhwani (eds.), *Organizations in Time: History, Theory and Methods*. Oxford: Oxford University Press, 192–216.

White, H. (1975). *Metahistory: The Historical Imagination in Nineteenth-century Europe*. Baltimore, MD: Johns Hopkins University Press.

Yates, J. (2014). Understanding Historical Methods in Organization Studies. In M. Bucheli and R. D. Wadhwani (eds.), *Organizations in Time: History, Theory, Methods*. New York: Oxford University Press, 265–283.

Yin, R. K. (2009). *Case Study Research: Design and Methods*. 4th edition. Thousand Oaks, CA: Sage.

Zald, M. (1993). Organization Studies as a Scientific and Humanistic Enterprise: Toward a Reconceptualization of the Foundations of the Field. *Organization Science*, 4, 513–528.

# 9

# STORIES AS SOCIAL ACTION
## Rethinking Narrative Studies of Organizing

*Tammar B. Zilber*

Narratives are by now a well explored phenomenon in various disciplines, including psychology (Muntigl, 2004; Ochs and Capps, 1996, 2001), sociology (Franzosi, 1998; Maines, 1993; Orbuch, 1997; Polletta et al., 2011; Richardson, 1990), anthropology (Maggio, 2014; Mattingly, 1998; Mattingly and Garro, 2001), criminology (Presser, 2009; Rajah et al., 2014), social work (Baldwin, 2013; Rutten et al., 2010), law (Amsterdam and Bruner, 2000; Cover, 1983; Ewick and Silbey, 1995, 2003; Farber and Sherry, 1993; Griffin, 2013), communication (Fulton, 2006; Hoffmann, 2010), political science (Boswell, 2013; Patterson and Monroe, 1998; Polletta, 1998, 2006; Polletta and Lee, 2006), and medicine (Charon, 2001, 2004; Kumagai, 2008).[1] In organization studies as well, especially after the linguistic turn, stories were given a central role, as "the great factories of meaning, creating it, transforming it, testing it, sustaining it, fashioning it, and refashioning it" (Gabriel, 2000: 4). It was probably the recognition of the importance of stories to organization culture in the early 1980s (e.g., Martin et al., 1983; for a review, see Giorgi et al., 2015) and for sensemaking in the early 1990s (e.g., Weick, 1995; for a review, see Maitlis and Christianson, 2014) that have been boosting the interest in, and legitimacy of, their study. As demonstrated in Figure 9.1, which depicts the growing number of articles published in top tier journals in the area of business and management that use either narrative or story as their topic,[2] and from various recent reviews (Boje, 2008; Czarniawska, 2004; Gabriel, 2000; Rhodes and Brown, 2005; Vaara et al., 2016), the interest in narratives has been growing with time.

While the empirical study of stories in and around organizations is very rich, it is also fundamentally limited. Two main perspectives can be discerned. In the first strand, researchers try to identify and build upon stories told by organizational members in the context of research interviews. Narratives are thus used to tap into organizations' members' experiences and understandings (e.g., their identities and the ways they make sense of organizational life). While in the first strand researchers try to stay close to the actors' experiences, in the second strand, researchers open up a larger epistemological gap between their understandings and members' actual experiential horizons. Researchers use "composite stories," that is build their own stories based on variety of data, and contemplate how those stories affect organizational dynamics.[3]

Still missing in these studies, however, are stories told spontaneously in everyday organizational lives. Methodologically, they are the most difficult to trace, especially given the preference of interview over observation data in qualitative research on organizing. Analytically,

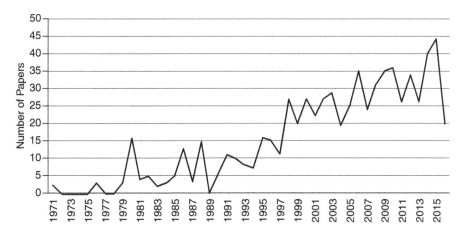

*Figure 9.1*   Number of Papers Using Narrative/Story as Their Topic

*Note*
Articles published in top tier journals in the area of business and management that use either narrative or story as their topic. Based on a Web of Science search, September 2016.

following stories in everyday life means moving away from understanding stories as mere capsules of meanings, towards their conceptualization as part of social actions and interactions. Crucial questions are then what stories do in organizations, not merely what they mean for organizational members. It is thus a "strong" approach for understanding narratives as it has the potential of avoiding collapsing them back into meaning, ideas, and sensemaking processes alone.

In this chapter, I make the case for, and elaborate upon, a "strong" narrative approach,[4] one that focuses on the study of stories as social action. I build on the distinction between "big" and "small" stories, recently developed within narrative psychology, in relation to the study of identities as life stories (Bamberg, 2006; Bamberg and Georgakopoulou, 2008; De Fina and Georgakopoulou, 2008; Georgakopoulou, 2007. For rebuttals, see Freeman, 2006, 2011). This distinction helps also in reviewing current studies of stories in organization studies – highlighting the preference toward "big" stories, and making the case for the study of "small stories," studying stories as social action. Further, I examine in detail a few examples of the study of stories as action, and use them to chart some paradigmatic, theoretical and methodological concerns for a "strong" narrative approach, the study of naturally occurring stories and their action in organizations.

## Big and Small Stories in Narrative Psychology

The interest in studying stories in and around organizations has been part of the "narrative turn" in the humanities and social sciences. Three decades after the diffusion of stories from literary studies into a variety of disciplines, "narrative remains an elusive, contested and indeterminate concept, variously used as an epistemology, a methodological perspective, an antidote to positivist research, a communication mode, a supra-genre, a text-type" (Georgakopoulou, 2006: 122). Indeed, there is much variety within narrative studies, in terms of paradigmatic stands (e.g., Spector-Mersel, 2010; Vaara et al., 2016) and research designs (e.g., Rosile et al., 2013). One important transformation in narrative psychology has been the move from text to practice

(De Fina and Georgakopoulou, 2008) or from "big" to "small" stories (Bamberg and Georga-kopoulou, 2008).

The debate around stories big and small as formulated in narrative psychology relates to its major concern – the conceptualization and study of individual identities (Bruner, 1986, 1990; Gergen and Gergen, 1987; McAdams, 1988, 1993). Narrative psychology aimed to introduce into psychology – a field dominated by the isolation of independent and dependent abstract variables and cause and effect models – an approach that underscores personal meanings, inten-tionality and phenomenological experience. In particular, according to narrative psychology, human beings are not aggregates of isolated variables (e.g., skills, attitudes, etc.) that either cause other effects or serve as effects of other causes. Rather, human beings are subjects located in specific times and places, who constantly try to make sense of their local worlds, and of their own individual identity within them. Human beings do so, argued narrative psychologists, through storytelling.

Narratives were thus understood mainly as a mode of cognitive functioning, different yet complementary to the paradigmatic or logico-scientific one (Bruner, 1986). Whereas the latter deals with formal, cause and effect reasoning, narrative knowing was portrayed as concerned with "human or human-like intention and action and the vicissitudes and consequences that mark their course. It strives to put its timeless miracles into the particulars of experience, and to locate the experience in time and place" (Bruner, 1986: 13). Whereas the paradigmatic mode asks for objective verification, narrative knowing leads to subjective good (or bad) stories, evalu-ated by their correspondence "to some perspective we can imagine or 'feel' as right" (Bruner, 1986: 52). Further, whereas the logico-scientific mode "is oriented outward to an external world," narrative knowing is oriented "inward toward a perspective and a point of view toward the world" (Bruner, 1986: 52). Narrative knowing was considered as having primacy over the scientific and paradigmatic mode in everyday processes of sensemaking (Polkinghorne, 1988: 1, 135, 155) and communication (Currie, 1998; Fisher, 1984, 1987).

People use stories to make sense of themselves, and to communicate those understandings to others. Storytelling allows people to bind together a sequence of temporally ordered events, "by some principal of logical coherence" (Franzosi, 1998), which turns them into a meaningful story (Polkinghorne, 1988: 131). Such identity work is never ending. We "write," tell, and "rewrite" stories to ourselves, as "we cannot live without searching for stories to give coherence to our lives" (Kirmayer, 1993: 180). Various versions of the identity story exist simultaneously. One's identity exists in between all these versions. As Havel (1989: 155) wrote: "I exist ... as the tension between all my 'versions', for that tension, too (and perhaps that above all), is me." In other words, "we actualize our selves through the activity of narrating. We use narrative as a tool for probing and forging connections between our unstable, situated selves" (Ochs and Capps, 1996: 29). Thus, "[identity is] a continuous process of narration where both the narrator[s] and the audience[s] are involved in formulating, editing, applauding, and refusing various ele-ments of the ever-produced narrative[s]" (Czarniawska-Joerges, 1997: 49). Further, such iden-tity work is context bound. People construct their stories within multiple contexts (Zilber et al., 2008): subjective (Bruner, 1986, 1990; McAdams, 1988; Sarbin, 1986), intersubjective (Gergen and Gergen, 1987), and in light of the "cultural stock of stories" available to them (see Bruner, 1990: 11, 33, 96; Mumby, 1993: 5; Polkinghorne, 1988: 107; Ricoeur, 1991: 76; Somers, 1994: 606).

The epistemological basis of narrative psychology was accompanied by a quite specific meth-odological toolkit, a "talking heads" method that allows for an exact recording of people's stories. Following the conceptualization of identity as narrative, most studies within narrative psychology used life-story interviews in their efforts to elicit interviewees to tell their identity story. This research design presumably allows the researcher to control the social event, and the interviewee to tell a "free" and full story (with more or less directing questions in a semi-structured interview format). Scholars using this research design acknowledged its limitations: Each

> particular telling … inspires distinct and only partially overlapping narratives, as inter-locutors link the telling to their particular lived and imagined involvements in the world … Each telling of a narrative situated in time and space engages only facets of a narrator's or listener/reader's selfhood in that it evokes only certain memories, con-cerns, and expectations.
>
> *(Ochs and Capps, 1996: 21–22)*

It was still assumed, however, that the collection of such a "big story" – a life story in its entirety through an artificial social event (the interview) – provides a very rich and generally authentic ("true") narrative of identity.

Lately, the study of such "big stories" came under attack. Big stories, so the critique goes, are the product of "research or clinical elicitation techniques" (Bamberg and Georgakopoulou, 2008: 377). While interview encounters produce prototypical narratives – rich, detailed and long retro-spective accounts of one's life – such a methodological and conceptual approach offers a narrow definition of the empirical object – stories, and in particular their actual use in people's lives.

Scholars pointed out the deep possible differences between "big" stories as told in interviews and "small" stories told naturally and spontaneously within everyday life. Studies in discourse and conversation analysis show that stories told in such natural situations are terse, partial, and co-narrated (Boje, 1991; Goodwin, 1984; Jefferson, 1978; Rühlemann and Gries, 2015). Fur-thermore, they function differently, for they are not only "tools of reflection" (Bamberg and Georgakopoulou, 2008; Georgakopoulou, 2006), as is the case within an interview, but rather they constitute personal and social action and interaction.

The difference between big and small stories have important implications for the "identifica-tion and analysis of narrative" (Georgakopoulou, 2007: vii). The move toward the appreciation, and exploration, of "small stories" entails a focus on naturally occurring stories, including

> narrative activities, such as tellings of ongoing events, future or hypothetical events, shared (known) events, but also allusions to tellings, deferrals of tellings, and refusals to tell. These tellings are typically small when compared to the pages and pages of tran-script of interview narratives.
>
> *(Georgakopoulou, 2007: vii)*

Further, in terms of attention to time, plot, and the dynamic dimensions of narratives, the big stories approach looks at fully fledged stories,

> a coherent temporal progression of events that may be reordered for rhetorical pur-poses and that is typically located in some past time and place. A plot line that encom-passes a beginning, a middle, and an end, conveys a particular perspective and is designed for a particular audience who apprehend and shape its meaning.
>
> *(Ochs and Capps, 2001: 51)*

By contrast, in the main, small story research looks at those stories that would have been missed or dismissed by a big story approach, looking at even "the smallness of talk … fleeting moments of narrative orientation to the world" (Georgakopoulou, 2007: vii). In a small stories approach, the focus is on "concrete sites of engagement in which small stories are negotiated" (Bamberg and Georgakopoulou, 2008: 380), on stories in interaction (De Fina and Georgakopoulou, 2008).

The call is thus made to shift from big to small stories, or from story-as-text to story-as-action. A move

> from a long-standing conceptualization of (oral, cf. natural, non-literary) narrative as a well-defined and delineated genre with an identifiable structure toward the exploration of the multiplicity, fragmentation, and irreducible situatedness of its forms and functions in a wide range of social arenas.
>
> *(De Fina and Georgakopoulou, 2008: 275)*

This call is by now apparent in a variety of disciplines building on discourse and socio-linguistic narrative analysis. It is about time for it to affect the study of stories in and around organizations.

## Big Stories in the Study of Organizations

In the main, empirical studies which built on a narrative paradigm fall into two categories. Some build on stories told by organizational members in the context of research interviews, or published stories (e.g., biographies) to tap into their representations of experiences, understandings, identities, and sensemaking. Others are based on "composite stories," that is, stories put together not by organization members but by the researcher, based on varieties of data sources (Currie and Brown, 2003). Both kinds, however, produce stories that "seem to float in a social vacuum. The voices echo in an otherwise empty world. There is an extraordinary absence of social context, social action, and social interaction" (Atkinson, 1997: 339).

Shamir et al.'s (2005) study of leaders' development is a good example of the first, interview- or biography-based narrative studies in organizations. Taking a life story approach to leadership (see also Shamir and Eilam, 2005), Shamir et al. (2005) analyzed life stories of leaders, in order to identify presumably universal and general themes of leadership development. As against the common tendency in the research literature to attribute leaders' influence to their psychological traits or behavior, the authors suggest that leaders' life stories are central to their influence. Leaders' life stories serve three main functions: They provide followers and others with much information to learn about and evaluate the leader; they provide the leader with a self-concept, which is pivotal to his/her ability to lead; and the telling of their life-stories is an important part of leadership. Using interviews with leaders, and published biographies of leaders, the authors identified four universal proto-stories of leadership development. The researchers treat these leadership stories as "depositories of meaning" (Gabriel, 2000: 15), focusing on their content alone. Following the logic of the small story critique, these stories are big but they lack grounding in everyday life. If indeed development stories of leaders are important, and are used by leaders in their interactions with followers and others, then they should be studied also as social action. To appreciate the work of leaders' stories, we need to follow them in action – as they are told, accepted, and negotiated in real-life situations. A new methodology should be adopted because interviews or biographies provide limited data for understanding the role of narratives in leadership.

Whereas biography- and interview-based studies are inherently limited in their ability to explore the social action of stories, fieldwork (and ethnographic) methods – especially observations and their analysis – seem more suitable for that end. Still, often even ethnography-based narrative studies seem to take a "weak" approach to narrative. Currie and Brown's (2003) study of managers' reactions to change interventions in Omega, a UK hospital, is a case in point. The researchers follow the individuals' and the group's stories by which middle managers "make sense of events in their working lives, and define their work identities" (Currie and Brown, 2003: 563). The study is based on more than three years of data collection that followed the process of change, and on a variety of data sources – interviews, observations, and archival. The findings are arranged into two "group stories," those of the middle and those of the senior managers. Yet, as the authors write, "the narratives were not related to us in their entirety by any single member of either group. Rather, the data we collected yielded narrative fragments that we have pieced together into coherent stories" (569). The two narratives are detailed and contrasted, and the change process is conceptualized in narratological terms, moving from "narrative imposition" by the senior managers, to "narrative resistance" by middle managers, and to "narrative confluence," a stage in which both narratives changed and became "less polarized" (576). This narratological depiction of the change in Omega highlights sensemaking and power relations. But while the authors claim that their study offers "a view of organizations as storytelling milieux, in which narratives play important collective sensemaking, identity-defining, hegemonic, and legitimatory roles" (579), in actuality they do not follow storytelling dynamic processes (actions and interactions) within the organization. They instead use a metaphor of storytelling to depict a change process. They assume, instead of actually explore, that organizational reality is enacted through stories people tell. They do not explore how the actual stories that were (if at all) told during the process were used by organizational members, how they were telling, negotiating, and retelling them as part of naturally occurring conversations taking place in the organization, and to what effect.

Sonenshein (2010) provides another good example of the "composite narrative" studies within our discipline. Once again, it is a study of change implementation, focusing on a Fortune 500 retailer. It is based on extensive fieldwork of 15 months, and so it includes "both retrospective and real-time data," including interviews, documents, archival records, observations, and a survey (482–483). It is the author who transformed fragments of stories he heard, mostly in the interview data, into "composite narratives" that "summarize collective constructions of meaning" (483). The findings are presented through those composite stories, contrasting two managers' narratives with four employees' narratives of the change, and offering a model of how those narratives influenced change implementation. Specifically, the author identified various types of narrated responses – ways by which employees reacted to managers' narratives. But while the author offers ample data to support the content of the six narratives he identifies, his analysis is presented as a generalized model of the process he observed, rather than a detailed following up of the various contexts, actions, and interactions within which the various narratives were socially used. Thus, the readers are not offered a clear analysis of how stories were told in real time, and how they were narrated, consumed, and reacted to in concrete situations.

A final example of the limitations of the "composite narrative" approach is Zilber (2007). Zilber collected data through ethnographic methods in a field-level event of the Israeli high-tech industry, following the 2001 financial crisis. Out of the rich discourses characterizing the proceedings of the event, she constructed three narratives that give different explanations for the crisis and its future implications. The three narratives were told by different actors in the field, cast different actors in the roles of leading and supporting heroes and villains, offered different plot lines, and built on different authorities and discursive tools. One, a unified and unifying story, was told openly, and two competing and conflictual stories were told in more subtle ways. Zilber uses the case to discuss the ability of narratives – through the manipulation of overt and covert meaning – to serve various and even conflictual meanings, and highlights the power relations and politics involved in telling stories. Still, those are composite stories, constructed from various data sources by the researcher. Readers do not get a clear understanding of how bits and pieces of the concrete stories were actually told, and rejected or accepted in real time.

These and other studies (e.g., Brown et al., 2008) all offer valuable insights regarding sense-making in organizational and field-level dynamics. Their use of narrative methods helps in highlighting the linguistic construction of reality on individual, group and organizational levels, and underscores its embeddedness in power relations among social actors. These contributions notwithstanding, in terms of the potential of a narrative approach, they fail to capture the social action of stories in organizational life. The limits of this approach have to do with the reliance on interview data (rather than naturally occurring stories), and on the reduction of stories observed in real time into mere content. In following the "big" stories, these studies represent then a "weak" version of a narrative approach for they avoid conceptualizing stories as social performance and as part of social actions and interactions. In the next section, I will exemplify the potential of a "strong" narrative approach that follows "small stories" and their social action.

## Small Stories in the Study of Organizations: From Text to Action

A "small stories," or "strong" approach to stories in and around organizations needs to go beyond treating stories "as texts to be analyzed for the meanings they express." Rather stories should be explored as "social performances that are interactively constructed, institutionally regulated, and assessed by their audiences in relation to hierarchies of discursive credibility." The move from studying stories to the study of storytelling entails capturing stories "in the contexts of their telling" (Polleta et al., 2011: 110). Let me provide examples of this move, and its potential, using some recently published papers on the role of stories in decision-making processes.

Abolafia (2010) studied decision-making at the Federal Reserve's Open Market Committee (FOMC). Using verbatim transcripts of FOMC meetings in the summer of 1992, the author explore the role of stories in FOMC's monetary policy making. Rather than exploring the content and structure of narrativized meanings, Abolafia explores the process of meaning construction through stories. Specifically, he outlines a three-stage process. In the first stage – abduction – participants try to move from "facts" to models. They select the relevant indicators to describe the economic situation, and try to explain them using existing economic models. In the second stage – plotting – there is a collective effort to construct a story, adding complexity and temporality. Through the story, participants try to bridge between the simplistic economic models, and the complexity of the reality they need to capture. In this stage, participants tell and re-tell the evolving story, evaluate it and re-phrase it, adding emphases that serve their own interests. This is a collective, cyclic and political process. In the third stage – selective retention – potential decisions that do not fit the evolving shared story are ruled out, and there is pressure to cohere around a consensual decision. In his model of narrative decision making, Abolafia (2010) uses "narrative" literally (not as a metaphor). Using verbatim transcripts of everything that was said in the meetings he analyzed, he was able to identify the very processes of narrative construction of reality. In the analysis he does not focus on the content of the discussions alone, but follows their dynamics, the ways stories were actually told and negotiated by participants. This is an example of a "strong" approach to narratives in organization for it examines how stories were told in a committee meeting, how they were mutually narrated and how they influenced decision making.

A similar "strong" narrative approach is reflected in another study of group decision making, albeit in a very different context. Gibson (2011a; see also Gibson, 2011b) studied decision making in the U.S. President Kennedy's Executive Committee of the National Security Council (ExComm) during the Cuban Missile Crisis. In that crisis, which unfolded in October 1962 and was part of the Cold War between the two world powers, the Soviet Union responded to the deployment of U.S. ballistic missiles in Italy and Turkey by deploying their own missiles in Cuba. ExComm deliberated throughout the crisis, in efforts to assess the U.S.'s possible lines of response, and their possible consequences. Many of these meetings were recorded, and Gibson used the verbatim transcripts to explore how a decision was reached in those tense and consequential discussions. Gibson (2011a) highlights the difficulty in decision making that is based on unclear and ambiguous forecasts of the future and the role of stories and storytelling in such circumstances. In the case of ExComm, stories were told not only about the past, but also about potential futures. The potency of the stories to influence action depended on various characteristics, including the epistemic authority of the narrators, the evaluations of the stories based on historical versus narrative truth, and the establishment of some "path-dependency" that will legitimize the story as credible. President Kennedy eventually decided in favor of a U.S. blockade over Cuba, although that decision carried much risk of a later need to attack against operational missiles. Exploring in detail the evolving shared future narrative that led to that decision, Gibson highlights how participants in the discussions needed to suppress its potential risks. This disassociation of the decision from its potential consequences was achieved through various narrative moves, like omission, self-censorship, ambiguation, uptake failure, and narrative interdiction.

By exploring the narrative dynamics of decision making, Gibson (2011a) demonstrates how stories actually work in real time. He follows how they were collectively constructed, grounded in vested interests and power relations, evolved through time, and, once stabilized, directed to a clear, and seemingly the only, plausible decision.

A final example of a "strong" narrative approach, one that explores stories in and around organizations as social action, is apparent in Martens et al.'s (2007) study of how stories told by entrepreneurs affect their success in raising funding for their initiative. Their study is based on financial and textual data on 169 firms in three high-tech sectors that went through an initial public offering (IPO) in a big U.S. stock exchange 1996–2000. Specifically, the authors analyzed the IPO prospectus – a binding legal text describing the firm, which has a narrative structure. They found that "effectively constructed stories" have specific characteristics. To begin with, such stories "construct unambiguous identities for entrepreneurial firms." They also offer just enough, but not too much, information, about how they plan to deal with risks: "elaborate how the proposed means of exploitation will attenuate risk (without providing overly complex explanations)." Finally, effective stories in this context balance between familiarity and innovation, by invoking "familiar elements to contextually ground those that are less familiar." All these narrative elements "do help entrepreneurs acquire the money they need to exploit identified opportunities" (Martens et al., 2007: 1125). In this study, Martens et al. (2007) explore the actual use of entrepreneurs' stories in the entrepreneurial resource acquisition process. They use real-time stories (in this case, texts that were part of the IPO process), and highlight their consequential characteristics.

## Concluding Remarks

The turn to a "strong" narrative approach and "small" stories may be seen in the context of a wider growing theoretical interest in performativity and practice in and around organizations, like actor-network theory and strategy-as-practice (i.e., Alcadipani and Hassard, 2010; Denis et al., 2007; Hodgson, 2005; Jarzabkowski et al., 2007; Lee and Hassard, 1999; MacKenzie and Millo, 2003; Nicolini, 2011; Tyler and Cohen, 2010; Vaara and Whittington, 2012. For a recent critique, see Cabantous et al., 2016). A narrative approach seems to be especially fit for such a focus (Fenton and Langley, 2011). Indeed, in this spirit, advocates of a "strong" narrative approach argue in favor of treating stories in and around organizations as social performance. This approach entails moving scholars' focus from understanding stories as linguistic structures that hold certain meanings to examining how stories work as social actions in a local context. The analysis thus adds to the study of content and of texts and the study of the acts of storytelling (Polletta et al., 2011). The new basic questions thus become how telling stories integrates into other organizational social dynamics, and to what extent telling stories is consequential to organizations and to organizations' members both in the short run and in the long run.

Still, moving from the study of stories to the study of storytelling is not simple. To begin with, it requires a deep paradigmatic shift. The "strong" narrative perspective entails a broad and clear social constructionist paradigmatic stand, which is still somewhat peripheral in our discipline (Amis and Silk, 2008). Further, it entails both methodological and theoretical shifts. Methodologically, qualitative studies tend to prioritize interview data over all other kinds of qualitative data (Atkinson and Delamont, 2006), but the study of stories as action necessitates the use of real-time data – whether in vivo and in situ, or through the use of verbatim transcripts. This kind of data is hard to collect or come by in organizations (Locke, 2011). Finally, it involves a theoretical shift that underscores the ways social action is worked out in organizations. Social action is a messy business, and so theoretical insights based on a "strong" narrative approach tend to offer a complex understanding of organizational processes, one that is fraught with conflicts, power relations, collective rather than individualistic explanations, unintended consequences, and local circumstances. All these stand in contrast to the more rational process models current in our field. Still, a "strong" narrative approach – while challenging – also holds much potential to revitalize our theories, moving from a normative to a more naturalistic understanding of organizations and making our theories and studies more relevant to the actual experiences of people in organizations.

## Acknowledgment

Writing was supported by the Leon Recanati Fund, and the Asper Center for Entrepreneurship and Innovation, both at the School of Business Administration, the Hebrew University of Jerusalem. Thanks to Raza Mir and Sanjay Jain for their helpful comments on an earlier version of this chapter. Special thanks to Yehuda Goodman for the ongoing discussion of the ideas articulated in this chapter.

## Notes

1 I use "narrative" and "story" interchangeably, notwithstanding some differential definitions and uses in literary theory and other disciplines.
2 Based on a Web of Science search, September 2016.
3 Apart from these empirical studies, attempts have been made to use narratives as an analytic model for theoretical thinking or organizational practice (e.g., Barry and Elmes, 1997; Lawrence and Maitlis, 2012; Pentland, 1999; Shipp and Jansen, 2011; Starkey and Crane, 2003; Tsoukas and Hatch, 2001).
4 After Langley (2009), who distinguished between "strong" and "weak" versions of process studies. I use "strong" and "weak" in a non-judgmental way. I acknowledge that both perspectives to narrative studies are valid, important, and serve different purposes. Still, they are different in terms of their paradigmatic basis, especially ontologically – relating to "strong" or "weak" constructivist stands.

# References

Abolafia, M. Y. (2010). Narrative construction as sensemaking: how a central bank thinks. *Organization Studies, 31*(3), 349–367. doi:10.1177/0170840609357380.

Alcadipani, R., and Hassard, J. (2010). Actor-network theory, organizations and critique: towards a politics of organizing. *Organization, 17*(4), 419–435. doi:10.1177/1350508410364441.

Amis, J. M., and Silk, M. L. (2008). The philosophy and politics of quality in qualitative organizational research. *Organizational Research Methods, 11*(3), 456–480. doi:10.1177/1094428107300341.

Amsterdam, A. G., and Bruner, J. (2000). *Minding the Law: How Courts Rely on Storytelling, and How Their Stories Change the Ways We Understand the Law and Ourselves.* Cambridge, MA: Harvard University Press.

Atkinson, P. A. (1997). Narrative turn or blind alley? *Qualitative Health Research, 7*(3), 325–344.

Atkinson, P., and Delamont, S. (2006). Rescuing narrative from qualitative research. *Narrative Inquiry, 16*(1), 164–172. doi:10.1075/ni.16.1.21atk.

Baldwin, C. (2013). *Narrative Social Work: Theory and Application.* Bristol: Policy Press.

Bamberg, M. (2006). Stories: big or small – why do we care? *Narrative Inquiry, 16*(1), 139–147. doi:10.1075/ni.16.1.18bam.

Bamberg, M., and Georgakopoulou, A. (2008). Small stories as a new perspective in narrative and identity analysis. *TEXT & TALK, 28*(3), 377–396.

Barry, D., and Elmes, M. (1997). Strategy retold: toward a narrative view of strategic discourse. *Academy of Management Review, 22*(2), 429–452. doi:10.2307/259329.

Boje, D. M. (1991). The storytelling organization: a study of story performance in an office-supply firm. *Administrative Science Quarterly, 36*(1), 106–126. doi:10.2307/2393432.

Boje, D. M. (2008). *Storytelling Organizations.* London: Sage.

Boswell, J. (2013). Why and how narrative matters in deliberative systems. *Political Studies, 61*(3), 620–636. doi:10.1111/j.1467-9248.2012.00987.x.

Brown, A. D., Stacey, P., and Nandhakumar, J. (2008). Making sense of sensemaking narratives. *Human Relations, 61*(8), 1035–1062. doi:10.1177/0018726708094858.

Bruner, J. (1986). *Actual Minds, Possible Worlds.* Cambridge, MA: Harvard University Press.

Bruner, J. (1990). *Acts of Meaning.* Cambridge, MA: Harvard University Press.

Cabantous, L., Gond, J. P., Harding, N., and Learmonth, M. (2016). Critical essay: reconsidering critical performativity. *Human Relations, 69*(2), 197–213. doi:10.1177/0018726715584690.

Charon, R. (2001). Narrative medicine: a model for empathy, reflection, profession, and trust. *Jama – Journal of the American Medical Association, 286*(15), 1897–1902. doi:10.1001/jama.286.15.1897.

Charon, R. (2004). Narrative and medicine. *New England Journal of Medicine, 350*(9), 862–864. doi:10.1056/NEJMp038249.

Cover, R. M. (1983). The Supreme Court 1982 term. Foreword: nomos and narrative. *Harvard Law Review, 97*(1), 4–69.

Currie, G., and Brown, A. D. (2003). A narratological approach to understanding processes of organizing in a UK hospital. *Human Relations, 56*(5), 563–586. doi:10.1177/0018726703056005003.

Currie, M. (1998). *Postmodern Narrative Theory.* New York: St. Martin's Press.

Czarniawska, B. (2004). *Narratives in Social Science Research.* London: Sage.

Czarniawska-Joerges, B. (1997). *Narrating the Organization: Dramas of Institutional Identity.* Chicago, IL: University of Chicago Press.

De Fina, A., and Georgakopoulou, A. (2008). Introduction: narrative analysis in the shift from texts to practices. *TEXT & TALK, 28*(3), 275–281.

Denis, J. L., Langley, A., and Rouleau, L. (2007). Strategizing in pluralistic contexts: rethinking theoretical frames. *Human Relations, 60*(1), 179–215. doi:10.1177/0018726707075288.

Ewick, P., and Silbey, S. S. (1995). Subversive stories and hegemonic tales: toward a sociology of narrative. *Law & Society Review, 29*(2), 197–226. doi:10.2307/3054010.

Ewick, P., and Silbey, S. (2003). Narrating social structure: stories of resistance to legal authority. *American Journal of Sociology, 108*(6), 1328–1372. doi:10.1086/378035.

Farber, D. A., and Sherry, S. (1993). Telling stories out of school: an essay on legal narratives. *Stanford Law Review, 45*(4), 807–855. doi:10.2307/1229198.

Fenton, C., and Langley, A. (2011). Strategy as practice and the narrative turn. *Organization Studies, 32*(9), 1171–1196. doi:10.1177/0170840611410838.

Fisher, W. R. (1984). Narration as a human communication paradigm: the case of public oral argument. *Communication Monographs, 51*, 1–22.

Fisher, W. R. (1987). *Human Communication as a Narration: Toward a Philosophy of Reason, Value, and Action.* Columbia, SC: University of South Carolina Press.

Franzosi, R. (1998). Narrative analysis: or why (and how) sociologists should be interested in narrative. *Annual Review of Sociology, 24,* 517–554. doi:10.1146/annurev.soc.24.1.517.

Freeman, M. (2006). Life "on holiday"? In defense of big stories. *Narrative Inquiry, 16*(1), 131–138.

Freeman, M. (2011). Stories, big and small: toward a synthesis. *Theory & Psychology, 21*(1), 114–121.

Fulton, H. (2006). *Narrative and Media.* Cambridge: Cambridge University Press.

Gabriel, Y. (2000). *Storytelling in Organization: Facts, Fiction and Fantasies.* Oxford: Oxford University Press.

Georgakopoulou, A. (2006). Thinking big with small stories in narrative and identity analysis. *Narrative Inquiry, 16*(1), 122–130.

Georgakopoulou, A. (2007). *Small Stories, Interaction and Identities.* Amsterdam and Philadelphia, PA: John Benjamins.

Gergen, K. J., and Gergen, M. (1987). Narratives as relationships. In R. Burnett, P. McGee, and D. C. Clarke (eds.), *Accounting for Relationships* (pp. 269–315). London: Methuen.

Gibson, D. R. (2011a). Avoiding catastrophe: the interactional production of possibility during the Cuban Missile Crisis. *American Journal of Sociology, 117*(2), 361–419. doi:10.1086/661761.

Gibson, D. R. (2011b). Speaking of the future: contentious narration during the Cuban Missile Crisis. *Qualitative Sociology, 34*(4), 503–522. doi:10.1007/s11133-011-9206-0.

Giorgi, S., Lockwood, C., and Glynn, M. A. (2015). The many faces of culture: making sense of 30 years of research on culture in organization studies. *Academy of Management Annals, 9*(1), 1–54. doi:10.1080/19416520.2015.1007645.

Goodwin, C. (1984). Notes on story structure and the organization of participation. In J. M. Atkinson and J. Heritage (eds.), *Structures of Social Action* (pp. 225–246). Cambridge: Cambridge University Press.

Griffin, L. K. (2013). Narrative, truth, and trial. *Georgetown Law Journal, 101*(2), 281–335.

Havel, V. (1989). *Letters to Olga: June 1979 – September 1982* (P. Wilson, Trans.). New York: Henry Holt.

Hodgson, D. (2005). "Putting on a professional performance": performativity, subversion and project management. *Organization, 12*(1), 51–68. doi:10.1177/1350508405048576.

Hoffmann, C. R. (ed.) (2010). *Narrative Revisited: Telling a Story in the Age of New Media.* Amsterdam and Philadelphia, PA: John Benjamins.

Jarzabkowski, P., Balogun, J., and Seidl, D. (2007). Strategizing: the challenges of a practice perspective. *Human Relations, 60*(1), 5–27. doi:10.1177/0018726707075703.

Jefferson, G. (1978). Sequential aspects of storytelling in conversation. In J. Schenkein (ed.), *Studies in the Organization of Conversational Interaction* (pp. 219–248). New York: Academic Press.

Kirmayer, L. J. (1993). Broken narratives: clinical encounters and the poetics of illness experience. In C. Mattingly and L. C. Garro (eds.), *Narrative and the Cultural Construction of Illness and Healing* (pp. 153–180). Berkeley and Los Angeles, CA: University of California Press.

Kumagai, A. K. (2008). A conceptual framework for the use of illness narratives in medical education. *Academic Medicine, 83*(7), 653–658.

Langley, A. (2009). Studying processes in and around organizations. In D. A. Buchanan and A. Bryman (eds.), *The Sage Handbook of Organizational Research Methods* (pp. 409–429). London: Sage.

Lawrence, T. B., and Maitlis, S. (2012). Care and possibility: enacting an ethic of care through narrative practice. *Academy of Management Review, 37*(4), 641–663. doi:10.5465/amr.2010.0466.

Lee, N., and Hassard, J. (1999). Organization unbound: actor-network theory, research strategy and institutional flexibility. *Organization, 6*(3), 391–404. doi:10.1177/135050849963002.

Locke, K. (2011). Field research practice in management and organization studies: reclaiming its tradition of discovery. *Academy of Management Annals, 5,* 613–652. doi:10.1080/19416520.2011.593319.

McAdams, D. P. (1988). *Power, Intimacy and the Life Story: Personological Inquiries into Identity.* New York and London: The Guilford Press.

McAdams, D. P. (1993). *The Stories We Live By: Personal Myths and the Making of the Self.* New York: William Morrow.

MacKenzie, D., and Millo, Y. (2003). Constructing a market, performing theory: the historical sociology of a financial derivatives exchange. *American Journal of Sociology, 109*(1), 107–145. doi:10.1086/374404.

Maggio, R. (2014). The anthropology of storytelling and the storytelling of anthropology. *Journal of Comparative Research in Anthropology and Sociology, 5*(2), 89–106.

Maines, D. R. (1993). Narrative's moment and sociology's phenomena: toward a narrative sociology. *Sociological Quarterly, 34*(1), 17–38. doi:10.1111/j.1533-8525.1993.tb00128.x.

Maitlis, S., and Christianson, M. K. (2014). Sensemaking in organizations: taking stock and moving forward. *Academy of Management Annals, 8*(1), 57–125. doi:10.1080/19416520.2014.873177.

Martens, M. L., Jennings, J. E., and Jennings, P. D. (2007). Do the stories they tell get them the money they need? The role of entrepreneurial narratives in resource acquisition. *Academy of Management Journal, 50*(5), 1107–1132.

Martin, J., Feldman, M. S., Hatch, M. J., and Sitkin, S. B. (1983). The uniqueness paradox in organizational stories. *Administrative Science Quarterly, 28*(3), 438–453. doi:10.2307/2392251.

Mattingly, C. (1998). *Healing Dramas and Clinical Plots: The Narrative Structure of Experience.* Cambridge: Cambridge University Press.

Mattingly, C., and Garro, L. C. (eds.). (2001). *Narrative and the Cultural Construction of Illness and Healing.* Berkeley and Los Angeles, CA: University of California Press.

Mumby, D. K. (1993). Introduction: narrative and social control. In D. K. Mumby (ed.), *Narrative and Social Control: Critical Perspectives* (vol. 21, pp. 1–12). Newbury Park, CA: Sage.

Muntigl, P. (2004). *Narrative Counselling: Social and Linguistic Processes of Change.* Amsterdam and Philadelphia, PA: John Benjamins.

Nicolini, D. (2011). Practice as the site of knowing: insights from the field of telemedicine. *Organization Science, 22*(3), 602–620. doi:10.1287/orsc.1100.0556.

Ochs, E., and Capps, L. (1996). Narrating the self. *Annual Review of Anthropology, 25,* 19–43.

Ochs, E., and Capps, L. (2001). *Living Narrative: Creating Lives in Everyday Storytelling.* Cambridge, MA: Harvard University Press.

Orbuch, T. L. (1997). People's accounts count: the sociology of accounts. *Annual Review of Sociology, 23,* 455–478. doi:10.1146/annurev.soc.23.1.455.

Patterson, M., and Monroe, K. R. (1998). Narrative in political science. *Annual Review of Political Science, 1,* 315–331. doi:10.1146/annurev.polisci.1.1.315.

Pentland, B. T. (1999). Building process theory with narrative: from description to explanation. *Academy of Management Review, 24*(4), 711–724.

Polkinghorne, D. E. (1988). *Narrative Knowing and the Human Sciences.* New York: State University of New York Press.

Polletta, F. (1998). "It was like a fever …": narrative and identity in social protest. *Social Problems, 45*(2), 137–159. doi:10.1525/sp. 1998.45.2.03x0163g.

Polletta, F. (2006). *It Was Like a Fever: Storytelling in Protest and Politics.* Chicago, IL: University of Chicago Press.

Polletta, F., and Lee, J. (2006). Is telling stories good for democracy? Rhetoric in public deliberation after 9/11. *American Sociological Review, 71*(5), 699–723.

Polletta, F., Chen, P. C. B., Gardner, B. G., and Motes, A. (2011). The sociology of storytelling. In K. S. Cook and D. S. Massey (eds.), *Annual Review of Sociology* (vol. 37, pp. 109–130). Palo Alto, CA: Annual Reviews.

Presser, L. (2009). The narratives of offenders. *Theoretical Criminology, 13*(2), 177–200. doi:10.1177/1362480609102878.

Rajah, V., Kramer, R., and Sung, H. E. (2014). Changing narrative accounts: how young men tell different stories when arrested, enduring jail time and navigating community reentry. *Punishment & Society – International Journal of Penology, 16*(3), 285–304. doi:10.1177/1462474514527148.

Rhodes, C., and Brown, A. D. (2005). Narrative, organizations and research. *International Journal of Management Reviews, 7*(3), 167–188. doi:10.1111/j.1468-2370.2005.00112.x.

Richardson, L. (1990). Narrative and sociology. *Journal of Contemporary Ethnography, 19*(1), 116–135. doi:10.1177/089124190019001006.

Ricoeur, P. (1991). Narrative identity. *Philosophy Today, 35*(1), 73–81.

Rosile, G. A., Boje, D. M., Carlon, D. M., Downs, A., and Saylors, R. (2013). Storytelling diamond: an antenarrative integration of the six facets of storytelling in organization research design. *Organizational Research Methods, 16*(4), 557–580. doi:10.1177/1094428113482490.

Ruhlemann, C., and Gries, S. (2015). Turn order and turn distribution in multi-party storytelling. *Journal of Pragmatics, 87,* 171–191. doi:10.1016/j.pragma.2015.08.003.

Rutten, K., Mottart, A., and Soetaert, R. (2010). Narrative and rhetoric in social work education. *British Journal of Social Work, 40*(2), 480–495. doi:10.1093/bjsw/bcp082.

Sarbin, T. R. (1986). *Narrative Psychology: The Storied Nature of Human Understanding.* New York: Praeger.

Shamir, B., and Eilam, G. (2005). "What's your story?" A life-stories approach to authentic leadership development. *Leadership Quarterly, 16*(3), 395–417. doi:10.1016/j.leaqua.2005.03.005.

Shamir, B., Dayan-Horesh, H., and Adler, D. (2005). Leading by biography: towards a life-story approach to the study of leadership. *Leadership, 1*(1), 13–29. doi:10.1177/1742715005049348.

Shipp, A. J., and Jansen, K. J. (2011). Reinterpreting time in fit theory: crafting and recrafting narratives of fit in medias res. *Academy of Management Review, 36*(1), 76–101.

Somers, M. R. (1994). The narrative constitution of identity: a relational and network approach. *Theory and Society, 23*(5), 605–649.

Sonenshein, S. (2010). We're changing – or are we? Untangling the role of progressive, regressive, and stability narratives during strategic change implementation. *Academy of Management Journal, 53*(3), 477–512.

Spector-Mersel, G. (2010). Narrative research: time for a paradigm. *Narrative Inquiry, 20*(1), 204–224.

Starkey, K., and Crane, A. (2003). Toward green narrative: management and the evolutionary epic. *Academy of Management Review, 28*(2), 220–237.

Tsoukas, H., and Hatch, M. J. (2001). Complex thinking, complex practice: the case for a narrative approach to organizational complexity. *Human Relations, 54*(8), 979–1013.

Tyler, M., and Cohen, L. (2010). Spaces that matter: gender performativity and organizational space. *Organization Studies, 31*(2), 175–198. doi:10.1177/0170840609357381.

Vaara, E., and Whittington, R. (2012). Strategy-as-practice: taking social practices seriously. *Academy of Management Annals, 6*, 285–336. doi:10.1080/19416520.2012.672039.

Vaara, E., Sonenshein, S., and Boje, D. (2016). Narratives as sources of stability and change in organizations: approaches and directions for future research. *Academy of Management Annals, 10*(1), 495–560. doi:10.1080/19416520.2016.1120963.

Weick, K. E. (1995). *Sensemaking in Organizations*. Thousand Oaks, CA: Sage.

Zilber, T. B. (2007). Stories and the discursive dynamics of institutional entrepreneurship: the case of Israeli high-tech after the bubble. *Organization Studies, 28*(7), 1035–1054. doi:10.1177/0170840607078113.

Zilber, T. B., Tuval-Mashiach, R., and Lieblich, A. (2008). The embedded narrative: navigating through multiple contexts. *Qualitative Inquiry, 14*(6), 1047–1069. doi:10.1177/1077800408321616.

# 10

# BRICOLAGE IN THE FIELD

## Experimenting in Ethnography

*Anne-Laure Fayard*

Ethnography seems to be in fashion these days (Van Maanen, 2011, 2015; Jarzabkowski et al., 2015) as suggested by the proliferation of ethnography-inspired or ethnography-labeled studies in organizational and information systems research. Some might argue, however, that many of these studies do not rely solely on ethnography's characteristic fieldwork. Long immersions have become rare, and some studies do not involve participant observations at all. Instead, they have been replaced with a mix of interviews, videos, texts, archival data, and online data. While these changes call into question whether such studies are ethnographies, I argue and try to demonstrate that ethnography is more than a set of methods; it is an epistemic stance that can be enacted through different practices. What makes a study ethnographic is not so much the methods but the stance that the researcher enacts.

It is important to remember that, in essence, ethnography demands continuous experimentation or ongoing bricolage in the field, where the ethnographer adapts her methods to the phenomena she studies. Hence, while the essential skills of observation and of uncovering patterns remain relevant, ethnographers today are required "to understand very complex, rapidly changing settings, where multiple activities are carried out by multiple actors with multiple agendas, relying on multiple, complex technologies" (Jordan, 1996: 201). These changes call for revisiting the traditional notion of the field and what it means to do fieldwork. I make no claims here about adequately describing new methods used in ethnography and its evolution. I present a personal vantage point deeply influenced by the various studies in which I have been involved and have always experimented.

## Ethnography as an Epistemic Stance

Instead of seeing ethnography as a given method or specific type of study, I view it as an epistemic stance,[1] a way of knowing enacted in practice and the kind of knowledge that results from that practice. Ethnography is about understanding others' perspective by attending to their context and practices as much as what they say. By developing "thick descriptions" (Geertz, 1973), ethnographers attempt to explain how these experiences represent a "web of meanings" (Geertz, 1973: 5) or the "cultural understandings" (Fayard et al., 2016a) in which people live. The encounter with the "foreign" is the very essence of ethnography (Agar, 1980), and this encounter is dynamic and iterative. We go and spend time in the field observing and asking questions. We then leave to reflect on the experience; we write memos and refine our questions. We then go back in the field to ask more questions and observe yet again before leaving to reflect even more.

Ethnography is experimental and deeply improvisational. Going in the field requires embracing ambiguity: We start by not knowing which questions to ask and by being ready to be surprised, and we continuously evolve and fine-tune our questions, poised to challenge our interpretations. It's in the field that we come to understand what we will need to learn next. There are neither recipes nor procedures for successful ethnography; at best, there are tricks of the trade (Becker, 1998) to help decide, depending on the study's specific context, how to proceed.

Ethnography aims to identify and uncover the emergent and local meanings of behaviors, interactions, and work practices, and this happens by "being there" through fieldwork or participant observation. At the core of ethnographic practice is fieldwork:

> Fieldwork usually means living with and living like those who are studied. In its broadest, most conventional sense, fieldwork demands the full-time involvement of a researcher over a lengthy period of time (typically unspecified) and consists mostly of ongoing interaction with the human targets of the study on their home ground.
>
> *(Van Maanen, 2011: 2)*

The ethnographer becomes the research instrument as she partakes in the daily activities and interactions of a given group or organization (Mauthner and Doucet, 2008; Van Maanen, 2011; Gluesing, 2013). Hence, doing ethnography is always personal because the data collected are dependent on the ethnographer's own experience (Van Maanen, 2011).

And time is of the essence for ethnographic understandings to emerge (Cefkin, 2013). Being there in the field and for an extended period of time is particularly important because what people say they do and think they do versus what they actually do are usually not the same (Geertz, 1973; Forsythe, 2001). It is only with systematic participant observation that these disparities become visible; it is only with long immersion in the field that tacit beliefs and knowledge may be uncovered (Gluesing, 2013; Forsythe, 2001). It also takes time to learn how to "see" and "hear," as well as to unlearn all we might believe as "outsiders" or what we might start to believe (and think we understand) when we begin spending time in the field.

Hence, traditionally, the ethnographic stance is associated with a view of ethnography (somewhat idealized, many would say, and increasingly difficult to enact, as I will argue) where the ethnographer, a lone wolf, immerses herself for a lengthy period of time within a specific community, group, or organization to do fieldwork. Some exemplary ethnographies are the fieldwork of anthropologists such as Geertz and Malinowski who spent an extended amount of time in "exotic" communities in Bali and Trobriand Island. In organizational studies, fieldwork is still presented as the lengthy immersion of a sole researcher in a somewhat "foreign" organizational context (e.g., Dalton, 1959; Kanter, 1977; Kunda, 1992; Orr, 1996; Weeks, 2003; Bechky, 2003; Anteby, 2008). However, such ethnographies are less frequent, and when they happen, they tend to be singular – "once in a lifetime," so to speak, and typically take the form of a dissertation.[2]

Beyond personal and institutional constraints (e.g., family life, tenure requirements, and the need to publish), changes in the phenomena that ethnographers of organizations study also explain the evolution of ethnographic practice and fieldwork. The field is no longer a single, local site but one that expands across multiple boundaries of geography, time, occupations, media, and technology. Ethnographers now study work distributed around the world across numerous teams and organizations whose many interactions are mediated by technology. Even when collocated, work heavily relies on communication technologies that limit what ethnographers can observe. Work in action often becomes invisible, and other data need to be collected, analyzed, and interpreted (Riopelle, 2013). If, in traditional ethnography, the primary research instrument is the ethnographer, it becomes harder to rely just on one individual and solely on participant observations because interactions are distributed and mediated by technology. This challenge becomes even more salient when the interactions studied take place (mostly) online.

## The Ethnographer as *Bricoleur*

Because ethnography is a local method that looks to uncover emergent local, emic meanings and work practices (Van Maanen, 2011), it cannot be procedural. It is more of a toolbox of methods that need to be adjusted, evolved, and adapted to a specific context. Methods are not fixed in stone but evolve over time in the field and across sites (Van Maanen, 2015). The ethnographer is a bricoleur, a Jill-of-all trades who engages in bricolage, defined by Lévi-Strauss as the process of creating or making from a diverse range of available things. She must creatively use and develop tools and methods that allow her to understand interactions and practices, uncover meanings and patterns, and make sense of them. As the phenomena that ethnographers study become more complex, more distributed, and less visible, they have to become more creative, even if it means moving away from what is thought of as the core practices of ethnography, such as observation and lengthy immersion. It might mean using video or other technology, collecting data from social media, having teams of ethnographers instead of a single individual, or shortening time spent in the field. In the following sections, I discuss three methodological adaptations – the use of video, team-based ethnography, and virtual ethnography – that have emerged in response to changes in the field. The list is not exhaustive; it reflects trends in the new methods and tools used by ethnographers, as well as some of my own experiments in the field.[3] (See Table 10.1 for a summary of the advantages and challenges of each adaptation and a description of the different forms they can take.)

### *Bricolage with Video*

More and more, video has become an investigative tool used by researchers in qualitative studies, particularly those that seek to understand multimodal interactions (Jewitt, 2012). Its use is not new:

> Ethnography has always been carried out with technology support, from Margaret Mead's notebook and film camera and the 40 pounds of video equipment I used to drag into the field in the 1970s and the 1980s, to the ubiquitous tape recorders that still allow us to catch interactions but now with increasing granularity.
>
> *(Jordan, 2013: 15)*

And, with the low cost of video cameras that have become lighter and less bulky, as well as the availability of video features on mobile phones and easy-to-use cheap or free editing software, the use of video in research has become more accessible (Jewitt, 2012). Researchers have used video for many years, especially in workplace studies (e.g., Jordan, 1996; Heath and Luff, 1992; Suchman and Trigg, 1991; Goodwin, 2000). For example, Jordan and her team (1996) used video to track communication between airlines' operations room and flight personnel, customer agents, baggage crew, etc. at a West Coast airport. They used seven cameras running at the same time in order to investigate how activities in each location affected those in others (Jordan, 1996). Communication scholars and other researchers interested in discourse analysis have also used video extensively to analyze ongoing communication processes and their role in organizations (Cooren et al., 2007; Goodwin and Goodwin, 1992).

The use of video in workplace studies has been particularly productive for researchers seeking to design new technologies and tools that support collaboration and communication (e.g., Jordan, 1996; Suchman and Trigg, 1991; Heath and Luff, 1992; Mackay et al., 1998). Many of these studies embrace the interaction-analysis approach, an interdisciplinary video-based analysis "for the empirical investigation of the interaction of human beings with each other and with objects in their environment" (Jordan and Henderson, 1995: 39).

Video analysis usually involves video recorded in conjunction with ethnographic fieldwork. During a preliminary fieldwork phase, researchers identify "interactional 'hot spots'" (Jordan and Henderson, 1995: 43) that they then record. In my own experience with video, I always combined it with participant observation. For the first six weeks of a study of air traffic controllers in Athis Mons air traffic control center near Paris's Orly Airport, for instance, we simply observed the controllers at work (Mackay et al., 1998). We then began to systematically videotape. We also took copious notes and asked the controllers many in situ questions during the taping and outside of it. These field notes proved to be crucial during the analysis of the video, and they were key to developing a cultural understanding of air traffic controllers' work practices.

The combination of videotaping and traditional fieldwork allows for a dialogue between the ethnographic data that provide general background and framing and the microanalysis of video that informs general ethnographic understanding. This approach is inductive and deeply empirical, following Geertz's advice (1973: 24) that theory should stay "rather closer to the ground than tends to be the case in sciences more able to give themselves over to imaginative abstractions."

Video data provides data that ethnographers may not have been able to capture in their notes, thus alleviating concerns about not being able to capture "everything." Video also invites experimentation with data analysis because it allows for multiple viewings[4] where other researchers can be invited to share different perspectives, thus enriching the interpretation. Study participants may also be invited to review the tapes or collages of video segments and to provide their own interpretations. For example, during our study of air traffic controllers, we edited video segments to reflect our interpretations of the resulting patterns and categories and shared them with participants to elicit their interpretations. This led to very rich conversations about work practices, and associated assumptions emerged. It also gave us the opportunity to ask for clarification and to gather complementary contextual information. Video can thus become a tool for engaging participants and articulating tacit knowledge.

While video has a lot of potential for ethnographers because it allows them to collect data simultaneously in different places and to create a shared repository that can be revisited and analyzed, it has, like any tool or method, limitations.[5] The representational bias of video has been discussed at length. Video is always a *re*-presentation; it is not an emic perspective. Participants do not necessarily see what is "shown" on the video nor do they see what researchers view when they look at it. It always requires some – in fact, several – layers of interpretation. Goldman and McDermott (2009: 101) argue that

> the power of video is not in what [the tapes] make easily clear, but in what they challenge and disrupt in the initial assumptions of an analysis. They are a starting point for understanding the reflexive, patterned ways interactions develop.

Video data becomes data through the interpretative act of researchers, similar to the interpretative act of the ethnographer making sense of her observations and field notes.

The representational bias also stems from the fact that videos always show just one aspect of the situation recorded from a certain perspective dependent on the camera's positioning. What might seem like researchers' technical decisions (e.g., where is the camera located? Is it a wide-angle view or a zoom? At what level is the audio set? Are there just one or several cameras?[6]) are far from insignificant because they define what is visible and what is audible. All the studies in which I used video (Mackay et al., 1998; Fayard, 2006; Fayard and Weeks, 2007) involved a lot of tinkering with the camera locations and angles. In all cases, the choices we made meant that some interactions were visible while others were hidden.

To address the representational bias, an option could be to have the actors carry the video. This was the aim of the SubCam ("subjective"[7] camera), a miniature, wearable, wide-angle video camera clipped onto a pair of glasses (Fayard and Lahlou, 1998) that recorded individual activity from the point of view of the user wherever he or she went. It was developed as part of a study of the impact of information technology on office work (Fayard and Lahlou, 1998). Originally, the research team experimented with fixed cameras but soon realized that the resulting videos mostly captured empty offices because the managers they studied were often outside their offices. To replicate Mintzberg's (1970) structured observation while being less intrusive, the SubCam was developed to collect participants' perspective.[8] Yet, even in this case, the videos were only a partial representation. Moreover, to be able to make sense of the videos, observational data were collected. Other researchers (Cooren et al., 2007; Meunier and Vasquez, 2008) have experimented with video shadowing[9] as another way to stay close to participants' perspective.

In video-based research, as in any fieldwork, researchers always have to play, improvise, and experiment with the use of videos, depending on the specific site or sites of their study. While the medium provides rich data (different and/or multiple perspectives), it becomes meaningful only during the interpretative process that occurs as a result of observations and interviews collected during the study.

### Teams for Studying Distributed Organizations and Phenomena

While ethnography was originally conceived as the act of a lone fieldworker, ethnographers have increasingly experimented with teamwork to develop deeper understandings of growing global, complex, and distributed phenomena (Marcus, 1995; Van Maanen, 2006; Jordan, 1996; Jarzabkowski et al., 2015). For example, to follow the rollout of programs and technologies from headquarters into different field organizations, Jordan's (1996) team chose to have two-ethnographer teams in a number of field sites simultaneously and a permanent team at headquarters. Similarly, Barley and Kunda (2006) teamed up in their multi-sited study of the market for temporary professionals when they studied contractors, clients, and three staffing agencies. This allowed them, they claim, to access "the global."

Jarzabkowski et al. (2015) experimented further by conducting global fieldwork in 25 organizations across 15 countries with a team of up to five members to explore the "global practice of reinsurance trading" (p. 9). They reflected on the challenges that emerge from global, team-based ethnography,[10] especially when it came to sharing data and developing a common understanding that went beyond each individual's perspective on the phenomenon. Team sharing is particularly difficult because it involves reflection, which is usually seen as a solitary activity (Barry et al., 1999; Jarzabkowski et al., 2015). To support team-sharing and collective reflection, Jarzabkowski et al. (2015) developed various practices, such as sharing in the field (via emails,

Skype, etc.), creating a common repository of data as well as norms and codes for note taking and analysis.

My personal experience with team-based ethnography originally began as a single ethnography of the culture of an international company, which grew into a project lasting seven years and including 30 studies of various geographies and units (Fayard et al., 2016a; Fayard and Van Maanen, 2015). As the original study expanded to include various sites, several post-docs[11] joined as research assistants involved in field and analytic work. These post-docs were involved in a company-wide comparative study across different geographies and segments that we conducted as part of this overall research project. That specific study lasted two years and involved 17 sites and more than 220 interviews, complemented by site visits and observations (at ten sites). Team ethnography in this case allowed us to have breadth. Like other team-based ethnographies (Jordan, 1996; Jarzabkowski et al., 2015; Barley, 1996), we met regularly, communicated frequently and reliably, developed codes and norms for team sharing, and established a common repository. Our meetings were essential in helping us share interesting hunches and predictions that we could then check in the field. They also helped us revisit our individual and group assumptions about the culture of the different sites we were studying.

Barley (1996)[12] also reported a team-based, multi-site ethnography where eight researchers (a sociologist, an anthropologist, five doctoral students, and an undergraduate) developed ethnographies of technicians' occupations. In that case, team ethnography did not aim to understand a distributed phenomenon. The goal was to develop a deep understanding of technicians' work by comparing and contrasting multiple occupations. The team chose "to emulate [a project overlay] structure by becoming experts in particular occupations within the context of a team that could bring individual ethnographers' expertise to bear on an array of comparative inquiries" (p. 414). Two products emerged from this collaborative work:[13] "emic ethnographies of individual occupations and etic analyses grounded in the comparison of emic data collected across multiple occupations" (p. 415).

In the cases discussed above, team-based ethnography emerged to develop a rich understanding of a phenomenon (e.g., distributed or global) that called for more than a solitary researcher. But collaborative ethnography does not completely erase the personal nature of ethnography, which always requires each ethnographer to, in some ways, "subject … the self – body, belief, personality, emotions and cognitions – to a set of contingencies that play on others" (Van Maanen, 2011: 219). From the coming together of multiple selves emerges various points of view that allow for rich and deep understanding, but this variety also makes reflection and sense-making more challenging (but not impossible) and, in some ways, more interesting as it becomes a collective practice. Team research and the use of communication technologies to support the work have substantially transformed ethnographic practice. The distinction between data collection, analysis, and write-up are blurred, and feedback from others is included from the beginning unlike traditional ethnography, where the ethnographer does not receive much feedback on her insights and interpretations until long after the fieldwork has been completed (Jordan, 1996).[14] In that sense, some might argue that these new practices have allowed " 'sense-making conversations' [to] become more inclusive and more substantial" (Jordan, 1996: 205).

## *Virtual Ethnography*

With the growing ubiquity of technology and the development of new media, technology-mediated communication has moved to the foreground of work even when collocated, thus making a large part of the work invisible (Riopelle, 2013: 39). In order to observe work in action, ethnographers need to pay attention to technology-mediated interactions and communications.

Moreover, the development of the Internet and new media has led to the rise of novel forms of organizing, especially for online communities such as OpenSource, Wikipedia, and online forums (O'Mahony and Lakhani, 2011), where technology is the main medium for interactions. Consequently, studies relying heavily on online data have flourished (e.g., Fayard and DeSanctis, 2010; O'Mahony and Ferraro, 2007; Scott and Orlikowski, 2014; Schultze, 2012; Vaast, 2007; Nardi, 2010), and a new form of ethnography – virtual or online ethnography (Hine, 2000) – has surfaced. These developments raise several issues for ethnography, particularly in terms of how the "field" – now mostly or partly text on a screen produced by collocated or distributed members – and "being there" are defined.

*Being there* is challenging even for ethnographers studying work in organizations where organizational members are collocated, because they often inhabit both physical and digital spaces, making it difficult for an ethnographer to observe work and interactions. Riopelle (2013) addressed this challenge in his study of a product innovation team in an automotive company composed of 298 staff distributed in various locations worldwide by combining conventional ethnography methods (i.e., observations and interviews) and those based in technology (emails, analytics). He reviewed 45,000 emails and created a dashboard of indicators that made the characteristics of virtual work among 2,000 people around the globe "visible." These insights then informed interviews and observations. Likewise, in a study of service designers, we complemented our interviews and observations with ongoing monitoring and analysis of service designers' websites, blogs, Twitter accounts, and LinkedIn groups (Fayard et al., 2017) to better understand the phenomenon at the community level (e.g., What issues were discussed? What stories were told?), as well as how service designers presented themselves to the public and potential clients.

Being there seems even more challenging when studying online communities where technology-mediated communication is the main form of interaction. *Virtual (or online) ethnography* has emerged as a new method, but it is more than that, I would argue: The qualifier "virtual" emphasizes the role of technology as the primary medium of interaction and the consequences it has for fieldwork.[15] Virtual ethnography, like traditional ethnography, consists of deep, long-term immersion in an online environment where the ethnographer seeks to understand the phenomenon from the point of view of the "natives" and to develop a rich account of a specific online world. But the "context" here is not a collocated, physical world. It is usually a web platform or virtual environment where people can create avatars, as in World of Warcraft or Second Life. For example, through long-term immersion as a participant observer in the community, Rheingold (1993) was able to provide a thick description of the WELL's (one of the first virtual communities) culture and norms of interactions. In his book, Rheingold describes his experience as one very similar to anthropologists who explore exotic places with fundamentally different communication norms. In her study of a discussion group used by soap opera fans, Baym (1995) started as a group member and was a participant observer for three years. She collected messages that she later analyzed; she also conducted interviews with other group members. Akin to any ethnography, the research focus continuously evolved as Baym spent time "in the field" and reflected on her insights, which led to a deep understanding of the social life and assumptions of the community. In another recent virtual ethnography, Nardi (2010) spent more than three years as a participant observer of World of Warcraft games in the United States and China. Nardi quickly realized in this case that she needed to mix observations of online interactions with observations of the offline interactions of players in Internet cafes in China.

My own study of the OpenIDEO community,[16] an open social innovation community (Fayard and Metiu, 2012; Fayard and Levina, 2015), nicely illustrates how "being there" can become multi-formed. The fieldwork for this study was originally online: I was a participant observer on all 22 challenges posted on the platform for nearly three-and-a-half years. I complemented those observations with interviews (formal and informal) with community members, sponsors, and members of the OpenIDEO team. I realized after a year that, as with other virtual ethnographies (e.g., Nardi, 2010), I needed to engage in offline observations to develop a broader understanding of the online community's context. For instance, when meet-ups inspired by OpenIDEO challenges sprang up in various cities, I participated in those in New York. As I regularly reflected on my participation in the community, it became clear that "the field" was amorphous and not tied to a specific "geography," even a virtual one. "Being there" therefore means "experiential rather than physical displacement" (Hine, 2000: 45). It is an engagement in a place constructed through the sociomaterial practices and interactions taking place in and afforded by the community's environment (Fayard, 2012). Being there still matters[17] in studies of online interactions and communities, but what "being there" means is hazy and open to constant redefinition, which does not necessarily mean being only online.[18]

Virtual ethnography is not a stable form but an evolving one that is adapting to new forms of online interactions. It began as text-based interactions and moved to include many forms of online engagement, such as multiplayer online games (e.g., World of Warcraft), a graphical world such as Second Life, social networking sites (e.g., Facebook, MySpace), blogging, and online forums (Hine, 2008). Being flexible and agile – important in all ethnographies – is crucial in virtual ethnographies because the notion of the field itself is radically altered: Its definition and how you get there are blurry and need to be continuously constructed and refined. For example, researchers often assume that there will be *one* online location, "the field," where interactions take place. Yet, they often end up realizing that the field expands offline (e.g., Internet cafés or other venues where people play World of Warcraft (Nardi, 2010), or meet ups where community members met to work on OpenIDEO challenges) and/or though the use of other media (messaging, Skype, Yammer, etc.). It is therefore important to keep in mind that " 'the field' is an epistemological rather than an ontological category: It is a state of mind" (Hine, 2004: 8). In response to changes in organizations that increasingly rely on technology, the emergence of new forms of organizations such as online communities, and the muddying of the physical and the virtual, "ethnography today is becoming a hybrid methodology" (Riopelle, 2013: 38).

## Concluding Remarks

Bricolage in the field has always been an important element of ethnography; today it is more essential than ever. As the phenomena studied by ethnographers become more global and distributed and thus less "visible" to the traditional lone observer, and as technology becomes as ubiquitous for those we study as for us, ethnographers have experimented with new methodological adaptations in the field. As with any method, each experiment has advantages and challenges (see Table 10.1). Rather than quibble over methods and tools to determine if they belong or are aligned with conventional ethnography, however, it is more fruitful to think of all methods as complementary to and supportive of enacting the ethnographic stance understood as improvisational and experimental.

Instead of trying to sort different methods and approaches – individual or team-based, handwritten or video-based observations, collocated or virtual – that may be seen as polar opposites, it is more productive to consider whether they allow us to enact an ethnographic stance, i.e., being there, being open to surprises, improvising and experimenting in response to hunches that surface in the field, and continuously engaging in the interpretative process. The generative power of the multiple experiments, tools, and formats we see emerging should be evaluated not

Table 10.1 Three Forms of Bricolage to Adapt to Changes "in the Field"

| Methodological Adaptations | Advantages | Challenges | Different Approaches and Exemplary Papers |
|---|---|---|---|
| Video ethnography | • "Seeing more" than what one can capture in one's notes.<br>• Capturing interactions from different angles or at the same time in different places.<br>• Data can be analyzed multiple times and by different people. | • "Sensory" overload including data management, coding, and sampling.<br>• Representational bias: Videos always show one aspect of the situation recorded. They need to be complemented with observations (and interviews).<br><br>They become meaningful data only through the interpretative process central to ethnography. | • One or multiple fixed cameras at various locations (Jordan, 1996; Suchman and Trigg, 1991; Heath and Luff, 1992; Goodwin, 2000; Mackay et al, 1998; Fayard, 2006; Fayard and Weeks, 2007).<br>• Mobile video.<br>• Shadowing: The first author spent 12 days in the field with a camera held at belly level, shadowing the head of the MSF (Médecins Sans Frontières) mission in the Democratic Republic of Congo (Cooren et al., 2007). See also Meunier and Vasquez (2008).<br>• Embarked video: Participants were asked to wear the SubCam for several days (Fayard and Lahlou, 1998). |
| Team-based ethnography | • Developing a deeper understanding of global distributed phenomena through multi-site ethnography.<br>• Multiplicity of perspectives that allows comparison of and contrast across cases. | Difficult to share data and develop a collective reflection and common understanding that goes beyond each individual's perspective. | • Multi-site ethnography with studies done by several individual researchers (Barley, 1996; Fayard et al., 2016c).<br>• Pairs of researchers engaged in a multi-site ethnography of a global phenomenon (Jordan, 1996; Jarzabkowski et al., 2015). |
| Virtual ethnography | • Access the invisible work and interactions that have become part of everyday life at work (even when collocated) and in occupations and communities.<br>• Study new forms of organizing, such as online communities. | What "being there" means can be amorphous because people use multiple communication media and as the boundaries between physical and digital spaces are increasingly blurred. | • Analyzing "invisible" work done online (Riopelle, 2013; Fayard et al., 2016b)<br>• Participant observation in online communities (Rheingold, 1993; Baym, 1995; Nardi, 2010; Fayard and Metiu, 2012). |

(solely) by their ability to address different questions more or less adequately but by the presence of the adventurous spirit of discovery offered by ethnography.

Current trends in organizational and information systems research and the questions they prompt are nothing new. They simply invite us as ethnographers to keep being reflective and remember that the field is always constructed through a social process. The field is similarly constructed during the research stage. Being in the field is not a stand-alone activity that takes place at the beginning of the project; rather, it is through the interpretative process that the scope of the project arises. This ongoing interpretative process (in and outside of the field, on the way, and in between) allows us to go beyond explaining the "results" of cultural production and to explain, or at least illuminate, the process of how a given state of affairs (the production) has been achieved and is sustained.

## Acknowledgments

This essay has emerged from ongoing conversations with my co-authors, research collaborators, and students, who have all helped me reflect on my research practice. Our research collaborations – explicitly mentioned or not in this chapter – have led me to better articulate my epistemological stance. In particular, I would like to thank Beth Bechky, Manos Gkeredakis, Austin Henderson, Natalia Levina, Wendy Mackay, Anca Metiu, John Van Maanen, and John Weeks. I am grateful to Wendy Mackay with whom I had my first experience of going into the field and who taught me many tricks of the trade. Austin Henderson was a great mentor in particular when it came to video analysis and being playful with different forms of ethnography. A special thank you to John Van Maanen, who has always been supportive of my experiments and who has pushed me to always be curious and reflective. Of course, a big thank you to all the people who I met, observed, and interacted with in the field. Without them, there would be no fieldwork!

## Notes

1 See Fayard et al. (2016c), for a discussion of ethnography as epistemology. For a definition and discussion of epistemic stance, see Fayard et al. (2016a: 3–5). While the notion of epistemic stance in that case is understood at the organizational level, the different elements of the concept are still useful to the argument presented in this chapter.

2 John Van Maanen made this point several times at conferences and in seminars.

3 I have also experimented with what we call "contract ethnography." For a discussion of this form of ethnography, see Fayard et al. (2016c).

4 For more on the practice of interaction analysis, see Jordan and Henderson (1995). On group analysis in particular, see pp. 44–47.

5 An important limitation that has been raised is what Snell (2011) calls the "sensory overload" of video data, which includes data management, coding, and sampling. Video-based research is indeed very time-consuming, and it is important to be well organized while collecting data. Another issue often discussed is the camera effect or the notion that the camera influences people so that they don't behave and interact "normally." In fact, as noted by Jordan and Henderson (1995) and Heath et al. (2010), and as I observed in all my studies involving video, people grow accustomed to the camera surprisingly quickly. It is also important to note that manipulating and controlling one's behavior can't be done at length without seeing how microbehaviors like head turns and gazes are often unconscious (Jordan and Henderson, 1995).

6 When studying a distributed MBA course between France and Singapore, I recorded what happened at both sites. Because I spent half the course at one location and half at the other site, this allowed me to "see" what happened in the location where I was not. Besides tinkering with the location of the camera, I also made the decision to start the video 40 minutes before the beginning of class, to keep it running during the break, and to leave it on for at least 15 minutes after class ended. I reasoned that

"the class" was not necessarily beginning (or ending, for that matter) at the time I officially "started" (concluded) it as per the official class schedule. Instead, it might start before, when students began arriving at both sites. The video link between the two classrooms was also started earlier and maintained during the break. Similarly, interactions during the break were considered class participation.

7  If arguably not "subjective," this point of view is a mobile one that allowed us to follow the journey of individual knowledge workers and to better understand their interactions. While it did not follow the wearer's gaze, the SubCam told us the direction that his or her head faced.

8  At the beginning of each study, I spent about half a day observing the work of a manager. Afterwards, I would give the SubCam to the individual, who would keep it for two weeks and who was instructed to wear it during the entire workday. Participants could switch off the audio recording or both the audio and video when issues of confidentiality arose. In this case, the video allowed us to follow the individual managers in a way we could not before, while giving them a sense of privacy.

9  For more on video shadowing, see Cooren et al. (2007), and Meunier and Vasquez (2008), who provide detailed descriptions of shadowing as well as insightful methodological and epistemological reflections on video used this way.

10  See Jarzabkowski et al. (2015) for a detailed discussion of the challenges faced by researchers engaged in team-based global ethnography.

11  Several post-docs joined and then left, so team composition shifted. It evolved to include two, three, and up to four members.

12  As noted by Barley (1996), there has been prior experimentation with teamwork, with occasional collaborations between ethnographers studying the same site (Becker et al., 1961; Strauss et al., 1964).

13  For specific details about the ways of working and tools used, see Barley (1996: 414–418).

14  See Jordan (1996) for a detailed discussion of the methods she developed with team members on various projects.

15  See Metiu and Fayard (2016) for a discussion of the consequences of virtual ethnography for the analysis and interpretation of data.

16  As of the summer of 2016, OpenIDEO has about 100,000 members in more than 150 countries, with 7,000 ideas posted (for a total of 36 challenges) and 50 local chapters distributed worldwide.

17  Hine (2008) reports distinctions between two possible methods for conducting virtual ethnographies: distanced or involved. Distanced ethnography is based only on the qualitative analysis of texts, images, and the observation – without participation – of social interactions in online environments. In contrast, in involved ethnography, the researcher actively participates in the community she studies.

18  The role of offline interactions for OpenIDEO illustrates the blurring of the virtual and physical noted in other studies of online communities. See O'Mahony and Ferraro (2007), and Fayard and DeSanctis (2005).

# References

Agar, M. (1980). *The Professional Stranger*. New York: Academic Press.

Anteby, M. (2008). *Moral Gray Zones: Side-Production, Identity, and Regulation in an Aeronautic Plant*. Princeton, NJ: Princeton University Press.

Barley, S. R. (1996). Technicians in the workplace: Ethnographic evidence for bringing work into organization studies. *Administrative Science Quarterly*, 41: 404–441.

Barley, S. R. and Kunda, G. (2006). *Gurus, Hired Guns, and Warm Bodies: Itinerant Experts in a Knowledge Economy*. Princeton, NJ: Princeton University Press.

Barry, C. A., Britten, N., Barber, N., Bradley C., and Stevenson, F. (1999). Using reflexivity to optimize teamwork in qualitative research. *Qualitative Health Research*, 9(1): 26–44.

Baym, N. K. (1995). From practice to culture on Usenet. In S. L. Star (ed.) *The Cultures of Computing*, 29–52. Sociological Review Monograph Series. London: Basil Blackwell.

Bechky, B. A. (2003). Sharing meaning across occupational communities: The transformation of knowledge on a production floor. *Organization Science*, 14: 312–330.

Becker, H. S. (1998). *Tricks of the Trade: How to Think about Your Research While Doing It*. Chicago, IL: University of Chicago Press.

Becker, H. S., Geer, B., and Hughes, E. C. (1961). *Boys in White: Student Culture in Medical School*. Chicago, IL: University of Chicago Press.

Cefkin, M. (2013). The limits to speed. In B. Jordan (ed.) *Advancing Ethnography in Corporate Environments*, 108–119. Walnut Creek, CA: Left Coast Press.

Cooren, F., Matte, F., Vasquez, C., and Taylor, J. R. (2007). A humanitarian organization in action: Organizational discourse as an immutable mobile. *Discourse and Communication*, 1(2): 153–190.

Dalton, M. (1959). *Men Who Manage*. New York: John Wiley.

Fayard, A.-L. (2006). Interacting on a virtual stage: The collaborative construction of an interactional video setting. *Information Technology and People*, 19(2): 152–169.

Fayard, A.-L. (2012). Space matters, but how? Physical space, virtual space, and place. In P. Leonardi, B. Nardi, and J. Kallinikos (eds.) *Materiality and Organizing: Social Interaction in a Technological World*, 177–195. Oxford: Oxford University Press.

Fayard, A.-L. and DeSanctis, G. (2005). Evolution of an online forum for knowledge management professionals: A language game analysis. *Journal of Computer-Mediated Communication*, 10(4). doi:10.1111/j.1083-6101.2005.tb00265.x.

Fayard, A.-L. and DeSanctis, G. (2010). Enacting language games: The development of a sense of "we-ness" in online forums. *Information Systems Journal*, 20: 383–416.

Fayard, A.-L. and Lahlou, S. (1998). The SubCam: A new tool for analyzing office work. In the *Video Proceedings of CSCW'98, Seattle, November 1998*.

Fayard, A.-L. and Levina, N. (2015). The orchestration of collaboration in an open innovation community. *Academy of Management*, Vancouver, August.

Fayard, A.-L. and Metiu, A. (2012). *The Power of Writing in Organizations: From Letters to Online Interactions*. Series Organization and Management. New York: Routledge.

Fayard, A.-L. and Van Maanen, J. (2015). Making culture visible: Reflections on contract ethnography. *Journal of Organizational Ethnography*, 1: 4–27.

Fayard, A.-L. and Weeks, J. (2007). Photocopiers and water-coolers: The affordances of informal interactions. *Organization Studies*, 28(5): 605–634.

Fayard, A.-L., Gkeredakis, E., and Levina, L. (2016a). Framing innovation opportunities while staying committed to an organizational epistemic stance. *Information Systems Research*. Online: March 28, 2016.

Fayard, A.-L., Stigliani, I., and Bechky, B. (2016b). How nascent occupations construct mandate: The case of service designers' ethos. *Administration Science Quarterly*, 62(2): 270–303. Online: September 1, 1–34.

Fayard, A.-L., Van Maanen, J., and Weeks, J. (2016c). Contract ethnography in corporate settings: Innovation from entanglement. In K. Eslbach and R. Krammer (eds.) *Handbook of Qualitative Organizational Research: Innovative Pathways and Methods*, 45–53. New York: Routledge.

Forsythe, D. (2001). *Studying Those Who Study Us: An Anthropologist in the World of Artificial Intelligence*. Palo Alto, CA: Stanford University Press.

Geertz, C. (1973). *The Interpretation of Cultures: Selected Essays* (vol. 5019). New York: Basic Books.

Gluesing, J. (2013). Being there: The power of conventional ethnographic methods. In B. Jordan (ed.) *Advancing Ethnography in Corporate Environments*, 23–37. Walnut Creek, CA: Left Coast Press.

Goldman, S. and McDermott, R. (2009). Staying the course with video analysis. In R. Goldman, R. Pea, B. Barron, and J. Derry (eds.) *Video Research in the Learning Sciences*, 101–114. New York: Routledge.

Goodwin, C. (2000). Action and embodiment within situated human interaction. *Journal of Pragmatics*, 32: 1489–1522.

Goodwin, C. and Goodwin, H. (1992). Context, activity and participation. In P. Auer and A. di Luzio (eds.) *The Contextualization of Language*, 77–100. Amsterdam: John Benjamins.

Heath, C. and Luff, P. (1992). Collaboration and control: Crisis management and multimedia technology in London Underground line control rooms. *Computer Supported Cooperative Work (CSCW)*, 1(1): 69–94.

Heath, C., Hindmarsh, J., and Luff, P. (2010). *Video in Qualitative Research*. London: Sage.

Hine, C. (2000). *Virtual Ethnography*. London: Sage.

Hine, C. (2004). Virtual ethnography revisited. Paper summary prepared for session on online research methods. Research Methods Festival, Oxford.

Hine, C. (2008). Overview: Virtual ethnography: Modes, varieties, affordances. In N. G. Fielding, R. M. Lee, and G. Blank (eds.) *Handbook of Online Research Methods*, 257–271. London: Sage.

Jarzabkowski, P., Bednarek, R., and Cabantous, L. (2015). Conducting global team-based ethnography: Methodological challenges and practical methods. *Human Relations*, 68(1): 3–33.

Jewitt, C. (2012). An introduction to using video for research. NCRM working paper. Institute of Education, London, March 2012.

Jordan, B. (1996). Transforming ethnography – reinventing research. In J. Schiestl and H. Schelle (eds.) *Groupware: Software für die Zukunft: Grundlegende Konzepte und Fallstudien*, 200–212. Marburg, Germany: Tectum Verlag.

Jordan, B. (ed.) (2013). *Advancing Ethnography in Corporate Environments*. 2nd edn. Walnut Creek, CA: Left Coast Press.

Jordan, B. and Henderson, A. (1995). Interaction analysis: Foundations and practice. *Journal for the Learning Sciences*, 4(1): 39–103.

Kanter, R. M. (1977). *Men and Women of the Corporation*. New York: Basic Books.

Kunda, G. (2006 [1992]). *Engineering Culture: Control and Commitment in a High Tech Corporation*. 2nd edn. Philadelphia, PA: Temple University Press.

Mackay, W., Fayard, A.-L., Frobert, L., and Médini, L. (1998). Reinventing the familiar: Exploring and augmented reality design space for air traffic control. In *Proceedings of ACM CHI '98 Human Factors in Computing Systems*, 558–565. Los Angeles, CA: ACM/SIGCHI; ACM Press.

Marcus, G. E. (1995). Ethnography in/of the world system: The emergence of multi-sited ethnography. *Annual Review of Anthropology*, 24: 95–117.

Mauthner, N. S. and Doucet, A. (2008). Knowledge once divided can be hard to put together again: An epistemological critique of collaborative and team-based research practices. *Sociology*, 42(5): 971–985.

Metiu, A. and Fayard, A.-L. (2016). Between text and context: Innovative approaches to the qualitative analysis of online data. In K. Eslbach and R. Krammer (eds.) *Handbook of Qualitative Organizational Research: Innovative Pathways and Methods*, 381–390. New York: Routledge.

Meunier, D. and Vasquez, C. (2008). On shadowing the hybrid character of actions: A communicational approach. *Communication Methods and Measures*, 2(3): 167–192.

Mintzberg, H. (1970). Structured observation as method to study managerial work. *Journal of Management Studies*, 7(1): 87–104.

Nardi, B. (2010). *My Life as a Night Elf Priest: An Anthropological Account of World of Warcraft*. Ann Arbor, MI: University of Michigan Press.

O'Mahony, S. and Ferraro, F. (2007). The emergence of governance in an open source community. *Academy of Management Journal*, 50(5): 1079–1106.

O'Mahony, S. and Lakhani, K. R. (2011). Organizations in the shadow of communities. In C. Marquis, M. Lounsbury, and R. Greenwood (eds.) *Communities and Organizations*, 3–36. Research in the Sociology of Organizations, vol. 33. Bingley, UK: Emerald.

Orr, J. (1996). *Talking about Machines: An Ethnography of a Modern Job*. Ithaca, NY: ILR Press/Cornell University Press.

Rheingold, H. (1993). *The Virtual Community: Homesteading on the Electronic Frontier*. Cambridge, MA: MIT Press.

Riopelle, K. (2013). Being there: The power of technology-based methods. In B. Jordan (ed.) *Advancing Ethnography in Corporate Environments*, 38–53. Walnut Creek, CA: Left Coast Press.

Schultze, U. (2012). Performing embodied identity in virtual worlds. *European Journal of Information Systems*, 23(1): 84–95.

Scott, S. V. and Orlikowski, W. (2014). Entanglements in practice: Performing anonymity through social media. *MIS Quarterly*, 38(3): 873–893.

Snell, J. 2011. Interrogating video data: systematic quantitative analysis versus microethnographic analysis. *International Journal of Social Research Methodology*, 14(3): 253–258.

Strauss, A. L., Schatzman, L., Bucher, R., Ehrlich, D., and Sabshin, M. (1964). *Psychiatric Ideologies and Institutions*. New York: Free Press.

Suchman, L. and Trigg, R. H. (1991). Understanding practice: Video as a medium for reflection and design. In J. Greenbaum and M. Kyng (eds.) *Design at Work: Cooperative Design of Computer Systems*, 65–90. Hillsdale, NJ: Lawrence Erlbaum.

Vaast, E. (2007). Playing with masks: Fragmentation and continuity in the presentation of self in an occupational online forum. *Information Technology & People*, 20(4): 334–351.

Van Maanen, J. (2006). Ethnography then and now. *Qualitative Research in Organizations and Management: An International Journal*, 1(1): 13–21.

Van Maanen, J. (2011 [1988]). *Tales of the Field: On Writing Ethnography*. 2nd edn. Chicago, IL: University of Chicago Press.

Van Maanen, J. (2015). The present of things past: Ethnography and career studies. *Human Relations*, 68(1): 35–53.

Weeks, J. (2003). *Unpopular Culture: The Ritual of Complaint in a British Bank*. Chicago, IL: University of Chicago Press.

# 11

# INNOVATIONS IN ORGANIZATIONAL ETHNOGRAPHY

## Being Them, Even without Trying

*Alexandra Michel*

Organizational ethnography has changed beyond recognition. In our knowledge economy, ethnographers have devised new methods to study new organizational forms. While ethnography has always been defined by immersion in an organization as the relevant field, approaches such as virtual ethnography (Hine, 2000), network ethnography (Howard, 2002), multi-site ethnography (Hannertz, 2003), and netnography (Kozinets, 1998) involve neither immersion nor a localized organizational setting. For example, because multi-site work requires the researcher to cover more settings, immersion is impractical, leading to a primary reliance on interviews (Hannertz, 2003). As new empirical developments challenge the localism that has been implicit in traditional conceptualizations of organizations, our basic assumptions about what constitutes organizational ethnography and how to conduct it are now becoming research tasks, raising the following questions:

1   What, if any, shared theoretical commitments should guide organizational *ethnographers*? "Doing ethnography" differs from "using ethnographic methods" (Green and Bloome, 1997). While the latter is guided by the appropriateness of the method to the empirical phenomenon, the former is also informed by overarching theoretical commitments, namely documenting an insider's perspective, which has traditionally been ethnography's "final goal" (Malinowski, 1922). Examining such commitments matters as new methods emerge. For example, if our goal remains to attain an insider's perspective, can we afford to do away with immersive observant participation and resort to "participation light" or to a primary reliance on interviews?

2   Are these theoretical commitments different for *organizational* ethnographers? Some new methods, such as multi-site ethnography, are borrowed from other disciplines, notably cultural anthropology (e.g., Marcus, 1995). But with the change to a knowledge-based environment comes not only a change in the object of ethnographic study, such as locally dispersed organizations, but also a different relationship for organizational ethnographers to their informants, as compared to the previous industrial economy and to cultural anthropology. Following the "crisis of representation" (e.g., Clifford and Marcus, 1986; Marcus

and Fischer, 1986), anthropologists have devised new methods partly because the anthropologist is separated from informants by an unbridgeable cultural gap, which challenged the goal of obtaining an insider's perspective through immersion. In contrast, organizational scholars do have the unique opportunity to achieve an insider's perspective because they resemble their informants in terms of socialization and can participate in similar organizational socialization processes. Should the organizational discipline reinvigorate the commitment of obtaining an insider's view through immersion ("Being There/Being Them"), even as it might recede into the background for other disciplines?

3    What types of innovations are necessary for organizational ethnography in response to a changing ethnographic object, while observing shared theoretical commitments? For example, given that we can no longer assume what the relevant setting is, namely a localized organization, at the very least we will need to devise methods that help us construct the relevant setting for each particular instance, such as methods that help us trace connections (Marcus, 1995). Without a theoretical commitment to obtaining an insider's perspective, it is easy to prioritize practicality, to "satisfice" (Falzon, 2009), and simply give up the goal of immersion. But given that organizational scholars can achieve an insider's perspective and given new types of organizational contexts, perhaps there are new and practical forms of immersion. The following first motivates and then answers these questions, using both theory and data from my research.

## The Changing Nature of Organizational Ethnography

Traditionally, ethnography has involved immersive inquiry in a setting ("the field"). Immersive means that the scholar enters the place where people live or work for a prolonged period of time and develops relations with them in order to achieve an insider's perspective. Ethnography refers both to the process of inquiry and the resulting written product. Even though ethnography is used across disciplines, it has been "at the heart of" (Marcus, 1994: 42) cultural anthropology, which has long had an explicit model of ethnography. Namely, the anthropologist spends about two years in a foreign society, with the goal to understand their entire culture and social life (e.g., Evans-Pritchard, 1951). Examples of such long-term exclusive engagement with one or rarely two cultural settings – "one scribe, one tribe" – include Boas's work on the Inuit people on Baffin Island, Malinowski's study of the Trobriand Islands and New Guinea, and Radcliffe-Brown's research in Australia. The prescribed immersion is in the service of the "final goal of anthropology," "of which the Ethnographer should never lose sight ... [which is] to grasp the native's point of view, his relation to life, to realize his vision of his world" (Malinowski, 1922: 25). Ethnography thus is about "Being There" (Geertz, 1988), which involves becoming so intimately familiar with a face-to-face community that one is close to "Being Them."

Organizational ethnography has its own tradition, which from the very beginning has admitted a wider array of models, as compared to cultural anthropology. Yet, similar to how ethnography has been defined traditionally in anthropology, organizational scholars believe that "fieldwork of the immersive sort is by and large definitional of the trade" (Van Maanen, 2006: 13), as is the commitment to understanding phenomena from the informants' point of view, that is, achieving an emic perspective. For example, "Being There/Being Them" is the title of a long-standing professional development workshop where organizational ethnographers reconvene on a yearly basis.

The defining of a uniquely *organizational* ethnography is a shared commitment to the organization as the relevant setting or field (Ybema et al., 2009: 4). The notion of the organization as the relevant field has been taken for granted, shaping ethnographic methods without being problematized. Standard textbooks and doctoral seminars teach ethnography as a matter of entering and "hanging out" in a field, such as an organization. Aspiring students learn how to navigate access, what kinds of roles to assume, including participation and observation, how to develop central informants, how to take fieldnotes that are "detailed, context-sensitive, and locally informed" (Emerson et al., 1995: 10), how long to observe, when and how to interview, and how to analyze findings.

It turns out, however, that far from context-free, these practices are contingent on specific ontological assumptions that, moreover, are becoming obsolete. When the notion of the organization as the relevant field falls, so do our notions of fieldwork. Specifically, organizational fieldwork depends on the assumption that there is a localized "field" that one can enter and where one can become an insider. Traditionally, fields have been envisioned implicitly as being bounded, assuming that "each culture, if not literally confined to an island, could be approached as if it were" (Faubion, 2001: 44). Fieldwork methods, such as "hanging out" and writing fieldnotes, assume a "mise-en-scene" (Marcus, 1997: 87), a term borrowed from filmwork: We assume that the field (1) is situated in a *place* and (2) spreads out in front of the fieldworker, similar to the arrangement in front of the camera.

Challenging organizational ethnography as we know it are new organizational forms, such as online communities, enabled by technology innovation. Because these organizations do not exist in one location, researchers cannot use the methods that we unproblematically associate with ethnography, such as entering and hanging out in an organization, requiring innovation, such as multi-sited fieldwork (Marcus, 1995) or network ethnography (Howard, 2002). These methods involve neither a localized organization nor the researcher's immersion. For example, Hannertz (2003) studied foreign correspondents in international locations. Following Marcus's (1995) prescription for multi-sited work, the field emerged during the study, as Hannertz discovered connections between geographically dispersed correspondents. Because the researcher needed to study multiple sites, he covered each site in less depth.

Similarly, Howard (2002) analyzed a professional community that supplies political campaigns with tools for coordinating volunteers, analyzing data, and shaping ideology. To study such "physically decentralized social networks made up of individuals who form a community but are not members of the same formal organization" (p. 553), an increasingly common phenomenon, he utilized a "network ethnography," which combines social network analysis and what he argues is ethnography, namely interviews and observing small group interactions at professional events or conferences, for example.

Green and Bloome (1997) distinguish between "using ethnographic methods," on the one hand, and, on the other hand, "doing ethnography." The former is driven primarily by methodological imperatives; the latter is also guided by overarching theoretical commitments, such as developing an empathetic understanding with informants through immersion. While both Hannertz (2003) and Howard (2002) were certainly using ethnographic methods, were they "doing ethnography?" And does it matter?

## Research Question 1: What, If Any, Shared Theoretical Commitments Should Guide Organizational *Ethnographers?*

Some scholars have defined ethnography in terms of its attributes, including the methods used. For example, Ybema et al. (2009: 5ff.) discuss the "key characteristics of ... organizational ethnography," including "(c)ombined fieldwork methods," being "(a)t the scene," uncovering "(h)idden and harsh dimensions," and featuring "(c)ontext-sensitive and actor-centered analysis."

While these are attributes of effective ethnography, they do not differentiate ethnography from other qualitative research. In fact, Ybema et al. (2009) use the term "ethnography" (p. 5) synonymously with using "ethnographic methods" (p. 6).

In contrast, I propose that there is something to be gained by making a distinction between (1) a methods-driven approach, in which the scholar draws from the ethnographic toolkit to use whatever method is appropriate for understanding an empirical phenomenon, and (2) "doing ethnography," in which the scholar also heeds distinctive theoretical commitments, including ontological commitments about the relevant object of organizational ethnography and epistemological commitments about the preferred methods for studying this object.

*Ethnography's ontological commitments.* One of ethnography's distinctive ontological commitments is that "it is concerned with the study and representation of culture (with a distinctively small c)" (Van Maanen, 2006: 13). Writing culture with a small c responds to the criticisms of the traditional American culture concept, as promulgated by Boas, Mead, and Benedict, who defined culture "as the worldview and ethos of a particular group of people" (Ortner, 2006: 112). This perspective has been criticized because it invites homogenizing and essentializing participants, for example, portraying "the Balinese" as if they had an essence that (1) is shared by all participants, as a "club of the like-minded" (Eagelton, 1983: 73), and (2) determined their behaviors. Written with a small c, culture is not a kind of thing that people "have," but a process, something that is "constructed (and construed)" (Van Maanen, 2006: 15), a perspective on culture that can be traced back to continental Europe, most notably Wittgenstein.

However, if we stopped with a definition of ethnography as concerned with the study and representation of culture, we would lose one of its central attributes, namely its unique positioning as "the most scientific of the humanities and the most humanistic of the sciences" (Van Maanen, 2006: 13). Something is humanistic when it is about the interests of people. Yet there are non- and even anti-humanistic approaches to culture, such as a structuralist approach in the tradition of Levi-Strauss, which "invert(s) humanist premises by prioritizing the structure over the subject" (Fox, 2003: 24), aiming "not to constitute but to dissolve man" (Levi-Strauss, 1966: 247).

In contrast to structuralism, ethnography's inalienable commitment centers on the person as product and producer of culture. *At the heart of doing ethnography is investigating the cultural shaping of persons.* Doing ethnography is aiming to generate "a special scientific description of a people and the cultural basis of their peoplehood" (Vidich and Lyman, 2000). Originating in cultural anthropology, this theoretical commitment is based on the interrelated insights that (1) human forms of life vary widely across cultures, and (2) different cultural formations entail different ways in which basic human functions ("peoplehood") manifest themselves. Far from essentializing the person, these insights promote studying the plasticity of persons, which is one of ethnography's distinct contributions to the social sciences.

*Epistemological commitments.* Ethnography's ontological commitment matters because it is associated with a set of methods that can generate a more accurate and comprehensive understanding of personhood, as compared to other approaches to human functioning, such as psychology. Ethnography features at least two interrelated epistemological commitments: (1) As a discipline, scholars seek out maximum variance in cultural context in order to discover the extent of human plasticity; (2) Through immersive participation, each scholar aims to undergo a self-transformation to facilitate *Verstehen* (Dilthey, 1914).

First, concerning the variance in cultural contexts, because traditional psychology assumes that basic human functioning does not depend on the context, research can be done on the person in isolation from the context. For example, psychologists study people in the "neutral" context of the laboratory, which, of course, is merely a highly specialized kind of context. As a result, psychologists only see human functioning in a narrow range of contexts, including familiar cultures and sub-cultures, such as the university students who fill out psychological questionnaires. Because psychologists do not actively seek out cultural variation, they do not generate the data that could challenge the discipline's assumptions about universality. Ethnography provides the necessary counterpoint.

For example, while psychologists have argued that human emotions fall into six universally valid types (Ekman, 1999), namely disgust, sadness, happiness, fear, anger, and surprise, by seeking out cultural variance, ethnographers have found states that do not correspond to psychological categories. For instance, *liget*, found in the Ilongot of the Philippines, a tribe of headhunters, was a sense of anger, heat, energy, and envy that manifested in behaviors such as sulking, slashing baskets, and, when it is fulfilled, decapitating men from other tribes, which, in turn, resulted in joyful celebration by the tribe (Rosaldo, 1980). More important than merely the variance from familiar types of emotions is the insight that *liget* had a social function at a particular, historically situated moment. When Rosaldo went back to the tribe after a few years, headhunting had stopped, thwarted by Philippine authorities, the tribe had been converted to Christianity, and, as a result, members exhibited a more placid set of emotional norms.

This example shows how ethnography cannot only give us a better understanding of the broad range in which human functioning can manifest, as compared to traditional psychology. It thereby also provides a more accurate understanding of what human functioning is, namely not the attribute of a person, but a mutual constitution of person and context: The context shapes people in ways that compel them to reproduce the focal context. At different cultural-historical moments, the Ilongot exhibited the distinct types of emotions that contributed toward the goals of the society. They exhibited aggression as headhunters and peaceful states as Christians. The notion of mutual constitution does not imply a contextual determinism. Quite the contrary, especially when applied to organizations, it opens up the opportunity to examine different types of contexts, compare their distinct effects on human functioning, and design more beneficial types of context.

Like ethnography, cross-cultural psychology compares cultural contexts. However, unlike ethnography, it often studies people in isolation from these contexts, for example, by administering paper and pencil tests to students from Eastern versus Western cultures (e.g., Nisbett et al., 2001). Cross-cultural psychology contributes to our understanding of human plasticity because it shows that human functioning differs across different contexts. However, because cross-cultural psychologists do not actually examine the relation between the person and the context, we do not understand what aspects of the context produce variation in human functioning. Consequently, we do not know how to influence human functioning by designing better contexts.

For example, cross-cultural psychologists assume that – but do not demonstrate how – Eastern and Western cultures differ because of relatively stable intellectual traditions, namely Confucianism versus Cartesianism, which, in turn, manifest in distinct social institutions that presumably shape all participants in similar ways. More recent cross-cultural approaches have moved away from the problematic assumption that large groups of people share one type of mindset, examining variety across subcultures. However, to attain a sufficiently granular understanding of how particular aspects of a culture shape participants, ethnography is indispensable, as demonstrated by Bourdieu's (1977) research on the Kabyle.

Bourdieu describes how Kabyle men climb and work up in trees, cutting down branches. The women sit at the bottom of the tree, picking up the branches. Because the activity locates them up in trees, men have a different vantage point on the world, as compared to the women whose gaze is confined to a narrow radius. Also, these different types of activity shape differential action potentials and embodied dispositions. Men gain upper body strength, an erect posture, and the propensity to initiate action, while women's muscles atrophy, their bodies become stooped, and they are conditioned to be reactive to cues from men.

This example indicates the mutual constitution of the person and the context. The person is shaped by the culture, including work, in ways that maintain the culture. Moreover, this shaping is holistic; it goes beyond affecting the "component parts" of persons (Lave, 2003) that psychology focuses on, such as mental concepts. It also includes embodied dispositions, such as posture and strength. Being about the cultural shaping of *persons*, ethnography is uniquely positioned to discover all of the aspects of the person that are affected by culture. The Kabyle example also shows that and how participants are shaped not only by large intellectual traditions, but also by the specific form of their daily activities. This matters. Because we can only with great difficulty influence large cultural traditions, focusing on this static sphere directs analytic attention away from those cultural aspects that we can influence, such as the particularities of work practices.

Bourdieu's practice theoretical approach illustrates that a commitment to studying the culturally shaped *person* makes no a priori assumptions about the extent of human agency. The analytic image of the person that could emerge from empirical research may well be a radically decentered one, such as Latour's (2005) flat ontology, in which the person is not a privileged agent, but merely contributes resources to action at the same level with non-human agents, such as tools. Ethnography's scientific humanism is not about artificially upholding a primacy for humans as agents. The scientific aspect is about empirically studying humans and their concerns. The humanistic commitment is about taking the side of persons, understanding how they affect and are affected by the world.

Ethnography's second epistemological commitment is self-transformation through immersive participation. Ethnography is based on the assumption that the ideal approach for understanding people is "actually taking part in the activity together with the people involved in it" (Winch, 1956: 31). This is what differentiates it from other types of naturalistic fieldwork, such as the study of flowers by a botanist. For example, while Malinowski (1922: 6) maintained that observation is central in studying cultures, including recording kinship terms and drawing out maps and plans, he insisted that observation merely yields "dead material" and "lacks flesh and blood" (p. 17). More important and the hallmark of ethnography is that fieldworkers not only attempt to record how insiders think and feel, but aim to self-transform by becoming part of informants' activities:

> I had to learn how to behave, and to a certain extent, I acquired "the feeling" for native good and bad manners.... I began to feel that I was indeed in touch with the natives, and *this is certainly the preliminary condition of being able to carry on successful field work.*
>
> *(Malinowski, 1922: 8; emphasis supplied)*

Immersion is essential for self-transformation and has two aspects. One, and often overlooked by organizational ethnographers, it means distancing oneself from one's culture of origin, such as academia. It "require[s] cutting oneself off from the company of other white men, and remaining in as close contact with the natives as possible, which really can only be achieved by camping right in their villages" (Malinowski, 1922: 6). Two, it means that one sometimes has "to put aside camera, note book and pencil, and to join in himself what is going on," for the purpose of enhanced *Verstehen*: Because of these "plunges into the lives of the natives ... their behavior, their manner of being ... became more transparent and easily understandable than it had been before" (Malinowski, 1922: 22).

In anthropology, the ideal of self-transformation through participation has been challenged, not because it is not desirable but because it may not be possible. The cultural distance between the anthropologist and the "native," used as Geertz (1976: 226) points out " 'in the strict sense of the term,' " is unbridgeable. Because anthropologists typically have not been born into the focal culture, they cannot experience the same formation processes as, and therefore never truly become, insiders. Also, Western ethnographers usually do not experience the same constraints as their informants (Bittner, 1973). This means that it is incorrect to understand the relation between the anthropologist and the informant as a type of personal attunement. It is more accurate to view it as an encounter between two distinct cultures, namely the native's culture and academia:

> However far from the groves of academe anthropologists seek out their subjects – a shelved beach in Polynesia, a charred plateau in Amazonia, Akobo, Meknes, Panther Burn – they write their accounts with the world of lecterns, libraries, blackboards and seminars all about them. This is the world that produces anthropologists, that licenses them to do the kind of work that they do, and within which the kind of work they do must find a place if it is to count as worth attention. In itself, Being There is a postcard experience.... It is Being. Here a scholar among scholars, that gets your anthropology read ... published, reviewed, cited, taught.
>
> *(Geertz, 1988: 130)*

While Geertz continued to uphold Malinowski's goal of seeing things from the native's point of view, he developed different means of doing so, contributing to ethnography's semiotic turn:

> [T]he ethnographer does not, and in my opinion, largely cannot perceive what his informants perceive. What he perceives – and that uncertainly enough – is what they perceive "with," or "by means of," or "through" or whatever word one may choose ... [namely] symbolic forms – words, images, institutions, behaviors – in terms of which ... people represent themselves to themselves and to one another.
>
> *(Geertz, 1976: 228)*

This crucial aspect, namely the extent of attunement possible between researcher and informant, has recently become different for *organizational* ethnographers, allowing them to realize traditional ethnographic commitments in ways that were never possible for anthropologists.

## Research Question 2: Are These Theoretical Commitments Different for *Organizational* Ethnographers?

I propose that even though these commitments have come under attack in cultural anthropology, spawning new methods, organizational ethnographers should reinvigorate them. Innovation in methods is needed here, too, as discussed in the next section. However, it should take a different form, as compared to cultural anthropology, tampered with traditional methods, most importantly self-transformative immersion.

*Why organizational ethnographers should reinvigorate traditional ethnographic commitments.* The recent change to a knowledge-based society has created a qualitative change in the extent to which organizational ethnographers can realize ethnography's ontological and epistemological commitments, as compared to cultural anthropologists and compared to what was possible during an industrial society.

For decades, the exotic cultures studied by cultural anthropologists presented the main opportunity for (1) obtaining variance in cultural contexts, that (2) was consequential in shaping participants' functioning. Industrial types of organizations were a less powerful shaping force because employees only worked for about 40 hours per week, leaving ample time for other socialization influences. In contrast, one of the defining attributes of contemporary knowledge work is the all-encompassing commitment it extracts from participants. Doctors, lawyers, consultants, bankers, and software engineers all regularly work up to 100 hours per week and are connected to work electronically 24/7, leaving less time to participate in other socializing institutions. These "greedy organizations" (Coser, 1967) thus function as "total institutions" (Goffman, 1961), making it possible for the ethnographer to isolate a person-shaping process that is relatively undiluted by competing socializing sources.

While knowledge-based organizations may be comparable to native societies in terms of influence on participants, studying these organizations has distinct explanatory advantages. Because they need to innovate in business models to keep up with their turbulent business environment, different organizations are likely to design different cultural practices, reflecting differences in their environment and competitive positioning. This means that, as a discipline, organizational scholars have the opportunity to observe a relatively broad variance in a subset of cultural practices that are important for socialization, while holding the overall cultural context stable. The fact that variation occurs against the backdrop of stability makes it easier to discern what causes variance in participant functioning, as opposed to the comparisons generated by cultural anthropologists, in which different cultures varied on a much greater number of dimensions, obscuring the causes of the observed variance in human functioning.

For example, my research tracks the incoming associates into two different Wall Street investment banks over time, observing how the different banks shaped participants in differential ways (e.g., Michel and Wortham, 2009). Because the participants, selected from the same schools, had experienced similar socialization processes, I could establish a shared baseline at entry against which to determine the distinct development trajectories of bankers who entered a different bank. Moreover, because the two banks were similar on many dimensions that could explain participants' development, it was possible for me to isolate those distinct practices in the two banks that caused the observed differential changes in participants.

Enhancing explanatory quality even further, the same organization may change business models and therefore cultural practice in a relatively short period of time, making it possible for the ethnographer to observe the change. Because native cultures change more slowly, anthropologists rarely witnessed qualitative cultural change during their observation time. In contrast to anthropologists, thus, through longitudinal research, organizational scholars can potentially observe how cultural change in organizations transforms participants. Observing culturally induced transformation processes offers deeper insight into the relation between culture and person, as compared to merely statically comparing different cultures ("Easterners versus Westerners") or subcultures and inferring what causes participants' distinct attributes: We understand what something is partly by seeing how it changes (Wertsch, 1991).

In fact, the organizational scholar sometimes can induce cultural change and observe outcomes and change processes, a feat that is more manageable in an organization, as compared to a native culture. Such control over the "independent variable," namely organizational culture, is ideal for offering high-quality explanations. Paired with ethnographic observation, this controlled design can yield deep insights into the cultural shaping of contemporary persons. For example, Perlow and Porter (2009) changed BCG's overwork culture by implementing a predictable evening off per week. The scholars could observe the beneficial effect of this change on both individuals and the organization. In addition, they could study the change process.

One surprising finding was that consultants initially resisted even this minimal change in work habits. They opposed the initiative even though it was mandated by the organization, had no negative impact on their work because colleagues could fill in, and could benefit them by allowing them to pursue private commitments, which was previously not possible because the consultants had been available to clients 24/7. This type of resistance, which goes against one's own interest without benefiting the community one identifies with, points to culturally shaped habit. Identifying unproductive cultural conditioning in these consultants is a contribution because knowledge workers perceive themselves and are perceived by scholars as autonomous (Davenport, 2005). Without a proper diagnosis of what causes unproductive behaviors, namely the organizational context, one cannot change them.

Even without a controlled design, contemporary knowledge-based organizations offer a unique vantage point on the "dependent variable," namely the cultural shaping of persons. In contrast to natives and to industrial workers, knowledge workers have shorter tenures in a given culture. The average executive career is about four years. This means that it is possible to ethnographically study a complete socialization cycle. The quotation marks around "independent variable" and "dependent variable" indicate that I use these terms merely for clarity in exposition. The concept of mutual constitution, which is central to my understanding of the cultural production of persons, makes such a variable-based perspective problematic, since the "independent variable," such as the organization's practices, cannot be analytically separated from the "dependent variable," such as the culturally shaped person, who reproduces the culture in action.

*Why organizational ethnographers should rededicate themselves to traditional immersion.* So far I have suggested that contemporary knowledge-based organizations are ideal objects for the traditional goals of ethnography, namely understanding the cultural shaping of the person. In addition, the change to a knowledge-based society also presents a unique opportunity for understanding this object with traditional ethnographic methods, namely self-transformation through immersion. One, because careers have become shorter in a knowledge-based economy, informants themselves are only temporary organizational members. It may therefore be possible for an ethnographer to participate in a culture for the same length of time as informants, experiencing the same cultural transformation processes.

For example, some consulting firms and banks offer temporary positions for undergraduates, such as a two- or three-year "analyst" position. These junior employees often work exceptionally long hours and are expected to forego outside commitments, a situation that does not change much for permanent employees (e.g., Padavic et al., 2013). Even permanent employees tend to have relatively short tenures due to up-or-out types of arrangements. For example, the average tenure of a McKinsey consultant is about two-and-a-half years (Quora, 2013). Similarly, about 44 percent of executives will stay with an organization for two to five years (BlueSteps, 2013).

More importantly, in contrast to anthropologists, organizational ethnographers are not separated from their informants by an unbridgeable cultural distance. Quite the contrary, because they are remarkably like their informants to begin with and because they can participate in the same types of transformation processes, they have the unique opportunity to truly "Be Them" if they invest in "Being There." In our modern knowledge economy, scholars and informants often have similar types of primary socialization. They might have attended the same schools and obtained the same degrees. In fact, organizational ethnographers sometimes were members of the culture that they subsequently study. For example, Leslie Perlow, who investigates management consultants, was a management consultant before she became an academic. Similarly, Kate Kellogg, who ethnographically explores healthcare organizations, was a member of healthcare organizations before she became an academic. I was an investment banker before I received my Ph.D. and started to study investment bankers ethnographically.

This shared socialization is an advantage for ethnographers. Scholars often, only half-jokingly, say that people study their hang-ups. A researcher who cannot discipline himself develops a theory about routines. A person who has trust issues develops theories about social contracts. Solving personally significant problems supplies part of the energy that following long-term research agendas requires. In contrast to such idiosyncratic motivations for research, shared socialization makes it likely that the ethnographer becomes interested in socially shared problems and, reflecting the power of the method, can articulate them, sometimes even before they become publicly recognized as problems. For example, Perlow's work on "time famine" was published in 1999. Almost a decade after her research was conducted, Deloitte named the "overwhelmed employee" as one of the most important trends in the contemporary workplace. This sequence in timing is also likely to reflect Perlow's choice of setting. Some knowledge-based firms, including consulting firms and banks, experience business-environmental trends earlier than other firms and devise practices that other firms emulate as they encounter the same trends.

One might argue that some of these opportunities come with equally important impediments. One reason for studying exotic cultures was that they rendered the familiar strange. By presenting us with alternative ways of social organizing and the resulting different ways in which humans could function, we could see aspects of our lives that were previously invisible, recognizing the supposed givens as design choices. In contrast, organizational scholars and the knowledge workers we are studying participate in the same cultural background, making this background less visible. For example, even though I was committed to studying the themes that presented themselves in the field, I did not notice bankers' overwork and the resulting deterioration in their health for a long time because I was working the same hours and, therefore, struggled with similar health issues. Both the hours and the resulting depletion were unremarkable to me.

Moreover, as I elaborate below, it turned out that precisely this aspect, which was invisible to me and to my informants, was the most consequential aspect for structuring the social fabric in which we participated. This is always true. Culture operates at different levels. For example, institutional scholars examine how people make choices based on rule setting, monitoring, and sanctioning. However, these choice processes represent surface levels of culture (Scott, 2008) that people are aware of and can therefore manipulate for their own advantage. The deeper, more powerful levels of culture are those that are invisible to people and that compel them to act in culturally consistent ways not out of choice, but because they cannot conceive otherwise. Self-transformative immersion is an ideal method for identifying these deep levels of culture because the scholar can use analytic tools to self-analyze in ways that cultural participants cannot. Especially when conducting multi-site work, analyzing the self gives the ethnographer the opportunity for more sustained observation that, moreover, can target private aspects of experience that informants might be reluctant to reveal.

Some have argued that these traditional commitments are out of touch with a changing reality:

> The ghosts of Malinowski and Geertz still haunt the theory and practice of ethnography.... These revenants constantly return, via contemporary traditionalists, to insist that the power of fieldwork is best, or only, derived from long-term immersion and encounter with "the native's point of view." ... Multi-site ethnography is seen to play fast and loose with such sticklers' understandings.... But, ... Ethnography should not still "be what it used to be."
>
> *(Kenway, 2015: 37)*

I agree with Kenway and other proponents of new approaches, such as multi-site fieldwork, that innovation is necessary. However, far from being an anachronistic formality, immersion has a new and indispensable function in a changing research context. I will illustrate both this function and the need for innovation with a case study from my research, as part of answering the last research question.

### Research Question 3: What Types of Innovations Are Necessary for Organizational Ethnography in Response to a Changing Ethnographic Object, While Observing Shared Theoretical Commitments?

For about 15 years, I have been studying the four cohorts of investment bankers who entered at the same time into two Wall Street investment banks. For the first two years, I conducted participant observation, for up to 100 hours per week, mirroring the bankers' schedule. The two-year immersion period is consistent with the traditional prescriptions of how long an anthropologist should study a focal culture (e.g., Evans-Pritchard, 1951). I continued the study beyond the initial two-year plan and agreement with the banks because I kept observing systematic changes in the bankers.

Since then, I have been studying the bankers through an average of four interviews per year plus limited participation observation, following them into new firms as they departed the banks (e.g., Michel, 2014). Doing so required two interdependent innovations in methods: (1) multi-site work to study how bankers diffused the banks' practices through the economy, yielding "thin" descriptions, balanced by (2) auto-ethnography that involved immersing myself into the same situation as the bankers. I used myself as an informant to whom I had continuous and deep access, yielding thick, emic descriptions of patterns on which the bankers could not self-report.

Through this combination of methods, I have been able to capture the dispersing object of my work without sacrificing deep understanding from the informants' perspective. Because of the intensive time demands of this methodology and because of how it transformed me as a researcher to fit my object, I also upheld the "one scribe, one tribe" norm. However, because of the fast-paced changes in my informants' lives, the attributes of the "tribe" members have changed radically during my observation time, affording me a similar transformation through immersion. Self-transformation through immersion takes on a new form in ethnography in contemporary knowledge-based organizations with important advantages for research, yet so far little methodological guidance.

*Multi-site work.* One research stream illustrates how the bankers' chronic overwork was shaped by and shaped a social fabric that extends beyond the banks, pointing to the need for multi-site research. First, similar to other professional service firms, such as management consulting firms, the two banks hired from top schools, selecting students who had both exceptional grades and demanding extra-curricular activities, a combination that indicates the individuals' high energy and stamina. The banks hired people out of college, as opposed to experienced individuals, and, moreover, hired "insecure overachievers" because these candidates were more "moldeable" (the banks' term). This means that the socialization processes that I wanted to observe had started with other institutions that I did not observe. This connection across socializing institutions is one illustration of Marcus's (1995) point that single-site research is insufficient because organizations are embedded in a larger system, requiring multi-site research with the goal to empirically establish connections between settings.

I started to conduct multi-site research when bankers left the banks, often because the intense work had caused body breakdowns. The average tenure in the banks was seven years; the average age 35. Illustrating the mutual constitution of person and cultural practice, partly because of this systematic and self-generated pattern of employee exhaustion, the banks organized differently, as compared to traditional organizations. Instead of hiring individual candidates for particular vacancies as they occurred, they hired in yearly cohorts, pumping in "fresh blood" as exhausted bankers predictably left. Using interviews and limited participant observation, I followed the bankers as they started to fan out into the economy, where they often assumed leadership positions in important organizations (Michel, 2014).

This diffusion of elite workers into the economy is not limited to my sample, indicating an important path to follow for future work. For example, Goldman Sachs places so many people into leading government positions that it is nicknamed "Government Sachs," supplying for example treasury secretaries such as Robert Rubin, Hank Paulson, and Timothy Geithner as well as important advisors, such as Stephen Friedman (Head of Foreign Intelligence Advisory Board), and governors, including Jon Corzine. Similarly, McKinsey is referred to as the "leadership factory" because alumni often become leaders in important organizations worldwide, for example, at some point supplying more than 70 CEOs of Fortune 500 firms (McDonald, 2013).

Marcus's (1995) approach to multi-site work is based on the trope of "following," establishing "chains, paths, threads, conjunctions, or juxtapositions of locations" (p. 105). While he suggested that one could follow many different analytic objects, including people, things, metaphors, stories, or allegories, I propose that a theoretical commitment to ethnography is about following the person. The humanistic aspect of ethnography centers on the person. It aims to understand how other things that circulate, such as categories, affect the person holistically, including those aspects neglected by psychology, including embodied dispositions. Moreover, the change that cultural circulation affects in the person often facilitates ongoing circulation (e.g., Bourdieu, 1977; Giddens, 1984): People develop the kinds of dispositions that reproduce the culture in action. This means that to understand cultural circulation comprehensively, we have to understand the acting subject, not as a privileged agent, but as the nexus for resources, such as categories, tools, and dispositions.

My research traced how the bankers carried their socialized dispositions into the economy, reproducing the bank's culture in the firms they joined next and thereby the culturally supporting dispositions in the firms' participants, with the unintended consequence of intensifying the work pace for everyone. For example, the bankers introduced a "results only" practice with the intention of freeing people from arbitrary standards and giving them autonomy to decide their own work pace and location. However, the unintended consequences were the opposite. Participants started to work much more because the results that they had to achieve were so high and because they competed against other high achievers. Moreover, instead of allowing participants more autonomy than in a setting that regulated working hours, participants now were regulated by more diffuse, pervasive, and compelling social controls, namely each other in the form of social comparison.

Participant observation was important because I could observe how and why the bankers' new workplaces changed over time to resemble the banks. Even though bankers recognized that they continued to work as hard as before, they did not recognize that this was because (1) through their actions, they were constructing the context that compelled this overwork and (2) that these consequential actions were not personal design choices, but dispositions that the banks had socialized into them. Because bankers could not self-report on these two aspects, interviews would not have been sufficient for discovering this societally important connection across sites and for tracking change processes in the cultural context and the persons.

Multi-site work can entail that the researcher covers each site in less depth (Hannertz, 2003; Marcus, 1995). This has been true for my research. I observed in a few different settings for a few days at a time, revisiting every three or four months. However, thinness in some aspect of the fieldwork can be balanced through immersion in other aspects. For example, the immersive aspects completed during the study's earlier years provided a different context for the subsequent, thinner observations. Through the early immersive observation, I had established a detailed sense for the object I was following, namely a specific form of person production through work. Without this baseline, it would have been more difficult to recognize that the diverse work situations that different bankers entered as they left the banks were variations on a theme. The multi-site work extended the earlier work by affording cross-site comparison. I could see if and how this pattern was reproduced and reproduced differently in different settings, allowing me to isolate more influences and generate a more complete process account.

For example, comparisons across international sites let me see the previously invisible role of the larger cultural context. In the U.S. firms, incumbents changed as a result of the new practices. Even workers who had previously not felt ambition for their jobs, prided themselves on and sustained long working hours. This was partly because of the new work practices, but also because the bankers tapped into a broader set of values that circulated in the national culture. Namely, U.S. workers valued "a strong work ethic" and respected and emulated the bankers who displayed it. This influence only became clear to me when some bankers joined and instituted "results only" practices in European companies. In contrast to the U.S. firms, working hours in these European firms did not escalate and, when they did, workers experienced protest from friends and family that caused the short bursts of overwork to level out and kept in check worker over-identification with work.

These findings, too, support Marcus's (1995) contention that the practices that happen in one site are really part of and structured by an overall lifeworld (Habermas, 1981) or cultural background (Dreyfus, 1999) of circulating meanings that the ethnographer has to discover empirically, rendering the traditional single-site approach deficient. However, the notion of the lifeworld also suggests, and the international example demonstrates, that one cannot merely follow one dimension, such as a metaphor or trope, because the elements of a lifeworld are mutually constituted. The meaning that one circulating cultural object has, such as the "results only" practice, depends on the other cultural objects into which it becomes embedded, such as the distinct culturally shaped work ethics. Persons are often the nexus at which this embedding takes place, as they enroll these resources in action, pointing toward the need for a "follow the person" multi-site strategy.

Moreover, the very notion of a lifeworld or cultural background implies that it is transparent to participants, which means that they cannot self-report on it. The U.S. participants did not understand that and why a practice that was designed to make them work less contributed to making them work more because it became enrolled with a culturally circulating respect for hard work. Some have argued that multi-site research depends more on interviews (e.g., Hannertz, 2003), as compared to traditional ethnographies, for reasons related to practicality. Yet the above logic suggests that interviews by themselves may be ineffective for getting at precisely those elements that multi-site work wishes to discover.

This deficiency became even more apparent during the later stages of my research, when some bankers left organizations altogether, forced by debilitating breakdowns, and embarked on a radical self-transformation for which I had no baseline through immersion and little attunement based on my own experiences, requiring me to experiment with additional and different types of immersion, namely auto-ethnography.

*Auto-ethnography.* Induced by sustained overwork, bankers experienced breakdowns soon after they had joined the new organizations that, for some, were debilitating, requiring them to stop working for a prolonged period of time. Because their illnesses were caused by a combination of stress and body suppression, bankers took up physical activity to heal. As their prolonged, forced absence made them outsiders to the professional organization-based work culture, they experimented with new ways of working and living, finding that their bodies functioned differently, compared to before and compared to the cultural norm. Bringing to physical activity their socialized ambition, problem-solving ability, and the financial resources they had secured through high-powered careers, individuals who had never considered themselves athletically capable became very good at demanding sports, such as marathons, mixed martial arts, mountaineering, and iron man races. Also, they did so relatively late in life, when we culturally expect people to decline physically, not boom; the bankers experienced this development as "aging backwards."

Again, the bankers were merely exhibiting a trend that can also be observed in society as a whole. For example, in such challenging sports as marathons, participants in their fifties and older constitute the fastest growing category (Helliker, 2012). This trend is culturally new because it depends on relatively recent affordances, such as new training and recovery technologies and the ability of knowledge workers to work independently, charging enough to get by on a radically reduced and flexible work schedule.

This example again demonstrates the mutual constitution of person and cultural context. With different cultural affordances, personhood manifests differently, down to the biological level. No other research approach besides ethnography has the theoretical commitment and methodologies to study this type of co-evolution of person and culture. The example also shows the importance of following the person. One can observe all the individual elements of this pattern – the new technology, the fact that affluent people in their forties and older become elite athletes, and such socially circulating categories as "Four-hour work week" – without understanding why only some of the people who could live like this and would benefit from living like this make use of these affordances.

Briefly, similar to what I found when the bankers were still at the banks, people do not discover opportunities for freeing themselves from destructive conditioning unless their biology forces them to, through breakdowns that force them to become cultural outsiders. This is another new and important affordance of ethnography in the context of contemporary knowledge-based organizations, as compared to cultural anthropology: Because organizational socialization can be as comprehensive as that of native cultures, but with shorter cycles, one sometimes has the opportunity to examine not only the cultural shaping of the person, but also how people can transcend (some of) it, not through will and reflection, but by becoming enrolled into a different set of cultural affordances.

Like the cultural objects that it examines, the practice of immersion functions differently in different contexts. In our contemporary knowledge-based society, the researcher can capitalize on the historically relatively new similarity between ethnographer and informant, for example, by choosing observant participation or auto-ethnography over the traditional participant observation, as I did for these later aspects of my work. Specifically, I sought out similar experiences to my informants, in addition to observing and interviewing. I did not aim to write a "confessional tale" (Van Maanen and Kolb, 1985), but I used myself as an informant to whom I had privileged access, writing down fieldnotes about my personal experiences, tacking back and forth between my and the bankers' experiences. In contrast to traditional auto-ethnographies (e.g., Ellis et al., 2011), my experience was merely an analytic tool for understanding what was socially shared. Through my training, I could access my own experiences better than my informants could theirs.

This illustrates another powerful attribute of ethnography in our contemporary society, namely the researcher's purposeful and potentially socially beneficial self-transformation through immersion. When Malinowski's diary was published after his death (1967), it showed that even though he learned how to behave like his informants, he kept experiencing them as different and inferior. In contrast, I immersed myself in life choices that I admired, such as the attempt to generate excellence in both knowledge work and athletics. Moreover, different from the forms of life in peculiar subcultures and exotic cultures, these life choices are also accessible and potentially beneficial for many others. Ethnography thus opens up a qualitatively different way for people, including researcher and readers, to transform themselves radically, not only from the inside out, through reflection, but from the outside in, by guiding people to participate in those social contexts that are likely to transform them positively.

# References

Bittner, E. 1973. Objectivity and realism in sociology. In G. Psathas (ed.), *Phenomenological Sociology* (pp. 109–125). New York: Wiley.

BlueSteps. 2013. How long is a senior-level executive's tenure? Online at www.bluesteps.com/blog/how-long-executive-tenure-infographic.aspx. Accessed April 24, 2017.

Bourdieu, P. 1977. *The Logic of Practice*. Stanford, CA: Stanford University Press.

Clifford, J. and G. E. Marcus (eds.) 1986. *Writing Culture: The Poetics and Politics of Ethnography*. Berkeley, CA: University of California Press.

Coser, L. 1967. Greedy organizations. *European Journal of Sociology*, 8: 196–215.

Davenport, T. H. 2005. *Thinking for a Living*. Boston, MA: Harvard Business School Press.

Dilthey, W. 1914. *Weltanschauung und Analyse des Menschen seit Renaissance und Reformation*. Gesammelte Schriften, vol. 2. Stuttgart: B.G. Teubner.

Dreyfus, H. L. 1999. *Being-in-the-World*. Cambridge, MA: MIT Press.

Eagleton, T. 1983. *Literary Theory: An Introduction*. London: Verso.

Ekman, P. 1999. Basic emotions. In T. Dalgleisch and M. Power (eds.), *Handbook of Cognition and Emotions* (pp. 45–60). Chichester: Wiley.

Ellis, C. T., E. Adams, and A. P. Bochner. 2011. Autoethnography: An overview. *Forum Qualitative Sozialforschung*, 12(1): 273–390.

Emerson, R. M., R. I. Fretz, and L. L. Shaw. 1995. *Writing Ethnographic Fieldnotes*. Chicago, IL: University of Chicago Press.

Evans-Pritchard, E. E. 1951. *Social Anthropology*. London: Cohen & West.

Falzon, M. A. (ed.) 2009. *Multi-Sited Ethnography: Theory, Praxis, and Locality in Contemporary Research*. Farnham, Surrey: Ashgate.

Faubion, J. D. 2001. Currents of cultural fieldwork. In P. Atkinson, A. Coffey, S. Delamont, J. Lofland, and L. Lofland (eds.), *Handbook of Ethnography* (pp. 39–59). London: Sage.

Fox, N. F. 2003. *The New Sartre: Explorations in Postmodernism*. New York: Continuum.

Geertz, C. 1976. From the native's point of view: On the nature of anthropological understanding. In P. Rabinow and W. M. Sullivan (eds.), *Interpretive Social Science: A Reader* (pp. 225–241). Berkeley, CA: University of California Press.

Geertz, C. 1988. *Work and Lives: The Anthropologist as Author*. Stanford, CA: Stanford University Press.

Giddens, A. 1984. *The Constitution of Society*. Berkeley, CA: University of California Press.

Goffman, E. 1961. *Asylums: Essays on the Social Situation of Mental Patients and Other Inmates*. Garden City, NY: Doubleday.

Green, J. and D. Bloome. 1997. Ethnography and ethnographers of and in education: A situated perspective. In J. Flood, S. B Heath, and D. Lapp (eds.), *A Handbook for Literacy Educators: Research on Teaching the Communicative and Visual Arts* (pp. 1–12). New York: Macmillan.

Habermas, J. 1981. *The Theory of Communicative Action*. London: Beacon Press.

Hannertz, U. 2003. Being there … and there … and there! Reflections on multi-site ethnography. *Ethnography*, 4: 201–216.

Helliker, K. 2012. Marathon runners stop aging out of the race. *Wall Street Journal*. October, 30. Life and Style Section: 1.

Hine, C. 2000. *Virtual Ethnography*. London: Sage.

Howard, P. N. 2002. Network ethnography and the hypermedia organization: New media, new organizations, new methods. *New Media Society*, 4: 550–574.

Kenway, J. 2015. Ethnography "is not what it used to be." Rethinking space, time, mobility, and multiplicity. In S. Bollig, M.-S. Honig, S. Neumann, and C. Seele (eds.), *MultiPluriTrans in Educational*

*Ethnography: Approaching the Multimodality, Plurality and Translocality of Educational Realities* (pp. 37–56). Bielefeld: Transcript.

Kozinets, R. V. 1998. On netnography: Initial reflections on consumer research investigations of cyberculture. In J. Alba and W. Hutchinson (eds.) *Advances in Consumer Research* (pp. 366–371). Provo: UT: Association for Consumer Research.

Latour, B. 2005. *Reassembling the Social: An Introduction to Actor-Network Theory*. Oxford: Oxford University Press.

Lave, J. 2003. The practice of learning. In S. Chaiklin and J. Lave (eds.), *Understanding Practice: Perspectives on Activity and Context* (pp. 3–34). New York: Cambridge University Press.

Levi-Strauss, C. 1966. *The Savage Mind*. Chicago, IL: University of Chicago Press.

McDonald, D. 2013. *The Firm: The Story of McKinsey and Its Secret Influence on American Business*. New York: Simon and Schuster.

Malinowski, B. 1922. *Argonauts of the Western Pacific*. New York: Dutton.

Malinowski, B. 1967. *A Diary in the Strictest Sense of the Term*. London: Routledge and Kegan Paul.

Marcus, G. E. 1994. After the critique of ethnography: Faith, hope, and charity, but the greatest of these is charity. In R. Borofsky (ed.), *Assessing Cultural Anthropology* (pp. 40–53). New York: McGraw-Hill Humanities. Social Sciences and World Languages.

Marcus, G. E. 1995. Ethnography in/of the world system: The emergence of multi-sited ethnography. *Annual Review of Anthropology*, 24: 95–117.

Marcus, G. E. 1997. The uses of complicity in the changing mise-en-scene of anthropological fieldwork. *Representations*, 59: 85–108.

Marcus, G. E. and M. Fischer (eds.) 1986. *Anthropology as Cultural Critique: An Experimental Moment in the Human Sciences*. Chicago, IL: University of Chicago Press.

Michel, A. A. 2014. Participation and self-entrapment: A 12-year ethnography of Wall Street participation practices' diffusion and evolving consequences. *The Sociological Quarterly*, 55: 514–536.

Michel, A. A. and S. E. F. Wortham. 2009. *Bullish on Uncertainty: How Organizational Cultures Transform Their Participants*. Oxford: Oxford University Press.

Nisbett, R. E., K. Peng, I. Choi, and A. Norenzayan. 2001. Culture and systems of thought: Holistic vs. analytic cognition. *Psychological Review*, 108: 291–310.

Ortner, S. 2006. *Anthropology and Social Theory: Culture, Power, and the Acting Subject*. Durham, NC: Duke University Press.

Padavic, I., R. J. Ely, and E. Reid. 2013. The work-family narrative as a social defense. *Gender and Work: Challenging Conventional Wisdom*. Harvard Business School. Online at www.hbs.edu/faculty/conferences/2013-w50-research-symposium/Documents/Gender_and_work_web_update2015.pdf.

Perlow, L. A. 1999. The time famine: Toward a sociology of work time. *Administrative Science Quarterly*, 44(1): 57–81.

Perlow, L. A. and J. L. Porter. 2009. Making time off predictable – and required. *Harvard Business Review*, 87(10): 102–109.

Quora. 2013. Why are employees loyal to McKinsey? Online at www.quora.com/Why-are-employees-loyal-to-McKinsey. Accessed April 24, 2017.

Rosaldo, M. 1980. *Knowledge and Passion*. Cambridge: Cambridge University Press.

Scott, W. R. 2008. Approaching adulthood: The maturing of institutional theory. *Theory and Society*, 37: 427–442.

Van Maanen, J. 2006. Ethnography then and now. *Qualitative Research in Organizations*, 1(1): 13–21.

Van Maanen, J. and D. Kolb. 1985. The professional apprentice: Observations on fieldwork roles in two organizational settings. In S. B. Bacharach and S. M. Mitchell (eds.), *Research in the Sociology of Organizations* (pp. 1–33). Greenwich, CT: JAI Press.

Vidich, A. J. and S. M. Lyman. 2000. Qualitative methods: Their history in sociology and anthropology. In N. K. Denzin and Y. S. Lincoln (eds.), *Handbook of Qualitative Research* (2nd edition) (pp. 37–84). Thousand Oaks, CA: Sage.

Wertsch, J. V. 1991. A sociocultural approach to socially shared cognition. In L. B. Resnick, J. M. Levine, and S. D. Teasley (eds.), *Perspectives on Socially Shared Cognition* (pp. 85–100). Washington, DC: American Psychological Association.

Winch, P. 1956. Social science. *The British Journal of Sociology*, 7(1): 18–33.

Ybema, S., D. Yanow, H. Wels, and F. Kamsteeg. 2009. Studying everyday organizational life. In S. Ybema, D. Yanow, H. Wels, and F. Kamsteeg (eds.), *Organizational Ethnography: Studying the Complexities of Everyday Life* (pp. 1–21). Los Angeles, CA: Sage.

# 12

# ETHNOGRAPHY AS WRITING

## How Creative Nonfiction Can Inspire Organizational Ethnographers

*Chahrazad Abdallah*

> A text must do more than awaken moral sensibilities. It must move the other and the self to action. Ethnography's future can only be written against the history of a radical democratic project that intends humane transformations in the public sphere.
>
> *(Denzin, 1997: xxi)*

In a postcolonial, post-industrial, and globalized world, in which conflict, inequality and climatic transformations are having unparalleled damaging consequences on the lives of the majority of humans on this planet, organizational scholars need to write ethnographic texts that commit to be useful means of experiencing the world for readers who are increasingly in need of engaged sensemaking. This chapter is rooted in an understanding of ethnography as an interpretive, critical, gendered, pragmatic, and ethical endeavor. It follows a long line of work in anthropology and sociology that considers writing not only to be a way of evocative representation but also a unique way of knowing, a method of inquiry conveying experiential and sensible knowledge (Denzin, 1997; Richardson, 2000a). How to write ethnographic texts to make them more vivid expressions of the researcher's lived experience in the field as well as more engaging symbolic texts with transformative potential is the aim of this chapter.

I will examine how creative nonfiction, defined as a literary movement, which uses some of the storytelling techniques of fiction to write about actual events, offers a new imaginative form of writing that provides narrative tools and techniques to make academic ethnographic writing less "flat, dry, and sometimes unbearably dull" (Van Maanen, 1988: 48). I argue in this chapter, following Narayan (2007), that creative nonfiction opens up a fertile ground to enrich ethnographic writing practice with more vivid and emotionally engaging texts. Attention to how ethnographic texts convince has been consistently called for during the past few years (Golden-Biddle and Locke, 1993; Jarzabkowski et al., 2014) but a need to enrich the narrative rather than just polish the arguments is critical. In this chapter, I will offer some suggestions as to how this can be done with the tools and techniques developed in creative nonfiction.

## Some Introductory Remarks on the Nature of Interpretive Ethnography

As a consequence of the "critical, interpretive, linguistic, feminist, and rhetorical turns" (Denzin, 1997: 3; Lather, 1993; Yanow and Schwartz-Shea, 2006) in social sciences, qualitative research in general and ethnography in particular face a number of challenges and crises (Prasad and Prasad, 2002a; Prasad, 2005). Two of the most important of these crises are a crisis in representation and a crisis in legitimation. The first crisis stems from the problem of representation within an objectivist and realist framework (a much debated issue in qualitative research – see Cunliffe (2011)) and the second one is related to the questioning of the "validity" of interpretive research. In this context therefore, there are continuous attacks on a practice of ethnography aimed at developing more experiential and sensible forms of knowledge. It is beyond the scope of this chapter to discuss these issues[1] although it is important to acknowledge their existence. Here, I proudly reaffirm an intellectual filiation with the work of a number of qualitative researchers that defend the development of and engagement with what Laurel Richardson termed "Creative Analytic Practice Ethnography" (or CAP ethnography) (Richardson, 2000a: 929). CAP ethnography[2] is both creative and analytic and is rooted in a conception of ethnography as both a scientific and aesthetic approach. For Richardson,

> Increasingly, ethnographers desire to write ethnography which is both scientific – in the sense of being true to a world known through the empirical senses – and literary – in the sense of expressing what one has learned through evocative writing techniques and form. More and more ways of representing ethnographic work emerge.
>
> *(2000b: 253)*

CAP ethnography is a way of producing academic texts that provide simultaneously a substantive contribution, a strong reflexive account, a subjective expression of a reality while demonstrating aesthetic qualities and hopefully a lasting impact on readers.

In a thought-provoking essay discussing the issue of representation in ethnographic writing, Humphreys and Watson (2009) for whom "ethnography is writing" (p. 40), show that ethnographic writing can take various forms ranging from what they call the "naive realistic" to the largely fictionalized. For them, writing ethnography is a craft and by no means a way of "telling the truth." Their contention with that last word comes from their Pragmatist understanding of representation that concerns mainly the attainment of an account that is "truer than other accounts to the extent to which it better informs human practices than do those other accounts" (p. 45). My aim in this chapter is, again, not to discuss matters of representation in ethnography, which have been rightly addressed at length elsewhere (Van Maanen, 1995), but to examine what Humphreys and Watson call a continuum of ethnographic writing form. I argue that despite a strong predominance in ethnographies of organizational phenomena of what Van Maanen (1988) termed "realist tales" (Cunliffe, 2015), there is a space, in fact, a need for other narrative forms of ethnographic writing that would provide richer, more engaged and more vivid accounts of "lived experience."

In recent years, despite an increased interest in ethnography in the field of organization studies, it appears that it is the use of *ethnographic approaches* – understood as a data collection technique relying mainly on observation – rather than ethnography – as the writing of lived experience aimed at understanding a particular "culture" – that is strongly prevalent (Bate, 1997; Cunliffe, 2015). In what follows, I first outline the main argument of the chapter for a defense of *ethnography as writing* by discussing its underlying articulations. I then introduce creative nonfiction as a literary movement that can provide a useful source of inspiration to aspiring or established organizational ethnographers in search of tools that can help them concretely improve their writing. I conclude the chapter with a discussion on the nature and impact of a renewed approach to ethnographic writing.

## Ethnography as a Translucent Method

Ethnography, or "the artful exploration of the human condition" (Brown and Thompson, 2013: 1155), is a method that "reflects a bedrock assumption held historically by fieldworkers that 'experience' underlies all understanding of social life" (Van Maanen, 1988: 3). It is

> a style of social science writing which draws upon the writer's close observation of and involvement with people in a particular social setting and relates the words spoken and the practices observed or experienced to the overall cultural framework within which they occurred.
>
> *(Watson, 2011: 206)*

Ethnography therefore *is* writing (Geertz, 1988; Humphreys and Watson, 2009). If ethnography is writing, then it is conveyed via a language (no matter which one – either the one chosen by the ethnographer or the one imposed on her by various institutional constraints[3]). According to Anderson (1987), language is never transparent; it is translucent. One cannot completely ignore the words but is always aware of them, of their sound, their "texture," what they invoke, what they convey. The experience of reading ethnography is also an experience of style. In Van Maanen's words, it is not possible to "erase the presence of and role played by emotion, presupposition, and artistry in ethnography" (1988: 12). Ethnography itself is therefore translucent. Readers can never go past the writing; the writing is what makes ethnography "truthful." Ethnography is a translucent method whose final aim is to convey meaning but which can never ignore the vessel on which this meaning travels.

In fact, ethnography is a "translucent" method on two levels: the first, just described, contends that one never just sees the words on the page; it is through these words that we get the meaning. Language is not a neutral medium, bridging us with the meanings we inscribe to something. It has a texture, it has a materiality to it; the words we choose convey certain meanings and make us "see" them in a particular way. The second level contends that if ethnography is representation of experience, then the writing can never be a "transparent" rendering of the researcher's experience. The way it is written is a "textured" evocation of that lived experience. In both cases, writing is what gives ethnographic accounts any relevance. In other words, issues of representation and legitimation might both be better addressed through better writing techniques.

Although as previously stated the aim of this chapter is not to discuss the idea of representation in ethnography and its corollary of "truthfulness" or "universal validity," there are a number of ideas that I would like to address here and that, in my opinion, constitute the theoretical bases for defending ethnography as a source of experiential, sensible, and subjective knowledge (the nature of that knowledge is also subject to debate as already mentioned but won't be the focus of this paper). The core argument here is that ethnography is not a realist exercise that can only rely on the ability of the ethnographer to lay her analytic insights on the page but an all-encompassing one that is aimed at conveying the "texture" of shared and lived experience. Ethnographic realism as the "approved genre within anthropology" (Marcus and Cushman, 1982: 29) – and by extension organization studies – is set aside for a more complex view of ethnography that is characterized by "the oddity of constructing texts ostensibly scientific out of experiences broadly biographical" (Geertz, 1988). The argument, which contends that ethnography is a translucent method that relies on writing to convey any sense of knowledge or understanding, has three main implications that are described here.

## There Is No Privileged Vantage Point for Observation and Therefore No "Truer," Detached, Neutral or "Objective" Representation in Ethnographic Accounts

*Tales of the Field*, Van Maanen's classic reflection on ethnography, was written as "a phenomenological war whoop declaring that there is no way of seeing hearing or representing the world of others that is absolutely universally valid or correct" (1988: 35).[4] With these strong words Van Maanen asserts a crucial point about the nature of ethnographic texts and their ultimate point. It is only by affirming that writing ethnography is a subjective and personal endeavor that the ethnographer can pay the attention that is due to how the writing provides a stronger sense of shared experience. To do so, talented ethnographers rely on various writing techniques that can be consciously or unconsciously (Humphreys et al., 2003) borrowed from other forms of writings around them. Their writing is more engaging and readers tend to naturally follow the "flow" of ideas and thoughts. For younger and less experienced ethnographers, writing is generally more challenging. They tend to struggle more to find a way to elegantly thread fieldwork, headwork, and textwork (Van Maanen, 2011).

## Ethnography Is about Developing Experiential Knowledge and Experiential Knowledge Is Personal and Subjective

Ethnography is an "interpretive craft" (Van Maanen, 2011: 219) and as such relies on the researcher's engagement with the phenomenon under examination to build a sense of understanding and to tentatively develop new knowledge. Ethnography is a profoundly personal endeavor that requires the researcher to immerse herself in a "culture" – with a distinctly small c nowadays as Van Maanen notes (2011: 218) – during a certain amount of time and to extract from it a form of narrative account that accurately represents her engagement with that culture. It is precisely in the "engagement with" that lays the source of any ethnographic insight rather than in the representation itself. Indeed, as stated earlier, forms of representations are numerous and are all a result of the subtle and complex chemistry of what the researcher does with the fieldwork and what the fieldwork has done to her. Knowledge rooted in shared experience is the result of a process of acquaintance, appropriation, assimilation, reinterpretation, and reflexivity and it is consequently distinctly personal. Once that premise is accepted, the focus should be removed from whether or not the ethnographic account is a representation of what "truly" happens in the field and move to the realization that if the researcher wants to be "truthful," then she must pay careful attention to how that engagement is conveyed in writing and with what descriptive power of evocation it is characterized.

## "Writing It" Is at the Heart of the Process and Improving the Writing Using Tools and Techniques from Nonfiction Can Be Liberating and Empowering

Since it is established that ethnography takes form in its writing, and that writing is a bricoleur's craft as well as an art form, it is thus possible to address style as an argument in and of itself (Anderson, 1987; Van Maanen, 1995). A sense of ethnographic style, contrary to what some may think, can be learned or at the very least practiced by relying on established literary tools and techniques developed by professional writers to improve their texts (on form and content).

In his very original *Aramis, or The Love of Technology*, Latour (1996) wonders about the "method" he should use to convey a sense of what he's seen and experienced while studying the demise and ultimate "killing" of Aramis, a Personal Rapid Transit (PRT) system in the Paris area. In the preface of the book, he interrogates himself on his writing choices:

> What genre could I choose to bring about this fusion of two so clearly separated universes, that of culture and that of technology, as well as the fusion of three entirely distinct literary genres – the novel, the bureaucratic dossier, and sociological commentary? … Everything in this book is true, but nothing in it will seem plausible, for the science and technology it relies upon remain controversial, open-ended.
>
> *(p. viii)*

He then goes on:

> Was I obliged to leave reality behind in order to inject a bit of emotion and poetry into austere subjects? On the contrary, I wanted to come close enough to reality so that scientific worlds could become once again what they had been: possible worlds in conflict that move and shape one another. Did I have to take certain liberties with reality? None whatsoever. But I had to restore freedom to all the realities involved before any one of them could succeed in unifying the others. The hybrid genre I have devised for a hybrid task is what I call scientifiction.

These long quotations show how an established social scientist cannot avoid the internal struggles of how to tell the story. Here, he comes up with his own hybrid form and arguably succeeds at it. Organizational ethnographers also face those dilemmas and are invited to continually reinvent their writing and ultimately their understanding of the world.

In what follows, I focus on creative nonfiction as a source of inspiration and support for organizational ethnographers who want to contribute to the "hybridization" of their academic writing to make it more lively, engaging, and powerful. I offer here that the use of creative nonfiction techniques as well as poetry, drama, performance text, or any other form of writing innovations will ultimately allow the field to experience a meaningful renewal.

## Creative Nonfiction or "Not Writing Straight"[5]

Creative nonfiction is a literary movement that uses storytelling techniques of fiction to write about actual events. According to Cheney (2001: 2) "creative nonfiction writers inform their readers by making the reading experience vivid, emotionally compelling, and enjoyable while sticking to the facts." Whereas I would dispute that there are such a thing as "facts" that can be unequivocally translated on a page and that the process of recording those "facts" is closer to what Geertz (1988) calls "faction" (collapsing fact and fiction within the same word), I would like to suggest that the set of literary tools and techniques developed in creative nonfiction can be of great help to ethnographers.

Creative nonfiction as a literary movement was initially coined "new journalism" in a seminal anthology edited in part by Tom Wolfe (Wolfe and Johnson, 1973) and further described as literary journalism, narrative journalism, long-form journalism, or, more recently, "new new journalism" (Boynton, 2005). This literary movement, rooted in a steady evolution of journalistic writing and a parallel reflection on the role of journalists and their responsibilities (Malcolm, 1990), offers an interesting and varied range of nonfiction writing practices that have steadily received critical acclaim as well as various prestigious journalism prizes (McPhee, 2000; Wright, 2006). Creative nonfiction has been discussed in a number of academic texts as a potential source of insight for organizational ethnographers (Van Maanen, 1988; Agar, 1995; Denzin, 1997). Agar (1995) for instance, declared that

> the new creative nonfiction writers despite their many differences, shared a new writing program – to blend the factual content and fiction form, to play the roles of both observer/reporter and tentmaker, to commit equally to artistic and empirical truth, and to research fact not as an end in itself but as a means to art.
>
> *(p. 117)*

The debate around the use of the term "creative" in academic writing is not the focus of this paper but it needs to be acknowledged and recognized since it generates considerable discomfort in academic circles where notions of "facts," "objectivity," or "methodological neutrality" are still held in an undisputed esteem. Here, and following the argument stated above about ethnography as subjective, experiential writing of culture(s), I tend to find, just like the writer Teju Cole, "the stern distinction between fiction and nonfiction odd … everything is a combination of what's observed, what's imagined, what's overheard, and what's been done before" (2014: 127). It is *narrated experience* that constitutes the heart of ethnographic writing and that narrated experience can take many forms and blur a number of boundaries between what is seen, what is recollected, what is implied, what is inferred, referred to, or even understood in the field. The creation of a unique space of narrative is what creative nonfiction techniques can help researchers with. The written text, whether we label it "creative" or "realist," is always the result of authorial will and framing.

The principles of creative nonfiction writing are particularly relevant to the "new," interpretive ethnography (Goodall, 2000) in that they suggest a more hybrid approach to narration in which writing genres are blurred and multiple narrative strategies are deployed. As a principle, creative nonfiction is based on a "show rather than tell" positioning despite giving authorial presence a considerable place. It is therefore not a question of "killing the author" but rather a matter of how, by acknowledging the author, we recognize the criticality of the engagement of this author with the field in the ultimate conveying of meaning and experience. Creative nonfiction as a literary movement has consistently engaged with wider issues in society, has refused a totaling reading of reality and, has constituted an extremely rich source of knowledge on contemporary society in the U.S. and the rest of the world (for a rich bibliography, see Boynton, 2005).

As previously discussed, various forms of organizational ethnographic writing exist: from realist, detached and dry accounts to more evocative ones, more engaging and closer to the fiction genre (it is interesting to note that a number of anthropologists, most notably, Barley (2000) are also fiction writers). The use of literary techniques borrowed from creative nonfiction can greatly help to develop more lively, intellectually stimulating, and thought-provoking forms of writing organizations. I will address in what follows the various techniques and tools that can be borrowed from creative nonfiction to contribute to renewing organizational ethnographic writing.

## "Tools of the Trade": How Creative Nonfiction Techniques Can Inspire Organizational Ethnographers

Academic writing has been at the center of the attention of a number of scholars in recent years (Colyar, 2009; Rhodes, 2009; Sword, 2012; Cloutier, 2016). The importance of writing style and its consequences on the research process and on the researcher herself is now recognized as critical. Yet, despite numerous calls to pay closer attention to the writing itself, the field of organization studies is still dominated by certain forms of methodologically driven writing templates (Langley and Abdallah, 2011) that contribute to the highly formulaic nature of the writing. Ethnographic texts are not immune to this and tend to be based on dry descriptions of systematic observations of meetings rather than more vivid accounts of an engagement with the field.

In nonfiction writing, however, the focus is strongly directed to descriptive evocative narratives of the field. Characters are described densely, alternative points of views are used to assert the writer's voice, and there are variously deployed narrative strategies. Facts are always considered to be social constructions and therefore always described from multiple angles. Facts are consequently not the basic unit of analysis, yet scenes or situations are. Blurring the lines of "genre" writing is also frequent. Moreover, the presence of a narrative arc is critical. In ethnography this would be akin to identifying the outline of the ethnographic account or its structure. Writing of that kind often relies on three general writing techniques mainly borrowed from social realist novels like those by Balzac, Gogol, Dickens, or Melville.[6] We present these techniques in what follows and identify some helpful writing "tips" for ethnographers.

## *Scene-by-Scene Construction*

A "scene" is based on a unity of time and place. The scene is a constitutive element of the narrative. It is usually manifested in a paragraph (or more) but its main role is to put the reader *into* the narrative. In ethnography, it provides a way of immersing the reader in a chosen "episode" and enabling her to be as close to the experiential accounts as possible. Scene selection is therefore critical to the unfolding of the narrative. In his book on writing, Hart (2011) suggests thinking of scenes as one would when developing a storyboard in filmmaking. The narrative is elaborated from the succession of scenes that ground the story from one "unity" to another.

Using scene-by-scene construction relies on very detailed descriptions of people, locations, interactions, and material surroundings. Descriptions must be clear and compelling and must offer an "image" of what is going on. Thinking visually of a scene is one of the techniques that has been repeatedly suggested to nonfiction writers (Hart, 2011). A scene is a location, a moment, a mood. The following excerpt from Michael Herr's (1977) *Dispatches* is a powerful illustration:

> I see a road. It is full of ruts made by truck and jeep tires, but in the passing rain they never harden, and along the road there is a two-dollar piece of tissue, a poncho which had just been used to cover a dead Marine, a blood-puddled, mud-wet poncho going stiff in the wind. It has reared up there by the road in a horrible, streaked ball. The wind doesn't move it, only setting the pools of water and blood in the dents shimmering. I'm walking along this road with two black Grunts, and one of them gives the poncho a vicious, helpless kick. "Go easy, man," the other one says, nothing changing in his face, not even looking back. "That's the American flag you gettin' your foot into."

For each scene, it is important to have a spatial reference point prior to an action reference point. The spatial reference point can be described in details using precise qualifiers or, symbolically, using metaphors, comparisons or even allusions. That process is what is usually referred to as "setting the scene." Actions can then be described (movements, dialogues, decisions) and woven into the spatiality of the scene. Social cues can help ground the action in its spatiality and provide very pertinent elements to get a sense of the lived experience of the ethnographer.

There is no need to describe people too precisely (unless this is what the ethnography examines) but certain critical elements can be extremely useful indicators of the social status or mental state of a participant. For instance, in her beautiful essay "On keeping a notebook," Joan Didion (1968) describes a woman's conversation with a cat ("she is talking, pointedly, not to the man beside her but to a cat lying in the triangle of sunlight cast through the open door") and her attire (plaid silk dress from Peck & Peck) and ends the paragraph with "the hem is coming down." That single descriptive element is surprising and unexpected but also a powerful cue about the state of mind of the woman in the silk dress. A strong attention to social manners, material surroundings, décor, details of clothing, furniture, gestures, voice changes, facial expressions, and mannerisms are key elements in the construction of a scene and end up forming the thread of the narrative.

The use of "narrative summaries" is also a helpful part of scene-by-scene construction and provides a nice way to keep the reader on track. They are used as an effective transitioning tool between scenes and help maintain the rhythm of the narrative. Constructing the narrative as a succession of scenes enables the ethnographer to develop that rhythm and choose its variations: sometimes, rhythm itself can be a major element of the completed narrative and give its own kind of account of the context. Depending on where the ethnography takes place, thinking of the rhythm of the scenes is also part of conveying a sense of the "texture" of the context itself. Good scenes contain narrative turns, dramatic tensions, paradoxes, irony, flashbacks or flash-forwards, narrative juxtapositions, and action. These various techniques can be used by organizational ethnographers to catch the attention of their readers and get them to dive into the narrative. Flash-forwards or foreshadowing techniques enable ethnographers to integrate the wider structure of the narrative within the writing itself and to "prepare" their readers for what's next. Consider this excerpt from Kessel (1954): "I only thought of sleeping. But I couldn't breathe under the mosquito nest. The room itself oppressed me with its huge sign: *Make sure you close the door*. I went outside to get some air" (my translation). In this passage, using a classic foreshadowing technique, the writer gets the reader only to think of one thing: what will happen when (not if) the narrator doesn't close the door. The passage grips readers' imagination and makes them want to read further in the text. In fact, it transforms the nature of the narrative into a much more engaging and enjoyable one.

If then, the ultimate "measure" of an ethnography's effectiveness is to get the reader to "be there" (Geertz, 1988), the construction and interlacing of scenes is a strong means to convey that sense of recognition and closeness. Being there is not the easiest thing to convey and despite numerous efforts, some more successful than others, organizational ethnographers would certainly benefit from a more vivid depiction of context and a more engaging narrative.

## *Dense Characterization*

The word "character" is strongly associated to fiction for most readers and less adventurous ethnographers could feel a certain discomfort with it. In nonfiction writing, character is critical to the unfolding of the narrative. In fact, characters make the narrative. Characters can take various forms in organizational ethnography; they can be people but also objects, relationships, or places. For instance, London, Paris, Berlin, and Los Angeles are characters in Garrett's (2013) exploration of hidden and secret urban spaces in contemporary metropolises, as is "Aramis," the PRT system, in Latour's (1996) *Aramis, or The Love of Technology*.

Character is often a key to the reader's interest. The ultimate goal is to develop characters to make them appear more "rounded" and less "flat." Burroway (1987) distinguishes these two types thus: "a flat character is one who has only one distinctive characteristic, exists only to exhibit that characteristic, and is incapable of varying from that characteristic. A round character is many faceted and capable of change." Good descriptions of characters are so effective that even within a restricted space, the writer can convey a lot of what a person is about. Consider for example, this brief passage from the Pulitzer-winning article *Una Vida mejor – A Better Life*, by journalist Anna Hull, published in the *Saint Petersburg Times* on May 9, 1999:

> She was 35, barely 5-feet tall in her sandals. Her pans of Tamales had gradually found their way to her hips. For a mother of eight, she was unusually mild-mannered. A hen would fall asleep in her hand as she drew the hatchet back to chop its neck.

Another good example is the following description by journalist Gay Talese (2015) of Frank Sinatra in a hotel bar

> Frank Sinatra, holding a glass of bourbon in one hand and a cigarette in the other, stood in a dark corner of the bar between two attractive but fading blondes who sat waiting for him to say something. But he said nothing; he had been silent during much of the evening, except now in this private club in Beverly Hills he seemed even more distant, staring out through the smoke and semidarkness into a large room beyond the bar where dozens of young couples sat huddled around small tables or twisted in the center of the floor to the clamorous clang of folk-rock music blaring from the stereo. The two blondes knew, as did Sinatra's four male friends who stood nearby, that it was a bad idea to force conversation upon him when he was in this mood of sullen silence, a mood that had hardly been uncommon during this first week of November, a month before his fiftieth birthday.

In ethnography, choice of character is key and again, does not have to be linked to particular people but more accurately to "actants" of the story to use a word borrowed from actor-network theory. As discussed, Latour's (1996) work is a perfect example of a hybridized ethnographic account that chooses to focus on very original "characters." Ultimately, it is characterization that constitutes an important process. It can be direct – a preferred form, more based on "thick" description – or indirect – via commentary or notes on character that may unfortunately convey, as a side effect, a sense of omnipotence of the narrator (Burroway, 1987).

Dense characterization is the closest nonfiction gets to the idea of "thick" description initially suggested by Geertz. Despite its ubiquity in written research accounts, thick description is often replaced in organizational ethnography by what Bate (1997), citing Wolcott (1995), calls "quick description." For him, ethnographic accounts end up being "yet another business case study or company history, a pale reflection of the 'experientially rich social science' envisaged by early writers like Agar (1980)." Thick description supposes a deep delving into the particulars in order to convey a more vivid sense of the context. Dense characterization is a thick description of the main "characters" chosen to be at the heart of the narrative, be they humans or not.

## *Voice and Style*

A central writing device in ethnography for Geertz (1988) is the construction of an authorial persona. Following the classic interrogations set up by Clifford (1983) on "how, precisely, is a garrulous, over determined, cross cultural encounter shot through with power relations …, composed by an individual author," anthropologists and more recently, organization ethnographers (Watson, 2011) have continued to struggle with these issues (Prasad and Prasad, 2002b).

For Clifford, one possible answer to his interrogation is a coherent presentation of an experiential, interpretive, dialogical and polyphonic process and a controlling mode of authority where the author is ultimately making a "strategic choice" (1983: 142) as to how the narrative accounts will take shape.

Voice attracts and holds readers regardless of the topic but voice is a slippery concept. For Hart (2011) voice is simply "the personality of the writer as it emerges on the page" (p. 64). Despite it being profoundly personal, institutional voice is also an important player in the writing of ethnography. By institutional voice, I particularly think of the set of institutional arrangements that constrain and have historically shaped the writing of ethnography in academia. This is particularly the case for journal-length ethnographies that are left with very little creative space to let the voice of the author come through. In that regard, Kunda (2013: 21) regrets that he has

> continuously noted and wondered about the extent researchers in the early stages of their careers, and graduate students in particular, feel, or are made to feel, that while they are granted the methodological license, and sometimes looseness of "qualitative methods" (a phrase that often replaces or refers to a watered down version of ethnography), the academic authority system (in terms of funding, supervision, publication requirements, and career options) compels them to limit their questions, choice of theory and writing style to those that enhance the chances of approval, funding and quick publication.

Despite these institutional constraints, it is still possible to have a voice if a number of elements are addressed: how much of themselves do ethnographers put into their writing? How controlled is the ethnographic written account? How willing are ethnographers to shift the boundaries of the field in their academic writing? All these questions need not be addressed at once but should be considered carefully by every ethnographer who wants to offer richer, more vivid and more engaging accounts of their fieldwork.

Mark de Rond's *The Last Amateurs* (2009) is a case in point. It is based on a one-year-long ethnography of the Cambridge rowing team, preparing for their annual boat race against Oxford. In his deeply personal account, he conveys the fears and the challenges faced by high performance teams while reflecting on issues of masculinity and identity. In this book, De Rond challenges his body whilst reflexively acknowledging its role in his ethnography: from a fascination with the athletes in the beginning of his fieldwork – which makes him aware of his physical limitations – to the daily contact with highly trained, testosterone-laden athletes and their ease with their own bodies which makes him highly self-conscious. The epic victory in the end eventually reconciles him with his own limitations and his own insecurities. This book-length ethnography enabled him to vividly convey these emotions and reflections through the use of precise scene descriptions and a distinctly personal voice.

Defending the importance of the ethnographer's voice in ethnographic writing does not preclude taking into account the multiplicity of voices from the field (research-setting voices as well as academic ones). Conveying the polyphony of the field is critical, yet it needs to be channeled via the voice of the ethnographer whose point of view should by no means be the ultimate reference point but should set the tone of the narrative. Narrative style is part of voice and is also important to consider. Voice and style can be a worry for young researchers in search of themselves and can arguably be less critical a few years down the line when experience and time have considerably lessened the ethnographer's anxieties. Nevertheless, to pay attention to voice, tone, and style is crucial in writing. Hart (2011) suggests that the more relaxed and fast-paced the writing, the clearer the voice. While not easy at first, free-writing first drafts can considerably help ethnographers to find their voice.

In the field of organization studies for instance, writers like James March, Karl Weick or Henry Mintzberg have very distinctive personal voices that are highly recognizable and that have been inspirational to many scholars of the field (Van Maanen, 1995). Indeed, Van Maanen urges organizational researchers to be more inspired by the writing of Weick, which is more literary, less formulaic, and much more engaging than the vast majority of what is published in the field (for an illustration, see Weick, 1993).

## Shifting the Boundaries of Ethnography: On Writing "New" Interpretive Texts

According to Bate (1997) there are four qualities to good ethnography. The first, expressiveness, is the "being there" quality or the ability to convey a sense of shared experience with the reader. It is entirely dependent on the writing, in fact, that quality is in the writing. Good examples are Kunda (1992) or Tracy Kidder's *The Soul of a New Machine* (1981). These texts are composed of rich descriptions of context and provide thoughtful analytical insights. The second quality is attention to detail. It is what Bate calls the mundanity or everydayness quality; what makes the reader delve into the text and build a rich imagery from it. Organizational ethnographers such as Barley (1983), for example, are good at conveying that sense of detail. The third quality to a good ethnography is an ability to convey plurality and polyphony. It is the ability to take multiple points of view into account and weave them together to form a rich narrative. A good example of that process, applied to an inherently pluralistic setting, is Fox's (1993) study of surgical ward rounds. Lastly, for an ethnography to be good, it needs to show insight, it needs to have a point and a punch line and prompt the reader to think. After all, isn't the main objective to contribute to developing more understanding and ultimately more knowledge?

Quality in ethnography is thus also a matter of taste. Some readers will favor accuracy, verisimilitude, or fidelity over evocativeness or aesthetic sense whilst others will want to get a strong sense of truthfulness to the shared experience. Good writing like good ethnography is not a matter of focus on one element or the other but more of a commitment to conveying experiential knowledge. In essence, "artful ethnography is evocative in addition to being factual and truthful"[7] (Van Maanen, 1988: 34) yet "ethnographic truths are partial, committed and incomplete" (Clifford, 1986: 103).

Whilst ethnographers need to acknowledge the boundaries of their "field of play" (Richardson, 1997) and the institutionalized standards of good ethnography (truthfulness, accuracy, authenticity) and whilst they need to be accountable to the people about whom they write and ultimately, to their readers by disclosing their writing process and the articulations of the ethnographic accounts (empirical and theoretical), it is still possible to play with these boundaries and creatively push them to make the writing more evocative of the richness of the field.

An important point needs to be made at this stage: The belief in the transformational potential of creative nonfiction techniques on the writing of organizational ethnographic accounts is in no way an invitation to "make things up." Creative nonfiction only implies here that creative license can be taken with the representational form of empirical data (Whiteman and Phillips, 2006) meaning that it is possible to represent the experience in different ways as opposed to the naïve belief in the possibility of "neutral" reporting of experienced phenomena. Using dialogue, scene and character descriptions or even choosing to focus on non-human characters is a powerful way of conveying a richer, deeper, more engaging account of experience leading to greater understanding and knowledge. The invention of situations is not advocated here.

However, a creative way of "displaying" ethnographic "data" or "telling the tale" is encouraged. For instance, Bazin (2011) condenses a six-month-long ethnography of a psychiatric hospital ward into a four-week "scenarized synthesis" (p. 5) in which he shows how the organizational practice of psychiatric diagnosis is institutionalized.

A number of "new," interpretive, and critical ethnographies were published in the wake of Clifford and Marcus's (1986) call to renew ethnographic writing in their seminal book, *Writing Culture*. As in anthropology and sociology, there was a marked interest within organization studies to develop the genre and try to convey subtler, more engaging accounts of organizational lives. Numerous studies are testament to this re-engagement with the field and to the need to consider much more carefully the wider historical and cultural context (Watson, 1994; Linstead, 1996; Morrill and Fine, 1997; Prasad and Prasad, 2002a; Kostera, 2007; Neyland, 2008). Organizational concepts such as control, identity, entrepreneurship, and strategy are increasingly studied using ethnographic approaches (Ahrens and Mollona, 2007; Humphreys and Brown, 2002; Bruni et al., 2004; Smets et al., 2015). Unfortunately, despite a plethora of new published papers, the writing seems not to have been considerably improved. In fact, it could be argued that because of the tougher institutional constraints that young researchers must face in contemporary university settings, the writing stiffened. It is time to pay a closer attention to it.

Despite the predominance in organizational research of the "realist" tale (Van Maanen, 1988; Cunliffe, 2015), I would like with this chapter to encourage students and young ethnographers to seriously consider other "tales." I do not advocate eliminating one tale for another (although I confess a personal preference) but I argue with Narayan (1999) that we need a multiplicity of narrative forms that inform one another when it comes to studying organizations. Using creative nonfiction writing techniques can inspire us to develop some of these multiple narrative forms and by the same token, to reinvent the writing of organizations. Focusing on writing more vivid ethnography that not only provides strong theoretical argumentative constructions but also engaging, appealing and compelling depictions of the "lives of others" is at the heart of this call. In times ridden with inequality and injustice, let's transform the "trained incapacities" (Burke, 1954) that make us see the world as determined by our theories of it into a strong, vivid, compelling, and critically engaged ability to write the world in its twisted beauty.

## Acknowledgment

I would like to thank Viviane Sergi for her insightful comments and continuous support during the writing of this chapter.

## Notes

1 Very good discussions are provided in Denzin (1997) and Richardson (2000a).
2 CAP ethnography includes different forms of ethnographic writings like auto-ethnography (Boyle and Parry, 2007), screenplay (Berbary, 2011), or performance texts (McCall, 2000). For a complete discussion, see Richardson (2000a).
3 For an interesting discussion about those constraints, see Kunda (2013).
4 For an insightful debate on the nature and transformations of ethnography and ethnographic research accounts and on a discussion of the "realist" position in qualitative research, see Denzin and Lincoln (1995).
5 This is borrowed from Weingarten's (2010) book, *The Gang That Wouldn't Write Straight: Wolfe, Thompson, Didion, Capote, and the New Journalism Revolution*.
6 Tolstoy also had a considerable influence. His later nonfiction writing in the early twentieth century and his masterpiece *War and Peace* have had a lasting impact on the literature (be it fictional or nonfictional) of the twentieth (and arguably twenty-first) century.

7 It is important to note here that ethnographers like John Van Maanen and Michael Agar, despite recognizing creative nonfiction's potential to improve narrative structures and writing practices generally, were also critical of it. See Van Maanen (1988: 128–132).

# References

Agar, M. (1980). *The Professional Stranger*. New York: Academic Press.

Agar, M. (1995). Literary journalism as ethnography: Exploring the excluded middle. In J. Van Maanen (ed.) *Representation in Ethnography*. Thousand Oaks, CA: Sage, 112–129.

Ahrens, T., and Mollona, M. (2007). Organisational control as cultural practice: A shop floor ethnography of a Sheffield steel mill. *Accounting, Organizations and Society*, 32(4): 305–331.

Anderson, C. (1987). *Style as Argument: Contemporary American Nonfiction*. Carbondale, IL: Southern Illinois University Press.

Barley, N. (2000). *The Innocent Anthropologist: Notes from a Mud Hut*. Long Grove, IL: Waveland Press.

Barley, S. (1983). Semiotics and the study of occupational and organizational cultures. *Administrative Science Quarterly*, 28(3): 393–413.

Bate, S. P. (1997). Whatever happened to organizational anthropology? A review of the field of organizational ethnography and anthropological studies. *Human Relations*, 50(9): 1147–1171.

Bazin, Y. (2011). *The Institutionalization of Organizational Practices: The Case of Psychiatric Diagnosis*. Ph.D. Thesis. Conservatoire National des Arts et Metiers (CNAM). Paris, France.

Berbary, L. A. (2011). Poststructural writerly representation: Screenplay as creative analytic practice. *Qualitative Inquiry*, 17(2): 186–196.

Boyle, M., and Parry, K. (2007). Telling the whole story: The case for organizational autoethnography. *Culture and Organization*, 13(3): 185–190.

Boynton, R. (2005). *The New New Journalism: Conversations with America's Best*. New York: Vintage.

Brown, A. D., and Thompson, E. R. (2013). A narrative approach to strategy-as-practice. *Business History*, 55(7): 1143–1167.

Bruni, A., Gherardi, S., and Poggio, B. (2004). Doing gender, doing entrepreneurship: An ethnographic account of intertwined practices. *Gender, Work & Organization*, 11(4): 406–429.

Burke, K. (1954). *Performance and Change*. Los Altos, CA: Hermes.

Burroway, J. (1987). *Writing Fiction: A Guide to Narrative Craft*. New York: Little, Brown.

Cheney, T. A. R. (2001). *Writing Creative Nonfiction: Fiction Techniques for Crafting Great Nonfiction*. Dordrecht: Springer Science and Business.

Clifford, J. (1983). On ethnographic authority. *Representations*, 2: 118–146.

Clifford, J. (1986). On ethnographic allegory. In J. Clifford and G. E. Marcus (eds.) *Writing Culture: The Poetics and Politics of Ethnography*. Berkeley, CA: University of California Press, 98–121.

Clifford, J., and Marcus, G. E. (1986). *Writing Culture: The Poetics and Politics of Ethnography: A School of American Research Advanced Seminar*. Berkeley, CA: University of California Press.

Cloutier, C. (2016). How I write an inquiry into the writing practices of academics. *Journal of Management Inquiry*, 25(1): 65–84.

Cole, T. (2014). Teju Cole by Aleksandar Hemon. *Artists in Conversation, BOMB Magazine*, 127.

Colyar, J. (2009). Becoming writing, becoming writers. *Qualitative Inquiry*, 15(2): 421–436.

Cunliffe, A. L. (2011). Crafting qualitative research: Morgan and Smircich 30 years on. *Organizational Research Methods*, 14(4): 647–673.

Cunliffe, A. L. (2015). Using ethnography in strategy-as-practice research. In D. Golsorkhi, L. Rouleau, D. Seidl and E. Vaara (eds.) *Handbook of Strategy as Practice*. 2nd edn. Cambridge: Cambridge University Press, 431–446.

De Rond, M. (2009). *The Last Amateurs: To Hell and Back with the Cambridge Boat Race Crew*. London: Icon Books.

Denzin, N. K. (1997). *Interpretive Ethnography: Ethnographic Practices for the 21st Century*. Thousand Oaks, CA: Sage.

Denzin, N. K., and Lincoln, Y. S. (1995). Transforming qualitative research methods: Is it a revolution? *Journal of Contemporary Ethnography*, 24(3): 349–358.

Didion, J. (1968). *Slouching towards Bethlehem*. New York: Macmillan.

Fox, N. J. (1993). Discourse, organisation and the surgical ward round. *Sociology of Health & Illness*, 15(1): 16–20.

Garrett, B. (2013). *Explore Everything: Place-hacking the City*. London: Verso Books.

Geertz, C. (1988). *Works and Lives: The Anthropologist as Author.* San Francisco, CA: Stanford University Press.

Golden-Biddle, K., and Locke, K. (1993). Appealing work: An investigation of how ethnographic texts convince. *Organization Science,* 4(4): 595–616.

Goodall Jr, H. L. (2000). *Writing the New Ethnography.* Walnut Creek, CA: AltaMira Press.

Hart, J. (2011). *Storycraft: The Complete Guide to Writing Narrative Nonfiction.* Chicago, IL: University of Chicago Press.

Herr, M. (1991[1977]). *Dispatches.* New York: Vintage.

Hull, A. (1999). Una vida mejor – A better life. *Saint Petersburg Times,* May 9, 1999.

Humphreys, M., and Brown, A. D. (2002). Narratives of organizational identity and identification: A case study of hegemony and resistance. *Organization Studies,* 23(3): 421–447.

Humphreys, M., and Watson, T. J. (2009). Ethnographic practices: From "writing-up ethnographic research" to "writing ethnography." In S. Ybema, D. Yanow, H. Wels and F. H. Kamsteeg (eds.) *Organizational Ethnography: Studying the Complexities of Everyday Life.* London: Sage, 40–55.

Humphreys, M., Brown, A. D., and Hatch, M. J. (2003). Is ethnography jazz? *Organization,* 10(1): 5–31.

Jarzabkowski, P., Bednarek, R., and Le, J. (2014). Producing persuasive findings: Demystifying ethnographic textwork in strategy and organization research. *Strategic Organization,* 12(4): 274–287.

Kessel, J. (1954). *La piste fauve.* Paris: Gallimard.

Kidder, T. (1981). *The Soul of a New Machine.* Boston, MA: Little, Brown.

Kostera, M. (2007). *Organizational Ethnography: Methods and Inspirations.* Lund: Studentlitteratur AB.

Kunda, G. (1992). *Engineering Culture: Control and Commitment in a High-tech Corporation.* Philadelphia, PA: Temple University Press.

Kunda, G. (2013). Reflections on becoming an ethnographer. *Journal of Organizational Ethnography,* 2(1): 4–22.

Langley, A., and Abdallah, C. (2011). Templates and turns in qualitative studies of strategy and management. *Research Methodology in Strategy and Management,* 6: 201–235.

Lather, P. (1993). Fertile obsession: Validity after poststructuralism. *Sociological Quarterly,* 34: 673–694.

Latour, B. (1996). *Aramis, or, The Love of Technology.* Cambridge, MA: Harvard University Press.

Linstead, S. (1996). Understanding management: Culture, critique and change. In S. Linstead, R. Grafton Small, and P. Jeffcutt (eds.) *Understanding Management.* London: Sage, 11–33.

McCall, M. M. (2000). Performance ethnography: A brief history and some advice. In N. K. Denzin and Y. S. Lincoln (eds.) *Handbook of Qualitative Research.* 2nd edn. Thousand Oaks, CA: Sage, 421–433.

McPhee, J. (2000). *Annals of the Former World.* New York: Macmillan.

Malcolm, J. (1990). *The Journalist and the Murderer.* New York: Vintage.

Marcus, G. E., and Cushman, D. (1982). Ethnographies as texts. *Annual Review of Anthropology,* 11(1): 25–69.

Morrill, C., and Fine, G. A. (1997). Ethnographic contributions to organizational sociology. *Sociological Methods & Research,* 25(4): 424–451.

Narayan, K. (1999). Ethnography and fiction: Where is the border? *Anthropology and Humanism,* 24(2): 134–147.

Narayan, K. (2007). Tools to shape texts: What creative nonfiction can offer ethnography. *Anthropology and Humanism,* 32(2): 130–144.

Neyland, D. (2008). *Organizational Ethnography.* London: Sage.

Prasad, P. (2005). *Crafting Qualitative Research: Working in the Postpositivist Traditions.* Armonk, NY: M. E. Sharpe.

Prasad, A., and Prasad, P. (2002a). The coming of age of interpretive organizational research. *Organizational Research Methods,* 5(1): 4–11.

Prasad, P., and Prasad, A. (2002b). Casting the native subject: Ethnographic practice and the (re)production of difference. In B. Czarniawska and H. Höpfl (eds.) *Casting the Other.* London: Routledge, 185–204.

Rhodes, C. (2009). After reflexivity: Ethics, freedom and the writing of organization studies. *Organization Studies,* 30(6): 653–672.

Richardson, L. (1997). *Fields of Play: Constructing an Academic Life.* New Brunswick, NJ: Rutgers University Press.

Richardson, L. (2000a). Writing: A method of inquiry. In N. K. Denzin and Y. S. Lincoln (eds.) *Handbook of Qualitative Research.* 2nd edn. Thousand Oaks, CA: Sage, 923–948.

Richardson, L. (2000b). Evaluating ethnography. *Qualitative Inquiry,* 6(2): 253–255.

Smets, M., Jarzabkowski, P., Burke, G. T., and Spee, P. (2015). Reinsurance trading in Lloyd's of London: Balancing conflicting-yet-complementary logics in practice. *Academy of Management Journal*, 58(3): 932–970.

Sword, H. (2012). *Stylish Academic Writing*. Boston, MA: Harvard University Press.

Talese, G. (2015). *Frank Sinatra Has a Cold*. Cologne: Taschen.

Van Maanen, J. (1988). *Tales of the Field: On Writing Ethnography*. Chicago, IL: University of Chicago Press.

Van Maanen, J. (1995). *Representation in Ethnography*. Thousand Oaks, CA: Sage.

Van Maanen, J. (2011). Ethnography as work: Some rules of engagement. *Journal of Management Studies*, 48(1), 218–234.

Watson, T. (1994). *In Search of Management: Culture, Chaos and Control in Managerial Work*. London: Routledge.

Watson, T. J. (2011). Ethnography, reality, and truth: The vital need for studies of "how things work" in organizations and management. *Journal of Management Studies*, 48(1): 202–217.

Weick, K. E. (1993). The collapse of sensemaking in organizations: The Mann Gulch disaster. *Administrative Science Quarterly*, 38: 628–652.

Weingarten, M. (2010). *The Gang That Wouldn't Write Straight: Wolfe, Thompson, Didion, Capote, and the New Journalism Revolution*. New York: Crown.

Whiteman, G., and Phillips, N. (2006). *The Role of Narrative Fiction and Semi-Fiction in Organizational Studies*. ERIM Report Series Research in Management. December.

Wolcott, H. F. (1995). Making a study "more" ethnographic. In J. Van Maanen (ed.) *Representation in Ethnography*. London: Sage, 57–73.

Wolfe, T., and Johnson, E. W. (1973). The new journalism. *The New Journalism: An Anthology*. New York: Harper and Row.

Wright, L. (2006). *The Looming Tower*. New York: Vintage.

Yanow, D., and Schwartz-Shea, P. (eds.) (2006). *Interpretation and Method: Empirical Research Methods and the Interpretive Turn*. Armonk, NY and London: M. E. Sharpe.

13

# ETHNOGRAPHIC IMAGES OF WORK

## Lessons from Journalism

*Jinia Mukerjee and Anca Metiu*

## Introduction

In the vast and eclectic field of organization studies, the mission of providing truthful and rich images of working people and of the work they do falls upon the shoulders of qualitative researchers, and especially on those of ethnographers. Images of work and workers are also common in journalistic accounts, albeit in a different form. In this chapter we provide a comparison between ethnography and journalism, identify their main similarities and differences, and provide suggestions about ways in which ethnographic reports of work can benefit from following several specific journalism practices.

Images of work that do justice to people's work lives have always been needed and consequential (Barley and Kunda, 2001). Scientific management (Taylor, 1911), the Hawthorne Studies (Roethlisberger and Dickson, 1939), practice theory (Orr, 1996; Bourdieu, 1977), were all predicated upon images of work provided by field researchers who took the time to describe and puzzle over the behaviors of people stooped over their wheelbarrows, work stations, agricultural fields, or copiers.

The recognition of these images' power to shape our understanding of work and organizations has increased over the past two decades. Barley and Kunda's (2001) strong call for truthful, nuanced images of work occurred at a time when several ethnographies were published and getting recognition. Barley and Kunda themselves, and their students were an influential group in this respect, as their work offered in-depth understandings of the dynamic interrelationship between roles, technologies, and organizing (Barley, 1986), of the types and patterns of managerial discourse (Barley and Kunda, 1992), of the knowledge transformation process needed for collaborations across occupational boundaries (Bechky, 2003), of the burnout associated with work heroics (Kunda, 1992). Ethnographies of work have enriched the understanding of identity (Kreiner et al., 2009; Elsbach and Kramer, 1996), routines (Feldman, 2000), innovative work (Dougherty, 1992, 2001; Hargadon and Sutton, 1997), worker resistance (Anteby, 2008), the use of communication technology by professionals (Mazmanian, 2013; Mazmanian et al., 2013) and much more. In terms of theoretical advancement and influence, such qualitative studies of work represent some of the most vibrant areas of organization studies.

Yet we can do better. For instance, emotions are an underlying dimension of most human activities; they form a large part of what goes on in organizations, and in people's minds and bodies while at work (Barsade and Gibson, 1998; Lazarus, 1991; Etzioni, 1988; Hochschild, 1975, 1979). Or, a lot of the studies of work are downplaying or downright ignoring this aspect. Understating the drama, attenuating the intensity of feelings, downplaying the absurdities and quirkiness observed while in the field, have become a way to make ethnographic work look more "scientific" and legitimate to the academic community. This is a loss, given the numerous outcomes, both organizational and individual, of emotions felt and expressed in organizations (Rafaeli and Sutton, 1989; Hochschild, 1979; Bandura, 1977).

Another realm that would benefit from more nuanced images of work are the new and rapidly evolving forms of work, such as distributed work within increasingly complex webs of collaborators, the infusion of technology in all types of work and contexts, and the rapid changes in the configuration of industries. Detailed accounts of these developments are needed if we want to accompany workers and employers in their quest for better and more meaningful work lives.

The larger economic and political context also needs to become more central in our accounts of work. The 2008 subprime crisis, the political tensions and refugee surges, the environmental threats, all affect people's work lives in ways that are barely understood. As Barley and Kunda (1992) argued, the boundaries around work organizations have always been porous – and this is not only in terms of alliances and inter-firm cooperation. Therefore, the studies of work will be richer when integrating the larger contextual aspects of people's entire lived experience as they have a bearing on their work and work practices. Studies of work–life boundaries and balance are useful; however, confining "life" to the sphere of the private and the family life is unrealistic: individuals dwell in much more than family life, their lives are interlaced with a myriad of larger contextual elements.

Journalism is one domain that is attuned to the lived experiences of people, to their emotions, to the nuances and changes in their lives. According to the American Press Institute, the goal of journalism is to "provide people with verified information they can use to make better decisions"; it is characterized by a series of practices, "the most important of which is a systematic process – a discipline of verification – that journalists use to find not just the facts, but also the 'truth about the facts'."[1] Journalism keeps us "informed of the changing events, issues, and characters in the world outside."[2] This attention to contextual changes, as well as journalism's ability to write both clearly and movingly, make journalism a good complement to qualitative research when it comes to providing work images that are truthful and rich.

A particular stream of journalism, "anthro-journalism," comes close to ethnography in its aim to produce in-depth reports that do justice to the complexity, subtlety, and emotional tones of human lives. Anthro-journalism has produced rich, truthful, and often moving accounts of welfare recipients (Susan Sheehan's "A welfare mother" in *The New Yorker*), drug users (Mike Sager's book *Stoned Again*), migrants (Isabel Wilkerson's book, *The Warmth of Other Suns*), nuclear war survivors (John Hersey's book, *Hiroshima*), to name just a few. Anthro-journalism achieves this through techniques that are partly similar to those of ethnography: long immersion in the field, multiple data sources, attunement to people's circumstances and feelings, and persuasive writing. It is these techniques of anthro-journalism than can enrich work ethnographers' toolkit.

## Journalism and Ethnography: Fraternal Twins?

Journalism and ethnography share the goal of providing truthful information about people and their worlds, as well as a main method – fieldwork involving interviews and observations, capturing life by "being there." In their endeavor to acquire a first-hand experience of what's going on, they observe, take notes, talk to people to understand the meaning they ascribe to their lives and their environment, witness routine behavior and happenstance, question and follow leads, listen patiently, rummage through documents and email records, try to get the backstory right, set the events against the larger context, sometimes make friends (and sometimes enemies), and then write up an account of what they saw and learned. In doing so, they learn quickly that their work is humbling, that they know little about the things that might have seemed obvious, that human beings often surprise, that details matter, that sensemaking comes through recording and not from judging (Harrington, 2003).

Skillful writing is central to both trades, as they only have words to inform and persuade. To achieve these ends, they build carefully constructed scenes, provide snippets of conversations and descriptions of nonverbal behavior, use rhetorical tools. While the quotes and vignettes from the field provide the reader with a sense of lived life, they also convey credibility: readers of both ethnography and journalism need to be convinced that the reports are not a personal opinion or interpretation, but a true depiction of characters and events.

Interpretation, of course, is never far. As Geertz (1973) says, ethnographic writings are "fictions, in the sense that they are 'sometimes made', 'sometimes fashioned' … not that they are false, unfactual or merely 'as if' thought experiments" (p. 15). Similarly, Van Maanen has remarked that "ethnographic data are constructions of other people's construction of what they and their counterparts say and do" (Van Maanen, 2011: 228). These assessments apply as well to journalism, which is also twice removed from the actual action. Journalists also interpret the data collected, but their fictions take the form of storytelling – and this is where the main difference between the two crafts lies.

While they share the main goal of providing truthful information, both crafts also have an additional task, as important as the first. Besides informing, journalism aims to change the readers' minds about people and events through storytelling – through the drama, conflict, and changes a particular set of characters undergo in particular circumstances. Ethnographers of work's other goal besides informing is to tell a theoretical story, to enter into a dialogue (and sometimes debate) with existing theory, and to explain how social theory should change on the basis of the reported findings. Ethnographic stories too have characters, change, and conflict, but these elements are in the service of a theoretically informed story.

## Storytelling versus Theoretical Contribution

The main difference in the types of stories written by journalists and ethnographers engenders several other distinctions. Thus, the two trades have different audiences. While journalistic writing can often boast a broad array of readers – ranging from fifth graders to students, managers, and politicians – ethnographic writing has a narrower audience, and often remains restricted to the academic community of scholarly skeptics.

To grab the attention of their broad readership, journalists rely on storytelling. They employ all the techniques that makes a story compelling – action, dialogues, descriptions, conflict or struggle, changes in the plot or drama; they infuse their stories with emotions, and utilize the narrative hook; they use direct, lucid language and poignant pictures that illustrate and impress. Emotional impact is often essential for a good piece of journalistic writing. As a journalist friend told us, "We need to grab the reader by the neck from the first word and keep him going, it has to be emotional; if not, it was not worth writing the piece in the first place" (Personal correspondence). Such writing not only urges engaged readership, but also has an impact on the way people think about the world in which they live. Remarkable examples include Carl Bernstein and Bob Woodward's reporting of the Watergate scandal in the realm of politics, and Barbara Ehrenreich's *Nickeled and Dimed: On (Not) Getting By in America* in the realm of work.

Ethnographers, on the other hand, are much less free in their reporting. While their writing is also rich in detail, it is often devoid of emotional appeal. The aim to produce a theoretical contribution makes the ethnographer interested in patterns and concepts, necessarily leaving less room for a tenacious focus on individuals and their unavoidable dramas and idiosyncrasies. Building a conflict, tracing characters' highs and lows, distilling a plot's twists, using a vivid narrative style all take second place to building a theoretical contribution, tracing patterns, defining constructs, and distilling mechanisms. The strict academic writing guidelines leave almost no room for surprise and revelation, or for picture usage.

Even the fieldwork that lies at the heart of both journalism and ethnography often takes very different forms. Thus, the amount of data needed for credible journalistic or ethnographic writing is dissimilar. Ethnographers spend months and even years in the field, use different data sources, and perform systematic comparisons between events, observations, and people. They often sieve through monumental piles of notes, memos, and interview transcripts to detect categories and concepts and refine their relationships. An ethnographic work has to demonstrate rigor (in terms of the reliability and validity of the findings) in order to be accepted by scholars as a worthy piece of research.

Journalists, on the other hand, tend to spend a limited time in the field (sometimes only days or even hours), and they may focus on only one person or occurrence. However, the focus on individuals and their plight can be sufficient for the purpose of writing a compelling story. Thus, a heart-rending account of a single mother's struggle to spend time with her young boy while juggling an erratic schedule can leave an indelible impact in the mind of the readers, even if it involves only one family (Kantor, *New York Times'* "Working anything but 9 to 5," 2014). Anthro-journalism of course involves extensive fieldwork; for example, Leon Dash's (1969) work for the *Washington Post*, which later turned into the book *Rosa Lee: A Generational Tale of Poverty and Survival in Urban America*, was based on four years of ethnographic work of following the life of a poor woman and her family.

The two trade's approach to fieldwork itself is somewhat different. Ethnography requires avoiding prejudgments about what is interesting and what is not before entering the field; a "fresh look" without any preconceived notion lies at the core of ethnography (Van Maanen, 2011). In contrast, journalists choose to investigate settings on the basis of their intriguing, even shocking nature; arousing readers' interest is a necessity and intended outcome, and invariably guides journalistic fieldwork.

These differences affect the way information is obtained during fieldwork. Journalists are never too reticent to ask provocative questions given their desire to provide the public something striking and revelatory, even sensational. Sometimes journalists can even obtain data in a way that can be seen by the scientific community as less than ethical. This doesn't, however, mean that journalists lack in ethics; the journalistic mantra that "truth needs to be uncovered, by any means" simply makes their sense of ethics different to that of an ethnographer; for a journalist, a hidden camera or tape-recorder to capture the exact words and gestures may be necessary to uncover (and then expose) the truth.

In contrast, after spending significant effort getting access to the field, ethnographers often take a cautious approach in their questioning. Their priority, in the first days in the field, is to safeguard confidence, avoid arousing suspicion, in the hope that over the following weeks and months subjects would themselves render needed sensitive information. These circumstances, along with the recommendation that their presence in the field be non-obtrusive, tend to teach ethnographers a very cautious approach to data gathering. The benefits in terms of reliable findings are clear; less so are the possible costs of the approach in terms of capturing natives' strong views and feelings.

Finally, journalists' credibility stems from the verifiability of the facts they report. To be credible, they often disclose the identity of their subjects. Although in some cases anonymity is unavoidable, in general, journalists are wary of anonymity; newspapers often have source and content checkers to verify a report before it is published. When asked how he protects the identity of his subjects, a journalist we interviewed replied in an exasperated voice:

> What do you mean protecting identity? Why on earth would you believe that I was telling you the truth if I didn't disclose you the background and the identity of the poor farmer who told me his story of being exploited for years by the land-owner? I could plain and simply be making up the whole story!
>
> *(Personal correspondence)*

Under conditions of verifiability, even a far-fetched story becomes trustworthy. Additionally, revealing subjects' identity is also liberating for the writing process as it allows for more candid descriptions of people and their emotions.

In contrast, the credibility of ethnographic accounts does not rely on revealing natives' true identities. Confidentiality agreements often ensure subjects' and organizations' anonymity, but ethnographers' empathy towards the natives also makes them loyal to those who received them in their midst and revealed their lives and experiences. The credibility of ethnographic accounts largely depends on the amount of time spent in the field, the rigorousness of data collection and interpretations, the ability to show vivid scenes and truthful images of people and their work, to provide an account of the natives' beliefs and perspectives, and of course on the phenomenological and theoretical insight gained by such deep commitments (Sanday, 1979; Van Maanen, 2011).

Although the strong resemblance of the actual process through which they obtain the material for their writing makes both ethnographers and journalists "workers in the same vineyard" (Fillmore, 1987: 1), the compelling demand from ethnographers to discover new phenomena, contradict the obvious, and advance social science has given rise to the opinion that ethnography is more than journalism (Bird, 2005; Harrington, 2003). To teach students some of the rigors of ethnographic work, journalism curricula have started incorporating anthropology and ethnography classes. The methodological rigors practiced by ethnographers (e.g., multiple data sources, triangulation, prolonged stay in the field, self-reflexivity in each step of the process, participant observation) are especially praised as having helped journalists provide in-depth and truthful accounts. Many journalists unequivocally acknowledge their debt to their training in anthropology and ethnography, which refined their ability to capture life and its events while staying true to "a feeling of the living experience" (Harrington, 2003: 91). At the same time, in good ethnographer practice, we should question the supposed intellectual superiority and methodologically austere status of our trade, and ask ourselves if there are things we can learn from journalism.

## What Can Ethnographers Learn from Journalists?

We have identified three main ways in which we as ethnographers can strengthen our work by adopting some of the techniques and practices used in anthro-journalism: attention to the emotional aspects of work, the use of narrative techniques, and incorporating the context in our analyses.

## Emotional Aspects of Work

Journalists, just as novelists, are masters at depicting the emotions of their characters, those given off by particular settings, and at evoking emotional responses in their readers. How do they do it?

### Detailed Description

Description has acquired a bad reputation in the academic world (Abbott, 2001; Yin, 1994). But description is primordial; there simply is no deep or systematic understanding without observation, without detailed renderings of people, places, behaviors, interactions, and interpretations. Journalists are often masters at precise, evocative description. Here is an excerpt from a *New York Times* article titled "Invisible child," written by Andrea Elliott (2013), which tells the story of a child living with her family in a decrepit shelter for the homeless; by giving minute details about the shelter, the text helps readers visualize the desolation of the place in which this family lives:

> The family's room is the scene of debilitating chaos: stacks of dirty laundry, shoes stuffed under a mattress, bicycles and coats piled high…. To the left of the door, beneath a decrepit sink where Baby Lele is bathed, the wall has rotted through, leaving a long, dark gap where mice congregate…. A few feet away, Dasani's legally blind, 10-year-old sister, Nijai, sleeps on a mattress that has come apart at the seams, its rusted coils splayed. Hand-washed clothes line the guards on the windows, which are shaded by gray wool blankets strung from the ceiling. A sticky fly catcher dangles overhead, dotted with dead insects.

Rarely do our accounts of people at work and of workplaces reach the same level of detail and emotional impact. And yet we do know that work groups and organizations are vast emotional fields (Huy, 2002; Kelly and Barsade, 2001; Fineman, 2000), sometimes splattered with joy and engagement (Kahn, 1990), often strewn with the bodies of emotionally depleted people (Kunda, 1992; Hochschild, 1979). Also, the people leading work organizations are as emotion-driven as anybody (Chatterjee and Hambrick, 2007). Yet our accounts of work and work relationships are rarely attuned to their emotional tones and dynamics. Even when emotions are present and consequential, they rarely take center stage. For instance, Alexandra Michel (2012) reports consultants' detailed recollections about how their bodies changed with their work and its demands. In some of our own work we were able to provide interactional detail on people working on an exciting, innovative product (Metiu and Rothbard, 2013). While there was a clear emotional undertone to both accounts, the descriptions of people and settings were not sufficiently detailed to conjure natives' emotional states.

### Visual Data

Journalists have long used visuals to create an emotional impact. The faces of the fire fighters in the aftermath of the 9/11 attacks told of emotions both complex and heart-breaking. More recently the faces of the refugees crammed on fortune boats in the Mediterranean tell of yet other stories of hope against hope, of despair and determination (see the *New York Times* 2015 series "Traveling in Europe's river of migrants"). The examples are abundant.

Visuals are not unknown to traditional ethnographic research; Bateson and Mead (1942) took extensive photos and films in their fieldwork for their research on Balinese culture, which comprised the main contents of their book *Balinese Character: A Photographic Analysis*. Yet our ethnographic accounts of work are remarkably devoid of actual images. The use of visual ethnography holds great promise though (Buchanan, 2001; Dougherty and Kunda, 1990), and we expect newer theoretical currents such as sociomateriality to use them extensively. Furthermore, work ethnographers can also borrow from rigorous visual methods used recently in research in marketing (Dion, 2007; Wallendorf and Arnould, 1991). Combining the rigor of these new methods with the emotional impact inherent in images will elicit a sensory experience of the contextual elements of work, enhance the representation of the emotional underbelly of work, and ultimately provide a richer and more truthful image of everyday work lives.

## Provocative and Sensitive Questions

Journalists do not hesitate to ask uncomfortable or confrontational questions to expose the truth and to dig deeper into their subjects' minds – their intentions, moves, and feelings. For example, in a CNN Democratic debate a journalist asked one of the socialist candidates: "A Gallup poll says half the country would not put a socialist in the White House. You call yourself a democratic socialist. How can any kind of socialist win a general election in the United States?"

Can ethnographers ever ask the "question that hurts" the way journalists do? How often do we ask questions such as: How did it feel when you got fired? What was your boss doing at the moment s/he was firing you? What was going on in your mind when you heard the news that the competitor company was threatening the existence of your organization? Asking such questions has the power to bring to the surface the emotions already experienced by organizational members (and often by the field researcher herself) but which would not be expressed in the absence of inquisitive questioning.

There are good reasons, of course, for ethnographers' reluctance to ask such questions, the most obvious of which is that their presence in the field is largely due to the management's and natives' acceptance. It may be dangerous to disrupt the sometimes fragile agreements by prodding too deeply into sensitive issues, or provoking emotional reactions in natives. The ephemeral yet pervasive aspects of the daily emotional lives and experiences of work can only be brought to light, and enrich organizational studies when ethnographers are ready to ask uncomfortable and irksome questions. Ethnographers could attempt such questioning in opportune moments, and perhaps in informal settings away from the workplace.

## Individuality and Backstory

More often than not journalists reveal the identity of the people and settings they report on; they reveal the backstory, publish the photos, depict the physical features, the tics, the particularities, all of which make characters and settings vivid for readers. Here is another excerpt from "Invisible child," which makes the child's individuality come alive in front of our eyes:

> Dasani is a short, wiry girl whose proud posture overwhelms her 4-foot-8 frame. She has a delicate, oval face and luminous brown eyes that watch everything, owl-like. Her expression veers from wonder to mischief.

Our accounts, however, are rarely populated with individuals with sparkles or tears in their eyes. Ethnographers usually do not reveal the identity of the people and the setting in which the fieldwork is conducted. A drawback of this practice is that when we designate people and organizations with pseudonyms, they seem less real, their story less potent, the drama less poignant. We see people engaged in the crisis of a failed collaboration, we see them intensely engaged in work effort, and apart from the obligatory "demographics table" we have no image of who they are (Metiu and Rothbard, 2013; Metiu, 2006).

Our suggestion is for ethnographers to strive for access to settings in which people will be freer to reveal their identities, and negotiate less anonymity. Such a step would make ethnographic work more truthful, transparent, and meaningful to the readers. Moreover, ethnographers would be less stifled with the anxiety of "giving away" the identity of their settings and their subjects when they write, which would make their writing more powerful.

## Narrative Style

Using a persuasive narrative style is yet another lesson that ethnography can learn from journalism. Although one of the primary goals of ethnography is to provide vivid images and descriptions of what is observed, felt and heard in the field, many ethnographic writings end up being firmly analytical, with dashes of facts, written in a well-established scientific format, with little attention to the style of writing. As Spradley lamented, ethnographers often write "without even feeling the importance of communicating in a way that brings the culture to life" (Spradley, 1979: 205). Hasty abstractions are quickly made, to display theoretical contribution. Such writing ends up as "the bare bones, the skeleton of knowledge, without the flesh ..." (Spradley, 1979: 211). One solution is turning to literary practices (Van Maanen, 1992) of the sort used by journalists. Far from detracting from the preoccupation with truth, meaning, and theory, such practices can enhance ethnographic accounts.

### Simple and Direct Language

Ethnographers are not the worst sinners among management scholars in terms of the amount of jargon used. Doing grounded theory keeps one's feet on the ground, as it were. Journalists, however, militantly safeguard direct, jargon-free language in their writing. Here is how the series "Traveling in Europe's river of migrants," written by Anemona Hartocollis (2015) in the *New York Times* starts: "It was the Danes who finally wore the Majid family down."

It could have been the beginning of a short story, of a novel. The sentence puts us square in the middle of the action, in a clear context, together with the Majid family. We want to know what happened to them before the Danes, and how come the Danes were able to wear them down. So we keep reading, engulfed in the story.

Journalists acquire the skills needed for such writing in the numerous writing courses that form the bulk of the journalism degree curriculum. They spend several semesters learning how to write well. Then they usually spend their initial working years reporting on mundane events and issues of daily life, thus developing the ability to write clearly, concisely, and quickly, using precise and vivid language. In addition, the journalism curriculum teaches attention to lexicons, syntax and rhetoric, recognizing voice, decoding the structure of a narrative, and reflecting on the power of storytelling (Harrington, 2003).

The social science curriculum on the other hand, by and large ignores the usefulness of such training. For people whose main job is to produce detailed, rich, precise images of work and workers, it is surprising that no more systematic training in writing is provided. Many ethnographers learn the craft in a more or less haphazard fashion, by themselves, and under the guidance of their advisors. Exemplary ethnographers also recognize the influence of reading good literature on their ability to provide nuanced, detailed, persuasive accounts of work and workers (Barley, 2006). To help future scholars acquire narrative skills, many Ph.D. programs have added writing courses and workshops to their curricula. Bolstering the curriculum of social science in graduate schools with training in writing (and reading literary texts) and encouraging future ethnographers to take writing workshops outside the social sciences (including creative writing) can greatly improve the quality of ethnographic writing.

## Voices from the Field

Journalists know how to provide the detail that speaks for itself and thus can dispense with the need for lengthy interpretation. Here is an image of the migrants from the *New York Times* article "Traveling in Europe's river of migrants":

> One young man ran sobbing across the room, pursued by a young woman in a hijab. He seemed to just want to be let go. The police tried to comfort him and let him sit on the floor near the door, head in his knees, whimpering.

In ethnographic writing, such observations from the field often get drowned in researchers' interpretation that explain the link between the data and the theories used to interpret them. Long vignettes from field notes that would give a sense of immersion are often chopped to fit the methodological standards or simply banned altogether. While such writing clearly points to the theoretical concepts and categories, it breaks the spell of details provided and prevents readers' immersion in the story.

Some work ethnographies do manage to convey the sense of action, movement, and energy so often brimming in real life. To draw the reader into this river of action, ethnographers sometimes choose to start their papers with powerful vignettes. Here is how a paper by Bechky starts:

> It is 6 a.m. when I arrive in Rittenhouse Square for the first scene of the shoot, as instructed by the location manager. Two people with their hoods up against the pouring rain are waiting at the edge of the pavement in front of a seafood restaurant: a woman on her cell phone and a tall man with a walkie-talkie in his hand. As I introduce myself, two trucks pull up to the curb and with a quick apology, the location manager and her assistant head off in opposite directions – one toward the trucks to tell them where to park, the other into the restaurant to talk with the owner. The back of the truck opens and purposeful-looking people equipped with headphones pour out. "Watch your back!" someone yells at me as they pass by, carrying wheeled equipment carts, lights and directors' chairs into the restaurant…. A day later, they have finished filming the commercial, and I comment to the location manager, "Yesterday morning seemed amazingly orderly for the first day of shooting." "We only have two days to do it," she replied, "We need to get things done right away."
>
> *(Bechky, 2006)*

By placing the vignette above at the very beginning of the paper, the author draws us into the setting, and raises in our minds the very question the study will answer – how do people manage to get their work organized so swiftly in this setting? Our suggestion is two-fold. First, ethnographers could strive to make the canon more flexible so as to allow for longer, rich vignettes. This will allow the reader to get a feel for the setting, the characters and their challenges, while also suggesting relevant social science questions. Second, we advise keeping the reporting of the data and the theoretical discussion separate, so as to allow readers a more direct feel for the setting studied.

## Author's Voice

Journalists are individuals roaming the earth in search of information and of stories. Their voices are heard, and often loudly, expressing their opinions, taking positions, advocating for various groups and causes. Their voices are also heard in their reports: first person accounts are common in both books and in shorter pieces. This is how Barbara Ehrenreich (2001) reports on her own experiences as a nickelled and dimed worker:

> I mumble thanks for the advice, feeling like I've just been stripped naked by the crazed enforcer of some ancient sumptuary law: No chatting for you, girl. No fancy service ethic allowed for the serfs. Chatting with customers is for the good looking young college-educated servers in the downtown capriccio and ceviche joints, the kids who can make $70–$100 a night.
>
> *(Ehrenreich, 2001: 35)*

Reporting in the first person reduces the distance between the actions and the account from two steps to only one; consequently, the characters and events are more vivid. Of course, ethnographers also have points of view and opinions; they also have undergone various experiences in the field; they also have feelings about the events and people they observe. Following sound methodological advice, they pay particular attention to the first days in the field, to initial impressions and emotions, because they're likely to match the natives' own. What they rarely do though is report these impressions and emotions. Accounts given in the first person such as Gephart's (1978) paper on status degradation, or that led through author's distinct voice such as Kunda's (1992) book on engineers, or Bechky's vignette above, are a rarity. In published papers, using the first person "I" in the methods or findings section feels like an act of bravery, and many ethnographers keep their voices for confessional pieces (Van Maanen, 2011; Kunda, 1992; Barley, 1990).

In our own work, we have been guilty by omission; for example, Metiu's comparative ethnography presented her with two very different settings: one dynamic, fast-moving, and hopeful, the other slow and marred by doubts about final success (Metiu and Rothbard, 2013). As soon as she arrived in the second site, she was struck by the much slower pace of walking in the hallways, and by the fact that at 5 pm she was the only one still in the site, typing her field notes; in the first project it was the ethnographer who felt guilty for leaving at 6 or 7 pm, fearful of missing some important interactions among those who were still working intensely. These stark differences were duly noted in field notes, used implicitly in analyses, but never reported as such. Part of the reason is that ethnographers of work are torn between reporting their own experiences in the field, and their scientific role with all its connotation of distance and objectivity. We submit that, far from undermining methodological rigor, reporting such personal impressions and hearing the ethnographer's voice, can serve as an additional, reliable data source.

## *The Larger Context*

Journalism's focus on extraordinary events puts it at the center of public life; it fuels and shapes public and political debates, monitors the social environment, acts as a medium of education and enlightenment, and often has a far-reaching impact on people's social reality (McNair, 2005). Journalists have brought down presidents with their stark revelatory stories, unraveled hidden corruption thus ending governments, demystified monarchies, exposed the darker social side of governmental policies, to name a few.

In contrast, work ethnographers are operating in the shadows of organizations. They are tolerated in routine situations, and rarely if ever get access to sites of conflict or significant decision-making. Of course, this attention to the routine, the understated, and the non-obvious is one of ethnography's main strengths. At the same time, settings that are linked to the larger dramas of our time also deserve our attention. As Elsbach and Bechky (2009) have explained, it is largely through attention to context that ethnography is able to generate theories and concepts that are specific, explanatory, and relevant. The contexts we study are consequential for our contributions to social science.

## Unusual Settings

It is journalists' duty to be present where the action is, so as to inform the public via reports and stories. A momentous social change such as the American welfare reform act of 1996 prompted Barbara Ehrenreich's (2001) *Nickel and Dimed: On (Not) Getting By in America*, a book that sheds deep light into the impact of the act on the life and work of low-wage workers in the U.S. The book had an enormous impact; regardless of criticism and controversy, it stirred a public debate around the minimum wage, and the hurdles faced by low-wage earners for their everyday survival. In her review of the book, Dorothy Gallaghar of the *New York Times* thanked the author "for bringing us the news of America's working poor so clearly and directly, and conveying with it a deep moral outrage and a finely textured sense of lives as lived" (Gallagher, 2001).

In a more recent context in which numerous workers struggle with hectic and unpredictable work schedules, the piece "Working anything but 9 to 5" (Kantor, *New York Times*, 2014) portrays the plight of a young single mother working at Starbucks. The image of the woman reading a story at bedtime to her son is meaningful and moving because such moments are rare and precious given her unpredictable work hours. The protagonist's schedule may be extreme, but the struggle to make time for loved ones in spite of one's work hours (translated, rather lifelessly, into the work–life balance concept in organization studies) is relevant to many other working parents.

It may never be the case that ethnographers are given field access when plants are closing or when work acquires a new meaning in a war zone. Field access is a great hurdle for work ethnographers, and this limits greatly their ability to study sensitive settings. At the same time, we view as promising the recent trend to work on extreme cases (Pratt, 2000; Pettigrew, 1990; Eisenhardt, 1989). For instance, qualitative studies of the free and open source software community have provided a series of insights into work motivation, collaboration, and governance (O'Mahony and Bechky, 2008; Lee and Cole, 2003; Von Krogh et al., 2003). Studying unusual, atypical settings can be illuminating both phenomenologically and theoretically.

## Ethnographic Teamwork

Journalists often work in teams comprised of other journalists, photographers or videographers, software layout designers, graphic artists. For instance, the *New York Times* piece "Traveling in Europe's river of migrants" was done collaboratively among a journalist, a photojournalist, and a videographer. The team produced a striking account of individuals, families, and destinies changing in the midst of danger and serendipity. We hear the migrants' voice, we see their faces, bodies, and gestures. We travel with them. Such an account could only be produced because the journalistic teams pooled their complementary skills.

Such collaborations among ethnographers are almost non-existent. The rare examples include ethnographers with similar skills who pulled their data together to produce insightful comparative studies. For instance, Bechky and Okhuysen (2011) combined data that they had separately collected in two different settings – film production crews and a SWAT team – for a comparative analysis to understand organizational responses to uncertainty and surprises. In a paper on contract workers, O'Mahony and Bechky (2006) combined data from two field studies that they had separately conducted – one on high-tech contract workers and the other on film projects – to show how people manage their careers in a context of temporary work projects. As these examples illustrate, collaborations among like-minded ethnographers can lead to rich and insightful studies that draw on the generative power of the comparative method. In the future ethnographers may also consider collaborating with experts with complementary skills, such as photographers or videographers, in order to produce truthful and rich images of work and workers.

## Conclusion

Ethnography and journalism are different trades whose specificities make each valuable. That they can spur each other on has been the argument developed in this chapter. Ethnographic accounts of work are deep and nuanced, based on extended field immersion, attention to the multiplicity of groups and perspectives in a particular setting, and with meticulous attention to patterns, routines, regularities. Ethnographers also take self-reflexivity seriously, striving to understand (and often even to report) how their position as observers of people and events may have affected their perceptions and interpretations. Anthro-journalism aims to emulate all these remarkable qualities (Harrington, 2003). At the same time, ethnographers can produce richer and truer accounts of work and workers were they to emulate journalists' attention to the emotional aspects of work, the use of narrative techniques, and stronger connections to the larger context. Ultimately, the theories thus developed by ethnographers will be all the more grounded and nuanced, their impact farther-reaching.

## Notes

1 See www.americanpressinstitute.org/journalism-essentials/what-is-journalism/makes-journalism-different-forms-communication/ (accessed February 13, 2017).
2 See www.americanpressinstitute.org/journalism-essentials/what-is-journalism/purpose-journalism/ (accessed February 13, 2017).

## References

Abbott, A. (2001) *Time Matters: On Theory and Method*, Chicago, IL: University of Chicago Press.
American Press Institute (2015) www.americanpressinstitute.org/journalism-essentials/what-is-journalism/makes-journalism-different-forms-communication/ (accessed October 9, 2016).
Anteby, M. (2008) *Moral Gray Zones: Side Productions, Identity, and Regulation in an Aeronautic Plant*, Princeton, NJ: Princeton University Press.
Bandura, A. (1977) Self-efficacy: Toward a unifying theory of behavioral change, *Psychological Review*, 84(2): 191–215.
Barley, S. R. (1986) Technology as an occasion for structuring: Evidence from observations of CT scanners and the social order of radiology departments, *Administrative Science Quarterly*, 31(1): 78–108.
Barley, S. R. (1990) Images of imaging: Notes on doing longitudinal field work, *Organization Science*, 1(3): 220–247.
Barley, S. R. (2006) When I write my masterpiece: Thoughts on what makes a paper interesting, *Academy of Management Journal*, 49(1): 16–20.
Barley, S. R. and Kunda, G. (1992) Design and devotion: Surges of rational and normative ideologies of control in managerial discourse, *Administrative Science Quarterly*, 37(3): 363–399.

Barley, S. R. and Kunda, G. (2001) Bringing work back in, *Organization Science*, 12(1): 76–95.

Barsade, S. G. and Gibson, D. E. (1998) Group emotion: A view from top and bottom, *Research on Managing Groups and Teams*, 1(4): 81–102.

Bateson, G. and Mead, M. (1942) *Balinese Character: A Photographic Analysis*, Special Publication of the New York Academy of Sciences, New York, 17–92.

Bechky, B. A. (2003) Sharing meaning across occupational communities: The transformation of understanding on a production floor, *Organization Science*, 14(3): 312–330.

Bechky, B. A. (2006) Gaffers, gofers, and grips: Role-based coordination in temporary organizations, *Organization Science*, 17(1): 3–21.

Bechky, B. A. and Okhuysen, G. A. (2011) Expecting the unexpected? How SWAT officers and film crews handle surprises, *Academy of Management Journal*, 54(2): 239–261.

Bird, S. E. (2005) The journalist as ethnographer? In E. W. Rothenbuhler and M. Coman (eds.) *Media Anthropology*, Thousand Oaks, CA: Sage, 301–308.

Bourdieu, P. (1977) *Outline of a Theory of Practice* (vol. 16), Cambridge: Cambridge University Press.

Buchanan, D. A. (2001) The role of photography in organization research: A reengineering case illustration, *Journal of Management Inquiry*, 10(2): 151–164.

Chatterjee, A. and Hambrick, D. C. (2007) It's all about me: Narcissistic chief executive officers and their effects on company strategy and performance, *Administrative Science Quarterly*, 52(3): 351–386.

Dash, L. (1969) *Rosa Lee: A Generational Tale of Poverty and Survival in Urban America*, New York: Basic Books.

Dion, D. (2007) Les apports de l'anthropologie visuelle à l'étude des comportements de consommation, *Recherche et Applications en Marketing*, 22(1): 61–78.

Dougherty, D. (1992) Interpretive barriers to successful product innovation in large firms, *Organization Science*, 3(2): 179–202.

Dougherty, D. (2001) Reimagining the differentiation and integration of work for sustained product innovation, *Organization Science*, 12(5): 612–631.

Dougherty, D. and Kunda, G. (1990) Photograph analysis: A method to capture organizational belief systems. In P. Gagliardi (ed.) *Symbols and Artifacts: Views of the Corporate Landscape*, New York: de Gruyter, 185–206.

Ehrenreich, B. (2001) *Nickel and Dimed: On (Not) Getting By in America*, New York: Metropolitan Books.

Eisenhardt, K. M. (1989) Building theories from case study research, *Academy of Management Review*, 14(4): 532–550.

Elliott, A. (2013) Invisible child. Girl in the shadows: Dasani's homeless life (part 1), *New York Times*, www.nytimes.com/projects/2013/invisible-child/#/?chapt=1 (accessed October 10, 2016).

Elsbach, K. and Bechky, B. A. (2009) Introduction: Research context and attention of the qualitative researcher. In K. D. Elsbach and B. A. Bechky (eds.) *Qualitative Organizational Research 2: Best Papers from the Davis Conference on Organizational Research*, Greenwich, CT: Information Age Publishing, 1–10.

Elsbach, K. D. and Kramer, R. M. (1996) Members' responses to organizational identity threats: Encountering and countering the Business Week rankings, *Administrative Science Quarterly*, 41: 442–476.

Etzioni, A. (1988) Normative-affective factors: Toward a new decision making model, *Journal of Economic Psychology*, 9: 125–150.

Feldman, M. S. (2000) Organizational routines as a source of continuous change, *Organization Science*, 11(6): 611–629.

Fillmore, R. (1987) Anthro-journalism, *Communicating Anthropology* [Fact Sheet] from The Center for Anthropology and Science Communications, www.siencessitescom/CASC/ajrf.html (accessed December 2, 2012).

Fineman, S. (ed.) (2000) *Emotion in Organizations*, London: Sage.

Gallaghar, D. (2001) Making ends meet. *New York Times*, www.nytimes.com/books/01/05/13/reviews/010513.13gallagt.html (accessed December 17, 2016).

Geertz, C. (1973) *The Interpretation of Cultures: Selected Essays* (vol. 5019), New York: Basic Books.

Gephart Jr, R. P. (1978) Status degradation and organizational succession: An ethnomethodological approach, *Administrative Science Quarterly*, 23: 553–581.

Hargadon, A. and Sutton, R. I. (1997) Technology brokering and innovation in a product development firm, *Administrative Science Quarterly*, 42: 716–749.

Harrington, W. (2003) What journalism can offer ethnography, *Qualitative Inquiry*, 9(1): 90–104.

Hartocollis, A. (2015) Traveling in Europe's river of migrants, *New York Times*, www.nytimes.com/interactive/projects/cp/reporters-notebook/migrants (accessed October 10, 2016).

Hochschild, A. R. (1975) The sociology of feeling and emotion: Selected possibilities, *Sociological Inquiry*, 45(2–3): 280–307.

Hochschild, A. R. (1979) Emotion work, feeling rules, and social structure, *American Journal of Sociology*, 85(3): 551–575.

Huy, Q. N. (2002) Emotional balancing of organizational continuity and radical change: The contribution of middle managers, *Administrative Science Quarterly*, 47(1): 31–69.

Kahn, W. A. (1990) Psychological conditions of personal engagement and disengagement at work, *Academy of Management Journal*, 33(4): 692–724.

Kantor, J. (2014) Working anything but 9 to 5, *New York Times*, www.nytimes.com/interactive/2014/08/13/us/starbucks-workers-scheduling-hours.html (accessed December 12, 2016).

Kelly, J. R. and Barsade, S. G. (2001) Mood and emotions in small groups and work teams, *Organizational Behavior and Human Decision Processes*, 86(1): 99–130.

Kreiner, G. E., Hollensbe, E. C., and Sheep, M. L. (2009) Balancing borders and bridges: Negotiating the work-home interface via boundary work tactics, *Academy of Management Journal*, 52(4): 704–730.

Kunda, G. (1992) *Engineering Culture: Control and Commitment in a High-tech Organization*, Philadelphia, PA: Temple University Press.

Lazarus, R. S. (1991) Cognition and motivation in emotion, *American Psychologist*, 46(4): 352–367.

Lee, G. K. and Cole, R. E. (2003) From a firm-based to a community-based model of knowledge creation: The case of the Linux kernel development, *Organization Science*, 14(6): 633–649.

McNair, B. (2005) What is journalism? In H. De Burgh (ed.) *Making Journalists: Diverse Models, Global Issues*, London: Routledge, 25–43.

Mazmanian, M. (2013) Avoiding the trap of constant connectivity: When congruent frames allow for heterogeneous practices, *Academy of Management Journal*, 56: 1225–1250.

Mazmanian, M., Orlikowski, W. J., and Yates J. (2013) The autonomy paradox: The implications of mobile email devices for knowledge professionals, *Organization Science*, 24: 1337–1357.

Metiu, A. (2006) Owning the code: Status closure in distributed groups, *Organization Science*, 17(4): 418–435.

Metiu, A. and Rothbard, N. P. (2013) Task bubbles, artifacts, shared emotion, and mutual focus of attention: A comparative study of the micro processes of group engagement, *Organization Science*, 24(2): 455–475.

Michel, A. (2012) Transcending socialization: A nine-year ethnography of the body's role in organizational control and knowledge workers' transformation, *Administrative Science Quarterly*, 56(3): 325–368.

O'Mahony, S. and Bechky, B. A. (2006) Stretchwork: Managing the career progression paradox in external labor markets, *Academy of Management Journal*, 49(5): 918–941.

O'Mahony, S. and Bechky, B. A. (2008) Boundary organizations: Enabling collaboration among unexpected allies, *Administrative Science Quarterly*, 53(3): 422–459.

Orr, J. E. (1996) *Talking about Machines: An Ethnography of a Modern Job*, Ithaca, NY: Cornell University Press.

Pettigrew, A. M. (1990) Longitudinal field research on change: Theory and practice, *Organization Science*, 1(3): 267–292.

Pratt, M. G. (2000) The good, the bad, and the ambivalent: Managing identification among Amway distributors, *Administrative Science Quarterly*, 45(3): 456–493.

Rafaeli, A. and Sutton, R. I. (1989) The expression of emotion in organizational life, *Research in Organizational Behavior*, 11(1): 1–42.

Roethlisberger, F. J. and Dickson, W. J. (1939) *Management and the Worker*, An Account of a Research Program conducted by the Western Electric Co., Hawthorne Works, Chicago, Cambridge, MA: Harvard University Press.

Sanday, P. R. (1979) The ethnographic paradigm(s), *Administrative Science Quarterly*, 24(4): 527–538.

Spradley, J. P. (1979) *The Ethnographic Interview*, New York: Holt, Rinehart and Winston.

Taylor, F. (1911) *The Principles of Scientific Management*, New York: Harper & Brothers.

Van Maanen, J. (1992) Displacing Disney: Some notes on the flow of culture, *Qualitative Sociology*, 15(1): 5–35.

Van Maanen, J. (2011) *Tales of the Field: On Writing Ethnography*, Chicago, IL: University of Chicago Press.

Von Krogh, G., Spaeth, S., and Lakhani, K. R. (2003) Community, joining, and specialization in open source software innovation: A case study, *Research Policy*, 32(7): 1217–1241.

Wallendorf, M. and Arnould, E. J. (1991) "We gather together": Consumption rituals of Thanksgiving Day, *Journal of Consumer Research*, 18(1): 13–31.

Yin, R. K. (1994) *Case Study Research: Design and Methods*, Thousands Oaks, CA: International Educational and Professional Publisher.

# PART III

# Contexts

# 14

# ANALYZING CHANGES IN ORGANIZATIONAL CULTURAL REPERTOIRES

*Davide Ravasi, Violina Rindova, and Elena Dalpiaz*

Research on cultural phenomena in organizations has been characterized by the co-existence of different research traditions, resting on different understandings of what culture is and how it should be studied (Schultz and Hatch, 1996; O'Reilly and Chatman, 1996; Morris et al., 1999; Giorgi et al., 2015).

An important line of inquiry, grounded in organizational psychology, has employed large-scale quantitative studies (e.g., Hofstede et al., 1990; O'Reilly et al., 1991) to capture how individually held values (belief structures defining appropriate ways to think and act) influence different types of organizational behavior (e.g., Luthans et al., 1985; Kirkman and Shapiro, 2001; Chatman and Spataro, 2005; Kirkman et al., 2009).

Another important research tradition, grounded in anthropology (Smircich, 1983) and organizational sociology (Morrill, 2008), has adopted an interpretive approach, and it has relied on in-depth, case-based, qualitative inquiry to explore how members construct understandings of their organizational life (e.g., Martin et al., 1983; Phillips and Brown, 1993) and how these understandings influence social processes in organizations (e.g., Barley, 1983; Kunda, 1992; Ravasi and Schultz, 2006). Scholars in this second tradition broadly share a view of organizations as "speech communities sharing socially constructed systems of meaning that allow members to make sense of their immediate, and perhaps not so immediate, environment" (Barley, 1983, p. 393). These scholars consider culture as residing in relatively shared cognitive structures (Harris, 1994; DiMaggio, 1997) that structure relationships inside the organization in terms of more abstract understandings of desirable or undesirable behavior that are commonly referred to as values (Schein, 1985). These cognitive structures manifest in more visible cultural forms, such as artifacts, stories, vocabularies, and even spaces, in formal organizational practices, such as policies, structures, and systems, as well as in informal practices, such as unwritten norms and conventions (Martin, 2002).

Early work on organizational culture conceptualized it as a relatively stable set of taken-for-granted norms, beliefs, and symbols that shape members' thoughts and actions in a coherent and predictable way, and provide the structural stability fundamental for the everyday functioning of an organization (see Schein, 1985). This view reflected ideas from cultural sociology portraying culture as acquired, often unconsciously, through socialization, and shaping action with a high degree of automaticity and predictability (Wrong, 1961).

Recent work in cultural sociology, however, increasingly views culture as a "toolkit" (Swidler, 1986, 2001) – a set of symbolic resources that individuals flexibly draw upon to support different strategies of action. Organizational scholars have embraced this approach in order to better understand the ways in which organizational members, as well as organizations employ cultural resources to accomplish diverse goals (see Harrison and Corley, 2011; Howard-Grenville et al., 2011; Rindova et al., 2011). Advocates of this perspective maintain that, contrary to a traditional understanding of culture as constraining action, individuals enjoy a relative degree of agency in the flexible interpretation and pragmatic use of the elements of a cultural system. They used the term *cultural repertoires* to refer to subsets of cultural resources that particular members have learned and deploy flexibly according to their goals and the situation (Weber, 2005; Rindova et al., 2011). While some scholars have emphasized the existence of *cultural registers* (Weber, 2005) to refer to subsets of cultural resources associated with specific fields, others have argued that organizations can proactively source cultural resources across fields to pursue novel goals and transform existing situations (Rindova et al., 2011).

Table 14.1 summarizes the key differences among the three perspectives: culture as individually held values, culture as shared norms and beliefs, and culture as toolkit.

From a methodological standpoint, research in the first tradition relies on quantitative analytical tools to measure individual-level values and attitudes and their diffusion within and across organizations (e.g., Cooke and Rousseau, 1988; Hofstede et al., 1990). Research in the second

*Table 14.1* Different Perspectives on Organizational Culture

|  | Culture as Individually Held Values | Culture as Shared Norms and Beliefs | Culture as Toolkit |
|---|---|---|---|
| Disciplinary roots | Psychology | Anthropology | Cultural sociology |
| Paradigmatic stance | Neo-positivistic | Interpretive | Interpretive |
| Where does culture reside? | *Individually held values:* Cultural differences are manifested in the differences in the average diffusion and intensity with which certain values are held | *Relatively shared mental structures* (assumptions and values): Cultural differences are manifested in different patterns of behavior and symbols (artifacts) | *Cultural resources:* Repertoires of concepts, symbols, rituals, etc. Cultural differences are manifested in access to and use of different repertoires |
| How does culture affect organizations? | Cultural values *define appropriate ways to think and act*, and influence individual organizational behavior and response to organizational policies | Cultural assumptions and values *influence how people make sense of their organizational reality* and *define appropriate ways to think and act* | Individuals *flexibly use cultural resources* to construct and account for individual "strategies of action" |
| How should culture be studied? | Experiments and/or surveys capturing individually held values through culturally neutral multi-item scales ("etic" approach) | Multiple methods (ethnographic observation, interviews, etc.) aimed at describing behaviors and beliefs in terms meaningful to organizational members ("emic" approach) | Systematic tracking of cultural concepts manifested in language, narratives and other texts, as evidence of use of resources from a repertoire |

tradition has also drawn on well-established guidelines for the ethnographic observation and analysis of cultures (e.g., van Maanen, 1979; Barley, 1990).

Application of the notion of culture as toolkit to the study of organizational cultures, instead, is still at an early stage of development. One set of methodological tools that has been identified as fruitful is the semiotic analysis of texts. Semiotic analysis has been used to map the cultural register of a field (Weber, 2005), and to show how pre-existing (oppositional) structures in semiotic codes can be used to trigger new sensemaking and mobilize different patterns of action. Semiotic analysis can be particularly useful in contexts where organizational, institutional, and societal contradictions are manifest, and cultural resources are used to express them and amplify them. While insightful, such analysis may be limited to contexts where comprehensive field-level data are available, and where field boundaries are clear. They may also provide limited means for capturing idiosyncratic organizational processes of sourcing and combining diverse cultural resources, and deploying them to pursue different strategies of action. To expand the methodological toolkit of research on cultural toolkits, in the remainder of the chapter we articulate some guidelines based on our own experience with analyzing longitudinal changes in the cultural repertoire of a single organization that led to substantive organizational changes (Rindova et al., 2011).

## Content Analysis of Texts and the Mapping of Cultural Toolkits

A central issue in the analysis of cultural toolkits is the identification and mapping of the "cultural resources" that constitute either a cultural register (field-level) or a cultural repertoire (organizational or individual levels). Swidler's initial conceptualization of cultural resources broadly included ideas, stories, rituals, symbols, worldviews, and other cultural manifestations (Swidler, 1986, 2001). Applications of Swidler's theory to the analysis of organizational culture operationalize this broad conceptualization by equating cultural resources to meaning structures – parings of concepts and the words that carry them (Weber, 2005) – informing organizational strategies, structures, and practices (see for instance, Harrison and Corley, 2011; Rindova et al., 2011).

Past research has used various forms of content analysis of texts to examine the concepts available to a given social group to organize knowledge in a particular domain. Weber (2005), for instance, used techniques from semiotic analysis to content analyze letters to shareholders and produce an accurate map of the elements of the register of the German pharmaceutical industry. Zilber (2006) content analyzed media coverage of high-tech and want ads of high-tech firms to show how the latter flexibly draw from the broader societal-level register reflected in press articles. Ocasio and Joseph (2005) showed how evolving governance practices in organizations mirrored the changing vocabulary used by the media.

Later research focused on organizational cultural repertoires, however, followed different methodologies. Harrison and Corley (2011), for instance, used naturalistic inquiry (Lincoln and Guba, 1985), based on a prolonged engagement with an organization and multiple sources of data, to uncover the exchange of cultural resources between the organization and its stakeholders. Following Swidler (2001), Howard-Grenville and colleagues (Howard-Grenville et al., 2011) used interviews to capture how informants "used" culture in three different sites as they attempted to bring new resources in the cultural repertoire of the organization. Canato et al. (2013) indirectly inferred the enrichment of a cultural repertoire from informants' spontaneous and flexible use of new concepts acquired as part of a change program aimed at modifying the culture of the organization.

These two approaches point to an important trade-off in the analysis of the use of cultural repertoires: Analyses that emphasize the relationship between organizational cultural repertoires and the broad field-level register seem less suited to the in-depth examination of cultural processes in organizations. First, these guidelines recommend an inductive, bottom-up mapping of a cultural register based on the observed usage of cultural resources by field actors. This approach requires a data source – such as letters to shareholders (Weber, 2005) or ads (Zilber, 2006) – that offers comprehensive and systematic access to actors' usage of these resources; such data sources, however, may not always be available. Also, collecting and analyzing data about all actors in a field may excessively burden a study focused on a single organization. Second, by assuming that cultural repertoires of actors will mirror the cultural register of their field, and by inferring the composition of the register from the observed use of resources, this approach may fail to capture resources that are used only by specific organizations and/or are drawn from other cultural registers (see Rindova et al., 2011). Finally, by focusing on discursive content, this approach may fail to capture the extent to which concepts are actually used as resources to pursue strategies of action, and whether they are used flexibly or not.

Our investigation of how Alessi, an Italian producer of high-design kitchenware, incorporated a variety of cultural resources from other domains to enrich its cultural repertoire and transform its strategies of action (Rindova et al., 2011) offered us the opportunity to counterbalance the approaches emphasizing field-level registers. In the published version of this study, space constraints prevented us from fully articulating and displaying all the analytical steps and the intermediate output that allowed us to make credible claims about the cultural processes we examined. We believe that articulating the steps we took in our analytical process may expand the methodological toolkit of cultural researchers interested in investigating organizational processes and strategies.

## Mapping an Organizational Cultural Repertoire and the Flexible Use of Resources in Strategies of Action

Our study tracked the enrichment of the cultural repertoire of Alessi over three decades. Our analysis revealed the gradual incorporation in the cultural repertoire of the organization of different and partly contradictory conceptualizations of products (as tools, as artwork, as toys), product value (functionality, form, consumption rituals, and emotional experience), and production (efficiency, authorship, and craftsmanship). It also enabled us to observe how these concepts had practical implications for the way products were designed, manufactured, and marketed. Ultimately, our analyses uncovered how different cultural resources inspired unconventional and versatile strategies of action manifested in the development of innovative product lines targeting different customer segments or diversifying into new product categories.

### *Data Collection*

Our study relied on multiple sources of data (see Table 14.2 for details). We used archival documents, mostly written by the organizational leader and its close collaborators, to track the concepts that were gradually incorporated in the organizational language and self-referential discourse to explain Alessi's purpose, identity, activities, and product lines. This source also helped us track changes in organizational practices and strategies of action, and link these changes with the evolving cultural repertoire. We used interviews with informants to triangulate and deepen our analysis of repertoire enrichment, and to document the use of new cultural resources in organizational practices.

*Table 14.2* Data Sources

| Source of Data | Type of Data | Use in the Analysis |
| --- | --- | --- |
| Corporate archive | **Books**<br>Published by Alessi between 1979 and 2006 in four categories:<br><br>1 Official corporate autobiographies (4)<br>2 Books on specific product development projects (16)<br>3 Books on designers (4)<br>4 Reports from workshops organized by Alessi (4). | Track changes in the cultural repertoire of the organization at different points in time, as organizational texts document the evolution of a repertoire without retrospective bias (Weber, 2005). |
| | **Catalogues**<br>70 commercial catalogues published between 1960 and 2007. | Gather detailed information regarding interpretation of product features and environment. |
| Interviews | **First round**<br>*Spring 2006–Fall 2007.* Twelve interviews with ten members of the company, including then CEO Alberto Alessi, his closest collaborators, and junior and senior managers across functions. Interviews lasted between one and four hours. All recorded and transcribed for a total of 159 pages. | Gather data regarding the organizational strategy, structures, and practices, their origins and evolution. |
| | **Second round**<br>*Spring 2008.* Eleven interviews with: (a) five members of the company, including two retired managers; (b) two designers.<br><br>*Fall 2008.* Three interviews with external design experts<br><br>All recorded and transcribed for a total of 150 pages. | Verify the timeline of the incorporation of different concepts in Alessi cultural repertoire, refine our emerging theoretical insights, contextualize the observed processes in terms of industry and design history. |
| | **Video-taped archival interviews**<br>Four open-ended interviews recorded by Alessi Museum in 1999 and 2001 with informants no longer available for in-person interviews: Carlo Alessi (Alberto's father and former CEO), Ettore Alessi (Alberto's uncle and former technical manager), and architects Carlo Mazzeri (first external designer to collaborate with Alessi) and Franco Sargiani (designer of logo and packaging in the early 1970s). | Triangulate facts and observations, gain additional understanding of the organization and the strategy prior to the change process and of the early years of the change. |

*continued*

*Table 14.2* Continued

| Source of Data | Type of Data | Use in the Analysis |
|---|---|---|
| Other archival sources | 1 Scholarly publications on Alessi written by art critics (Casciani, 1996), business historians (Casciani, 1996; Sweet, 1998), and design (Verganti, 2006) and management scholars (Moon et al., 2003; Salvato, 2003, 2006), as well as scholarly publications on design history in general (Branzi, 2004; De Fusco, 2002).<br>2 Industry reports on the household industry.<br>3 Specialized media, such as architecture and design magazines (*Domus*, 1965–; *Ottagono*, 1965–; *Casabella*, 1970–; *Modo*, 1984–; *Abitare*, 1970–1979), the oldest household industry magazine (*Articoli casalinghi e Piccoli Elettrodomestici*, 1969–1980), and various Italian and American household magazines (various issues in the 1980s and 1990s). | Triangulate facts and observations, enhance validity of insights, contextualize observed process in terms of industry and design history. |

*Source*: Rindova et al. (2011). A cultural quest: A study of organizational use of new cultural resources in strategy formation. *Organizational Science*, 22(2): 413–431.

## Data Analysis

Our analysis combined coding techniques from grounded theory building (Locke, 2001) with longitudinal case analysis (e.g., Pettigrew, 1990; Yin, 1994). The former helped us systematically capture and track the emergence of new "concepts" in how organizational leaders made sense of Alessi, its goals, practices, products, and stakeholders across three decades. The latter helped us track the flexible use of these concepts to inspire and develop new strategies of action, and capture the difficulties associated with the simultaneous implementation of their contradictory implications. For the sake of clarity, we discuss our analysis in sequential steps, while in reality, we followed an iterative process traveling back and forth between the data and the emerging theoretical structure (Locke, 2001).

*Step 1: Longitudinal reconstruction of events.* As is common in case-based research (Yin, 1994), our first step was the creation of a long (over 100 pages) and detailed chronological description of Alessi's history, from its founding in 1921 to late 2006. While not directly related to the mapping of the cultural repertoire of the organization, this first step was fundamental to establishing a clear timeline of Alessi's changing strategy and the historical, social, and organizational contexts that surrounded it. In this step, we not only familiarized ourselves with the changes and the context, but began to observe key junctures and important events. We used these observations to repeatedly revisit the analysis of cultural resource incorporation and use discussed below.

*Step 2: Mapping the enrichment in the cultural repertoire.* In the next step, we set out to accurately map changes in the cultural repertoire of the organization between 1970 and 2006. In this step, we followed the guidelines for the analysis of cultural toolkits (Weber, 2005) discussed in the introduction. We content analyzed all corporate texts (books, book chapters, and transcripts of speeches, for a total of more than 300 pages of text) written by or reporting the statements of Alberto Alessi (the grandson of the founder, who initiated cultural changes and led the organization for over three decades) and his collaborators.

Two important points are worth noting about this step in the analysis. Frist, our purpose in this step was not to map the entire repertoire of Alessi at any point in time. Instead, we sought to capture the addition of new concepts into the repertoire. Second, we were not looking to document the frequency of use of specific terms, but to capture the emergence of broader meaning structures reflected in the language. Accordingly, we used sentences or paragraphs, rather than individual words, as coding units. We initially used in vivo codes (van Maanen, 1979), that is either the actual terms used in the texts or a simple descriptive phrase. In a subsequent iteration, we grouped multiple specific textual expressions into first-order codes, while still keeping our codes close to the language used by organizational members (see also Gioia et al., 2012). To illustrate, we grouped expressions containing references to design activity as "commercial art" or linking products to the "same figurative and expressive value of architectures" under the first-order code "design as artistic activity." Two researchers conducted this open-coding step independently and generated the first-order codes, resolving occasional differences through discussion.

A further iteration involved all three researchers evaluating similarities in first-order codes and suggesting more abstract, theoretical labels, attempting to capture the broader, more fundamental meaning structures (concepts) that guided action at Alessi. To illustrate, we grouped the first-order codes "product form as expression of artistic language" and "formal innovation" under the more general second-order code (concept) "value of form." This concept was also connected to specific examples from interviews and archival data that associated product success with product form rather than function. Unprompted use of concepts by our informants during the interviews provided ecological validity for the text-based coding process, as well as an indication that these were not simply the ideas of the organizational leader and his collaborators but cultural resources that organizational members currently used.

As we coded corporate texts, we noticed that most of the new concepts that were introduced in the organizational vocabulary were explicitly associated to theories or practices from other domains of action, namely the fine arts, crafts, anthropology, and psychoanalysis. In a final stage of coding, then, we organized the second-order codes (concepts) into four clusters, associated to what we provisionally interpreted as the cultural registers of these four domains. We recoded our interviews to identify explicit statements that our informants made regarding the source of inspiration for the concepts and found numerous and very specific references to the cultural registers associated with these concepts. For instance, informants associated concepts such as "emotive involvement," "products as toys," and "products as vehicles for fantasy" to specific psychoanalytical theories that the organization had deliberately exposed itself to in search of concepts to guide its thinking and action.

In a next step, we reviewed extant theoretical work in the four domains uncovered in our clusters to assess the fit of the concepts we identified with the concepts associated with these registers by experts in these domains. Thus, while our concepts were inductively developed from the specific texts that Alessi produced to reflect on its strategy, in this step, we linked these concepts to broader cultural registers to confirm the association. However, we did not impose any expectations about the registers that Alessi might have been using on the open coding of cultural resources. In fact, uncovering the sourcing of cultural resources from multiple cultural registers was one of the surprising findings of our study.

Table 14.3 shows an excerpt of the working table we produced, linking evidence (fragments of texts), first-order and second-order codes, and summarizing corroborating evidence from academic literature. Figure 14.1's maps of the concepts that enriched the cultural

Table 14.3 Mapping the Enrichment of the Cultural Repertoire: Concepts, Selected Evidence, and Theoretical Corroboration [Excerpt]

| Second-Order Codes (Concepts) | First-Order Codes and Selected Evidence | Theoretical Corroboration from Past Research |
|---|---|---|
| Concepts from the Arts Register | | |
| Products as artworks | Design as artistic activity | Artworks are the results of the coordinated activities of all people and organizations (artists, galleries, museum curators, organizations that produce the work) whose cooperation is necessary for that artwork to occur as it does and whose agreement defines what can be claimed artwork and its value (Becker, 1974, 1982). |
| | "By reducing the dimension of his/her project without changing its linguistic elements, [the210architect] is able to transfer on the object the same figurative and expressive power of his/her architectures" (A. Alessi, 1985, quoted in CA30). | |
| | "Luckily, there also exists a second way of intending design … which one can define as design understood as art" (A. Alessi, 1992, CA8). | Artworks can be reproduced without losing their artistic character (Clignet, 1979). |
| | Industrial products as contemporary art | |
| | "[We believe] that today industrial subspecies of 'objects of art' can exist, and are becoming strong, typical, necessary and representative forms of contemporary visual art" (Mendini 1989, CA21). | |
| | "Because of its language and its communicative elements, Branzi's kettle can be appreciated, and indeed was appreciated, perhaps by the modern art lovers" (A. Alessi, 2001, CA33). | |
| Authorship | Artist freedom | Artists are free to interpret (Becker, 1974) and break with (Crane, 1989) artistic conventions to produce unique and different artworks. Artistic talent is inferred by inspection of an artist's work (Becker, 1982, p. 14), but, in some cases, signature is the only element to make a work an artwork. |
| | "Artwork … cannot be subjected to the same constraints and evaluation criteria of usual products" (Scarzella, 1985, CA30). | |
| | "[The design of Sottsass's] cutlery … required some phases of hot processing, which is unusual for these objects. At the end, he [Sottsass] won, and the cutlery set was presented exactly as he wanted it" (A. Alessi, 1989, quoted in CA25). | |
| | Value of signature | |
| | "We spotted an interesting market segment for author-marked cutlery sets, free for the marketing logic that price couldn't exceed 500,000 liras" (Polinoro, 1989, CA25). | |
| | "This kettle [9091] was the first author-kettle, heralding a new season of kettle ideas for ourselves as well as for many other kettle manufacturers" (A. Alessi, 2002, CA2). | |

| Value of form | Formal innovation | Aesthetics defines what is art, and consists of concepts and arguments that justify classifying things as "beautiful," "artistic," or good or bad forms of artistic expression. These systems of arguments are then applied by critics to arrive at a judgment of worth about a given work, which in turn produces reputation for work and artist, which is then taken into account by audience and distributor when they have to choose/support a work (Becker, 1982). Being beautiful or exhibiting other narrow formal properties, and expressing the point of view of the artist are some of the categories which count toward something being art (Gaut, 2007). |
| | "An aspect of [Alessi's] research in these years [the 1980s] is the design of objects of high formal content and highly expressive" (Scarzella, 1985, CA30). | |
| | "[In steel objects] form is the only element one can play upon to denote diversity" (Scarzella, 1985, CA30). | |
| | *Form is more important than function* | |
| | "An object [5070 oil cruet] with a specific use, whose extraordinary commercial success does not depend at all upon its functionality but upon … [its] distinguished image, even at the cost of diminished function" (Scarzella, 1985, CA30). | |
| | "La Comica is an object with a high-impact design … in which the image has a strong prevalence on the function …, and perhaps here lies its commercial success" (Polinoro, 1989, CA25). | |
| | *Product form as expression of artistic language* | |
| | "Graves had a great capacity of blending very different formal inspirations and of materializing them in a single and distinctive language" (A. Alessi, 1989, quoted in CA25). | |
| | "What I was more interested in in Starck's designing practice was the proximity of his designing method to the method of the artistic creation" (A. Alessi, 1989, quoted in CA25). | |

**First-Order Codes**

**Second-Order Codes (Concepts)**

**Registers**

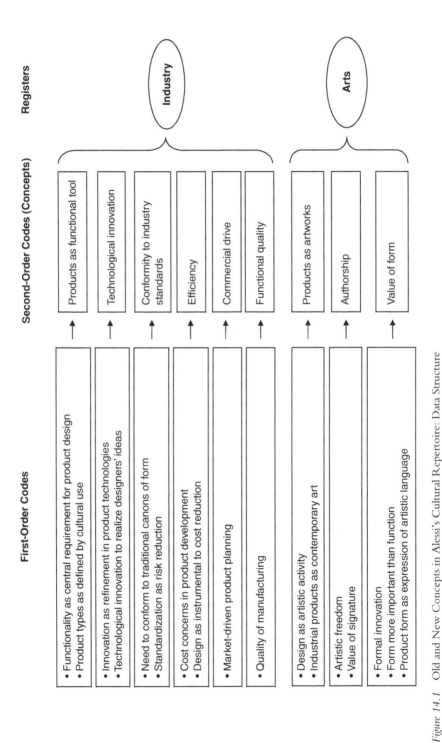

- Functionality as central requirement for product design
- Product types as defined by cultural use

→ Products as functional tool

- Innovation as refinement in product technologies
- Technological innovation to realize designers' ideas

→ Technological innovation

- Need to conform to traditional canons of form
- Standardization as risk reduction

→ Conformity to industry standards

- Cost concerns in product development
- Design as instrumental to cost reduction

→ Efficiency

- Market-driven product planning

→ Commercial drive

- Quality of manufacturing

→ Functional quality

**Industry**

- Design as artistic activity
- Industrial products as contemporary art

→ Products as artworks

- Artistic freedom
- Value of signature

→ Authorship

- Formal innovation
- Form more important than function
- Product form as expression of artistic language

→ Value of form

**Arts**

*Figure 14.1*  Old and New Concepts in Alessi's Cultural Repertoire: Data Structure

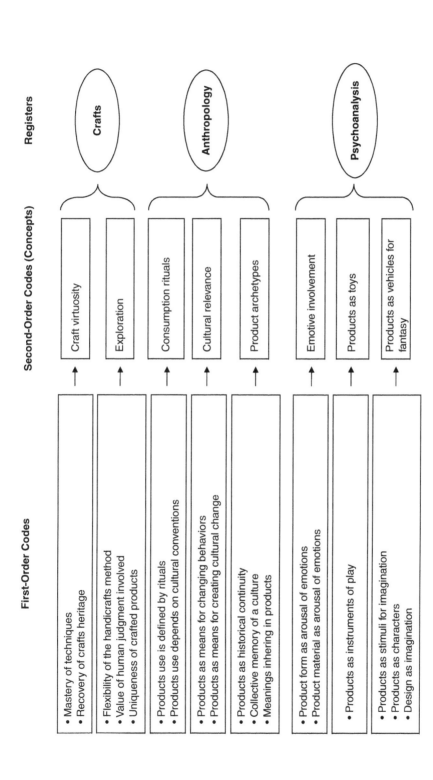

**First-Order Codes**

- Mastery of techniques
- Recovery of crafts heritage

- Flexibility of the handicrafts method
- Value of human judgment involved
- Uniqueness of crafted products

- Products use is defined by rituals
- Products use depends on cultural conventions

- Products as means for changing behaviors
- Products as means for creating cultural change

- Products as historical continuity
- Collective memory of a culture
- Meanings inhering in products

- Product form as arousal of emotions
- Product material as arousal of emotions

- Products as instruments of play

- Products as stimuli for imagination
- Products as characters
- Design as imagination

**Second-Order Codes (Concepts)**

Craft virtuosity

Exploration

Consumption rituals

Cultural relevance

Product archetypes

Emotive involvement

Products as toys

Products as vehicles for fantasy

**Registers**

Crafts

Anthropology

Psychoanalysis

*Figure 14.1*  Continued

repertoire of Alessi between 1970 and 2006, and the register from which they were borrowed.

By keeping track of when a concept first appeared and later featured in corporate texts, we could distinguish concepts that had a long-lasting influence from concepts that made only occasional appearance and were therefore dropped from our analysis. The latter were usually concepts, such as "ecological sustainability," that had no connections with other concepts in the evolving repertoire, and did not belong to any of the four registers. Longitudinal tracking also indicated that concepts from the four registers were introduced in four waves, usually through dedicated texts (see Figure 14.2 for a timeline of events).

Corporate texts explicitly related other concepts to the register of the household industry – or industrial manufacturing more generally (also mapped in Figure 14.1) – often highlighting the opposition between these concepts and new ones borrowed from other registers. We collected these concepts in a fifth cluster (see Table 14.4), and, in a further analytical step, we proceeded to map these oppositions more accurately, and examine their implications for organizational action.

*Step 3: Mapping oppositions among old and new cultural resources.* Archival data and interview data suggested that some concepts were viewed by organizational members as having contradictory implications for action. This observation led to another round of coding, in which we mapped the contradictions between concepts belonging to different registers. Past research used semiotic techniques to map "logical oppositions" between concepts (Weber, 2005; see also Weber et al., 2008; Tavory and Swidler, 2009). Our analysis focused on cultural resources in use in the organization; accordingly, we inferred oppositions from explicit statements in corporate texts and interview statements. Oppositions, in this sense, were not logically derived from external semiotic structures, but reflected how organizational members made sense of their reality. The outcome of this phase was a table tracking all the oppositions we encountered in our data base, along with selected evidence (fragments of text) (see Table 14.5), and a figure offering an overview of the opposing relationships among concepts from the five cultural registers of industry, arts, crafts, anthropology, and psychoanalysis (see Figure 14.3).

This observation was theoretically important because it pointed to the problematic nature of importing resources from other registers, and supported the view of Alessi's organizational culture as a repertoire to be flexibly used, rather than an ordered and internally coherent system of norms and beliefs.

*Step 4: Tracking the use of cultural resources in development initiatives.* A major next step of the analysis was to link the new concepts in Alessi's repertoire to organizational action. Iterating between archival sources and conversations with key informants, we identified 22 product development initiatives through which the transformation of the organization from producer of high-quality serving tools in stainless steel to a diversified producer of a broad range of objects for the house – designed by the most famous international architects and designers – was carried out. Corporate texts described these initiatives in depth and presented them as important milestones of Alessi's recent history. For each initiative, we tracked the concepts that corporate texts used to illustrate its rationale and the underlying philosophy, the changing practices associated with it (e.g., the use of graphic designers to develop products, or artisanal workshops to produce them), and the strategic innovations it introduced (e.g., new products segments or new target users). This analysis produced a table linking concepts, practices, and strategies, which was essential in documenting and analyzing how new cultural resources were used flexibly to pursue new strategies of action.

*Step 5: Relating concepts and changes in organizational practices.* Archival and interview data contained rich evidence that the new concepts introduced in the organization throughout the years were not merely aimed at projecting an appealing image to external audiences, but were

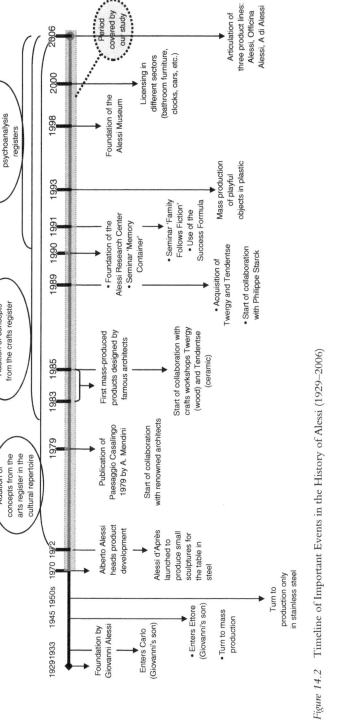

*Figure 14.2*  Timeline of Important Events in the History of Alessi (1929–2006)

*Table 14.4* Baseline Concepts from the Industry Register

| Second-Order Codes (Concepts) | First-Order Codes and Selected Evidence |
| --- | --- |
| Products as functional tools | *Functionality as central requirement for product design*<br>When one designs a bowl, for example, it has to meet simple functional needs – being able to hold fruit, for example (1996, CA23).<br><br>From a technical point of view, objects for hotels have properties and needs that are quite different from those of domestic objects: They have to be more resistant, more solid, heavier, and respond to complex functional needs (1985, CA30). |
| Technological innovation | *Innovation as refinement in production technologies*<br>In this company there has always been, and it was still very alive in those years, the idea of being at the technological forefront in the field of stainless steel cold-work. To put this in simple terms, we had the ambition of holding true to the statement: "What Alessi cannot make with stainless steel cannot be made by anyone else" (ID19). |
| Conformity to industry standards | *Need to conform to existing standards*<br>Design for the hotel industry is often a design without much personality, in order to allow people to substitute these objects easily. … Both in hotels and restaurants there are slightly different objects that do not belong to the same sets (ID18).<br><br>*Standardization as risk reduction*<br>Large-scale industry tends to work as far as possible from [creativity], because that is a risky area … but this means that all cars are the same (2001, CA33). |
| Efficiency | *Cost concerns in product development*<br>The preparation of molds [for steel objects] is highly elaborate and very expensive … implying the necessity to produce on a large scale to amortize investments for tools (1985, CA30).<br><br>*Design as instrumental to cost reduction*<br>[Interpreting design as an instrument of technology] tends to reduce its role as a means to help industry produce more rapidly and at a lower cost (2006, CA3). |
| Product quality | *Quality of manufacturing*<br>Top quality products are in our company's DNA (2006, CA3).<br><br>Quality means how products are polished, how they are finished. Our trays did not have sharp edges (ID22).<br><br>*Quality of materials*<br>Imitations of our products are much less expensive, but you can easily notice the difference, especially for plastic products: the quality of other producers' products is clearly inferior to ours (ID 9). |
| Commercial potential | *Market-driven product planning*<br>Large-scale industry is not concerned to make products of high aesthetic and cultural quality, they want to make popular products (2001, CA33).<br><br>Alessi and Mendini decided to … produce a new pot set that could target a … much larger market than that for "The Orion's Belt" (1989, CA25). |

*Table 14.5* Oppositions among Concepts from Different Cultural Registers [Excerpt]

| Opposition among Concepts | Analytical Observation | Selected Evidence |
| --- | --- | --- |
| *Arts Register vs. Industry Register* | | |
| Products as artworks vs. product as tool | Attempts to endow household objects with artistic and expressive value require the involvement of "artists" in the design process, who do not concern themselves with the functionality of their creations. | The freest expression of trends and scenarios is undoubtedly art, which neither has, nor claims to have, any immediate purpose or function (Mendini, quoted in Casciani, 1996). [Working with pure artists was difficult] because an artist's idea is not geared toward a usable object. Typically, it is more of an abstract or a decorative type of object. I mean, it is hard to think of having an artist design a coffee maker (ID19). |
| Value of form vs. product as tool | The exploration of new formal languages and the search for highly characterized product forms frequently occur at the expense of functionality. | What I was more interested in in Starck ... was the proximity of his designing method to the method of the artistic creation: ... the creation of objects where the function is secondary to the objects' expressive values (1989, CA25). "100% Make-up" was a provocative operation ... that was meant to highlight an opposite attitude to the one of the functional school of design.... They were emphasizing also the importance of ... the artistic-decorative aspect of the objects (ID14). |
| Authorship, Products as artworks vs. efficiency | Designer "authors" are allowed to realize their own ideas, which increases both production costs and market risk. | By pursuing creativity in advance of economic ... considerations, Alessi is a rare beast indeed ... [It] propagates a new way of working: "Our philosophy does not put economics or mass production first" (Sweet, 1998, p. 3). When I saw that squared aluminium pot I said: "I'd rather go home than work on that thing. Do you want to make a museum piece? Go ahead ...! We can hand-make ten of them without having to build the machines, ... and put one in the museum in New York ..., but I am not building the equipment and all that stuff" (ID22). |
| Authorship vs. commercial considerations | Designers' ideas characterized by original, complex forms are faithfully developed, even at the expense of the commercial considerations. | I can't stand the commercial pressure ... to produce uninspired, low-profile design. I prefer on the contrary to work with the most cultivated ... designers (1993, 34). The idea [for the Nuovo Milano set] was to keep on producing an author-marked cutlery set free from the traditional marketing logic (1989, CA25). |

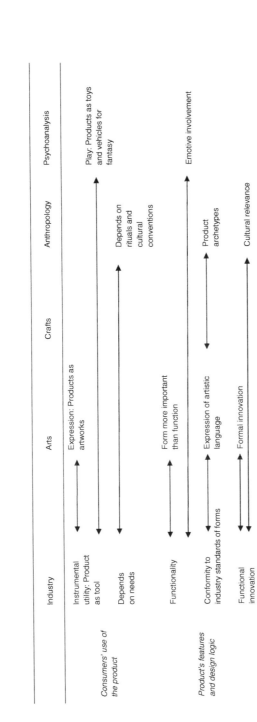

*Figure 14.3* Mapping Oppositions among Concepts from Different Cultural Registers

used internally to guide changes in practices and in some organizational structures. In fact, much of the archival material we used had been developed and used primarily, an informant explained, to "acculturate" organizational members by discussing new practices and the concepts that inspired them.

In a further analytical step, then, we built on the analysis of development initiatives to systematically map the relationships between concepts and practices. We first mapped all the new practices introduced in the organization since 1970, broadly grouping them in three areas – product development, manufacturing, and marketing and distribution. We then went back to our data to retrieve all the co-occurrences of references to concepts and practices in the corporate texts – or, in other words, all the fragments of text that explained practice change in terms of the new concepts. We created three separate tables to catalogue new practices in product development, manufacturing, and marketing and distribution, respectively, and link them to concepts from the four cultural registers (see Table 14.6 for an excerpt from one of these three tables). We also generated three visual representations of the timeline of changes in organizational practices in the three areas showing how these changes roughly co-occurred with the incorporation of new concepts in the repertoire (see Figure 14.4 for an example).

*Step 6: Documenting consequences for organizational strategies of action.* In a final round of analysis, we examined the effects of these new practices on Alessi's product market strategies in terms of the type of products it produced, the customer segments it served, and the resources it used to develop and manufacture products for these segments (materials and types of designers). In tracing these changes, we observed that practices across three broad areas (development, production, marketing and distribution) resulted in chains of actions that constituted new strategies of action through which Alessi sought to compete in the market place. These new strategies led the organization into new product categories, new customer segments, and into technologies based on new materials. They also redefined the bases of its competitive advantage – from high product quality and efficient manufacturing to aesthetic and cultural innovation. To map these outcomes, we developed yet another working table showing how each new development initiative contributed to introduce new concepts in the repertoire, alter organizational practices, and push strategic innovation in different directions (see Table 14.7). Through these analyses, we were able to describe the cultural resources Alessi used and their effects on various practices and diverse set of strategic outcomes, with a high degree of granularity.

## Conclusions

Research on organizational cultural repertoires has just begun to explore the implications of the adoption of a culture-as-toolkit perspective to the analysis of organizations. While more established perspectives rely on consolidated methodological conventions, methods adopted by past studies of organizational cultural repertoires are still varied. They range from comprehensive content analyses of large bodies of text to map the whole register of a field, to in-depth, qualitative case analyses to unpack the processes that underlie the organizational acquisition and use of cultural resources.

In this chapter, we have proposed an approach to the study of organizational cultural repertoires that balances the accurate mapping of the portion of the repertoire interested by the focal cultural processes (in our case, the incorporation of resources from a different register), with the systematic examination of the practical implications of the cultural resources involved in these processes. Our approach addresses two issues that are crucial for the adoption of a culture-as-toolkit perspective, as opposed to the more traditional ones.

Table 14.6 New Practices Implementing New Concepts in the Cultural Repertoire: Product Development [Excerpt]

| Practices | Implemented Concepts | Representative Quotations in the Data |
|---|---|---|
| Collaboration with acknowledged artists (1972–)<br><br>Responsibility for product design shifts from the technical office to external collaborators: not only industrial designers, but also graphic designers, architects, decorators, etc. | Products as artworks | "In the early 1980s, Alessandro Mendini suggested to use architects because architecture is the mother of arts, and every artistic movement starts from here" (ID3).<br><br>"[For the 100% Make Up project] 100 designers have been selected worldwide. They represent different areas of creativity: architects, designers, graphic designers, artists, fashion designers and other creative people belonging to alternative cultures" (1992, CA20). |
| Designers, names are explicitly identified as "authors" of specific products. | Authorship | "[The great idea that changed Alessi was] to bring in all of those personalities from the design world.… If the designer had an important name, it was an important name who works for Alessi" (ID22).<br><br>"Working with these [artists] … came from the awareness that these were people with something more, people who were able to confront the company's technology and goals in an innovative way, originating truly special products – special not in the sense of being bizarre or strange, but different, newer than anything else on the market" (ID25). |
| The collaboration with these artists is aimed at stimulating innovation in product form and at incorporating new styles and languages reflecting contemporary trends. | Value of form | "One of the aspects of … these years [the 1980s] is the project of objects with high formal content and very expressive. Hence, the role of the designer is fundamental, who, in the case of Alessi, is not anymore only the technician, but also the architect. Nonetheless, by reducing the dimension of his/her project without changing its linguistic elements, he/she is able to transfer on the object the same figurative and expressive power of his/her architectures" (1983, CA30). |
| Efforts to faithfully implement designers' ideas (1972–)<br><br>The task of the technical office becomes "translating" designers' ideas into manufacturable objects. The realization of designers' ideas has priority over production and sale-related concerns. | Authorship | "The feasibility study sometime can modify a project. As it should have happened in this case because his [Sottsass's Nuovo Milano Cutlery Set] cutlery, very rounded and with large differences in thickness, required some phases of hot processing, which is unusual for these objects. At the end, he [Sottsass] won, and the cutlery set was presented exactly as he wanted it" (1989, CA25).<br><br>"We [technicians] are not allowed to put limits on design: 'This is my [designer's] design, if you like it that's how it is, and if you don't like it, goodbye'" (ID21). |
| Technicians are expected to preserve designers' original forms, even at the expense of functionality or efficiency. | Value of form | "Architects are expected to investigate in experimental terms on the form of objects of use. For this reason, there are no constraints related to concrete aspects and necessities of production" (1985, CA30).<br><br>"The company … [is] a free place of linguistic research, to be offered to architects and designers, where they could elaborate and propose experimental … forms" (1983, CA22). |

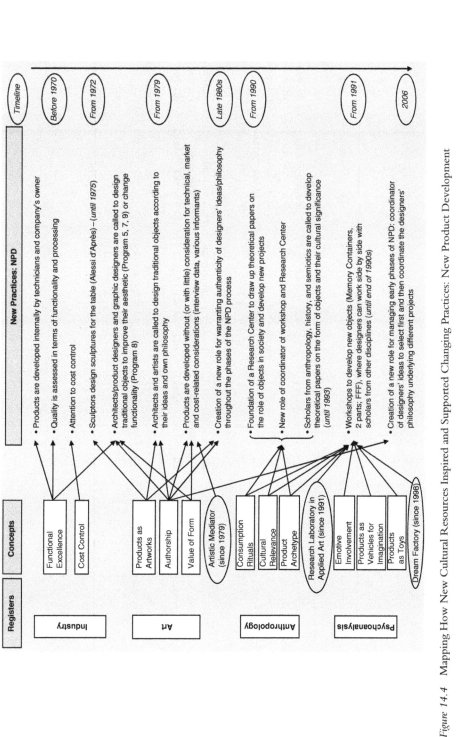

*Figure 14.4* Mapping How New Cultural Resources Inspired and Supported Changing Practices: New Product Development

Table 14.7 Linking Practices to New Strategies of Action [Excerpt]*

| Development Initiatives | Related NPD Practices | Related MFG Practices | Related MKTG Practices | Changes in Competitive Scope | Changes in Competitive Advantage |
|---|---|---|---|---|---|
| Alessi d'Après Industrial production of art objects on a large scale | Collaboration with sculptors, efforts to preserve artists' ideas (PRODUCTS AS ARTWORKS, AUTHORSHIP) | Large-scale production (EFFICIENCY) | Product commentaries, relationships with cultural institutions (PRODUCTS AS ARTWORKS), segmentation of retail | A new product category (art multiples), entry in an unfamiliar industry (art), addressing the ordinary home segment | Relatively low cost (for an art object) based on industrial production |
| Officina Alessi Engagement in the production of highly experimental and artful objects | Collaboration with external designers, efforts to preserve their ideas (AUTHORSHIP, VALUE OF FORM, EXPLORATION) | Small-scale (PRODUCTS AS ARTWORKS), craftsman's techniques, collaboration with craftsman's workshops (CRAFT VIRTUOSITY) | New catalogue, product commentaries, establishment of relationships with cultural institutions (PRODUCTS AS ARTWORKS), segmentation of retail | Expansion into new client segments (museums and design lovers) | Search for differentiation coming from original product forms and concepts, and the signature of an acknowledged artist |

*Note*
* Concepts driving a new practice are indicated in capital letters.

First, while mapping the evolving repertoire of the organization, we pay particular attention to tracking contradictions between cultural resources. One of the key differences between a view of culture-as-norms and a view of culture-as-toolkit is the idea that organizational cultures are constituted by a multitude of resources, the implications of which for thought and action are partly incompatible or outright contradictory. When studying cultural processes, therefore, accounting for these tensions and contradictions is crucial to justify the adoption of a culture-as-toolkit as opposed to a more traditional perspective. Further, unlike past studies that had mapped logical oppositions based on semiotic analysis (Weber, 2005), we captured tensions and contradictions from informants' accounts of the practical or symbolic implications of different cultural resources for the performance of specific organizational practices.

Second, our approach combined content analysis with a longitudinal case analysis to account for the substantive and strategic implications of the use of new cultural resources in organizations. Using content analysis of texts to map cultural repertoires may be questioned on the grounds that the results of this analysis may reflect corporate rhetoric rather than reality. The concepts uncovered by this analysis, in other words, may capture the discursive resources used by official corporate spokespersons to portray and justify organizational action, rather than the meaning structures that inspire and motivate choices (for a distinction between the discursive and practical-motivational modes of culture and cognition, see Vaisey, 2009). By linking the concepts resulting from content analysis to the changes in practices and strategies highlighted by case analysis, instead, our approach offers reassuring evidence of actual use of these cultural resources to envision and pursue new strategies of action.

# References

Barley, S. R. 1983. Semiotics and the study of occupational and organizational cultures. *Administrative Science Quarterly*, 28: 393–413.

Barley, S. R. 1990. Images of imaging: Notes of doing longitudinal fieldwork. *Organization Science*, 1(3): 220–247.

Becker, H. S. 1974. Art as a collective action. *American Sociological Review*, 39: 767–776.

Becker, H. S. 1982. *Art Worlds*. Berkeley, CA: University of California Press.

Branzi, A. 2004. *Il Design Italiano, 1964–2002 (Italian Design, 1964–2002)*. Milan: Mondadori Electa.

Canato, A., Ravasi, D., and Phillips, N. 2013. Coerced practice implementation in cases of low cultural fit: Cultural change and practice adaptation during the implementation of Six Sigma at 3M. *Academy of Management Journal*, 56: 1724–1753.

Casciani, S. 1996. *The Art Factory*. Milan: Editrice Abitare Segesta.

Chatman, J. A., and Spataro S. A. 2005. Using self-categorization theory to understand relational demography-based variations in people's responsiveness to organizational culture. *Academy of Management Journal*, 48: 321–331.

Clignet, R. 1979. The variability of paradigms in the production of culture: A comparison of arts and science. *American Sociological Review*, 44: 392–409.

Cooke, R., and Rousseau, D. 1988. Behavioral norms and expectations: A quantitative approach to the assessment of organizational culture. *Group and Organizational Studies*, 13: 245–273.

Crane, D. 1989. Reward system in avant-garde art: Social networks and stylistic change. In A. W. Foster and J. R. Blau (eds.) *Arts and Society: Readings in the Sociology of the Arts*. Albany, NY: State University of New York Press, 261–276.

De Fusco, R. 2002. *Storia del Design Italian (History of Italian Design)*. Roma: Editori Laterza.

DiMaggio, P. J. 1997. Culture and cognition. *Annual Review of Sociology*, 23(1): 263–287.

Gaut, B. 2007. *Art, Emotion and Ethics*. Oxford: Oxford University Press.

Gioia, D. A., Corley, K. G., and Hamilton, A. L. 2012. Seeking qualitative rigor in inductive research: Notes on the Gioia methodology. *Organizational Research Methods*, 16(1): 15–31.

Giorgi, S., Lockwood, C., and Glynn, M. A. 2015. The many faces of culture: Making sense of 30 years of research on culture in organization studies. *Academy of Management Annals*, 9(1): 1–54.

Harris, S. G. 1994. Organizational culture as individual sensemaking: A schema-based perspective. *Organization Science*, 5: 309–321.

Harrison, S. H., and Corley, K. G. 2011. Clean climbing, carabineers and cultural cultivation: Developing an open-systems perspective of culture. *Organization Science*, 22(2): 391–412.

Hofstede, G., Neuijen, B., Ohayv, D., and Sanders, G. 1990. Measuring organizational cultures: A qualitative and quantitative study across twenty cases. *Administrative Science Quarterly*, 35: 286–316.

Howard-Grenville, J., Golden-Biddle, K., Irwin, J., and Mao, J. 2011. Liminality as cultural process for cultural change. *Organization Science*, 22: 522–539.

Kirkman, B. L., and Shapiro, D. L. 2001. The impact of cultural values on job satisfaction and organizational commitment in self-managing work teams: The mediating role of employee resistance. *Academy of Management Journal*, 44: 557–569.

Kirkman, B. L., Chen, G., Farh, J.-L., Chen, Z. X., and Lowe, K. B. 2009. Individual power distance orientation and follower reaction to transformational leaders: A cross-level, cross-cultural examination. *Academy of Management Journal*, 52: 744–776.

Kunda, G. 1992. *Engineering Culture: Control and Commitment in a High-tech Corporation*. Philadelphia, PA: Temple University Press.

Lincoln, Y., and Guba, E. 1985. *Naturalistic Inquiry*. Beverly Hills, CA: Sage.

Locke, K. 2001. *Grounded Theory in Management Research*. London: Sage.

Luthans, F., McCaul, H. S., and Dodd, N. G. 1985. Organizational commitment: A comparison of American, Japanese, and Korean employees. *Academy of Management Journal*, 28: 213–219.

Martin, J. 2002. *Organizational Culture: Mapping the Terrain*. Thousand Oaks, CA: Sage.

Martin, J., Feldman, M., Hatch, M., and Sitkin, S. 1983. The uniqueness paradox in organizational stories. *Administrative Science Quarterly*, 28: 438–453.

Moon, Y. E., Dessain, V., and Sjoman, A. 2003. *Alessi: Evolution of an Italian Design Factory*. Cambridge, MA: Harvard Business Review Case Collection.

Morrill, C. 2008. Culture and organization theory. *The Annals of the American Academy of Political and Social Science*, 619: 15–40.

Morris, M. W., Leung, K., Ames, D., and Lickel, B. 1999. Views from inside and outside: Integrating emic and etic insights about culture and justice judgment. *Academy of Management Review*, 24: 781–796.

Ocasio, W., and Joseph, J. 2005. Cultural adaptation and institutional change: The evolution of vocabularies of corporate governance, 1972–2003. *Poetics*, 33(3–4): 163–178.

O'Reilly, C., and Chatman, J., 1996. Culture as social control: Corporations, cults and commitment. In B. Staw and L. Cummings (eds.) *Research in Organizational Behavior*, vol. 18. Greenwich, CT: JAI Press, 157–200.

O'Reilly, C., Chatman, J., and Caldwell, D. 1991. People and organizational culture: A profile comparison approach to assessing person-organization fit. *Academy of Management Journal*, 14: 487–516.

Pettigrew, A. M. 1990. Longitudinal field research on change: Theory and practice. *Organization Science*, 1(3): 267–292.

Phillips, N., and Brown, J. L. 1993. Analyzing communication in and around organizations: A critical hermeneutic approach. *Academy of Management Journal*, 36: 1547–1576.

Ravasi, D., and Schultz, M. 2006. Responding to organizational identity threats: Exploring the role of organizational culture. *Academy of Management Journal*, 49: 433–458.

Rindova, V., Dalpiaz, E., and Ravasi, D. 2011. A cultural quest: A study of organizational use of new cultural resources in strategy formation. *Organizational Science*, 22: 413–431.

Salvato, C. 2003. The role of micro-strategies in the engineering of firm evolution. *Journal of Management Studies*, 40: 83–108.

Salvato, C. 2006. Micro-foundations of organizational adaptation: A field study in the evolution of product development capabilities in a design firm. Unpublished dissertation, Jonkoping International Business School.

Schein, E. H. 1985. *Organizational Culture and Leadership* (1st edition). San Francisco, CA: Jossey-Bass.

Schultz, M., and Hatch, M. J. 1996. Living with multiple paradigms: The case of paradigm interplay in organizational culture studies. *Academy of Management Review*, 21: 529–557.

Smircich, L. 1983. Concepts of culture and organizational analysis. *Administrative Science Quarterly*, 28: 339–358.

Sweet, F. 1998. *Alessi: Art and Poetry*. London: Thames and Hudson.

Swidler, A. 1986. Culture in action: Symbols and strategies. *American Sociological Review*, 51: 273–286.

Swidler, A. 2001. *Talk of Love: How Culture Matters*. Chicago, IL: University of Chicago Press.

Tavory, I., and Swidler, A. 2009. Condom semiotics: Meaning and condom use in rural Malawi. *American Sociological Review*, 74(2): 171–189.

Vaisey, S. 2009. Motivation and justification: A dual-process model of culture in action. *American Journal of Sociology*, 114: 1675–1715.

Van Maanen, J. 1979. The fact of fiction in organizational ethnography. *Administrative Science Quarterly*, 24(4): 539–550.

Verganti, R. 2006. Innovating through design. *Harvard Business Review*, 84(December): 114–122.

Weber, K. 2005. A toolkit for analyzing corporate cultural toolkits. *Poetics*, 33: 227–252.

Weber, K., Heinze, K. L., and DeSoucey, M. 2008. Forage for thought: Mobilizing codes in the movement for grass-fed meat and dairy products. *Administrative Science Quarterly*, 53(3): 529–567.

Wrong, D. H. 1961. The oversocialized conception of man in modern sociology. *American Sociological Review*, 26(2): 183–193.

Yin, R. K. 1994. *Case Study Research*. Beverly Hills, CA: Sage.

Zilber, T. B. 2006. The work of the symbolic in institutional processes: Translations of rational myths in Israel high tech. *Academy of Management Journal*, 49(2): 281–303.

# 15

# QUALITATIVE APPROACHES FOR STUDYING INNOVATION AS PROCESS

*Raghu Garud, Hans Berends, and Philipp Tuertscher*

This chapter articulates various options for qualitatively conducting research on innovation as process. Although this quest seems straightforward, it is far from the case. Several questions must first be addressed including: *What is innovation? What is process? And, what exactly is qualitative?* It seems there are more questions than we can productively address in this short piece. Notwithstanding this challenge, even an overview of key issues can generate an informed opinion on qualitative approaches to the study of innovation as process. Consequently, we briefly explore each term to explicate how we use them.

## Explicating Terms

### *What Is Innovation?*

Everyday, in our personal and professional lives, we innovate. Nothing matters more to our success and our survival – and yet we struggle with our understanding of the process of innovation. Sometimes it is messy; sometimes it is elegant; usually it is both and more. Our difficulty in grasping the process of innovation is vexing. Successful innovation brings us joy and confidence and well-being. It generates long-term sustainable growth. Once we've tasted this wonderful experience, we want to experience it again – but we are frequently confounded. The process is nonlinear, and it cannot be managed in traditional ways. By following our best practices and instincts, we can generate a *Post-it Note* or a valuable new pharmaceutical like imiquoimod, or we can hit a dry hole.

*(Coyne, erstwhile Senior Vice President of Research and Development at 3M Corporation, 1999: vii)*

In this observation, we see at least two meanings of the term innovation. One is that of an outcome (what Coyne refers to as "successful innovation"). Indeed, most think of innovations as novel "things" that have value in use. However, the process whereby such outcomes emerge is yet another meaning associated with innovation. And, as Coyne noted, even though we all desire successful outcomes, "we struggle with our understanding of the process of innovation."

So, what lies "under the hood" of the innovation engine? Coyne offers a clue in his observation "The process is nonlinear, and it cannot be managed in traditional ways." Indeed, Coyne's observation from the field is backed by research that details the complexities of innovation (e.g., Dougherty and Dunne, 2011; Garud et al., 2013). The process is full of ups-and-downs, false starts and dead-ends, partial victories and triumphs as bits and pieces of phenomena combine and recombine as innovation journeys unfold (Van de Ven et al., 1999).

Even as scholars accumulated such insights on the process of innovation, underlying innovation dynamics have changed. For most of the twentieth century, a dominant model of innovation conceptualized the process of innovation as one involving new product introductions during eras of ferment followed by relatively long eras of incremental change (Tushman and Anderson, 1986; Utterback and Abernathy, 1975). However, with the advent of digital technologies, the frequency of new product introductions, updates, and extensions has increased to such an extent that the boundaries between product generations have blurred (Garud et al., 2008; Yoo et al., 2012). In such a world, it is no longer sufficient to think about the *process of innovation* demarcated by a beginning and an ending. Instead, *innovation itself is a continual unfolding process* (Garud et al., 2017).

## What Is Process?

We begin with a distinction that Mohr (1982) offered between variance and process. With variance, "the precursor (X) is a necessary and sufficient condition for the outcome (Y)" (Mohr, 1982: 37). In contrast, a process is: "a series of occurrences in a sequence over time so as to explain how some phenomenon comes about" (Mohr, 1982: 9). Distinguishing such a view from a variance view, Mohr noted, "The predominant flavor of a process model is that of a series of occurrences of events rather than a set of relations among variables" (Mohr, 1982: 54). The sequence of events matters, as evident in Mohr's observation,

> what comes out of a probabilistic process depends on what goes in, and what goes in almost always depends on what came out of a former one, so that their order must be faithfully rendered within the model.
>
> *(Mohr, 1982: 59–60)*[1]

The view of process as a sequence of events representing changes in things is one way of understanding the emergence of phenomena over time. Things interact with one another to generate events that can be observed (Morgeson et al., 2015). These events, when placed in chronological order, can generate an explanation of how phenomena unfold. For instance, a person could be inflicted with malaria if a mosquito that has already acquired the parasite bites him or her. But, if a mosquito first bites a person and then acquires the parasite, malaria is not the outcome. In other words, the sequence of events matters.

The temporal sequence of events as changes in things based on substantive metaphysics is one view of process (Van de Ven and Poole, 2005). Process metaphysics (Rescher, 2005) offers another. Process metaphysics views phenomena as unfolding journeys that materialize things along the way. Rescher (1996: 27) clarified that "process philosophy does not – or need not – deny substances (things), but sees them as subordinate in status and ultimately inhering in processes." In the management field, Langley et al. (2013) highlighted the differences between process and substance views on phenomena by observing,

> process and temporality … can be viewed from different ontologies of the social world: one a world made of things in which processes represent change in things (grounded in a substantive metaphysics) and the other a world of processes, in which things are reifications of processes (Tsoukas and Chia, 2002) (grounded in process metaphysics).

Not surprisingly, these two ontological positions have their epistemological counterparts. Chia and Langley (2004) noted,

> The first perspective appears dominant in much of organizational and social scientific research, and tends to be pragmatic, empirically grounded, and analytical in orientation. The latter perspective has been primarily conceptual, strongly informed by strands of process philosophy, theology and the humanities at large, following especially the lead of philosophers such as James, Whitehead, Bergson, and Deleuze.... *While the first perspective helps us observe and empirically research process, the latter enables us to appreciate the sui generis nature of process. Each one has its own strengths and weaknesses.*
>
> *(Emphasis added)*

We have deliberately emphasized the last part of Chia and Langley's (2004) observation to highlight the difficulties involved in empirically investigating phenomena from a perspective that embraces process metaphysics. Rescher's (1996: 37) observation offers one way to do so. He noted, "we humans understand change owing to the fact that *we experience change* in ourselves: we act or do things, and things happen to us" (emphasis added). From this, an empirical approach to process metaphysics is to study and report change as experienced by those engaged with phenomena.

Synthesizing observations across Mohr (1982) and Rescher (1996), for the purpose of this paper we propose two positions on how researchers might empirically study innovation as process. These are *process as observed* by researchers, and *process as experienced* by actors in the field. We do not advocate one position over the other. Instead, we want to leave it to researchers to decide which approach they would like to choose for their projects depending on their goals and the questions they want to address.

Indeed, our investigation of papers that have qualitatively examined innovation processes highlights that some scholars have chosen hybrid approaches. Hybrid approaches are consistent with the utility of embracing a paradox inherent in organizing – namely, organizational phenomena are substances and processes at the same time. As Einstein noted in his discussion of wave–particle duality in physics,

> It seems as though we must use sometimes the one theory and sometimes the other, while at times we may use either. We are faced with a new kind of difficulty. We have two contradictory pictures of reality; separately neither of them fully explains the phenomena of light, but together they do.
>
> *(Einstein and Infeld, 1938: 279)*

## *What Is Qualitative?*

Many in our discipline tend to distinguish qualitative research by comparing it with quantitative research (Cornelissen, 2016; Golden-Biddle and Locke, 2007). Some think that the latter is research conducted with numbers whereas the former is research conducted with texts. Others conceptualize qualitative research as being exploratory and quantitative research as confirmatory. In this regard, Eisenhardt et al. (2016: 1115) equate qualitative research ("cases, interpretivist studies, and ethnography") with inductive theory building.[2] Furthermore, they note:

> Inductive research on grand challenges is more likely to flourish with multiple approaches, something that is difficult when authors must follow specific templates.

A good example is requiring authors to follow a particular writing format which Pratt (2009) cautions against. An illustration is mandating a data structure figure. While this device may make sense for some studies, it is a force-fit for others, as its authors note (Gioia, Corley and Hamilton, 2013). In fact, given that a "data structure" displays names such as for categories or concepts and themes or constructs, but often lacks actual data, its usefulness seems modest.

Our views on the distinctive domain of qualitative process research may already be evident in the moves we have made and the turns that we have taken. For us, qualitative means appreciating the richness of phenomena by considering their relational (e.g., the bits and pieces constituting activities) and temporal (e.g., sequences, patterns, and temporal experiences of those involved) contexts. As relationality and temporality are progressively "endogenized," we step away from the realm of data and information generated by using pre-determined categories and criteria, to the realm of meaning and interpretation of phenomena as observed and experienced (Bruner, 1991). The latter implicates notions of quality endogenous to situated experiences, and not those imposed from the outside.

## Options for Conducting Qualitative Research on Innovation as Process

Now that we have explicated our positions on some of the key terms that form the basis for this paper, we now provide specific examples of research from the innovation management literature for illustrative purposes (Table 15.1). The columns in Table 15.1 highlight various variance and process options. From our investigation of published pieces from a range of journals, we found that process options lay across a spectrum. At one end is research based on *process as observed* as a sequence of events. At the other end is research based on *process as experienced* by those involved. And, there are hybrids in-between. The examples we offer, while indicative of the onto-epistemology positions of each approach, clearly spill over to the other approaches (see Table 15.2 for more details).

Following Allison (1971: 8), we offer a number of caveats as to how our exposition of the research ought to be read. First, each position in Table 15.1 is a "caricature, or a strawman." But, caricatures can be useful, as they allow one to think of ideal types and, in turn, hybrids. Second, fitting in empirical work into these positions is necessarily Procrustean. Phenomena, like the research studies we review, are richer than any theory or method, and can be approached from multiple onto-epistemological positions. Moreover, it is impossible to do justice to all the details of the methods used and the theories employed in the articles we reviewed. Indeed, our objective is not to conduct a comprehensive review, nor is it to offer extensive notes on how to design a study, gather data, analyze it, and report findings. Instead, our review is meant to serve a cartographic role, directing the attention of readers to different methods and theories used in process-oriented studies. Finally, in any research effort, there is always a creative leap (Klag and Langley, 2013; Weick, 1989) that cannot be fully explicated, nor should this be codified, in our opinion.

### *Variance Approaches*

Continuing with the distinction offered by Mohr (1982) between variance and process, we begin our exploration with studies conducted from a variance perspective. Although qualitative approaches can be used for provisional theory testing (Glaser and Strauss, 1967), here we focus on exploratory studies that inductively generate hypotheses, which can then be tested across

Table 15.1 Innovation Process Inquiry Approaches

| | Variance | Process | | |
| --- | --- | --- | --- | --- |
| | | Process as Observed | ← In-between → | Process as Experienced |
| Objectives | Generate theory by identifying efficient causation between independent and dependent variables moderated and mediated by others. | Identification of a pattern in the progression of sequence of events to appreciate innovation as a complex unfolding and emerging process involving multiple actors with different frames of reference and different levels of inclusion. | Contextualize innovation journeys and identification of motivations and strategies that were involved in framing the innovations as they emerged. | Appreciate innovation as a human endeavor involving a plenum of agencies; forces scholars to ask values-based questions as to what innovation is, for whom, and for what purpose. |
| Methods | Theoretically sample entities with different outcomes and then compare and contrast them to inductively understand potential causes for the differences. | Identify events either in one string or multiple strings and look for patterns such as resonance between these strings and occasions when these strings become entangled to generate new events. | A historical contextualized account based on publicly available data on events and experiences of the participants. | Track experiences through ethnographic approaches and/or following the narratives of the actors involved. |
| Examples | Brown and Eisenhardt (1997) | Garud and Van de Ven (1989) | Hargadon and Douglas (2001) | Garud (2008) |
| | Block et al. (2016) | Reymen et al. (2015) | Tuertscher et al. (2014) | Deken et al. (2016) |

Table 15.2 Details of the Methods Used in the Papers Reviewed

| | Variance | Process | | |
| --- | --- | --- | --- | --- |
| | | Process as Observed | ← Hybrid → | Process as Experienced |
| Research design | Brown and Eisenhardt (1997)<br>• Grounded theory generating inductive insights<br>• Multiple case design (9 cases) using replication logic (Yin, 1993)<br>• Cases treated as independent experiments<br>• Theoretical sampling<br>Block et al. (2016)<br>• Grounded theory-building<br>• Multiple–case study (Eisenhardt, 1989) | Garud and Van de Ven (1989)<br>• Single case<br>• Follow the actors and events<br>• Ongoing journey<br>• Principle of symmetry – not to evaluate any event in and of itself<br>Reymen et al. (2015)<br>• Theoretical sampling (Gerring, 2007)<br>• Multiple cases<br>• Determining beginning and end of journey | Hargadon and Douglas (2001)<br>• Single, revelatory case [(Yin, 1993)]<br>• Historical analysis (Kieser, 1994)<br>Tuertscher et al. (2014)<br>• Longitudinal study focusing on critical technological controversies (Latour, 1987)<br>• Embedded case design (Yin, 1993)<br>• Zooming in and zooming out to identify micro-mechanisms and understand their role in the overall | Garud (2008)<br>• Immersion in collective "events"<br>• Abductive<br>• Multiple such events, but not replicative logic<br>Deken et al. (2016)<br>• Aim at theory elaboration (Vaughan, 1992)<br>• In-depth longitudinal study of single case (two years)<br>• Narratives of episodes as embedded unit of analysis |

*continued*

Table 15.2 Continued

| | Variance | Process | | |
|---|---|---|---|---|
| | | Process as Observed | ← Hybrid → | Process as Experienced |
| Data collection | Brown and Eisenhardt (1997)<br>• Incorporated data from two to three levels of management hierarchy<br>• Also incorporated impact of company- and industry-level forces<br>• Real-time observations and retrospective data (interviews, questionnaires, secondary data)<br><br>Block et al. (2016)<br>• Semi-structured interviews with CEOs and business unit managers<br>• Triangulation with archival data such as annual reports (Yin, 1993), to mitigate retrospective bias (Huber and Power, 1985)<br>• Interviews with academic experts and industry experts | Garud and Van de Ven (1989)<br>• Archival and real time (five years+)<br>• From multiple sources including interviews, trade journals, attendance at conferences, scientific journals, strategic business meetings at 3M etc. [(Garud and Rappa, 1994)]<br>• Events generated from this intensive immersion into the thick of things<br><br>Reymen et al. (2015)<br>• Retrospective interviewing (Huber and Power, 1985)<br>• Focus on significant events (Chell, 2004)<br>• Triangulation to ensure multiple data sources per event (Yin, 1993)<br>• Creation of event lists to enhance reliable recollection of retrieval (Belli, 1998) | Hargadon and Douglas (2001)<br>• Archival data<br>• Compilations of primary data including documentation of observed events as well as experiences by involved actors (inventors, investors, and consumers)<br>• Secondary histories of Edison and the gas lighting industry<br><br>Tuertscher et al. (2014)<br>• Twenty years archival data (meeting minutes, presentations, reports, emails, and personal notes)<br>• Unobtrusive data collection (Webb and Weick, 1979): data were generated and archived by actors in real time for their own purpose<br>• Archival data was complemented with six years of contemporary data (observations and interviews) | Garud (2008)<br>• Ethnographic<br>• Archival<br>• Gather the bits and pieces at conferences (photographs, visiting cards, drafts of communiqués, edits, narrative snippets, rumors, etc.)<br><br>Deken et al. (2016)<br>• Ethnographic methods<br>• Observations of various meetings, captured in field notes<br>• Formal and informal interviews with stakeholders<br>• Documents produced and used in routines<br>• Focus on actions as constitutive elements of routines (Feldman and Pentland, 2003) |

| | Brown and Eisenhardt (1997) | Garud and Van de Ven (1989) | Hargadon and Douglas (2001) | Garud (2008) |
|---|---|---|---|---|
| Data analysis | • Grounded theory building (Glaser and Strauss, 1967)<br>• First writing individual case studies and then comparing across cases to construct conceptual framework (Eisenhardt, 1989; Miles and Huberman, 1994) | • Analysis of events within and across tracks [Van de Ven and Poole, 1995]<br>• Patterns such as FDA cycles<br>• Identification of critical events that shaped industry emergence | • Historical analysis of the interplay between design, innovation, and institutions<br>• Focus on concrete details and actions of particular situations to understand the larger systems of meaning reflected in them (Geertz, 1973) | • Collage work that involved:<br>• Looking at the lived experiences of the many different people and the translation of many different things and activities (texts, instruments, sub-events) at these conferences<br>• And juxtaposed against extant insights from relevant literature (e.g., isomorphism, collective fields, translation, immutable mobiles, etc.) |

| | Block et al. (2016) | Reymen et al. (2015) | Tuertscher et al. (2014) | Deken et al. (2016) |
|---|---|---|---|---|
| | • Structured and iterative theory building approach<br>• Open coding of interview data, with some codes derived from literature<br>• Combination of codes into common themes and aggregate dimensions (Gioia et al., 2013)<br>• Assess inter-rater reliability of coding<br>• Comparison of four cases on aggregate dimensions (Miles and Huberman, 1994)<br>• Establish causal link of aggregate dimensions to innovation outcome, captured in propositions | • Uniform definition of events [(colligation, Abbott, 1984)]<br>• Iterative creation of event lists that document the chronology of cases (Van de Ven and Poole, 1990)<br>• Creation of coding scheme to code distinct events (Poole et al., 2000)<br>• Moving averages of event types<br>• Identifying turning points as embedded unit of analysis (Lichtenstein et al., 2006)<br>• Identifying necessary conditions for turning points (Mohr, 1982)<br>• Within case analysis and cross-case analysis | • Analysis of technological challenges encountered over time and how they were addressed<br>• Considered events as important occurrences within a larger flow (Van de Ven, 1992), visualized in diagrams to get holistic understanding (Langley, 1999)<br>• Coding for thematic content and patterns (Miles and Huberman, 1994) to identify emergent themes and explanations, corroboration with latent semantic analysis (Deerwester et al., 1990) and scientometrics (Callon et al., 1986)<br>• Validation of explanations by pattern matching across embedded cases (Trochim, 1989) | • Identify routines as patterns of action from event list<br>• Identify episodes of routine performances, written as narratives (Langley, 1999)<br>• Use of coding to develop categories of "routine work" used in episodes (Van Maanen, 1988)<br>• Analysis of breakdowns in episodes (Sandberg and Tsoukas, 2011)<br>• Analyzing dependencies across episodes to acknowledge temporal connectedness (Pettigrew, 1990)<br>• Visualization of patterns (Langley, 1999) |

continued

Table 15.2 Continued

| Variance | Process | | |
| --- | --- | --- | --- |
| | *Process as Observed* | *← Hybrid →* | *Process as Experienced* |
| **Reporting of findings** | Brown and Eisenhardt (1997)<br>• Only reporting of cross-case comparisons (individual case stories were not reported)<br>• Differences on the "dependent variable" were juxtaposed against different patterns of the explanatory features, mostly summarized and stylized using tables<br><br>Block et al. (2016)<br>• General introduction of phenomenon<br>• Sequential discussion of five propositions on determinants<br>• Presentation of evidence for each of four cases<br>• Integrated causal model | Garud and Van de Ven (1989)<br>• Description of chronology of events within and across tracks [[Langley, 1999]]<br>• "Petri-net" inspired diagram of industry emergence<br><br>Reymen et al. (2015)<br>• Graphs representing moving averages and turning points<br>• Tables with turning case per case<br>• Examples, supported with quotes<br>• Integrated model<br>• Illustration of model with history of one case | Hargadon and Douglas (2001)<br>• Description of chronology of events within and across tracks [[Langley, 1999]]<br>• Combined with quotes and narratives describing how contemporary actors experienced unfolding events<br>• Table with timeline of key events<br><br>Tuertscher et al. (2014)<br>• Narrative of unfolding of process<br>• Zooming into the process to explain micro-mechanisms<br>• Quotes to convey to readers how actors experienced process<br>• Zooming out to show overall process<br>• Illustrations and diagrams to visualize complex relational data<br>• Diagram of process model | Garud (2008)<br>• Narrative style of relational and temporal unfolding and becoming<br>• Zooming in and zooming out<br>• Photos and textual documents from the conferences shown so as to bring the readers into these conferences<br><br>Deken et al. (2016)<br>• Narratives of selected episodes<br>• Iterative telling and showing<br>• Diagram of process model |

*Note*
We have inserted citations to references used by the authors within parentheses (). Early articles employed many of these methods; only, they did not cite articles, as they were not in print at that time. Consequently, we have now inserted some cites using brackets [].

large-sample studies. Such variance research could generate "process" models that consider innovation variables such as "innovation speed" or "adoption," and the links between them. Driving such inductive research are considerations such as theoretical sampling, replication logic, generalizability, and inter-rater reliability. These issues are in no particular order, nor is the list comprehensive.

**Two templates.** Scholars have been using two major templates to induce theoretical insights (see Langley and Abdallah, 2011, for a comparison between the two approaches). With the "Eisenhardt" method, several cases (typically six to eight) are theoretically sampled so as to establish variations across the dependent variables (such as success or failure) and then rich case studies are written to inductively understand the potential causes for the variations in the dependent variables. In contrast, with the "Gioia" method, researchers develop a corpus of data typically based on interviews from one or more settings, which they then interpret using open and axial coding. This effort results in a "data structure" comprising first-order and second-order categories, and possibly overarching theoretical categories (Gioia et al., 2013). The first-order level captures informant-centric terms/codes and a second-order level denotes researcher-centric theoretical themes and dimensions (Rheinhardt et al., forthcoming). This approach generates an inductive model that establishes the interrelationships (typically causal) between the second-order categories.

*Overview of study 1:* Brown and Eisenhardt (1997) conducted a study to generate insights on phenomena that did not conform to the then predominant model of punctuated change. In their own words, Brown and Eisenhardt (1997: 2)

> chose grounded theory building because of [their] interest in looking at a rarely explored phenomenon for which extant theory did not appear to be useful. In such situations, a grounded theory-building approach is more likely to generate novel and accurate insights into the phenomenon under study than reliance on either past research or office-bound thought experiments (Glaser and Strauss, 1967).

As per the hallmarks of this "Eisenhardt" method, the authors chose a multiple-case research design that permitted a "replication logic" (Yin, 1994) in which the cases were treated as a series of *independent* experiments that confirmed or disconfirmed emerging conceptual insights. A comparison of successful and less successful firms showed that successful multiple-product innovation (a) blends limited structure around responsibilities and priorities with extensive communication and design freedom to create improvisation within current projects; (b) relies on a wide variety of low-cost probes into the future, including experimental products, futurists, and strategic alliances; and (c) links the present and future together through rhythmic, time-paced transition processes. Generalizability is a hallmark of this method, as these findings can be tested in other large-sample-based studies.

*Overview of study 2:* Block et al. (2016) used the "Gioia method" to induce new theory on "user-manufacturer diversification." The authors identified four cases where firms started out as user-innovators and then extended their operations to manufacture and sell the products of their innovative efforts even to competitors. In other words, these firms diversified vertically by supplying their products to others, including competitors, besides using them for their own purposes.

The authors' inductive theory development effort focused on finding explanatory variables for this outcome. Interview data were analyzed by creating a "data structure" with interview quotes, combined codes, and aggregate dimensions. Findings were summarized in a model of five antecedent variables that predict initiation and stability of user-manufacturer diversification. For instance, one of their propositions is as follows:

A continuous stream of user innovations from the core business leads to the accumulation of deep user need and solution knowledge, which in turn favors the move toward and the success of user-manufacturer diversification through supplying product innovation ideas and generating absorptive capacity for external user needs.

Presumably, one would test this proposition (and the others) by regressing the extent to which user-manufacturer diversification is successful (the dependent variable) against the extent to which a business continues to offer a stream of user innovations (as the independent variable) mediated by the accumulation of knowledge on user needs and solutions.

**Summary.** The two examples we have chosen are exemplary. One, based on realism, generates insights by comparing across cases. The other, based on interpretivism, generates insights from a single case, based on interpretations offered by those involved. Both use constant comparison as an analytical technique to induce generalizable propositions. Both approaches offer models that establish causal explanations between categories that were inductively derived from grounded theorization. However, the use of the word "process" in these studies differs from the use of the term "process" as development, as noted by Van de Ven and Poole (1995: 512):

> Our developmental view of process should not be confused with two other uses of process in the management literature. Here [the latter], process refers to either (1) the underlying logic that explains a causal relationship between independent and dependent variables in a variance theory or (2) a category of concepts of organizational actions (e.g., rates of communications, work flows, decision-making techniques, or methods for strategy making). *These concepts or mechanisms may be at work to explain an organizational result, but they do not describe how these variables or mechanisms unfold or change over time.*

*(Emphasis added)*

## Process Approaches

These observations serve as a transition to notions of process that lie closer to those articulated by Mohr (1982) and Rescher (1996). Such an approach structures and analyzes data over time, rather than across cases or constructs. We will discuss various approaches ranging from studies exemplifying process as observed, to process as experienced. We also explore hybrids that embrace the substance/process duality. For each approach, we provide examples to illustrate the methodological diversity that exists.

**Process as observed.** One approach is to identify the *events* that unfold in-between idea conception (which marks a beginning) and commercialization (which marks an ending). The significance of any single event is not readily evident in and of itself. Instead, and consistent with Mohr's suggestions, an innovation journey is understood by finding patterns in a sequence of events. Indeed, such sequencing of events in-between beginnings and endings generates a rich understanding of the challenges involved in taking an idea from conception to commercialization (Van de Ven et al., 1999).

*Overview of study 1:* Research from the Minnesota Innovation Research Program (MIRP) offers one such event sequence approach. Events were conceptualized as changes in ideas, people, transactions, contexts, and outcomes as expressed by participants involved with innovation journeys (Van de Ven et al., 1999). In addition, considerable contextual data were gathered from sources such as articles in trade and scientific journals, media articles, interviews, ethnographic observations, patents, etc. (Garud and Rappa, 1994). These data made it possible for the researchers to track the progression of events across several categories of interest. For instance, one study on the emergence of the cochlear implant industry (Garud and Van de Ven, 1989) examined the sequence of events across various industry ecosystem categories that had been generated by researchers by iterating between literature and data. Figure 15.1 is a depiction of a sequence of events unfolding across multiple industry ecosystem sub-elements tracks. Clearly, it looks complicated, and so it should, as the emergence of an industry ecosystem is not a straightforward linear process, which is precisely what we were trying to show with this figure.

This effort led to further analysis driven by questions such as, *What happened within a track? How did the events in one track influence events in another? When did events across tracks become entangled?* The researchers found that one sequence of events dominated all the others. Companies had to follow a sequence of events to conduct clinical trials of their devices, as the widespread acceptance of any product in the marketplace is conditional upon receiving pre-market FDA approvals. The interaction of this sequence of events with others (across proprietary product

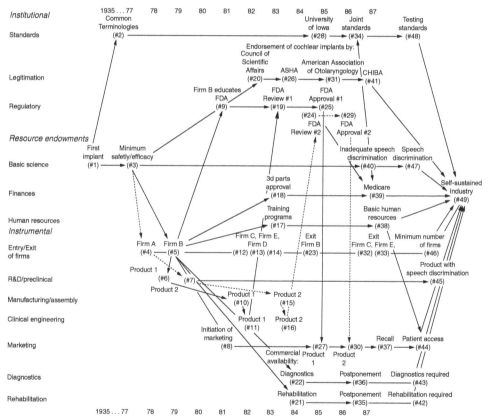

Note: Each new product has to pass through the FDA route twice before receiving FDA approval for commercial sale. First, for an investigational device exemption (IDE) which permits the researcher to conduct clinical trials, and second, for approval for marketing the device on a commercial basis (PMA). So far, the FDA has granted 6 IDEs and 2 PMAs. The paths connecting R&D and FDA for the IDEs have not been shown as this complicates the chart enormously. The PMA route is the most significant and important of the two and has been shown for the two products with PMA.

*Figure 15.1*  Sequence of Events in the Emergence of the Cochlear Implant Industry

*Note*
This figure shows events that unfolded across different tracks during the emergence of the cochlear implant industry as it appears in Garud and Van de Ven (1989).

development and market acceptance tracks) created a particularly difficult environment for firms. For instance, efforts by multiple firms to develop different kinds of cochlear implants generated considerable ambiguity (Garud and Van de Ven, 1992). As firms continued with their efforts to seek FDA approvals, others would pre-announce the future availability of superior devices. As a result, potential users took a "wait-and-see" attitude (what Rosenberg, 1982, has labeled "anticipatory retardation") resulting in sales that were less than anticipated. In addition, members of the deaf community rejected cochlear implants, as these devices threatened their culture. Eventually, the entanglement of events across the tracks led to the self-destruction of the emerging cochlear implant industry.

*Overview of study 2:* Whereas the cochlear implant study from MIRP examined events across tracks, the paper by Reymen et al. (2015) on the drivers of the innovation process in new ventures looked within one track. Specifically, they asked, *How do innovators decide what to do next, and how to move forward?* In this regard Sarasvathy (2001) proposed an effectual logic wherein actors start from their existing means to conceive potential ends and contrasted it with causal logic wherein actors take goals as primary and then select means. Reymen et al. (2015) reasoned that decision making is an iterative process with outcomes of one effort creating the conditions for new actions and decisions (Sarasvathy and Dew, 2005). To explore this empirically, the researchers reconstructed the histories of nine technology-based ventures by tracking events (defined as actions or decisions taken by the entrepreneurial team). Following procedures explicated by Poole et al. (2000), all events were coded for effectuation and causation dimensions using a detailed *coding scheme* and checking for inter-rater reliability.

The coded event sequences allowed the researchers to map the use of causation and effectuation over time showing that innovators typically relied more on effectual decision making early in the process and causal decision making later. The analysis also revealed that ventures made notable decision-making shifts along the journey. Further analysis revealed that these "turning points" were triggered by changes in stakeholder pressures, market uncertainty, and resource constraints. Overall, this analysis enabled the refinement and blending of process models to understand subtle changes in the use and combination of logics.

**Summary.** The two examples provide a deeper understanding of processes as observed during innovation journeys. One explores events across tracks within one context, whereas the other, within a single track across contexts. Both subscribe to the notion of symmetry in reporting and theorizing about successes and failures (Bijker et al., 1987). Although opening up the innovation black box, the event sequence approach that underlies both studies does not fully capture the journey as experienced by the participants. To understand how this could be accomplished, we examine other studies that embrace an experience-based view.

**Process as experienced.** The objective of such research is to appreciate innovation as a human endeavor. Experiences cannot be reduced to atomistic events, but instead must be understood as relational-temporal complexes that are formed and re-formed through actors' attempts at generating meaning. A strategy is to track experiences through ethnographic methods, and by following the narratives of the actors involved. Findings are reported in the form of "thick descriptions" of experiences (Geertz, 1994; Jarzabkowski et al., 2017). We provide two examples.

*Overview of study 1:* The first study is a spillover of one of the studies from the MIRP program. It is a study of how actors involved in the development of cochlear implants experienced their journeys during collective engagements. In this study, "events" are not changes in ideas, people, transactions, and outcomes *over* time (i.e., a departure from existing affairs), but instead a gathering of people and things *within* time (i.e., convergence of humans, artifacts, symbols, etc.).[3] Among other activities, it is during such moments that people express themselves formally and informally, articulate their positions publicly and privately, engage with one another intensely, produce communiqués that may serve as speech acts, and demonstrate their products. Consequently, such gatherings are prime occasions for researchers to appreciate the experiences of the people involved.

This ethnographic study captures the narratives of the actors involved during and across conference settings. A researcher always enters phenomena "in the middle" (i.e., *mid res*), an actor-network theory position that this study explicitly adopts. Translation rather than diffusion characterizes the links that are made, broken, and constituted between social and material elements (Callon, 1987). Insights are abduced (Pierce, 1965) by juxtaposing the bits and pieces of lived experiences reported by participants and observed/recorded by the researcher against the bits and pieces of observations from academia. We show an example of such *collage work* in the form of a picture and text, which are reproduced from this study (Figure 15.2).

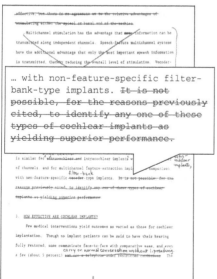

*Figure 15.2*   Demonstrations and Texts at Cochlear Implant Conferences

Notes
The first image is a photograph of demonstration activities unfolding during the XIII Otolaryngology Conference appearing in Garud (2008).
The second image is a copy of text that was circulated and edited to create an "immutable mobile" appearing in Garud (2008).

**Overview of study 2:** The second study examines an automotive company's 15-year journey to extend its automobile products with information-based services (e.g., using sensors measuring vehicle performance to advise drivers on fuel efficiency). One researcher followed the development of this program over two years using ethnographic methods (observing formal meetings and informal conversations, having interviews with all key actors involved, and collecting documents and artifacts). The company had well-established product development routines that resembled stage-gate processes (Cooper, 1990). Building on the performative perspective (Feldman and Pentland, 2003), these routines were not studied as entities or stable structures but as ongoing accomplishments in which some performances got temporarily stabilized (e.g., a new "tree routine"). Yet, there were differences in how the actors experienced the novelty of the program based on their past experiences, interests, and future aspirations. What some experienced as a necessary divergence from existing ways of working was considered by others as just a "sloppy performance." Such differences in how actors experienced current events in light of past routine performances appeared problematic, as routines were a means to engage and enroll other actors. Moreover, novel approaches appeared to have consequences for "downstream" routines (e.g., purchasing routines). Consequently, innovators had to anticipate intertemporal consequences for others. Overall, this study illustrates how experiences (comprising actions and events) stretch beyond discrete moments to invoke the past and the future.

**Summary.** Both studies use ethnographic methods to appreciate the lived experiences of the participants. This places an additional burden on researchers. What should they report and how? Any over-theorization does violence to the lived experiences of those involved. At the same time, reporting the raw experiences of innovation participants without any editorial work is also problematic as such an assemblage can clearly overwhelm readers.

Here, we see two different strategies employed by the authors of the two papers we reviewed. The first paper offers a *collage* of the experiences (as narrated by those in the field and observed by the researchers) juxtaposed against insights from academia. Such *collage work* by researchers must have some degree of internal coherence and some degree of external resonance with its audiences (both practitioners and academicians) so as to establish verisimilitude (Bruner, 1991). The second also takes a relational perspective, but the experiences of those involved are not presented as a collage. Instead they are used to develop an analytical scheme of different types of routine work to develop a process model of progression and breakdowns.

**Hybrid approaches.** In between process-as-observed and process-as-experienced approaches are studies that are hybrids. These are typically historical studies based on publicly available data (see Vaara and Lamberg, 2016, for different historical approaches for example). Specifically, they demonstrate how historical accounts can be used to "zoom in and out" (Nicolini, 2009) to open up the innovation black box. In doing so, they contextualize innovation journeys by identifying the motivations and strategies of engaged actors who took decisions and framed innovations as they emerged. Such studies are becoming all the more feasible with the availability of digital traces of what happened when, and who was involved (Garud et al., 2008; Pink et al., 2015). We believe that such techno-ethnography will become all the more prevalent over time (e.g., see Manning and Bejarano, 2016, on crowdfunding campaigns).

**Overview of study 1:** The paper by Hargadon and Douglas (2001) examines actors' framing based on historic data on the emergence of electrical lighting. The authors make a case for historical case studies, as they provide a perspective that covers the decades often necessary to observe an innovation's emergence and stabilization. At the same time, historical studies offer opportunities to examine emergent processes. Exploring innovations carefully highlights "the reciprocal links between the concrete actions of innovators and the social forces of the institutions they overturn" (Hargadon and Douglas, 2001: 480).

The authors note the possibility of distortion of facts and stories over time, or the problem that arises when concrete details that shape and constitute actions are not available or neglected. However, to the extent that events are well documented, as was the case with Edison's introduction of incandescent lighting, it is possible to examine the concrete details and actions of particular situations to understand the larger systems of meaning reflected in them. Indeed, the authors drew on data from a wide range of sources including compilations offering primary data on Edison's early efforts and newspaper accounts, secondary histories of Edison, and histories that tracked technological changes covering the demise of the gas industry and the concurrent rise of the electric industry.

This approach is well suited for the question asked on the interactions between institutions and innovations. Normative, cultural and regulatory institutions provide forces for continuity, whereas innovations act as forces for change. How these two forces interact provides an interesting tension that this paper explores. Other examples of historical studies include Leonardi's (2010) history of innovation in automotive safety testing, and several studies contained in the *Social Construction of Technological Systems* book (Bijker et al., 1987), such as Pinch and Bijker's (1987) story of the emergence of bicycles. The authors in this book locate themselves at unfolding moments in time during innovation journeys, so that their accounts could be written from the point of view of the actors who did not know future outcomes.

***Overview of study 2:*** The second paper is a longitudinal study of critical events that unfolded over a 20-year period during the development of the ATLAS Experiment at CERN. The longitudinal analysis, which was based on archival data (generated in real-time by participants) led to an understanding of how "cycles of contestation and justification" made it possible for interdependent groups of scientists to make co-oriented technological choices in the development of this complex system.

To understand the process from the perspective of the people involved, the authors analyzed controversies they identified from meeting minutes, emails, and personal notes of scientists involved, much of it maintained in electronic form. Such zooming in (Nicolini, 2009) with the help of electronic records helped the authors make sense of the experiences of the people involved. To enable this analysis, the authors also zoomed out to establish connections between different events, which were not readily apparent by merely studying one temporal sequence. For example, such an approach made it possible to identify diachrony in the use of ideas that were not immediately useful but turned out to be solutions to problems encountered in a different context later.

**Summary.** These two studies show how it is possible to understand innovation processes as observed and as experienced simultaneously. Following Pepper (1942), events that have unfolded and their sequences provide the context for subsequent unfolding of actions. Both studies take a historical approach, which makes it possible to examine events over a period of time. In both cases, because experiences were recorded, the authors of these papers were able to report actors' experiences. In the ATLAS study, these included the experiences of the many different scientists and engineers from around the world. The Edison case, in contrast, examined how a central actor framed the innovation to deal with institutional forces. A comparison across the two highlights the increased demands being placed today on scholars to articulate the qualitative methods they used.

## How Should We Decide Which Approach to Use?

Paraphrasing Korzybski (1958), the map that has emerged so far based on the various alternatives that we have reviewed is clearly not the territory. As may be evident, it is impossible to cover all the nuanced details of the many different qualitative studies on innovation processes in this short piece. More importantly, our investigation of the articles highlights that there is no one method that suffices to fully understand innovation as process. Which then begs the question: *How should researchers decide which method to use?*

Clearly, what the researcher wants to know is one consideration. This is typically evident in the research questions asked. If the questions pertain to the causal factors underlying the emergence of innovation as outcomes, a variance approach is probably best suited for the purpose at hand. Exploring efficient causation between independent and dependent variables results in the generation of testable hypotheses and generalizable knowledge. However, if questions center on *how* innovation unfolds and/or the experiences of the people involved, then process methods might be more appropriate. For instance, tracking events and/or the narratives of the people involved can offer a contextualized understanding of the motivations and experiences of those engaged with innovation journeys.

In sum, the kinds of questions researchers pose (in variance or process terms for instance) influence their methods. Science and technology studies (STS) scholars note that the reverse is also true. That is, the methods we use to probe the world around us constitute and reinforce the assumptions that we have about phenomena, which Latour and Woolgar (1979) labeled "moments of inversion," i.e., rather than neutral mediators of the world as experienced, these methods constitute and reinforce the assumptions that we have about phenomena.

In other words, ontology and epistemology come in packages, and thus serve as a second consideration in the choice of methods. Researchers must be reflexive about such packages, as otherwise there is a potential for a mismatch between ontology and epistemology when the methods employed to explore phenomena are not suited for addressing the ontological positions implicit in the questions raised. One example is what Thompson (2011: 759) labeled the "fallacy of reification."

> Reification describes the attribution of entitative existence to processes – or transforming a social construct (such as an institution) into a thing with unquestioned, separable ontological existence and "phantom objectivity" (Lukács, 1967). Such a fallacy is described as a form of ontological drift since the ontological claims have drifted out of alignment with the appropriate epistemological lens.

In other words, the fallacy of reification occurs when researchers subscribe to process ontology, but use methods from an entity/substance epistemology. For instance, a study rooted in process ontology (e.g., innovation process being non-linear) that captures ups and downs of the innovation process by a survey item measuring the level of "bumpiness" could lead to a fallacy of reification. At the same time, there might also be a tendency to subscribe to entity/substance ontology while employing methods from a process epistemology. Thompson (2011: 760) noted that such misapplications generate a "fallacy of processification."

The scholarly conversation that researchers want to join is a third consideration in the choice of methods to employ. Problems may emerge when critics/reviewers subscribing to one onto-epistemology evaluate a study based on another. In other words, there might be a mismatch in the quality criteria in use by the authors as opposed to those used by reviewers. For instance, critics/reviewers who use criteria from variance theory may not favorably receive studies that document innovations as experienced. To accommodate the former, researchers may be tempted to adopt variance methods even while subscribing to process ontology (see Arend et al., 2015, for such a recommendation). But, such a "fallacy of reification" ends up contorting the phenomenon of innovation as process (Garud and Gehman, 2016). Instead, those who subscribe to innovation as process must more forcefully articulate their onto-epistemological assumptions such as "verisimilitude" (Bruner, 1991), and the value of stories (Dyer and Wilkins, 1991), thereby signaling the criteria that must be applied to evaluate their scholarship.

A fourth consideration is axiology. Whereas ontology refers to our assumptions about phenomena, and epistemology about how we know phenomena, axiology refers to the values involved in our knowing, i.e., the ethics and aesthetics of the research we conduct (Rescher, 2005). For instance, is there a case to be made that innovation scholars have focused their attention to frame and address innovation studies around firm survival, and in the process ignored the wider ramifications of continual innovation on communities and societies at large? Posed in a different way, has the relentless process of creative destruction (Schumpeter, 1942) now resulted in destructive creation? Axiological considerations suggest that researchers must examine how their research methods and findings impact the communities they study, given that inquiry about phenomena can end up constituting them. Such performativity can be problematic, as it could do violence to the lived experiences of the people. Consequently, researchers must generate some reflexivity about the theories they deploy and methods they use.

## Looking Back to Move Forward

Our examination of some of the past research reveals a variety of qualitative methods available to study the many different facets of innovation. We found that, even within a specific onto-epistemological package, researchers have to apply methods creatively to do justice to their settings. Going further, new research questions on innovation as distributed processes may require a re-examination of existing methods. In addition, researchers must consider the value statement implicit in the research they conduct from any specific onto-epistemological package.

For instance, looking forward, we might see more research that is reflexive of the values embedded in the onto-epistemological approaches we adopt. The recognition of grand challenges (Colquitt and George, 2011; Ferraro et al., 2015) such as sustainability and the innovations that ensue call for research that examines the lived experiences of the people involved. Such research efforts are all the more possible, given the availability of digital traces of people's experiences recorded on online social media, which can help researchers understand the experiences of people from all walks of life, including those at the bottom of the pyramid (Prahalad, 2006). In our opinion, onto-epistemological positions such as actor-network theory (Callon, 1987; Latour, 2005), narratives (Czarniawska, 1998; Vaara et al., 2016), and design approaches (Boland et al., 2008; Liedtka, 2015) that have the capacity to embrace the substance–process duality are required to capture the gradual but steady shifts that different communities can make and are making in meeting grand challenges such as sustainability.

## Acknowledgments

Each author has contributed significantly to the development of this paper. We thank Mohammad Rezazade Mehrizi for his comments on an earlier draft of this paper. We offer a special note of thanks to Sanjay Jain and Raza Mir for their comments on an earlier version of this paper. We also thank many colleagues and collaborators who have influenced the ideas in this paper including Robert Chia, Joep Cornelissen, Fleur Deken, Joel Gehman, Marleen Huysman, Peter Karnoe, Arun Kumaraswamy, Ann Langley, Anup Nair, Barbara Simpson, Hari Tsoukas, Andy Van de Ven, members of the KIN Research Group at VU Amsterdam, and the Process Organization Studies (PROS) community that convenes each year in one of the Greek Islands to discuss and debate process research. The responsibility for the views expressed in this paper lies with its authors.

# Notes

1 The distinction offered by Mohr obscures a complication that arises because of the polysemy associated with the term "process." The specific complication arises because scholars who conduct variance studies also use the term "process" when referring to models establishing causality between independent and dependent variables.

2 Our views on these issues are as follows. The qualitative/quantitative dimension is orthogonal to the inductive/deductive dimension. Data mining and pattern recognition can be driven by an inductive logic, for instance, and the provisional tests of a hypothesis using qualitative data (Yin, 1994) can be based on deductive logic. Besides, most research is a combination of induction, deduction and abduction.

3 The data collected during MIRP studies were such that they could allow for analysis from multiple onto-epistemological perspectives.

# References

Abbott, A. 1984. Event sequence and event duration: Colligation and measurement. *Historical Methods: A Journal of Quantitative and Interdisciplinary History*, 17(4): 192–204.

Allison, G. T. 1971. *Essence of Decision: Explaining the Cuban Missile Crisis*. Boston, MA: Little, Brown and Company.

Arend, R. J., Sarooghi, H., and Burkemper, A. 2015. Effectuation as ineffectual? Applying the 3E theory-assessment framework to a proposed new theory of entrepreneurship. *Academy of Management Review*, 40(4): 630–651.

Belli, R. F. 1998. The structure of autobiographical memory and the event history calendar: Potential improvements in the quality of retrospective reports in surveys. *Memory*, 6(4): 383–406.

Bijker, W. E., Hughes, T. P., and Pinch, T. J. (eds.). 1987. *The Social Construction of Technological Systems: New Directions in the Sociology and History of Technology*. Cambridge, MA: MIT Press.

Block, J. H., Henkel, J., Schweisfurth, T. G., and Stiegler, A. 2016. Commercializing user innovations by vertical diversification: The user-manufacturer innovator. *Research Policy*, 45(1): 244–259.

Boland, R. J., Collopy, F., Lyytinen, K., and Yoo, Y. 2008. Managing as designing: Lessons for organization leaders from the design practice of Frank O. Gehry. *Design Issues*, 24(1): 10–25.

Brown, S. L. and Eisenhardt, K. M. 1997. The art of continuous change: Linking complexity theory and time-paced evolution in relentlessly shifting organizations. *Administrative Science Quarterly*, 42(1): 1–34.

Bruner, J. 1991. The narrative construction of reality. *Critical Inquiry*, 18(1): 1–21.

Callon, M. 1987. Society in the making: The study of technology as a tool for sociological analysis. In W. E. Bijker, T. P. Hughes, and T. J. Pinch (eds.), *Social Construction of Technological Systems*. Cambridge, MA: MIT Press, 83–104.

Callon, M. N., Law, J., and Rip, A. 1986. *Mapping the Dynamics of Science and Technology: Sociology of Science in the Real World*. London: Macmillan.

Chell, E. 2004. Critical incident technique. In C. Cassell and G. Symon (eds.), *Essential Guide to Qualitative Methods in Organization Studies*. London: Sage.

Chia, R. and Langley, A. 2004. The first Organization Studies summer workshop: Theorizing process in organizational research (call for papers). *Organization Studies*, 25(8): 1486.

Colquitt, J. A. and George, G. 2011. Publishing in AMJ – Part 1: Topic choice. *Academy of Management Journal*, 54(3): 432–435.

Cooper, R. G. 1990. Stage gate systems: A new tool for managing new products. *Business Horizons*, 33(3): 44–53.

Cornelissen, J. P. 2016. Preserving theoretical divergence in management research: Why the explanatory potential of qualitative research should be harnessed rather than suppressed. *Journal of Management Studies*, 54(23): 368–383.

Coyne, W. E. 1999. Foreword. In A. H. Van de Ven, D. E. Polley, R. Garud, and S. Venkataraman, *The Innovation Journey*. New York: Oxford University Press, vii–viii.

Czarniawska, B. 1998. *A Narrative Approach to Organization Studies*. Thousand Oaks, CA: Sage.

Deerwester, S., Dumais, S., Furnas, G. W., Landauer, T. K., and Harshman, R. 1990. Indexing by latent semantic analysis. *Journal of the American Society for Information Science*, 41(6): 391–407.

Deken, F., Carlile, P. R., Berends, H., and Lauche, K. 2016. Generating novelty through interdependent routines: A process model of routine work. *Organization Science*, 27(3): 659–677.

Dougherty, D. and Dunne, D. D. 2011. Organizing ecologies of complex innovation. *Organization Science*, 22(5): 1214–1223.

Dyer, W. G. and Wilkins, A. L. 1991. Better stories, not better constructs, to generate better theory: A rejoinder to Eisenhardt. *Academy of Management Review*, 16(3): 613–619.

Einstein, A. and Infeld, L. 1938. *The Evolution of Physics*. Cambridge: Cambridge University Press.

Eisenhardt, K. M. 1989. Building theories from case study research. *Academy of Management Review*, 14: 532–550.

Eisenhardt, K. M., Graebner, M. E., and Sonenshein, S. 2016. Grand challenges and inductive methods: Rigor without rigor mortis. *Academy of Management Journal*, 59(4): 1113–1123.

Feldman, M. S. and Pentland, B. T. 2003. Reconceptualizing organizational routines as a source of flexibility and change. *Administrative Science Quarterly*, 48(1): 94–118.

Ferraro, F., Etzion, D., and Gehman, J. 2015. Tackling grand challenges pragmatically: Robust action revisited. *Organization Studies*, 36(3): 363–390.

Garud, R. 2008. Conferences as venues for the configuration of emerging organizational fields: The case of cochlear implants. *Journal of Management Studies*, 45(6): 1061–1088.

Garud, R. and Gehman, J. 2016. Theory evaluation, entrepreneurial processes, and performativity. *Academy of Management Review*, 41(3): 544–549.

Garud, R. and Rappa, M. A. 1994. A socio-cognitive model of technology evolution: The case of cochlear implants. *Organization Science*, 5(3): 344–362.

Garud, R. and Van de Ven, A. H. 1989. Technological innovation and industry emergence: The case of cochlear implants. In A. H. Van de Ven, H. L. Angle, and M. S. Poole (eds.), *Research on the Management of Innovation: The Minnesota Studies*. New York: Harper and Row, 489–535.

Garud, R. and Van de Ven, A. H. 1992. An empirical evaluation of the internal corporate venturing process. *Strategic Management Journal*, 13: 93–109.

Garud, R., Gehman, J., Kumaraswamy, A., and Tuertscher, P. 2017. From the process of innovation to innovation as process. In A. Langley and H. Tsoukas (eds.), *The Sage Handbook of Process Organization Studies*. Thousand Oaks, CA: Sage, 451–465.

Garud, R., Jain, S., and Tuertscher, P. 2008. Designing for incompleteness and incomplete by design. *Organization Studies*, 29(3): 351–371.

Garud, R., Tuertscher, P., and Van de Ven, A. H. 2013. Perspectives on innovation processes. *The Academy of Management Annals*, 7(1): 775–819.

Geertz, C. 1973. *The Interpretation of Cultures*. New York: Basic Books.

Geertz, C. 1994. Thick description: Toward an interpretive theory of culture. In M. Martin and L. C. McIntyre (eds.), *Readings in the Philosophy of Social Science*. Cambridge, MA: MIT Press, 213–231.

Gerring, J. 2007. *Case Study Research: Principles and Practices*. Cambridge: Cambridge University Press.

Gioia, D. A., Corley, K. G., and Hamilton, A. L. 2013. Seeking qualitative rigor in inductive research: Notes on the Gioia methodology. *Organizational Research Methods*, 16(1): 15–31.

Glaser, B. and Strauss, A. 1967. *The Discovery of Grounded Theory: Strategies for Qualitative Research*. Chicago, IL: Aldine.

Golden-Biddle, K. and Locke, K. 2007. *Composing Qualitative Research*. Thousand Oaks, CA: Sage.

Hargadon, A. B. and Douglas, Y. 2001. When innovations meet institutions: Edison and the design of the electric light. *Administrative Science Quarterly*, 46(3): 476–501.

Huber, G. P. and Power, D. J. 1985. Retrospective reports of strategic-level managers: Guidelines for increasing their accuracy. *Strategic Management Journal*, 6(2): 171–180.

Jarzabkowski, P., Lê, J., and Spee, P. 2017. Taking a strong process approach to analyzing qualitative process data. In A. Langley and H. Tsoukas (eds.), *The Sage Handbook of Process Organization Studies*. Thousand Oaks, CA: Sage, 237–253.

Kieser, A. 1994. Why organization theory needs historical analyses: And how this should be performed. *Organization Science*, 5(4): 608–620.

Klag, M. and Langley, A. 2013. Approaching the conceptual leap in qualitative research. *International Journal of Management Reviews*, 15(2): 149–166.

Korzybski, A. 1958. *Science and Sanity: An Introduction to Non-Aristotelian Systems and General Semantics*. Lakeville, CT: Institute of General Semantics.

Langley, A. 1999. Strategies for theorizing from process data. *Academy of Management Review*, 24(4): 691–710.

Langley, A. and Abdallah, C. 2011. Templates and turns in qualitative studies of strategy and management. In D. D. Bergh and D. J. Ketchen (eds.), *Building Methodological Bridges*, Research Methodology in Strategy and Management, 6. Bingley, UK: Emerald, 201–235.

Langley, A., Smallman, C., Tsoukas, H., and Van de Ven, A. H. 2013. Process studies of change in organization and management: Unveiling temporality, activity, and flow. *Academy of Management Journal*, 56(1): 1–13.

Latour, B. 1987. *Science in Action: How to Follow Scientists and Engineers through Society*. Cambridge, MA: Harvard University Press.

Latour, B. 2005. *Reassembling the Social*. New York: Oxford University Press.

Latour, B. and Woolgar, S. 1979. *Laboratory Life: The Social Construction of Scientific Facts*. Beverly Hills, CA: Sage.

Leonardi, P. M. 2010. From road to lab to math: The co-evolution of technological, regulatory, and organizational innovations for automotive crash testing. *Social Studies of Science*, 40(2): 243–274.

Lichtenstein, B. B., Dooley, K. J., and Lumpkin, G. T. 2006. Measuring emergence in the dynamics of new venture creation. *Journal of Business Venturing*, 21(2): 153–175.

Liedtka, J. 2015. Perspective: Linking design thinking with innovation outcomes through cognitive bias reduction. *Journal of Product Innovation Management*, 32(6): 925–938.

Lukács, G. 1967. Reification and the consciousness of the proletariat. In G. Lukács (ed.), *History and Class Consciousness*. New York: Pegasus, 240–269.

Manning, S. and Bejarano, T. A. 2016. Convincing the crowd: Entrepreneurial storytelling in crowdfunding campaigns. *Strategic Organization*. https://doi.org/10.1177/1476127016648500.

Miles, M. B. and Huberman, A. M. 1994. *Qualitative Data Analysis: An Expanded Sourcebook*. Thousand Oaks, CA: Sage.

Mohr, L. B. 1982. *Explaining Organizational Behavior: The Limits and Possibilities of Theory and Research*. San Francisco, CA: Jossey-Bass.

Morgeson, F. P., Mitchell, T. R., and Liu, D. 2015. Event system theory: An event-oriented approach to the organizational sciences. *Academy of Management Review*, 40(4): 515–537.

Nicolini, D. 2009. Zooming in and out: Studying practices by switching theoretical lenses and trailing connections. *Organization Studies*, 30(12): 1391–1418.

Pepper, S. C. 1942. *World Hypotheses: A Study in Evidence*. Berkeley, CA: University of California Press.

Pettigrew, A. M. 1990. Longitudinal field research on change: Theory and practice. *Organization Science*, 1(3): 267–292.

Pierce, C. S. 1965. *Collected Papers of Charles Sanders Peirce, vols. 1–8*. Cambridge, MA: Belknap Press.

Pinch, T. J. and Bijker, W. E. 1987. The social construction of facts and artifacts: Or how the sociology of science and the sociology of technology might benefit each other. In W. E. Bijker, T. P. Hughes, and T. J. Pinch (eds.), *The Social Construction of Technological Systems: New Directions in the Sociology and History of Technology*. Cambridge, MA: MIT Press, 17–50.

Pink, S., Horst, H., Postill, J., Hjorth, L., Lewis, T., and Tacchi, J. 2015. *Digital Ethnography: Principles and Practice*. Thousand Oaks, CA: Sage.

Poole, M. S., Van de Ven, A. H., Dooley, K. J., and Holmes, M. E. 2000. *Organisational Change and Innovation Processes: Theory and Methods for Research*. Oxford: Oxford University Press.

Prahalad, C. K. 2006. *The Fortune at the Bottom of the Pyramid*. Upper Saddle River, NJ: Wharton School Publishing.

Pratt, M. G. 2009. From the Editors: For the lack of a boilerplate: Tips on writing up (and reviewing) qualitative research. *Academy of Management Journal*, 52(5): 856–862.

Rescher, N. 1996. *Process Metaphysics: An Introduction to Process Philosophy*. New York: SUNY Press.

Rescher, N. 2005. *Value Matters: Studies in Axiology*. Frankfurt: Ontos Verlag.

Reymen, I. M. M. J., Andries, P., Berends, H., Mauer, R., Stephan, U., and van Burg, E. 2015. Understanding dynamics of strategic decision making in venture creation: A process study of effectuation and causation. *Strategic Entrepreneurship Journal*, 9(4): 351–379.

Rheinhardt, A., Kreiner, G. E., Gioia, D. A., and Corley, K. G. Forthcoming. Conducting and publishing rigorous qualitative research. In C. Cassell, A. L. Cunliffe, and G. Grandy (eds.), *The SAGE Handbook of Qualitative Business and Management Research Methods*. Thousand Oaks, CA: Sage.

Rosenberg, N. 1982. *Inside the Black Box: Technology and Economics*. Cambridge: Cambridge University Press.

Sandberg, J. and Tsoukas, H. 2011. Grasping the logic of practice: Theorizing through practical rationality. *Academy of Management Review*, 36(2): 338–360.

Sarasvathy, S. D. 2001. Causation and effectuation: Toward a theoretical shift from economic inevitability to entrepreneurial contingency. *Academy of Management Review*, 26(2): 243–263.

Sarasvathy, S. D. and Dew, N. 2005. New market creation through transformation. *Journal of Evolutionary Economics*, 15(5): 533–565.

Schumpeter, J. A. 1942. *Capitalism, Socialism, and Democracy*. New York: Harper & Row.

Thompson, M. 2011. Ontological shift or ontological drift? Reality claims, epistemological frameworks, and theory generation in organization studies. *Academy of Management Review*, 36(4): 754–773.

Trochim, W. 1989. Outcome pattern matching and program theory. *Evaluation and Program Planning*, 12: 355–366.

Tsoukas, H. and Chia, R. 2002. On organizational becoming: Rethinking organizational change. *Organization Science*, 13(5): 567–582.

Tuertscher, P., Garud, R., and Kumaraswamy, A. 2014. Justification and interlaced knowledge at ATLAS, CERN. *Organization Science*, 25(6): 1579–1608.

Tushman, M. L. and Anderson, P. 1986. Technological discontinuities and organizational environments. *Administrative Science Quarterly*, 31(3): 439–465.

Utterback, J. M. and Abernathy, W. J. 1975. Dynamic model of process and product innovation. *Omega: International Journal of Management Science*, 3(6): 639–656.

Vaara, E. and Lamberg, J.-A. 2016. Taking historical embeddedness seriously: Three historical approaches to advance strategy process and practice research. *Academy of Management Review*, 41(4): 633–657.

Vaara, E., Sonenshein, S., and Boje, D. M. 2016. Narratives as sources of stability and change in organizations: Approaches and directions for future research. *The Academy of Management Annals*, 10(1): 495–560.

Van de Ven, A. H. 1992. Suggestions for studying strategy process: A research note. *Strategic Management Journal*, 13: 169–188.

Van de Ven, A. H. and Poole, M. S. 1990. Methods for studying innovation development in the Minnesota Innovation Research Program. *Organization Science*, 1(3): 313–335.

Van de Ven, A. H. and Poole, M. S. 1995. Explaining development and change in organizations. *Academy of Management Review*, 20(3): 510–540.

Van de Ven, A. H. and Poole, M. S. 2005. Alternative approaches for studying organizational change. *Organization Studies*, 26(9): 1377–1404.

Van de Ven, A. H., Polley, D., Garud, R., and Venkataraman, S. 1999. *The Innovation Journey*. New York: Oxford University Press.

Van Maanen, J. 1988. *Tales of the Field: On Writing Ethnography*. Chicago, IL: University of Chicago Press.

Vaughan, D. 1992. Theory elaboration: The heuristics of case analysis. In C. C. Ragin and H. S. Becker (eds.), *What Is a Case? Exploring the Foundations of Social Inquiry*. Cambridge: Cambridge University Press, 173–202.

Webb, E. and Weick, K. E. 1979. Unobtrusive measures in organizational theory: A reminder. *Administrative Science Quarterly*, 24(4): 650–659.

Weick, K. E. 1989. Theory construction as disciplined imagination. *Academy of Management Review*, 14(4): 516–531.

Yin, R. K. 1993. *Applications of Case Study Research*. Thousand Oaks, CA: Sage.

Yin, R. K. 1994. *Case Study Research: Design and Methods* (2nd ed.). Thousand Oaks, CA: Sage.

Yoo, Y., Boland, R. J., Lyytinen, K., and Majchrzak, A. 2012. Organizing for innovation in the digitized world. *Organization Science*, 23(5): 1398–1408.

# 16

# WHATDDYA KNOW?

## Qualitative Methods in Entrepreneurship

*Ted Baker, E. Erin Powell, and Andrew E.F. Fultz*

As entrepreneurship researchers deeply interested in qualitative methods, we are happy about the current state of the art and the prevalence of good work in elite entrepreneurship and general management journals. We are also a bit concerned about what appear to us as the beginnings of some trends that might limit the continued flourishing of qualitative entrepreneurship research. Mostly, however, we are optimistic and excited about possibilities for improving our understanding of entrepreneurship through the development and embrace – by authors, reviewers and editors – of a broader range of approaches to qualitative research.

This chapter is presented in three acts: Landscape, Suggestions and the Music of Qualitative Research. First, we set the groundwork by briefly describing the recent prevalence and patterning of scholarly entrepreneurship research. We contrast how many qualitative versus quantitative entrepreneurship papers and how many qualitative versus quantitative non-entrepreneurship papers have been published in an important set of journals during the last decade. We do this by comparing two five-year periods: 2006–2010 and 2011–2015. We also more closely examine a subset of qualitative entrepreneurship papers that focus on either organization creation or founder-run organizations, providing brief descriptions and some discussion of characteristics and patterns in this work within and across journals. Second, drawing on our experience doing and trying to publish qualitative research in entrepreneurship and as reviewers and editors of this work, as well as upon conversations with our colleagues in similar roles, we provide a somewhat impressionistic review of what we see as some important themes and issues in contemporary qualitative work in entrepreneurship. Third, we try to express some of the personal joy and sense of human connection that can come from doing this sort of work, and proffer a little bit of advice for people considering trying to make this kind of music.

### Part I: The Landscape

As shown in Table 16.1 (please see Appendix for methodological details), entrepreneurship's overall share of publications in general management journals (excluding *Organization Studies*) held steady between 11 to 12 percent during the ten years we examined, with qualitative entrepreneurship papers representing 3 percent across both periods. In *Organization Studies* (OS), entrepreneurship's overall share was 9–10 percent, but with qualitative papers representing most of this. In the entrepreneurship journals, the share of qualitative papers increased slightly from

Table 16.1 Empirical Paper Summary

| | Qualitative Entrepreneurship | | | | Quantitative Entrepreneurship | | | | Qualitative Non-Entrepreneurship | | | | Quantitative Non-Entrepreneurship | | | | Totals | |
| --- | --- | --- | --- | --- | --- | --- | --- | --- | --- | --- | --- | --- | --- | --- | --- | --- | --- | --- |
| | 2006–2010 | | 2011–2015 | | 2006–2010 | | 2011–2015 | | 2006–2010 | | 2011–2015 | | 2006–2010 | | 2011–2015 | | 2006–2010 | 2011–2015 |
| Mgmt* | 27 | 3% | 32 | 3% | 70 | 9% | 77 | 8% | 164 | 20% | 193 | 20% | 543 | 68% | 660 | 69% | 804 | 962 |
| E'ship** | 42 | 13% | 65 | 16% | 276 | 87% | 354 | 84% | – | | – | | – | | 28 | 16% | 318 | 419 |
| OrgStudies | 16 | 9% | 16 | 7% | 1 | 1% | 4 | 2% | 125 | 74% | 179 | 79% | 28 | 16% | 28 | 12% | 170 | 227 |

Notes

* Academy of Management Journal, Administrative Science Quarterly, Journal of Management Studies, Organization Science.
** Journal of Business Venturing, Entrepreneurship Theory & Practice, Strategic Entrepreneurship Journal.

13 to 16 percent between the two periods. We take these patterns to represent stability overall in entrepreneurship's share of papers published in leading journals, in the balance between quantitative and qualitative papers and in the distribution across general management versus entrepreneurship journals. Among the general management journals, there was a substantial drop-off (not shown in the table) in entrepreneurship papers published in *Administrative Science Quarterly*, with 17 entrepreneurship papers published during the first five-year period (five qualitative) and four entrepreneurship papers published during the second five-year period (one qualitative). Increases across the other general management journals balanced out this decline in the overall numbers. We suspect that the level of stability we observed likely reflects the overall legitimation and institutionalization of entrepreneurship as a field of research.

Table 16.2 focuses on only the subset of entrepreneurship papers that utilize qualitative methods and represent the traditional and still predominant research focus on organization creation and/or founder-controlled ventures (e.g., excluding corporate entrepreneurship and most institutional entrepreneurship, but including a broad range of contemporary topics such as social entrepreneurship, gender and entrepreneurship, entrepreneurial identity, and entrepreneurship in the Global South). Table 16.2 contrasts the general management (*including* OS, which did not differ greatly from the other general management journals for these comparisons) and entrepreneurship journals across the two periods in terms of whether or not qualitative entrepreneurship papers develop propositions and also in terms of whether they offer justifying text about why qualitative methods were appropriate (see discussion below). The most striking pattern in Table 16.2 is that papers in the entrepreneurship journals are much more likely than the general management journals to offer both propositions and justifying text. One possible interpretation is that offering propositions is methodologically legitimating because they create a connection to the hypotheses common in quantitative theory-testing papers. Similarly, justifying is an explicit attempt to claim methodological legitimacy.

Table 16.3 examines the same set of papers as Table 16.2, comparing the prevalence of five common qualitative methods cites. In terms of methodological approaches tied to organization studies, papers drawing on Eisenhardt and her colleagues (e.g., Eisenhardt, 1989; Eisenhardt and Graebner, 2007) remain highly influential in both the management and entrepreneurship journals, appearing in 67 percent of the papers in Table 16.2 over ten years, and garnering more than 25 percent of all cites to these five sets of authors. Work by Gioia and colleagues (e.g., Gioia *et al.*, 2013) is growing in importance in both the management and entrepreneurship journals. Overall, this body of work is dominated by cross-case analysis of multiple cases (Eisenhardt, 1989) and by the development of grounded theory. It is therefore perhaps unsurprising that "standard" references for this sort of work from outside of organization studies, including various

*Table 16.2* Qualitative Entrepreneurship, Creation/Founder Summary (*N* = 98)

| | Propositions (Yes) | | | | Justification (Yes) | | | |
|---|---|---|---|---|---|---|---|---|
| | *2006–2010* | | *2011–2015* | | *2006–2010* | | *2011–2015* | |
| Mgmt* | 5 | 38% | 5 | 29% | 5 | 38% | 8 | 47% |
| E'ship** | 12 | 48% | 22 | 51% | 15 | 60% | 29 | 67% |

*Notes*
\* *Academy of Management Journal, Administrative Science Quarterly, Journal of Management Studies, Organization Science, Organization Studies.*
\*\* *Journal of Business Venturing, Entrepreneurship Theory & Practice, Strategic Entrepreneurship Journal.*

Table 16.3 Qualitative Entrepreneurship, Creation/Founder Summary (N=98 papers and 250 citations)

| | Eisenhardt et al. | | Gioia et al. | | Glaser + Strauss et al. | | Miles et al. | | Yin | | Totals | |
|---|---|---|---|---|---|---|---|---|---|---|---|---|
| | 2006–2010 | 2011–2015 | 2006–2010 | 2011–2015 | 2006–2010 | 2011–2015 | 2006–2010 | 2011–2015 | 2006–2010 | 2011–2015 | 2006–2010 | 2011–2015 |
| Mgmt* | 10 29% | 12 22% | 2 6% | 6 11% | 10 29% | 15 27% | 6 17% | 9 16% | 7 20% | 13 24% | 35 | 55 |
| E'ship** | 18 28% | 26 27% | 0 0% | 5 5% | 20 31% | 25 26% | 9 14% | 17 18% | 17 27% | 23 24% | 64 | 96 |
| Papers citing this author 2006–2015 | 67% | | 13% | | 71% | | 42% | | 61% | | | |

Notes

* Academy of Management Journal, Administrative Science Quarterly, Journal of Management Studies, Organization Science, Organization Studies.
** Journal of Business Venturing, Entrepreneurship Theory & Practice, Strategic Entrepreneurship Journal.

publications by Glaser, Strauss, Miles, Huberman and Yin, remained strongly represented throughout the ten-year period.

## Part II: Impressions, Concerns and Some Suggestions

Is qualitative research in entrepreneurship different in any meaningful way from qualitative research in other areas of organization studies? In many cases, probably not. But here we suggest a few ways that some entrepreneurship research seems different, and use this to motivate and contextualize claims and conjectures about where qualitative research in entrepreneurship stands and where it is going. We start by providing a stylized characterization of a range of research relationships between researchers, research instruments, and people and organizations being studied.

To understand the contrast we wish to draw, consider an organizational researcher doing primary quantitative data gathering using a structured questionnaire. The questionnaire is an object separate from the researcher, containing standardized items to be asked in a consistent way. It is administered to "respondents" or "informants" who are typically describing aspects of an organization which is itself an object separate from the respondents. Schematically, the research relationships look something like the following:

Researcher ↔ Questionnaire ↔ Respondent ↔ Organization

The key relationships here are between the questionnaire and the respondent, assessed in terms of validity, and between the respondent and organization, assessed in terms of respondent knowledge. The researcher–questionnaire relationship is presumed to be standardized such that the characteristics of the researcher do not matter and the researcher effectively disappears.

In qualitative research, in contrast, to a varying degree, "the *researcher is the* instrument" (Lofland *et al.*, 2006: 3; Patton, 1990; Rew *et al.*, 1993; Strauss and Corbin, 1998). This is true to a larger extent in ethnographic and observational studies and to a lesser extent when data gathering takes place using structured interview protocols. Thus, the research relationships change to the following:

(Researcher = Instrument) ↔ Respondent ↔ Organization

Moreover, when studying the creation of new and founder-dominated ventures, it is also often fair to say that the entrepreneur is – initially – the organization.[1] Hannan and Freeman (1989: 81), for example, describe startups as "little more than extensions of the wills of dominant coalitions or individuals; they have no lives of their own." Indeed, the process through which the organization may become an entity understandable as separable from the founder is itself theoretically and practically important. Schematically, the research relationship condenses to something like the following:

(Researcher = Instrument) ↔ (Founder = Organization)

The crucial relationship here is therefore that between the researcher and the founder.

Here, we briefly explore several aspects of this stylized depiction and use it to comment upon some aspects of the state of the art in qualitative entrepreneurship research.

The first point is that the "connection" between the researcher and the founder can be crucial. To the extent that the organization really is an extension of the founder, failure to connect in a meaningful way with the founder will severely limit what the researcher can learn.

It is, of course, possible to connect meaningfully in a wide variety of ways. We have frequently been treated as confidantes and as therapists, helping founders to make their own ethical and practical sense out of what they are doing. Founders sometimes seem to hope (despite disavowals) that we will take the role of free strategy consultants and sources of cheap student labor and access to university resources. Occasionally we are treated as "clueless academics" to be educated and – sometimes, eventually – just as good listeners.

Any of these roles can be pathways to the sorts of connections that allow founders to tell us what they believe to be true, enable us to see things that would otherwise remain hidden and allow us to be able to ask uncomfortable questions. We have seen clearly how processes of building connections over time through multiple interactions allow for learning things that will otherwise remain opaque. For example, in one case of being treated as clueless academics, even after many hours of interviews and observation, an elderly founder was still not prepared to share with us any financial documents. But he eventually came to trust us as confidantes, first opening up about a life-threatening medical issue and subsequently providing detailed documentation on his personal and business finances.

As in other relationships, sometimes connections and trust come more quickly. In one remarkable case (Baker *et al.*, 2003), a husband and wife founder team mistook one of us for their banker and came to an initial discussion armed with financial records and statements "proving" that they needed additional money for working capital to support increased accounts receivable. Informed of the mistake, the couple relaxed and laughingly began telling us the history of the business. Less than an hour later, they asked, "Do you want to see what we are really going to do with the money?" They then brought us into a locked room in the basement that contained the Rube Goldberg-looking prototype into which they wanted to invest money borrowed on the pretext of growing the existing business. Such trust may also come very slowly or not at all, based on any number of issues either idiosyncratic to the relationship or based on other factors such as race, class, age, gender and other demographic and social differences. Several times, we have had founders willing to show or tell us different things depending on whether one of us, the other, or both were present.

This suggests that in qualitative research on founders and their firms, the nature of the research instrument is partly constructed by the nature of the relationship between the researcher and the researched. Even if strong researcher–founder connections emerge, the idiosyncratic nature of such relations means it is not enough to assume that another researcher would learn the same things. The more general issue is that the relationship between researcher and founder may strongly shape what is and isn't shared and therefore what is learned. At the same time, the founder and the new venture may be changing in fluid ways. Moreover, the research instrument changes as the researcher learns more about the context, adds cases and begins to formulate new theoretical ideas that shape the ongoing research project and process.

The rationale behind well-designed research instruments and structured protocols in deductive work suggests that many different researchers can get highly comparable results across a variety of different respondents, providing some promise of both validity and replicability. However, the researcher as relationship-formed instrument lacks consistent application of questionnaire items, validated scales and bodies of "measurement" theory that can lend validity in a mechanical way to the "data" that are generated using other instruments (Pedhazur and Schmelkin, 1991). To complicate matters further, emerging and young private founder-run organizations leave very limited archival traces and public records of the sorts that abound for many established corporate entities. This means that researchers trying to validate and contextualize what they learn from observing and talking with founders must often scramble to get access to financial and legal records, contracts, emails, friends, neighbors, suppliers, customers and employees of founders (Powell and Baker, 2014). These sources of data will likely differ across cases, making direct comparison unlikely. While in most scientific research, a well-structured methods section is presumed to provide the basis for testing replicability, the subjectivity and idiosyncratic social relations inherent in the ongoing construction of the research instrument make this an unrealistic goal in much qualitative entrepreneurship research. Instead, the goal must be to establish a different sort of trust between the author and reader, a trust which must first be negotiated between author, reviewers and editors.

At a more general level, we suspect with apprehension that some form of epistemological anxiety over the apparent idiosyncratic and subjective elements of what we have just described may be leading to certain counterproductive behaviors in the research and publication process. This anxiety shapes the behavior of authors, reviewers and editors and probably even readers of published papers. We suspect the effects of this epistemological anxiety are exacerbated by long-standing – though we believe outdated (Baker and Welter, 2014) – concerns about the legitimacy of entrepreneurship research as a field (Shane and Venkataraman, 2000). We speculate that epistemological anxiety and this underlying sense of illegitimacy have combined to drive authors, reviewers and editors at elite journals to compensate by eagerly embracing only the most established and middle-of-the-road approaches to qualitative research in entrepreneurship.

## Huddling in a "Small Tent"

Arguably, qualitative research in entrepreneurship published in elite journals (and perhaps management research more generally) has taken a fairly small tent approach, embracing a small group of well-proven approaches (e.g., Eisenhardt, 1989; Eisenhardt and Graebner, 2007; Gioia *et al.*, 2013) and largely excluding others. As shown in Table 16.3, of the 98 qualitative papers focused on organization creation or founder-run ventures, 67 percent drew on Eisenhardt methods references and 61 percent drew on Yin, overwhelmingly in support of cross-case comparative research. In full disclosure, we are also happily part of this majority in much of our own work. Despite calls for use of a broader array of qualitative methods (Bansal and Corley, 2011; Pratt, 2009), entrepreneurship (and perhaps management more generally) researchers, even including people who do qualitative work primarily, seem too often to be remarkably narrow in their assessment of what constitutes an acceptable method. Encouraging a broadening of approaches, Bansal and Corley (2011) went so far as to provide an illustrative list of other sorts of methods that they, as (at the time) the two editors responsible for qualitative papers at AMJ, would welcome, while quoting with shared concern Tracy's (2010: 837–838) comment that "Despite the gains of qualitative research in the late 20th century, a methodological conservatism has crept upon social science over the last ten years." We have largely eschewed methodological experimentation and perhaps innovation as well, as broadly suggested by the concentration of methods cites described in Table 16.3. In terms of being able to get a paper through the review process, unfortunately, this makes complete sense. Using methods that are well-known and perceived as legitimate makes it easier for reviewers and editors to have a positive gut-level response to papers, while doing anything else makes it easier for them to have a correspondingly negative gut-level response. This is self-reinforcing, because the small tent approach means that most of us perceive as novel even approaches that are well-known in other fields.

Why is this methodological narrowness a concern? First, and most broadly, because available acceptable methods shape what questions can be asked and answered in our journals and thus what we can learn. Second, and closely related, because we believe that our theories and understanding of entrepreneurship are far from good enough yet to bar the door, a priori, to any qualitative methodology that might generate interesting and useful new insights. Third, because if we are not open to new qualitative methods, there is no process for improving their rigor through use or for reviewers and editors to develop expertise and judgment regarding more or less rigorous use of anything even locally novel. Fourth, as we will discuss in the next two sections, methodological narrowing may be on a dangerously reductive path in which the semi-structured interview becomes the de facto standard for doing qualitative research in entrepreneurship, with the data that interviews generate therefore forming the narrow standard for what counts as an evidentiary basis for published work.

### *Narrowing the Evidentiary Basis: The Valorization of Utterances*

One response to the epistemological anxiety of qualitative research in entrepreneurship seems to us to be driven by the desire to minimize, in a straightforward way, the very existence of the researcher as instrument. One way to do this is by privileging founder utterances as the supreme – and sometimes seemingly the only – form of data treated as evidence. Think of it this way: if everything the researcher claims is going on is supported by a series of illustrative quotes taken as evidence, it is almost like the entrepreneur is speaking directly to us as readers, seemingly eliminating the messy idiosyncrasies and subjectivity of the relation between the researcher and the researched. Perhaps this is why so many researchers and reviewers seem to grasp tightly onto the notion of "in vivo codes" from interview transcripts as the first level of data analysis. Another reason may be that the elevation of quotes provides a rationale for qualitative research that relies entirely or nearly entirely on (often relatively brief) interviews, which after all, produce mostly only utterances. As we've seen with the best research applying the Gioia method (see Gioia *et al.*, 2013, for an impressive list), semi-structured interviews can be the basis for profound insights. But in many other cases, a series of quotes is a thin reed on which to build the thick descriptions and empathic understanding on which much good qualitative research rests. This becomes a more serious problem if a narrowing methodological focus on the primary evidence produced by semi-structured interviews – quotes – becomes the de facto standard for what counts as evidence for many authors and reviewers. This, unfortunately, appears to be taking place.

What should potentially "count" as evidence in our research? Cultural anthropology and the notion of a researcher's deep embeddedness in another culture provide an extreme example of understanding and explaining what is going on based on evidence, interpretation and human understanding that draws on much more than quotes (Malinowski, 1922). Somewhat closer to home, consider Van Maanen's (2011: 177–178) reflections on the overestimation of the role of fieldnotes in ethnographic research, embracing not only written documentation but the researcher as instrument as fundamental sources of understanding:

> The heavy glop of material we refer to as fieldnotes is necessarily incomplete and insufficient. It represents the recorded memory of a study perhaps, but it is only a tiny fraction of the fieldworker's own memory of the research period.

Van Maanen's perspective throws into relief the broad range of data that can constitute the materials of qualitative research. A researcher who spends time, pays attention and connects with founders and all the messy data that surround them learns things that can be neither learned nor "evidenced" simply, or sometimes at all, by any array of things that a person or persons said. Empathic understanding, well-known in the Weberian methodological concept of *Verstehen*, is far from fully dependent on answers to what an interviewer asks or things that are overheard. The persistent call to qualitative researchers to "make your data available" mostly by supporting every inference by a set of pertinent quotes, is therefore oftentimes misplaced.

This can be illustrated in principle with very simple and direct examples. During a study of textile entrepreneurs (Powell and Baker, 2014) several founders told us during interviews how strongly they were personally connected to their employees. Spending time with and without them in their factories made abundantly clear that this meant very different things across their firms, ranging from reciprocal warmth to near ridicule. Trying to understand the differences between the words and the lived reality shaped the direction in which we took the research. Several founders also extolled the "green" virtues of their firms. The time we spent in their production facilities allowed us to see – in one case – that the noxious chemicals they claimed to have banished long before were in fact still in use and that a new batch had been mixed just days before. This helped open us up to exploring the dynamics of identity aspirations and the construction of ideological narratives.

In another study, gaining late access to many months of emails gave the lie to the frontstage (Goffman, 1959) consensus that founders were constructing in both discussions with one another and in some interviews (Powell and Baker, in press). Absent access to this trove, the "positive" quotes we had recorded would have taken on a very different meaning. We were only made aware of and given access to the emails through months of having built up connections and trust with the founders. Or, imagine a study of entrepreneurial improvisation (Baker *et al.*, 2003) in which the researcher observes multiple occasions during which a founder makes – or even just describes – ad hoc solutions to problems and gives the appearance through body language, facial expression, tone of voice and enthusiasm to relish these episodes. But they never say anything like, "I enjoy improvising." Is this enough evidence to later "code" them as someone who enjoys improvisation? What if the founder instead appears consistently to be morose when engaging in or describing improvisation, but they proffer, "I do it so much, I guess I must really like fixing things on the fly?" Would it be reasonable to label them an improv aficionado?

In addition, the meaning of an utterance is often not readily understandable by someone who was not there, especially if it is taken out of context as in a table of quotes. We recently observed a case in which authors attempted to contextualize quotes in tables by embedding them in short snippets describing the scenario in which the quote was generated. Reviewer response was strongly negative, with one reviewer suggesting the quotes should be able to stand alone and that the contextualization was an attempt to manipulate the reader into hearing the quote the way the authors did. We'd prefer not to imagine a starker example of the methodological reification of utterances. Quotes can be extremely illuminating, perhaps especially when contextualized as part of a narrative showing how the lived experience of those being researched fits with the process and mechanisms of a theory being developed or extended. But the notion that tables of decontextualized quotes consistently represent a superior form of evidence seems quite suspect and potentially pernicious.

Apparently helping to legitimate the valorization of quotes in the eyes of some authors and reviewers is a misinterpretation of the Gioia methodology's focus on respecting those who are being studied. It seems unfortunate if this, or Pratt's (2009: 857) compelling advice to do work that "honors the worldview of informants," could become the basis for some dysfunctional narrowing of what represents strong evidence to nothing but sound bites. As Gioia and colleagues (2013) explain, what they describe as "first-order codes" is based on Strauss and Corbin's (1998) notion of "open coding," applied to a context in which data comes primarily from semi-structured interviews. It is useful to remember that Strauss and Corbin (1998) developed their notion of open coding to apply to studies drawing on a very wide range of data sources, including but not at all limited to what people say. It honors those we study to embrace their lived experience and worldviews more holistically than quotes allow.

## *Taking Comfort in Templates*

Amplifying the anxiety over idiosyncrasy, subjectivity and legitimacy is the absence of an agreed upon formulaic approach for presenting qualitative research. For example, many of us feel like we know to a large extent what a normal quantitative paper is supposed to "look like" for mainstream journals. This includes the ordering of the sections and the relationship between introduction, theory and hypothesis development, methods and data, results and discussion. Despite the small tent approach described above, however, there has still been much less of an obvious consensus about what is normal for qualitative work. Unfortunately, in our opinion, this may be changing. Indeed, a number of accomplished scholars with profound expertise in qualitative methods have recently expressed concerns about the possibility that the broad variety of useful approaches to doing qualitative research might be reduced to a much narrower acceptable "style" (Bansal and Corley, 2011) or "boilerplate" (Pratt, 2009) or "template" for doing or presenting qualitative research (Eisenhardt *et al.*, 2016), and have argued in favor of resistance against this narrowing. When they published their methodological guidance, Gioia and colleagues (2013: 25), expressed concern "that organizational researchers seem to be applying the methodology as a template, or ... to be treating it as a 'formula,'" worrying that inappropriate use of their approach "sacrifices the benefits of qualitative research's flexibility in applying different approaches to fit different phenomenological needs." We see this as an increasing problem in entrepreneurship research.

In particular, we have seen that scholars inexperienced with qualitative work or seeking shortcuts may have incentives to fool themselves into thinking that the mode of presentation and the mode of discovery and theorizing are the same. Many students and researchers have what we consider a reasonably accurate perception that doing qualitative research is often time consuming and difficult. As well, many researchers (authors and reviewers) have far more extensive training in design and methods for doing theory-testing quantitative research than for doing qualitative research. Nonetheless, and probably for good reason (Eisenhardt *et al.*, 2016), many people want to try their hands at qualitative work. Given this scenario, it is easy to understand why would-be qualitative researchers might be highly motivated to find "shortcuts" both to learning and doing qualitative methods. Pressures to publish quickly and a perception that promotion and tenure committees may not fully appreciate the high risk–reward ratio and time consuming nature of good qualitative research, compound these pressures. We have recently seen a proliferation of papers submitted to entrepreneurship journals that present the "data structures" suggested in the Gioia method, but that seem not to have followed the underlying methodology or done the hard work of developing the insights the data structures are supposed to support.

The good news is that most of these simulacra of the Gioia methodology papers do not seem to be making it past reviewers. The process of developing rigor through use for a qualitative method may be working well in this case. We remain concerned, however, that this may not prevail. As the Gioia methodology gains rapidly in popularity, it is easy to imagine not only authors looking for shortcuts, but also reviewers and editors being "fooled" by papers that follow the template and "look right." This seems particularly likely among reviewers with limited experience in qualitative research. While we have frequently seen scholars decline to review a paper because they are unfamiliar with a quantitative analytic technique, almost everyone appears to believe that they can effectively review qualitative research. During a recent conversation about this with someone we expected to be sympathetic, the response was along the lines of: "So what? This is just theory building anyway, right? If someone comes up with a good idea, what difference does it make whether it came from the data?" This suggests how little resistance to evisceration of serious qualitative research and in some cases how little appreciation for differences between profound and perfunctory work may exist in the reviewer community at large. We hope that this is not the case.

Finally, we express a concern that may appear as more of a quibble, but which we think nicely reflects our need as a community of scholars to understand the value of a more diverse set of perspectives and methodologies.

## *Accepting a Defensive Posture*

As noted above, we found that 57 of 98 founder/creation papers using qualitative methods included explicit justifications for why qualitative methods were appropriate for a study or its research questions. These typically take something like the following form: "Given the limited state of theory/knowledge about X, an inductive approach to developing grounded theory was deemed appropriate." Most quantitative papers, in contrast, appear to require no such explicit global justification, but instead are more likely to describe why some specific modeling strategy was chosen. The need for justification often seems to be treated as if qualitative approaches have only some narrow applicability – perhaps during some brief "exploratory" window – for any research topic. This seems completely wrong to us. One way to see this is to consider other "justifying" text that qualitative researchers might use. For example: "Given that our understanding of X has become too narrow while chasing incremental increases in R-squared, there is an overwhelming need for qualitative research to bring life to this topic." Or, "Given that researchers in this area have long been unable to move beyond crude null hypothesis testing, grounded theory development was particularly fruitful in providing and refining fundamental theoretical insights."

Better yet, let's put the shoe on the other foot and imagine what sorts of text we might expect were the onus of justifying methodology placed on quantitative researchers. This seems particularly important in a field such as entrepreneurship in which most of our theories are in relatively early stages of development and where "deductively" generated hypotheses are likely to have a somewhat loose relationship with existing theory and also to be extraordinarily imprecise in terms of predicting the magnitude of effects. Perhaps our goal as a research community should rather be something like:

> The interplay of qualitative and quantitative research in prior studies of X allowed us to formulate precise and contextualized hypotheses, which guided our gathering of appropriate longitudinal data and allowed us to deductively craft nuanced quantitative hypotheses and to test them for accuracy.

In any case, it would seem that the rationale for either qualitative or quantitative research should be based on the results and contributions to knowledge it generates, with neither requiring any special justification.

## Part III: Extending the Instruments Metaphor: The Music of Qualitative Research

Underlying our essay is the notion of the researcher as instrument. This is useful as a contrast to instruments such as survey questionnaires or experimental protocols. It is limited, however, in that it implicitly characterizes researchers as passively responding to signals of various sorts that impinge on them in the field. At the risk of being accused of a play on words, we want to explore extending the "instrument" as sensor metaphor to the notion of an "expressive instrument," by using simple musical imagery.

First, we imagine the social worlds we study as governed by sheet music that we cannot read directly, but that we can only attempt to decipher and understand through our empirical research and theorizing. In this world, musical instruments are tools for interpreting and trying to express to an audience some understanding of the written score. From this perspective, any given study using a particular methodology represents a single attempt to portray this social world in music using a single instrument. It seems obvious that no such performance is likely to capture either the richness of any social world or to give us a firm grasp on the sheet music that – from this perspective – represents the underlying reality that science should seek to discover and portray in our theories. Even from this nicely deterministic perspective, a curious scientist would want to encourage a barrage of performances, both by single instruments and voices and by bands, orchestras and choruses. The popularity of the electric guitar or the violin or the synthesizer would not itself be taken as evidence of superior access to or expression of truth. And good science would even encourage and embrace the construction of new instruments, new tunings and new musical forms.

Second, let's relax the assumption that there is actually some underlying sheet music or score that shapes the social worlds we study in deterministic ways,[2] but instead imagine that these worlds are to some extent improvised in unpredictable ways through complex interactions infused with ongoing meaning making and interpretation. Understanding such worlds would presumably call for greater openness to a wide range of instruments, styles and research-performances. Classical interpretations of old standards, including songs of structure and function versus agency, power, domination and emancipation would remain with us and would also generate new music, but even those who grew up listening to these on vinyl would resist the urge to say about the new sounds, "that's not music."

Our rationale for this musical interlude is partly to end on a more upbeat note than the worries we have expressed. But it is also to offer some practical advice for those entrepreneurship researchers who would choose to immerse themselves in the social worlds they seek to study. Try for a moment to think of yourself as an instrument. For many scholars, being a qualitative researcher is itself an important identity that infuses their professional and sometimes their personal lives. From this perspective, questions about who you are and who you want to be shape your "theoretical sensitivity": how you are able to respond to the various signals that impinge on you in the field. They also shape the music you try to play and how effectively you express what you have learned. This has several direct, highly pragmatic implications.

First, you need to nurture your sense of empathy toward people in the social worlds you want to study. It may help to begin to develop a sense of what it is like to be "studied," to be an object of interest to you as a researcher. Although we have a great deal of theory on responses to questionnaire items, we have much less theory (at least in organization studies) on responses to having a fieldworker around. In the end, you can be critical of the behavior or performance of those you study, but if you are incapable of generating empathy while you study them, much of the score and the improvisations that shape these social worlds are likely to remain invisible to you.

Second, from the beginning (and in our experience at all times), you are simultaneously learning to become and to play an instrument while iteratively gathering and interpreting data. You may be one of the lucky prodigies born with perfect pitch and the voice of an angel. But maybe not. In the latter case, you need to accept (we hope joyfully) that it takes a lot of work and practice for most people to become adept at good qualitative research. Perhaps partly because of the structure of academic training, becoming even a little bit competent seems to take longer for qualitative research than it does for quantitative work. Or maybe it just appears this way because the studies themselves seem to take longer from initial conception to publication. Thus, you also have to nurture patience, which can be particularly difficult in the face of a ticking tenure clock.

Third, the authors we cited above demanding respect for the people and social worlds we study are on high ground both methodologically and morally. Again, this holds even if in the end we develop a critical perspective. If you choose to enter into the lives of those you study in even a small way, you will as a "sensing" instrument see, hear, feel and sometimes even smell (think textile dyeing) aspects and patterns of their lives and interactions with others in this social world. It's all data. We think it is useful for you to think of your responsibility as an "expressive instrument" to provide an adequate account of who they are and how they live and work in this world.

Fourth, you are responsible for keeping yourself as an instrument – in both senses – calibrated and in tune. We have learned from experience that it is easy to get completely drawn into and overwhelmed by what you are studying.[3] You cannot live two lives simultaneously, one focused on another social world and one focused on your own. Get enough sleep. Exercise. Eat well. Attend to your own existing relationships as well as those you are building with the people you are studying. Realize (this is hard) that almost no one – including those you are studying and your friends and loved ones – will find what you are discovering or the process of discovery as interesting as you do. The one exception may be if you are lucky enough to have a research partner who finds every little thing you are learning just as interesting as you do (the metaphor here is "this study is our baby, isn't it the cutest and best baby ever?!").

Finally, as you develop grounded theory, you are likely not only to become convinced that it is in some deep way true, you may also come to see everything about the world through this lens. This can be incredibly fun as well as intellectually rewarding. Don't get addicted. Improving both your theoretical sensitivity and your ability to express yourself in a way that resonates with others requires a broader perspective. Read broadly, including fiction, watch movies and plays. Hang out with people who share none of your theoretical, methodological or identity commitments. Remember, that as an expressive instrument, you will also have an audience – sometimes different or competing ones – needing to hear practical and theoretical implications that may challenge but must also fit within their sense of the world if they are to be moved by the music of your narrative. Become a better instrument so you can enter another social world with even more gusto than the last.

## Appendix

1    We selected five high-quality general management journals that had the reputation for publishing qualitative research: *Academy of Management Journal*, *Administrative Science Quarterly*, *Journal of Management Studies*, *Organization Science* and *Organization Studies*. We also selected three high-quality entrepreneurship journals: *Entrepreneurship Theory & Practice*, *Journal of Business Venturing* and *Strategic Management Journal*. For each journal we examined ten years of papers, grouped into two five-year periods, 2006–2010 and 2011–2015. Because *Organization Studies* publishes a higher percentage of qualitative studies than we anticipated, we report on it separately. In total, we examined 2,900 empirical articles.

2    Because we are particularly interested in the traditional view of entrepreneurship as being about organization-creation and founder-run ventures, we looked more closely at qualitative entrepreneurship papers that focused on these closely related topics. We report on these comparisons in Tables 16.2 and 16.3.

3   Overall our coding of articles was relatively inclusive and was based on the full text of articles rather than on abstracts. For Table 16.1, we included a wide variety of phenomena, including but not limited to founders, venture creation, corporate, institutional and social entrepreneurship as well as incubators, opportunity discovery/construction, venture capital and IPOs if the focus was in any way on entrepreneurship. If an author said they were doing entrepreneurship research or if they claimed contributions to entrepreneurship research or if they described their setting as focused on entrepreneurship and suggested this setting was important to the study, we coded the study as entrepreneurship. As is commonplace in other reviews of entrepreneurship research (Aldrich and Baker, 1997), we did not include population-level studies such as those rooted in population ecology, as entrepreneurship research.

     Similarly, if an author said that they were doing qualitative research or if our reading of the methods section suggested they were, even if they did not adopt this label, we coded the paper as qualitative. We included two entrepreneurship papers using fuzzy set Qualitative Comparative Analysis as qualitative papers. We decided to exclude "mixed methods" papers claiming both qualitative and quantitative methods from all counts. While in a few cases these papers really performed both qualitative and related quantitative studies, in many more cases the "qualitative methods" were limited to a few exploratory interviews at the service of grounding or illustrating claims in what was primarily a quantitative paper.

## Notes

1 Both the "researcher" and the "entrepreneur" can be plural; the overall point still holds.
2 We are intentionally avoiding using the terms "epistemology" and "ontology" here, but our suggestion of different roles for the sheet music is intended to suggest that our recommendations can make sense to researchers with a variety of commitments about how the social world "really is" and how we should understand it.
3 This should not be confused with the old racist and colonialist notion of "going native."

## References

Aldrich H. E. and Baker, T. 1997. Blinded by the cites? Has there been progress in entrepreneurship research? In Donald L. Sexton and Raymond W. Smilor (eds.) *Entrepreneurship 2000*. Chicago, IL: Upstart, pp. 377–400.

Baker, T. and Welter, F. 2014. Bridges to the future: challenging the nature of entrepreneurship scholarship. In Baker, T. and Welter, F. (eds.) *The Routledge Companion to Entrepreneurship*. London: Routledge, pp. 3–18.

Baker, T, Miner, S. and Eesley, D. 2003. Improvising firms: bricolage, retrospective interpretation and improvisational competencies in the founding process. *Research Policy*, 32: 255–276.

Bansal, P. and Corley, K. 2011. From the editors: the coming of age for qualitative research: embracing the diversity of qualitative methods. *Academy of Management Journal*, 54: 233–237.

Eisenhardt, K. M. 1989. Building theories from case study research. *Academy of Management Review*, 14: 532–550.

Eisenhardt, K. M. and Graebner, M. E. 2007. Theory building from cases: opportunities and challenges. *Academy of Management Journal*, 50: 25–32.

Eisenhardt, K. M., Graebner, M. E. and Sonenshein, S. 2016. From the editors: grand challenges and inductive methods: rigor without rigor mortis. *Academy of Management Journal*, 59: 1113–1123.

Gioia, D., Corley, K. and Hamilton, A. 2013. Seeking qualitative rigor in inductive research: notes on the Gioia methodology. *Organizational Research Methods*, 16: 15–31.

Goffman, Ervin. 1959. *The Presentation of Self in Everyday Life*. New York: Anchor.

Hannan, M. T. and Freeman, J. 1989. *Organizational Ecology*, Cambridge, MA: Harvard University Press.

Lofland, J., Snow, D., Anderson, L. and Lofland, L. 2006. *Analyzing Social Settings: A Guide to Qualitative Observation and Analysis* (4th ed.). Boston, MA: Wadsworth.

Malinowski, B. 1922. *Argonauts of the Western Pacific: An Account of Native Enterprise and Adventure in the Archipelagoes of Melanesian New Guinea*. London: Routledge & Sons.

Patton, M. Q. 1990. *Qualitative Evaluation and Research Methods*. Thousand Oaks, CA: Sage.

Pedhazur, E. J. and Schmelkin, L. P. 1991. *Measurement, Design, and Analysis: An Integrated Approach*. Hillsdale, NJ: Erlbaum.

Powell, E. E. and Baker, T. 2014. It's what you make of it: founder identity and enacting strategic responses to adversity. *Academy of Management Journal*, 57(5): 1406–1433.

Powell, E. E. and Baker, T. Forthcoming. In the beginning: identity processes and organizing in multi-founder nascent ventures. *Academy of Management Journal*, in press.

Pratt, M. 2009. From the editors: for the lack of a boilerplate: tips on writing up (and reviewing) qualitative research. *Academy of Management Journal*, 52(5): 856–862.

Rew, L., Bechtel, D. and Sapp, A. 1993. Self-as-instrument in qualitative research. *Nursing Research*, 42(5): 300–301.

Shane, S. and Venkataraman, S. 2000. The promise of entrepreneurship as a field of research. *Academy of Management Review*, 25(1): 217–226.

Strauss, A. and Corbin, J. 1998. *Basics of Qualitative Research, Techniques and Procedures for Developing Grounded Theory* (2nd ed.). Thousand Oaks, CA: Sage.

Tracy, S. J. 2010. Qualitative quality: eight "big-tent" criteria for excellent qualitative research. *Qualitative Inquiry*, 16: 837–851.

Van Maanen, J. 2011. *Tales of the Field: On Writing Ethnography* (2nd ed.). Chicago, IL: University of Chicago Press.

# 17

# DOING QUALITATIVE RESEARCH ON EMERGING FIELDS AND MARKETS

*Nina Granqvist, Galina Kallio, and Heli Nissilä*

## Introduction

There has been a proliferation of research on market and field emergence since the 2000s. The numerous literatures exploring this topic include institutionalist approaches (Lounsbury et al., 2003; Maguire and Hardy, 2006; Maguire et al. 2004), market categories (Glynn and Navis, 2013; Granqvist et al., 2013), sociotechnical approaches and actor-network theory (Garud and Karnøe, 2003), the sociology of expectations (van Lente, 2012; Borup et al., 2006), and practice theoretical perspectives (Araujo et al., 2008; Callon, 1999; Gomez and Bouty, 2011). Studying this topic is both important and interesting because it helps us to cast light on how novelty becomes instituted, a phenomenon that is fundamental to the social sciences in general. Research has provided insight, for example, on how new meanings and understandings take shape by negotiating and probing the boundaries of field or categories (Granqvist et al., 2013; Navis and Glynn, 2010), how new ideas and cultural meanings are collectively mobilized so that they gain in momentum and influence (Lounsbury et al., 2003; Weber et al., 2008), how expectations become materially embedded in activities and artifacts related to emerging innovation and technology (van Lente, 1993), and how new practices take shape through mundane and routinized activities performed in organizations and at their boundaries (Bapuji et al., 2012; Gherardi and Perrotta, 2011).

Market and field emergence is a complex topic of research. The related processes typically extend over a long period of time across multiple levels of analysis and several groups and communities of actors that often adjoin many existing fields. All this is characterized by ambiguity regarding the "object" of emergence, the shared meanings and boundaries that the participating communities come to shape, and the duration and outcome of the process, combined with a multiplicity of interaction. Emergence is thus an elusive object to trace, posing multiple challenges for empirical research.

The first such challenge relates to timing of the fieldwork and its implications for data collection. The great majority of studies explore emergence after the fact. As a result, researchers most often make use of retrospective rather than real-time data. Consequently the challenge is then how to gain a sufficiently fine-grained understanding of occurrences that have taken place in the past, taking into consideration the role of post-hoc rationalizing.

The second challenge is operationalizing the object of research. Existing studies almost never trace "emergence" but rather, it is a context in which particular processes occur. The main challenge is to understand "what is this a case of" – what exactly is the phenomenon under study. A multitude of different concepts can be used when framing such research, including field, market, institution, practice, network, social movement, discourse, and meanings and frames.[1] Each of these concepts is grounded in a broader literature and explains different aspects and processes. Moreover, studies of emergence often cross levels of analysis. For example, all previously mentioned concepts can be analyzed at the micro, meso, or macro levels, thus compounding the challenge confronted in focusing the study. Understanding one's own onto-epistemological approach, attention to the kind of data at hand, meticulous analyses, and often several rounds of revisions are required to find clarity in these issues.

The third challenge is how to structure and write up the findings. Events and actions should be mapped chronologically in order to trace how a market or a field has developed over time. However, coding for themes and patterns in the data is required to uncover explanations of specific phenomena. Elegantly combining the two requirements – narrating the flow of events and presenting the analytical categories – can be challenging.

In this chapter we explore and provide insight on the issues discussed above. Table 17.1 summarizes the key insights and recommendations. Our aim is to provide support and a conceptual and practical toolbox for researchers who are engaging, perhaps for the first time, in empirical research on emerging fields and markets. We also wish to initiate a broader discussion on how to study emergence by making use of a broader set of existing methods, and developing new methodology for future research.

## What Is Emergence, and Emergence of What?

In the social sciences it is rather difficult to talk about the emergence of a market or a field in any absolute terms. The object of emergence is not coherent and clear-cut such that all observers would perceive it in the same way. Rather, there are multiple points of view and interpretations of what, in this case, a field or a market consists of. This chapter assumes a social constructivist perspective in addressing emergence. By this we mean that "all claims to knowledge, truth, objectivity or insight are founded within communities of meaning making" (Gergen, 2001: 2).

*Table 17.1* Summary of Insights and Recommendations

*Starting the fieldwork*
Considering the timing of the fieldwork – what is the current stage of development?
Using both real-time and retrospective data
Considering the level of engagement with the field: Archival data – interviews – observation – ethnography

*Operationalizing the research object*
Understanding researcher's own onto-epistemological approach
Approaching emergence as a context for research rather than an object of inquiry
Identifying the phenomenon to be explained
Assessing possible data collection methods and access to data sources
Reflecting and deciding upon the level of analysis

*Analyses and reporting the findings*
Abduction: Iterative process of analyzing the data and identifying potential conceptual frameworks
Typical structures for findings: Chronological narrative, analytical categories, combination
Accounting for "success bias" and seeming linearity in developments
Justifying and co-constructing analyses and conceptual positioning during the review process

This approach accentuates that people make sense of their experiences through lenses or frameworks provided by their contexts and communities, and meanings and interpretations are negotiated within them. In a similar manner, researchers co-construct an object of inquiry together with informants, by drawing from various data sources. The quality of the study depends on the breadth and quality of the data and the depth of analysis. Taken together, the data and analyses allow researchers to uncover possible explanations and assume multiple points of view, informed by specific scholarly communities of meaning making.

Within sociological approaches both fields and markets are understood as "socially constructed arenas" where a variety of participants engage in repeated interaction and share a common meaning system (Fligstein and Dioun, 2015: 67). Scott and Meyer (1994: 56) define organizational fields as domains of social action – "communities of organizations that partake of a common meaning system and whose participants interact more frequently and fatefully with one another than with actors outside the field." Markets, in turn, can be broadly understood as socio-economic entities – exchange structures between suppliers and demand-side actors (DiMaggio, 1984). They have been seen to comprise institutions, networks, performances, fields, practices, and cultures (Beckert, 2010; Fligstein and Dauter, 2007; Kjellberg and Helgesson, 2007), and engage several actors, such as suppliers, customers, governments, and workers. It is no surprise that studies using such broad concepts frequently overlap.

At its core, studying emergence is about exploring complex processes with an open ending – processes that take place in multifaceted interaction among objects, actions, and events (Senge, 1990) over a long period of time. Observers can only see that a coherent field of action has emerged after the fact. Previous studies on field or market emergence usually explore some form of action and collaboration (e.g. Lawrence et al., 2002) – new relationships take shape between actors, new understandings emerge that connect previously isolated entities together, new objects take form through these interactions. Empirical studies have explored shared new meanings, practices, and actor roles during the emergence of an organizational field around recycling (Lounsbury et al., 2003; Walker et al., 2014) or the formation of producer identities, the establishment of an exchange infrastructure, and the gradual sharing of values around the market for grass-fed beef (Weber et al., 2008). In other words, scholars need to explore what produced the outcome in question, and draw from literatures such as collaboration, identities and identification, labeling, categorizing, frames and social movements for focused explanations. We discuss the process of framing the study briefly in the following section as it forms a key aspect for focusing analyses.

## Starting the Fieldwork

In preparing for fieldwork, researchers need to account for several issues. In this section we provide some ideas on how to get started – how to map what is going on and how to understand what the "case" in question is about. To gain further insight and provide examples, Table 17.2 summarizes some key studies. It outlines their theoretical framing, the empirical phenomena addressed by them, the level of analysis, the data sources, and the analytical methods and briefly presents the findings and contributions. We will discuss these aspects further in this section and in the remainder of the chapter.

### *Timing of the Fieldwork and the Nature of Data*

What researchers can observe and, thus, what data collection methods are appropriate, depend on the phase in the development of the field or market during the fieldwork. Typically, a

*Table 17.2* Examples of Studies in Market and Field Emergence

| | Theoretical Framing | Empirical Phenomenon | Level of Analysis | Data Sources | Method for Analysis | Findings |
|---|---|---|---|---|---|---|
| *Garud (2008)* Conferences as venues for the configuration of emerging organizational fields: The case of cochlear implants | Field-configuring events, sociology of associations | Conferences as venues for configuring emerging fields | Micro-interactions in the field | Participatory observations on three conferences and their preparatory efforts, interviews and archival data | Real-time collection and analysis of data, grounded analysis | Conferences are prime venues in field emergence and act as sites for generating consensus for one approach over another and achieving institutional closure |
| *Gomez and Bouty (2011)* The emergence of an influential practice: Food for thought | Practice-theory | Emergence of a new practice in an existing field | Practice level, field-level | Interviews, observations, media, Michelin guides | Real-time data in the form of interviews and observations (habitus-level of analysis), media (agent-field-level analysis), Michelin guide database (analyzing emergence of the new practice in the field) | A strong habitus of a key chef influenced the emergence of a practice of using vegetables in Haute Cuisine and helped in its adaptation at the field level |
| *Granqvist, Grodal and Woolley (2013)* Hedging your bets: Explaining executives' market labeling strategies in nanotechnology | Market categories, symbolic management | Use and adoption of nanotechnology label during the market category emergence | Executives' labeling practices | Interviews, archival materials | Qualitative inductive methods through iterative coding. Identification of labeling strategies and label uses. | Identifying types of labelling strategies: claiming, hedging and disassociating. Mapping label use in terms of firms' actual capabilities. Developing a framework for executives' labeling strategies in emerging market categories. |

| Reference | Concept | Research focus | Perspective | Data | Analysis | Findings |
|---|---|---|---|---|---|---|
| *Maguire and Hardy (2006)* The emergence of new global institutions: A discursive perspective | Discourses and emerging regulatory institutions | Relationship between the new environmental discourse of "precaution," legacy discourses and institution building related to the Stockholm Convention on Persistent Pollutants | Interplay between discourses, objects, concepts and subject positions; institutional effects of discourses; field-level | Texts from the formal negotiating process including official reports and attempts to influence the evolving text; observations on three meetings, 40 interviews with state and non-state actors involved in the negotiations | Constructing a discursive event history by appointing texts to chronological events; iteration between theory, themes and data starting from theory-driven categories; comparison of two discourses related to their object, concept and subject positions; analysis of texts by four key actors and institutional contributions of distinct discourses | New institutions emerge out of a discursive struggle between a new discourse and established legacy discourses. In this struggle actors use their authority to create overlaps and interactions between the new and the legacy discourses, and as a result the meanings of both discourses are altered. |
| *Maguire, Hardy and Lawrence (2004)* Institutional entrepreneurship in emerging fields: HIV/AIDS treatment advocacy in Canada | Institutional entrepreneurship | Activities in the emergence of a field for HIV advocacy; specifically practices of consultation and information exchange | Micro-dynamics in institutional entrepreneurship | Semi-structured interviews with pharmaceutical companies and community organizations, observations at meetings, documents such as agendas, personal notes, and presentations | Constructing a chronology on field emergence, analyzing the degree of change, identifying key roles and activities that generated the outcomes, identification of broad themes in the data, and reducing the themes into precise categories | Three activities related to institutional entrepreneurship were central: (1) the occupation of subject positions that bridge different stakeholders; (2) theorization of new practices; and (3) institutionalization of new practices by creating linkages to routines and values |

*continued*

Table 17.2 Continued

|  | Theoretical Framing | Empirical Phenomenon | Level of Analysis | Data Sources | Method for Analysis | Findings |
|---|---|---|---|---|---|---|
| *Martin and Schouten (2014)* Consumption-driven market emergence | Actor network theory, consumer culture theory | Emergence of a market for a new type of motorcycle sports | Practices, group-level interactions | Ethnographic observations of events, 24 interviews, archival material | Actor-network analysis, analyzing the role of humans and non-humans, translations | A market emerged through a three-stage process of translation, namely consumer innovation; assembling a community; catalyzing and legitimizing a market |
| *Weber, Heinz and DeSoucey (2008)* Forage for thought: Mobilizing codes in the movement for grass-fed meat and dairy products | Social movements, economic sociology, institutional theory | Emergence of markets for grass-fed meat | Social movement | Interviews, observation, movement publications, websites, online discussion forums, news articles, reports | Abductive; iteration between pre-existing theories and data. First stage analysis: semiotic codes, second stage: empirically grounded themes | Binary semiotic codes influence framing of the movement; market creation happens through establishment of three components: entrepreneurial producers, producer community, market exchange |

researcher observes that something "new" is happening and that it is a meaningful object for study. At this stage the field is often fairly advanced – it has some level of legitimacy or it may be publicly contested and therefore visible. Scholars often produce stylized, bracketed, and "clean" accounts because they typically trace developments retrospectively, moving backwards from the current situation – an outcome. This makes the process seem fairly linear. As a result, lived experiences, messiness, and trials and errors are seldom detected by the radar and do not appear in published papers. This also gives rise to a "success bias" – researchers tend to study those fields and markets that have "made it" and thus overlook many more ideas and activities that failed to gain traction and have thus vanished into the dustbin of history. Hence research covers only the tip of the iceberg, leaving much of the emergence process invisible.

In terms of data, to gain understanding on what has happened up until the current point in time, and what is now going on, there is a need for both real-time and retrospective data. Retrospective data refer to empirical materials that interpret past events at a later point in time from the perspective of current understandings. For example, in interviews informants look back and tell what happened as they recall it at the moment of the interview – with certain bracketing of what are meaningful developments in the flow of actions and events. These recollections might not be representative of how things unfolded and how various participants engaged and understood the field or the market at the time. Such accounts tend to rationalize past events and overlook trial and error, dead ends, and a variety of events that may have had a major impact.

Hence it is also necessary to collect real-time data to complement the retrospective data. Archival materials, such as news stories and reports, provide "real-time" accounts of how certain events were understood. These data are also relatively easy to access. Moreover, researchers may sometimes be "lucky" and enter the field in an early phase of emergence, when some activities may be evident although their outcomes remain unknown. Prominent forms of real-time data collection are observation and (other) ethnographic methods in which the researcher engages with the field and is able to trace and follow developments in situ.

### *Considering Theoretical Framing – What Is This a Case of?*

A theoretical framing defines the key concepts of the paper, lays out the studies that have addressed the phenomenon under inquiry, and discusses the central processes and explanations identified by the previous research. Moreover, a theoretical framing outlines gaps in extant research and elaborates on how the study at hand can develop novel understanding.

In inductive, qualitative work, a theoretical framing becomes fully developed at a fairly late stage of the research process. Prior to developing a coherent framing, researchers have typically conducted extensive fieldwork and data analysis and written multiple versions of the empirical findings. Although they usually have assumptions on relevant theoretical concepts at the outset, these are revised and often rejected during the process. Extensive analyses of the data are frequently required to fully grasp "what is this a case of" – that is, what is the empirical phenomenon to be explained, and what are the appropriate concepts and literatures.

Usually a study draws on or advances more than one theoretical discussion. For example, a study may connect practice theory and institutional theory while simultaneously enhancing understanding within a specific niche of practice theory (Gomez and Bouty, 2011; Gherardi and Perrotta, 2011). Alternatively, a study may bring together literatures on categories, market creation, and social movements to explain processes that happen during emergence (Weber et al., 2008).

Choosing the level of analysis is important because it has a major impact on what literatures and explanations are relevant and what theoretical framings can be adopted. Emergence initially happens at the margins among only a few people, after which a broader mobilization takes place among certain collectives or communities (Granqvist and Laurila, 2011; Maguire et al., 2004). The level of analysis can thus vary from tracing the emergence of novel practices at the micro-social level to mapping collective mobilization through social movements and the framing of meaning (Lounsbury et al., 2003).

## *How to Get Started with Data Collection*

All fieldwork initially seeks to make sense of what is going on, which may be a daunting task. Writing event histories by studying archival materials such as reports and news stories, partici-pating in public events, and conducting pilot interviews are effective ways to identify the key players, determine the current status of development, and ascertain the direction in which the field is heading. Based on a pilot study, researchers can begin to make sense of the observed phenomenon and elaborate "what is this a case of." They can also identify the methods most appropriate for collecting data while also accounting for the timing of the fieldwork.

## Methods for Data Collection

The extant empirical research has employed multiple methods for data collection, typically including a combination of interviews, observation, and archival material (e.g., Gomez and Bouty, 2011; Weber et al., 2008). Each method for data collection has its own particular strengths. Interviews – the most common source of data in studies of this kind – are crucial to access motives, meanings, and cultural frames as experienced and narrated by informants. Textual and archival material – web pages, media reports, or texts produced by the informants them-selves – support an understanding of *what* is going on and *why*. Observation is a prime method for studying *how* actions (e.g., organizing a protest, encounters among producers and consum-ers) are carried out in situ and how interaction between actors unfolds. To capture an emergent phenomenon, multiple data sources are usually needed.

## *Interviews*

Interviews usually form the primary data set for analysis. As discussed above, interviews usually contain both real-time and retrospective elements, in other words, informants tell about both past and current developments. Explorative interviews are appropriate for familiarizing oneself with the object of inquiry whereas thematic interviews provide more focus on specific themes. A combination of these allows novelty to emerge while keeping the focus on the topic identi-fied. We discuss some aspects of whom and how to interview below.

### *Who to Interview?*

Any process of emergence involves people from different participating communities with varying interests and points of view. These include researchers, firms with an offering in an emerging field or market, funders, venture capitalists, governmental agencies, activists, and NGOs. Moreover, to gain a better understanding of history, institutional and political environ-ments, and existing trends and cultures, it may be beneficial to include other stakeholders such as employees of city councils or local government, representatives of research institutions, the media, or related industries. Deciding who to interview may be challenging, as observed phenomena often intersect with many existing fields, markets, and institutions.

Finding informants is an emergent process in its own right. Along with increasing under-standing of the object of inquiry new actor groups and, thus, potential informants also become visible. Snowball "sampling" – asking informants to suggest other informants – also serves this end. The search should employ a variety of means in order to ensure a broad range of partici-pants. For example, silenced and marginal groups can provide information on paths not taken and the related power dynamics.

## How to Interview – Explorative and Thematic Interviews

There are a multitude of approaches to interviewing. We address two approaches here – the explorative and the thematic – which are particularly effective in tracing participants' experi-ences of the field. Explorative interviews are usually a good way to begin data collection. As the emerging domains may be new to both researchers and practitioners, an overall understanding is important. In exploratory interviews it is essential to avoid forcing the frameworks or desired explanations of the researchers on the informants. Researchers should instead ask open questions that allow practitioners themselves to explore what is currently happening and explain what is important or interesting from their vantage point. After initiating conversation around the topic, it is helpful to use short and open questions such as "how did that happen?", "what happened then?", "why was this so?", and "tell more about this." The aim is to understand the topic or issue as much from the informant's perspective as possible, and provide space for authentic nar-ratives. While this is a generic guideline applying to qualitative interviews beyond the topic of field and market emergence, this approach is particularly relevant to the study of emergence as there may be little existing material on which to draw and interviews may act as sites for sense-making and "producing" the field.

A clearer focus gradually emerges during data collection. Thematic, semi-structured inter-views allow coverage of certain key themes while keeping the overall interview format flexible. In thematic interviews, a researcher crafts a set of questions under a few major themes. Each theme is opened with a broad, open question that allows the informant to talk freely about the issue. More specific questions follow. The aim is still to enable "natural talk" – but also to address themes considered important by the researcher. For example, a theme can be to explore the role of public financing during emergence. Then the entry question could be "How do you perceive the role of public financing in this field?" Follow-up questions – such as those described in the above paragraph – can be used to prompt more natural talk. Thematic interviews allow scoping into more specific questions based on the interests of researchers. Themes and lists of questions provide support and comfort. However, not all themes will be relevant for the informant and hence it is necessary to allow room for new themes and issues to emerge. In sum, thematic interviews also require flexibility from the researcher.

When planning thematic interviews, it is useful to consider what kind of interview questions would best trigger narratives on the emergence of novelty, as opposed to the mere narration of static themes, opinions, and current situation (Senge, 1990). For instance, it is useful to ask ques-tions that urge thinking over long time spans and contrasting the past with the present and the anticipated future. One way to gain access to stories of this kind is to ask what specific changes have occurred with regard to a given topic, how the present situation differs from the past, and what visions and expectations the informants have concerning the future. Moreover, people typically have vivid memories of events and situations in which they were closely involved and tend to narrate them in detail.

Finally, a major factor in the emergence of fields and markets is how people maintain estab-lished meanings and practices in their everyday life and make use of new ones. In tracing these meanings and practices, it is important to differentiate between what people actually *do* as opposed to what they *say*. Interviews can be used to trace novel practices. Though it may be hard to get informants to talk concretely about their routines, there are techniques for achieving this end. First, conducting interviews in surroundings familiar to an informant may promote more "authentic" speech. Second, in order to form a better understanding of practices from the perspective of practitioners, it is important to ask concrete and very practical questions on how work tasks are being practically accomplished, along with inquiring why they are accomplished in that particular way (for more information, see e.g., Gherardi, 2012). Overall, questions should be focused on matters in which informants have primary experience and in which they do not need to speculate overly on the motives or perceptions of other actors.

## Archival Materials

Archival materials rarely serve as the only source of data in studies on field and market emergence. Instead, researchers typically use them as an additional data source that can either be analyzed in detail or used for testing and validating interpretations. Archival materials are also useful for creating event histories and they represent a snapshot of how some issues were understood at a particular point in time. Moreover, archival materials are usually easily accessible through websites and various archives.

This type of data may consist for example of news articles, reports by field participants, reports and analyses by consultants, emails, discussions on social media, and video materials. News articles are a common source of data that provides insight into the public discussions of an emerging issue. Hence, they can be helpful in gaining understanding of the level of public interest in an issue over time and in revealing important turning points in the emerging field. News articles are also useful because they may provide a longitudinal data set on the research topic. When analyzing news articles, the researcher may, for instance, focus on the number of news stories published over time on a specific topic, the tone of the articles (whether the news is generally positive or negative), and actors and groups that have been active over time.

As opposed to public news media, reports typically represent the perspectives of specific legitimate actors in a novel field, such as NGOs and governments. Reports usually present specific points of view and interests; they aim to forward policies or mitigate risks and often project expectations for future development. It is also worthwhile to explore what video materials may be available on a topic. Social events are often available on Internet video services and can offer an opportunity to complement observational data with minimal effort.

The email lists of various participating communities are a further interesting data source. Such distribution lists offer a perspective into interaction between actors and can thus provide "backstage" information on the topic. Similarly, social media can provide a useful platform for tracing interaction between engaged actors. This data source is still underused in studies on emergence and will provide many opportunities for future research. Ethical research standards must, however, be kept in mind – quoting non-public or semi-public social media discussions may require permission.

As a general rule of thumb for the use of all archival materials, it is important to consider who produced the data and when, and the original purpose of the data. Careful reflection of these issues enables the researcher to make informed decisions on the role and value of different kinds of data sets and how best to use them in developing findings and constructing arguments.

## *Observation and Ethnography*

Observation is commonly used as an additional method in studying the emergence of fields and markets, complementing interviews and archival materials (Gomez and Bouty, 2011; Weber et al., 2008). It is a form of real-time data collection and allows, for instance, tracing of micro-interaction, which includes conversation, collaboration, and routine work tasks. Observation also allows following the use and appropriation of material objects such as technology and spaces and the emergence of new types of action.

In particular, public events such as conferences and workshops are typical sites for observation in many studies (e.g., Garud, 2008; Granqvist et al., 2013; Hardy and Maguire, 2010; Nissilä, 2015). In such events, "people from diverse organizations … assemble periodically … to announce new products, develop industry standards [and] construct social networks" (Lampel and Meyer, 2008). These events provide a rather easy access to observing activities involved in field emergence. They also provide understanding of the key participants and allow access to basic knowledge on the topic of interest through keynote talks and other presentations. Such organized events also provide a setting for gathering vast amounts of other data, including archival data (reports, participant lists, and presentation and marketing materials that are normally made accessible through websites or mailing lists) or engaging in informal chats or "ethnographic interviews" (Flick, 2009: 169). These encounters may also offer an opportunity for arranging regular interviews with event participants.

Further, participation in events may give access to private accounts and interaction, thereby enabling an insider perspective (see e.g., Garud, 2008). Beyond formally organized field-level events, there are also closed meetings among core members. Having access to such gatherings can provide valuable data on developments and debates occurring "backstage." This provides the researcher with further understanding and the possibility to make specific claims.

However, observation has been rarely used as the primary source of data. Ethnography refers to a set of methods – and more broadly to a practice – for studying a phenomenon inductively from the perspective of participants (Barley, 1996; van Maanen, 1988). The main difference between an ethnographic study and more "conventional" qualitative research with some observation is the level of engagement with the object of inquiry. Ethnography is a demanding approach because it typically requires a scholar to become an "insider" in order to gain cultural understanding and capture the experiences of the people under study. This is achieved by observing everyday practices over extensive periods of time in the field and conducting several informal interviews. Also, gaining access to the field at the right time and in the right situation may be hard – following people "in action" requires permission from those being observed. Perhaps the easiest way to gain access is to use the existing networks of researchers. In the absence of such contacts, a pilot study may help in building relationships with key people and gaining trust.

Ethnographic observation is also a demanding method because it is learned through trial and error. To avoid the main errors, fieldwork should be prepared in advance by considering *what* to observe and *how*. This allows a focus on, for example, interaction, language use, routines, shared patterns of doing, or use of places and materiality. Generating observational data also includes various techniques to "record" the data. Entering the field with a notebook and open mind and observing the phenomena from close up is the conventional approach. It may be possible to record ad hoc interviews, take pictures, record videos, and use other material such as meeting notes, presentations, or concrete products generated at the time of the fieldwork. Participation in social media allows online observation. Obviously not all of the data will be of equal importance, but in the early stage of the fieldwork the focus of the study may not yet be fully clear. Thus, collecting a wealth of empirical material allows more leeway. Well-written field-notes are filled with detail, personal experience, and interpretation, which will also enable use of creative interpretive methods such as narrative writing later on.

In sum, ethnographic methods such as observation facilitate a more concrete and experiential understanding of what is happening in the field – something that remains hidden when using only written materials or interviews.

## The Data Analysis Process

As discussed earlier, this paper assumes a social constructivist perspective to field and market emergence. Qualitative research is ideally inductive; theories are built from the data without imposing pre-existing theoretical frameworks. In practice, however, research is abductive; interpretations of the data are tied to pre-existing assumptions and frameworks and data analysis and conceptual development proceed iteratively as the researcher constantly seeks better explanations for observations (Dubois and Gadde, 2002). The process of data analysis is therefore one of construction in which the author engages with a variety of empirical materials and conceptual frameworks to interpret observations. It is inherent to such iterative methodology that analysis begins by making sense of what is happening; researchers devise a theoretical framing for the empirical findings by going back and forth between empirical data and various literatures. Specific research questions can be posed only at the end of this process. The research questions and the related theoretical framing and research gaps finally define "what is this a case of" – what particular approach or perspective the study produces. Abductive qualitative analysis is not dedicated to studying emerging fields and markets but used to explore a variety of social processes (see e.g., Zietsma and Lawrence, 2010).

Iterative analyses often lead to the following type of analytical process. The first stage relates to making sense of the field and occurs through immersion during data collection. Usually a researcher makes an assumption – for example, the emergence of nanotechnology is similar to that of biotechnology with industry networks and collaborations playing a key role. Empirical work, however, takes the research in unpredictable directions and often provides an unexpected focus for the inquiry. During the fieldwork and analyses, the researcher needs to abandon many preconceptions and allow novel insight to emerge. Methods for data collection and analysis need to support such gradual development of understanding and focus.

To immerse in and order the data, researchers often write extensive narratives about what they observe. These are usually chronological and make sense of the unfolding of actions and events and the relationships between them over time. Chronology tables are often used to create event histories and "bring order to the chaos." Such chronologies and chronological narratives may also be based on field notes describing for example relationships between actors and mapping their roles in an emerging domain based on observations at various social gatherings and on newspaper stories and reports.

This exposure may offer initial understandings of what the study is about in more specific terms, providing an initial analytical framework. Once such an understanding is taking shape, a more detailed coding of the data may begin, for example by coding only a part of the data set in order to test the emerging framework. This type of "pilot coding" may lead to reiteration of the key concepts and informs a more focused coding of the data. Although not always applicable, a typical approach is the Gioia-model for the process of data analysis (Gioia and Thomas, 1996; Gioia et al., 2013). According to this model, the researcher first categorizes the data through first-order analysis based on concepts that appear in the data and using the words and concepts of the informants. This is followed by a second-order analysis in which the researcher aggregates the first-order concepts into "themes," and third into "aggregate dimensions" (Gioia et al., 2013). Data categorization of this kind is useful for identifying themes and patterns in the data set and facilitates analytical insight. Through such analyses, researchers may develop models and frameworks that clarify relationships between various concepts. This may provide new or revised understandings of the social processes that relate, in this case, to field and market emergence. Data tables are a means for displaying the original data and supporting the identified analytical categories.

When a study is submitted to an academic journal, the review process typically gives rise to new rounds of iterative coding and focusing. Moreover, reviewers often challenge the researcher's interpretations. Producing a journal article therefore becomes a joint process of construction where the ideas presented are reflected and reified against a particular body of knowledge, as interpreted by the reviewers and negotiated during the review process.

## Reporting the Findings

There are several possible ways to present findings. Most studies addressing emergence fall under two main types – chronological order or analytical categories type structure. Writing a chronological narrative of how the emergence process has unfolded is an essential part of all such studies and provides readers with important background information. Beyond this, institutional studies in particular present chronologically ordered findings where the developments occur in stages. They are usually supported with a chronology table presenting the order and timing of the key events (for examples, see Granqvist and Laurila, 2011; Lounsbury et al., 2003; Navis and Glynn, 2010). In such studies researchers "bracket" the developments within a field or market into stages that are distinct from each other in terms of, for example, prevailing norms and values, activities, or produced outcomes. Such studies capitalize on an extensive historical analysis of a variety of materials and trace the process of emergence and the flow of events and actions and the relationships between actions and concepts over time.

Another typical option is Gioia-style analysis, which provides themes or categories that structure the findings. In this approach, the starting point is to use the aggregate dimensions as the headings in the findings section and then explain the key dynamics and show the data that supports the argument under these sections. More recently, studies have begun to address interaction between the aggregate dimensions and the outcomes that they produce (see Granqvist and Gustafsson, 2016; Zietsma and Lawrence, 2010, for examples). In these studies the outcomes provide the key sub-headings for the findings section and the analysis opens up how such outcomes emerged in interaction with the key analytical concepts.

However, these two types are somewhat idealized – the findings sections usually contain elements of both the chronological and analytical category type elements. For example, nearly all institutional studies on field emergence provide event chronologies as they are very informative on the development of a novel field or market. This provides a backdrop for understanding the ensuing analysis. Also, in chronologically structured empirical sections there is an analytical lens that structures the narrative and present analytical constructs that connect to one another in the flow of time. On the other hand, studies with structures based on analytical categories may provide a chronological order for facets of the analyses (see e.g., Granqvist and Gustafsson, 2016).

Finding a suitable structure for the findings section is an iterative process in which researchers are forced to experiment. Also, it is important during this process to check that the analyses also account for counterfactuals and "success bias" by exploring other possible development paths and outcomes. This may be helpful to avoid overly linear and deterministic explanations. In sum, a findings section takes shape by making sense of the object of the inquiry and determining the key constructs and how they relate to one another, chronologically and conceptually, and how they contribute to the explanation. In writing analyses this often requires several experiments with the structure and consideration of alternatives.

## Conclusions

Studying the emergence of fields and markets is a topic of much interest and continued relevance among scholars in management studies. This chapter outlined some of the key challenges for qualitative empirical work in the research area, including the timing of the fieldwork and identifying appropriate data collection methods, the challenges posed by operationalizing the object of research and tracing "what is this a case of," analyzing data, and writing up the findings. The extant body of research shows that qualitative studies are best suited to tracing changes in actions, meanings, and materiality that relate to a variety of aspects of field and market emergence.

However, there is still much room for further contributions. Studies to date rely mostly on interviews and archival data sources. Though challenging, participative data collection methods such as observation and ethnography allow direct observation of the unfolding actions and events and are the most promising means for tracing the various micro-processes of emergence. Such real-time participative methodology is perhaps best suited for following the emergence of novel practices and forms of organizing, changing meanings, and actor roles as they relate to new practices and emerging routines and the appropriation of materiality such as new technology and spaces.

In sum, we called for further research on some fundamental processes behind emergence. How people engage in new action and how they, through this action, come to develop new practices, value systems, and relationships is not yet fully understood. Also, there has been less research on the role of materiality in market and field emergence; here observational methods could bring new insight. Future research should also take up a diverse range of both exciting and more mundane contexts of emerging social action. While studies have looked into major new movements, it is also important to explore how minor changes in mundane practices and routines over time can give rise to novelty.

## Note

1 In this chapter, we use concepts of fields and markets throughout as they are the most typical for the research.

## References

Araujo, L., Kjellberg, H., and Spencer, R. (2008). Market practices and forms: Introduction to the special issue. *Marketing Theory*, 8(1), 5–14.

Bapuji, H., Hora, M., and Saeed, A. M. (2012). Intentions, intermediaries, and interaction: Examining the emergence of routines. *Journal of Management Studies*, 49(8), 1586–1607.

Barley, S. R. (1996). Technicians in the workplace: Ethnographic evidence for bringing work into organizational studies. *Administrative Science Quarterly*, 41(3), 404–441.

Beckert, J. (2010). How do fields change? The interrelations of institutions, networks, and cognition in the dynamics of markets. *Organization Studies*, 31(5), 605–627.

Borup, M., Brown, N., Konrad, K., and Van Lente, H. 2006. The sociology of expectations in science and technology. *Technology Analysis & Strategic Management*, 18(3–4), 285–298.

Callon, M. (1999). Actor-network theory: The market test. *The Sociological Review*, 47(S1), 181–195.

DiMaggio, P. J. (1984). The nonprofit instrument and the influence of the marketplace on policies in the arts. In W. McNeil Lowry (ed.) *The Arts and Public Policy in the United States*. Englewood Cliffs, NJ: Prentice-Hall, 57–99.

Dubois, A., and Gadde, L.-E. (2002). Systematic combining: An abductive approach to case research. *Journal of Business Research*, 55(7), 553–560.

Flick, U. (2009). *An Introduction to Qualitative Research*. Los Angeles, CA: Sage.

Fligstein, N., and Dauter, L. (2007). The sociology of markets. *Annual Review of Sociology*, 33, 105–128.

Fligstein, N., and Dioun, C. (2015). Economic sociology. In J. D. Wright (ed.) *International Encyclopedia of the Social and Behavioral Sciences*. Amsterdam: Elsevier. [Online].

Garud, R. (2008). Conferences as venues for the configuration of emerging organizational fields: The case of cochlear implants. *Journal of Management Studies*, 45(6), 1061–1088.

Garud, R., and Karnøe, P. (2003). Bricolage versus breakthrough: Distributed and embedded agency in technology entrepreneurship. *Research Policy*, 32(2), 277–300.

Gergen, K. J. (2001). *Social Construction in Context*. London: Sage.

Gherardi, S. (2012). *How to Conduct a Practice-based Study: Problems and Methods*. Cheltenham, UK: Edward Elgar.

Gherardi, S., and Perrotta, M. (2011). Egg dates sperm: A tale of a practice change and its stabilization. *Organization*, 18(5), 595–614.

Gioia, D. A., and Thomas, J. B. (1996). Identity, image, and issue interpretation: Sensemaking during strategic change in academia. *Administrative Science Quarterly*, 41(3), 370–403.

Gioia, D. A., Corley, K. G., and Hamilton, A. L. (2013). Seeking qualitative rigor in inductive research notes on the Gioia methodology. *Organizational Research Methods*, 16(1), 15–31.

Glynn, M. A., and Navis, C. (2013). Categories, identities, and cultural classification: Moving beyond a model of categorical constraint. *Journal of Management Studies*, 50(6), 1124–1137.

Gomez, M. L., and Bouty, I. (2011). The emergence of an influential practice: Food for thought. *Organization Studies*, 32(7), 921–940.

Granqvist, N., and Gustafsson, R. (2016). Temporal institutional work. *Academy of Management Journal*, 59(3), 1009–1035.

Granqvist, N., and Laurila, J. (2011). Rage against self-replicating machines: Framing science and fiction in the US nanotechnology field. *Organization Studies*, 32(2), 253–280.

Granqvist, N., Grodal, S., and Woolley, J. L. (2013). Hedging your bets: Explaining executives' market labeling strategies in nanotechnology. *Organization Science*, 24(2), 395–413.

Hardy, C., and Maguire, S. (2010). Discourse, field-configuring events, and change in organizations and institutional fields: Narratives of DDT and the Stockholm Convention. *Academy of Management Journal*, 53(6), 1365–1392.

Kjellberg, H., and Helgesson, C. F. (2007). On the nature of markets and their practices. *Marketing Theory*, 7(2), 137–162.

Lampel, J., and Meyer, A. D. (2008). Guest editors' introduction. *Journal of Management Studies*, 45(6), 1025–1035.

Lawrence, T. B., Hardy, C., and Phillips, N. (2002). Institutional effects of interorganizational collaboration: The emergence of proto-institutions. *Academy of Management Journal*, 45(1), 281–290.

Lounsbury, M., Ventresca, M., and Hirsch, P. M. (2003). Social movements, field frames and industry emergence: A cultural-political perspective on US recycling. *Socio-Economic Review*, 1(1), 71–104.

Maguire, S., and Hardy, C. (2006). The emergence of new global institutions: A discursive perspective. *Organization Studies*, 27(1), 7–29.

Maguire, S., Hardy, C., and Lawrence, T. B. (2004). Institutional entrepreneurship in emerging fields: HIV/AIDS treatment advocacy in Canada. *Academy of Management Journal*, 47(5), 657–679.

Martin, D. M., and Schouten, J. W. (2014). Consumption-driven market emergence. *Journal of Consumer Research*, 40(5), 855–870.

Navis, C., and Glynn, M. A. (2010). How new market categories emerge: Temporal dynamics of legitimacy, identity, and entrepreneurship in satellite radio, 1990–2005. *Administrative Science Quarterly*, 55(3), 439–471.

Nissilä, H. (2015). Conferences as sequential arenas for creating new sustainable fields. *Industry and Innovation*, 22(1), 209–228.

Scott, W. R., and Meyer, J. W. (1994). *Institutional Environments and Organizations: Structural Complexity and Individualism*. Thousand Oaks, CA: Sage.

Senge, P. M. (1990). *The Fifth Discipline*. New York: Doubleday.

Van Lente, H. (1993). *Promising Technology: The Dynamics of Expectations in Technological Developments.* PhD Thesis, University of Twente, Enschede, 1993.

Van Lente, H. (2012). Navigating foresight in the sea of expectations: Lessons from the sociology of expectations. *Technology Analysis and Strategic Management*, 24(8), 769–782.

Van Maanen, J. (1988). *Tales of the Field: On Writing Ethnography.* Chicago, IL: University of Chicago Press.

Walker, K., Schlosser, F., and Deephouse, D. (2014). Organizational ingenuity and the paradox of embedded agency: The case of the embryonic Ontario solar energy industry. *Organization Studies*, 35(4), 613–634.

Weber, K., Heinze, K. L., and DeSoucey, M. (2008). Forage for thought: Mobilizing codes in the movement for grass-fed meat and dairy products. *Administrative Science Quarterly*, 53(3), 529–567.

Zietsma, C., and Lawrence, T. B. (2010). Institutional work in the transformation of an organizational field: The interplay of boundary work and practice work. *Administrative Science Quarterly*, 55(2), 189–221.

# 18

# METHODOLOGICAL GUIDELINES FOR THE STUDY OF MATERIALITY AND AFFORDANCES

*Paul M. Leonardi*

## Introduction

Technological artifacts are central to the organizing process. In fact, it seems unlikely that organizing could occur without their aid. Ethnomethodologists like Garfinkel (1967) routinely observed how humans organized micro-level interactions with each other based on their relationships to objects. Symbolic interactionists such as Goffman (1959) showed that objects like doors and pots helped to define people's roles and, because roles have social elements, their relationships with others (for a wonderful analysis of the role of materiality in Goffman's work see Pinch (2010)). And today, scholars who study organizations that are purely "virtual" describe how the communication technologies through which people communicate with one another and the technological infrastructures that support their shared files are key to enabling these new forms of networked organizing (Belanger and Watson-Manheim, 2006; Chudoba et al., 2005). Technological artifacts are not accoutrements for organizations; they are constitutive of the organizing process.

This chapter explores the methodological challenges associated with the study of technological artifacts. It does so by focusing on materiality. "Materiality" is a term used across many disciplines in the social sciences and it means many things. Even within the field of organization studies the term has come to be used in a variety of ways and is not always applied exclusively to technological artifacts like tables, doors, assembly lines, computers, or software; it is also often used in relationship to conceptual artifacts like routines, discourses, and institutions. Yet unlike such conceptual artifacts, technological artifacts are typically made of actual materials that are limited by the laws of physics on what they are able and not able to do. The key problem associated with studying the materiality of a technological artifact is that one needs to account for not only the materials out of which it is made, but also the fact that, like conceptual artifacts, those materials (and the way they shape use) only come to matter in certain instances and at certain times. Consequently, organizational researchers are in need of a methodological approach to the study of the materiality of technological objects that does three things.

First, such an approach needs to account for the physical limits of the materials out of which the artifact is fashioned. This is important because not all materials invite, encourage, or enable the same types of uses. Materials are limited in their capacity to be used in particular ways and these limitations matter for the ways that technological artifacts can be used and can become a core part of the organizing process. I call this first step "accounting for materials."

Second, it must account for the ways that the matter of an object is activated at a given point in time by those who approach it. I say "approach" here because perceptions of the utility of that matter are often activated simply when individuals think about how they will use the technological artifact in their work – even before they actually start exploring its features directly. In the interplay between perception and exploration people come to define the materiality of the object in the sense of its utility for action. Thus, I term this second step, which consists of how technological objects inhere in a social system and come to matter for users, "accounting for materialization."

Third, a comprehensive approach to the study of the materiality of technological artifacts must account for the various ways that such artifacts constitute or reconstitute the organizing process. In other words, technological artifacts probably do not matter much for organizations unless their properties are activated in ways that shape the dynamics of organizing. Following this logic, a third step in an approach to the empirical exploration of technological artifacts involves "accounting for materiality."

In what follows, I discuss these three steps in depth and offer some guidelines for how researchers might go about examining the role that materiality plays in the organizing process. I argue that these steps are chronological and cumulative; insights from one step aid us in our ability to answer the questions germane to the next step. Performing all three steps in the analysis of qualitative data collected about technological artifacts is essential for linking materiality to the organizing process.

## Steps Toward an Accounting of Materiality and Organizing

### Step 1: Accounting for Materials

All technological artifacts are made from materials of some kind. Physical artifacts like tables, doors, chairs, whiteboards, and file cabinets are made out of fairly easily identifiable materials. Those materials matter for the way technological artifacts behave and how they can be used. I have the students in an undergraduate class that I teach break into teams. Each team is assigned one of three chairs that happen to be present in the classroom. I ask for a volunteer from each team who is not afraid of heights and, once these volunteers are selected, I ask them to stand on the chairs. One of the chairs is made of steel, one is made of wood, and the third is made of a fairly pliant plastic. Each time I ask the students to stand on the chairs, the person who stands on the plastic chair remains on it for only a few seconds before he or she hops off. When I ask why the person hopped off the answer is almost always the same: "The seat is bending way too much and I felt like I was going to break it."

Then I have the students go back to their groups and I assign the groups three new chairs. These chairs are more interesting than those in the first group. Instead of being made from just one material, all three chairs are made from various materials. One has plastic arms and a fabric seat over an aluminum frame. Another has mesh backs and wheels. The third is made of steel. It is very tall and heavy, and it has a wooden seat. I ask the groups to list all of the things they could do with the chair to which they are assigned. The lists are always fascinating. Of course, students from each of the groups indicate that they can use their chairs for sitting. Sometimes, all three groups indicate that they can use their chairs to prop open a door. But the differences in perceived use are much more interesting. The group assigned to the chair with the aluminum frame says that they could use it to break the window in the room in case of a fire. The group with the heavy metal chair always laughs because their chair is much too heavy to pick up and swing at a window. The group with the chair with the mesh back say that they could cut the mesh back off and use it to catch fish or fashion it into a bag. The members of the other groups laugh because the materials out of which their chairs are made do not permit fishing or bag carrying. Finally, the group with the heavy metal chair suggests that their chair could be easily used as a step for reaching high objects given that it is so sturdy. The other groups talk about how difficult it would be to stand on their chairs because they are not sufficiently weighted for such an activity.

This simple exercise illustrates, quite succinctly, that the materials out of which a technological object are created matter in important ways. They matter because some uses are simply impossible or very difficult to achieve due to the materials used in their construction. This idea that materials matter significantly in the way an object works is by no means new. Pickering (1995) discusses this notion in quite a bit of detail when he argues that the materials that scientists use to capture physical phenomena in the laboratory (as well as the phenomena themselves) often resist scientists' attempts to manipulate them. The word resist implies an agency on the part of an artifact's materials, and the source and function of such material agency is a primary concern of Pickering's book. But one need not move into discussions of agency to account for the importance of an object's materials in shaping the way a technological artifact can be used.

Kallinikos (2012) cleverly reminds us that although materials are core to the essence of technological artifacts, those materials can be arranged or shaped in various "forms" and that those forms affect our ability to use those artifacts in certain ways. The student groups in my class typically pick up on this point quite easily as well. For example, the first two chairs have some amount of plastic in them. But only in the second chair is the plastic formed into wheels at the bottom of each leg. The students invariably suggest that the chair with wheels is very useful for moving objects from one place to another or for moving people from one location to the next. The groups assigned to the chairs without wheels have never talked about using their chairs as dollies with which to move objects. What is clear from this exercise is that materials can have various degrees of utility based on the forms into which they are cast. In a parlance more recognizable to people who study technological objects, we might call materials crafted into certain forms "features." The meshed vinyl backing of the chair is a feature, as are its plastic wheels and its plastic arms. Put together, those features constitute a particular technological artifact that looks different and can be used for different purposes than another technological artifact that we might call by the same name; in this case a chair.

If the combination of materials and form results in a feature, and a technological artifact is comprised of a set of features, it becomes easy to see how important those materials are in helping to shape how those technological artifacts can and may be used. The examples I have given of chairs made from plastic, wood, and steel are quite basic, but they illustrate the point rather clearly. Advanced, digitally based, technological artifacts are made out of materials too. I have argued elsewhere (Leonardi, 2010) that although those materials are often harder to see and harder to define than for artifacts in the physical realm they are no less important in the constitution of a technological artifact. What is more complicated though, is that the materials themselves are often not the limiting factor in people's use of the technological artifact; it is the agency of the software routines that are built on those materials that are. Take for example a digital technological artifact that has been thoroughly researched in the organization sciences: the Group Decision Support System (GDSS). This digital software is designed to assist groups in decision-making tasks. The software has a number of features. Poole and DeSanctis (1992) carefully listed these features and described why the designers of the particular system they studied created these features and what those features were expected to do. One might say that the code that produced those digital features was a material in its own right because, like wood, steel, or plastic, it enabled certain activities but forestalled others. The "anonymous voting" feature, for example, was programmed in a way so as to limit users from seeing who entered what comment into the system. Unless the user re-wrote the code (tantamount to swapping the steel frame for a wood frame on a chair) he or she could not see who was behind a particular vote. But although that code may be seen as a material unto itself, it was not the only material at play in producing the feature. The code was compiled by a compiler in a machine with an integrated circuit (semiconducting chip) and a certain amount of memory. The compiler works as it does because the integrated circuit and the memory enable it to do so – different processors and different memory results in different possibilities for compiling code. The "materials" out of which the compiler was created as well as the more physical materials, like silicon, out of which the integrated circuit is created, all play a role in the production of the "anonymous voting" feature and what it is able to do.

Faulkner and Runde (2012) have been among the researchers most active in theorizing this relationship between the digital and material features of an object. They have argued that many digital materials (like code) sit on top of other physical materials (like integrated circuits) that are their bearers. That physical materials are bearers for digital materials makes it complex to understand exactly what materials matter in which ways when we focus our research attention on digital artifacts. I have argued elsewhere (Leonardi, 2011) that what is probably most important in this arena in the digital realm is to focus on the agency of the technological features with which people work. By material agency I mean the things that a feature does that are not completely within the user's control. Material agency is a useful analogue to physical materials in the digital world because both concepts direct our attention to the things that a technological artifact can or cannot do vis-à-vis the materials out of which it is created.

As this discussion makes clear, accounting for the materials of a technological artifact should constitute the first step in a methodological procedure aimed, ultimately, at exploring the role of materiality in organizing. To be able to conduct such an account means that the researcher will need to immerse him or herself in an understanding of how a particular technological artifact is created. The analysis will need to uncover:

1   What are the materials out of which the object is made?
2   How are those materials arranged into particular features?
3   What do those features do or not do?

After these three questions are answered, the researcher will be able to have an understanding of the potential limits of the technology before people in a particular social context begin to make perceptions of that technological artifact and begin to use it in their work. Without this understanding, it would be too easy to slip into an ultra-constructivist viewpoint and begin to assume that users could do anything they wanted with the technological artifacts in which they work. Understanding real constraints upon opportunities action is crucial for good empirical explanations of the role of materiality.

## *Step 2: Accounting for Materiality*

Understanding the materials constituting the technological artifacts with which people work is but the first step in understanding the role of materiality in organizing. The second step is to uncover the ways in which people perceive those materials and begin to make use of them. This is the step in which we venture into discussions of materiality directly. To do so requires untangling at least two terms used in the literature: materiality and sociomateriality.

In recent years, scholars have begun to use various terms to describe the way that materiality becomes entangled with people's everyday practices. Perhaps the most popular term used in the organization sciences is "sociomateriality." Orlikowski and Scott (2008: 456) have argued that: "The portmanteau 'sociomaterial' (no hyphen) attempts to signal [an] ontological fusion. Any distinction of humans and technologies is analytical only, and done with the recognition that these entities necessarily entail each other in practice." Drawing on Barad's (2007) discussion of agential realism, Orlikowski and Scott make an argument for an ontology that treats technological artifacts and the people who use them as constitutively intertwined. This ontological position privileges a relationship between people and things that, following logic laid out by Bruno Latour (2005), is only demarcated by scholars attempting to make claims about what counts and what does not from within a particular disciplinary point of view. From this perspective, it seems more accurate to say that sociomateriality is a way of being than it is to claim that it is a phenomena or a process that one could study.

From such an ontological position, the concept of sociomateriality should remind researchers that although materials matter (Step 1), materials are always interpreted, accessed, and used by people. That is, materiality is activated through people's encounters with it. In that sense, it is difficult to argue at an ontological level, that people and technological artifacts are inherently separate. Barley (1988) made a very similar claim nearly three decades ago when he argued that any time a technological artifact is produced or used it is transformed from a material into a social object. What Barley was implying was that as people use technologies they engage in practices that are sociomaterial – that are defined mutually and reciprocally both by the person and the artifact. Following this logic, I have argued elsewhere (Leonardi, 2012) that practices are sociomaterial in that they are spaces in which human agency and material agency (or perhaps more simply, materials) are imbricated with one another.

So, if sociomateriality is an ontology, is there something out there called "sociomateriality" that we can also study empirically? I don't think so. Technological artifacts cannot have sociomateriality, but they can have materiality. Recognizing the tenets of an ontology of sociomateriality, to say that an artifact has a certain materiality is to recognize that its materials are produced, interpreted, and used by people within a social context. In other words, saying that an artifact has materiality is to say that its materials are being merged, entangled, imbricated, mangled, or (insert the preferred verb here) with people's experiences, goals, norms, or culture in ways that make it difficult to define the technological artifact apart from its context of production or use.

From a methodological standpoint, perhaps the most important concern related to materiality, then, is to explore how materiality is produced. If materials (Step 1) play a key role in shaping if and how people use a technological artifact (Step 2), understanding how the fusion between artifacts and people occurs should be the researcher's focus in this second step. How might one do this?

Over the past few years, I have argued that perceptions of affordance and constraint are primary mechanisms through which materiality is produced (Leonardi, 2011, 2012, 2013). Other scholars have begun to make similar claims about the usefulness of focusing, empirically, on affordances and constraints for explaining how materiality emerges at the intersection between people and a technological artifact's materials (Faraj and Azad, 2012; Majchrzak et al., 2013). There are multiple ways to conceptualize affordances. In an effort to explain how animals perceive their environments, James Gibson (1986: 127), a perceptual psychologist, suggested that people, surfaces, and objects all offered certain "affordances" for action:

If a terrestrial surface is nearly horizontal ... nearly flat ... sufficiently extended ... and if its substance is rigid ... then the surface *affords* support.... It is stand-on-able, permitting an upright posture for quadrupeds and bipeds.... Note that the four properties listed – horizontal, flat, extended, and rigid – would be *physical* properties of a surface if they were measured with scales and standard units used in physics. As an affordance of support for a species of animal, however, they have to be measured *relative to the animal*. They are unique for that animal. They are not just abstract physical properties (emphasis in original).

In Gibson's formulation, people do not interact with an object prior to or without perceiving what the object is good for. As he suggests, the physical (or material) properties of an artifact exist apart from the people who use them, but they are infused with meaning "relative to the posture and behavior of the animal being considered" (1986: 127–128). The concept of affordance is useful in explaining why human and material agencies become imbricated: Artifacts have material properties, but those material properties afford different possibilities for action based on the contexts in which they are used. Although the material properties of an artifact are common to each person who encounters them, the affordances of that artifact are not. Affordances are unique to the particular ways in which an actor perceives materiality. To this end, Gibson (1986: 134) offers an explanation of the relationship between materiality and affordances:

The psychologists assume that objects are composed of their qualities ... color, texture, composition, size, shape and features of shape, mass, elasticity, rigidity, and mobility.... But I now suggest that what we perceive when we look at objects are their affordances, not their qualities. We can discriminate the dimensions of difference if required to do so in an experiment, but what the object affords us is what we normally pay attention to.

Because materiality can provide multiple affordances, it is possible that one artifact can produce multiple outcomes.

Norman (1990, 1999) suggests an alternative view of affordances. He argues that good designers purposefully build affordances into artifacts to suggest how its material properties should be used. Norman (1990: 9) seems to suggest that affordances are intrinsic properties of artifacts and that the role of design is to make affordances easily perceptible to would-be users:

Affordances provide strong clues for the use of their materials. Plates are for pushing. Knobs are for turning. Slots are for inserting things into. Balls are for throwing or bouncing. When affordances are taken advantage of, the user knows what to do just by looking: no picture, label, or instruction is required.

For Norman, affordances are "designed-in" properties of artifacts. The goal of an affordance is to signal to the user what the technology can do and how it is to do that thing. To do this, designers must make affordances easy to perceive: "The designer cares more about what actions the user perceives to be possible than what is true" (1999: 39). Users are important to Norman insomuch as they can identify a technology's affordances; however, they play little role in creating affordances. Instead, affordances are created strategically (if she is good at her job) by the designer. In this formulation, Norman's argument is different than Gibson's in that he claims affordances do not change across different contexts of use; rather, they are always there waiting to be perceived.

In somewhat of a middle ground position between these two prior views, Hutchby (2001) emphasizes the relational character of affordances. In his view, affordances are not exclusively properties of people or of artifacts – they are constituted in relationships between people and the materiality of the things with which they come in contact. In this formulation, materiality exists independent of people, but affordances do not. Because people come to materiality with diverse goals (Pickering's useful operationalization of human agency) they perceive a technology as affording distinct possibilities for action. For Hutchby, the affordances of an artifact can change across different contexts even though its materiality does not. Similarly, people may perceive that an artifact offers no affordances for action, perceiving instead that it constraints their ability to carry out their goals. In short, people have perceptions, artifacts have materiality, and affordances or constraints are created when people construct perceptions of an artifact's materiality. Thus, as proponents of Hutchby's view in the IS and management literatures have recently emphasized, because affordances are relational – existing between people and an artifact's materiality – artifacts can be used in myriad ways and have multiple effects on the organization of work (Fayard and Weeks, 2007; Zammuto et al., 2007).

To follow the ontological position advocated by proponents of sociomateriality – that the distinction between people and artifacts is analytical only – the relational view of affordances would seem to provide researchers the most benefits. This is because the relational view recognizes that technological artifacts are made of materials that do not change across their context of use, but that place limits on the kinds of things people can do. And, it also recognizes that what that technological artifact ultimately affords someone the ability to do depends on what the person wants to do in the first place. To put this statement into relief, consider the example of the students evaluating the various chairs I bring into class. Every student agrees that every chair I bring affords sitting. When their goal is to sit, they look at the materials out of which the chair is made and make a determination (perhaps consciously, but not always) that the materials will aid them in accomplishing their goal (which is to sit). As their goals are filtered through their understanding of the material properties of the artifact they construct a perception of what that object will afford. Although some students eventually come to see that some chairs could afford the catching of fish and other chairs can afford the breaking of glass, they do not normally construct perceptions of those affordances unless I design the assignment in such a way that encourages them to do so. The materials of the technological artifact are a necessary, but not a sufficient condition for the construction of all possible affordances.

In fact, those materials themselves may be insufficient in every case. Just because the class will come and immediately sit in a chair does not mean that they have actively, in that moment, constructed a perception that the material out of which those chairs are made afford sitting. But rather, the materials arranged into particular forms, have, over time, become embedded in a common stock of cultural knowledge as technological artifacts that afford sitting. In this way, culture tells us what something affords, rather than our direct interpretation of materials and forms. Affordances (or constraints) are therefore a joint production between materials and cultural practices that eventuate in the construction of perceptions.

What this means for researchers who are interested in the study of materiality is that in addition to examining and explaining the materials out of which a technological artifact (Step 1) are constructed, they need to next examine how those materials merge with the social context around them to produce people's perceptions about what a technological object affords them to do or constrains them from doing (Step 2). To be able to account for materiality in this way means that the researcher will need to answer the following questions:

1    What social or cultural institutions have shaped a person's goals?
2    How do those goals mediate the interpretations people make about what a technological artifact's materials can or cannot do?

3    Why did or did not people perceive alternative affordances or constraints based on the actual possibilities offered by the materiality itself (uncovered through answering the questions in Step 1 above)?

After these three questions are answered, the researcher will be able to understand how the technological object has become a social object. In other words, they will be able to articulate the ways in which the material and the social are intertwined. What is so important about this point (especially when compared to the results generated in Step 1 above) is that they will also be able to see what other affordances and constraints could have been produced based on the materials out of which the technology's features are built. In knowing alternate possibilities, the researcher will be able to provide a strong explanation for what features of the social context called forth perceptions of particular materials and not others, leading to a more robust explanation of what the materiality of the technological artifact is in that particular moment.

## Step 3:  Accounting for Materialization

There are many technological artifacts that are used by people to conduct their work and to interact with others. As discussed above, each of those technological artifacts is made of its own materials (Step 1) and achieves its own materiality by virtue of the way that those materials become enmeshed in the social fabric of the organization as people come to view the technological artifact as providing certain affordances for or constraints on action (Step 2). But not all technological artifacts necessarily come to affect the organizing process. To use a basic example, a technological artifact like a table can be made from many different kinds of materials. Being made of wood, metal, or plastic likely has little affect on whether someone perceives a table as affording support for writing during a meeting. The cultural conventions of most offices, and the fact that tables are situated in conference rooms, mean that meetings get carried out in roughly the same way regardless of the materials out of which a table is made. It is certainly possible that when those materials are crafted into certain forms – say a round table or a rectangular table – that form may have some subtle influence on the meeting (like whether someone is emboldened to play the role of the leader because the rectangular table has a head and someone can sit at it and assume a leadership role), but it is unlikely that those subtle differences have dramatic impacts on the organizing process. Thus, to understand the relationship between materiality and organizing, researchers must move past documenting the materials out of which technological artifacts are constructed and past the affordances those artifacts provide to accounting for the ways that those affordances come to matter in the organizing process. In other words, the third step in the analysis of materiality is to explore how technological artifacts come to matter – how they materialize in ways that constitute the organizing process.

This issue of materialization first became salient to me when I conducted a study of computer support technicians who were given a new technological artifact to help them track and respond to customer problems (Leonardi, 2007). All the computer support technicians in the organization had worked there for some time, but they had all worked in different departments. The new IT manager decided that they would work more efficiently if they were organized into one function, so he pulled them all out of their project teams and created a new "support" function within the department. These technicians who had never worked together before now had offices located in the same hallway. They were also responsible for working together to decide who should respond to what user problems and to document the resolutions they created. These technicians used a great many advanced information technology artifacts in their work. They had a number of diagnostic tools that they used regularly and some had developed specific scripts to help users with common problems. There were several large file storage systems that they managed, and they also worked with a good deal of hardware – computers, printers, mice, cell phones, etc. From the point of view of the technicians, and from my point of view as the researcher, this new technology implemented to help them track customer repair requests was nothing special.

Because these technicians did not know each other well, they were unsure who amongst them had the expertise they needed to help solve problems. What they did know about each other, though, was who was the most senior among them. When they ran into user problems that they could not solve on their own, they thus turned to their colleagues who were the most senior for help. The new technology that the team was using for tracking customer repair requests had features (materials arranged into particular forms) that enabled technicians to (1) describe the customer job request, (2) assign the job request to another technician to complete, (3) document the problems that they solved, and (4) see what jobs that they and other technicians had been assigned as well as the documentation that they and other technicians wrote to summarize the resolution of a problem. When they first began to use the technology, technicians constructed an affordance that the technology was good for assigning others jobs (they only noticed and used the first two features). But over time, a number of shifts happened in their work roles that enabled the group to begin to perceive the affordance for documenting completed jobs and, importantly, for using the documentation of completed jobs to make determinations about who should be assigned to complete which jobs. It was not until this affordance as a "job assignment tool based on past documentation" was constructed that the technology began to materialize as an important component of the organizing process. To assign each other jobs based on the documentation that they wrote, the technicians had to read the documentation carefully. In reading the documentation, they began to form impressions about who had what expertise amongst their colleagues. Quite quickly, the technicians stopped seeking advice from colleagues who were most senior when they ran into their own problems and started seeking advice from technicians who had written about solving a related job better than any other technician whose documentation they had read. It so happened that those technicians with the best documentation were the most junior in the department. Thus, in a period of just under six months, this new, seemingly inconsequential technology had upended the status hierarchy of the group. Technicians' advice networks changed completely and the most senior technicians grew upset that people were no longer seeking their advice and counsel. One technician was so upset that she quit and the whole department's performance ratings plummeted as a result.

This case provides an illustrative example of one technological artifact among many that had consequences for the organizing process. But even this technological artifact's earliest days in the organization were unremarkable; it, by itself, had no consequence for the organizing process. It was not until its materials were activated through the construction of particular affordances that its effects on the organizing process began to materialize. Put another way, materials and materiality themselves have little bearing on the organizing process unless something helps them to materialize.

Cooren (2015: 310) reminds us that the word "material" comes

> from the Latin root "materia," which means the "substance from which something is made" or the "origin, source, or mother." For instance, when we ask someone "what's the matter?", we usually want to know what is the origin or source of what seems to be happening in a given situation. In other words, we want to know what substantiates – that is, what literally stands under – what is taking place.

To say that something materializes is to acknowledge that it has produced some substantial effect, something of consequence. Not all materials or all materiality materializes in ways that bring it into a central role in the organizing process. All of those other technological artifacts that technicians used day in and day out did not materialize in the way that the technology for tracking customer support requests did. And even that technological artifact did not materialize for quite some time. Thus, to extend the study of materials and materiality one must look for what technological artifacts do in the process of organizing.

As organizational scholars, we would only seem to care about materiality, writ large, if it matters for organizing. The examples presented above suggest that certain technological artifacts do not naturally matter more than others, but that their effects on the organizing process materialize at certain points. Why they materialize at those points and not at others, or not at all is the main question that guides the third step in the analysis of materiality.

Researchers who are interested in materiality's role in organizing must therefore move beyond the analysis proposed in Steps 1 and 2 to account for the materialization process. To be able to account for materialization, the researcher will need to answer the following questions:

1   In what ways are existing patterns of organizing dependent upon the materiality of certain technological artifacts?
2   Why do certain forms of organizing produce a social context in which a technological artifact's materiality can materialize in ongoing streams of action and interaction?
3   How have the affordances produced by a new technology sustained, altered, or transformed the way that people act and interact with each other?

Answering these questions will help the researcher to speak with confidence about why materiality matters for organizing. As I have summarized above, it would be difficult for a researcher to arrive at answers to these questions without first accounting for materials themselves and then accounting for the way that materiality is produced. Performing these two steps will provide the researcher with sufficient knowledge to be able to then argue with confidence about why certain organizing processes related to technological artifacts operate as they do, when they do.

## Conclusion

Today, many students of organizing are beginning to recognize that technological artifacts are part and parcel of the organizing process. To understand how, when and why they matter requires exploring their materiality in some depth. This insight is particular important given the broad acceptance of the ontological stance of sociomateriality – that artifacts do not stand outside the organizing process, but that they are part of it.

But despite such recognition, we have very few methodological guidelines for studying materiality. In this chapter I have argued that to study materiality, writ large, involves three related steps of analyses. The first step is to account for the materials out of which a technological object is produced. Understanding these materials – their possibilities and limitations – is essential for being able to describe with any specificity the ways that technological artifacts matter for organizing. The second step is to account for materiality. Materials only have potency if they are called for in action in some way. I have argued that people call them forth as they construct perceptions of their affordances and constraints. Because the construction of affordances and constraints involves a relationship between materials and people, affordances can be seen as the mechanism by which the social and the material worlds become entangled. The third step is to account for the way in which technological artifacts materialize in the organizing process.

This means that researchers must explore when and how particular affordances come to shape the patterns of action and interaction that define the organizing process. Unless technological artifacts materialize into patterns of action and interaction, they cannot be said to be constitutive of organizing.

In outlining each of these three steps, I have generated a number of questions that will guide researchers' analyses. These questions are certainly not exhaustive, but are meant to guide coding and analysis of qualitative data. Answering these questions will require researchers to first generate data in ways described so well by Eisenhardt and Ott (this volume), Ozcan et al. (this volume), and Fayard (this volume), and to then analyze those data with the kinds of approaches outlined by Garud et al. (this volume), Erickson (this volume), and Wadhwani and Decker (this volume). The questions outlined for each of the three steps serve as linchpins between data and analysis: they direct researchers' attention to specific occurrences in the data so that they can perform a full accounting of each step. Taken together, then, the analyses produced in each step should help scholars to make precise and useful statements about the role that technological artifacts play in organizing.

# References

Barad, K. (2007). *Meeting the universe halfway: Quantum physics and the entanglement of matter and meaning.* Durham, NC: Duke University Press.

Barley, S. R. (1988). Technology, power, and the social organization of work: Towards a pragmatic theory of skilling and deskilling. *Research in the Sociology of Organizations, 6*, 33–80.

Belanger, F., and Watson-Manheim, M. B. (2006). Virtual teams and multiple media: Structuring media use to attain strategic goals. *Group Decision and Negotiation, 15*, 299–321.

Chudoba, K. M., Wynn, E., Lu, M., and Watson-Manheim, M. B. (2005). How virtual are we? Measuring virtuality and understanding its impact in a global organization. *Information Systems Journal, 15*(4), 279–306.

Cooren, F. (2015). In medias res: Communication, existence, and materiality. *Communication Research and Practice, 1*(4), 307–321.

Faraj, S., and Azad, B. (2012). The materiality of technology: An affordance perspective. In P. M. Leonardi, B. A. Nardi, and J. Kallinikos (eds.), *Materiality and organizing: Social interaction in a technological world* (pp. 237–258). Oxford: Oxford University Press.

Faulkner, P., and Runde, J. (2012). On sociomateriality. In P. M. Leonardi, B. A. Nardi, and J. Kallinikos (eds.), *Materiality and organizing: Social interaction in a technological world* (pp. 49–66). Oxford: Oxford University Press.

Fayard, A.-L., and Weeks, J. (2007). Photocopiers and water-coolers: The affordances of informal interaction. *Organization Studies, 28*(5), 605–634.

Garfinkel, H. (1967). *Studies in ethnomethodology.* Englewood Cliffs, NJ: Prentice Hall.

Gibson, J. J. (1986). *The ecological approach to visual perception.* Hillsdale: NJ: Lawrence Erlbaum.

Goffman, E. (1959). *The presentation of self in everyday life.* Garden City, NY: Doubleday Anchor.

Hutchby, I. (2001). Technologies, texts and affordances. *Sociology, 35*(2), 441–456.

Kallinikos, J. (2012). Form, function, and matter: Crossing the border of materiality. In P. M. Leonardi, B. A. Nardi, and J. Kallinikos (eds.), *Materiality and organizing: Social interaction in a technological world* (pp. 67–87). Oxford: Oxford University Press.

Latour, B. (2005). *Reassembling the social: An introduction to actor-network theory.* Oxford: Oxford University Press.

Leonardi, P. M. (2007). Activating the informational capabilities of information technology for organizational change. *Organization Science, 18*(5), 813–831.

Leonardi, P. M. (2010). Digital materiality? How artifacts without matter, matter. *First Monday. 15*(6), Available from: www.uic.edu/htbin/cgiwrap/bin/ojs/index.php/fm/article/viewArticle/3036/2567.

Leonardi, P. M. (2011). When flexible routines meet flexible technologies: Affordance, constraint, and the imbrication of human and material agencies. *MIS Quarterly, 35*(1), 147–167.

Leonardi, P. M. (2012). Materiality, sociomateriality, and socio-technical systems: What do these terms mean? How are they different? Do we need them? In P. M. Leonardi, B. A. Nardi, and J. Kallinikos (eds.), *Materiality and organizing: Social interaction in a technological world* (pp. 25–48). Oxford: Oxford University Press.

Leonardi, P. M. (2013). When does technology use enable network change in organizations? A comparative study of feature use and shared affordances. *MIS Quarterly, 37*(3), 749–775.

Majchrzak, A., Faraj, S., Kane, G. C., and Azad, B. (2013). The contradictory influence of social media affordances on online communal knowledge sharing. *Journal of Computer Mediated Communication, 19*(1), 38–55.

Norman, D. A. (1990). *The design of everyday things*. New York: Doubleday.

Norman, D. A. (1999). Affordance, conventions, and design. *Interactions, 6*(3), 38–43.

Orlikowski, W. J., and Scott, S. V. (2008). Sociomateriality: Challenging the separation of technology, work and organization. *The Academy of Management Annals, 2*(1), 433–474.

Pickering, A. (1995). *The mangle of practice: Time, agency, and science*. Chicago, IL: University of Chicago Press.

Pinch, T. (2010). The invisible technologies of Goffman's sociology from the merry-go-round to the internet. *Technology and Culture, 51*(2), 409–424.

Poole, M. S., and DeSanctis, G. (1992). Microlevel structuration in computer-supported group decision making. *Human Communication Research, 19*(1), 5–49.

Zammuto, R. G., Griffith, T. L., Majchrzak, A., Dougherty, D. J., and Faraj, S. (2007). Information technology and the changing fabric of organization. *Organization Science, 18*(5), 749–762.

# 19

# WORKING, BEING, AND RESEARCHING IN PLACE

## A Mixed Methodological Approach for Understanding Digital Experiences

*Ingrid Erickson*

## Introduction

While I have not understood it for much of its duration, my entire academic career has focused on trying to understand what happens when individuals engage with technology while inhabiting physical space. By definition, this places technology users on two planes simultaneously – the digital and the physical. As a researcher, one can observe them on either plane separately – looking at what they do in the physical space or what they produce in the digital space, but the challenge comes in understanding how these two sets of activities form a whole synthetically. How I have come to acquire the competence to assess this whole effectively (or even adequately) is what I will expand on in detail in this chapter. I present a story of developing both observational skills as well as a certain comfort level with digital data. As personal as this narrative may be, I will also argue that a combined perspective, built on rich qualitative techniques as well as an appreciation and manipulation of digital data, is one that organizational scholars should embrace as our phenomena of interest become ever more sociotechnical with the adoption of information and communication technology. Becoming sociotechnical researchers in this vein requires us to expand our methodological palette in ways that may also put us in conversation with a wider array of interdisciplinary methods and collaborators.

My focus on the digital-physical practices of individuals is an example of the need for perspectival width. These practices cannot help but abut a set of distinct, yet interrelated, scholarly concerns, which give necessary contextualization to what is observed and how it is shared in the scholarly marketplace. The first scholarly area in which my research becomes unavoidably entangled involves both the discussion of as well as the adoption of shifting social norms brought about by the widespread adoption of mobile devices. This topic is exemplified by research documenting the rising use of cellphones in public spaces and the ways that this became institutionalized during the 2000s (Fortunati, 2005; Green, 2002; Humphreys, 2005; Katz and Aakhus, 2002; Ling and Campbell, 2010). Thus, to engage in research that explores individuals' digital-physical practices is often to engage, in parallel, in the emergent discourse about how mobile devices are shaping modern society.

A second area of concern to which my research abuts involves the potential impacts on individual and collective privacy wrought by all of this locative (i.e., tagged with geographic metadata) sharing. Privacy is a particularly salient consideration when individuals share their location in real time (via posted media), but it is fast becoming a social and professional matter as new technology affords governments and/or employers that ability to track citizens and/or workers (Dourish, 2003; Levy, 2016; Rodriguez Garzon and Deva, 2014). The third area in which my research must be conversant involves new forms of geography, namely the ways that new digital-physical practices link to a long history of tracking spatial mobility and documenting the experience of place (Ciolfi and Bannon, 2005; Dourish, 2006; Kelley, 2011). How we experience place, document it, or traverse through it can be – and often is – changed with a connected device in our hands or pockets. As such, what at first may seem a research focus on organizing can quickly morph into something about space and place – areas that we are not well trained to comment on in our management-focused training.

Less directly connected to the topic of digital-physical practices, but an important contextual factor regarding it, involves the dynamics of online community (Baym, 2007; Yuqing Ren et al., 2007). In most occurrences, individuals engaged in posting on the go or emailing on the bus are involved in social activity of one sort or another. Trying to understand the social import of locative praxis means that my work engages not only with other organizational scholars, sociologists, and anthropologists who study collective behavior, but also with those in the field of "social computing" (Olson and Kellogg, 2014), who design and research systems that support the collective behavior I often observe. Admittedly caricatured, social computing researchers aim to understand collective phenomena so that they can be better human-centered designers (Dourish, 2007; Grudin, 1988); they try to create effective environments, tools, applications, and the like that support social, communal interaction. Whereas being in conversation with social scientists has the virtue of progressing the understanding of new forms of mediated social interaction, being in conversation with designers requires one to be much more agile in producing actionable outcomes. Often these two goals can be at odds with one another.

Ultimately, this preamble seeks to assert that the contextual space conjured by bringing the digital and the physical together is complex and, by its very nature, highly interdisciplinary. Parts of this world codify my investigations as progressing "organizational" or "social" scholarship, while another sifts my findings for progressive design interventions. What gives me satisfaction as a researcher – when I have recovered from twisting this way and that depending on the audience – is that all of the communities I am engaged in accept my contention that neither people nor technology are the primary force in shaping sociotechnical relationships. To adopt this neutral stance means that the data need to speak the loudest, not the conceptual frame.

For the remainder of this chapter, I will discuss my mixed reality as a researcher of the digital and physical from the vantage point of my own crisscrossed history of disciplines, levels of analysis, and methodological perspectives, I attempt only to weave a web among a set of interesting, disparate parts; as such, I can promise nothing solidly coherent or stolidly fixed. As I have learned – often the hard way – questions that find themselves in institutional conceptual spaces such as the one I describe above often elude conclusiveness.

## Studying the Products of Place

My first foray into the convergence of the digital and the physical took shape as a focus on users of social media and their reasons for linking digital posts to physical places (Erickson, 2008, 2010a, 2010b). The ability for a social media user to "geotag" (i.e., connect to location-based metadata) a shared piece of media was enabled by the introduction of geographical positioning system (GPS) technology into mobile devices and social media in the mid-2000s. However, noting an uptick in this practice did not explain users' rationale for doing so – and it was this gap in explanation that intrigued me. My initial dissertation work chose to probe this open question by sampling users in two types of social media communities: microblogging and photo sharing. Data for this research was gathered in 2006 and 2007, which is an important milestone to note as it primarily preceded the introduction of the iPhone, which was released to much acclaim on June 29, 2007. Prior to the iPhone, if one wanted to geotag a photograph or, even more rare an occurrence, a tweet, it had to be done manually with a dedicated piece of hardware that captured longitude and latitude coordinates in sync with timestamps. Therefore, my subjects, who were early in the transition to locative media, chose to geotag their media with intention; for them, the addition of geographic metadata was a dedicated act. I sought to understand more about how this intentional connection between the digital and the physical rendered their posted media into something more meaningful. It was my initial hunch that something larger was going on – namely, the emergence of a new set of practices that were making possible a new type of digital production of space and place. I sought to explore these practices by exploring the relationship between people's digital artifacts and the new spatial arrangements and relationships they appeared to engender (Ames and Naaman, 2007; Özkul and Humphreys, 2015).

Obviously, the "products of place" I ended up exploring were constrained by the design of the tools that were available at the time. In the case of microblogging, I chose to contrast some of the newest media of the day: Jaiku and Twitter for microblogging and Flickr for photo sharing. Jaiku, a Finnish-born mobile application designed by former Nokia employees, was an application that combined the ability to make a textual microblog post and to precisely geotag it. (By contrast, Twitter at the time only "located" posts based on the user's declared location, irrespective of the individual post's location.) If you have never heard of Jaiku, that may be due to the fact that it was purchased by Google in 2007 soon after its launch in 2006 and promptly killed off. In my research design, the complement to Jaiku, chosen because it did not enable ready or obvious geotagging, was Twitter – at that time a rather new entry to the social media marketplace. Both tools were limited to less than 150 characters, although Jaiku at that time did allow the inclusion of images, while Twitter did not.

When studying photo sharing, I chose to look within one tool, the prevailing photo-sharing tool of the time: Flickr. Flickr was started by Stewart Butterfield and Caterina Fake (as Ludicorp) in 2004 and then subsequently purchased by Yahoo! in 2005. Methodologically, Flickr provided me as a researcher with a ready comparative. Photos posted by its users could be cataloged a variety of ways: structurally (i.e., by being associated with different personal or collective groups), semantically (i.e., by being tagged with desired keywords), and geographically, both formally and informally. By formal, I mean that individual photographs could be affixed with a precise geotag, pegging it to a very specific location. Either a user could do this by uploading metadata on their own, perhaps captured as machine data on a camera or specialized device, or a user could select a location by dragging a photo manually onto a Google map representing the world. Using this method, the location of a photo would be attached to the image at the level of granularity of the map – that is, a person could attach the location of an exact street corner by zooming into that level of detail or could "drop" into a country at a grosser level of granularity.

Informal geotagging is really not geotagging in the technical sense at all. Rather, this means that a microblogger or a photo sharer uses a formal place name in his or her post for a particular reason. For example, a person might tweet something like, "Looks like it's going to rain in New York City tonight." This links the tweet to a specific location. The same would be true of a Flickr user if they titled or described a posted photo with a formal location name like "Sunrise over San Francisco." Because it is also possible to put photos into groups in Flickr, I also counted an image as informally geotagged if it was put in a group with a formal location name, i.e., London Pictures. A person studying locative behavior in social media today might address this formal and informal divide differently given today's automated tools for geotagging, perhaps even discounting all of the informal means of connecting a piece of media to a physical place altogether. At the time, however, things were not so easy, so accounting for place-related intentions of all types was an important strategy for me in addressing my research ambitions.

Focusing on microblogging and photo sharing allowed me to look at two things in particular: one, which pieces of media were being given locative treatment; and two, why the individuals engaging in this practice were motivated to do so. In order to address the first point, I needed to engage in an analysis of the artifacts that were being shared. All of this I did by hand, meaning that I did nothing to scrape the digital data off the Internet so that I could manipulate it digitally (nor at the time was I able to do so with my extant technical skills). Instead, naively but with passion, I created screenshots from all of these sources and analyzed them as if they were visual artifacts. For the microblog posts, I made note of the words when looking for place names; I also noted the metadata, including the username of the poster and the timestamp. For posted images in Flickr, I again looked for place names, but my focus was primarily on the geographical metadata as this was the means, as stated above, by which users could most effectively connect their artifacts to physical locations.

To address the question of motivation, I conducted 70 interviews with individuals that were active in posting in these social media forums. I conducted 20 interviews each with users who used geographical tagging in Jaiku and Flickr, and, as a control, conducted 15 interviews each with Twitter users and users who did not post in Flickr using geographical metadata or categorization. My interview protocol included questions about personal practices within each tool as well as the reasons why each participant engaged in the practices that they did.

Analysis of these counts and categorizations was centered on identifying patterns in both the interviewees' stories as well as the products that they made in their respective digital environments. Building on inductive rounds of analysis, it also became clear that certain motivations were paired with certain types of artefactual patterns. In the end, drawing on Orlikowski and Gash's concept of "technological frames" (Orlikowski and Gash, 1994) as well as Miller's notion of "genre as social action" (Miller, 1984), my interpretations of artifacts and interview transcripts revealed three clear genres of what I came to call "socio-locative practice."

Key to my findings was the fact that social media was used to support social interaction, even though many of the locative practices that I discovered were highly individuated. Take, for example, the genre I came to call "self-in-place." The motivation behind this practice was to create a place-based history of one's movements across time, like a map-based diary. Mostly occurring via the posting of geolocated images, the resulting record acted most like a personal archive. Yet rarely was this diary kept private; in certain instances, it was even publicly promoted. In other words, the archival records my subjects created of and primarily for themselves typically became a social record of geographical association and mobility. People could point to their prior association with a place (e.g., "Yes, I have been to Rome") and, because these self-in-place photo reels were chronologically organized, could also account for the extent of their mobility (e.g., "Yes, I'm a frequent world traveler"). Not only was the digital production of place engaged in by these Flickr users a commentary on a physical location, but it became clear to me in my analysis that it also acted as a form of personal metadata – a geolocated timestamp that could be reintroduced or resurfaced as needed or desired.

The other two genres I identified were more overtly social in their generic qualities. The first of these was also predominant in Flickr, but not exclusive to this social media environment. This is the socio-locative genre that I refer to as "curated documentary," which is a recognizable artefactual pattern that people use to share something specific about a geographical location with others – a practice that is particularly akin to the way a curator would put together an art exhibition. As such, these postings were almost always collections of media. For instance, one subject that I interviewed, a geographer by training, was interested in the ways that the history of Point Reyes, an area north of San Francisco, was being lost, so she set about to document the history (or indicators of that history) that was still remaining. Her aim in posting and scrupulously documenting her uploaded photographs was to highlight and precisely locate evidence of this diminishing past. Another subject found fit to document all of the security cameras in Washington, DC – an activity that not only put him in the role of curator, but also in the role of citizen activist. Flickr was the medium through which he could make his own public service messages.

Finally, my combined method of artifact analysis and interviews produced evidence of a third genre, that of "proxy broadcasting." We recognize this activity today as the rather pedestrian activity that people engage in when they post simultaneous transmissions from a place-based event, like an Apple product release press conference. Yet back in 2007, when the immediacy of tools like Twitter and Jaiku was relatively new, proxy broadcasting of this ilk was a more distinct locative practice. According to my interviewees, the motivation for engaging in this practice was, like the self-in-place genre, to link themselves to a specific location, but in quite obvious contradistinction to morph the stated aims of this first genre. Instead of focusing on the self, a poster engaging in this practice sought to become an invisible conduit to transmit the broadcast of a place-based activity beyond its physical origins. Indeed, this last genre of socio-locative communication was only visible by recognizing that this practice occurred in a clustering of posts that occurred in short succession of one another. The first post in the sequence would announce the physical location of the salient activity, and the posts that followed would fill in detail. Like a pointillist painting, the individual dots of media transmission were meant to be consumed in aggregate so that re-located whole they could be reassembled and consumed by an off-site recipient.

Close scrutiny of post content reveals evidence of a subgenre within the larger genre category of proxy broadcasting that I came to call "citizen broadcasting." Like proxy broadcasting, this practice was also tied to a physical location and transmitted without reference to the poster's identity, emotional state, or other aspects of themselves. What distinguishes this practice from the other is the civic intentionality behind the transmission. Individuals would choose to post information that they felt was beneficial to other members of that geographic community, such as weather related warnings, traffic conditions, or other hyper-localized events. There was no desire for self-identification in these posts, rather a highlighting of civic duty and/or neighborliness. These posters used location to reinforce the geographic boundaries of an imagined shared community (i.e., we are all members of the same community affected by this tornado warning or leaky gas main), whereas in the case of proxy broadcasting, the location identified something that was – by definition – non-shared and which could come to have meaning only through the deft curation of transmissions made by the broadcaster him or herself.

In sum, doing research on locative media practices in microblogging and photo sharing enabled me to see social media as a means for distributed individuals to produce space and place in ways that they had not been able to before. At the time of my data collection, these new types of digital production were beginning to organize new types of social interaction. In turn, social media tools were morphing from their original capacities to merely host social interaction into platforms for merging the digital and the physical. Geotags at the ready, I found that people were engaging in producing their own interpretations of the physical contexts in which they found themselves – in making "products of place."

## Studying Practices in Place

Moving forward in my academic career, a desire to refine the insights born of my graduate research began to grow within me. The questions that I was beginning to pursue, particularly as I (re)turned more pointedly to the study of work, pushed against my prior emphasis on production "of" place and came to rest more on practices "in" place. In one way, I would say that I continued my interest in how people produce place online, but in my new investigations these productions moved past representations of place and became constructions *in* place – constructions that were made possible by the affordances of digital ecosystems as well as features of the specific location itself. As the physical place became more central in its contextual complexities surrounding practices, however, it became much less evident for its traditional geographic features. One could say that my eye had turned away from formal descriptions of place altogether and was now aimed squarely on understanding the way that its particular characteristics supported an entirely different set of practices, namely mobile work (Erickson et al., 2014; Erickson and Jarrahi, 2016).

Indeed, the desire to study place-based practices came into being as my research moved toward studying mobile workers (de Carvalho et al., 2011; Mark and Su, 2010; Middleton, 2009; Ciolfi, 2013; Su and Mark, 2008). This is a category of workers who use mobile devices to accomplish their work while primarily working on the go. This is a rising proportion of the work force in the United States, and likely in other industrialized contexts, as knowledge work becomes a more and more dominant part of the globalized economy (Barley and Kunda, 2006; Bechky, 2006; Florida, 2014; Wajcman, 2014). Many knowledge workers are valued for their expertise and, as such, often move to where work is rather than having work come to them. That said, a particular subset of mobile knowledge workers identify themselves as "location-independent." Often called digital nomads (Hart, 2015; Spinks, 2015), these workers can conduct their work anywhere in the world, without the need for face-to-face interaction of any kind. This group often celebrates their freedom from fixed locational constraints by blurring their work/life boundaries in exotic locations around the world – places that others might consider vacation destinations.

A challenge in studying mobile workers is that mobility is not strictly confined to one type of work or a limited set of industries. It occurs throughout different types of knowledge work – that is, work that is not typically in fixed, manufacturing settings – so it can be difficult to define a particular sample of workers to study. This has been a somewhat difficult challenge when seeking funding to support extended research and it has also raised an issue with regard to the nomenclature used to isolate (and contribute to) relevant literature. As a side project, I am currently engaging with colleagues to understand the way that this type of work is emically described by workers themselves. Looking to Twitter as a source of contemporary discourse, we are mining hashtags to discover trends in contemporary parlance. This work is currently in process, but it does suggest in its early stages that digital nomadism, mentioned above, is the term *du jour*. That said, other suggestive terms like #coffice and #workinplace suggest that the location of work, even if momentary and makeshift in its construction, is still on the minds of workers as they go through their daily professional lives. If we are to understand the nuanced dimensions of mobile work types and practices of all kinds, we will eventually need to distinguish different types of professional patterns from one another. This current side project is an initial attempt to do this inductively by looking at the labels used by workers (and associated commentators themselves) to describe their experiences, environments and challenges. Continued discourse analysis in this area certainly needs to continue being done.

This study aside, the bulk of the research that I have conducted to date with regard to mobile knowledge workers looks at the question of how they accomplish their work while on the move. This query forefronts a key concern of the modern worker, namely how one maintains a networked connection to the digital services that enable him or her to communicate and collaborate with others. Given this focus, we have come increasingly to look at infrastructure as a vital part of knowledge work. By infrastructure, we mean both the large technical systems such as electricity and transport systems described by Hughes (1987) as well as what has come to be called "knowledge" or "information infrastructure" – those combinations of hardware and software, coupled with the norms that direct their common use, that enable work to happen in the modern age (Edwards et al., 2013; Finn, 2013; Monteiro et al., 1994). This latter view of infrastructure draws on prior work studying scientific cyberinfrastructures, particularly their sociotechnical natures, in the field of science and technology studies (Ribes and Lee, 2010; Star and Ruhleder, 1996).

Infrastructure is present in my collaborative research in the different assemblages or ensembles of tools that individuals put together to do their work (Mainwaring et al., 2005; Oulasvirta and Sumari, 2007; Sawyer et al., 2014). We have come to discover the extent of and creative intention behind these assemblages in our interviews when we have our participants dump out the contents of their bags, describing which items they always carry with them and why. Standard answers typically include laptops and mobile devices, but also stray into omissions as well. For example, many of our interviewees nowadays do *not* carry an external means to connect to the Internet (i.e., portable hotspot) on the presumption that they will be able to connect via Wi-Fi using a free or commercially available service at any location. Indeed, it was the rare interviewee that ever had to resort to using a tethered connection from a phone to use a laptop.

Looking at individual toolsets allows a researcher to open up interesting second lines of questioning, for instance questioning where this faith in the constant availability of an Internet connection derives as in the case above. Probing in this way, we discovered that most workers have a mental map of locations in mind where they know they can find accessible infrastructures (sometimes Wi-Fi, sometimes electricity). This knowledge becomes embedded in worker practices and ends up directing the choices of workers as they traverse specific locations over and over again. Workers' mental maps are a secondary area of research ripe for further investigation within organizational studies.

This point of insight also reveals a divide between people who traverse the same area repeatedly and people that travel more extensively between cities or other locations. The inability to possess precise, localized knowledge tends to mean that these individuals include different things in their travel kit; instead of relying on the infrastructural virtues of known territory, they rely on the virtues of recurring standards or patterns to plan their journeys (Egyedi, 2001; Vertesi, 2014). For example, larger airports now provide access to electricity (often in concert with the ability to order food or drink) in ways that were rare even five years ago. Certain airlines also reliably provide travelers access to USB ports through which they can recharge most mobile devices. Despite these new points of access, one of our subjects reports that she still carries two laptops on coast-to-coast flights – what we would identify as a type of digital assemblage – because together these two computers provide her power for the entire journey when used sequentially. Comparing local and distributed practices in this way showcases different sets of knowledge that workers possess, which would have been difficult to discover without starting from a simple accounting of tools in a bag. At the same time, this research method helped us to understand how workers creatively leverage a widely varying set of affordances present (sometimes latently) in today's common information and communication technologies.

Our interviews also helped us understand not only the means but also some of the oft overlooked reasons why maintaining access to infrastructure is so important for workers today. Previous studies in the early days of mobile device adoption in business showcased how expectations of professionalism became institutionalized around the extended temporal access to workers that BlackBerries and like devices provided (Mazmanian et al., 2013; Wajcman et al., 2009). Now, a decade on, it would be difficult to identify what traditional working hours are – at least in the United States (Perlow, 2012). Part of this reality is in response to the rise of flexible working arrangements, in which many workers are no longer responsible for being in attendance at a workplace, only for executing deliverables on time (Schultze and Boland, 2000; Spinuzzi, 2015). In a similar vein, employment arrangements have also begun to loosen during the last few years, with a rising number of contingent and contract workers making up modern workforces. Together, these two shifts mean that many more workers are now temporary and off-site. As a result, managers have had to find different ways of assessing the competency and productivity of their workers. This assessment gap is definitely on the minds of our interviewees and comprises one of the main motivations they express for navigating connectivity on the move. According to them, maintaining a reputation as a productive, collaborative, and efficient worker is akin to coming into the office early and staying late in an earlier era. Today's equivalent might be summarized as never appearing to be stymied by connectivity difficulties.

A fundamental component of mobile work is that one is prone to encounter many more boundaries in one's traversal of different contexts than one would if they worked in a fixed location (Mark and Su, 2010). Consider the movements of one of our interviewees who runs her own business in New York City. As an architect and designer, Megan needs to be on site at multiple client locations throughout a typical day to pitch proposals, conduct assessments, and deliver products. In other words, she needs to travel around Manhattan on a nearly daily basis. During these excursions, she also needs to direct and communicate with her small staff, some of whom work at a co-working space, but who themselves are often in transit as they fulfill their own responsibilities for the company. In a city like New York, it is rather likely that you will be able to receive a cell signal for any service provider that you elect to use in nearly any location you find yourself, which may not be the case in a more remote region. But, as yet, this does not include the subway, which is a popular way of getting around town. So, if one needs to be on a call or otherwise be connected to the Internet when in transit, then one's options for transportation need to adjust in turn. Have a conference in the half an hour between meetings? Then better hail a cab.

Once Megan arrives on site, it is typical for her to bring and use her laptop for two key reasons. First, the products of her trade are highly visual and require specialized software that is not standard for mobile devices (at least those that run on Android or iOS software). Second, given the importance of design and visual presentation in her business, both she and her clients prefer to look, see, and discuss the artifacts they are sharing in a meeting on a bigger screen. This not only renders the details of Megan's work more evident, but allows her clients to identify errors or ask questions more proactively. Thus, the choice of tools in Megan's toolkit goes beyond mere personal preference; what she carries with her possesses a professional logic. This logic may not be as readily identifiable as a photographer and her camera, but when one looks more closely and probes a bit more intensively these latent strategic selections become more understandable, oftentimes for the subject as well as the researcher.

Laptop in hand, Megan is not yet done negotiating infrastructural boundaries. If she needs to access a file or website that requires her to be connected to the Internet, she faces another infrastructural boundary – this time in the form of organizational policy. In order to use the local organization's Wi-Fi network, she must negotiate access. Sometimes this is easily done; sometimes not. For instance, who is the correct person to provide this access? Is this a request that should be made officially or is it something that can get dealt with more informally? The answer to either of these questions often requires speculation into the future by both parties: will this contractor be engaged with the organization well into the future such that official access may be the prudent option or is the professional relationship between provider and client likely to be short term only? To avoid this conversation altogether, Megan sometimes thinks ahead and downloads all of her required documents locally, but this also means that it is more difficult to engage in unexpected forms of impromptu collaboration or to go off script. As this scenario suggests, it is increasingly the case that working together, even when co-located, requires the ability to get online.

Finally, all of these activities, whether on a mobile phone or a laptop, require that a device be charged and ready to be used. This may sound inconsequential, but it is not when one is rarely in a fixed location throughout the course of a day. For Megan, power (both electrical and interpersonal!) is part of her reputation. To maintain the image of an astute professional, she must always be thinking ahead about how she can leverage a location for the infrastructural resources it provides. One can observe an interesting pattern occurring as she hops from one meeting location to the next. In order to arrive charged and ready to go at Meeting B, she will often tarry behind (if possible) once Meeting A has concluded, perhaps in the same conference room in which Meeting A took place (especially if there is remaining time booked for the room). Lagging behind in Location A so that she can arrive ready to go in Location B (often across town) is a pre-emptive strategy on her part because she knows how imperative it is for her to make a powerful first impression – or to continue the organized and "charged up" (literally and figuratively) reputation that is so important for her to acquiring a continuing stream of work. Arriving at a meeting without power is considered a consequential lack of preparedness or seeming disorganization – like failing to catch a typo on your first PowerPoint slide. Forgivable, certainly, but also suggestive of a lack of attention to important details, which can make all the difference in today's competitive professional marketplace.

How do I know these things? With Megan, in particular, I have spoken with her several times in formal interview situations, but I also followed her as she traversed from Grand Central Station to a meeting at the United Nations to a co-working place in lower Manhattan. I was able to observe not only her interesting "infrastructuring practices" (see a more extensive treatment of these insights in Erickson and Jarrahi, 2016), but also her effect on other people as she was engaging in this work. Observations sandwiched by interviews is a very effective method for identifying not only the "invisible work" (Star, 1999; Star and Strauss, 1999; Suchman, 1996) that comprises an extensive part of mobile knowledge work, but also for understanding its import from the point of view of one's participant. The whys give flesh to the observations in very important ways, particularly in these fast-changing professional environments.

Take, as another evocative example, an insight gleaned from observation coupled with conversation: another of our subjects showed us both her laptop and the bag that she carries it in. A young woman in her twenties whose work involves a particular aspect of web development, Shannon told me that these artifacts have particularly important symbolic power in the professional environments in which she is actively engaged. Notably, these environments tend to be dominated by men and tend to have masculine cultures – though not exclusively as her persistent employment in this area can attest. One way that she signals her competence is via the age and model of her computer; if it is too old or missing a certain feature or piece of software, it suggests – like the electric power example above – a certain lack of adroitness or acumen.

As such, even though her work tasks might not demand the need for upgraded processing power, her professional community does. For women in the male-dominated computing field, proving oneself professionally is an ongoing feat of adjustment and skill.

Shannon's computer bag also possesses associative meaning. This feminine, leather holdall was purchased by her, she told me, to suggest a seriousness and a professionalism to others. While she prefers a backpack to carry her possessions while she travels from meeting to meeting, it, combined with her young age, would assert an image that lacked the impression of professional accomplishment – something too close to the student presentation of self (Goffman, 1959) that she has only recently moved beyond. Again, merely noting these possessions as a qualitative observer is not enough to understand them: one needs to understand them contextually, which only an emic explanation can do.

In our study of mobile workers, many people gave us detailed accounts of the lengths to which they go to maintain an active connection to their colleagues and managers; we also observed some of these intentional – and some unwittingly habitual – practices in situ. As a scholar, I am now in the process of taking these findings and putting them within a larger socio-economic context. With the rise of flexible work arrangements both in the United States and abroad, workers are becoming accustomed to selling not only their expertise but also their professionalism itself. An increasing component of a professional reputation is "infrastructural competence," namely possessing the knowledge to maintain a constant and visible connection – or the perception of a constant and visible connection – to one's colleagues, clients, and employers (Mazmanian and Erickson, 2014). Navigating access to infrastructure to maintain this apparent seamlessness is a worker's way of professional code switching or, perhaps more accurately put, "performing" professionalism. In other words, they are exercising a calm and connected front stage while furiously attending to all the necessary infrastructural machinations behind the scene.

Indicators of professionalism also include the possession of "symbols of competence." Laptops and computer bags, powered devices and presentation typos are increasingly standing in as quick and easy proficiency proxies, whereas in former days, estimations of competence relied on more fulsome assessments done by full-time managers. As a pertinent backdrop to the contemporary experience of work, the shift away from permanent workforces toward the acceptance (and coordination) of contingent, contractual ones changes what and how we need to collect and analyze our data.

## Mixing Things Up

What can we observe by looking at the *products of* place? We can see important trends in cultural discourse, noteworthy new patterns of knowledge production, and creative acts of appropriation and legitimation. What can we observe by looking at *practices in* place? We see the agility of actors who cultivate strategies and draw on knowledge to make their activities as smooth as they can be. Observation and conversation reveals what is occurring and helps to answer the question(s) of why it is important. In both cases, I, as a researcher, observe what is happening by identifying repeated patterns, but only when I complement these data with the proclamations and explanations of my subjects – through interviews – do I see those data in fuller light. This is not a declaration that the interview is or should be the preeminent method for my research, but that it helps to complete the picture in ways that observation alone cannot.

Increasingly, as can be seen by my explanations above, it is difficult to obtain anything near a sense of completeness by coupling interviews with physical and artifactual observation alone. Digital practices in physical spaces have always created a hybrid data zone which needs to be investigated; my early forays into the space, while naively ambitious, now appear to fall well short of even a semi-complete mark. Moving forward in my own research, both in pursuit of new research questions but also in line with my collaborators and research community, I am beginning to embrace a mixed methodological approach – one, in particular, that relies on trace data.

Trace data looks beyond the human-made productions of space – such as the geotagged photographs or intentionally "located" tweets comprising my earlier research efforts – to things that are the non-intended by-products of using digital tools (Whelan et al., 2016; Freelon, 2014; Geiger and Ribes, 2011; Howison et al., 2011). In some cases, this "digital exhaust" is seen as highly problematic, raising significant privacy and control concerns for workers (Krontiris et al., 2014; Martin and Shilton, 2016a, 2016b; boyd and Crawford, 2012; Floridi, 2014; Mai, 2016). Without minimizing these efforts, there is also a case to be made that trace data can reveal important new patterns for understanding humans' relationship(s) with technology. Without this type of granular data, we researchers cannot easily detect hidden connections between locations and actions, which matters because different locations possess different infrastructural fingerprints. Nor could we see organizational or individual practices at their more genetic level, including, for instance, what environmental cues trigger certain responses or what sequences of action get repeated most often by different types of workers.

It should be forthrightly stated that my argument for a mixed methodological approach – one particularly centered on the utility of digital trace data as a complement to traditional field research – does not negate the virtues of the methods I've explained earlier. Indeed, trace data can never reveal the motivations behind an action, never extrapolate the contextual conditions that make a worker's practices of reputational professionalism persist and endure. Yet, when coupled with exploratory conversations, observations, and artifact analysis, trace data can prove quite a rich medium both for detailed research pattern recognition and participant auto-reflection. While my own work has not yet veered down this particular path, several of my colleagues with close research interests have found that collected trace data elicits an entirely new set of commentary from subjects when they are allowed to see and contemplate it. Looking at timestamps, for example, can help a participant remember significant, if interstitial, events that shed light on their own invisible work. Mapping activities is an interesting research analysis in and of itself, but when presented to a subject, it can trigger stories or reveal evidence of strategies that in previous conversations or observations went unnoticed.

They key insight that I want to impress here is that much of what counts for professional and organizational praxis today cannot be understood without the collection and analysis of trace data. Observable practices will always be important to study as will digital artifacts, but the combination of the two increasingly requires this mixed methodological approach. This is particularly true when confronting the challenge of understanding modern forms of work. We inhabit spaces as workers, but our work is not confined to those spaces – it comes and goes and we need to understand how, why, and when this happens and, even more importantly, what this mobile set of activities truly comprises.

As such, there are several methods-based challenges I want to call out as I close out this essay. First, we organizational scholars need to become better programmers and quantitative analysts. By this I mean that trace data is not easy to obtain without some technical skill, and, because it comes in larger quantities than the average qualitative scholar may be used to, it requires some type of statistical analysis to render it appropriately comprehensible. Short of acquiring these skills ourselves, we need to become friendly and collaborative with disciplinary colleagues that possess these skills or with a few cousins from different disciplines who may bring their skills (and insights) to the questions at hand.

Second, we need to work to bring down the wall between the quantitative and qualitative camps within our community (and related communities). This divide feels less and less meaningful when considered from the vantage point of modern forms of organizing – from the micro to the macro. Empirical complexities of the sorts that I have described throughout this chapter will not be satisfied, let alone sufficiently understood, by maintaining a strict barrier between methodological types. Of course, I know that I am not the first to suggest and promote an embrace of mixed methods; many studies engage in this type of work and have positively influenced the field already. But too often this research orientation is the exception, not the rule.

In tandem, we need to become more deft reviewers of work that does not fit neatly into known categories. Increasingly, I find my work being reviewed by scholars who strongly identify with one methodological perspective at the expense of all others, which sets me up nicely if I am recognized as kin but bodes poorly if not. These artificial allegiances leave us all ill equipped to see the merits in generative, if interstitial, investigative spaces. Scholars plumbing these murky depths deserve talented and dedicated reviewers that are willing to take a chance on what may be a nascent research genre, while all the while holding fast to their own learned conception of rigor. To become such a person means being a type of progressive fundamentalist – a type as yet all too rare in our own scholarly environs.

Relatedly, we also need to continue promoting methodological diversity in our conferences and journals. The questions of the age require as many hands on deck as they can get, so it behooves the larger goal of knowledge production to embrace and learn from one another rather than cordoning off investigative areas to normative methods (i.e., digital trace data is the intrinsic domain of computational, quantitative research approaches). In making this comment, I am thinking explicitly about how we can demote the lofty goals of some data scientists who believe that the large caches of data they now possess will enable them to answer any question or address any issue that someone cares to throw at them. In this same spirit of diversity, it is incumbent on us as mixed methodologists to quash these hubristic boasts not only with logic but a trail of robust research evidence as well.

In the future, I will continue to look beyond the edges of what is obvious when researching the intersections of work and technology. This requires not only my well-trained eye, my curious conversational interviewing style, and the interpretive lens I bring to bear on tweets, Google documents, and the like. It also requires playing with code, running regressions, and looking at clusters of timestamps and other machine data that put the practices and the products of place within their native digital environment. We must look to this environment as something that can bear fruit for the continuing quest to understand social and organizational dynamics instead of a mere collection of binary code best attended to by others. Acquiring this hybrid agility for an organizational scholar who also claims membership amongst the ranks of those who study social computing is a challenge to develop and maintain, but like the subject it enables me to address, I find it a summons worth heeding.

## References

Ames, M., and Naaman, M. (2007). Why we tag: Motivations for annotation in mobile and online media. In *Proceedings of CHI 2007* (pp. 971–980). San Jose, CA: Association for Computing Machinery (ACM).

Barley, S. R., and Kunda, G. (2006). *Gurus, Hired Guns, and Warm Bodies: Itinerant Experts in a Knowledge Economy*. Princeton, NJ: Princeton University Press.

Baym, N. K. (2007). The new shape of online community: The example of Swedish independent music fandom. *First Monday, 12*(8). doi:http://dx.doi.org/10.5210/fm.v12i8.1978.

Bechky, B. A. (2006). Talking about machines, thick description, and knowledge work. *Organization Studies, 27*(12), 1757–1768.

boyd, d., and Crawford, K. (2012). Critical questions for big data: Provocations for a cultural, technological, and scholarly phenomenon. *Information, Communication and Society*, *15*(5), 662–679.

Ciolfi, L. (2013). Space and place in digital technology research: A theoretical overview. In S. Price, C. Jewitt, and B. Brown (eds.), *The Sage Handbook of Digital Technology Research* (pp. 158–173). London: Sage.

Ciolfi, L., and Bannon, L. J. (2005). Space, place and the design of technologically-enhanced physical environments. In P. Turner and E. Davenport (eds.), *Spaces, Spatiality and Technology* (pp. 217–232). Dordrecht: Springer.

de Carvalho, A. F. P., Ciolfi, L., and Gray, B. (2011). The making of nomadic work: Understanding the mediational role of ICTs. In M. M. Cruz-Cunha and F. Moreira (eds.), *Handbook of Research on Mobility and Computing: Evolving Technologies and Ubiquitous Impacts* (vol. 1, pp. 381–396). Hershey, PA: IGI Global.

Dourish, P. (2003). What we talk about when we talk about context. *Personal and Ubiquitous Computing*, *8*(1), 19–30.

Dourish, P. (2006). Re-space-ing place: "Place" and "space" ten years on. In *Proceedings of the 2006 20th Anniversary Conference on Computer Supported Cooperative Work* (pp. 299–308). New York: ACM.

Dourish, P. (2007). Responsibilities and implications: Further thoughts on ethnography and design. In *Proceedings of the 2007 Conference on Designing for User eXperiences* (pp. 25:2–25:16). New York: ACM.

Edwards, P. N., Jackson, S. J., Chalmers, M. K., Bowker, G. C., Borgman, C. L., Ribes, D., ... Calvert, S. (2013). *Knowledge Infrastructures: Intellectual Frameworks and Research Challenges*. Retrieved from http://deepblue.lib.umich.edu/handle/2027.42/97552 (retrieved November 15, 2014).

Egyedi, T. (2001). Infrastructure flexibility created by standardized gateways: The cases of XML and the ISO container. *Knowledge, Technology & Policy*, *14*(3), 41–54.

Erickson, I. (2008). The translucence of Twitter. *Conference Proceedings: Ethnographic Praxis in Industry Conference*, *2008*(1), 64–78.

Erickson, I. (2010a). Documentary with ephemeral media: Curation practices in online social space. *Bulletin of Science, Technology & Society*, *30*(6), 387–397.

Erickson, I. (2010b). Geography and community: New forms of interaction among people and places. *The American Behavioral Scientist*, *53*(8), 1194–1207.

Erickson, I., and Jarrahi, M. H. (2016). Infrastructuring and the challenge of dynamic seams in mobile knowledge work. In *Proceedings of the 19th ACM Conference on Computer-Supported Cooperative Work and Social Computing* (pp. 1323–1336). New York: ACM.

Erickson, I., Jarrahi, M. H., Thomson, L., and Sawyer, S. (2014). More than nomads: Mobility, knowledge work, and infrastructure. In *Proceedings of the European Group for Organizational Studies Colloquium, Rotterdam, Netherlands*.

Finn, M. (2013). Information infrastructure and descriptions of the 1857 Fort Tejon earthquake. *Information & Culture*, *48*(2), 194–221.

Florida, R. (2014). *The Rise of the Creative Class – Revisited: Revised and Expanded*. New York: Basic Books.

Floridi, L. (2014). Open data, data protection, and group privacy. *Philosophy & Technology*, *27*(1), 1–3.

Fortunati, L. (2005). Mobile telephone and the presentation of self. In R. Ling and P. E. Pedersen (eds.), *Mobile Communications* (pp. 203–218). London: Springer.

Freelon, D. (2014). On the interpretation of digital trace data in communication and social computing research. *Journal of Broadcasting & Electronic Media*, *58*(1), 59–75.

Geiger, R. S., and Ribes, D. (2011). Trace ethnography: Following coordination through documentary practices. In *2011 44th Hawaii International Conference on System Sciences (HICSS)* (pp. 1–10). IEEE.

Goffman, E. (1959). *Presentation of Self in Everyday Life*. New York: Anchor Books.

Green, N. (2002). On the move: Technology, mobility, and the mediation of social time and space. *The Information Society*, *18*(4), 281–292.

Grudin, J. (1988). Why CSCW applications fail: Problems in the design and evaluation of organizational interfaces. In *Proceedings of the 1988 ACM Conference on Computer-supported Cooperative Work* (pp. 85–93). New York: ACM.

Hart, A. (2015, May 17). Living and working in paradise: The rise of the "digital nomad." *The Daily Telegraph*. Retrieved from www.telegraph.co.uk/news/features/11597145/Living-and-working-in-paradise-the-rise-of-the-digital-nomad.html (retrieved November 24, 2016).

Howison, J., Wiggins, A., and Crowston, K. (2011). Validity issues in the use of social network analysis with digital trace data. *Journal of the Association for Information Systems*, *12*(12), 767.

Hughes, T. P. (1987). The evolution of large technological systems. In W. E. Bijker, T. P. Hughes, and T. Pinch (eds.), *The Social Construction of Technological Systems* (pp. 51–82). Cambridge, MA: MIT Press.

Humphreys, L. (2005). Cellphones in public: Social interactions in a wireless era. *New Media & Society*, 7(6), 810–833.

Katz, J. E., and Aakhus, M. (2002). *Perpetual Contact: Mobile Communication, Private Talk, Public Performance.* Cambridge: Cambridge University Press.

Kelley, M. J. (2011). The emergent urban imaginaries of geosocial media. *GeoJournal*, 78(1), 181–203.

Krontiris, I., Langheinrich, M., and Shilton, K. (2014). Trust and privacy in mobile experience sharing: Future challenges and avenues for research. *IEEE Communications Magazine*, 52(8), 50–55.

Levy, K. E. C. (2016). Digital surveillance in the hypermasculine workplace. *Feminist Media Studies*, 16(2), 361–365.

Ling, R., and Campbell, S. W. (2010). *The Reconstruction of Space and Time: Mobile Communication Practices.* New Brunswick, NJ: Transaction Publishers.

Mai, J.-E. (2016). Big data privacy: The datafication of personal information. *The Information Society*, 32(3), 192–199.

Mainwaring, S. D., Anderson, K., and Chang, M. F. (2005). Living for the global city: Mobile kits, urban interfaces, and ubicomp. In *UbiComp 2005: Ubiquitous Computing* (pp. 269–286). Berlin: Springer.

Mark, G., and Su, N. M. (2010). Making infrastructure visible for nomadic work. *Pervasive and Mobile Computing*, 6(3), 312–323.

Martin, K., and Shilton, K. (2016a). Putting mobile application privacy in context: An empirical study of user privacy expectations for mobile devices. *The Information Society*, 32(3), 200–216.

Martin, K., and Shilton, K. (2016b). Why experience matters to privacy: How context-based experience moderates consumer privacy expectations for mobile applications. *Journal of the Association for Information Science and Technology*, 67(8), 1871–1882.

Mazmanian, M., and Erickson, I. (2014). The product of availability: Understanding the economic underpinnings of constant connectivity. In *Proceedings of the SIGCHI Conference on Human Factors in Computing Systems* (pp. 763–772). New York: ACM.

Mazmanian, M., Orlikowski, W. J., and Yates, J. (2013). The autonomy paradox: The implications of mobile email devices for knowledge professionals. *Organization Science*, 24(5), 1337–1357.

Middleton, C. A. (2009). Do mobile technologies enable work–life balance? In D. Hislop (ed.), *Mobility and Technology in the Workplace* (pp. 209–224). New York: Routledge.

Miller, C. R. (1984). Genre as social action. *The Quarterly Journal of Speech*, 70(2), 151–167.

Monteiro, E., Hanseth, O., and Hatling, M. (1994). *Developing Information Infrastructure: Standardization vs. Flexibility.* Working Paper 18 in Science, Technology and Society, University of Trondheim, Norway.

Olson, J. S., and Kellogg, W. A. (eds.) (2014). *Ways of Knowing in HCI.* New York: Springer.

Orlikowski, W. J., and Gash, D. C. (1994). Technological frames: Making sense of information technology in organizations. *ACM Transactions on Information Systems*, 12(2), 174–207.

Oulasvirta, A., and Sumari, L. (2007). Mobile kits and laptop trays: Managing multiple devices in mobile information work. In *Proceedings of the SIGCHI Conference on Human Factors in Computing Systems* (pp. 1127–1136). New York: ACM.

Özkul, D., and Humphreys, L. (2015). Record and remember: Memory and meaning-making practices through mobile media. *Mobile Media & Communication*, 3(3), 351–365.

Perlow, L. A. (2012). *Sleeping with Your Smartphone: How to Break the 24/7 Habit and Change the Way You Work.* Boston, MA: Harvard Business Review Press.

Ribes, D., and Lee, C. P. (2010). Sociotechnical studies of cyberinfrastructure and e-research: Current themes and future trajectories. *Computer Supported Cooperative Work: CSCW: An International Journal*, 19(3–4), 231–244.

Rodriguez Garzon, S., and Deva, B. (2014). Geofencing 2.0: Taking location-based notifications to the next level. In *Proceedings of the 2014 ACM International Joint Conference on Pervasive and Ubiquitous Computing* (pp. 921–932). New York: ACM.

Sawyer, S., Crowston, K., and Wigand, R. T. (2014). Digital assemblages: Evidence and theorising from the computerisation of the US residential real estate industry. *New Technology, Work and Employment*, 29(1), 40–56.

Schultze, U., and Boland, Jr, R. J. (2000). Place, space and knowledge work: A study of outsourced computer systems administrators. *Accounting, Management and Information Technologies*, 10(3), 187–219.

Spinks, R. (2015, June 16). Meet the "digital nomads" who travel the world in search of fast Wi-Fi. *The Guardian*. Retrieved from www.theguardian.com/cities/2015/jun/16/digital-nomads-travel-world-search-fast-wi-fi (retrieved November 24, 2016).

Spinuzzi, C. (2015). *All Edge: Inside the New Workplace Networks*. Chicago, IL: University of Chicago Press.

Star, S. L. (1999). The ethnography of infrastructure. *The American Behavioral Scientist, 43*(3), 377–391.

Star, S. L., and Ruhleder, K. (1996). Steps toward an ecology of infrastructure: Design and access for large information spaces. *Information Systems Research*, 7(1), 111–134.

Star, S. L., and Strauss, A. (1999). Layers of silence, arenas of voice: The ecology of visible and invisible work. *Computer Supported Cooperative Work: CSCW: An International Journal, 8*(1–2), 9–30.

Su, N. M., and Mark, G. (2008). Designing for nomadic work. In *Proceedings of the 7th ACM Conference on Designing Interactive Systems* (pp. 305–314). New York: ACM.

Suchman, L. (1996). Supporting articulation work. In R. Kling (ed.), *Computerization and Controversy: Value Conflicts and Social Choices*, 2nd edition (vol. 2, pp. 407–423). Boston, MA: Academic Press.

Vertesi, J. (2014). Seamful spaces: Heterogeneous infrastructures in interaction. *Science, Technology & Human Values, 39*(2), 264–284.

Wajcman, J. (2014). *Pressed for Time: The Acceleration of Life in Digital Capitalism*. Chicago, IL: University of Chicago Press.

Wajcman, J., Bittman, M., and Brown, J. E. (2009). Intimate connections: The impact of the mobile phone on work/life boundaries. In G. Goggin and L. Hjorth (eds.), *Mobile Technologies: From Telecommunications to Media* (pp. 9–22). London: Routledge.

Whelan, E., Teigland, R., Vaast, E., and Butler, B. (2016). Expanding the horizons of digital social networks: Mixing big trace datasets with qualitative approaches. *Information and Organization, 26*(1–2), 1–12.

Yuqing Ren, Kraut, R., and Kiesler, S. (2007). Applying common identity and bond theory to design of online communities. *Organization Studies, 28*(3), 377–408.

# 20

# METHODS AND CHALLENGES OF CONDUCTING RESEARCH IN SUBSISTENCE SETTLEMENTS

*Srinivas Sridharan*

The qualitative research tradition in organizational studies has made an important contribution to organizational research methods. By exploring phenomena embedded in contexts and offering the reader intimacy with informants' experiences, it has helped to diversify organizational inquiry toward revealing more textures and hues in the way managers and organizations work. These are worthy gains. However, a casual review of qualitative research reported in organizational scholarship suggests that the fieldwork largely tends to be conducted within organizational settings rather than in the settings of the markets that those organizations serve.[1] As a result, whilst qualitative research based on a researcher's journey into organizations potentially brings rich insights from their interactions with ideas, people, and experiences in those settings (Bansal and Corley, 2011), it has some limitations.

First, managers are not consumers; they cannot know the experience of consumption in its full socio-cultural scope, and yet consumption-centric insight is critical to properly assess the effectiveness of an organization's market offerings and processes (Foxall et al., 1998). Hence, it is logical that research fieldwork must extend into the market contexts where customers and channel partners experience and test products and services embedded in market realities. Second, the bounded fieldwork means that the insights would likely fail to transcend the "managerial perspective" and its inescapable focus on organizational effectiveness. At a time when critiques of studying the pursuit of narrow economic objectives over the good of society abound (e.g., Tsui, 2013), operating within this limitation is untenable. It is also inconsistent with Lewin's (1946) argument that a key path to building social theory is to unravel social problems in the field.

Nowhere does this issue take as much relevance as in the recent, so-called base-of-pyramid (BoP) research agenda, where organizations under study tend to be engaged in making and delivering products and services to the world's poorer people. Regardless of the underlying intent to create social good, managers simply would not understand the psychology of an impoverished and illiterate consumer living in conditions of precarity and subalternism (Varman and Belk, 2008). Yet, vast swathes of humans live in communities of subsistence settlements all over the world in this very manner (e.g., homeless, and in slums, favelas, shanties, peri-urban spaces, and migrant enclaves). Unless organizational scholars adopt such subsistence communities as fieldwork sites in their research, it is impossible to develop an informed body of scholarship about the business contribution to the BoP.

In this chapter, I address this issue and present some insights based on personal and proximal experience conducting fieldwork in subsistence settings over the past eight years. The personal experience components are: a six-year program of research on entrepreneurship in an Indian urban subsistence settlement (2009–2014), and a three-year program of participatory action research in peri-urban informal settlements of three small Pacific island countries (2013–2016) (Barrington et al., 2017). The proximal experience components, conducted by two of my doctoral students, are two six-month studies of smallholder agricultural system members in two African countries – Uganda (2012) and Zimbabwe (2014). As these are diverse settings across three continents and with different research questions and investigation approaches pursued over a period of time, I hope to draw from them insights that can be broadly applicable to organizational scholars wishing to conduct fieldwork in subsistence environments.

## Subsistence Market Contexts

In the past two decades, the context of emerging markets has especially fascinated organizational researchers (Burgess and Steenkamp, 2006; Hoskisson et al., 2000). This corresponds to the rapid expansion of globalization as a fundamental force in society, and affecting markets (Levitt, 1993). Further, scholars have reckoned that in most emerging market countries, people living at subsistence income levels visibly aspire to an improving quality of life, but that "these often go unnoticed by marketplace actors and institutions" (Blocker et al., 2013, 1196). Given a rising consumer culture globally, for better or for worse, poor people often interpret desired lifestyles and identities to be achievable through accessing modern goods and services (Miller, 2001). However, conventionally these aspirations have not been legitimate considerations in the strategies of large resourceful firms that make these products and services.

In recent years, owing to exhortations by influential scholars like Prahalad (2005) and Hart (2005) and pioneering compilations like Viswanathan and Rosa (2007) and Rangan et al. (2007), firms are beginning to come around to the need for them to reliably serve consumption needs in subsistence market segments. However, it remains that their methods are varied, and their pursuit can prove to be a minefield of ethics, social justice, and local capacity development vs. exploitation, thus meriting ongoing critical examination by market and organizational scholars. Lacking a critical perspective, organizational solutions can at times become bigger problems than the problems they set out to solve. A substantial reason for this lies in the radically different nature of life in subsistence contexts than what organizational managers would be familiar with. First, these tend to be communities of largely low-literate individuals and families earning minimal incomes ($1–$5 a day, much of which can be uncertain), and often living in substandard housing and polluted conditions. Second, their economic activities happen largely in an informal economy, shorthand to indicate that these economic activities occur outside the framework of public policy and private sector institutions (Hart, 1973). In fact, they particularly occur within slums and peri-urban informal settlements, i.e., impoverished residential areas in cities, often on illegally occupied land and without property rights, which have proliferated at a rapid rate globally. Peri-urbanization results in conflicts in the most basic needs and resources such as water, energy, sanitation, and solid waste management (UNCTAD, 2015). So, an organization seeking to engage would have its task cut out.

## Subsistence Market Contexts as Field Settings for Organizational Research

Given that organizations need ongoing input from organizational scholarship to help them address subsistence market contexts in their planning and strategy, let us consider the fieldwork options available to organizational scholars in a quest to build informed scholarship in this area.

A first option, and closest to status quo, would be to conduct subsistence research within organizations, researching managerial attitudes and plans towards engaging with subsistence populations (for an example, see Ramachandran et al., 2012). It is the easiest option to execute. Depending on the research question, it could also be an appropriate course of action. However, would this type of research adequately capture and reflect the needs, psychology, and aspirations of the prospective customers and partners of the firm? Given that such needs can often be in opposition to managerial priorities, it seems a pertinent question to ask. Further, when an organizational scholar works in the familiar confines of organizations, what is the likelihood she would experience moments of *perplexity* about the source phenomenon of poverty (Rabinow, 2007)? To be studying nuances of a phenomenon that the world and its nations and policy makers are continually perplexed about and to not encounter moments of perplexity would raise significant epistemological questions.

A second option is that this research could be conducted in the field, researching directly the interventions implemented by organizations. The numerous case studies reported in the BoP literature largely follow this option (see London, 2009 or Prahalad, 2005, or a review of the BoP literature by Kolk et al., 2013). For instance, Mair et al. (2012) study the work of Bangladesh Rural Advancement Committee (BRAC), often acknowledged as the world's largest NGO. Their data comprise interviews conducted intermittently over six years, in several villages where BRAC rolled out its interventions. Although conducted in the field and wide-ranging in scope, their data collection exercise focuses explicitly on BRAC's proprietary work in the areas of education, social development, human rights, and the ultra poor program. This has the effect of keeping the insights anchored on the focal market institution, which raises a fundamental question of ontology. If poverty and subsistence comes to be understood primarily through the lens of what the NGO has framed its longstanding work to be based on, then the scholar's understanding of the nature and scope of the phenomenon is at risk – the multidimensionality of poverty, its intersectionality with other issues such as gender, caste, and literacy, and the extent to which life experiences are mediated by market methods. Finally, this type of fieldwork can become vulnerable to a market success bias, i.e., because the fieldwork would, to an extent, have to be set in a context where a market intervention has worked successfully, what is understood may only be representative of a very small proportion of subsistence phenomena. The more pervasive scenario of market failure may stand ignored.

This brings us to the third option, i.e., research conducted in situ deep within subsistence communities, researching their ground realities and lived experiences without regard to whether they are a reflection of specific market interventions. This option allows the researcher to observe the experience of consumption in its full socio-cultural scope. Csikszentmihalyi (2000) refers to consumption as the energy a person expends to improve their quality of life by exchanging something of value for objects that satisfy their human needs. In poverty, unquestionably consumption is restricted, and likely to impart a felt level of deprivation, which can only be understood when doing research in situ. Second, in most developing countries, the middle-class consumer is increasingly similar to a globally standardized consumer stereotype, thus leaving poor people to be the last remaining repositories of localized culture (Venugopal and Viswanathan, 2015) from whom organizations can learn something new. Finally, as subsistence populations constantly live on the edge of chaos and co-evolve with their environments in surprisingly innovative ways, the learning that can be uncovered through in situ research could prove invaluable input to an organization's market offerings and its organizational thinking.

Not that this option is without disadvantages. For starters, it is very difficult to execute fieldwork of this nature on a sustainable and long-term basis, and if not done on that basis, it could yield little by way of meaningful data. However, keeping in mind the advantages just specified, in the remaining sections of this article, I report on a program of research conducted using this third type, and elaborate on the methods used, insights found, and lessons learned.

## Method

### *Case Study Analysis of Three Case Studies*

1 *2009–2014 – Six-year program of research on entrepreneurship in an Indian urban subsistence settlement.* I initiated this research program in 2009 in Chennai, India, when I conducted a survey of subsistence entrepreneurs to understand how they use social networks to aid marketplace navigation. My basis to pursue this question was that a bulk of the development literature had by then begun to revere the value of social networks and social capital as a local resource for collective action and progress in developing countries (Mosse, 2006). It was important to me to ask this question in a marketplace context. For example, knowing how this sociability impacted consumption and entrepreneurship skills may throw light on policy making in the consumer interest relevant to subsistence contexts. Understanding the specific mechanisms, by which sociability imparts its impact, can enable organizations to embed their market methods within the local social fabric in a strengthening way rather than market logic supplanting the enduring informal courtesies. However, after beginning with this motive and in this specific manner, I allowed my research question to broaden over the subsequent years to an overall inquiry of entrepreneurial behavior in an impoverished settlement of what was a large city of a developing country. This broadening allowed me to employ various research methods rather than a single one, and formulate a larger research vision – one that sought to understand and document the social-spatial configurations of market opportunities available to poor populations in a globalized, urbanized world.

2 *2012 and 2014 – Two survey studies of smallholder agricultural system members in two African countries – Uganda and Zimbabwe.* Aided by the above-mentioned evolution in research vision, I involved myself in a second set of investigations via the work of my doctoral students. First, in 2012, one of my students set out to investigate small exporting firms from Kenya and Uganda, who were participating in global food chains as producers and exporters. Being net food exporters in commodities like maize, small (and often near-subsistence) exporting firms in these two countries were being increasingly integrated within global chains, changing a long history of solely engaging in neighboring regional trade. Her quest was to understand how they were being affected by global supply chain trends as they strove to achieve sustainable exporting performance as well as contribute to the economic growth of their countries. She surveyed 595 firms, mostly concentrated in Kampala and Nairobi. Later, in 2014, another doctoral student set out to examine the market participation of smallholder farmers in Zimbabwe. Motivated by recent shifts in agricultural policy favorable to this segment, but troubled by the continuing ineffectiveness of removing barriers to markets, she wished to study the farmers' market engagement in a farmer-centric manner and whether it entailed a sustained pattern and meaningful exchange much beyond the neighboring market. Set against the backdrop of a unique and countrywide land reform

movement, her study uncovered the relative impacts of conventional market access initiatives versus variables such as market orientation and market literacy reflecting the marketing mindset of the smallholder. She surveyed over 500 smallholder farmers in the rural hinterlands of Zimbabwe.

3   *2013–2016 – Three-year program of participatory action research in peri-urban informal settlements of three small Pacific island countries.* This project was initiated by virtue of obtaining a large research grant from the Department of Foreign Affairs and Trade, Australia, to understand and foster conditions under which sustained and self-determined water, sanitation and hygiene (WaSH) solutions could emerge in impoverished peri-urban Pacific island communities.[2] Urban migration had substantially increased city populations in Melanesian countries, and a mix of housing affordability and conflict-prone land tenure issues had led to a rapid growth in informal settlements. As these were typically on the urban fringes, unplanned, and illegal, they lacked basic infrastructure. Most settlements lacked connections to mains water and sewerage lines and could not access local city council solid waste collection programs. Over three years, and as a multi-country, multidisciplinary team of academics and NGOs, we worked with six informal settlements that had a self-identified desire to improve their WaSH situation. We used a participatory action research process, where the communities and enabling actors (local government departments, NGOs, universities) became co-researchers alongside our team. We explored WaSH from the lens of marketing exchange systems, and investigated how the access and use of WaSH products and services can influence individual and community well-being. As an action research project, the work included efforts in fostering conditions under which new actions and institutions could emerge.

## Research Findings

I now present the insights gained from engaging in these three separate subsistence fieldwork exercises. The insights are organized around four organizing themes – preparing for the research, conducting the research, disseminating research findings to the community, and publishing from the research (see Figure 20.1). Within each organizing theme, several issues are detailed, representing specific stand-alone issues for scholars to consider.

## *Preparing for the Research*

It is a common cultural maxim among the qualitative scholarly community that the essence of great fieldwork is "being in the moment." However, ironically it is not feasible to achieve this without adequate prior preparation and foresightful planning, often many months in advance. For subsistence research, preparation is also the aspect that imposes the biggest learning curve in the organizational researcher's toolkit.

### *Methods – Scientific vs. Aesthetic*

In preparing for conducting fieldwork in subsistence contexts, a key and early decision centers on the question of what one hopes to glean through fieldwork, and thus choice of research method. The basic options are clear enough: a scientific, evidence-based approach, or a subjective, empathetic, and critical approach, loosely positioned as positivist-quantitative versus constructionist-qualitative. If the pursuit is a specific understanding of a specific phenomenon, then the research approach will need to be bounded, controlled, and driven by a need for

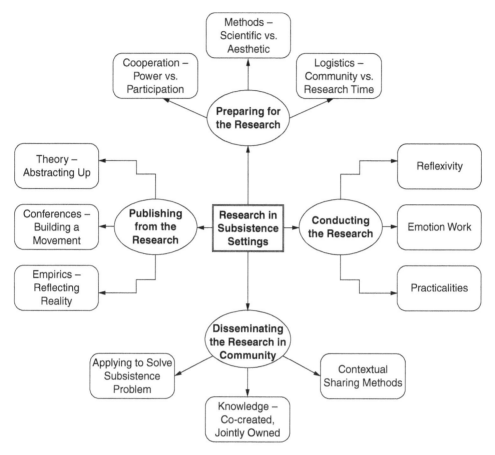

*Figure 20.1* A Framework for Fieldwork-based Research in Subsistence Market Contexts

scientific determinism. Both my doctoral students' projects embodied this approach. For example, my doctoral student knew she wanted to assess the market strategies and practices of Zimbabwean smallholder farmers on a number of specific dimensions. To her, the quest was to reveal for policy makers a sharper and multidimensional indicator of farmer engagement with market methods than the ones that were prevailing until then. She even named one of her constructs as *market mobility* in particular comparative reference to the prevalent economic concept of economic mobility, and ended up arguing that her variable added better value on a policy maker's dashboard of economic progress. Given her research question, it was imperative that she decided very early on to adopt a deterministic data collection approach (in this case, surveys). In contrast, in my India work I had decided early that I wanted to focus on marketplace exchange experiences of local subsistence entrepreneurs. I wanted to learn about their methods, strategies, coping mechanisms, growth aspirations, and how they adapted to the business outcomes they experienced. I reasoned that the subsistence entrepreneurial context was not easily quantifiable and required a grounded construction of theory, as well as developing, testing, and retesting emerging ideas in situ. Thus my emphasis was on qualitative methods.

However, beyond the simple quantitative–qualitative distinction, there are some further nuances worth considering. For example, I also decided early that I wanted to develop an interpretation that would be shared by my research participants, research associates, and myself and my academic colleagues. This was in turn because my pursuit was for a holistic understanding of the marketplace lives and experiences of participants, which was impossible for me to develop unilaterally. Given I had to embrace the potential co-creation of knowledge with multiple stakeholders, my research method planning had to go beyond the conventional quantitative–qualitative dichotomy, and to a consideration of what Denzin (2000) calls *"aesthetic" research*, or conducting social science research as an aesthetic process. In its simplest form, an aesthetic methodological orientation entails demonstrating a deep commitment to the research participants (rather than to theory) and contextualizing the depictions of individuals, events, and institutions (Dixson et al., 2005). I illustrate with our WaSH work in the Pacific islands.

As explained earlier, it was a priority for us in this research that communities wore the hat of co-researchers alongside our team, rather than merely be research subjects. Accordingly, a couple of years into the project, there was a breakthrough development when one community group wrote out a proposal to the local city council entirely on their own, requesting financial assistance for a sanitation training workshop that they had conceptualized. This came to pass after two years of sustained interactions between the research team and the community, involving numerous interim activities like physical, psychological and social systems mapping at household and community levels, and action planning and prioritization sessions. The team also resisted the urge to refine the proposal because the English was not great, preferring to preserve the community ownership of the proposal down to language and format. The point of this illustration is to highlight that the aesthetic approach is a *mindset* that takes the scholar much beyond just an operational affiliation with qualitative or ethnographic methods. For example, the proposal presented as it was, to the city council, along with a supporting cover letter from the research team, reflects the idea of the "aesthetic whole" espoused by Lawrence-Lightfoot (1983) in her pioneering "portraiture" methodology. An aesthetic whole offers space for the perspectives and voices of the researcher as well as the research participant, much as a portrait is at once a reflection of the lived reality of the subject of the portrait and of the portraitist's presence in the process. Eventually the community received a global NGO's support for their proposed workshop (even though the city council declined to support), and in this process, we were able to form what Dixson et al. (2005, 18) refer to in the language of aesthetic research as "empowering partnerships between the researcher and participants."

The aesthetic approach holds much promise for organizational research, and in particular for subsistence fieldwork settings because of its communal, dialogic function (Finley, 2014) and its potential for establishing new spaces for projecting previously subjugated voices. As Chambers (1995) points out, the poor have very different views of their poverty than those that professionals impose upon them. In particular, the approach allows the surfacing of participant views based on their (1) felt meanings, (2) lived experience, (3) sensory experience of the world around them (Warren, 2008). Often these experiences have an external trigger. For example, when our respondents spoke of lives lived alongside open drains, amidst dwindling neighboring mangroves, or under the constant threat of police harassment, they were speaking of an embodied, sensory mode of experience and the life judgments they have formed based on these. One needs to go much beyond the in-depth interview to be able to surface these *aesthetic* experiences. For further advice on how to implement an aesthetic orientation in fieldwork, one good place to begin would be the critical-arts based research tradition, outlined in Finley (2014); and another would be its place in organizational research, outlined in Warren (2008).

## Cooperation – Participation vs. Power

All fieldwork in subsistence settings relies on the local community offering its cooperation. However, cooperation when offered is far from a simple issue. The researcher would have to think long and hard about the notions of power, participation, and the control of knowledge, before entering the fieldwork stage.

First, subsistence individuals earn minimal incomes and possess sparse assets. As such, any vote of confidence toward cooperating with a research team can tend to have strings attached, such as an expectation that the research team will offer them monetary compensation for their time. When this is the case, there can be unanticipated consequences that can skew the nature of participation that the community offers to the research process, and this needs to be thought through before the actual fieldwork begins.

In one community in the Pacific islands, it was pre-arranged that the community women would cook and provide us lunch on the three days we visited their community, in return for our paying them a "catering fee" at market rates. To them, such compensation at market rates represented windfall revenue, and was the quid pro quo for agreeing to participate in the research. However, several unanticipated consequences arose out of this arrangement. First, the lunch overshadowed proceedings such that a few women, deemed key stakeholders, went missing almost two hours prior to lunch to attend to the cooking. This was likely a reflection of their concern for our physical well-being and their desire to be good hosts. However, not only did this deplete the participation per se, but it also overpowered the need for honest conversations on some of the research topics – i.e., some respondents were being extra nice and thus avoiding providing negative opinions on anything. I also later sensed that the lunch provision had been somewhat taken over by the relatively well-off people within the community, something that development economists would call "elite capture" (Platteau, 2004). This view is evident in this phrase from my field notes of a specific fieldwork day:

> Miranda was standing inside her HUGE kitchen. Worth noting that it is a separate structure altogether from her house, which is a two-storey construction (although the lower level is just storage). Her house is clearly a well-off house relatively with an amazing garden and a newly dug well.

Second, subsistence communities tend to be physically and socially isolated from mainstream communities, which can breed a sense of social inferiority (Chambers, 1995). Under such a circumstance, their participation in research can be fragile, and as such the research program needs to have a carefully planned empowerment strategy embedded within it. The following is a quote from one respondent in our Pacific work (after almost three years of working in that community):

> There were I think two Professors from the [local university]. I talked with them. Sit with them. Eat with them. Because what I think is only the upper people they can talk to, but once the door opened from WASH … I realized that everyone is people! Everyone can talk with everyone. Can talk with the Prime Minister … because when we stay in areas like this we just look down on ourselves. I always looked down on me because I stay here. But once you came in I start to realize that we can be going up to the Parliament, to the Prime Minister and tell them about this settlement.

Because of the power differential, all aspects of the research and data collection would need to be planned ahead toward creating shared involvement, control, and power among researchers and participants. Not only is this an important *preparatory* aspect so that the fieldwork can go smoothly, but it is also an important *end goal*, i.e., all subsistence research should ideally aim to strengthen local identities and capacities by the time the researchers have to leave.

### Logistics – Community vs. Research Time

A third aspect of preparing for subsistence fieldwork worth elaborating on is the matter of logistics (Desai and Potter, 2006). This begins with the selection of a fieldwork site.

In my work in India, I had chosen a local community center and the office of a local NGO as the physical sites of my interviews in several of my early field trips. Over a period of time, I realized that this decision was inducing a specific bias into my research. Although I had designed this such that participants could enter a "neutral" space and speak in an unfettered manner, this also had the effect of somewhat divorcing the lived reality of their marketplace work from their responses. It is a tough one to resolve, as it is not easy to situate the interaction in their livelihood space for a range of reasons, including the potential for social undermining by family members. Carefully thinking about the research question and the importance it would place on completely in situ interactions vs. an arms-length distance from the workplace site would be an important aspect of preparation.

Second, as life in subsistence is hard toil, it is generally unreasonable to expect research participants to show up exactly when and how the researcher has planned it to be. Further, depending on country and regional context, the cultural view of time can be very different to what the researcher is used to. The south Pacific islands are known to be some of the most idyllic places on earth, and we were constantly reminded of the different view that people of this region take to time. This quote from one of my research colleagues after her fieldwork illustrates:

> As is pretty normal for all of our community workshops, community members were late and I think we started about 40 minutes behind schedule. This is an ongoing issue with this workshop as we are trying to cram so much in!

Evidently, we as a research team had planned for a day choc-a-bloc with activities and intended progress. This reflected our need to get things done in specific fieldwork episodes. Clearly, we were on "research" time whereas our research participants were on "daily life" time, and the two did not synchronize perfectly.

In finding solutions to both the above problems, a very useful task in the preparation stage would be developing local contacts for research assistance as well as community navigation. Both of these tasks tend to go far beyond how the researcher would have originally visualized them. In the work of my students, research assistance has involved becoming a quasi-respondent because the respondent's poor eyesight made it impossible for them to sign the consent form, etc., finding ways to make people in a hurry stay back and provide meaningful responses, and braving a dust storm during the interviewing process. Clearly, problems are to be expected in conducting research in harsh environments, but preparing ahead by enlisting effective research assistance can be a powerful way to overcome some of the challenges.

## Conducting the Research

As important as prior preparation is, as mentioned earlier, what forges great fieldwork in qualitative research at the end of the day is that which gets done in the field. Conducting the fieldwork in subsistence settings therefore merits its own elaboration, and I do so here along three dimensions – reflexivity of the researcher, moral and emotional aspects, and overcoming practical challenges.

## Self-Reflexivity

Fieldwork in general requires a large degree of reflexivity by the researcher, which is at a minimum, a critical investigation of how their individual self has affected and been affected by the research process (Pillow, 2003). In subsistence settings, this reflexivity will expand significantly, as much soul-searching can become triggered. The fieldwork experience will throw up complex existential questions about one's own life in contrast with those of the research participants, and how that is affecting what is researched and how interpretations are made. The aesthetic method orientation, discussed earlier, enables the researcher to effectively acknowledge her/his own presence in the research. In comparison to conventional qualitative philosophies, the aesthetic orientation would demand comprehensive reflexivity – physical, psychological, emotional, and spiritual (Dixson et al., 2005).

After my first fieldwork in India, I came away to my place of residence and work (at the time, Canada) with many fundamental questions. The most vexing one was an existential question: if observing and studying subsistence consumers and entrepreneurs in my hometown in India is what I wanted to do as a researcher, then what was I doing living and working in Canada? This question grew very loud and led to numerous other sub-questions: was this the right research for me? Was I qualified to conduct this type of fieldwork? Did I need to turn into an anthropologist to do this work? Did the fact that I spoke in the local language with my research participants confer any special advantages? Was I right in focusing on market-based phenomena? Was I fair in asking things of my participants and walking away without imparting any knowledge about running a business, despite being a business professor? Eventually, a researcher will have to confront and answer for herself these types of questions when doing fieldwork in subsistence settings.

Other than the existential type, there are several learning-type reflections to be done as well, after every field trip. For example, three simple questions my colleagues posed to themselves after every fieldwork trip to the Pacific islands were: What have I learnt? What have I not learnt? Have my experiences overcome my "belief traps"?

## Emotion Work

Examining life experiences that can trigger intense emotional episodes for the researcher undergirds subsistence research fieldwork. This must raise relevant questions for the scholar preparing for fieldwork in a subsistence setting. How will I ensure that I am empathetic to the research participant? What is my plan to try and stay un-swayed by either extremes of what I may possibly experience – i.e., overwhelming negativity upon seeing squalor and deprivation everywhere and rose-tinted romanticism upon seeing initiative and aspiration among the poor? More broadly, qualitative research is largely about the researcher gaining a view of the world through the eyes of the research participant. Hence it has been argued that the qualitative researcher "should experience research both intellectually and emotionally" (Gilbert, 2001, 9). As such, some scholars have portrayed qualitative research as "emotion work" (Dickson-Swift et al., 2009). Emotion work generally refers to the work involved in dealing with the emotions of others (Hochschild, 1979). Researchers are generally not trained for the emotional quotient of such situations. So, for qualitative researchers who find themselves in considerable amounts of personal interactions, it is important that they develop some understanding of how the research can emotionally affect the researcher.

An example will illustrate. While interviewing entrepreneurs in India in the office of a local NGO that had been working with this community, two of the participants broke down while narrating their lives and experiences. One was a male in his early forties, a very successful entrepreneur who had built two different businesses and acquired enough wealth to be counted in the middle class, employed four others, and lived and worked in the city. The other was female, in her early thirties, struggling to make ends meet, living rurally, and having migrated back home after an unsuccessful decade as a migrant family in a neighboring state. Two people leading very different lives, only one of them outwardly vulnerable, but both breaking down mid-interview. Despite knowing that I was going to speak with significantly underprivileged people, these episodes still affected me emotionally. Perhaps it was because they were my countrymen, perhaps it was because we were in the same age cohort, or perhaps I carried a gender bias into the process in not expecting the male to shed tears. I did not know whether I should listen in silence vs. offer words of consolation vs. channel my superior education, global experience, and upper-middle-class living status to offer some specific consulting advice to improve the business. In the end, I did an awkward mix of all three. Much later, I reasoned that I could view the research process as establishing a space where people who constantly feel economically marginalized and subjugated find a moment to express their voice, and that I could simply listen in silent empathy. I concluded that I was not going to commit to being openly emotional or making a special effort to conceal my feelings as some kind of "research method" philosophy. There are enough advantages and disadvantages of each approach that adopting one as a gestalt philosophy would be missing the point.

It is worth noting that when the research involves sensitive topics, the specter of emotions looms larger. In projects on food and agriculture, conversations around hunger have been very uncomfortable, and in projects on sanitation, conversations around open defecation have been difficult. Basic needs toward living a minimally decent life can be thwarted in subsistence settings, causing an assault on one's dignity. Talking about such issues can release raw emotions. Finally, it is also worth noting that the longer one takes to build rapport with people in the research site and the more comprehensive this process is, the greater toll it is likely to take on emotions once the fieldwork phase is completed, and leaving the site becomes an ordeal. One respondent remarked to me once:

> You guys are so cool; I have never met anyone like you in my life before, wanting to come and talk to us, help us, and even eat the food we prepare for you.

It was difficult to go, knowing that in a way, we had raised this person's expectations in life to a level she had previously not realistically considered, and that she now had to cope with this higher self-expectation in a world around her that may not have otherwise changed. This, in fact, has been my most recurring emotional dilemma throughout all of my research in subsistence settings.

## Practicalities

Finally, the practical everyday challenges involved in conducting subsistence fieldwork are a legitimate consideration of their own.

*Fieldnotes.* This is a first practical dimension to consider. Writing fieldnotes is standard practice in virtually all qualitative research traditions (Emerson et al., 1995). It induces some pragmatism into an otherwise philosophical research process. Fieldnotes enable the researcher to record what happened in the field right after the event without the additional intellectual burden of having to make sense of what happened. Having said that, it is not entirely without any interpretive effort, and as such fieldnotes have been called "the secret papers of social research" (Van Maanen, 1988, 223). However, engaging in this activity in the context of subsistence research is not entirely straightforward. Some special issues present themselves and cause complexity.

For instance, a lot happens in a day in a subsistence setting and although my goal was generally only to research marketplace phenomena, there have been many fieldwork days when I would have also observed a street fight, a sloganeering mob, or a funeral procession. There was always a choice to be made about what I focus on in writing fieldnotes. On the one hand, these events did not seem central to the phenomena I was researching. On the other hand, there was always a feeling they were relevant. As an entrepreneur running a teashop on the street where the fight broke out, would my respondent's business not be affected in any way (my years of watching street fights in Indian movies suggest otherwise)? As a flower seller in that locality, would my respondent's business not be impacted by the fact that someone in that locality had died and was taken in procession bedecked with many garlands' worth of flowers? Is it not conceivable that she would have sold the bereaved family some of those flowers? In settings that can saturate the senses, this type of choice and a challenge to research honesty can become excruciating. If a researcher lives in a developed country and visits a developing country for fieldwork, she will have observed a lot of phenomena from the moment she gets off the plane to the moment before fieldwork starts, which may influence what the researcher notices during fieldwork.

*Photographs.* Scholars have called for organizational researchers to consider and increase the use of photographic research methods (Ray and Smith, 2011). However, within the first couple of field trips, I found that I had to put the camera away – my photography of what were generally conditions of squalor were visibly paining research participants even though they had given consent for it. This can create a big dilemma. On the one hand, because of the researcher's inevitable lack of familiarity with subsistence settings, the camera would seem to be an indispensable recording tool, and yet on the other hand, too much reliance on it could dull the sense of observation as well as cause frictions when one least expects it. Discussing clearly with research assistants ahead of time, and steering clear of photographing children can go a long way in solving this issue.

Finally, working in a less-than-comfortable environment, health and safety become significant issues. In India, dengue has been a very real threat in the past few years, and when working in communities near open sewers or clogged water bodies, the mind tended to remain distracted and wary of mosquitoes. There is no real way to sanitize the situation or to conduct the work elsewhere.

## *Disseminating Findings to Subsistence Communities*

Sharing the results of analysis with research participants is perhaps the most important step in an overall trust-building process of working with subsistence communities. People give of their valuable time to researchers, and whilst the process in itself may be cathartic for some, there is always a general expectation that the researcher will come back to them with some helpful advice for their lives. As such, when a researcher decides to share their analysis and the theory they have constructed, this generally proves highly empowering for the community. In our Pacific work, as it was a three-year project conducted in several sequential and iterative phases, it proved important to always present something to the communities about what had emerged from the previous rounds of study. Often this can cause difficulty, as the researcher may not necessarily have had the time to complete a formal data analysis. Nevertheless, it is not so much the substance of the feedback but rather the act of giving feedback that communities look for. When offered in dialogic fashion, the communities make their own interpretation of the findings anyway.

On one occasion, I had gone into the field armed with some feedback I had prepared from analyzing data from a previous field visit. I had synthesized five key themes – individual initiative, health, social ties, spirituality, and livelihoods. During the visit, I shared specific findings within each theme, with the view that this discussion would serve as a logical springboard for future prioritization and action. Rather suddenly, one woman stood up and declared: "we are very proud of our spirituality." At first, I mildly acknowledged it in the manner that one normally does to comments that are emotionally based but unrelated to the subject at hand. But half an hour later, I was witnessing the entire group animatedly discussing spirituality as a particular strength of their community, and deciding to use that as the platform for all future action relating to water and sanitation. I would have never made this connection as a theorist. But that is the connection the community made. And they acted on it too. They subsequently organized fundraisers in their church group toward sanitation projects, and went on to do several initiatives that connected spirituality with sanitation.

Sharing findings with community members directly also preserves the honesty in the relationship. Informing the participants that the researcher will be using the same key findings in an abstracted fashion to publish in academic journals allows the participants to feel included in the process as well as to feel a sense of pride that they have been able to understand and process that which is going to be published in the high world of academia. After all, it is their phenomena that are being published, and sharing findings with the community also somewhat helps alleviate intellectual inequalities. The best principles of qualitative and action research traditions would suggest sharing findings in ways that the community can put to use on an immediate basis (e.g., the finding of social capital in a community could be shared toward an objective of collective action in cleaning a drain); and in ways that resonate with participant lives and experiences (e.g., depending on literacy and engagement levels, the use of plays, stories, discussion groups, workshops, etc. could be useful rather than be restricted to documents and reports).

## Publishing from the Research

As personally satisfying as it may be to engage in fieldwork in subsistence environments, it cannot be a significant career pursuit for organizational scholars unless such research can be published in academic journals recognized and valued by peers and university departments. I reiterate my earlier argument that the original impetus to conduct this type of research should ideally arise from acknowledging the inevitable knowledge gaps in organizational theory about subsistence marketplaces. As such, this research cannot be significant unless it can help plug these gaps and further build and inform organizational theory. Toward this, I offer some insights along three themes – abstracting theory from data, staying true to empirical reality, and building a movement through conferences.

### Theory – Abstracting Up

Given that organizational scholars will generally have no personal experience of poverty and the pain associated with it, the primary theoretical task is one of discovery. My experience of the last eight years leads me to conclude that the ideal way to approach this task is to start small and stay real to the phenomena being observed on the ground, consistent with the view that a theory is initially just a rough approximation of social reality (Wells, 1993). Given the immense complexity of life in subsistence conditions, focusing one's analysis on a very small part of consumer or entrepreneur activity can still offer a significant discovery pathway.

For example, eight years ago, I asked the fairly narrow research question: how do subsistence consumers use their social networks to aid in navigating the marketplace? Based on my first couple of field trips, I discovered that they used social networks for a range of marketplace tasks, such as acquiring product information and comparing deals. Not terribly novel or exciting, except that along the way I also discovered that they were not relying on social networks per se, but on what I became compelled to call "a web of trust." I discovered that subsistence consumers were building, over time, a personal network of trustworthy, informative, and reciprocating individuals; much more than a social network in the sense commonly understood in organizational research. Once a small but novel discovery is made, it is feasible to follow, over the years, a sequence of testing and retesting the veracity of this discovery, correcting as necessary, and then progressing to the gold standards of theorizing, i.e., explanation and prediction. I did just that, and ended up explicating and publishing a series of studies of "social capital in subsistence marketplaces," focusing on one or two dimensions per manuscript (e.g., informative, interactive, embedded, symbiotic, and transformative). I could not necessarily call it social capital in every manuscript, and for that matter, I did not interpret it in this way early on. But given that my quest was always to test or extend a small sliver of insight from every previous study, I eventually reached a position where I could look back and integrate the various studies and findings as an overall social capital thesis.

A second option to build theory from subsistence research relatively risk-free is to try to replicate in the subsistence context, some major and relevant findings in one's discipline. For example, to go with my interest in consumer behavior, I was also initially piqued by the question of how firms should organize their marketing activity in subsistence settings. I dusted off an early but famous contingency theory of marketing structure published in my discipline's top journal (Ruekert et al., 1985), and proceeded to test some of its tenets in the Indian subsistence context. For such a comprehensive and well-compiled theory, I found no tests and replications of it in the literature. In fact, my discipline has been historically culpable in this aspect – in 1,120 empirical papers published in the major marketing journals as of 1994, there were a mere 20 theoretical extensions and no exact replications (Hubbard and Armstrong, 1994). Similarly, within a few years, I tested parts of another major theory in my discipline, the commitment-trust theory of relationship marketing (Morgan and Hunt, 1994). Upon reflection, I would say that these avenues of theory building based on testing or extending well-known theories allowed me a soft landing in the major journals. It would be troublesome if one stopped there, but as a starting point or launchpad, it would be a perfectly reasonable strategy.

Another strategy is to construct the research program in a phased approach (McGrath and Brinberg, 1983). For example, the period 2006–2011 for me was all about laying groundwork for sustained study of subsistence markets (Viswanathan et al., 2010). Subsequently the period 2011–2016 has been the time for more intensive investigations and theory building (Sridharan et al., 2014). This approach has allowed many an idea to marinate over time, eventually proving to be genuine and useful additions to the literature. Whether they would have been of similar value, had they been rushed into peer review, is unclear. In this line of work, it is better to see one's work as a series of projects rather than a series of papers.

## Empirics – Reflecting Reality

A next issue meriting some elaboration is the challenge of one's empirical content accurately reflecting the lived reality in subsistence settings. In fact, abstracting upward from detailed data describing phenomena in subsistence settings to a level of theory acceptable to management and marketing journals raises a problem. I will illustrate with one example. In one instance, I had reached the point where a large number of research participants had recounted their stories with one common thread running through – starting very early in the morning and ending their day very late. This quote illustrates:

> My husband will get up at 3 in the morning and go for Koyambedu market … back by 5:30. Then we divide and he opens the shop by 6. Later till night 11 our shop will be open…. We don't close the shop in the afternoon, after cooking I come and take care of the shop…. He has to get up at 3 and till 11 we have to toil. He has no rest.

I was quite convinced that this incredible, body-numbing daily routine had not been recognized in the market-based, BoP literature on poverty. The BoP literature told stories of enterprise and aspirations and hard work, but I had never gotten from it the sense that subsistence entrepreneurs were trapped in a cycle of a 20-hour workday involving incredible physical labor and requiring immense mental strength, and often over 20 years or more. My field observations reminded me of the stark descriptions of the laboring class I had read in Thorstein Veblen's 1899 classic, *The Theory of the Leisure Class*. I settled upon the concept of *daily drudgery* as something that hangs on the subsistence entrepreneur's life like a blanket of fog that won't disperse – life goes on beneath the fog and everyone is busy running around and achieving things, but the fog is there … always. I elaborated to fill in some detail – for example, the travel/transit time for the above participant included the early morning rise and travel to get the supply of lemons, as well as the later morning and early evening rounds to supply lemons to juice shops and to collect payment from them; similarly the mental strain pertains to the constant vigil needed to mollify belligerent customers, as well as to avoid overextending one's space or legitimacy, to check on supply quality and supplier honesty; it may even extend to more subtly felt strain such as the misgiving over not being able to go out either for pleasure/recreation or for more official matters such as parent–teacher meetings; the environmental stress pertains to the constant heat and dust of the pavement as well as to more temporary circumstances of heavy rains, flooding, etc.

Armed with all this, I proceeded to conceptualize *daily drudgery* as a construct and imbue it with adequate theoretical dimensions. When presented to a journal along with a cluster of other constructs embedded in an overall framework of marketplace experiences, this was one of the first constructs to be shot down. The objection raised was, "In what way is this useful to organizations seeking to serve and partner with subsistence markets? We are not in the business of anthropological research." Scholars pursuing fieldwork in subsistence settings should be prepared for this battle, and make up their minds about the extent to which they would fight it. On the one hand, they will face reviewers who would say "you have interesting data here, but little insight," and on the other hand, other reviewers would say "this is a weird concept, you are better off calling this stress, which is something more readily understood." The bottom line for the researcher should be to reflect the lived reality as accurately as possible.

## *Conferences – Building a Movement*

For academics that wish to work in subsistence research contexts, presenting their work at conferences has to be a critical component of the overall research strategy. Although a routine part of every academic's professional life, because this line of work is generally seen as highly risky and activist rather than academic, conferences can help build a social movement that ultimately paves the way for equivalent chances of publishing one's research that might otherwise not happen. I touch upon three issues related to this.

First, participation in conferences in an ongoing manner can enhance the dialogic validity of subsistence research (Anderson et al., 2007), i.e., building the evidentiary basis and the sharpening of assumptions used in the research through dialogue with peers. Conferences offer opportunities to have critical discussions and debates about the research findings and conclusions, explore any inconsistencies and biases, and frame and reframe the research in better positions vis-à-vis the literature. For example, in early conferences, it became clear to me that going forward I would have to make a definitive choice between the adjectives "subsistence," "BoP," "subaltern," and "impoverished." Each had become a sub-field within my discipline and carried its own baggage, and professional survival (read publishability) demanded developing a clear affiliation.

Second, it can be very useful to "leave home," i.e., go beyond the conferences of one's own academic discipline and reach out to those of other disciplines. My initial attempts to present my work at my own disciplinary conference gained a lot from parallel attempts to also present at the Academy of Management (AoM) annual conferences. The AoM had a much more developed community of BoP scholars at the time, and given our complementary vantage points of organization-level vs. market-level analyses, I profited from some very useful exchanges. Over time, I would also visit conferences of engineering, public health, and international development disciplines and further gain from this broadening out.

Third, it can be highly enriching to develop greater interactions with the conference world outside the United States. Odd as this may sound, the fact of the matter is that US scholars dominate business school research and, by extension, BoP/subsistence research anchored in business schools. What this can do is to result in an American theory of poverty/subsistence without us even realizing it. After the first few years when I mostly presented at US conferences, I began venturing out further and reaped rich dividends. In a period of five or so years, I presented my work in conferences in South Africa, Australia/New Zealand, India, and Sri Lanka. All this while, there were pioneering conferences in the US, building a movement around subsistence research within marketing. While that is great for an individual researcher to be a part of, it is also easy to slip into another comfort zone of a community that appreciates one's work by default, and hence it is important to venture outward as well.

## Conclusions

In conclusion, conducting fieldwork-based research set in human subsistence settlements presents many challenges and opportunities, and demands deep reflection and long-range planning. In this chapter, I have elaborated on four basic themes – preparing for the fieldwork, conducting fieldwork, sharing research findings with subsistence communities, and planning for academic returns from such work. Across the themes, a couple of fundamental issues merit some repetition here.

First is the notion of being multidimensional in one's research methods. Investigating phenomena in subsistence settings requires at a minimum, integrative thinking across qualitative and quantitative methods, but usually a lot more than that, such as incorporating an aesthetic orientation and participatory and action research methods. Second, navigating the moral challenges inherent in subsistence research is imperative. There will be a huge power distance between researcher and researched; sensitive topics will abound; and building rapport and leaving the research site at the end present special moral challenges. One solution I would offer to tackle both above challenges is to approach research from the vantage point of a cross-disciplinary, cross-cultural research team rather than that of an individual researcher. I personally underwent this transition. From being a market-based scholar researching what I perceived to be market-based issues, in my most recent Pacific project, I was just one of eight researchers – a team that included besides myself, a public health scientist, an environmental engineer, a health geographer, an economist, and community researchers. The diversity in the team induced diversity in methods, as well as allowed a more comprehensive approach to moral challenges. And finally, the resistance that one could potentially face from one's academic reviewing community should not be underestimated. Instead, there should be a carefully planned strategy to overcome it, which may include building multiple academic communities, refining one's work across several conferences and friendly feedback episodes, and persevering in one's ideas and theorization.

## Notes

1 A 2016 search on Google Scholar for the terms "qualitative" and "organizational" to both appear in the title of an article yields 335 articles, whilst a search for the terms "qualitative" and "markets" to jointly appear yields only 64 results. Further, the latter set has at least a third of the articles belonging to the specific notion of capital markets rather than an analysis of markets per se from an organizational lens.
2 Funded by the Australian Government Department of Foreign Affairs and Trade, Australian Development Research Awards Scheme, project number: 201200898.

## References

Anderson, Gary L., Kathryn Herr, and Ann Sigrid Nihlen (2007), *Studying Your Own School: An Educator's Guide to Practitioner Action Research*, Thousand Oaks, CA: Corwin Press.

Bansal, Pratima, and Kevin Corley (2011), "From the Editors: The Coming of Age for Qualitative Research," *Academy of Management Journal*, 54(2), 233–237.

Barrington, D. J., J. Bartram, S. Meo, S. G. Saunders, K. F. Shields, S. Sridharan, and R. T. Souter (2017), *Fostering Water, Sanitation and Hygiene (WaSH) Marketing Exchanges Using Participatory Processes: A Guide for Working with Residents of Informal Settlements in the Pacific*. Brisbane: International WaterCentre.

Blocker, Christopher P., Julie A. Ruth, Srinivas Sridharan, Colin Beckwith, Ahmet Ekici, Martina Goudie-Hutton, José Antonio Rosa, Bige Saatcioglu, Debabrata Talukdar, Carlos Trujillo, and Rohit Varman (2013), "Understanding Poverty and Promoting Poverty Alleviation through Transformative Consumer Research," *Journal of Business Research*, 66(8), 1195–1202.

Burgess, Steven M., and Jan-Benedict E. M. Steenkamp (2006), "Marketing Renaissance: How Research in Emerging Consumer Markets Advances Marketing Science and Practice," *International Journal of Research in Marketing*, 23 (December), 337–356.

Chambers, Robert (1995), "Poverty and Livelihoods: Whose Reality Counts?" *Environment and Urbanization*, 7(1), 173–204.

Csikszentmihalyi, Mihaly (2000), "The Costs and Benefits of Consuming," *Journal of Consumer Research*, 27(2), 267–272.

Denzin, Norman K. (2000), "Aesthetics and the Practices of Qualitative Inquiry," *Qualitative Inquiry*, 6(2), 256–265.

Desai, Vandana, and Robert B. Potter (2006), *Doing Development Research*. London: Sage.

Dickson-Swift, Virginia, E. L. James, Sandra Kippen, and Pranee Liamputtong (2009), "Researching Sensitive Topics: Qualitative Research as Emotion Work," *Qualitative Research*, 9(1), 61–79.

Dixson, Adrienne D., Thandeka K. Chapman, and Djanna A. Hill (2005), "Research as an Aesthetic Process: Extending the Portraiture Methodology," *Qualitative Inquiry*, 11(1), 16–26.

Emerson, Robert M., Rachel I. Fretz, and Linda L. Shaw (1995), *Writing Ethnographic Field Notes*, Chicago, IL: University of Chicago Press.

Finley, Susan (2014), "An Introduction to Critical Arts-Based Research: Demonstrating Methodologies and Practices of a Radical Ethical Aesthetic," *Cultural Studies Critical Methodologies*, 14(6), 531–532.

Foxall, Gordon R., Ronald Earl Goldsmith, and Stephen Brown (1998), *Consumer Psychology for Marketing*, vol. 1, London: Cengage Learning EMEA.

Gilbert, K. R. (2001), *The Emotional Nature of Qualitative Research*, London: CRC.

Hart, Keith (1973), "Informal Income Opportunities and Urban Employment in Ghana," *Journal of Modern African Studies*, 11(1), 61–89.

Hart, Stuart (2005), *Capitalism at the Crossroads: The Unlimited Business Opportunities in Solving the World's Most Difficult Problems*, Philadelphia, PA: Wharton School Publishing.

Hochschild, Arlie Russell (1979), "Emotion Work, Feeling Rules, and Social Structure," *American Journal of Sociology*, 85(3), 551–575.

Hoskisson, Robert E., Lorraine Eden, Chung Ming Lau, and Mike Wright (2000), "Strategy in Emerging Economies," *Academy of Management Journal*, 43(3), 249–267.

Hubbard, Raymond, and J. Scott Armstrong (1994), "Replications and Extensions in Marketing: Rarely Published but Quite Contrary," *International Journal of Research in Marketing*, 11(3), 233–248.

Kolk, Ans, Miguel Rivera-Santos, and Carlos Rufín (2013), "Reviewing a Decade of Research on the 'Base/Bottom of the Pyramid' (BOP) concept," *Business & Society*, 53(3), 338–377.

Lawrence-Lightfoot, S. (1983). *The Good High School*. New York: Basic Books.

Levitt, Theodore (1993), "The Globalization of Markets," in Robert Z. Aliber and Reid W. Click (eds) *Readings in International Business: A Decision Approach*, Cambridge, MA: MIT Press, 249–266.

Lewin, Kurt (1946), "Action Research and Minority Problems," *Journal of Social Issues*, 2(4), 34–46.

London, Ted (2009), "Making Better Investments at the Base of the Pyramid," *Harvard Business Review*, 87(5), 106–113.

McGrath, Joseph E., and David Brinberg (1983), "External Validity and the Research Process: A Comment on the Calder/Lynch Dialogue," *Journal of Consumer Research*, 10(1), 115–124.

Mair, Johanna, Ignasi Martí, and Marc J. Ventresca (2012), "Building Inclusive Markets in Rural Bangladesh: How Intermediaries Work Institutional Voids," *Academy of Management Journal*, 55(4), 819–850.

Miller, Daniel (2001), "The Poverty of Morality," *Journal of Consumer Culture*, 1(2), 225–243.

Morgan, Robert M., and Shelby D. Hunt (1994), "The Commitment-Trust Theory of Relationship Marketing," *Journal of Marketing*, 58(3), 20–38.

Mosse, David (2006), "Collective Action, Common Property, and Social Capital in South India: An Anthropological Commentary," *Economic Development and Cultural Change*, 54(3), 695–724.

Pillow, Wanda (2003), "Confession, Catharsis, or Cure? Rethinking the Uses of Reflexivity as Methodological Power in Qualitative Research," *International Journal of Qualitative Studies in Education*, 16(2), 175–196.

Platteau, Jean-Philippe (2004), "Monitoring Elite Capture in Community-driven Development," *Development and Change*, 35(2), 223–246.

Prahalad, C. K. (2005), *The Fortune at the Bottom of the Pyramid: Eradicating Poverty through Profits*, Upper Saddle River, NJ: Wharton School Publishing.

Rabinow, Paul (2007), *Reflections on Fieldwork in Morocco*, Berkeley, CA: University of California Press.

Ramachandran, J., Anirvan Pant, and Saroj Kumar Pani (2012), "Building the BoP Producer Ecosystem: The Evolving Engagement of FabIndia with Indian Handloom Artisans," *Journal of Product Innovation Management*, 29(1), 33–51.

Rangan, Kasturi V., John A. Quelch, Gustavo Herrero, and Brooke Barton (2007), *Business Solutions for the Global Poor: Creating Social and Economic Value*, San Francisco, CA: John Wiley & Sons.

Ray, Joshua L., and Anne D. Smith (2011), "Using Photographs to Research Organizations: Evidence, Considerations, and Application in a Field Study," *Organizational Research Methods*, 15(2), 288–315.

Ruekert, Robert W., Orville C. Walker Jr, and Kenneth J. Roering (1985), "The Organization of Marketing Activities: A Contingency Theory of Structure and Performance," *Journal of Marketing*, 49(1), 13–25.

Sridharan, Srinivas, Elliot Maltz, Madhubalan Viswanathan, and Samir Gupta (2014), "Transformative Subsistence Entrepreneurship: A Study in India," *Journal of Macromarketing*, 34(4), 486–504.

Tsui, Anne S. (2013), "The Spirit of Science and Socially Responsible Scholarship," *Management and Organization Review*, 9(3), 375–394.

United Nations Conference on Trade and Development (UNCTAD) (2015), *Science, Technology and Innovation for Sustainable Urbanization Report*, Geneva: United Nations.

Van Maanen, John (1988), *Tales of the Field: On Writing Ethnography*, Chicago, IL: University of Chicago Press.

Varman, Rohit, and Russell W. Belk (2008), "Weaving a Web: Subaltern Consumers, Rising Consumer Culture, and Television," *Marketing Theory*, 8(3), 227–252.

Venugopal, Srinivas, and Madhubalan Viswanathan (2015), "Developing Customer Solutions for Subsistence Marketplaces in Emerging Economies: A Bottom-Up 3C (Customer, Community, and Context) Approach," *Customer Needs and Solutions*, 2(4), 325–336.

Viswanathan, Madhubalan, and Jose A. Rosa (2007), "Product and Market Development for Subsistence Marketplaces: Consumption and Entrepreneurship beyond Literacy and Resource Barriers," in José Antonio Rosa and Madhubalan Viswanathan (eds) *Product and Market Development for Subsistence Marketplaces*, Bingley, UK: Emerald, 1–17.

Viswanathan, Madhubalan, Srinivas Sridharan, and Robin Ritchie (2010), "Understanding Consumption and Entrepreneurship in Subsistence Marketplaces," *Journal of Business Research*, 63(6), 570–581.

Warren, Samantha (2008), "Empirical Challenges in Organizational Aesthetics Research: Towards a Sensual Methodology," *Organization Studies*, 29(4), 559–580.

Wells, William D. (1993), "Discovery-oriented Consumer Research," *Journal of Consumer Research*, 19(4), 489–504.

# PART IV

# Journeys

# 21

# "BLINDED BY THE LIGHT" OR "SEEING THE LIGHT"?

## Journeys of Positivist Scholars into Qualitative Inquiry

*Glen E. Kreiner, Derron G. Bishop, and Aparna Joshi*

What is it like to do qualitative research for the first time? People come to qualitative research from a variety of paths. Some were trained in qualitative methods at the beginning of their scholarly careers, whereas others begin qualitative inquiries later in their careers. Given the lack of formal qualitative training in most management doctoral programs, it is not surprising that many individuals have shied away from ever taking on a qualitative study. Without such formal training or seeing it done up close, it is quite difficult to begin a journey into seemingly rough waters. And, yet, we see many examples of scholars who for many years have published quantitative and positivist[1] research suddenly – or sometimes slowly – turning to qualitative projects. In addition to those who ultimately publish qualitative research, there are countless others who have considered doing so. Indeed, in our discussions with many scholars over the years we have found many "closet" admirers of qualitative research – quantitative researchers who confess to us that they have always wanted to do a qualitative study.

This chapter is written with two primary audiences in mind – (1) quantitatively oriented scholars who are considering or beginning journeys into qualitative research, and (2) those of us who have been working in qualitative areas but who would like to consider the journeys we and others have taken into this arena. (Perhaps we also have an even loftier goal should this chapter find its way into the hands of someone skeptical of qualitative research, to encourage them to reconsider their stance and ultimately incorporate qualitative work into their portfolio.) Our overarching goal, then, is to explore the process of conducting qualitative research from the vantage point of those who came to qualitative research after or while also being trained in and using quantitative methods. Indeed, our chapter is based on discussions with such scholars and their insights into learning qualitative methods.

We title our chapter to refer to two ways a scholar might experience his or her foray into qualitative work. On the one hand, we might feel "blinded by the light" because a qualitative orientation can seem very overwhelming – even jarring – compared to the procedures, assumptions, and logics used in quantitative research. (We know of many scholars who have wanted to try qualitative research, but have been deterred because of the time intensiveness and/or a lack of understanding about how to conduct it.) On the other hand, we often feel as though we are "seeing the light" upon immersing ourselves in qualitative data and realizing qualitative methods' tremendous potential for practice and theory building. We hope this chapter will help those who might have been worried about being *blinded by the light* to take another look and perhaps be inspired by those who *see the light* in qualitative inquiry. Indeed, we are encouraged by the considerable increase of qualitative research in top journals and the increasing diversity of the methods used – both in management and the social sciences more broadly (Bansal and Corley, 2011; Gergen et al., 2015). We hope that editors of journals who have typically not embraced qualitative research will work to systematically include interpretive studies in those journals, e.g., by bringing qualitative scholars onto their editorial boards and encouraging authors to submit their work.

## Our Approach

Each author of the chapter comes with a very different vantage point regarding their history with qualitative methods. Glen Kreiner had no graduate coursework in qualitative methods but started a qualitative research project during his doctoral studies because he was intrigued by the approach and his advisor was supportive (see Ashforth et al., 2007 for one happy result of that project). Glen thoroughly enjoyed the qualitative world and now primarily conducts grounded theory research (although he also publishes conceptual and quantitative work). Although Aparna Joshi had a qualitative methods course in her doctoral program, she published conceptual and quantitative research for many years before taking on her first grounded theory study, which is currently in the review process. Having enjoyed that experience, she has now taken on other qualitative studies. Derron Bishop is a new faculty member and has been trained in both quantitative and qualitative methods. Before beginning his doctoral program, he had many years of industry experience (e.g., in instructional design, project management, consulting) which gave him multiple lenses on viewing the world through both quantitative and qualitative inquiry. He now conducts primarily qualitative research.

To practice what we preach, we decided to inquire of 11 scholars who had been trained as quantitative researchers but had also, usually later, conducted qualitative studies. Some of these individuals actually became primarily qualitative scholars (like Glen's path); others simply added some qualitative work into their portfolio of methods (like Aparna's path). We also interviewed scholars who had conducted both qualitative and quantitative work throughout their careers (like Derron's path). We intentionally sampled individuals who fit these profiles. Frankly, we also asked people because they were our co-authors and/or because of their very interesting qualitative work. We make no claims of having followed rigorous theoretical sampling procedures.

We gathered insights through email exchanges and audio-recorded interview conversations. We thank each of these individuals for the time they shared with us and for their conscientious answers. In addition to gathering data from others, we also answered the questions ourselves in order to be reflexive about our work (Haynes, 2013). After gathering these data, we each read through all the responses and created categories to distill relevant themes. Below (and in Table 21.1) we report on the themes that appeared most important and insightful to us, and we interweave a travel metaphor to help cohere the themes together. We asked questions about surprises encountered when starting qualitative research; initial/early insights into how qualitative differed from quantitative; what needed to be "undone" or "relearned" when switching to qualitative research; and what individuals wish they had known upon starting in qualitative research. These, of course, are not orthogonal topics, and we found considerable overlap across the answers.

*Table 21.1* Supporting Data for Themes

| Theme | Sample Quotes |
| --- | --- |
| *Question 1 – Surprises Encountered Learning Qualitative Research* | |
| How fun and rewarding qualitative research is | I think the joys and benefits of doing qualitative research … include the sheer "interesting-ness" of analyzing the data, the richness of that data, the deeper understandings of "what is really going on" from analyzing the data, and so on. I would not trade my experiences in qualitative research, primarily because … qualitative research can capture the tensions and paradoxes that humans experience on a daily basis, the competing and oscillating contestation of discourses and courses of action in ways that survey participants choosing numbers on a scale simply cannot. – Mathew Sheep |
| | It's not always easy or possible to see the entire path and end of the journey, nor should it be that way. That's part of the fun of it as you step into the shoes of other people and start to see, feel, and think a little as they do. Then when themes, a model, and an overall theoretical "sense" starts emerging, you get another big jolt of fun! – Derron Bishop |
| | I've actually considered getting a custom bumper sticker that says "I'd rather be coding." The joy of sitting down with a transcript to code – ahhh. And the fun of the joint coding meetings with my co-authors – some of the most fun I've had, professionally speaking. We don't just analyze data; we talk, we eat, we sing. I get *paid* for this? – Glen Kreiner |
| Qualitative work is harder than expected | It is incredibly enjoyable, but surprisingly hard to conduct! I think many people assume that it is "easier" than quantitative research. But I have not found that to be the case at all. Perhaps that is because it is more open-ended. – Cristina Gibson |
| | I remember thinking that, since qualitative data doesn't involve numbers, it was going to be easier to "find" results. In reality, of course, the fact that qualitative data doesn't involve numbers means that in some cases it's much *harder* to find results, because often it's not obvious that the data are (or aren't) supporting your interpretation of them (numbers are much more cut and dried). – Chad Murphy |
| | Grounded theory is so hard, and it's scary…. It's a little more wide open. What's hard about it is trying to understand your research questions and figuring that out. – Vilmos Misangyi |
| Lack of formulas/ diversity of approaches | I suppose the biggest relearning was that qual is far less formulaic than quant, meaning that it's not just a case of following the cookbook…. A good example is the construction of the paper itself. In quant, there is a clear formula: intro, hypotheses, methods, results, discussion. In qual, the intro is usually the last thing I now do because you don't know how to frame the paper until you've analyzed the data. And although all papers are essentially exercises in story-telling (nonfiction, that is!), it requires a more artful touch in qual: what data to present, in what sequence. – Blake Ashforth |
| | First, I was surprised at the sheer number and breadth of qualitative methods. To this day, it continues to surprise me that I read papers in which the authors claim rather vaguely to have conducted an "inductive qualitative analysis" in their methodology section – with no further explanation of process or mention of what kind of qualitative analysis that might be. – Mathew Sheep |

*continued*

*Table 21.1* Continued

| Theme | Sample Quotes |
|---|---|
| Degree of change throughout the process | The process of qualitative methods can become very nerve-wracking. Sometimes, I wonder – what is the story going to be? Is the research question going to change? Is this study ever going to lead anywhere? ... What you thought you were going to study – much less find – often changes during the course of the study. Rarely in quantitative studies does the entire research question or complete literature change. In qualitative studies, such changes can occur with great regularity even in the review process. – Brett Smith |
| | Another pleasant surprise is that qual is less cut and dried than quant. There are many implicit decisions during the process of data collection (e.g., should I probe on this issue? should I talk to this promising guy, even though he's a bit outside my sampling plan?), data coding (is this an example of X or Y? should we split this code into two codes?), and writing it up (what to include, how to structure the flow). While this complexity can be overwhelming, the constant challenge makes it very engaging. – Blake Ashforth |
| *Question 2 – Differences between Quantitative Training and Qualitative Inquiry* | |
| Qualitative research brings you closer to the people/ phenomena | I absolutely love getting to know people – individually and collectively – through qualitative methods. Some key informants of mine have become friends over time. But even the individuals who maybe I just have an hour-long interview with can have a deep effect on me. I've been deeply moved by interviews I've conducted – sometimes even to tears. What a blessing to be able to get to know people and try to see the world from their vantage point. Quant methods just don't allow me to do that. – Glen Kreiner |
| | To me the main difference was a more in-depth engagement with the research context. Where the quant approach seemed sterile in contrast the qual approach seemed more down and dirty with the research setting. – Aparna Joshi |
| Different paradigms matter | The major tension revolves around the assumption of reality being grounded in something objective "out there" or something subjective within people's minds, which affects how to go about studying that reality ... and how to share one's understanding of that reality with others. – Derron Bishop |
| | I began to see it in its own right, with its own set of scientific rules and philosophical beliefs.... There are multiple paradigms that in turn influence multiple "right ways" of doing qualitative. I could have saved myself much grief if I'd known what "rules" I was breaking. – Stephen Humphrey |
| *Question 3 – Things to "Undo" or "Relearn" from Quantitative Training* | |
| Allow for organic, non-linear, emergent story | For feasibility purposes, it can be important to go into a project with a meaningful research question and methodological approach. Yet it's equally important to stay open to insights, possibilities, and opportunities that emerge. Some people have likened qualitative research to finding a needle in a haystack. Sometimes, it can feel like that. But at times I also wonder if the challenge can also be about picking from among numerous needles in a needlestack (especially when many others are also helping with the picking). – Derron Bishop |
| | It seems you are being completely open in your general research question and almost purposely trying to ignore what we, as scholars, know about the topic. – David Sluss |

*Table 21.1* Continued

| Theme | Sample Quotes |
| --- | --- |
| Undo the need for speed – qualitative research takes time | It soon became apparent that qual tends to take a lot longer than quant. With quant, you pull together some measures, send out a survey (or two or three), and run the analyses. Simple! With qual, every interview and every observational period is time-consuming, and then coding can take forever as well. – Blake Ashforth |
| | It is a lot more consuming than I expected it to be. Not only was I surprised by the time and energy required to think about the right questions for the interview protocol, but I was also surprised by the amount of time and energy needed across the entire process of interviewing, coding, and drawing links across different themes has, for me at least, required almost complete immersion. – Tiffany Johnson |
| Be prepared for considerable back-end work | While working with quantitative data such as survey data, there is a great deal of time and effort that go into the research design. Yet, once the data is collected and scrubbed, the data analysis is relatively more straight-forward. You know the kind of variables and therefore the kinds of tests to run. While the results may not always be what you want or the reviewers may ask you to run a number of other tests, you essentially know through some preliminary analysis whether or not you have found what you expected. [With qualitative research], once some of the initial data is collected – say many interviews deep – there is often this moment of panic. There is this thought, "What am I going to do with all of this information? How on earth am I going to try to make sense out of any of these mountains of conversations?" … You are not sure what you have found. – Brett Smith |
| | I've seen several students who are drawn to qualitative research collect a bunch of data and then get stuck because they get overwhelmed by the vastness of it, not sure what story to tell or how what they have advances the literature. – Teresa Cardador |
| *Question 4 – What We Wish We Knew When We Started* | |
| Need to practice good data management from the onset | I also wish I'd realized how easy it is to be overwhelmed by the data. Given that a one-hour interview can easily lead to a 15-page (single-spaced) transcript, the data tend to quickly mount. Thus, you've got to be really organized from the outset, otherwise you'll soon drown in the data – and, as I've unfortunately discovered, you may lose track of some (e.g., whatever happened to interview #4?) – Blake Ashforth |
| | I have learned to keep better track of my data and theoretical insights from the outset (e.g., take the time to create a naming standard for files and use it; write memos when thoughts occur to you). Time pressures can seem to get in the way, but it saves time in the end. – Derron Bishop |

*continued*

331

*Table 21.1* Continued

| Theme | Sample Quotes |
|---|---|
| Ideal personal attributes/skills | I wish I had a lot more patience and a little more confidence. While quantitative papers can take a long time to move from idea to publication, qualitative papers tend to be longer by orders of magnitude. This is not for the faint of heart – and may not be the only or best approach for someone who is constantly preoccupied by the ticking of the tenure clock. – Brett Smith |
| | An artistic bent can be tremendously helpful for the qualitative research, more so than for quantitative. I like to think of qualitative research – grounded theory in particular – as the fusion of science and art. It's clearly social science; there are rigorous procedures to investigate the phenomena and analyze the data. And yet it's also art; a "spark of creativity" is necessary in making the leap between a big pile of data and a model grounded in that data. – Glen Kreiner |
| Consider diversifying your portfolio with quantitative and qualitative projects | I would suggest to less experienced researchers that they work on a mix of qualitative and quantitative projects. The complexity and enormity of qualitative analysis can slow down the process significantly, especially for an inexperienced qualitative researcher … Working on a mix of projects will allow students to get the qualitative experience and training, but still ensure that they are prepared for the market. – Teresa Cardador |
| | It may be useful to consider a portfolio of projects – of which some of those projects are qualitative. – Brett Smith |

*Question 5 – Final Travel Tips: Advice for Doing Qualitative Research*

| | |
|---|---|
| Take the trip! | Given the openness to qual methods, which was scarce even a decade ago, I wish I had started earlier. But back when I started my career the advice was to stick with quant as it was less risky in terms of publishing. Today of course award-winning papers in our top journals are often qualitative and there are more and more submissions to journals like AMJ which has tripled the number of its qualitative associate editors. I guess I wish I had known that the methods would eventually be more widely accepted and ultimately viewed as acceptable and not necessarily more risky than any other methodology. – Aparna Joshi |
| | Qualitative research is rewarding and fascinating, so my advice would be to keep following that passion! – Teresa Cardador |
| Make sure qualitative is the right trip to take | I observed a phenomenon in the wild that I hadn't seen before and, at that time, no one else was emulating. Given that there wasn't a theoretical or empirical tradition for investigating the phenomenon, and there really was only one organization engaged in the activity, I knew of no way to study it using quantitative methodology. Moreover, I could not see how to bring it into a lab and see what emerged, as I didn't really understand the nuance from the outside. As such, I felt the only way into this project was to undertake a qualitative approach. – Stephen Humphrey |
| | It can come across as vague and not well-founded unless the researcher is very clear from the outset which qualitative method of analysis is to be used – with an unobstructed view of philosophical assumptions informing the research questions asked and research processes followed. – Mathew Sheep |

*Table 21.1* Continued

| Theme | Sample Quotes |
| --- | --- |
| Find a guide for the journey | Find a mentor or co-author who has been down this path. While an apprenticeship model is always useful in learning how to conduct research, it may be even more important in the application of qualitative methods. A guide who has been through the process and who understands the twists and turns of the research and publication process using qualitative methods in top-tier management journals is invaluable. – Brett Smith |
| | Work with fun co-authors with qualitative research experience. – Chamu Sundaramurthy |
| Be rigorous! | The challenge, however, is in battling the idea that I'm not being "rigorous" or "scientific." I'm not talking about convincing reviewers or editors – this is an internal battle. – Stephen Humphrey |
| | "Qualitative research" can become one of those trite terms that lacks useful meaning (like "leadership," "culture," or "change") unless specified well beyond that. – Mathew Sheep |

## Q1: Surprises Encountered Learning Qualitative Research

Entering the qualitative research world can be filled with surprises – both in a positive and in a negative sense. A predominant theme was how surprised people were at how fun and engaging qualitative work can be. But there were myriad challenges as well. Indeed, some people expressed a great deal of anxiety and dread about the qualitative research journey calling it sometimes "uncomfortable" and even "nerve-wracking." As one noted, "It's a learning experience, and I definitely feel like I'm walking on a tightrope (and I don't like heights!)" and another told us, "I also feel a discomfort and tend to be tentative in terms discussing and making inferences from qualitative findings. Quantitative research gives an illusion of definitiveness…. I still do not feel a sense of comfort with qualitative methods." To be sure, we three authors resonated with both the ups and downs reported by those we heard from – qualitative methods can be time-consuming, mysterious, and draining. And, yet, qualitative research can also be enjoyable and rewarding.

*How fun and rewarding qualitative research is.* There was widespread enthusiasm among our informants for engaging in qualitative methods. Words like "fun," "amazing," "love," "passion," "incredibly enjoyable" permeated what they wrote and told us. As Blake Ashforth noted:

> Most important, qual[2] research is fun! As social scientists, we're all voyeurs at heart, trying to understand what people are experiencing. Having conversations ("inter-views"), being nosy ("probing responses"), and rubbernecking ("nonparticipant obser-vation") are our tools of the trade. And, you're learning constantly. What's not to like?

*Qualitative work is harder than expected.* Most of our scholars openly view qualitative research as highly challenging, and no-one called it easy, whether those challenges were initially seen (like an obviously raging river) or not (like a calm river with powerful undercurrents). Part of the difficulty comes in dealing with the complexity and enormity of data. In addition to the enormous quantity of data that can be involved in qualitative research, good qualitative data has other challenging features, namely "complexity" and "richness." This is both a blessing and a curse. On the one hand, rich data is the lifeblood of qualitative research and allows for new theory and insights to be found. As Mathew Sheep noted, "Without rich data, the 'aha' moment will not come." On the other hand, such richness and complexity can leave one in a frozen daze (too many winding and interconnected paths to follow and make sense of). As Teresa Cardador noted about the analytic process, "You are moving between theory and data, constructing your framework, and deciding what 'story' your data tell. I have felt, and have seen several students, absolutely crippled by the complexity and enormity of this process."

Another key point at which the challenge of qualitative research becomes apparent is when reporting the research for publication. The challenge is two-fold. First, because of the complexity and richness of the data, many possible stories can be told and other team members and reviewers may all see and want to tell a different story. Thus, there may be too many "navigators" on the journey. As Cristina Gibson noted, "There are so many possible frames, perspectives, and ideas that can be explored. Making a convincing case that you have arrived at the most important and impactful representation of the data is very challenging." And while it may be tempting to try to tell an all-encompassing story, the result of doing so is often that everyone then perceives the result to be too thin and inadequate.

*Lack of formulas/diversity of approaches.* Although many best practices have emerged in qualitative research (e.g., Lincoln and Guba, 1985; Elsbach and Kramer, 2016; Cassell et al., forthcoming), our informants highlighted the variety of qualitative methods and how the qualitative research process can be flexible and adaptive. Further, as Pratt (2007) noted, there is a lack of a boilerplate in writing and reviewing qualitative methods. Scholars we interviewed pointed out the dual-edged sword of this issue – that qualitative research can be freeing on the one hand but paralyzing on the other. Being in the quantitative research world may prompt people to especially desire and appreciate the more adaptable, free flowing, and theoretically "broad" nature of qualitative research; however, such open-endedness can leave people wondering which of the countless possible paths to follow. "At least in quant, you know what your general hypothesis is," notes Vilmos Misangyi. And Cristina Gibson explained:

> There seem to be many more options for how to craft the research and report it, in the qualitative tradition. And if you are conducting mixed-methods, this is even more true! And this is both the beauty and the curse! It is beautiful because then you can use an emergent, iterative, flexible process, and there are many creative options to explore. But it can also be a curse, because there will likely be many opinions as to how you should or could do it differently.

And Brett Smith articulated:

> I think one of the biggest surprises was the lack of formulaic methods. Compared to quantitative methods where we are provided formulas, assumptions, and rules, qualitative methods had much less of a formulaic approach. At first, this can feel a bit unsettling especially as a new researcher who is trying to do things correctly. At first, the rules of how to do quantitative methods provides a sense of security – a blanket that may help defend you from the reviewers (or your dissertation committee). However, as time goes on, these same rules begin to feel more and more like a straight-jacket by constricting the range of questions you can explore and manner in which they can be explored. It limits your research "motion." … In some ways, it assumes you know

what you are going to find and then you go out to test or find it. By comparison, the qualitative approach leaves many more degrees of freedom.... It also allows for much greater serendipity in the process. As a new researcher, this is rather uncomfortable – and it doesn't feel like the strict research protocol in which we have supposedly been trained.

*Degree of change throughout the process.* Another surprise mentioned by many of our scholar informants was that qualitative research not only allows for – but often even demands – that you change course and make key decisions *throughout* the research process. The entire focus of the study may turn out to be quite different at the end of the study after the "real" story has emerged. This is in clear distinction to most quantitative approaches in which the majority of "big picture" decision making is made up front in the design of the study. In qualitative work, one has the flexibility (and even imperative) to "pivot" toward the most interesting theoretical story after immersing in the phenomenon of interest. As Linda Treviño put it:

> What I learned was that you could begin with a broad research question rather than a theory-based hypothesis. I really liked that especially because it seemed to provide more opportunity to contribute new knowledge in areas where we knew little and I've always been drawn to that type of research question.... Research questions were broader and even open to change as the research progressed. I liked the iterative process ... I particularly liked that the data informed the process as it unfolded. One was not "stuck" with the initial research question and design. It could evolve.

Glen recalls several occasions when students and faculty co-authors doing their first qualitative study would ask, often sheepishly, some variant of the question, "Is it *okay* to change our protocols after a few interviews?" It was almost as though the thought was so foreign – so "wrong" to change once you started. Invariably, however, each of these students and co-authors ultimately felt quite liberated to be able to be nimble and "pivot" to respond to emerging themes. This ability helps the qualitative scholar stay true to the population being studied, by responding to how *they* see the world rather than being stuck with one's initial preconceptions.

## Q2:  Differences between Quantitative Training and Qualitative Inquiry

Our second question asked our informants to consider differences between their quantitative training/experiences and what they learned when first taking on a qualitative project. Their responses were quite telling in that they revealed not only methodological differences, but practical, paradigmatic, and stylistic ones as well. Of course, much has been written about the differences between quantitative/positivist and qualitative/interpretive research, and a thorough review of those differences is beyond the scope of this chapter (for excellent treatments on this topic, see Gioia and Pitre, 1990; Lee, 1998; Lincoln et al., 2011). Instead, we focus on how our informants framed these differences as they discovered them while doing qualitative work.

*Qualitative research brings you closer to the people/phenomena.* One of the hallmarks of qualitative work is that it allows you to get considerably closer to the individuals, organizations, cultures, and phenomena you want to study. Indeed, as Evered and Louis (1981) put it, qualitative work typically emphasizes the "insider" approach instead of the "outsider" approach. This advantage was a key "payoff" for those embarking on qualitative research, not just for intellectual/academic reasons, but personal and interpersonal reasons as well. As Tiffany Johnson explained to us:

Hearing from one person about their work experiences during the interview stays with you – you think about their comments through the rest of the day (and sometimes even longer than that). And as soon as their memory begins to fade, their transcript has been completed, and you dive right back into their experiences, only to be further inundated by their world through their words. And that's just one person ... over time, you've collected information from tons of informants (hopefully) with unique yet similar experiences.... As you write about a theme, key quotes from informants pop up in your head, and you can literally hear them say the statement and/or visualize the words on the transcript. Their stories never leave you and that, at times, can be exhausting – yet paradoxically, energizing.

*Different paradigms matter.* Doctoral programs have no shortage of training in positivist paradigms – it is clearly the dominant approach, at least in North American management programs. Indeed, most business schools do not require a qualitative methods course of their management students, leaving most to cobble together some training from faculty members and/or other colleges on campus. One important implication of this is that students often lack an understanding of foundational paradigmatic differences that underpin different approaches to research. Consequently, when a quantitatively trained student embarks on a qualitative study, they often lack an understanding of how a different paradigm affects myriad decisions about the project – from design to data and from analysis to writing. This deficit can have important consequences throughout the project, as David Sluss told us:

As a deductive researcher, we are trained to think about mediators and moderators. Moderation leads one to think about how particular groups of people might differ and thus experience the mediation (or process) differently. Inductive research is not really set up to "find moderation" per se. As a result, I have struggled to let go or undo looking for moderation in my qualitative/inductive data as findings. Instead, the focus seems to be more on process.

## Q3: Things to "Undo" or "Relearn" from Quantitative Training

Our third question probed our informants to think about habits, mindsets, or urges that they developed from quantitative research that they now believed they had to undo or relearn when doing qualitative research. This question was sparked in part because Glen routinely hears from students who are learning qualitative methods (in a methods seminar) report that the course is pulling them to undo many assumptions that they had about an overall worldview as well as how to approach research.

*Allow for organic, non-linear, emergent story.* In contrast to quantitative methods, wherein the researcher creates hypotheses based on the literature, most qualitative methods urge an exploratory approach to the data to uncover an emergent story that would not have been predicted a priori. This more organic and non-linear approach is something that several of our scholar informants reported having to undo from their quantitative training. Vilmos Misangyi explained that for him, the hardest part of the transition from quantitative to qualitative was

letting go of your hypotheses and looking for support of your hypotheses; to me, good qualitative research is ... being brave enough to wade in and letting the data speak ... you let go of being married to any particular theoretical viewpoint. That is really, really hard.

Indeed, the notion that the story comes *later* can be seen as rather shocking to newcomers to qualitative work. Our colleague Stephen Humphrey, who recently conducted his first qualitative project, put it this way:

> There have been several "ah-ha" moments for me. As a person trained in laboratory research, I was conditioned to put an extreme amount of effort into understanding the theory before conducting the study – if you don't know the theory (and hypotheses) that you want to test, you cannot design an effective lab study.... Teams research in the lab is a one-shot experience, where success or failure is generally predicated on your ability to design a competent study. In contrast ... the qualitative approach allowed me to immerse myself entirely in the context and let the phenomenon emerge. It is telling that the manuscript being produced from this study is focused on a construct we never asked the informants about, yet which they all discussed on their own. This is truly a game-changer for me.

*Undo the need for speed – qualitative research takes time.* A second theme noted by many of our informants was that they had to recalibrate their expectations regarding how long it takes to do a high-quality inductive research project. Part of this stems from the labor intensive data collection and analysis, and part of it stems from time needed for ideas to percolate. Linda Treviño commented on the latter, telling us, "I have found that the story emerges for me over time. I have to give myself time for my brain to bring together the different pieces into a model that works and represents the data." Reflecting on the time commitment of various phases of qualitative project, Aparna reflected:

> Aah – time for some hard truths.... Yes the biggest challenge was overcoming the "need for speed." With a quant project once you have a robust finding, the paper unfolds naturally and can congeal into a working draft pretty quickly. But it's a little different with a qual project, to put it mildly. It takes a while to sift through the data – frankly it's just a ton of reading to distill some themes. And those themes may change through research meetings, etc. So the most salient part of this journey for me was to acquire a certain Zen about the process.

Importantly, there are perceived payoffs to the time commitment inherent in most qualitative research designs and the patience required of the researcher; these payoffs include more interesting stories, a closer tie to the phenomena studied, and a better theoretical contribution. As Chad Murphy explained:

> Qualitative research doesn't necessarily move very quickly, and so the key is to be patient with the findings. I think quantitative research can breed a kind of impatience with data – e.g., if the numbers aren't there, then let's move on to something else. For this reason, it was hard for me at first to be patient with qualitative data – I just wanted the results NOW! The more patient I've been, though, the more clearly I can think about the data and the better the end result seems to be. But that was (and continues to be) one of the more difficult aspects of qualitative research for me.

*Be prepared for considerable back-end work.* Closely related to the time-consuming nature of qualitative research was that our informants noted their surprise at how much time needed to be allocated to the later stages of the research project compared to quantitative work. Although some people mentioned challenges beginning with initial design (e.g., "involves the same level of thinking and rigor on the front-end design"), more often the challenge of qualitative research was seen as existing on the back-end. (One can imagine starting down an apparently simple-looking river, but ending up wondering "How did we end up here? Where are we? How do we get out of here?") As noted above, one of the surprises for those taking on qualitative research is that changes are allowed and encouraged to appropriately adapt throughout the research process. While that affords the scholar a great deal of flexibility, it also implies that one needs to be prepared for considerable "back-end" work during and after data collection. This is in stark contrast to most quantitative methods wherein the analytic process is relatively quick after data collection. Some even compared it to the experience of being lost on a journey. Indeed, one key point at which the challenge of qualitative research apparently starts becoming obvious is after collecting some data, as noted by Teresa Cardador:

> In quantitative research, much of the "work" is done upfront. Knowing the literature well enough to generate hypotheses based on theory, compiling appropriate measures, ensuring that you are conforming to high standards in your methodology, etc. Once all of this has been done and you have your data, it should simply be a matter of testing your hypotheses. However, with qualitative research, I have found the reverse to be true. The real "work" begins after data collection and upon theoretical saturation.

## Q4: What We Wish We Knew When We Started

Given that all of our scholar informants had conducted at least one qualitative study, and several of them have been doing qualitative work for many years, we wanted to see what things they wished they had known when they started qualitative work. These insights, we believed, could be particularly useful for scholars considering or just beginning qualitative projects.

*Need to practice good data management from the onset.* We heard various stories about lost data, overwhelmed researchers, and those who felt stymied by the sheer volume of data generated by most qualitative methods. Hence, one recurring theme was the lament that individuals didn't realize how important data management would be – particularly the need to start off the project well, in order to manage and leverage the data. Most of our informants use some kind of qualitative software (such as NVivo) but others prefer the "old fashioned" approach of themes and quotes on paper and/or note cards. Regardless of how high- or low-tech the process, starting off and staying organized with the data is tremendously helpful. As Tiffany Johnson told us:

> I've learned the importance of managing the data as it comes in. From the moment data is collected, it is important to keep track of the source of the data, new codes, new interview questions, emerging linkages between codes, etc. This makes tracking any of the changes made to protocols and codes a lot simpler when it's time to write up the manuscript.

*Ideal personal attributes/skills.* Perhaps at this point you are again self-assessing whether or not to take on a qualitative project. You may, in fact, be asking if you have a skill set that fits. Some elements in the responses from sample researchers did point to certain core competencies and attributes that are helpful for doing qualitative work. In fact, responses to the questions above such as patience or simply "being more Zen," suggest that there might be some underlying dispositions that explain our sample researchers' forays into the qualitative world. These included patience, artistic flair, and tolerance for ambiguity. Indeed, some researchers noted that they wished, looking back, that they had had "a lot more patience and a little more confidence … and [undertaking qualitative research] may not be the only or best approach for someone who is constantly preoccupied by the ticking of the tenure clock" (Brett Smith). Linda Treviño highlighted another key attribute, tolerance to ambiguity, noting:

> I'd like to say that, in order to love this and do it well, you need to have a high tolerance for ambiguity and love to "muck around" in the qual data. It is a very different process from quant design and methods.… If you don't enjoy this ambiguous process, stick with the traditional stuff.

(On a somewhat self-congratulatory note, Glen, Derron and Aparna promptly claimed extremely high ratings on tolerance to ambiguity!)

Our informants' responses lead us to highlight another core characteristic of qualitative research – the blending of art and science. Serendipity arising from human activity, insights that are suddenly "seen," and human creativity appear to be an important key to furthering knowledge. The need to be artful in one's process surprised (and even brought discomfort to) some researchers whose training in quantitative methods emphasized a more mechanical and formulaic approach to research – assumptions that had to be "undone" to some degree. An important turn of perspective appears to involve developing a deep appreciation for the implications of the human element in research (e.g., research designs involve human values and choices; research reports are an exercise in nonfiction "story telling"). Indeed, a recent experience in Glen's qualitative methods class illustrates this point: Denny Gioia, who started his career as an engineer, was the guest speaker for the day, and he noted that one of his biggest revelations many years ago when starting inductive research was that he could no longer hold onto the assumptions of physical science and especially the existence of one "reality" when studying organizations. Instead he soon recognized that when investigating *people*, he needed to account for their social constructions and the existence of multiple versions of reality. (See Denny's essay in this volume for further elaboration on this theme.)

*Consider diversifying your portfolio with quantitative and qualitative projects.* As noted, Glen took on his first qualitative project during his doctoral program, although his dissertation was quantitative. He has since conducted conceptual, qualitative, and quantitative research during his career. Part of this was because he enjoys all three, and part of it was to "diversify the research portfolio," a way to do the qualitative research you love but also "hedge your bets" and produce (quicker) quantitative research for career purposes. Indeed, we noted a theme of pragmatism underlying the choice of qualitative work across our sample of researchers. As noted above, qualitative research tends to take more time than quantitative, and this can have significant (negative) effects for such events as getting a job and tenure/promotion, especially at schools that do not recognize (and compensate for) the temporal implications of doing qualitative research. As Linda Treviño noted, reflecting back:

> I've done both for my entire career but, because of the perceived difficulty of publishing qual work in top journals early in my career, I focused on the quant work in order to get tenure and promotion. I still do a little of the quant now but am mostly focused on the qual work now which I much prefer.

Hence, this hybrid approach to one's research portfolio might be a pragmatic strategy for those who want to conduct qualitative research but are also concerned about the career implications of doing so exclusively.

## Q5: Final Travel Tips: Advice for Doing Qualitative Research

Like all good explorers/trailblazers, those who have made the qualitative research journey can make the journey easier for those who follow. Such it is with our informants. Although the qualitative research journey can be chaotic and non-linear, it may be helpful to consider these final "travel tips" as you undertake qualitative research.

*Take the trip!* You might be hesitant to start the journey, especially given the warnings we've discussed above. But the resounding sentiment of our scholar informants was to encourage others to try it out. As Cristina Gibson noted:

> If they are ready for the challenge, I'd like to encourage researchers to give qualitative a try, and even more specifically, to consider mixed-methods, which might be a more comfortable fit initially, if they are new to qualitative research. It is so incredibly powerful!

Mathew Sheep adds, "It is worth every bit of effort…. The reward is generating or elaborating new constructs and theory, not just testing yet another (how many can there possibly be?) variation of extant constructs."

*Make sure qualitative is the right trip to take.* While we encourage scholars to take the trip we also caution against embarking on the journey in haste. People begin qualitative work for many reasons – sometimes curiosity, sometimes habit, sometimes as an escape from quantitative work. But one must ensure that a qualitative study is the most appropriate one for the research questions at hand. As Teresa Cardador noted:

> Your method should always fit your research question. I can't tell you how many qualitative papers I have reviewed for journals that report findings that could be predicted from existing theory or don't build new theory in a meaningful way. Sometimes a qualitative approach is the way to go, and sometimes it's not. Combining qualitative research with some quantitative research may help you to derive greater theoretical insight, as well as develop a well-rounded program of research. So I guess I would say – be methodologically omnivorous!

*Find a guide for the journey.* It's commonly noted among qualitative scholars that this kind of research is not easily learned by simply reading textbooks and finding a few exemplary articles to emulate. There are countless decisions that need to be made during a qualitative project, yet *how* to make those decisions can't always be prescribed in textbooks, largely because there are so many contingencies involved. Hence, finding a guide of some sort – a mentor, a co-author – can be immensely helpful to teach you the process of decision-making in qualitative work. As Blake Ashforth explained:

> If I'd done much more up-front reading on qual methods and actually talked to some qual researchers, I could have saved myself some rookie mistakes…. Like any good chef, qual requires you to exercise judgment at every step of the process. This is partly why it's very helpful to learn as a protégé, as you can see tacit knowledge in action.

To this point, Aparna notes that her journey into the qualitative world would not have been nearly as rewarding if she had not sought out an expert as a collaborator (even controlling for her high tolerance to ambiguity).

*Be rigorous!* While qualitative research is prime territory for methodological flexibility and new discoveries, taking short-cuts can lead one directly into metaphorical quicksand. Achieving legitimacy and trustworthiness can be challenging when designing the study and reporting qualitative data. (For strategies, see Golden-Biddle and Locke, 1993; Lincoln and Guba, 1985; Rheinhardt et al., forthcoming). Reviewers may be skeptical of qualitative research or have certain standards (commonly accepted or perhaps their own) for how to do qualitative research. As Teresa Cardador noted:

> [One] thing that has surprised me is how much I have had to defend a qualitative approach. In the years I've been doing qualitative research, I've seen a big growth in acceptance, but it still surprises me that many people think of qualitative research as "descriptive," "exploratory," or not "empirical."

And as Stephen Humphrey told us was on his mind when doing qualitative work:

> Oh – and will I be accepted by the cool kids? It is easy for me to see a path to publication with my quant research, because I can write a manuscript that looks like published manuscripts, using the same methodology, analyses, etc. I've done it before, so I am "in-group." Will I use the language wrong when writing up the qual study? Will the editor give me the benefit of the doubt when the flaws in my paper are revealed? We've got a fine "imposter syndrome" going on here.

As several researchers noted to us, the legitimacy problem appears to have become better over the years. We fully expect the trend to continue, with increasingly more top journals institutionalizing processes to assure a place for rigorous qualitative work.

## Conclusion

To conclude, let us return to where we started. Our goal was to help inspire – or perhaps less grandiosely, nudge – those who might be considering forays into qualitative research. These stories of scholars like you show some of the promises and pitfalls of qualitative inquiry. It is a difficult but rewarding journey, not unlike ascending a mountain to get to the spectacular views above. We also hoped to remind qualitative scholars of their own journeys into this arena, perhaps stimulating some self-insight into your own growth as a scholar. Even for the experts in qualitative work, there is always much to be learned from each other as we share our stories – both triumphs and failures, both gains and setbacks – and so we encourage more discussions such as this one among our qualitative researcher peers. We should encourage each other to take a developmental stance on our work, thinking about how to help a new generation of qualitative researchers learn (and improve) the craft.

Qualitative research disproportionately wins best paper awards, in part because it tells us riveting stories, in part because it is well suited to ground-breaking research, and in part because it brings us closer to important organizational – and human! – phenomena. It has been said that to work is to relate, and qualitative research helps us relate to those we study at work. Beyond the somewhat intellectual reasons of contributing to theory and knowledge, qualitative research helps us connect to other people, which contributes to our sense of humanity. What greater goal could there be?

In summary, we hope this chapter has encouraged and enabled more of our fellow researchers to put the qualitative journey on their map. Bon voyage!

# Notes

1 Of course, much qualitative work takes a positivist stance. For reasons of parsimony we oversimplify the world by loosely referring to positivist/quantitative or interpretive/qualitative leaning scholars.
2 We note that many of our informants used the informal term "qual" for "qualitative" and "quant" for "quantitative," which are commonplace abbreviations. To preserve the in vivo text, we have retained the original language.

# References

Ashforth, B. E., Kreiner, G. E., Clark, M. A., and Fugate, M. 2007. Normalizing dirty work: Managerial tactics for countering occupational taint. *Academy of Management Journal*, 50: 149–174.

Bansal, P. and Corley, K. 2011. From the editors: The coming of age for qualitative research: Embracing the diversity of qualitative methods. *Academy of Management Journal*, 54: 233–237.

Cassell, C., Cunliffe, A., and Grandy, G. (eds.) Forthcoming. *Sage Handbook of Qualitative Business and Management Research Methods*. London: Sage.

Elsbach, K. D. and Kramer, R. M. 2016. *Handbook of Qualitative Organizational Research: Innovative Pathways and Methods*. New York: Routledge.

Evered, R. and Louis, M. R. 1981. Alternative perspectives in the organizational sciences: "Inquiry from the inside" and "inquiry from the outside." *Academy of Management Review*, 6: 385–395.

Gergen, K. J., Josselson, R., and Freeman, M. 2015. The promises of qualitative inquiry. *American Psychologist*, 70(1): 1–9.

Gioia, D. A. and Pitre, E. 1990. Multiparadigm perspectives on theory building. *Academy of Management Review*, 15: 584–602.

Golden-Biddle, K. and Locke, K. 1993. Appealing work: An investigation of how ethnographic texts convince. *Organization Science*, 4: 595–616.

Haynes, K. 2013. Reflexivity in Qualitative Research. In Symon, G. and Cassell, C. (eds.) *Qualitative Organizational Research*. London: Sage, 72–89.

Lee, T. W. 1998. Tensions between qualitative and quantitative traditions. In *Using Qualitative Methods in Organizational Research*. Thousand Oaks, CA: Sage, 5–14.

Lincoln, Y. and Guba, E. 1985. Establishing trustworthiness. In *Naturalistic Inquiry*. Beverly Hills, CA: Sage, 289–331.

Lincoln, Y. S., Lynhma, S. A., and Guba, E. G. 2011. Paradigmatic controversies, contradictions, and emerging confluences, revisited. In Denzin, N. K. and Lincoln, Y. S. (eds.) *Handbook of Qualitative Research*. Thousand Oaks, CA: Sage, 97–128.

Pratt, M. G. 2007. Fitting oval pegs into round holes: Tensions in evaluating and publishing qualitative research in top North American journals. *Organizational Research Methods*, 11: 481–509.

Rheinhardt, A., Kreiner, G. E., Gioia, D. A., and Corley, K. Forthcoming. Conducting and publishing rigorous qualitative research. In Cassell, C., Cunliffe, A. and Grandy, G. (eds.) *Sage Handbook of Qualitative Business and Management Research Methods*. London: Sage.

# 22

# APPRECIATING EMERGENCE AND SERENDIPITY IN QUALITATIVE RESEARCH

## Resisting the Urge to Follow Set Plans

*Rene Wiedner and Shaz Ansari*

In academic research, and perhaps more generally in modern society, we often face pressures to plan everything we do in detail. As we know from project and change management, many implementation issues can be more effectively addressed, or even avoided, with detailed planning. However, we also know that many issues cannot be predicted upfront (e.g. Balogun, 2006). Moreover, and perhaps more importantly for our argument, potential *opportunities* may arise during the implementation process that may be impossible to anticipate (e.g. Plowman et al., 2007). In fact, detailed planning may even inhibit our ability to identify and utilize emerging opportunities (cf. Mintzberg, 1991).

Such awareness of unpredictable opportunities is especially important in the context of qualitative research. Instead of testing hypotheses, the objective is to understand a phenomenon in rich detail, preferably from several angles. It entails exploration and therefore confronting the unknown. Obviously, we should prepare for such an expedition. Rather than running around aimlessly, we define objectives, if only to reassure ourselves (and others!) that we know what we are doing and where we are going. Not having a clear sense of direction can generate anxiety that we naturally tend to suppress.

In addition to the psychological benefits of planning, there are many forces that encourage us qualitative researchers to clearly specify our methods, theoretical foundations and potential contributions, as we discuss below. One could even argue that many researchers (ourselves included) could be accused of partially distorting what we actually do and how we report our research. For instance, we may generate research proposals for potential sponsors that bear little resemblance to the publications we eventually produce; we craft methods sections in peer reviewed journal articles that may not accurately reflect the messiness of the process we tried to manage; when asked during our fieldwork by colleagues, research subjects and others what we are specifically investigating, we may either pretend that we have a very clear idea or we come up with an answer that we think others might want to hear; we may say that, unlike quantitative researchers, we do not attempt to generate causal explanations – although, knowingly or unknowingly, we often try to do just that; we may put our research subjects at ease by telling them that we are not interested in any sordid details – although we may secretly or indirectly try our best to somehow get at them. Of course this list of potential distortions is not exhaustive, and others have problematized these and other issues in the past (e.g. Fine, 1993).

The aim of this chapter is not to criticize researchers for generating or contributing to these distortions. Instead of criticizing, we will use the space provided to argue that successful qualitative research is dependent not solely on accommodating these forces to seem systematic, orderly and methodical but, crucially, also on *resisting* them.

Resisting can be quite straining and it is easy to give up, especially when we follow mentors', supervisors' or peers' sound advice that we need to *focus* in order to produce something substantive and potentially more publishable. However, just as nurses who become managers may need to overcome the often seemingly overwhelming urge to care in order to grant their subordinates the necessary freedom to fulfil their roles (Lalleman et al., 2016), we too must be prepared to let go – and preferably know why, when, and how to do so.

Congruent with this notion of the value of letting go, our aim in this chapter is to provide an understanding of some of the benefits of adopting an emergent research design. By 'emergent research design' we do not mean starting with a completely blank slate in terms of the empirical phenomenon, theory and/or methods when entering the field. Such a strategy may, or may not, be useful or even possible. Indeed, while many qualitative researchers routinely claim to use 'grounded theory' (Corbin and Strauss, 2015), it is extremely difficult to do so in practice, and many do so only ritualistically and without using its procedures correctly.

Instead, we are referring to the ability and willingness to continuously respond to emerging puzzles, ideas and insights in a flexible manner which, in turn, depends on the adoption of a highly reflexive stance towards our theories, empirical surroundings and methodologies. It involves the search not just for answers but also, importantly, for profound questions throughout the entire research process. This constant search within research, when acknowledged at all, is often simply referred to as the 'iterative process of data collection and analysis' in publications but even the importance of this iterative process is rarely made explicit.

We believe it is beneficial for the scholarly community to take an emergent research design seriously rather than simply treat it as an aberration or collection of mistakes that may ultimately and unwittingly contribute to important and interesting theoretical insights that are accepted as worthy of publication by our academic peers. In other words, we want to question (implicit) assumptions that adopting an emergent research design is either the result of poor preparation, or that it is inherently riskier than adhering to a very clearly defined and circumscribed research question that guides the actual study from beginning to end.

We do this in the remainder of this chapter by contemplating relevant risks and potential rewards and presenting confessional tales about our own research projects. Overall, we hope that this can contribute to a greater understanding of the 'iterative process of data collection and analysis' by showing that there is (or can be) method in the madness. We begin by considering several forces against the adoption of an emergent design in academic research.

## Forces against Emergence

A hallmark of scientific research is methodological rigour. Experiments should be controlled. And yet, advances in chemistry and other disciplines have often arisen by accident. For instance, the fact that the compound sildenafil can lead to an erection was a completely unexpected discovery in trials that were meant to show its effectiveness in treating cardiovascular disorders. Recognizing an opportunity, Pfizer subsequently developed Viagra – a hugely successful drug (de Rond and Thietart, 2007). Similarly, a completely unanticipated service (text messaging or SMS) created a transformation in the industry as consumers adopted SMS despite the fact that it had very limited functionality. Thus, although the industry had promoted Internet browsing in its quest to make telephony data-centric, it was text-based social communication that diffused widely and shaped the change in mobile telephony (Ansari and Phillips, 2011). So, what stops us from (metaphorically speaking) developing our own, world-changing Viagras or SMS? Let us tackle this question by considering our interactions as researchers with several stakeholder groups, including (in no particular order) financial sponsors, academic peers, research subjects, employers and ourselves.

## *Financial Sponsors*

Research projects generally require funding. To attract funding, we often need to spell out our research objectives in some detail in research proposals. Sponsors, understandably, want to know how their grants are being used and for what purpose. They are rarely happy to write blank cheques. In return for financial sponsorship we agree to focus on a particular topic and utilize particular methods.

However, tension between the proposed plan and action may arise as the actual research unfolds. This can have several reasons. For instance, we may have liberally translated what we actually want to do in order to appeal to financial sponsors who have a limited understanding and interest in our specific academic endeavours. In Carlile's (2002) terms, we have to negotiate syntactic, semantic and pragmatic boundaries (i.e. different languages, understandings and inter-ests). This requires some flexibility which, of course, carries the risk that sponsors may be unhappy if their expectations are at odds with the ultimate results. Depending on our assessment of the importance of satisfying sponsors, this risk may not be worth it and so we might attempt to stick as closely as possible to what we have proposed. On the other hand, there always exists the risk that sponsors will not be satisfied with the results, no matter how closely proposals and results are aligned. However, if our methods do not substantially diverge from the proposal then we can at least say that we have adhered to the contract.

An explanation that is more central to this chapter for the divergence between the official plan that sponsors have received and the actual study is that, as the study progresses, and as we engage in the iterative process of data collection and analysis, we may realize that our original research question or framing is somehow at odds with the insights we are gaining. Our attempts to make sense of the data raise new questions that we were previously unable to consider. We are then faced with a choice: we can either continue down the path that is laid out on the map that we have previously generated (or that has been generated for us) or we begin exploring without completely relying on the map. Exploration can undoubtedly be a risky affair as we simply do not know what we will find. Even if the map does not guarantee interesting findings, it at least may offer some comfort by giving us a sense of direction (cf., Weick, 1995, p. 54) – a point we will come back to when considering interactions with ourselves.

In summary, we might want to stick to our plans rather than alter them to explore new, potentially more interesting avenues, in order to avoid having to engage in potentially difficult discussions and negotiations with our sponsors. Similar forces against adopting an emergent research design are at play when we consider our interactions with our academic peers, as we explore next.

## *Academic Peers*

Our ability to demonstrate that we have conducted high-quality research is largely dependent on persuading our academic peers. This is especially the case when submitting our research outputs to peer-reviewed academic journals. Our reviewing peers need to be convinced that our methods are robust and, ideally, that repeating the study would result in the same findings. It would seem pertinent to plan the study very carefully and follow through on this plan instead of making changes along the way. Any changes in our methods should, in theory, require a new plan.

Matters of reliability and validity are, of course, relatively less ambiguous with regard to quantitative research. As we know, qualitative research – especially in the case of ethnographies – is an inherently messy process. The data that we generate in interviews and observational fieldwork is always situation specific and our analysis techniques and employed categories are necessarily based on ontological and epistemological assumptions that we should try to, but can never fully, explicate. Nevertheless, we must conform to certain standards that are based on dominant paradigms, templates (Flyvbjerg, 2006) and word limits. The proliferation of the 'Gioia method' (Gioia et al., 2013) and the method of comparative case studies (Eisenhardt, 1989) are examples providing guidance through standardization and codification.

Moreover, while a description of the actual research process may offer important learning opportunities, these are usually reserved for confessional tales that, if made public at all, are published separately (e.g. Barley, 1990; Van Maanen, 2011). To paraphrase a former journal editor who shall remain unnamed, a methods section is a retrospective description of how the study would ideally be conducted if the authors had the chance to do it all over again. Methods sections, just like all other sections of a paper, can change considerably as a consequence of a detailed and lengthy review process that may call for the collection of further data or trigger the revision of the research question and/or analytic techniques. Ironically, the 'perfect' methodology that ultimately appears in the published article is almost impossible to achieve without actually undergoing such an arduous process of trial and error.

To be fair, reporting the actual messiness and complexity we encounter during our studies may not only be hard to accomplish, but may make our papers less readable or even less comprehensible – an outcome hardly any writer would intentionally wish for. In this world of information overload, pervasive social media, decreasing attention spans and increasing competition for what people actually get to read, it makes sense to 'clean up' our papers and edit out, if not disguise and conceal the messiness that often underlies what we produce.

Additionally, the mismatch between what we actually did and what ends up in print may be related to impression management that goes beyond simple conformity with publication standards. We may feel that revealing how we essentially only figured out what our research was about when we actually completed it may undermine our attempts to appear as authoritative scholars to editors and reviewers. We all tend to respect some level of honesty and humility. But we also tend to respect authority. Harnessing the latter might be a safer bet because we generally do not want to risk giving the impression that we are bumbling fools (or at least that, in some respects, we relied on serendipity rather than detailed planning during our study), especially to those who we are trying to impress. Of course, editors and seasoned reviewers know this. Impression management is part and parcel of the scholarly publication game.

In summary, we may think that justifying an emergent research design to our academic peers (including reviewers and readers) is difficult and that the more this can be avoided, the better.

## Research Subjects

Importantly, impression management is not necessarily limited to our dealings with financial sponsors and academic peers. It is just as likely to emerge when dealing with prospective 'informants' or 'research subjects'. Interestingly, the fact that informants may engage in impression management by telling researchers what they think they want to hear is already well-known (e.g. Alvesson, 2003; Bourdieu, 1996), while the fact that researchers do the same is rarely explicitly acknowledged. 'I'm exploring what is going on' is not the type of statement a non-academic interviewee expects to hear from a serious scientist/researcher. Surely, the researcher is drawing on a substantial and well-defined body of knowledge to be able to capture data that undergoes some form of statistical analysis in order to tell us how some variable is unequivocally related to another.

A telling example of this type of assumption is when one of the authors recently approached someone in the music industry and requested a semi-structured interview. After much reluctance the contact agreed to participate. The researcher then asked when would be a good time to conduct the interview. The simple response was: 'send it to me'. After explaining that the interview was not a survey, all communication stopped. Perhaps the individual was simply uncomfortable talking to a researcher or unable to find a convenient time but it appears that a survey was more readily accepted as a method of collecting data than a semi-structured interview, at least in the context of an academic study. Similarly, several attempts to explain the (admittedly rather vague) objectives of a qualitative study during an interview to a medical doctor (who probably associated rigorous research with randomized controlled trials (Pope and Mays, 1995)) were followed by a puzzled look and the comment 'I still don't understand what you're doing'.

Additionally, as others have pointed out, we gain research subjects' trust and – especially in the context of ethnographic studies – sometimes even become close friends, only to subsequently betray them (Beech et al., 2009). Although our objective is to generate theoretical insights and advance knowledge rather than attract media attention we know that to increase our chances of publication and thereby further our careers (and satisfy our employers, as discussed below) our outputs need to somehow stand out.

As qualitative researchers we rely on prose rather than on demonstrating statistical significance or mathematical equations. Essentially the story is all we have and we know that it needs to seduce readers and motivate continued reading. Especially in our field of management it is rare – and therefore potentially interesting – to read explicit examples about people making fools of themselves or engaging in what might be interpreted as dubious behaviour. Actually writing these things about our research subjects, even when anonymized, is of course very risky for the simple reason that it might jeopardize their and others' willingness to participate in future studies.

Adopting an emergent research design arguably amplifies these risks: if researchers stick closely to their plans, then these supposedly atypical occurrences of deviance or stupidity (cf. Alvesson and Spicer, 2012) can simply be ignored. If they, instead, pay attention to, and become interested in them, then these occurrences may substantially influence subsequent data collection and analysis. Rather than having awkward discussions with research subjects it might be easier simply to develop a clear plan and stick to it.

## Employers

As mentioned above, our performance as academic researchers is largely tied to persuading academic peers of our theoretical contributions. Ultimately, however, we need to convince not only our peers but also our employers that we are generating value. Academic institutions (especially business schools) tend to measure us in terms of the number of recent publications in highly ranked and selective, peer-reviewed journals. This pressure to produce does not favour many iterative rounds of exploration and re-examination of ever-expanding data sets, proliferating concepts and analytical angles that may eventually appear in books. It instead encourages us to draw boundaries around specific sub-projects and move on to the next if we are not confident about our ability to quickly use them as a basis for papers in specific journals. We are thereby arguably driven to 'search' rather than 're-search'.

## *Ourselves*

Finally, and as also already noted above, departing from carefully laid plans may induce anxiety. We arguably all strongly value ontological security and try to avoid ambiguities and uncertainties. Why make life unnecessarily difficult for ourselves? Ultimately, making changes during our study amounts to self-questioning and criticizing. By recognizing that we cannot come up with definitive answers to our questions (or even definitive questions!) and that theoretical saturation is only ever temporary, we risk postponing our results indefinitely.

## Emergent Research Design: A Risky Affair?

It would seem from all of the above that adopting, and being honest about adopting, an emergent research design is a highly risky affair. We may end up disappointing financial sponsors; we may jeopardize our chances of getting our papers accepted by revealing our flaws; we may get caught up in endless epistemological debates with others and ourselves; we risk feeling helpless or confused by not having a clear plan; we risk failing to convince potential informants to participate in our studies as a result of not living up to scientific ideals or stereotypes; we risk betraying our informants and jeopardizing their willingness to engage in future studies; we may get caught up in details that could distract us from achieving our research objectives.

All of this suggests it may be better to 'play it safe' and choose the seemingly less risky alternative of closely following a predefined research design (whether qualitative or quantitative). And yet, as Pettigrew (2012) has argued, the odds favour the risk taker in research. But is the alternative really less risky? Ultimately, we have to ask ourselves which strategy is more or less likely to result in desirable outcomes. And to do this we have to ask what these desirable outcomes are. The answer will undoubtedly differ from researcher to researcher but in the space available we would like to consider three fairly basic and obvious research related outcomes, namely (1) having access to data that are deemed interesting by academic peers and therefore stand a reasonable chance of being publishable in reputable outlets, (2) furthering our own intellectual development and (3) being ourselves motivated to continue researching a phenomenon.

With regard to the first point, and as already alluded to above, it is no secret that having access to a very rich data set about an exciting empirical phenomenon increases the chances that a submission to a journal will not be rejected. So, how can we get our hands on an interesting data set?

One approach is to start by being attentive to specific empirical phenomena that may initially seem difficult to explain (such as by regularly scanning news reports), choose one of them, conduct an in-depth literature review, spot the theoretical 'gap', prepare a research proposal, attempt to gain access to relevant data, analyse the data using 'informed speculation' (i.e. theorizing) and publish the (hopefully) interesting and even better, counter-intuitive findings that provide readers with an idea or a way of seeing that they had not previously entertained. This problem-driven research starts by identifying an empirical problem encountered in the world and seeking and understanding real-life problems that drive the choice of a theoretical frame. In contrast, in a paradigm-driven research, questions are derived from within a theoretical frame by identifying 'gaps' in the existing literature, and then seeking empirical phenomena that could help address these gaps (Lounsbury and Beckman, 2014). Both approaches need to offer a distinctive theoretical contribution whatever the starting point may be.

Conducting research in such a structured way – whether problem driven or theory driven – is risky for a large number of reasons, not least because we may not gain access to important, and potentially highly sensitive, data about the exciting phenomenon (such as a scandal). Moreover, despite our best efforts to spot the theoretical gap before collecting data, we may not be able to frame our findings in a way that reviewers accept as a distinctive theoretical contribution. Even if we do manage to gain access to all relevant documentation about the particular phenomenon we are investigating (such as judicial proceedings) we may need assistance to understand and interpret much of the data. For this purpose, we may be dependent on interviews with 'informants'. Yet, the issues associated with memory loss and retrospective sensemaking are well known (e.g. Danneels, 2011, p. 4). Indeed, readers often find direct observation and in situ interviews more persuasive.

This results in a paradox: in order to do 'good research' we need to carefully plan our study and be as specific as possible about our objectives to gain approval from funding bodies, ethics committees and the like. Moreover, both the planning process and gaining relevant approvals take time. However, once the researcher is ready to begin the study the interesting phenomenon will probably already have passed. Hence, 'good' research may generate uninteresting or 'poor' results. In addition, a key strength of qualitative data is often to be able to generate more innovative, less formulaic research (Reinecke et al., 2016).

One way around this time lag issue is to switch to quantitative methods – a strategy that is not uncommonly recommended at some business schools to PhD students and junior faculty members in order to maximize research output. Yet, we know that some of the most impactful publications are based on qualitative studies and that there are very good reasons that some of us are drawn to qualitative methods, such as a strong interest in understanding specific and complex dynamics.

An alternative strategy exists that may be perceived as even riskier than the qualitative approach outlined above: to immerse oneself in a particular setting early on, meticulously collect data, be attentive to initially incomprehensible phenomena, and follow these up with an iterative process of directed data collection and analysis; hypotheses are generated and 'tested' on the fly. In other words, there is the possibility of adopting an emergent research design as an alternative avenue to using a standardized recipe. Such an approach reduces the time lag between the interesting findings and data collection to the point that they may intersect and even turn the traditional research process on its head: from the wealth of primary data that has been collected, multiple research questions may emerge afterwards. This, of course, is not too different from quantitative forms of research that start by compiling data series and subsequently explore relationships between them. However, the qualitative researcher benefits from hopefully having access to very fine-grained ('rich') data and a very detailed appreciation of some of the complexities associated with the particular setting.

Gradual and deep immersion in the field, rather than a short and well-planned visit, allows a researcher to follow up on observations that may seem odd and difficult to explain. The simplistic map that initially served as a guide may be discarded, or at least temporarily ignored, in order to explore the paths that we were unaware of. By trying to explain things that initially do not make sense to us we increase the chances that we may come across something that our peers also find intriguing. Not branching out is thus riskier with regard to being able to generate something that our academic peers may consider 'interesting' (Davis, 1971). Obviously, frequent following up requires a lot of time and effort. But so does every meaningful enterprise.

In summary, adopting an emergent research design may actually be the least risky method of gaining access to interesting data. However, given our discussion of reporting our methods above, is it risky to reveal what we have actually done to reviewers (or others in our scholarly community who may judge us)? In this respect, it is worth pointing out that there have been increased calls by journal editors for researchers to make the methods they employed more transparent. Seasoned qualitative reviewers know that most qualitative studies – even when they begin with a clearly defined research question – tend to take unexpected turns along the way. They know that qualitative researchers often do not know where they will end up and that this iterative process poses immense challenges. Hence, they can generally tell when the description of the methods sounds too neat to be true and may actually appreciate honest attempts to spell out how the study really unfolded. Moreover, a very detailed description – even if it does not end up in the final version of a paper (and may be left in an initial submission for the appendix) – represents useful data for reviewers that not only helps them assess the trustworthiness of claims but also the innovativeness of the researchers.

Thankfully, there is also increasing recognition in our field that there is no 'boilerplate' or accepted template for writing up and reporting qualitative research (Pratt, 2009) and that variation in the tools, techniques and processes adopted provides scope for multiple ontological and epistemological assumptions to co-exist (Morgan and Smircich, 1980). The value of the recognition and acceptance of such diversity also ties into our next point, namely furthering our own intellectual development, as we discuss below.

We have argued above that generating insights is not just a means to an end but can be regarded as an end in itself. In other words, we may derive satisfaction from our own learning experiences. Furthermore, we know that the most effective method of learning is by reflecting on our own successes and failures. Unfortunately, not having much to hold onto and being free to explore is likely to result in uncomfortable mistakes and setbacks. Luckily in our field, this rarely results in life threatening experiences. By trying out new methodological approaches, considering new theoretical angles and exposing ourselves to new empirical settings (or areas within them), we have the ability to learn so much more than we could by following a pre-defined plan. As Robert Chia (2014) has noted, research, if done conscientiously, involves searching again, again and again.

Doing research in this way alters it from being simply a means of generating one or several publications about the particular topic to helping us thrive intellectually and increase our ability to respond effectively to new challenges. It is the ability to know how and when to improvise that sets leaders apart from others (Barrett, 2012), whether in management, the arts or – as we are trying to argue – academic research. Additionally, recognizing that we can never reach closure and that something new is always potentially lurking behind the corner helps us appreciate complexity and counteract narrowmindedness.

Of course, the fact that we learn most when we let go of preconceived ideas (including plans), experiment (or improvise) and, crucially, reflect upon experiences, is very well-known in theories of learning and change (Argyris, 1999; Schön, 1983). Notably, and linking back to our discussion regarding the ability to disseminate our insights, the honest reporting of the research process may also provide learning opportunities for reviewers.

With regard to our third desirable outcome for academic researchers, namely being motivated to continue researching a phenomenon, it is often said that doing research can be a very lonely, and perhaps dull, affair. We may over time come to the conclusion that what we set out to study is not that interesting to us after all. However, as one informant (an experienced manager in the public sector) once noted to one of us, even a meeting that can seem like a complete waste of time will tend to provide 'a nugget of information'. Seeking and following up on interesting avenues, even if these are not entirely aligned with our initial objectives, can help us stay curious and motivated without abandoning the field. This means that we not only increase the risk of having something interesting to report to our peers but also of actually enjoying the process (even if it may be a very bumpy ride at times). By embracing the possibilities of an emergent research design we may avoid the potentially painful realization that what we set out to do is not resulting in interesting findings and that redirection is called for. Hence, the adoption of an emergent research design may actually at times be more comforting than reliance on a previously generated map – especially when we realize that the map may actually blind us from the very interesting phenomena that surround us.

## Rene's Confessional Tale

Having discussed some of the risks and opportunities associated with the adoption of an emergent research design, we will now illustrate some of the above-mentioned points with confessional tales of our own. The first one deals with Rene's research on organizational change in public healthcare and begins like this:

In July 2010 the UK government announced controversial plans to fundamentally reform one of the largest organizations (or organizational systems) in the world – the National Health Service (NHS). The proposal was titled 'Liberating the NHS' (DH 2010) and sought to shift responsibilities for providing publicly funded healthcare services from the government to local groups of clinicians and allow 'any willing provider', including private companies, to bid for contracts to deliver these services.

This announcement gained widespread media attention for several reasons: first and foremost, it was regarded by many as a step towards the privatization of the cherished public healthcare system. Second, several commentators drew attention to potential ethical issues if medical doctors[1] were put in charge of managing the healthcare system. It was argued that they would have an incentive to reduce patients' access to expensive services, thereby conflicting with their objective of providing them with the best possible treatments. Even doctors themselves largely opposed this added responsibility. Third, such a major form of organizational restructuring (which involved abolishing hundreds of existing organizational entities and replacing them with new ones), was acknowledged as incurring very high transition costs and uncertainty.

What immediately attracted my attention – based on my interests in organizational restructuring and strategic change implementation – was the plan to hand over responsibilities for managing healthcare budgets (and manage contracts with healthcare service providers, such as hospitals) from local and regional government bodies run by civil servants to consortia run by groups of general practitioners (GPs) across the country. This seemed to me to be a case of an attempt to implement co-optation (cf. Selznick, 1949) on an unprecedented scale and was sure to trigger somewhat unpredictable dynamics.

The most obvious type of study to conduct in this context (from a healthcare management research point of view, which generally favours quantitative methods) would be to compare some healthcare service measures before and after the implementation of reforms and then provide a verdict on whether the reforms appeared to be contributing to positive or negative outcomes. However, such a study would neglect the actual transition process and require the gathering of data once the changes had settled. Moreover, given the frequency of organizational restructuring in the NHS, it was unclear whether a steady state would ever transpire. Additionally, it would be virtually impossible to attribute any outcomes to these specific organizational changes. Finally, it was unclear whether these reforms were actually going to be implemented at all.

I was more interested in understanding how stakeholders would respond to the reform announcements and how these responses could begin to influence their work. I thought it might be interesting to see (in some detail) how doctors and non-clinical managers would negotiate their roles and responsibilities with regard to managing local healthcare systems and whether the actual practice of healthcare systems management (including contract management) would change or remain stable as a result.

Without a clearly defined research question and theoretical framing in mind, and having very little a priori knowledge about the NHS and healthcare contract management, I initially set out to do four things: (1) find out as much as possible about the empirical context and phenomenon, namely the NHS and healthcare contract management, (2) start building a network of potential informants, (3) capture developments and responses related to the planned reforms via interviews, news reports and attending relevant events, and (4) read up on organizational change theories in order to help me make sense of my data and identify potential theoretical contributions.

Yet, after having conducted over a dozen interviews and collected data from a variety of other sources I had the feeling that I did not really know what healthcare contract management entailed in practice. A lot of jargon was used that I was initially unable to decipher. This was frustrating. At the same time, it was also strangely motivating: I thought that once I did actually 'get it' I would be able to share the details of this largely unknown but tremendously important practice – involving the management of over £100 billion and responsibility for the provision of healthcare services for a population of over 50 million people – with the world. I, perhaps naively, believed that this would already represent an important contribution to the social sciences and that this alone (apart from any sophisticated theoretical contribution) therefore warranted my perseverance. My desire to know as much as possible about healthcare contract management – in terms of both the details and the wider context – eventually led to me spending several months 'shadowing' (Czarniawska, 2007) a few contract managers (i.e. following them around for entire work days), while also reading many books and articles dealing with the history of the NHS and contract management.

At some point I reached what we could call the 'sweet spot' for empirical research: I was familiar enough with the empirical context so as not to be completely overwhelmed with information. Importantly, I had also not yet 'gone native'. This meant that there were still plenty of things that seemed odd or strange to me, which I saw as opportunities that had to be explained, thereby potentially resulting in a theoretical contribution of some kind. Moreover, I had by now gained some trust from influential informants, which allowed me to follow up on interesting avenues.

I did not know it at the time but what ultimately helped me most was following up on a comment by one contract manager who I had been shadowing for several months. She noted that her relationships with members of local healthcare service providers had always been very positive, which contrasted markedly with her colleagues who were dealing with local community care services. 'How so?' I asked. She then told me that community care contract meetings were so difficult that attendees could be seen crying in the corridor afterwards. Now, this I had to see! Subsequent interviews with people involved in community care contract management referred to a 'messy divorce' between the organizations involved. This was something I began to follow up and try to explain. It simply did not make a lot of sense to me. Furthermore, by examining what was going on in multiple service areas I was able to compare and contrast developments across them (resulting, for instance, in Wiedner et al., forthcoming).

Finding answers to the puzzling divorce was not easy. This was complicated by the fact that several individuals who were directly involved in managing the apparently dysfunctional inter-organizational relationship appeared to be reluctant to share information with me. Again, this reluctance made me even more curious, resulting in attempts to gain as much information from as many sources as possible. These attempts resulted in my increased awareness that a whole host of complex issues existed that I could not possibly hope to understand completely. However, this awareness alone arguably increased my confidence in the specific arguments I later discussed with co-authors and presented in submissions to conferences and academic reviewers.

Moreover, what initially looked like obstacles to data collection turned out to be opportunities. For instance, throughout my research I did not have a car. Yet, many healthcare management meetings took place at relatively remote locations and often without teleconference facilities. I essentially had two choices – either not attend the meetings in person (and rely on documents and recollections from – not necessarily open – participants) or ask participants if anyone could offer me a lift. These car rides turned out to be hugely beneficial for my research – they offered the ability to establish social bonds with potential informants, gain an understanding of what was actually on their minds, and gather initial feedback from them on my own interpretations of events.

Ultimately the transfer of budget responsibilities from civil servants to doctors became part of an interesting empirical setting that served as a background; it did not explicitly form part of the research questions that ended up in papers. In fact, what I had originally thought would be most interesting, namely how medical doctors become contract managers, turned out to be rather predictable with hindsight: most continued to work as doctors and were content to let experienced contract managers continue to deal with contract issues. This is not to say that I would not have been able to generate theoretical contributions if I had continued to focus on this particular issue. However, if I had done so I would have missed out on other interesting opportunities that I personally was more excited about and therefore probably invested more energy in.

In other words, this experience does not simply demonstrate that I was lucky to find interesting things in the field that then allowed me to construct theoretical contributions. It highlights that an emergent research design provides the flexibility to follow potentially interesting developments and suggests that the ability to identify and follow such paths is enhanced by immersing yourself in the field, coupled with a high degree of attentiveness. It requires a willingness to explore relatively hidden paths and continuous scanning of, and learning about, the terrain to find them, rather than adopting a narrow focus.

## Shaz's Confessional Tale

The second story deals with how consumers in the UK collectively contributed to the institutionalization of the practice of text messaging, and how this affected the field of mobile telephony (Ansari and Phillips, 2011). As a PhD researcher, I entered the field to explore how change occurred there. Without a clearly defined research question and theoretical framing in mind, and having very little a priori knowledge about mobile communications, like Rene, I also set out to find out as much as possible about the empirical context, identify potential informants, capture developments via interviews, archival data and attending relevant events, and read up on relevant theories in order to identify potential theoretical contributions.

Around 2000, in the wake of stagnating revenues from voice-based telephony, the industry sought new ways to increase the 'average revenue per user' (ARPU) by introducing sophisticated data-based mobile services via the new Wireless Application Protocol (WAP) system. This was seen by members of the field as a natural extension of mobile telephony that would make the Internet mobile and widely accessible However, although WAP was intended as the first major mobile data service to provide direct access to Internet content and to take over from voice telephony as the main source of industry growth, it had very limited success. Instead, it was a completely unanticipated service that created a transformation in the industry as consumers adopted SMS (text messaging) despite the fact that it had very limited functionality and that it had not even been intended for consumers. Although consumers did not develop the product that enabled text messaging, they built innovative practices around it that became highly institutionalized over time as the standard solution to their communication needs. While the entire industry was focused on WAP and 3G technologies, text messaging signalled a change in the nature of mobile communication from the 'spoken word' to the 'written message' that happened 'behind the backs' of the industry. The 'ugly duckling' of second-generation mobile telephony turned out to be the biggest consumer-driven 'killer application' (main source of profit) for the mobile telephony industry even though it had not been initially promoted by the industry.

At the time of the study that spanned seven years, I talked to almost every stakeholder in the field – mobile network operators, virtual operators, handset manufacturers, suppliers, trade journals, regulatory agencies, industry associations, content providers, standards bodies, other supporting and related organizations, and consumers – business and private – who depended on the system and related technologies to communicate wirelessly. Yet, even after having conducted dozens of interviews and collected data from a variety of other sources I had the feeling that I did not really know what had really driven the diffusion and institutionalization of this practice. After exploring several blind alleys, I was still wedded to the 'diffusions of innovation' framework given my familiarity with that literature at the time, and was simply unable to 'see' the phenomenon through a different lens. Everyone in the industry I spoke to wanted to talk about WAP and mobile Internet and while they acknowledged the importance of texting, given that they hadn't purposefully promoted it, they didn't have much to say about how it actually got there. Clearly, few were interested in talking about a development for which they could take little if any credit.

A few lone voices, however, stood out: one senior executive admitting that the industry had 'failed to spot' SMS's potential that had simply diffused behind the industry's backs, and another describing it as a 'blindspot'. A few analysts' reports I read also confirmed this perspective. Thus, it was only through continued and ongoing engagement in the field and being open to emergent and serendipitous developments that my co-author and I began to identify the role of consumers that industry respondents rarely talked about and that, as was evident from the literature review, had also been neglected in theories of institutional change.

Yet observations in the field (and occasionally informal discussions) of consumers in various settings such as trains, malls and cafés allowed me to gain a first-hand view of how consumers used texting in their day-to-day activities. Thus in a manner I sort of stumbled upon focusing on the active role of consumers – an actor that is often the focus of attention in the field of marketing but much less so in the field of organization theories, and in particular institutional theory.

As I got deeper into studies of change in institutional fields, it became apparent that these studies had paid scant attention to consumers despite acknowledging them to be a key constituent of a field. At the time, focusing on consumers in institutional theory had seemed unwise. We had realized that bringing consumers 'back in' was a thorny intellectual move relative to the foundations of institutional theory that argued against an overly narrow focus on how consumer preferences shape markets.

A return to these earlier approaches was risky as against focusing on the efforts of other formally organized field constituents as had been the dominant ideological orientation in institutional theory. However, I noticed that there was little contestation against this innovation as is usually seen when more organized actors come into conflict, such as when new entrants threaten to capture part of the incumbents' turf or when regulators pass laws that undermine incumbent domination. I then realized that consumer-led field changes may not necessarily be characterized by contestation to the same degree as industry-led changes. It also became evident that innovative consumer activities are driven by more personal goals such as the search for autonomy and identity or the solution of practical problems but their collective even if uncoordinated activities can lead to institutional change in a field. This yielded the key theoretical focus – consumer-led institutional change.

The paper eventually published in *Organization Science* (Ansari and Phillips, 2011) in retrospect appears to have been motivated by a clearly articulated theoretical issue – understanding the under-theorized role of consumers in fomenting field-level change as a general neglect of consumers in institutional theory has tended to obscure the dynamics of how consumers' activities impact organizational fields. While this question appears to be clearly motivated and well-articulated in the paper, it was, unsurprisingly, the outcome of a long, drawn out, iterative and messy process in trying to understand a key change in this field.

The process was far from linear, mechanical, or straightforward. Interestingly, an earlier version of the paper based on the same data had been rejected after going through three rounds of revision in the *Academy of Management Journal*. Clearly, my co-author and I had been unable to come up with a convincing research question and theoretical motivation as we vacillated between the literature on the diffusion of innovations and institutional change and had been unable to convince the editors and the reviewers despite being given multiple opportunities to do so. Yet a reflection of this admittedly frustrating and hugely disappointing experience (the news of the paper's rejection arrived by email on New Year's Eve) made it clear that the effort did not go in vain. Our ability to articulate alternative explanations and paths not taken, learning from theoretical framings tried and discarded, and deep (even if in the end disappointing) engagement with the review process at AMJ, arguably helped us increase credibility to transparently acknowledge how initial analytical choices were ill-suited and thus, adapted in subsequent iterations, led to revising earlier interpretations. Some of these arguments were not included in the final published version at *Organization Science* but were part of the open and frank communication we had with the reviewers and the editor in the response letters, and arguably helped us increase the credibility of our approach.

The key point here is not that I was simply lucky to find interesting things in the field that then allowed me to appropriately frame the findings and offer novel theoretical contributions. Rather, it highlights that an emergent research design opens up the possibilities to follow potentially interesting leads that may crystallize through deep immersion, sensitivity and open-mindedness. These insights suggest a process approach to academic research, where like other complex processes, such as innovation (Garud et al., 2011), human development (Reinecke and Ansari, 2015) and strategy (Mintzberg, 1978), it is complex, uneven, disorderly, and non-linear and does not follow a natural trajectory or a logic set in advance. Unanticipated and unexpected developments that emerge during the research journey can conspire to change various parameters even as a journey unfolds and require continual adaptation even as one has to 'close out' or 'freeze' the process. This can yield novel research directions and theorization (Alvesson and Kärreman, 2007).

## Conclusion

In this chapter we have argued for explicitly acknowledging the merits of adopting an emergent research design. We have noted that what often turns a research project into something extremely interesting is rarely made explicit in research outputs. Instead, vague references to an 'iterative process' of data collection and analysis are often made. This, perhaps, removes idiosyncratic aspects of a study that may be deemed irrelevant in terms of demonstrating theoretical contributions. However, this exclusion serves to mystify the methodological process and downplay the central importance of being both very attentive to our surroundings and being willing and able to exploit new, and potentially hitherto neglected or underexplored, avenues.

However, we also want to be clear that we do not advocate an 'anything goes' attitude that replaces planning, preparation and analytical rigour. Clearly, planning serves several important purposes, not least with regard to ensuring that we do not get completely lost or overwhelmed as we explore many alleys. Moreover, we do need to keep in mind the opportunity costs of following up everything that may be interesting because we have a limited amount of time and face other resource constraints. By following many paths, we, of course, run the risk of ultimately having only very little to say about many things instead of gaining a very deep understanding of a particular issue or phenomenon. We necessarily need to manage this risk. Nevertheless, we should treat every supposed 'cul de sac' as a learning experience rather than a waste of time. Dead ends signal new paths to be pursued.

Finally, we must acknowledge that a researcher may simply be very uncomfortable with an emergent research design or, despite extensive training, find it difficult to be constantly attentive to emergent research avenues. Certain research techniques are clearly not for everyone.

In conclusion, we suggest that an emergent research design offers potentially high rewards and that some of the biggest risks can be effectively managed. In other words, good research, whether formally planned or emergent, ultimately comes down to preparation, training, and skilled execution, rather than luck. Importantly, we argue that an emergent research design (when adopted carefully) is not necessarily riskier than the alternative of closely following a predefined research design. In fact, we have stressed that in many respects it appears to be less risky in terms of generating outputs that we are satisfied with. However, it does require resistance. And, as we all know, resistance necessarily entails effort.

## Note

1 It became obvious very quickly that only certain types of clinicians, namely medical doctors, would be expected to represent 'clinicians' (which include a number of occupational groups, including nurses), given their status in the healthcare field.

## References

Alvesson, M., 2003. Beyond neopositivists, romantics, and localists: A reflexive approach to interviews in organizational research. Acad. Manage. Rev. 28, 13–33.

Alvesson, M., Kärreman, D., 2007. Constructing mystery: Empirical matters in theory development. Acad. Manage. Rev. 32, 1265–1281. https://doi.org/10.2307/20159366.

Alvesson, M., Spicer, A., 2012. A stupidity-based theory of organizations. J. Manag. Stud. 49, 1194–1220. doi:10.1111/j.1467-6486.2012.01072.x.

Ansari, S., Phillips, N., 2011. Text me! New consumer practices and change in organizational fields. Organ. Sci. 22, 1579–1599. https://doi.org/10.1287/orsc.1100.0595.

Argyris, C., 1999. *On Organizational Learning*, 2nd ed. Blackwell Business, Oxford.

Balogun, J., 2006. Managing change: Steering a course between intended strategies and unanticipated outcomes. Long Range Plann. 39, 29–49. doi:10.1016/j.lrp. 2005.02.010.

Barley, S. R., 1990. Images of imaging: Notes on doing longitudinal field work. Organ. Sci. 1, 220–247.

Barrett, F. J., 2012. *Yes to the Mess: Surprising Leadership Lessons from Jazz*. Harvard Business Review Press, Boston, MA.

Beech, N., Hibbert, P., MacIntosh, R., McInnes, P., 2009. But I thought we were friends? Life cycles and research relationships, in: Ybema, S., Yanow, D., Wels, H., Kamsteeg, F. (eds.), *Organizational Ethnography: Studying the Complexities of Everyday Life*. Sage, London, pp. 196–214.

Bourdieu, P., 1996. Understanding. Theory Cult. Soc. 13, 17–37.

Carlile, P., 2002. A pragmatic view of knowledge and boundaries: Boundary objects in new product development. Organ. Sci. 13, 442–455. doi:10.1287/orsc.13.4.442.2953.

Chia, R., 2014. Reflections on the distinctiveness of European management scholarship. Eur. Manag. J. 32, 683–688. doi:10.1016/j.emj.2014.06.002.

Corbin, J., Strauss, A., 2015. *Basics of Qualitative Research: Techniques and Procedures for Developing Grounded Theory*, 4th ed. Sage, Los Angeles, CA.

Czarniawska, B., 2007. *Shadowing: And Other Techniques for Doing Fieldwork in Modern Societies*. Copenhagen Business School Press, Copenhagen.

Danneels, E., 2011. Trying to become a different type of company: Dynamic capability at Smith Corona. Strateg. Manag. J. 32, 1–31. doi:10.1002/smj.863.

Davis, M. S., 1971. That's interesting: Towards a phenomenology of sociology and a sociology of phenomenology. Philos. Soc. Sci. 1, 309–344.

de Rond, M., Thietart, R.-A., 2007. Choice, chance, and inevitability in strategy. Strateg. Manag. J. 28(5), 535–551. https://doi.org/10.1002/smj.602.

DH, 2010. Equity and excellence: Liberating the NHS (White Paper) [Online]. www.dh.gov.uk/en/Publicationsandstatistics/Publications/PublicationsPolicyAndGuidance/DH_117353 (accessed 12 December 2011).

Eisenhardt, K. M., 1989. Making fast strategic decisions in high-velocity environments. Acad. Manage. J. 32, 543–576. https://doi.org/10.2307/256434.

Fine, G. A., 1993. Ten lies of ethnography: Moral dilemmas of field research. J. Contemp. Ethnogr. 22, 267–294. doi:10.1177/089124193022003001.

Flyvbjerg, B., 2006. Five misunderstandings about case-study research. Qual. Inq. 12, 219–245. doi:10.1177/1077800405284363.

Garud, R., Gehman, J., Kumaraswamy, A., 2011. Complexity arrangements for sustained innovation: Lessons from 3M Corporation. Org. Stud. 32, 737–767.

Gioia, D. A., Corley, K. G., Hamilton, A. L., 2013. Seeking qualitative rigor in inductive research notes on the Gioia methodology. Organ. Res. Methods 16, 15–31. https://doi.org/10.1177/1094428112452151.

Lalleman, P. C. B., Smid, G. A. C., Lagerwey, M. D., Shortridge-Baggett, L. M., Schuurmans, M. J., 2016. Curbing the urge to care: A Bourdieusian analysis of the effect of the caring disposition on nurse middle managers' clinical leadership in patient safety practices. Int. J. Nurs. Stud. 63, 179–188. doi:10.1016/j.ijnurstu.2016.09.006.

Lounsbury, M., Beckman, C. M., 2014. Celebrating organization theory. J. Manage. Stud. 52, 288–308.

Mintzberg, H., 1978. Patterns in strategy formation. Manage. Sci. 24, 934–948.

Mintzberg, H., 1991. Learning 1, Planning 0: Reply to Igor Ansoff. Strateg. Manag. J. 12, 463–466.

Morgan, G., Smircich, L., 1980. The case for qualitative research. Acad. Manage. Rev. 5, 491–500. doi:10.5465/AMR.1980.4288947.

Pettigrew, A. M., 2012. Context and action in the transformation of the firm: A reprise. J. Manag. Stud. 49, 1304–1328. doi:10.1111/j.1467-6486.2012.01054.x.

Plowman, D. A., Baker, L. T., Beck, T. E., Kulkarni, M., Solansky, S. T., Travis, D. V., 2007. Radical change accidentally: The emergence and amplification of small change. Acad. Manage. J. 50, 515–543.

Pope, C., Mays, N., 1995. Reaching the parts other methods cannot reach: An introduction to qualitative methods in health and health services research. BMJ 311, 42–45.

Pratt, M. G., 2009. For the lack of a boilerplate: Tips on writing up (and reviewing) qualitative research. Acad. Manage. J. 52, 856–862.

Reinecke, J., Ansari, S., 2015. When times collide: Temporal brokerage at the intersection of markets and developments. Acad. Manage. J. 58, 618–648.

Reinecke, J., Arnold, D. G., Palazzo, G., 2016. Qualitative methods in business ethics, corporate responsibility, and sustainability research. Bus. Ethics Q. 26, xiii–xxii. doi:10.1017/beq.2016.67.

Schön, D. A., 1983. *The Reflective Practitioner: How Professionals Think in Action*. Temple Smith, London.

Selznick, P., 1949. *TVA and the Grass Roots: A Study in the Sociology of Formal Organization*. University of California Press, Berkeley, CA.

Van Maanen, J., 2011. *Tales of the Field: On Writing Ethnography*, 2nd ed. University of Chicago Press, Chicago, IL.

Weick, K. E., 1995. *Sensemaking in Organizations*. Sage, Thousand Oaks, CA.

Wiedner, R., Barrett, M., Oborn, E., forthcoming. The emergence of change in unexpected places: Resourcing across organizational practices in strategic change. Acad. Manage. J.

# 23

# REPORTING AFTER THE SUMMIT

## Getting Ethnographic Research into Print

*Katherine Chen*

### Introduction

Some of you are beginning your ethnographic journey, deciding whether to conduct research by observing or participating in an organization or similar setting. Some of you are already partway through your journey. You are developing a research question, gaining access to your field site, forming relationships with people, taking field notes on activities, or analyzing your field notes. Several of you are perched at the summit, admiring the view after a long stint or multiple rounds of collecting and analyzing data. You are contemplating your descent back to society. To share your discoveries with the wider community, you need to write and publish your ethnographic research.

While each step of ethnographic research is challenging, navigating the descent is the most treacherous. Exhilarated but exhausted, some researchers fall into a crevasse of serving other responsibilities, never to emerge, or they hibernate in the hypnotic cold, never to wake. Whether filed away in computers or cabinets, these adventurers' work has not circulated to a larger audience, where the scholarly community and public can learn from these adventurers' journeys.

As a researcher, your duties include completing a final leg of the journey: communicating your findings and the significance of understanding your phenomenon. By disseminating your research, students and the public can learn from your work, and other researchers can engage with your work, build upon it, or perhaps even refute it and discover new paradigms. You want to share why you went on this journey, what you found along the way, and why knowing this is important.

While your journey will not follow the same route as my journey, you will pass similar milestones. I am an ethnographic researcher with several peer-reviewed articles, both single-authored and co-authored, in academic journals. I have also published an award-winning book. These publications examined the growth of the organization behind the Burning Man event, an annual temporary arts community that as of 2015, drew about 67,500 persons to camp together in the Nevada Black Rock Desert. In addition to interviewing organizers and members about their experiences and perspectives, I studied this organization by observing daily office activities, organizers' meetings, volunteer trainings, and gatherings; I also conducted participant-observations as a volunteer for the Burning Man organization and as an attendee of 13 Burning Man events.

Using my experiences of conducting this research, I describe the final steps of the ethnographic journey: getting research through peer review and into print. First, I recommend reading other researchers' peer-reviewed publications, not only to learn the content, but also the craft of writing. I then describe where researchers publish and how they tend to sequence their publications. Next, I overview several conditions conducive to productive writing. I then show the writing process for one of my journal manuscripts. Finally, I review what should appear in each section of a journal manuscript.

## Getting into Print

### *Read Published Work to Understand both Craft and Content*

As a fledging author, you should not only read to learn, but also to understand the craft of writing and publishing. When reading, examine how authors communicate their content – their publications should state a research question and articulate their thesis or central research claim. Moreover, authors should explain the importance of understanding their phenomena, answering the "so what?" question.[1]

When reading, consider how researchers deploy the ethnographic method. Ethnographic research of organizations is particularly effective in revealing the everyday activities that most people take for granted. Ethnographies expose the "black box" or "inner" workings of organizations, where members cooperate – or are at odds – when collectively pursuing goals. For example, organizational ethnographers have studied:

- why employees worked hard for little compensation (Burawoy 1979),
- how corporations operated as fiefdoms, rather than meritocratic bureaucracies (Jackall 1988),
- how corporate culture energized or burned out employees (Kunda 1992),
- how self-managing teams recreated and internalized coercive control (Barker 1993),
- how routines both constrained and enabled workers (Leidner 1993),
- how organizations' charisma encouraged entrepreneurialism among members (Biggart 1989),
- how organizations thrived (vs. died) with collectivist-democratic practices (Rothschild and Whitt 1986),
- and even how vindictive workers punished annoying amusement park visitors by "accidentally" slapping their seatbelts or splitting up parties on rides (Van Maanen 1991).

More recently, organizational ethnographers have explored:

- how an elite business school inculcated students with certain values via the absence of open discussion (Anteby 2013),
- how a university and a corporation simultaneously eroded and upheld inequality with diversity measures (Berrey 2015),
- how store clerks handled class distinctions with customers (Hanser 2008),
- how medical staff resisted policy reforms in hospitals (Kellogg 2011),
- how professional facilitators inadvertently restricted deliberation processes (Lee 2015),
- how casino workers labored under surveillance (Sallaz 2009),
- and how workers enforced safety measures on oil rigs (Ely and Meyerson 2010).

When reading, examine how authors present their material. For example, what kinds of style do authors use to share their "tales"?[2] How do the authors sequence their argument – for instance, do they rely upon a chronological order, typologize their phenomena into categories, or follow persons or composites of persons? Disciplinary conventions shape how authors present their data. For instance, anthropologists share extensive descriptions and elaborate justifications for studying "up." Sociologists intersperse short and long quotes with interpretative commentary and explain how their data speaks to larger phenomena.

## *Find Out Conventions about Publishing*

As you read, decide how to target your publications. My publication approach was unconventional, reflecting my choice of topic and research site and disciplinary specialty as a sociologist. In my field, ethnographers usually first publish one or more journal articles, followed by a book that includes content from these journal articles along with other previously unpublished content. Partly, this sequence is pragmatic, as having at least one peer-reviewed publication can increase the chances of landing a tenure-track academic position.[3] Even community colleges and teaching-intensive institutions are pushing their faculty to publish sooner and more frequently for both tenure and promotion.

Institutions and departments vary in their preferred publication types, with most prioritizing publications where editors and peer reviewers (typically, researchers with methodological and/or substantive expertise in the manuscript's area) have given feedback on whether a manuscript should be published and how these manuscripts could improve. In business schools, peer-reviewed articles in management journals are the norm, but some business schools also recognize books published by university presses for tenure and promotion. Some departments in disciplines such as anthropology prefer that their faculty publish peer-reviewed monographs with university presses, while other departments prioritize peer-reviewed articles in particular journals. Departments, programs, and schools also have different metrics for how they count single-authored versus co-authored publications; some also consider the "quality" of publications based on a variety of metrics. Where you will spend your academic career – or where you aspire to move next – will factor into the kinds of publication venues that you target.

With a post-doctoral appointment followed by a tenure-track assistant professorship in a sociology department, I focused on writing my book manuscript first.[4] This involved fully rewriting my dissertation manuscript, including nine months spent reframing the introductory chapter, along with years spent in peer review and revisions. With my book in print, I switched to writing shorter manuscripts for peer-reviewed journals, and I continued to conduct follow-up field research. Focusing on the book first was a risky, "eggs in one basket" strategy since a manuscript can take years to emerge as a book: a press editor must first decide whether to send a manuscript out for review or to desk reject it; reviewers must agree to write their reports recommending publication or not; if invited to revise based on reviewers' comments, the author's revisions can take months, and these revisions must be reviewed again; the press's board must vote on whether to move forward with the publication. After the copy-editing of the page proofs and the indexing of the manuscript, the book goes to print. Since university presses release books just twice a year, in the spring and fall, authors have to time these last steps accordingly.

In comparison, some peer-reviewed journals have a quick turn-around time, with editors determining whether to send manuscripts out for review, soliciting reviewers, and then deciding whether to accept or reject manuscripts based on the reviewers' comments and assessments within several months. However, at other journals, manuscripts can languish, especially when editors have difficulties finding qualified, willing reviewers. Editors typically give reviewers between three weeks to three months to share their comments and assessments of a manuscript's merits; nonetheless, since peer review depends on volunteer efforts, tardy reviewers and laggard editors can easily add six months to a year to the review process. If editors reject the revised manuscripts, researchers must start the submission process anew, elongating the publication process.

In short, the process of publication is uncertain, as journals and university presses can operate at expedient or glacial speeds. Thus, it is essential to set up conditions that facilitate constant writing. This way, you can regularly submit manuscripts to publication outlets, generating a pipeline of writings in various stages of production.

## Dedicate Time to Write

We see researchers presenting at conferences or colloquiums, teaching in the classroom, participating in administrative meetings and committees, or conducting research in an archive, lab, or field. However, how researchers write and publish is usually invisible to budding researchers and the public. Since we are rarely privy to the moments when researchers write, novice researchers don't know how to do it or have misconceptions about the writing and publication process. Worse, we must unlearn bad habits, such as "binge" writing by penning a large number of pages in occasional bursts, forgoing sleep, and neglecting loved ones and friends.

Fortunately, several guides detail how productive scholars approach writing and publication. From Boice's (2002) and Zerubavel's (1999) handbooks, I learned to write in smaller chunks on a regular basis.[5] At the time, my most productive writing was scheduled in the morning. After writing, I could prepare and teach classes and handle service responsibilities with a lighter conscience, rather than experiencing existential dread about unfulfilled writing commitments. Moreover, scheduled, routine writing does not require inspiration or motivation. In fact, experienced researchers specifically advise against waiting for inspiration (Boice 2002, Zerubavel 1999). Productivity is a self-reinforcing waterwheel: productivity elicits productivity. By following a routine of constant practice, people are more likely to experience successful outcomes (cf. Chambliss 1989), which for researchers, involves sharing their findings.

## Find a Supportive Community

Few academics flourish in isolation.[6] Ideally, researchers should find or develop a community of people who can give constructive feedback on drafts and offer support. One common way of connecting with other researchers is to travel to a community, such as an annual conference or a weekly or monthly seminar.[7] Some researchers form or join groups that regularly meet in person (or virtually) to provide feedback on drafts. In the writing groups that I've joined or cofounded, two presenters circulate their drafts of a journal manuscript, book chapter, or memos on on-going research about a week before the gathering. When the group meets, members discuss what worked well in the manuscripts and how to improve the manuscripts. Oftentimes problems in other people's manuscripts are similar to your own, but are easier to solve collectively! Participants can also use writing groups as an accountability device when they set writing goals and report their progress back to the group (Silvia 2007). Your institution may offer resources – space, course releases, and paid facilitators – to support such writing groups.

## *Experiment*

Writing often involves constant experimenting and tinkering, including searching for appropriate literatures, reorganizing arguments, or fine-tuning the framing. By viewing my writings as drafts that I could always refine through the page proofs stage, I could avoid fixating on perfecting the first few pages. Other researchers perform similar Jedi mind tricks like calling writing "editing" to make writing less daunting.

Start each writing session by saving a new file of the previous draft; in the file label, include that day's date to differentiate that version from prior drafts. By saving a new document, you can return to older versions of that document when you need to resurrect content or references. Excised scraps – of which you will have many, if you revise enough – could seed future manuscripts.

## *Decide on Your Target Audience*

How you frame and present your work depends on your target audience. If you are presenting an unfamiliar phenomenon, you will need to spend more effort explaining your work. Since readers were not as familiar with Burning Man as they are now, I had to devote more space to explaining my phenomenon and its relevance to understanding organizations more generally.

Finding journals that are a good fit for your manuscript and timeline entails additional effort. One approach is to see where researchers who have similar interests as yours have published. Another is to look at the journals where your manuscript's cited articles appear. Read the "scopes and aims" sections of journals – usually available on journals' websites – and examine who is on their editorial board. When considering potential publication venues, ask other researchers about their experiences; this will allow you to gauge how long the review process might take at a particular venue. Allow additional time for revision and review, especially if editors change or if you experience life-changing events such as a new job or new addition to the family. For more predictability, target special issues about a relevant topic in journals; since special issues have set submission and publication deadlines, you're more likely to get a timely response. When submitting your manuscript, suggest potential reviewers, as journal editors may not have the time, expertise, or networks to corral appropriate reviewers. Even if the journal editors don't invite your suggested reviewers, your suggestions can help editors categorize your manuscript, increasing the chances that a qualified and interested reviewer will evaluate your work.

## An Example of a Journal Article Publishing Path

To illustrate the variegated paths that publications can take, I describe my experiences with writing and publishing one of my favorite papers, "Charismatizing the routine: Storytelling for meaning and agency in the Burning Man organization" (Chen 2012). This journal article emerged from the last substantive chapter that I wrote for my dissertation. This chapter's development into an article shows how a researcher can delve into open-ended, rich ethnographic data.

When conducting my observations, I hadn't planned on studying storytelling. However, while examining my field notes, I noticed that during meetings and get-togethers, members swapped stories that helped explain or clarify unfamiliar organizational guidelines and norms for newcomers and long-timers. They also shared experiences, including triumphs over adversity and otherwise forgotten moments, creating collective memories that were richer than the official organizational history documented on the website and by the media.

My field notes documented storytelling occasions like the following. At a training meeting, volunteer coordinator Molly Tirpak invited experienced volunteer managers to recount examples of how they handled instances of when "you got what you wanted or didn't want." A manager at the commissary, which served meals to workers and volunteers at the Burning Man event, told listeners how she handled a missing food delivery. Since they didn't have the time to replace these provisions by driving several hours back and forth from the nearest city, she decided to reassign volunteers to new tasks and tap the creative potential of her volunteers to make do with what they had:

> I had a huge job [managing] 35 workers.... One of the U-Hauls didn't make it, and that [vehicle] had the main dishes. I didn't know what to do. I had to go off and write down what to do ... I gave new jobs and new duties. They all had come up [with ideas about how] to deal with main food.

To underscore the story's point about how coordinators and volunteers needed to be flexible, Burning Man organizer Harley Dubois added, "This is very important to Burning Man: things change."[8]

My interview transcripts also showed how people discussed and, at times, contested stories and their interpretations, underlining how storytelling helped develop shared meaning among persons. For example, interviewee Naomi Pearce told the origins of Burning Man's first theme camp, which inspired subsequent campers to decorate or host interactive activities around a central motif, as follows:

> But the way I heard it was this guy ... decorated his camp in ... Christmas decorations ... and wore a Santa suit and played the same tape [*hums "Sleigh Bells are Ringing" song*] all weekend long, and the deal was that you could come into his tent and enjoy a free glass of eggnog, but you had to eat the fruitcake first, and that's like the whole conversation starter ...
>
> You've got to give the man some serious credit to wear a Santa suit in the middle of desert at the end of August.... Pretty soon, you've got people using stuff that's familiar to them, like the armed disgruntled postal workers were actually armed disgruntled postal workers.[9]

During her interview, organizer Harley Dubois countered this widely circulated story with two examples of what she felt were the true progenitors of theme camps:

> The first time that I saw what I thought was a theme camp would be rudimentary compared to what Peter Doty did [with Xmas Camp], but it was like only the year before that, and that was the co-founder Jerry James ... [he] built himself a little house to live in while he was out there, but it was like the perfect picture, little pitched roof, perfectly square idealized child's rendering of a house ... he would invite people into his house ...
>
> Somebody else used to have ... some kind of military vehicle and ... a full tea set ... and you could swing by and have a cup of tea, and he would be out there in his military wear with everything that you could possibly imagine, the most elegant military ... British feeling set-up with this fine china and great silver.[10]

Dubois acknowledged the Christmas Camp story's appeal and resonance, commenting "I actually would like to get it out of text on the [Burning Man] website, but I've never been successful at doing that because it makes a good story."[11]

When I realized how important this storytelling was in this organization, I investigated what other researchers had published about storytelling. At the time, I couldn't find much literature on storytelling in organizations, so I looked for articles in sociology and other disciplines, including the humanities. From these searches, I found definitions of stories and narratives that differentiated stories from other kinds of phenomena.

Using what I had learned from the literature, I wrote an analysis of storytelling, but I felt dissatisfied. This initial analysis described what people were collectively doing, but it lacked analytic oomph. While I had many examples of storytelling and how stories were used, I didn't yet have a term to describe what people were doing. By coining terms, researchers can identify and name phenomena that might otherwise be taken for granted – for example, Kanter (1977) devised the term *tokenism*, in which a person isn't treated as an individual but rather as a representative for an entire minority group, and Hochschild ([1983] 2003) named the *second shift* for the housework and childcare done after a workday. More importantly, I was not sure about how to frame my findings; I still had to figure out what puzzle my research addressed and which audiences to target.

While rewriting my dissertation as a book manuscript, I made the difficult choice to exclude the chapter on storytelling because it didn't address my book's research question. I knew that this long and unwieldy section required much rewriting to make it worth reading, so I set it aside to rework as a separate journal article. Having additional time and distance allowed me to more fully develop my concepts and to revise the manuscript for a journal format. I continued tinkering with the draft when not working on other manuscripts and presented my evolving drafts for feedback at a conference and at several writing groups. These occasions helped me revise the draft's framing, or its central argument and the literatures that it addressed. During the question and answer period following one conference presentation, a colleague suggested that I revisit Max Weber's ([1947] 1966, [1947] 1968) routinization of charisma; this suggestion helped me frame the draft's orienting puzzle, as I elaborate in my next paragraph. In addition, a writing group colleague encouraged me to divide the ballooning chapter into two. I split the chapter into two manuscripts, which immediately made the content more manageable.[12] This split was an important one because journal articles' word limits only allow for the thorough exposition of one idea. Scrawling in the margins of my paper, another writing group colleague asked whether I had to cite all of the literature on storytelling. After this admonishment, I re-focused the literature review with an argument, and I more purposefully decided which citations to include or exclude.

These suggestions and subsequent rewritings all contributed to my "eureka" moment. While mulling over what Burning Man members were doing with storytelling, I finally realized that their efforts inverted a process that afflicts organizations. Weber's ([1947] 1968) concept of routinization of charisma describes how collectivities bound together by a charismatic leader face a dilemma: these groups risk falling apart when their leaders depart or their leaders' charisma erodes. To continue, members can formally organize. However, the rules and routines introduced by formal organization can proliferate, such that rationalization drives out meaningful experiences. In the Burning Man organization, people including the organizers, complained or joked about the introduction of bureaucratic practices. I discovered that in sharing stories, Burning Man members were trying to reinvigorate their organizing efforts with meanings that were otherwise lost or subsumed by rationalization. With this revelation, I returned to the literature. I first checked whether other researchers had developed a similar concept of "charismatizing the routine." I then delved into Weber's writings about charisma, as well as other scholars' analyses of his concept, and pursued extensions of his concept by other researchers.

Now that I had a named concept, I revisited my data. I also noticed another source of data that didn't exist when I originally conducted my ethnographic research and interviews: stories contributed by Burning Man attendees to the Burning Man website. This website's stories offered additional insight into experiences aimed at a wider audience, the general public. After completing my content analysis, in which I coded these additional stories for themes, I revised the manuscript.

When deciding where to submit my manuscript, I followed the example of another ethnographer by selecting a journal that specialized in qualitative sociological research. I submitted the manuscript with a cover letter summarizing my research question and findings to the journal editor. After receiving a "revise and resubmit" decision that invited me to make revisions for re-evaluation, I set up an Excel spreadsheet of the comments and suggestions and decided how to respond. I made many of the requested revisions, keeping track of those in my spreadsheet. As I neared the completion of the revisions, I drafted a comprehensive letter to the editor summarizing and excerpting the changes made. I also explained when reviewers' suggestions were not relevant. This letter is crucial, as some editors and reviewers use it to assess whether the revised manuscript is publishable or requires more work. Depending on the number of changes made, this letter can take a full day or more to write, so do allocate time for this step. For additional ideas of how to address reviewers' and the editor's suggestions, I also ran my revisions and summary letter by my writing group.

After some back and forth with the journal editor, my revised paper was accepted. The paper made its way through the copy-editing process to the first set of page proofs. At this stage, the copy-editor asked for clarification of a definition (an unusual request, as most copy-editors focus on grammar, spelling, and formatting, rather than content) and corrections of misspellings and inconsistent citations and references. Since copy-editing can introduce new errors, this final stage of proof-reading requires vigilance when researchers are often most exhausted and exasperated with working on their manuscripts. However, it is one of the final steps signaling the end. As a nice flourish, the journal for my article asked for a photograph to include as the cover image of that issue, allowing me to share an image from my collection. After this long journey, the article was finally published.

For me, getting the article into print wasn't the end of the journey. After this publication appeared, I was invited to present what I had learned to practitioners, some of whom organize their own events, informal groups, and organizations that are modeled on Burning Man principles and practices in communities around the world. At a workshop training for leaders of regional off-shoots of Burning Man and a local event, I ran sessions on how to use storytelling to cohere collectives. My publications have also led to invites to give presentations before local and international academic audiences as well. Through the grapevine, someone will occasionally let me know that my writings have inspired people to consider and even implement alternative organizing practices. This impact is gratifying, as one of my original motivations for researching and writing about an unconventional organization was to show how alternatives to conventional bureaucracies exist and how these can thrive.

## What Goes into a Journal Article?

Ready to forge your own path from the summit, in anticipation of sharing your vista with the larger community? Here, I show what goes into the different sections of an article. While I cover elements in the order that they appear in journal articles, some sections are easier to write first than others, and I have noted these accordingly. I also strongly recommend reading and following the steps outlined in Belcher's (2009) *Writing Your Journal Article in 12 Weeks: A Guide to Academic Publishing Success*.

## Communicate One Major Idea

What goes into a journal article? Because journals have strict word limits, you will need to focus on one major idea, with two to three supporting components. A more nuanced gamut of impressions and introspection might better fit a monograph.

## Provide an Evocative and Descriptive Title

Your title should allude to your findings and contain keywords to help readers find your article. Your data may provide a memorable subtitle. For one publication, I included a phrase drawn from a content analysis of exchanges on an electronic bulletin board: '"Plan your burn, burn your plan": How decentralization, storytelling, and communification can support participatory practices' (Chen 2016). For me, composing the title is usually one of the last inspired steps in the writing process.

## Overview Your Paper in the Abstract

The abstract, which overviews your research question, methods, findings, and contributions, is most effectively completed after you have finished writing the draft. Potential reviewers and readers may scan this section before deciding whether to review your paper or read your full manuscript.

## Introduce Your Phenomena, State Your Thesis, and Clarify Your Contributions in the Introduction

This is another section that will fully coalesce after you have written the body of the paper. Nonetheless, draft this section, as you will always refine it later. Here, you introduce what you think your research question is, along with your phenomena. The framing of your question is important and will draw the most scrutiny – reviewers will consider whether you are addressing the right literature, or perhaps answering another question. They will also assess whether your framing fits the journal, so pitching your contributions appropriately is important. Clearly state your thesis or the take-away statement that you wish readers to remember after reading your manuscript.

Close the introduction with your manuscript's contributions. Unsure what your contributions are? Read Verba's (2010) advice about writing grant proposals; Verba's presentations of paradigms about how researchers make their contributions is applicable to journal and book writing. Most people elect to *extend* existing theories and research or examine an area they feel has been *underexplored*. Fewer people *refute* existing theories or prior research, as this is a high-risk (but potentially high-reward) move. Some people may decide to *apply a theory from one field to another area* – this approach requires familiarity with literature from other areas.

One final tip: you can showcase your ethnographic work at the introduction's start. I like beginning my articles with a quote from an interview or a vignette drawn from my field notes. These immediately immerse readers in the manuscript's puzzle, so that they have a concrete example that shapes their understanding of the phenomenon.

## Position Your Paper via the Literature Review

The literature review is where you converse with prior works. Treat the literature as a generative catalyst; do not allow the literature to limit your best ideas (Becker 1986). Reviewers may ask you to include additional citations – sometimes of their own publications – into this section. While you may not always agree with these suggested citations, you can use them to understand how readers are categorizing your work and adjust accordingly.

## *Explain Your Methods*

The methods section is often the easiest section to write; thus, this is a "low stakes" section where you can start drafting your manuscript. Write this section as soon as possible to document how you undertook the research, as details about what you did, when, and how you did it will start to fade with time. Describe your field site with enough context to orient readers for subsequent sections. Help readers understand how your research is useful for understanding your puzzle.

If you are submitting your manuscript to a generalist journal, or even to a qualitative journal, your reviewers and editor may ask that you explain your methods in great detail. Or, they may even ask you to comply with positivist standards that are inapplicable to your study and research question. Keep abreast of the methods literature so that you can cite appropriate readings about ethnographic methods, when needed.

## *Flesh Out Your Findings*

The findings section contains the meat of the paper, with both your analysis and examples drawn from your data. Use subheaders to help orient readers to points that support your thesis. Unfortunately, your ethnographic data may exceed some journals' word limits. To save space, such journals favor tables that excerpt illustrative quotes into categories. However, such tables can decontextualize the data. When presenting quotes, provide enough details and analysis so that readers don't have to puzzle through, or worse, make alternative explanations.

## *Wrap Up in the Conclusion*

The conclusion is a daunting section to write, as deciding how to end the manuscript is fraught with myriad possibilities and the pressure to wrap up your work with memorable take-away points. Start by revisiting the research question and thesis. Share implications for other settings, and describe areas that other researchers might explore.[13] I sometimes end my conclusion with a vignette or quote from my data to underscore my thesis.

## *Revise and Rewrite – Up to a Point*

Typically, manuscripts go through several revisions before they are published. But, at some point, rewriting must end, so that you can submit the manuscript for review. For perfectionists, wordsmithing can become obsessional. This has an opportunity cost of working on other projects, spending time with family and friends, and attending to important responsibilities, and can impact your abilities to land a position, secure tenure, and earn a promotion. Most importantly, you are depriving your community of the chance to learn from your findings. For perfectionists and procrastinators, a set deadline is helpful. A new cache of data or another idea can always be reserved for exploration in another manuscript. With the peer review process, you will always rework your drafts, sometimes much more than you anticipate.

## Deal With the Inevitable Rejection

If you are regularly submitting manuscripts for peer review, at least one or more of your manuscripts will be rejected, for a variety of reasons. The academic profession involves fielding rejections (or worse, efforts spent repeatedly revising a manuscript, followed by rejection). Nonetheless, rejection can catalyze clearer and more substantive writing. After making revisions, you may find your paper published in a higher ranked journal, with an appreciative audience.

Note that even luminaries' manuscripts are rejected – a few might even tell you about these experiences over consolation drinks at a conference. If your manuscripts are always rejected, have a trusted colleague or two go over reviewers' comments to sort out what you could change, whether it's where you submit your manuscripts or how you have structured your manuscript.

## Get the Word Out

When your journal article is in print, the journey isn't over yet! After celebrating, let people know about your publication. For those who cannot directly access your article (some journals have costly paywalls for nonsubscribers), upload a preprint version to your personal website, institution's website, or a sharing website. Send your publication with a thank you note to colleagues who have given you feedback. Update your website and social media. Your institution may feature your publication on their website and social media. Send a note to relevant blogs, asking the bloggers if they can let readers know about your publication, or, better yet, ask if you can write a guest post showcasing your publication.[14]

If you think your research is newsworthy or of interest to the general public, work with the public relations team at your university and press to see if you can summarize your findings in layperson terms for journalists. Be prepared to answer questions right away by phone or email, as journalists have a short turnaround time with their deadlines. Some researchers get additional training, sponsored by their institutions or at their own expense, to write op-eds, and the university or press public relations team might be able to help with placing these articles. Check with your professional association, as their staff may connect you with journalists seeking experts to interview for their articles in magazines, newspapers, and blogs.

## Help Other Researchers on Their Journeys

As a published ethnographer, you have the expertise to share your craft via teaching and writing. This is especially important since the standards for ethnography are not universally shared and are often misunderstood and contested. Participate in discussions about how to conduct and appropriately evaluate ethnographic works. Agree to peer review other scholars' manuscripts in a timely manner – for the academic commons to thrive, everyone must contribute via peer review. Finally, as you teach and write, share ethnographic journeys with future generations, as I have done here. Your journey may even inspire others to forge their own paths.

## Notes

1 For some studies, answering this "so what?" question may be obvious or easy. For other studies of seemingly esoteric phenomena, readers need help understanding the salience of that research. Elsewhere, I discuss how to show the relevance of extreme cases, in which "unusual" research settings elucidate phenomena that obscured in more conventional sites (Chen 2015).

2 Van Maanen's ([1988] 2011) *Tales of the Field* is a seminal text for understanding different ways that researchers can present ethnographic data.

3 While a few academics can land tenure-track positions without any publications, these are rare situations. When weighing job applicants' merits, hiring committees are more likely to seriously consider those with peer-reviewed publications.

4 Germano (2008) has a helpful guide for how to publish a peer-reviewed book with a university press.

5 Zerubavel (1999) describes other actionable steps, such as using a calendar to cross off days not available due to other commitments, working backwards from deadlines to estimate how much time to allocate to a draft, and setting up a color-coded folder filing system to track progress of drafts.

6 Notable exceptions include the Russian mathematician Grigory Perelman, whose seclusion nonetheless led to a prize-winning discovery.

7 A few may visit individual colleagues – the Hungarian mathematician Paul Erdös, who did not have a home or family, stayed with a colleague long enough to co-write a paper and ask for a recommendation of who to visit next. During his 83-year-long lifespan, he generated 1,475 papers (Hoffman 1998).

8 Observation of lead training, July 5, 2001, San Francisco.

9 Interview with Naomi Pearce, December 1, 2000, Albany.

10 Interview with Harley Dubois, December 21, 2001.

11 Interview with Harley Dubois, December 21, 2001.

12 The second manuscript covered how storytellers used storytelling to elicit attention to their interests and otherwise overlooked organizational histories; I published this research in a specialty journal as "Storytelling: An informal mechanism of accountability for voluntary organizations" (Chen 2013).

13 Reviewers will undoubtedly suggest ideas for future studies that would fit this section.

14 Here, I plug the orgtheory blog, where I am a regular contributor, which accepts guest posts. Professional associations also have their own blogs or listservs.

# References

Anteby, M. (2013) *Manufacturing Morals: The Values of Silence in Business Education*, Chicago, IL: University of Chicago Press.

Barker, J. R. (1993) 'Tightening the iron cage: Concertive control in self-managing teams', *Administrative Science Quarterly*, 38(3): 408–437.

Becker, H. S. (1986) *Writing for Social Scientists: How to Start and Finish Your Thesis, Book, or Article*, Chicago, IL: University of Chicago Press.

Belcher, W. (2009) *Writing Your Journal Article in 12 Weeks: A Guide to Academic Publishing Success*, Thousand Oaks, CA: Sage.

Berrey, E. (2015) *The Enigma of Diversity: The Language of Race and the Limits of Racial Justice*, Chicago, IL: University of Chicago Press.

Biggart, N. W. (1989) *Charismatic Capitalism: Direct Selling Organizations in America*, Chicago, IL: University of Chicago Press.

Boice, R. (2002) *Advice for New Faculty Members: Nihil Nimus*, Needham Heights, MA: Allyn and Bacon.

Burawoy, M. (1979) *Manufacturing Consent: Changes in the Labor Process under Monopoly Capitalism*, Chicago, IL: University of Chicago Press.

Chambliss, D. F. (1989) 'The mundanity of excellence: An ethnographic report on stratification and Olympic swimmers', *Sociological Theory*, 7(1): 70–86.

Chen, K. K. (2012) 'Charismatizing the routine: Storytelling for meaning and agency in the Burning Man organization', *Qualitative Sociology*, 35(3): 311–334.

Chen, K. K. (2013) 'Storytelling: An informal mechanism of accountability for voluntary organizations', *Nonprofit and Voluntary Sector Quarterly*, 42(5): 902–922.

Chen, K. K. (2015) 'Using extreme cases to understand organizations', in K. D. Elsbach and R. M. Kramer (eds.) *Handbook of Qualitative Organizational Research: Innovative Pathways and Methods*, New York, NY: Routledge, 33–44.

Chen, K. K. (2016) '"Plan your burn, burn your plan": How decentralization, storytelling, and communification can support participatory practices', *The Sociological Quarterly*, 57(1): 71–97.

Ely, R. J. and Meyerson, D. E. (2010) 'An organizational approach to undoing gender: The unlikely case of offshore oil platforms', *Research in Organizational Behavior*, 30: 3–34.

Germano, W. (2008) *Getting It Published: A Guide for Scholars and Anyone Else Serious about Serious Books*, Chicago, IL: University of Chicago Press.

Hanser, A. (2008) *Service Encounters: Class, Gender, and the Market for Social Distinction in Urban China*, Stanford, CA: Stanford University Press.

Hochschild, A. R. ([1983] 2003) *The Second Shift*, New York: Penguin.

Hoffman, P. (1998) *The Man Who Only Loved Numbers: The Story of Paul Erdös and the Search for Mathematical Truth*, New York: Hyperion Books.

Jackall, R. (1988) *Moral Mazes: The World of Corporate Managers*, New York: Oxford University Press.

Kanter, R. M. (1977) *Men and Women of the Corporation*, New York: Basic Books.

Kellogg, K. C. (2011) *Challenging Operations: Medical Reform and Resistance in Surgery*, Chicago, IL: University of Chicago Press.

Kunda, G. (1992) *Engineering Culture: Control and Commitment in a High-Tech Corporation*, Philadelphia, PA: Temple University Press.

Lee, C. W. (2015) *Do-It-Yourself Democracy: The Rise of the Public Engagement Industry*, New York: Oxford University Press.

Leidner, R. (1993) *Fast Food, Fast Talk: Service Work and the Routinization of Everyday Life*, Berkeley, CA: University of California Press.

Rothschild, J. and Whitt, J. A. (1986) *The Cooperative Workplace: Potentials and Dilemmas of Organizational Democracy and Participation*, New York: Cambridge University Press.

Sallaz, J. (2009) *The Labor of Luck: Casino Capitalism in the United States and South Africa*, Berkeley, CA: University of California Press.

Silvia, P. J. (2007) *How to Write a Lot: A Practical Guide to Productive Academic Writing*, Washington, DC: American Psychological Association.

Van Maanen, J. ([1988] 2011) *Tales of the Field: On Writing Ethnography*, 2nd ed., Chicago, IL: University of Chicago Press.

Van Maanen, J. (1991) 'The smile factory: Work at Disneyland', in P. J. Frost, L. F. Moore, M. R. Louis, C. C. Lundberg, and J. Martin (eds.) *Reframing Organizational Culture*, Newbury Park, CA: Sage, 58–76.

Verba, C. (2010) 'Writing fellowship proposals: The predissertation stage proposal'. Online. Available at: www.gsas.harvard.edu/images/stories/pdfs/scholarly_pursuits_writing_fellowship_proposals_pre-diss. pdf (accessed 5 July 2016).

Weber, M. ([1947] 1966) 'The types of authority and imperative co-ordination', in *Max Weber: The Theory of Social and Economic Organization*, ed. T. Parsons, trans. A. M. Henderson and T. Parsons, New York: Free Press, 324–423.

Weber, M. ([1947] 1968) 'The nature of charismatic authority and its routinization', in *Max Weber on Charisma and Institution Building*, ed. S. N. Eisenstadt, Chicago, IL: University of Chicago Press, 48–65.

Zerubavel, E. (1999) *The Clockwork Muse: A Practical Guide for Writing Theses, Dissertations, and Books*, Cambridge, MA: Harvard University Press.

# 24

# REASONING WITH QUALITATIVE DATA

## Balancing a Theoretical Contribution

*Saku Mantere*

When we first get acquainted with the world of scholarly publishing, receiving our first decision letter from a journal or attending a publishing workshop taught by a more senior colleague, most of us are struck by the importance of making a *theoretical contribution*. It's quite surprising how important such contributing is made to be, really. The intuition I at least had when I entered the business was that the quality of a publication largely hung on the shape and implementation of empirical research design, that is, was the data large, of good quality and from a sexy company. I was convinced that great papers were built on great methodological designs. Yet, funnily enough, while it would be unfair to say that such methodological concerns are insignificant, the make or break issue in whether most manuscripts ultimately get accepted and read seems to be whether the authors manage to influence a particular theoretical program by having something novel and interesting to say.

This chapter is about how theoretical contributions are made. I will draw mainly on my experiences in writing, reviewing and editing scholarly papers, as well as in teaching qualitative research to doctoral and master's students in Europe and North America. This is reflected in the writing style, which I will attempt to keep pretty close to the ground. Readers interested in the background assumptions for my arguments will find a more rigorous take in the two papers that I have co-authored with Mikko Ketokivi on reasoning in organizational research (Ketokivi and Mantere, 2010; Mantere and Ketokivi, 2013).

I have never had an easy time publishing my qualitative papers. This is not to say that hypothesis testing is easier to publish than qualitative work: getting published in good journals is hard. But qualitative work has its idiosyncratic challenges. Most processes involve seemingly endless rounds of complete rewrites, and the best outcome one often dares to hope for is another major revision request with a high risk of failure. I have a sense that most of my colleagues would report a similar sentiment and those who don't are blessed, inexperienced or dishonest. The good news is that for the most part, I seldom feel that the published argument, despite being radically different from the one I initially submitted, is worse in its first formulation.

"Reversal of strategic change," a paper I published in the *Academy of Management Journal* with Henri Schildt and John Sillince in 2012 was perhaps the clearest example from all my work where the argument changed framing radically through the process of revisions. The first manuscript that was submitted was about the role of narratives in organizational identity change. The final manuscript has neither narratives nor identity it; it's a strategic change paper. The final manuscript has a pretty clear contribution on how thinking about the change experienced by one relatively small branch of Finnish government could influence thinking about change endeavors that get canceled before realization. Most importantly, the first version of the manuscript did not have a theoretical contribution, but the final product did.

Indeed, it would seem that few qualitative papers are like Baby Jesus: perfect in every way from the moment of conception.[1] Papers seem to reach maturity in the review process. Sadly, as editor and reviewer, I have also perceived a growing tendency of writing papers for the review process rather than for publication; a practice which the economist Bengt Holmström has compared with showing up at the Metropolitan Opera and expecting to be taught how to sing.

## Contribution as a "Sweet Spot" between Data, Theory and Argument

Theoretical arguments are derived from empirical data through reasoning. Reasoning lies somewhere between the domains of methodology and theory; it has cognitive, computational and rhetorical aspects (see Ketokivi and Mantere, 2010; Mantere and Ketokivi, 2013). Reasoning is foundational to argumentation, and thus at the heart of scientific enterprise, because argumentation fuels critical discourse. Argumentation consists of presenting "reasons" for scientific claims, for which scholars seek acceptance from their peers in adding to the body of knowledge (Toulmin, 2003). Reasoning is by nature hard because human beings are more comfortable intuiting ("thinking fast") than reasoning ("thinking slow") (Kahneman, 2011).

Reasoning about qualitative data involves working with three core components: your data, the argument you present, and the theoretical discourse in which you seek to make that argument. The resulting triangle (Figure 24.1) is the playing field that you face when you are called upon to make a point. Typically, you face this challenge when you defend a thesis or revise a paper: you will not get far if all three elements are not present in your work at least at some level.

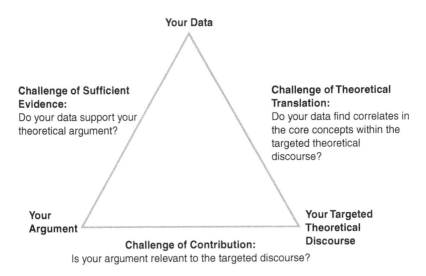

*Figure 24.1* Challenges in Reasoning with Qualitative Data

If your research design is not strong enough to warrant examination, you don't get to play. If your argument is so unclear that is it not visible, same thing.

And if there is no sense of a theoretical discourse, there is little hope that your arguments can reach an interested audience. But I say this with some reservations. There are those that claim the field is too preoccupied with theory and that hurts us. Those papers that make relevant arguments with sufficient empirical support but without theoretical translation are thus interesting. I have seen very few of those but I know people think they do exist and that such papers, because they are free from dogmatic beliefs inherent to theoretical programs, can be particularly innovative. Some people feel that cross-disciplinary work is also hampered by our over reliance on theory. New journals have been founded with the intent of capturing such papers, most notably the *Academy of Management Discoveries*. Established institutions such as the *Strategic Management Journal* are now allowing for what they call empirical contributions alongside theoretical ones. It may be that a new genre of writing will emerge out of these efforts and for the better; for now, this is my story and I stick to it. I am saying no theoretical framing, no contribution in our field.

The end points of the triangle themselves are a bit hard to pin down. What is a good argument? What constitutes a good theoretical framing? The figure starts to make a whole lot more sense when you turn your attention to the edges between the end points. A part of what makes a good argument is sufficient evidence: the edge that lies between your argument and your data. Do you have data to warrant your argument (Ketokivi and Mantere, 2010)? Qualitative data is complex and often ambiguous; how do you prove your point?

The other edge, leading out of your argument, to your targeted theoretical discourse presents the challenge of relevance; even if you manage to spell out your findings in the terminology of that theory, is that going to be novel or interesting to the participants in that research program? Will you be able to convince scholars in that program that they do not already know what you claim, or even worse, that they have disputed your claims?

Between your data and the theoretical discourse lies the challenge of theoretical translation. Often, again due to the complexity of qualitative data, many stories can be told, depending on which discourse one targets. During the revisions on our 2012 *AMJ* article with Henri Schildt and John Sillince, we debated about whether our story at hand should be told in the context of sensemaking, framing, identity, organizational change or organizational knowledge. This is because our cases surprise us: we could not have imagined what we would end up writing about when we were producing the data. Organizations do not behave the way we expect them to and often the really interesting story emerges to address questions pertaining to a different theory than anticipated.

## How to Avoid Getting Paralyzed by One Challenge

Meeting all challenges is not a simple matter of checking off boxes one by one. The requirements tend to conflict. Indeed, I have found that revising papers involves taking steps back while taking steps forward. You fix one thing and end up being criticized for a problem that was not there before. This is because you get sucked in by one of the challenges presented in Figure 24.1 and fail with the others. I have tried to illustrate this tendency in Figure 24.2. It suggests that making a contribution involves not only satisfying a number of challenges, but often trying to satisfy one challenge may cause one to fall short of satisfying another.

Metaphorically, the three sides of the triangle can be thought of as magnetic bars, and the scholar as a metal ball. The scholar's job is to avoid getting sucked in by one of the challenges, being paralyzed by the pull of one of the bars. There is a "sweet spot," a point of equilibrium

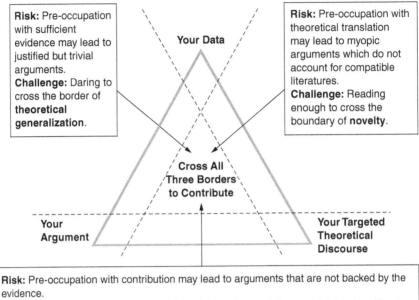

*Figure 24.2*   Problems Caused by Being Preoccupied with One Challenge

between the three forces that cancel each other out at the center. That's where you'll find your theoretical contribution.

Figure 24.2 introduces three demands for a theoretical argument, and three "borders" which illustrate that pre-occupation with any of the three demands tips the argument off balance. If you cross all borders, you are at least close to equilibrium and getting your story accepted. If you veer past one border, you risk getting stuck and unable to satisfy the remaining challenges. Game over. Start again. It is not uncommon with qualitative work to cross one border (say that of relevance) to find oneself back behind another border (typically sufficient evidence). With support from reviewers and a promising enough project, you may even get another chance to make things right. And if not, there is always the next journal.

## Border of Best Explanation

Between your argument and your targeted theoretical discourse lies the border of best explanation. We often find a cool story of great theoretical resonance to meet our findings. What remains is the discomfort of saying whether we can in all honesty claim that the story is the best explanation for what we see in our data. Best explanations are arguments that do most justice to the data among several competing explanations (Lipton, 2004). The only way to meet this challenge is to interrogate your data in a way that opens up alternative explanations and gives them a fighting chance alongside your shiny story. This is the difference between strong abduction and weak abduction; case studies tend to be explained by multiple arguments but looking at just one rarely provides a very strong argument (Mantere and Ketokivi, 2013).

Manuscripts fall into this trap during, rather that at the outset of the process of revisions. Authors try to come up with general and novel explanations and forget to check they make sense against their data. They get in trouble as they find that their newly minted theoretical arguments fail to be supported by their data; they fall prey to the lure of contribution and fail to pass the border of best explanation. This has happened to me more than once, I find that it is easy to get carried away and find myself struggling to find support for the argument I would like to make.

We have a natural tendency for theorizing, and once we find the courage and do the reading, we like making bold statements. This is wonderful, but also a risk; the challenge of best explanation is real. Your best friend against this risk is doubt. Our tendencies towards hasty generalization and over-interpretation are tempered by doubt (Locke et al., 2008). Doubt is so helpful for reasoning because it pushes us to re-examine our interpretations, address counter arguments, and revise our arguments up until the point that we feel confident that we at least believe them ourselves; I don't find much use for the word "truth," but if using it makes you happy, knock yourself out and say "up until the point that our arguments are true."

Doubt can lead to anxiety, in particular among students and junior colleagues who are learning the ropes. Yet, as texts ranging across the pragmatism of Charles Sanders Peirce (1878) to the hermeneutics of Hans-Georg Gadamer (1975) to influential methodological accounts in our field by authors such as Locke et al. (2008) or Alvesson and Kärreman (2007) demonstrate, doubt can be the single most important asset in scholarly reasoning.

## Border of Theoretical Generalization

Manuscripts that get revision requests often cross the border of best explanation at least more or less, but fall short of crossing two others. Such papers provide a credible explanation of data but fail to rise above the specifics of the case. First round submissions tend to be pretty focused on data and claims are thus not well rooted in theoretical language. The challenge of theoretical generalization boils down to the simple question: "What is it that management and organization scholars know about management and organizations (and *not* just about your often anonymous case organization) after reading your paper that they did not know before?" There is a whole lingo for masking this lack of argument in sentences like "we have provided a *rich* and *nuanced* account of X," or "we have *shown how* (i.e., rather than *argued that*) X is more complex than previously thought of." If you glue in a learned review of some theoretical discourse to begin your story, some journals let you get away with that. The ones I tend to like to read don't.

I have found that first submissions of papers – including those written by myself – are rarely strong on theoretical contribution. Rather, they pass the bar of entering the review process by virtue of showing a data set which appears rigorously produced, and arguments that are supported by that data set. The arguments that *are* made, while not particularly strong or novel, do pass as best explanations of that data due to the competent presentation of their authors (Figure 24.2). But the arguments themselves are often vague or lack ambition. This is often an indication of a pre-occupation with the problem of sufficient evidence.

Crossing this border involves daring. Mintzberg (1979) has called it "taking a creative leap." Not all authors are able to cross this boundary and some papers fail because their arguments are limited to explaining what the author sees in the data. Theoretical argumentation is founded on interpretation of the data, and all interpretations are to an extent incomplete, somewhat biased and potentially unfair. As such, the only risk-free choice is to abstain from theorizing and never cross the boundary of theoretical generalization.

## *Border of Novelty*

The failure in novelty relates to a preoccupation with finding a theoretical framing for one's findings, but doing this too soon, in too much haste and/or with too narrow a focus. The idiom "give me a hammer and I will treat all my problems as if they were nails" hits close to the mark in many cases. Scholars get lost in trying to explain their findings with their favorite theory and while the story may be novel to a small group of researchers, researchers from neighboring research programs find the lack of novelty disturbing and the argument myopic. The challenge of novelty is a particularly salient issue in the study of organizations due to the multi-paradigmatic nature of the field. If you look at the publication records of many senior scholars known for their qualitative research (say Kathy Eisenhardt, Ann Langley or Steve Barley), you tend to see contributions to various theoretical programs. Contributions are made into *a* theory, but over longer periods of time, scholars may contribute to various theories. This also suggests that when faced with empirical data, such scholars can draw from a rich source of explanations, and make sure that similar contributions are not made in a neighboring research program.

The trouble is that scholars tend to specialize. Junior scholars typically have the challenge of reading enough to get a sense of the opportunities in various literatures. To cross the border, one needs to stop just trying to explain what you see in the data in theoretical terms. This is often our first instinct when somebody says theoretical contribution – "hey, I will write my story in the language of some theory." The bar for providing a theoretical generalization that way is way too low; your story lacks ambition! The real challenge is to ask what your data can deliver for the needs of a particular theoretical discourse, and beyond its narrow confines. That is, the conundrum should ultimately not be empirical ("how can theory help to explain what I see in my case?") but theoretical in nature ("how can my data help a theoretical program to advance?"). Reading helps in making sure that the research program where you choose to locate your findings is not a limitation, but indeed the best explanation for your findings.

## Discussion

Figures 24.1 and 24.2 are founded on the assumption that authors have done their basic homework. The game described in Figure 24.2 in particular makes sense in the context of papers that have a fair chance of being published in the first place. It goes without saying that papers with weak research designs or data sets, or papers that are so poorly written that their arguments are not visible at all, have poor chances of survival; in such cases there is very little to balance: one flies out of the playing field altogether. Such papers are, and should be, typically desk rejected by editors and not face the review process at all.

What I have left out is the process of negotiating with reviewers. This is intentional. While reviewers and editors often offer valuable advice, an approach to conduct a revision as satisfying the reviewers' demands is often a kiss of death for a manuscript. Reviewers tend to point to important problems and areas of potential underpinning the argument, but the responsibility for finding these fundamental challenges ultimately lies with the author, not with the reviewers or editor.

I have focused on the activities or reasoning from qualitative data. I do not wish to suggest, however, that the challenges are somehow limited to qualitative data. One student of mine at a Ph.D. seminar on qualitative research complained: "but I'm better at math!" What I assume she meant was better at math than at making interpretations. With some forms of analysis, math gives us powerful tools to see regularities and patterns in our data. But what explains those regularities and patterns is as much a matter of interpretation as it is with qualitative data. Regardless of whether you are analyzing numbers, or turning text into numbers followed by analysis, or work with text alone, you face the challenge of interpretation that lies at the heart of any theoretical enterprise. There are multiple competing explanations for an empirical finding (Lipton, 2004). I have written this chapter to help you navigate this challenge.

## Note

1 I borrowed the analogy from Henry Mintzberg who has used it to challenge the planning conception of organizational strategy.

## References

Alvesson, M., and Kärreman, D. (2007). Constructing mystery: Empirical matters in theory development. *Academy of Management Review, 32*(4), 1265–1281.

Gadamer, H. G. (1975). *Truth and Method*, trans. W. Glen-Dopel. London: Sheed and Ward.

Kahneman, D. (2011). *Thinking, Fast and Slow*. London: Penguin Books.

Ketokivi, M., and Mantere, S. (2010). Two strategies for inductive reasoning in organizational research. *Academy of Management Review, 35*(2), 315–333.

Lipton, P. (2004). *Inference to the Best Explanation*. New York: Routledge.

Locke, K., Golden-Biddle, K., and Feldman, M. S. (2008). Perspective – making doubt generative: Rethinking the role of doubt in the research process. *Organization Science, 19*(6), 907–918.

Mantere, S., and Ketokivi, M. (2013). Reasoning in organization science. *Academy of Management Review, 38*(1), 70–89.

Mantere, S., Schildt, H. A. and Sillince, J. A. (2012). Reversal of strategic change. *Academy of Management Journal, 55*(1), 172–196.

Mintzberg, H. (1979). An emerging strategy of "direct" research. *Administrative Science Quarterly, 24*(4), 582–589.

Peirce, C. S. (1878). How to make our ideas clear. *Popular Science Monthly, 12*(January), 286–302.

Toulmin, S. E. (2003). *The Uses of Argument*. Cambridge: Cambridge University Press.

# 25

# "STANDING ON [TRANSPARENT] SHOULDERS"

## Applying Open Source Approaches to Qualitative Management Research

*Andrew J. Nelson*

We did not call our software "free software," because that term did not yet exist, but that is what it was. Whenever people from another university or company wanted to port and use a program, we gladly let them. If you saw someone using an unfamiliar and interesting program, you could always ask to see the source code, so that you could read it, change it, or cannibalize parts of it to make a new program. – Richard Stallman, Open Source Pioneer.

*(Stallman 1999, p. 53)*

In the 1960s and 1970s, researchers in both academic and corporate computer labs widely shared their computer code with one another (Lerner and Tirole 2002) – a practice that some scholars point to as critical for the development and diffusion of key software packages and even for the growth of entire technology-based fields (e.g., Nelson 2015). In response to the growth of proprietary software in the 1980s and 1990s, this sharing-based approach became codified in what has been termed "open source" software – software "that is made freely available to all" (von Hippel and von Krogh 2003, p. 209. Fitzgerald (2006) and West and Lakhani (2008) offer finer-grained definitions of open source).

A key dimension of open source software is the General Public License (GPL) or "copylefting" (as opposed to copyrighting); whereas the goal of copyright "is to restrict unauthorized use, copying, distributing, modifying, and performing," the goal of copylefting "is to allow these same activities" and to "restrict proprietary appropriation" to protect openness (O'Mahony 2003, p. 1186. See also Stallman 2002). The power of open source lies not merely in free distribution, but especially in the opening up of the "insides" of a program – the "source code" – to enable others to examine, build upon, enhance, and redistribute changes to this source code. In turn, the GPL specifies that these enhancements and changes must also be released under an open source model, thus perpetuating the system of open sharing.

Much inquiry in the academic literature has explored the benefits of open source software, the reasons for individuals and organizations to contribute to open source projects, and the challenges that open source development can encounter (e.g., Bogers et al. 2010; Lakhani and von

Hippel 2003; Lerner and Tirole 2002; O'Mahony 2003; West and Gallagher 2006). Yet academic publishing in management, and in many other fields, resembles the proprietary software model much more than the open source one. In fact, many academic publications about open source are published, ironically, in journals that claim copyright and that distribute this content only to those who pay high fees (Sample 2012). Moreover, academic publications in management rarely share raw data or full details of all analyses openly, nor do they encourage other authors to freely exploit and build upon these data in generating their own studies. In short, most management research falls far short of open source standards.

This chapter considers how qualitative management research might apply open source approaches, alongside the benefits and difficulties that scholars may encounter by doing so. I begin by highlighting three key challenges in social science research, focusing on features of qualitative research that can render it particularly problematic. The ensuing section then describes how an open source approach to qualitative management research can address these issues. The next section discusses various challenges that this approach is likely to encounter, along with potential ways to address them. Finally, the last section reflects more generally on the implementation of these suggestions, including individual incentives and needed changes in field-wide norms.

## The Challenge of Cumulative Research and Reproducibility

Transparency is the cornerstone of social science. Academic discourse rests on the obligation of scholars to reveal to their colleagues the data, theory, and methodology on which their conclusions rest. Unless other scholars can examine evidence, parse the analysis, and understand the processes by which evidence and theories were chosen, why should they trust – and thus expend the time and effort to scrutinize, critique, debate, or extend – existing research?

*(Moravcsik 2014b, p. 48)*

Currently, qualitative management researchers, like other social scientists, typically share final products – "findings" in the form of articles or books. (Sometimes, they share working papers with select colleagues and others, too.) The consumers of these products, who are primarily other researchers, understand the broad contours of the process that generated these findings – e.g., identification of a research question, gathering data, analysis of data, etc. Yet the details of this process typically are described in stylized and abbreviated form in a methods section, and the raw data themselves are rarely shared. For example, in a survey of 488 randomly-selected empirical researchers in economics and management, Andreoli-Vesbach and Mueller-Langer (2014, p. 1621) found that just 12 (2.5 percent) share data "in a comprehensive and clear way," 82 (16.8 per cent) sporadically share data, and 394 (80.7 percent) neither share data nor provide any indications of whether the data is available. (The authors do not distinguish, however, between qualitative and quantitative data in their study.) As Schwab and Starbuck (2017, p. 132) described the situation, "Data are a 'black box,' a term that denotes a system having unobservable inner workings."

A first challenge with this approach is that it can hinder cumulative research that builds upon particular data. In the natural sciences, researchers often work with common elements, systems, or data, or they can access specialized materials in biological resource centers or other data libraries that enable different researchers to build upon the same set of "inputs" (e.g., Furman and Stern 2011; Mathae and Uhlir 2012). This access enables findings to build upon one another, fulfilling Isaac Newton's oft-quoted claim, "If I have seen further, it is by standing on the shoulders of giants." By contrast, management studies build upon one another *theoretically* (though even here, authors, editors, and reviewers place a premium on novel theoretical contributions rather than cumulative theory per se). Yet the lack of sharing of data means that these studies rarely build upon one another *empirically*. If cumulative empirical (and theoretical) work is what enabled Newton's advances, then the lack of cumulative empirical work in management may slow the advance of the field overall.

A second challenge with the lack of sharing data and analytic processes is pedagogical. When scholars share only the final products of their research endeavors, the process by which they moved from initial idea, through data collection and analysis, to the presented outcome is unclear. In qualitative management research, specifically, there are a wide variety of empirical approaches and an ongoing need to understand their application, commonalities, differences, advantages, and disadvantages (e.g., Eisenhardt et al. 2016). Open sharing of the twists and turns of the research process can help to educate others as to how exactly an author conducted her study, enabling others to take a similar approach to different settings or data (or to apply a different approach to the same setting or data). Such sharing could also help towards establishing norms of what constitutes high-quality work and could build community among researchers who employ similar approaches. Indeed, the sharing of manuscript drafts in Ph.D. seminars indicates that understanding the details of the research process, including how a paper changes over time, is *very* valuable. As Barley (2016) advised qualitative researchers, "It is valuable to force ourselves to try to be as explicit about what we've done as possible."

A final challenge, and one that has received considerable and growing attention, concerns the believability of findings or outputs themselves. As Moravcsik (2014b, p. 48), quoted above, asked, "Why should [scholars] trust … existing research?" Indeed, a number of questions have emerged around the reproducibility of work in both the natural and social sciences. For example, a recent survey published in *Nature* found, "More than 70% of researchers have tried and failed to reproduce another scientist's experiments, and more than half have failed to reproduce their own experiments" (Baker 2016, p. 452). Similarly, a 2016 article in *Slate* titled "Everything is crumbling" reported, "A 'reproducibility crisis' in psychology, and in many other fields, has now been well-established. A study out last summer tried to replicate 100 psychology experiments one-for-one and found that just 40 percent of those replications were successful" (Engber 2016. See also Ioannidis 2005; Sarewitz 2016; Simmons et al. 2011). In the field of strategic management, Goldfarb and King (2016, p. 167) examined 300 papers in top journals and estimated "that if each study were repeated, 24–40 percent of significant coefficients would become insignificant at the five percent level." They guess that "for about half of these [studies], the true coefficient is very close to 0. The remaining coefficients are likely directionally correct but inflated in magnitude."

One response to this crisis has been the establishment of groups focused on reproducing scientific findings. For example, the Center for Open Science – a non-profit organization dedicated to research inclusivity and transparency – established "reproducibility projects" in psychology and cancer biology, attempting to replicate results published in leading journals (Center for Open Science 2016; Bartlett 2012). Similarly, in 2014 the Association for Psychological Science (APS) announced the creation of a "Registered Replication Report" – "a planned-out set of experiments, conducted by many different labs, in the hopes of testing a single study that represents an important research idea" (Engber 2016). One of APS's first targets was a foundational experiment on self-control that spawned hundreds of follow-on studies. Yet the replication attempts showed no signs of the effect reported in the foundational experiment (Engber 2016).

Of course, efforts to build upon or reproduce findings are fraught with difficulty. In qualitative management research, archival sources that are accessible in theory may be difficult to track down. Moreover, it can be impossible to access original interviews or field notes from ethnographic observations. In reflecting on these problems, Moravcsik (2014b, p. 48) noted:

> In a recent graduate seminar, my students found that even in the most highly praised mixed-method work, many sources (often 20% or more) could not be located by any means, including contacting the author. Even when sources can be identified, often the time, trouble, and translation difficulties required to get them impose prohibitive costs.

Often, qualitative research also draws on large volumes of disorderly data. Even if these raw data are made available, sorting through them to replicate analyses or to conduct a new study could require unreasonable effort. For all of these reasons, qualitative research may be especially subject to concerns about its veracity and the ability of others to build upon, extend or reimagine the empirics that inform its findings. How, then, might qualitative management researchers alter their practices to address these concerns?

## Open Source Scholarship as a Solution

A move towards open source approaches in management research can enable both replicability and cumulative research, while sowing confidence in research results and enabling others to learn from how a scholar approached a project and research question. For these reasons, disciplines related to management are already moving toward increased openness. For example, the American Economic Association (AEA) requires authors of accepted empirical papers to post "data, programs, and other details of the computations sufficient to permit replication" to the AEA website (AEA 2016). Of course, these data are overwhelmingly quantitative, so the concerns are somewhat different than in the case of qualitative research.

Political science, too, has moved toward open source, with several journals signing on to the Data Access and Research Transparency initiative (DA-RT). Building on King's (1995) admonition for research transparency, DA-RT requires authors to place data in a trusted digital repository, accessible to the community; to make the analytic procedures employed a matter of public record; and to cite data and analytic procedures with a title, version and persistent identifier (Alvarez 2014, Wilson 2014). In signing on to DA-RT, one journal, *The Political Methodologist*, issued the following statement:

> The social sciences receive little respect from politicians and segments of the mass public. There are many reasons for this, including:
>
> - we are not very good about translating our work to the public
> - many believe that our research is just common sense and so all we offer is opinion
> - and many distrust us as pointy-headed academics.
>
> A partial solution to building trust is to increase the transparency of our claims and this is why *The Political Methodologist* is signing on to DA-RT.
>
> *(The Political Methodologist 2014)*

As the DA-RT approach suggests, open source social science can consist of two key elements: (1) open sharing of data, both used and unused, and (2) open sharing of the process used for analyzing data, including reasons for employing these particular processes and changes made over time (e.g., "versioning").

## Sharing Data

The simplest approach to sharing data consists of posting it to a publicly accessible website. For example, the website that accompanies my book, *The Sound of Innovation* (www.thesoundof innovation.com), includes PDF scans of 634 archival documents that informed my account. (It also includes spreadsheet files with the quantitative data used in companion research articles, but these are beyond the scope of this chapter.) Importantly, these PDF scans include not only 176 documents directly referenced in the book, but also 458 documents that I read but did not directly incorporate. Qualitative research can be subject to the critique that authors simply "cherry pick" those sources or quotes that best support their argument (Moravcsik 2014b). By posting all data collected or consulted, authors enable others to directly assess whether such biases are present – and they facilitate others to use data that may otherwise lay fallow. (There are an additional 29 archival documents referenced in *The Sound of Innovation*, however, that are not posted due to confidentiality concerns – a point that I take up below.) Alongside this sharing, a fully open approach would also explain how the data were collected and how the author established boundaries around the collection process – explaining, in short, which data were collected, consulted, and used, and why.

The website for *The Sound of Innovation* also includes a section organized by chapter and footnote. This approach enables readers to trace footnotes directly to the supporting document. For example, a reference to an email to Steve Jobs can be traced to a PDF of the actual email, enabling readers to digest the full message and to discern the broader context in which the excerpted quote appeared.

This kind of direct linkage between quoted sources and publicly accessible archival documents mirrors the active citation approach proposed by Moravcsik (2012). Active citation (AC) consists of:

> A system of digitally-enabled citations linked to annotated excerpts from original sources. In the AC format, any citation to a contestable empirical claim is hyperlinked to an entry in an appendix appended to the scholarly work (the "Transparency Appendix" (TRAX)). Each TRAX entry contains four elements, the first three required and the last one optionally:
>
> 1    a short excerpt from the source (presumptively 50–100 words long);
> 2    an annotation explaining how the source supports the underlying claim in the main text (of a length at the author's discretion);
> 3    the full citation;
> 4    optionally, a scan of or link to the full source.
>
> *(Moravcsik 2014a)*

Of course, these approaches are all the more powerful when combined with open sharing of the final publication itself. On this front, management research has made much more progress. For example, the Social Science Research Network (SSRN) – a service devoted to the widespread, timely, and inexpensive distribution of social science research – provides open access to more than 560,000 papers by more than 310,000 authors (SSRN 2016). New open access journals such as PLOS ONE facilitate rapid peer review and release articles under a Creative Commons license, which offers free and immediate access and reuse. MIT Press, among other publishers, has released some of its books under a Creative Commons license, too (e.g., Nelson 2015; von Hippel 2005).

Such efforts stand to be bolstered by government pressure. For example, the European Union recently set a target of making all scientific papers freely available by 2020 (Enserink 2016). Similarly, in 2013 the White House Office of Science and Technology Policy directed federal agencies with more than $100 million in R&D expenditures

> to develop plans to make the published results of Federally funded research freely available to the public within one year of publication and requiring researchers to better account for and manage the digital data resulting from Federally funded scientific research.
>
> *(Stebbins 2013)*

These moves towards making final research products – papers and books – freely available are welcome and valuable. Yet these efforts need to be accompanied by open sharing of both data and analyses, too, to be considered fully open.

## *Sharing Analysis*

An open approach to qualitative management research would also share the analysis process – essentially, how one went from source materials to the presented account. Gioia et al. (2013, p. 18) describe the initial reviewer reaction to the Gioia and Chittipeddi (1991) paper as, "Great story! Good writing! Incisive thinking! But how do we know you haven't just made up an interesting interpretation?" Greater transparency helps to show how the authors moved from data to interpretation.

One key aspect of process transparency concerns the order in which a researcher consulted documents or sources. For example, some historians (e.g., Elton 2002) have argued that archival materials must be approached chronologically, in order to match the sequence in which the subjects themselves may have encountered or engaged with the events that documents reflect or record. The implication is that approaching source documents in another order would alter the interpretation reached. In turn, process transparency suggests that an author should explain exactly how he or she approached the data, and why.

Of course, the methods sections of qualitative papers already address the goal of process transparency, in part. For example, the popular "Gioia methodology" outlines a data structure consisting of a first-order analysis, "which tries to adhere faithfully to informant terms"; a second-order analysis that attempts to identify emerging themes and more general theoretical concepts "that might help us describe and explain the phenomena we are observing"; and aggregate dimensions that further "distill the emergent 2nd-order themes" (Gioia et al. 2013, p. 20. See also Glaser and Strauss 1967). The Gioia methodology provides insight into the sensemaking underlying the move from raw data to analytic categories. Yet the accounts offered in published articles are almost always sanitized "final" versions (Starbuck 2016), unlike the time-stamped comments and versions present in open source software – the latter of which enable one to see exactly how a project and associated interpretations unfolded over time.

Here, approaches such as open notebook science are informative (Priem 2013). In this model, scholars immediately and openly share their experiments *as they unfold*, thus publicizing the process itself in real-time, including missteps and failed experiments. This approach need not be limited to the natural sciences either. For example, Rice University historian Caleb McDaniel describes the process of open notebook history, which adopts the same ethos of transparency and versioning. In McDaniel's experiment with open notebook history, which accompanies development of a book manuscript, he runs an open wiki that publicizes his notes, automatically tracks changes to them, and enables comparisons between versions. A companion site posts a number of primary sources (McDaniel 2013).

Silberzahn and Uhlmann (2015) describe a similar crowdsourced approach. Inspired by a colleague's reanalysis and reinterpretation of one of their own studies, they devised an experiment in which 29 teams of researchers answered the same research question with the same data set. The various teams reached dramatically different conclusions. Yet they also engaged in dialogue as the process unfolded, questioning one another's approaches and refining their methods accordingly. As Silberzahn and Uhlmann (2015, p. 191) describe it, "the teams were essentially peer reviewing each other's work before even settling on their own analyses." The result was not a uniform answer to the research question, but rather an appreciation for "how conclusions are contingent on analytical choices" and the creation of "a safe space in which they [authors] can vet analytical approaches, express doubts, and get a second, third, or fourth opinion" (Silberzahn and Uhlmann 2015, p. 191).

Finally, it should be noted that there can be benefits to sharing the analysis procedure with informants themselves as a project unfolds. Indeed, a hallmark of open source approaches to software is that they involve not only sharing but also "co-creation," as multiple people come together to develop and maintain a software package. For example, management scholars might share both original archival documents and their emergent interpretations with informants in order to get informants' reactions and interpretations. Such sharing can jog memories, unearth inconsistencies and, especially, unveil alternative explanations offered by those coming from a different perspective. As McDaniel (2013) describes the benefits:

> By inviting others to see our work in progress, we also open new avenues of interpretation, uncover new linkages between things we would otherwise have persisted in seeing as unconnected, and create new opportunities for collaboration with fellow travelers. These things might still happen through the sharing of our notebooks *after* publication, but imagine how our publications might be enriched and improved if we lifted our gems to the sunlight *before* we decided which ones to set and which ones to discard? What new flashes in the pan might we find if we sifted through our sources in the company of others?

A key technique that I employed in writing *The Sound of Innovation*, for example, was to review archival documents – letters, emails, office memos, and the like – with my informants as I interviewed them, and to circle back to them to share my own evolving interpretations and analysis. The point was not to ensure that my interpretation matched theirs, but rather to leverage different interpretations as opportunities to stir reactions and to unearth additional perspectives. This real-time sharing approach also mirrors a key perspective in historical research in which emphasis is placed on interpretations rather than determining supposedly unbiased "facts" (c.f., Carr 1961; Evans 2001; Kirsch et al. 2014; Martin 2004).

As this discussion outlines, open source qualitative management research could, in its purest form, consist of full and open sharing of *everything* – used data, unused data, rationale, analyses, missteps, versions, etc. – with *everyone* at *every time*. In turn, such openness can lead to richer and more multiplex interpretations, can seed future cumulative contributions, and can assuage doubts about the veracity of the published interpretation.

## Several Challenges – and a Few Potential Solutions

Although there are clear benefits to such openness, it also entails significant costs and confronts serious challenges. A first and obvious challenge concerns the permission required to post information. In many cases, a researcher may not be allowed to openly share primary data. For example, institutional review boards (IRBs) sometimes require or encourage the anonymity of subjects and/or the protection of any information revealed in an interview, observation, or other qualitative data gathering exercise.

Sometimes, the protections required may be extreme. For example, Kirsch (2009) describes the "Brobeck Archive," which includes records from the now-defunct San Francisco law firm Brobeck, Phleger, & Harrison. The records contain "a diverse range of client data, as well as information related strictly to the administration of the partnership – minutes of partner meetings, operating and financial information about the firm, billing and accounting records, and other digital ephemera" (Kirsch 2009, p. 360). Understandably, making such rich qualitative data available for research purposes encounters a number of concerns with confidentiality for clients, law firm personnel, and others with whom these clients and personnel interacted. The solution, sanctioned by a U.S. Bankruptcy Court judge, is a closed archive, in which access takes place "in an on-site, non-networked, institutional setting, and only for enumerated purposes" (Kirsch 2009, p. 363). Thus, the data are made available, as in an open source model, yet access is controlled to address the confidentiality concerns.

Another potential solution to confidentiality concerns is to use secondary data that are already published or available in one form or another. For example, my investigation of scientific sharing practices uses oral histories with biotechnology pioneers that were conducted and published by U.C. Berkeley's Bancroft Library (Nelson 2016). Anthony et al. (2016) use interviews published in a trade magazine between 1975 and 1985 to assess user perceptions of music synthesizers during these same years, when the synthesizer was a new technology. Because such data are intended for publication, confidentiality concerns have typically been addressed already. (Oddly, as Kirsch et al. (2014, p. 235) note, archival sources "have been largely ignored by organizational researchers," despite their ability to provide new perspectives and their generally wider availability and dissemination.) Another advantage of using these data is that they can avoid retrospective bias and can sidestep the objection that the author manipulated the interview questions, since the author was not, by definition, involved in the interview. Archives, however, are usually controlled by another entity, such that an author cannot post copies of such materials. A key in using such data, therefore, is to point the reader or fellow researcher towards how to easily access these materials. For example, the Bancroft Oral Histories used in Nelson (2016) are easily accessible on a public U.C. Berkeley website.

A related challenge is the desire to protect informants' privacy. Both primary data and archival documents can contain information that may not be appropriate to share openly, such as salary data, social security numbers, evidence of illicit behavior, and potentially embarrassing reflections. In fact, the Academy of Management Code of Ethics (2006, p. 3) states, "It is the duty of AOM members to preserve and protect the privacy, dignity, well-being, and freedom of research participants." Archivists, of course, already wrestle with the question of how to protect privacy while facilitating access, and management researchers would be well-served to seek their counsel. One middle-ground approach is to signal that such information exists, but not to post it publicly – thus signaling information for future researchers to use while not ignoring privacy considerations.

A third challenge is that the expectation of non-publication can ensure a certain candor from informants. This candor may be lost if informants know and agree that information revealed in an interview or ethnography will be public. One way to address this concern is to initially follow the path of anonymity. Then later, it may be possible to reassess with a given informant whether publication might be acceptable. Indeed, I have often been struck by how interviewees' initial trepidation at sharing fades when I (privately) share with them the interview transcript and they realize that their fears of over-revealing or "sounding stupid" were unfounded. Informants may also agree to publication of portions of interviews or observations, while not fully sharing more confidential parts, or to publication that anonymizes all identifying information. These actions, of course, also need to be carefully coordinated with an IRB. The general idea, however, is to explore with informants and IRBs how some benefits of open sharing may be realized even as the goal of preserving informants' interests remains dominant.

A fourth challenge is that sharing and documentation – especially in the extreme forms described above – require a great deal of work. Even in the open source software world, documentation and support are key challenges (e.g., Lerner and Tirole 2002). Academic researchers may not have the resources needed to scan copies, create public directories and codebooks, and design and publish web pages. This challenge can be addressed, in part, by writing support for open sharing into grants. It may also be possible to leverage existing infrastructure, such as the Qualitative Data Repository (QDR) at Syracuse University. The QDR "makes available diverse guidance and resources to help researchers to prepare their data for sharing via QDR, and to access and make use of data projects stored in QDR" (Syracuse University 2016). Yet as I argue below, unless overall publication incentives change and open sharing is increasingly valued, simply addressing the resource requirements is unlikely to change behavior.

A fifth challenge is that extreme openness and transparency can destroy the flow of an article or book, emphasizing process at the cost of highlighting the novel insights gleaned from a study. Noting this concern, Eisenhardt et al. (2016) argue:

> There can be too much transparency, especially when journal space is precious. Analysis details require particular care because most authors have false starts, and travel a messy, episodic, and non-linear path to creative insight that is hard to describe or even remember…. Further, readers lose track of the critical methods features when there is extraneous detail, and may become distracted from the theory which is the central concern of journals like AMJ.

Although there is obvious value to analysis details, as argued throughout this chapter, these concerns are serious and must be weighed against the benefits to be derived from openness. Openness, however, need not be at odds with readability, focus, and journal space. For example, one approach is to put data and analyses on accompanying websites (e.g., in the form of an online appendix) rather than in the main body of the text. In the electronic version of *The Sound of Innovation*, for example, one can read the full text straight through, as with a traditional book; or, one can hover over footnotes to reveal additional comments and can follow numerous external links, as noted, to get mired deep in the original source material. In traditional paper journal formats, however, issues of space and reader engagement can be more difficult to resolve.

Finally, there is a question of when to post materials. Qualitative data collection represents a major investment of time and resources on the part of a researcher. Thus, it is reasonable to expect that a scholar should have the first-use right to exploit these data before sharing them with others. An obvious solution is to wait for public posting until a manuscript is published. Yet waiting can also make it difficult to take advantage of the inputs from others in the actual research process. (Recall, for example, McDaniel's open notebook history.) Moreover, when researchers plan to write multiple papers from the same data, lags between initial publication and data posting can pose serious dilemmas.

## Moving toward Open Source: Incentives, Barriers, and Preliminary Conclusions

Open source has transformed software production and maintenance, constituting a viable and, in some cases, dominant alternative to proprietary software. The same ethos of openness, transparency, and communal sharing could similarly transform qualitative management research. This approach would quiet concerns about reproducibility and, of greater excitement, enable the data and analyses underlying management research to become more collective products and benefit a wider range of researchers.

Moreover, the benefits to open source scholarship may accrue not only to the field as a whole, but also to individual researchers. Research in open source software has found that contributors participate for both internally and externally oriented reasons (Lakhani and von Hippel 2003; Lerner and Tirole 2002; O'Mahony 2003). Internally, such contributions can be fueled by a desire to "have fun" and to act altruistically. Externally, participation can enable one to increase his or her contributions and can lead to peer recognition that improves one's standing in the field and enhances career prospects. Lerner and Tirole (2002, p. 214) argue that these benefits are greater when the contribution is more visible to the relevant audience, more impactful on performance, and more informative about the individual contributor's talent.

These same motivations extend from open source software to social science research. For example, as Alvarez (2014) notes:

> By providing well-documented replication materials [authors] are increasing the likelihood that another scholar will download their materials and use them in their own research, which will likely generate a citation for the replication materials and the original article they come from. Or a colleague at another university will use well-documented replication materials in their methods class, which will get the materials and the original article in front of many students.

In turn, this enhanced author profile may result in new collaboration or employment opportunities for an author. Bolstering Alvarez's argument, emerging evidence indicates that open access papers are more highly cited than traditional "paywalled" papers in the journals that require a fee for access (Archambault et al. 2016).

Moves towards open source social science are already underway. Many economics journals require data to be publicly available. Many political science journals have signed on to the DA-RT initiative, which requires both data and analytic procedures to be publicly shared. Among management journals, *Management Science* (2016) "encourages (but does not require) the disclosure of data" through posting on a website, and both the *Strategic Management Journal* and the *Academy of Management Discoveries* encourage replication studies. The Academy of Management Code of Ethics (2006, p. 6) reads, in part, "In keeping with the spirit of full disclosure of methods and analyses, once findings are publicly disseminated, AOM members permit their open assessment and verification by other responsible researchers." Finally, initiatives such as the Qualitative Data Repository provide infrastructure for open sharing of data.

Despite this progress, however, the barriers remain significant. First, openness can be extremely difficult and even well-intentioned efforts can fall short. Throughout this chapter, I have referenced *The Sound of Innovation*, a book project in which I explicitly hoped to take an open approach. Yet I failed to gain permission to openly publish many interviews; my notes on some analytic decisions are weak or missing altogether; and I missed numerous opportunities to crowdsource both data and interpretations.

A second and more serious concern is that the individual incentives to engage in openness remain limited. Tenure and promotion decisions, and other measures of individual and institutional research activity and quality, are based on traditional (e.g., proprietary) journals and do not reward efforts to make data and analyses widely available. For scholars without tenure – who are racing to meet norms of publishing a certain number of articles in "A" management journals – none of which require or even encourage the degree of openness displayed in open source software, the pursuit of openness may be a far-removed concern. Indeed, Andreoli-Versbach and Mueller-Langer (2014) found that voluntary data sharing significantly increases with academic tenure, indicating that traditional tenure guidelines may be misaligned with openness.

As a first step towards addressing this challenge, some "existence proofs" – examples of scholars who have, in fact, received the "prizes" of academia, such as citations, tenure, and/or enhanced prestige – could be very influential. Overt statements of support by senior scholars can also signal that openness is both welcomed and valued. For example, Grote (2017, p. 2) reports on a meeting of two dozen organizational psychologists in senior roles ("heads of department, board members of funding agencies and executives of professional organizations"), who published a statement committing to "promote open source methods, resources and training." What is ultimately needed, however, may be a transformation of norms in management research as a whole, rewarding researchers not only on the basis of their findings and stated contributions, as is the case today, but also on the basis of their contributions to process and data. Although shifts in academic publishing culture are a very challenging proposition (Starbuck 2016), they may be the best hope for spurring a broad move towards open source inspired scholarship.

Here, too, qualitative management research may draw insights from the open source movement in software. To many observers, as late as the 1990s it was unfathomable that open source software could come to challenge the dominance of the proprietary model pursued by behemoths like Microsoft. Yet today, open source dominates many software applications, such as web servers, and even Microsoft contributes to open source efforts (Ovide 2012). Thus, there exists a model of bottom-up activism and engagement for transforming the practice and dominance of openness in a field. As qualitative management research grows in both prominence and prevalence, open source approaches promise to have an increasing positive impact on the field of management as a whole. And as scholars engage in ongoing discussions about the future of management research and its role in the world, open source may prove to be a source of inspiration for both the practice of research and the transformation of the academy.

## Acknowledgments

I thank Bill Starbuck and the editors for detailed comments and suggestions on an earlier version of this chapter. This work also reflects insights gleaned from conversations with David Kirsch, Caleb McDaniel, and Woody Powell.

## References

Academy of Management. 2006. Academy of Management Code of Ethics. February 2006. Available at: http://aom.org/uploadedFiles/About_AOM/Governance/AOM_Code_of_Ethics.pdf.

Alvarez, R. Michael. 2014. Improving research transparency in political science: Replication and political analysis. *The Political Methodologist* 22(1): 9–11.

American Economic Association (AEA). 2016. Data Availability Policy. Available at: www.aeaweb.org/journals/policies/data-availability-policy.

Andreoli-Versbach, P., and F. Mueller-Langer. 2014. Open access to data: An ideal professed but not practised. *Research Policy* 43(9): 1621–1633.

Anthony, C., A. Nelson, and M. Tripsas. 2016. "Who are you? I really wanna know": Product meaning and competitive positioning in the nascent synthesizer industry. *Strategy Science* 1(3): 163–183.

Archambault, Éric, Grégoire Côté, Brooke Struck, and Matthieu Voorons. 2016. Research impact of paywalled versus open access papers. OAnumbr 1: 1–5. Available at: www.1science.com/oanumbr.html.

Baker, Monya. 2016. 1,500 scientists lift the lid on reproducibility. *Nature* 533(7605): 452–454.

Barley, Steve. 2016. Confessions of a mad ethnographer. In Kimberly D. Elsbach and Roderick M. Kramer, eds., *Handbook of Qualitative Organizational Research: Innovative Pathways and Methods*. New York: Routledge, pp. 465–476.

Bartlett, Tom. 2012. Is psychology about to come undone? *The Chronicle of Higher Education*. April 17, 2012.

Bogers, M., A. Afuah, and B. Bastian. 2010. Users as innovators: A review, critique, and future research directions. *Journal of Management* 36(4): 857–875.

Carr, E. H. 1961. *What Is History?* London: Penguin.

Center for Open Science. 2016. https://cos.io.

Eisenhardt, K., Melissa Graebner, and Scott Sonenshein. 2016. Grand challenges and inductive methods: Rigor without rigor mortis. *Academy of Management Journal* 59(4): 1113–1123.

Elton, G. R. 2002. *The Practice of History*, 2nd ed. Oxford: Blackwell.

Engber, Daniel. 2016. Everything is crumbling. *Slate*. March 6, 2016.

Enserink, Martin. 2016. In dramatic statement, European leaders call for "immediate" open access to all scientific papers by 2020. *Science*. May 27, 2016.

Evans, R. J. 2001. *In Defence of History*. London: Granta.

Fitzgerald, B. 2006. The transformation of open source software. *MIS Quarterly* 30(3): 587–598.

Furman, J. L., and S. Stern. 2011. Climbing atop the shoulders of giants: The impact of institutions on cumulative research. *The American Economic Review* 101: 1933–1963.

Gioia, D. A., and Chittipeddi, K. 1991. Sensemaking and sensegiving in strategic change initiation. *Strategic Management Journal* 12(6): 433–448.

Gioia, D. A., K. G. Corley, and A. L. Hamilton. 2013. Seeking qualitative rigor in inductive research notes on the Gioia methodology. *Organizational Research Methods* 16(1): 15–31.

Glaser, B. G., and A. Strauss. 1967. *The Discovery of Grounded Theory: Strategies for Qualitative Research*. Chicago, IL: Aldine.

Goldfarb, B., and A. A. King. 2016. Scientific apophenia in strategic management research: Significance tests and mistaken inference. *Strategic Management Journal* 37(1): 167–176.

Grote, Gudela. 2017. There is hope for better science. *European Journal of Work and Organizational Psychology* 26(1): 1–3.

Ioannidis, J. P. 2005. Why most published research findings are false. *PLoS Med* 2(8): e124.

King, G. 1995. Replication, replication. *PS: Political Science & Politics* 28(3): 444–452.

Kirsch, D. A. 2009. The record of business and the future of business history: Establishing a public interest in private business records. *Library Trends* 57(3): 352–370.

Kirsch, D., M. Moeen, and R. D. Wadhwani. 2014. Historicism and industry emergence: Industry knowledge from pre-emergence to stylized fact. In Marcelo Bucheli and R. Daniel Wadhwani, eds., *Organizations in Time: History, Theory, Methods*. Oxford: Oxford University Press, pp. 217–240.

Lakhani, K. R., and E. von Hippel. 2003. How open source software works: "Free" user-to-user assistance. *Research Policy* 32(6): 923–943.

Lerner, J., and J. Tirole. 2002. Some simple economics of open source. *The Journal of Industrial Economics* 50(2): 197–234.

McDaniel, W. Caleb. 2013. Open notebook history. May 22, 2013. Available at: http://wcm1.web.rice.edu/open-notebook-history.html.

*Management Science*. 2016. Submission guidelines. Available at: http://pubsonline.informs.org/page/mnsc/submission-guidelines.

Martin, G. 2004. *Past Futures: The Impossible Necessity of History*. Toronto: University of Toronto Press.

Mathae, Kathie Bailey, and Paul F. Uhlir, eds. 2012. *The Case for International Sharing of Scientific Data: A Focus on Developing Countries: Proceedings of a Symposium*. Washington, DC: National Academies Press.

Moravcsik, Andrew. 2012. Active citation and qualitative political science. *Qualitative and Multi-Method Research* 10(1): 33–37.

Moravcsik, Andrew. 2014a. One norm, two standards: Realizing transparency in qualitative political science. *The Political Methodologist* 22(1): 3–9.

Moravcsik, Andrew. 2014b. Transparency: The revolution in qualitative research. *PS: Political Science & Politics* 47(1): 48–53.

Nelson, Andrew J. 2015. *The Sound of Innovation: Stanford and the Computer Music Revolution*. Cambridge, MA: MIT Press.

Nelson, Andrew J. 2016. How to share "a really good secret": Managing sharing/secrecy tensions around scientific knowledge disclosure. *Organization Science* 27(2): 265–285.

O'Mahony, S. 2003. Guarding the commons: How community managed software projects protect their work. *Research Policy* 32(7): 1179–1198.

Ovide, Shira. 2012. Microsoft dips further into open-source software. *Wall Street Journal*. April 16, 2012.

Priem, Jason. 2013. Scholarship: Beyond the paper. *Nature* 495 (March 28): 437–440.

Sample, Ian. 2012. Harvard University says it can't afford journal publishers' prices. *The Guardian*. April 24, 2012. Available at: www.theguardian.com/science/2012/apr/24/harvard-university-journal-publishers-prices.

Sarewitz, Daniel. 2016. Saving science. *The New Atlantis* (Spring/Summer): 5–40.

Schwab, Andreas, and William H. Starbuck. 2017. A call for openness in research reporting: How to turn covert practices into helpful tools. *Academy of Management Learning & Education* 16(1): 125–141.

Silberzahn, R., and E. L. Uhlmann. 2015. Crowdsourced research: Many hands make tight work. *Nature* 526(7572): 189–191.

Simmons, Joseph P., Leif D. Nelson, and Uri Simonsohn. 2011. False-positive psychology: Undisclosed flexibility in data collection and analysis allows presenting anything as significant. *Psychological Science* 22(11): 1359–1366.

Social Science Research Network (SSRN). 2016. Social Science Research Network: Frequently Asked Questions. Available at: www.ssrn.com/en/.

Stallman, Richard. 1999. The GNU operating system and the free software movement. In C. DiBona and S. Ockman, eds., *Open Sources: Voices from the Open Source Revolution*. Sebastopol, CA: O'Reilly Media, pp. 53–70.

Stallman, R. 2002. *Free Software, Free Society: Selected Essays of Richard M. Stallman*. Boston, MA: Free Software Foundation.

Starbuck, William H. 2016. 60th anniversary essay: How journals could improve research practices in social science. *Administrative Science Quarterly* 61(2): 165–183.

Stebbins, Michael. 2013. Expanding public access to the results of federally funded research. White House Office of Science and Technology Policy. February 22, 2013. Available at: www.whitehouse.gov/blog/2013/02/22/expanding-public-access-results-federally-funded-research.

Syracuse University. 2016. Qualitative Data Repository: Guidance and resources. Available at: https://qdr.syr.edu/guidance.

*The Political Methodologist*. 2014. Reproducibility and transparency. December 5, 2014. Available at: https://thepoliticalmethodologist.com/2014/12/05/reproducibility-and-transparency/.

von Hippel, E. 2005. *Democratizing Innovation: The Evolving Phenomenon of User Innovation*. Cambridge, MA: MIT Press.

von Hippel, E. V., and G. von Krogh. 2003. Open source software and the "private-collective" innovation model: Issues for organization science. *Organization Science* 14(2): 209–223.

West, J., and S. Gallagher. 2006. Challenges of open innovation: The paradox of firm investment in open source software. *R&D Management* 36(3): 319–331.

West, J., and K. R. Lakhani. 2008. Getting clear about communities in open innovation. *Industry and Innovation* 15(2): 223–231.

Wilson, Rick K. 2014. Reproducibility and transparency. *The Political Methodologist* 22(1): 2–3.

# PART V

# Frontiers and Reflections

# 26

# ENGAGING WITH THE VISUAL

## Opportunities for Qualitative Organizational Researchers

*Catherine Cassell*

## Introduction

The presence of visual media is increasingly apparent in our everyday working lives, ranging from the amount of time people spend looking at pictures on mobile devices to the billboard advertisements that bombard us whilst commuting to work. We know that visual images have a powerful impact, and in some cases have led to the collective definition of events that have triggered subsequent changes in history. Examples include the iconic photographs capturing the plight of the Vietnamese people during the Vietnamese or American war; the photographs of the aeroplanes crashing into the Twin Towers on 9/11 (Stiles, 2004); and more recently in Europe, the shocking images of a young drowned Syrian boy on a Turkish beach that led to a massive swell of public support throughout Europe for the plight of refugees (*The Guardian*, 2015). Given the impact of the visual, it is not surprising perhaps that there is now a general trend in the social sciences towards exploring the use of visual methods of data capture and analysis. Although previously under-explored in organization and management research (Meyer et al., 2013; Davison et al., 2012), Bell and Davison (2013) suggest that things are now changing and whereas previously the emphasis upon the linguistic turn had led to visuality typically being neglected, this is now being re-addressed in organization and management studies.

Whereas the term *visual* indicates what the human eye is visually capable of seeing, *visuality* refers to "how vision is constructed in various ways" (Rose, 2012: 2), hence enabling an exploration of how what we see may be socially and culturally constructed. An indication of this visual turn is the increased resources available for qualitative management and organizational researchers interested in such methods (e.g. Invisio: http://in-visio.org/) and the special issues on visual methods that have been produced by different journals (e.g. *Accounting, Auditing and Accountability Journal*, 2009; *Qualitative Research in Organizations and Management*, 2012; *Organizational Research Methods*, 2017). Indeed the expectation would be that a compendium such as this one would certainly include a chapter that considers the visual aspects of qualitative research. As Davison et al. (2012) suggest, visual methods particularly lean towards qualitative analysis. Although some have tried to do statistical analysis via the content analysis of images, visual images tend to be resistant to quantitative translation.

There is an extensive literature that focuses upon the analysis of a range of different types of visual images in the public domain and here there is more advice for the qualitative researcher than there is about the generation of new visual research data (Vince and Warren, 2012). This is partly because the analysis of such images has underpinned a range of arts and social sciences disciplines including the history of art, anthropology, sociology, semiotics, communication and media studies, and psychology (Meyer et al., 2013). Images that have been studied include photographs and paintings (Strangleman, 2004); annual reports (Davison, 2010); web images (Pritchard and Whiting, 2015); films (Hassard and Buchanan, 2009; Griffin et al., 2016); cartoons (Hardy and Phillips, 1999); stock photographs (Pritchard and Whiting, 2015); together with management tools such as PowerPoint (Kaplan, 2011) and visual maps (Cummings and Wilson, 2003). Research can also use multiple sources of images in the same study (e.g. Buchanan, 2001).

Visual stimuli are used in the qualitative research process in four different ways. First there are those that can be generated by the researcher for the purpose of their research. Examples include photo documentary (Buchanan, 2001; Czarniawska, 2010) or video ethnography (Llewellyn, 2014; Hassard, 2009; Toraldo et al., 2016; Clarke, 2011). Second, visual images can be participant-generated such as photo-elicitation (Slutskaya et al., 2012; Cassell et al., 2016) or collages (Plakoyiannaki and Stavraki, forthcoming 2018). Third, there are images that the researcher can analyse that are already in the public domain such as photographs (Parker, 2009) or film (Griffin et al., 2016) or 3D phenomena such as fashion, architecture or sculpture (e.g. Woodward, 2008). Fourth, there are images that are presented to research participants, such as cartoons or inkblots where they are asked for their interpretations of the image (e.g. Butler et al., 2014). Research projects can of course draw upon a combination of these uses (e.g. Bell, 2012; Pritchard and Whiting, 2015).

In seeking to map the opportunities available for qualitative management and organizational researchers wishing to engage with the visual, I have chosen here to focus specifically upon those where images are specially produced for a research project: the first two approaches outlined above. In what follows, I look at some of the research that has been conducted using these different types of visual methods and then offer a commentary about some of the challenges and key issues faced by those engaging with this type of research. My aim is to provide an introduction to the domain and the different kinds of research possibilities available to entice the reader who may not be familiar with visual methods to engage with some of the exciting opportunities they offer.

## Research Using Researcher-Generated Images

There has been a long history within qualitative research of researchers generating visual data from their observations. Indeed this underpins the ethnographic traditions that have had an important role to play in the development of qualitative organizational research. Approaches where the researcher generates the images tend to be referred to as documentary approaches (Meyer et al., 2013). Here, by way of example, we consider two such approaches: photo documentary and video ethnography.

### Photo Documentary

Rose (2012: 298) suggests that "In photo-documentation, a researcher takes a carefully planned series of photographs to document and analyse a particular visual phenomenon." Photographs can be understood as contributing to a research endeavour in a variety of different ways. Some authors claim that they are an accurate record of what is in front of the camera, represent reality, and therefore can add a precision to data analysis (Collier, 1967). However others would argue that the photograph itself is not a static and accurate account, rather it is the different meanings attributed to photographs that matter (Becker, 1995) and photographs can have multiple meanings.

Photographs are used by researchers in a variety of ways, for example to enrich the data that is captured from other sources or to facilitate the holistic interpretation of results (Meyer et al., 2013). For example Czarniawska (2010) enriches her account of an urban project in Rome with the inclusion of "photo reportage" to trace events. In another study, Buchanan (2001) draws on both photo documentary and photo elicitation to understand the complexities involved in the re-engineering of a hospital. The initial stage of the project involved a process mapping of the elective surgical in-patient process which was presented to staff both in a flow diagram and a detailed written account. At the final stage of the research the steps in the patient trail were documented photographically on 150 plus transparency slides. When these were shown to staff during a feedback session they provided an opportunity for staff to comment on what was missing from the characterization of the process. As Buchanan (2001: 162) summarizes: "The additional data revealed through photo-research methods concerned a combination of highly significant details of work processes and considered reflections on work activities" which had not been elicited through individual interviews, even when people had been asked to describe these processes in detail. In this way the method offered a particularly novel form of respondent validation where respondents could comment on the researcher's interpretation of the process and its success in capturing the intricacies required.

Meyer et al. (2013) suggest that there is little of this type of research within the management and organizational field, though the studies noted above highlight some of the possibilities of photo documentary by the researcher, not just in terms of accessing respondent feedback, but also as another important source of data. However, as Hinthorne (2014) argues, it is important that photographs are read in conjunction with other sources of data collected by the researcher as, like transcripts or field notes, they offer only a partial account of a research investigation.

## *Video Documentary*

An alternative to researchers taking photographs is researchers producing videos as part of their research. This methodological approach is usually conducted within an ethnographic context because of the emphasis upon seeing individuals within their natural settings. Hassard (2009: 270) points out how the British tradition of ethnographic documentary has been deployed to offer "grounded sociological insights into the 'real world' of institutions and occupations." In tracing a range of developments that typically follow the style of ethnographic documentaries that have been broadcast on British television, he highlights how at various times British television audiences have been bombarded with *cinema vérité* or film-truth where the video-maker or researcher seeks to capture the meaning or essence of how people experience work or organization.

A key issue here, as with photographs, is the extent to which these documentaries are representative or actually show "the truth." Clearly such documentaries are edited by TV producers or researchers and are therefore constructed in the same way as other social artefacts, so although researchers use them as a way of capturing data they clearly represent the researcher's view of the research topic and their interpretations of what is important. This in itself is only a problem if one is wedded to the commitments of a positivist philosophical stance where we would expect the researcher to be a neutral collector of data. In other philosophical traditions of qualitative research such as interpretivist approaches, we would assume that not only would the researcher have an impact upon the data collected but also that they would reflexively account for that impact in any write-up (Duberley et al., 2012).

## *Video Ethnography*

Whereas video documentary focuses upon understanding work and organization within a given context, video ethnography focuses instead upon the detailed micro-analysis of recordings of everyday interactions in practice. As such, it is clearly informed by ethnomethodology and conversational analysis approaches where the focus is upon everyday talk and interaction (Whittle, forthcoming 2018). Hence this kind of video analysis must be seen as both qualitative and interpretive (Knoblauch, 2012). Although a recent addition to organization and management studies (Llewellyn and Hindmarsh, 2010), video ethnography is increasing in use because of the opportunities it offers to provide insights into micro-practices. Moreover, the requisite equipment has now become readily available, inexpensive and easy-to-use. A number of authors have pointed out that an important aspect of video recording is that it enables the study of multimodality (Toraldo et al., 2016; Jarzabkowski et al., 2015), where the various different modes of semiotic systems through which people engage – for example gestures, talk and text – can all be captured. As Toraldo et al. (2016) highlight, comparing different insights across modalities offers potentially more complexity of understanding than would be achieved using a single modality.

Toraldo et al. (2016) suggest that there are three alternative uses of video within qualitative research. The first is as a source of raw data to examine the real-time behaviour of actors producing rich material for subsequent qualitative coding. The second is to use video as a form of triangulation (Jick, 1979) where data from different sources can be cross-referenced and validated. The third is to use video as a "reflective artefact" (Toraldo et al., 2016). Here through conversations between the researchers and the participants as they watch the recorded data, participants can reflect upon the meanings of their behaviours and actions and share these reflections with the researcher. This process has been described as "zooming with" by Jarrett and Liu (2016) to distinguish it from "zooming in" – video studies that focus upon the detail of interactions – and "zooming out" – where studies focus upon those interactions in context.

Examples of where video analysis is used in our field include the domain of strategy as practice (Samra-Fredericks, 2010; Jarzabkowski et al., 2015); embodied cognition (Gylfe et al., 2016); entrepreneur behaviour (Cornelissen and Clarke, 2010; Clarke, 2011); and studies of service work (Llewellyn, 2014). In all cases it is argued that video enables us to see the phenomenon as it is done, as lived experience, and the fine granularity of behaviours. An example is Llewellyn's (2014) study of age norms in service work. In a study of counter workers in an art gallery, Llewellyn highlights how they negotiate discussions regarding the age of customers when there are different entry prices for different groups, for example adults, children and senior citizens. In order to explore how customers are positioned in relation to age-based norms, the study focuses upon a micro-analysis of customer interactions generated through 16 hours of interactions at the payment counter over three days and recorded by a digital camera. Through this micro-analysis Llewellyn demonstrates how assumptions about age are played out through everyday organizational activities. He argues that in terms of methods, the visual turn has prioritized photographic images but they tend to prioritize the analyst's gaze, having been taken at a particular place and time. Hence they can present a "static and silent account" of organizational life (Llewellyn 2014: 169) whereas video offers other opportunities.

To take another example, Clarke (2011) reports on a visual ethnographic study of three entrepreneurs in the early stages of venture commercialization where video recordings were part of a multi-qualitative ethnographic study. Her findings showed the wide range of visual symbols used by entrepreneurs to gain legitimacy, for example settings, props, dress and expressiveness. Clarke concludes that "entrepreneurs can become skilled cultural operators who use their skills to give sense to others through visual symbols about what they are and what they represent"

(Clarke 2011: 1387). Such conclusions would be hard to achieve without the access to multi-modal aspects of behaviour enabled by video recording. Finally, Luff and Heath (2012: 275) highlight that there are "still a great many unresolved analytic and methodological challenges facing researchers who utilise audio–visual materials." They suggest that, although guidance has focused upon ethical concerns and access, some of the technical and practical choices, such as what and how to record need to be critiqued in more detail.

## Research Using Participant-Generated Images

Rather than focusing upon instances where the researcher generates the research data, another set of visual methodologies rely upon the research participant to generate the data, for example photographs or drawings. Hence the content of the data collected is selected by the participants, though the focus will be determined by the researcher in terms of the research question. We now consider some of the different types of data that can be elicited from research participants.

### *Photo Elicitation*

Within the field of management and organization studies there is an increased reporting of studies that include photo elicitation as a methodological tool. Indeed it has been argued that the opportunity of generating rich qualitative data from the use of photographs has great potential for organizational and management researchers (Harper, 2002; Warren, 2002; 2008; Hurdley, 2007). Rose (2012) suggests that there are four key strengths of photo elicitation as a data collection method. First, it enables a range of different insights into a given phenomenon from different perspectives. For example, Cassell et al. (2016) point out how in seeking to understand participants' experiences of work–life balance, photo elicitation was particularly useful in that it both enabled a range of diverse interpretations of the concept to be surfaced and revealed the complexities associated with managing work–life conflicts on a daily basis.

This focus upon the everyday is the second strength identified by Rose (2012). As Shortt and Warren (2012: 31) point out when we give an individual a camera: "we are forcing them to think about the everydayness of the things that surround them that they are probably unlikely to think about if we simply asked them about themselves." This type of everydayness can then be explored in more detail in a follow-up interview.

The third strength of photo elicitation identified by Rose is that the method has a positive impact on the power relationship between researchers and the researched in that the researched in choosing what to photograph are defining what is important about a given phenomenon. Within the social sciences literature more generally there are examples of where photo-elicitation methods have been used with groups that are typically hard to reach or difficult to access, for example socially excluded Black youth (Wright et al., 2010) and adults with mental illness (Fullana et al., 2014). Not only is the technology now more easily available in that many people own a mobile camera phone but also photographs are a way of capturing phenomena in real time and are less restrictive than other methods of data collection (Ray and Smith, 2012). As Stiles (2004: 127) suggests: "Digital technology has transformed pictures from an elitist knowledge domain protected by artists, photographers and graphic designers into a mass medium."

A fourth strength identified by Rose (2012) is the distinctive collaboration in photo elicitation techniques between the researcher and the researched. Here the participant engages in dialogue in collaboration with the researcher to uncover details encapsulated within photographs taken in the field (Harper, 2002). Combining visual and verbal methods allows the researcher to disentangle social phenomena, further observing the purpose, existence and meaning of social categories, bodies and items within photographs. This can often provide the researcher with access to new unexpected data providing alternative ways to talk about, reflect upon and thus understand social phenomena (Warren, 2008). Furthermore, Cassell et al. (2016) identify the potential of the method for enabling reflective practice on behalf of the interviewees as a form of the "zooming with" identified earlier (Jarrett and Liu, 2016).

Ray and Smith (2012: 311) reviewed the use of photographs within the organizational field and concluded, "We believe that photographic research holds great promise for investigating organizational phenomena – especially tracking internal processes and change over time as well as accessing multiple levels of understanding." The range of topics covered by photo-elicitation studies is diverse. For example, Guell and Ogilvie (2015) asked 19 participants to produce photographs that captured their everyday commuting practices. More than 500 images were produced by the participants and the authors note that participants tend to produce positive rather than negative images of their commuting experiences. Slutskaya, Simpson and Hughes (2012) conducted photo-elicitation interviews with butchers and suggested that the use of photographs encouraged working-class men who are not usually accessible to researchers to talk about issues such as the physicality of their work. Warren (2006) asked individuals working in a hot-desking environment to take photographs of their desks as part of a larger ethnographic study of workplace aesthetics. Vince and Warren (2012) note the inventory function of the camera in this instance when objects or artefacts not noticed by the participant can be identified by the researcher when part of the photograph and consequently discussed with the participant.

Shortt and Warren (2012) also point to the potential of photograph elicitation to draw attention to the performative aspects of work. In their study, hairdressers were asked to take photographs of spaces that were meaningful to them at work and said something about their "personalities" at work. The photographs were discussed in follow-up interviews four weeks later. The authors argue that the camera enabled both researchers and participants to be sensitized to the performative nature of identity construction.

## Participant Drawing

Apart from the elicitation of photographs, research studies have also been based upon eliciting drawings from participants. According to Vince and Warren (2012), the use of drawing in organization and management studies can be traced back to the late 1980s. Encouraging participants to draw has been used particularly within the fields of management and organizational development and change. For example Meyer (1991) outlines how Zuboff (1988) asked clerical workers to take pictures of how they felt about their jobs both before and after the implementation of a new computer system. In an investigation of the role of emotions in the change process in public sector organizations Broussaine and Vince (1996) asked 86 managers from six different organizations to produce a drawing that expressed their feelings about change at work. This exercise was followed up in a number of different ways to explore individual, team, inter-group and senior managers' interpretations of the pictures. Similar to the reflexive properties of photo-elicitation and video analysis identified earlier, in this study the authors report that the managers themselves were surprised by the strength of emotions that were captured by the drawings.

Pictures have also been a crucial part of soft systems approaches, for example through the drawing of "rich pictures" of the organization (Checkland, 1981; Walsh and Clegg, 2004) where the intention is to identify through the drawing how different parts of the system are interconnected. In terms of management development, the elicitation of pictures has also been used to see how new and experienced researchers view research and other researchers (Bryans and Mavin, 2006). Bryans and Mavin (2006) argued that a distinctive feature of the method was that in engaging students in a discussion about the skills and qualities they would need to be good researchers it encouraged them to start to think reflexively. In my own teaching practice I have also used this technique alongside metaphor elicitation with doctoral students at the commencement of their studies. In groups I ask the students to think of a metaphor that represents how they see the research process and summarizes their views about becoming a doctoral researcher. In groups they then start to explore and develop the metaphor through drawing a picture of it. Having used this technique over many years I find it is a playful and enjoyable way of surfacing and discussing student's concerns as they start to embark upon their doctoral process. Typical metaphors and pictures drawn are that of a mountaineer climbing a mountain and an explorer in the desert or outer space. Pictures usually contain within them a pictorial representation of the hazards and hindrances along the way, but hint to some joyful achievement at the end.

This method has also been used in the field of identity research (Stiles, 2004). For example, Stiles (2004) asked research participants to complete a *free-drawn personality metaphor image* by asking them to imagine that their organization had its own personality and to do a rough sketch to try to explain to someone who couldn't read or write what the organization looked like. He then followed this up with a series of focus groups where the discussion was about the extent to which the images captured the organization. The images concerned were of different international business schools, though Stiles suggests that the personality metaphor is sufficiently flexible and easy to use in any organizational setting with which people are familiar. Stiles (2004) concludes that as with photograph elicitation, it is best that the researcher does not assume an expert status and interpret the drawing without the commentary from the participants as there are potentially many different interpretations. He also suggests that this may be a useful technique when investigating strategy, given that many managers are so familiar with techniques like SWOT that they tend to stifle creativity, whereas this approach encourages a range of diverse and creative interpretations.

## *Elicitation of Other Images*

A range of other visual images have been elicited from participants as the basis of qualitative data collection. Examples include collages, timelines and video diaries. Plakoyiannaki and Stavraki (Forthcoming, 2018) discuss the methodological and interpretive opportunities associated with collages (Norris, 2008; Butler-Kisber and Poldma, 2010) as a form of qualitative inquiry. Adopting a postmodernist perspective they suggest that "collage is an artistic structure of heterogeneous elements that can capture the contradictions of modern life" (Plakoyiannaki and Stavraki, forthcoming, 2018: 6). In their study participants were given paper, paste, magazines and scissors and completed individual collages after they had visited an exhibition with the aim of contributing to an understanding of consumer's responses to the exhibition. This type of research is rare within the management and organizational field yet more prevalent in marketing, advertising and consumer research where arts-based approaches are beginning to have an impact.

Another method that has been used for research projects where chronology is important is the visual timeline (Mazzetti and Blenkinsopp, 2012; Sheridan et al., 2011). Mazzetti and Blenkinsopp (2012) used a visual timeline co-generated by the researcher and the participant to explore issues of organizational stress. In an individual interview, participants were presented with a large sheet of flipchart paper and a selection of coloured pens. Participants were asked to start the timeline when they had first started thinking about their careers and then to add key events. They were also asked about how key events had been appraised and coped with. Hence the timeline design itself was facilitated by questions from the researcher. Once a timeline was finished it was reviewed by the researcher and the participant. The researchers suggest that the timeline offered "added value" beyond traditional qualitative methods because as well as facilitating participants working out the chronology of events it enabled more insights into the complexity of stress, appraisal and coping by offering a more holistic picture (Mazzetti and Blenkinsopp, 2012: 661).

A final method that has just started to be used in the management and organizational field is the video diary; "an exciting addition to the ethnographic repertoire" (Brown et al., 2010: 434). Although previously used in consumer research (Brown et al., 2010; Sunderland and Denny, 2002), the opportunities offered by what has been called an "autovideography" method (Belk and Kozinets, 2005), together with the decreasing cost of the technology, have made the method attractive to management and organizational researchers. One example is the work of the Digital Brain Switch project (see www.scc.lancs.ac.uk/research/projects/DBS/research-studies/video-diaries-interviews/) who are investigating work–life balance in the digital age. In the project participants were provided with a camcorder and asked to keep a video diary for a week where they focused upon incidences of switching between life and work boundaries and how technology may have facilitated this. Their recordings were then reviewed by the research team. At a follow-up interview participants were asked to reflect upon and discuss a small number of the video excerpts as chosen by the project team. This produces an interesting methodological issue in that although the individual participant is fully in control of what is recorded and what is presented to the researchers, the researchers then edit the video recordings provided to select the excerpts to discuss with participants. This has particular implications for reflexivity (see Whiting et al., 2016).

Given the options for the use of video diaries that have been afforded by advances in communication technologies, we would expect to see more research using video diaries in the future. Brown et al. (2010) suggest that for a video diary study to be successful the important elements are rapport between the researcher and the researched; researcher empathy; time; and regular contact between the researchers and the researched. It is interesting to note that these success factors are all rooted in the relationship between the researcher and their participants. Indeed the longitudinal element of such research means that ongoing relationship maintenance is even more important than may be the case, for example, in an interview study. Once again, the commitments of this kind of research design are aligned with those of traditional ethnographic approaches.

In summary, Table 26.1 provides some examples of the ways in which visual methods have been used in management and organizational research. It is important to note that these are only examples and that there are myriad other possibilities offered by visual methods, some yet to be explored.

## Discussion

Within this discussion section I briefly explore and summarize some of the different challenges and key issues that have emerged from the account above. First, many of those who use visual methods highlight the importance of them being used alongside other methods of qualitative data collection and analysis (e.g. Luff and Heath, 2012; Simpson et al., 2014). For example, Simpson et al. (2014: 198) position photo-elicitation methods as part of an ethnographic strategy that also relies upon ethnographic field notes, observation and interviews. In their study the photographs were used as a "fixed caption of a moment in time." In a similar way Cassell et al. (2016) used photograph elicitation to capture critical incidents of work–life balance which were

*Table 26.1* Some Examples of the Uses of Visual Methods in Organizational Research

| *Analysis of Existing Images* | *Images Generated for the Research* |
| --- | --- |
| *By researchers* | |
| Management tools (Kaplan, 2011; Cummings and Wilson, 2003) | Photo documentary (Buchanan, 2001; Czarniawska, 2010) |
| Films (Hassard and Buchanan, 2009; Griffin et al., 2016) | Video ethnography (Llewellyn, 2014; Hassard, 2009; Toraldo et al., 2016; Clarke, 2011) |
| Paintings (Strangleman, 2004) | Video documentary (Hassard, 2009) |
| Annual reports (Davison, 2010) | |
| Web images (Pritchard and Whiting, Forthcoming, 2018) | |
| Cartoons (Hardy and Phillips, 1999) | |
| Photographs (Parker, 2009) | |
| 3D phenomena such as fashion or architecture (Woodward, 2008) | |
| *By the researched* | |
| Cartoons (Butler et al., 2014) | Photo elicitation (Slutskaya et al., 2012; Shortt and Warren, 2012; Cassell et al., 2016) |
| Photographs (Pritchard and Whiting, 2015) | Participant drawing (Zuboff, 1988; Broussaine and Vince, 1996; Walsh and Clegg, 2004; Bryans and Mavin, 2006) |
| | Collages (Plakoyiannaki and Stavraki, Forthcoming, 2018) |
| | Video diaries (Brown et al., 2010; Whiting et al., 2016) |
| | Visual timelines (Mazzetti and Blenkinsopp, 2012) |

then discussed in interviews and Czarniawska (2010) took her own photographs as a form of "photo reportage" alongside the use of other data collection methods to enable the tracing of events. The advantages of using multiple qualitative methods in this way go beyond any procedural desire for data triangulation to offer a richer picture of the phenomenon under study.

Second, there is evidence that using visual data can lead to a different relationship between the researcher and the researched. In the cases where images are elicited from research participants, it is clear that they enjoy engaging in the research process (Shortt and Warren, 2012; Brown et al., 2010; Cassell et al., 2016). Such engagement also creates additional opportunities for reflection and reflexivity from both the researchers and the researched (Cassell et al., 2016; Pink, 2001; Whiting et al., 2016), and powerful emotions can be associated with the research process (Broussaine and Vince, 1996). For the participant, they may be more in control of the research situation and be able to set the agenda (e.g. photo-voice, Warren, 2005) than may be typical in other research designs. There is also the issue of potentially making the researcher's role more open and democratic. For example, developments in digital photography have enabled the possibilities for mass observation such as the Mass Fashion Observation project conducted by researchers and students at Nottingham Trent University where trained student researchers photograph and interview people at public sites with the aim of creating through collaborative research a massive textual and visual data set. Woodward (2008: 870) highlights the potential of such projects to re-construct how we think about the research relationship: "As the research relationship is always embedded in a wider context and given how rapidly digital technologies are evolving, by definition the complex web of interactions that comes to constitute research relationships will also evolve rapidly."

Third, one of the key challenges in engaging with visual methods is the link between visual methods and theorization (Bell and Davidson, 2013). Davison et al. (2012) suggest that there are a number of reasons why the visual presents a distinctive set of theoretical challenges because of both the diverse set of visual images available for analysis and the variety of possible interpretations of those images. This also presents different theoretical opportunities for visual researchers, for example Meyer et al. (2013) outline how visual studies in organization and management studies have been used to apply, elaborate or extend theory. Hence visual methods can have a variety of roles to play in both theory testing and development, depending on the ontological stance of the researcher, though a plurality of options may lead to more complexity.

Fourth, closely linked to the challenge of theorization is that of how to analyse visual data. Within the literature a range of different types of analysis have been used and the choice of analytic strategy is very much influenced by the research question and the philosophical stance of the researcher. For example, those using micro-analysis of video excerpts tend to use conversation analysis (e.g. Jarrett and Liu, 2016). The choice of analytic tool is also complicated by the issue that in some cases images are not being analysed on their own but rather alongside the text created from an interview or some other data collection source, for example Warren's "image-text" approach to the presentation of data (e.g. Warren, 2002) where text is analysed alongside the relevant image (Vince and Warren, 2012).

In summarizing some of the different analytic choices available, the types of content analysis used for visual images are similar to those of other qualitative approaches where the emphasis is upon counting frequencies (Krippendorf, 1980). Relying on the development of a coding frame, it enables quantitative analysis of image content leading to the potential replicability of a given methodology. Different forms of thematic analysis such as template analysis (King, 2012) have also been used to analyse visual data. For example, Simpson et al. (2014) in their ethnography of refuse collectors used thematic analysis of elicited photographs together with data from other sources such as interviews to create their analysis of the meanings they attributed to their work. Another long-established approach for analysing the visual is semiotics where the focus is upon how an image conveys a message and the plurality of meanings that an image may hold (Plakoyiannaki and Stavraki, forthcoming 2018). Here, images are seen as polysemous in that they have multiple interpretations. Other authors have analysed images from a psychoanalytic perspective. For example Warren (2012) highlights how the concept of "image" occupies a central place in psychoanalytic thinking and suggests that psychoanalytic theorizing can bring a collective understanding to how images are viewed. This approach has been particularly used in exploring the meaning of film images, for example feminist critiques of Hitchcock films (see Rose, 2012). Informed by the history of art, images can also be critiqued through compositional analysis (see Rose, 2012). Other forms of analysis are those associated with the linguistic turn, for example discourse and rhetorical analysis (e.g. Hardy and Phillips, 1999).

Fifth, something experienced by qualitative researchers more generally relates to the ongoing challenge of seeking credibility for qualitative research in the management and organizational domain (Cassell and Symon, 2012). Bell and Davison (2013) suggest that there is still some resistance to the use of visual research. From a positivist perspective which still dominates much of business and management research (Symon et al., 2016), there will be questions about the scientific rigour of the collection and analysis of visual data. This can lead to a range of difficulties in publication and consequent career development, issues of which are explored in other chapters in this volume.

A final important issue is that of ethics. Researchers using visual methods have drawn attention to some of the distinctive ethical challenges with these approaches. For example Rose (2012) and Vince and Warren (2012) note that with the use of photo elicitation there are complex ethical issues such as the ownership rights of the interpretive elements of visual images which although produced by participants are nevertheless jointly interpreted as part of a collaborative dialogue between the researcher and participant. There is also the complex issue of consent when individuals are the subject of photographs. Wiles et al. (2012) consider the ethical challenges of anonymization in visual methods. In a study of how visual researchers manage such issues they highlight the tension between paternalism and agency. Some researchers argued that anonymization of images was important as a way of protecting informants (paternalism), whereas others argued that some respondents wanted to be visible, and may have taken part in a research project because they wanted to be seen (agency). Hence anonymizing them within the images was denying them that opportunity. Therefore even amongst visual researchers there are different stances taken to what are fundamental ethical issues. These complexities offer legal and ethical concerns when it comes to the publication of images (Bell and Davison, 2013). Furthermore, the advancement of new technologies creates a new and distinctive set of issues around digital ethics (Whiting and Pritchard, Forthcoming, 2018). Hence this is an area of ongoing debate.

## Conclusions

Within this chapter I have highlighted just some of the methods of visual data collection available to qualitative management and organizational researchers. Before finishing, it is important to consider what future developments may have in store for those who wish to conduct their qualitative research using visual methods. One issue is that with changing communication technologies, new opportunities regularly occur to investigate images. Digital video technology is also developing at a rapid rate with most households now having a webcam with a computer where videos can be recorded and uploaded to a researcher (Murthy, 2008), hence offering a new range of research options. Similarly web images are an area of potential investigation where there is currently little management or organizational research (Pritchard and Whiting, 2015). Another particularly significant area for potential development is the smart phone, the potential of which has yet to be fully explored by qualitative researchers (Garcia et al., 2015).

In conclusion, the generation of visual images by the researcher or research participant has much to offer the qualitative management and organizational researcher. As a recent convert myself through a photo elicitation study, I have been overawed by the power of the visual to produce both interesting and rich data from research interactions. Moreover, discussions with research participants around how images can be interpreted provide an additional set of insightful data. For those readers who have not yet used visual methods I would urge you to go out, explore and enjoy.

# References

*Accounting, Auditing and Accountability Journal.* 2009. Volume 22, issue 6, special issue on Visual perspectives on accounting and accountability, ed. S. Warren and J. Davison.

Becker, H. 1995. Visual sociology, documentary photography, and photojournalism: it's (almost) all a matter of context. *Sociology*, 10(1–2): 5–14.

Belk, R. W. and Kozinets, R. V. 2005. Videography in marketing and consumer research. *Qualitative Market Research: An International Journal*, 8(2): 128–141.

Bell, E. 2012. Ways of seeing death: a critical semiotic analysis of organizational memorialization. *Visual Studies*, 27(1): 4–17.

Bell, E. and Davison, J. 2013. Visual management studies: empirical and theoretical approaches. *International Journal of Management Reviews*, 15: 167–184.

Broussaine, M. and Vince, R. 1996. Working with metaphor towards organizational change. In C. Oswick and D. Grant (eds.) *Organizational Development: Metaphorical Analysis*. London: Pitman, 57–72.

Brown, C., Costley, C., Friend, L. and Varey, R. 2010. Capturing their dream: video diaries and minority consumers. *Consumption, Markets and Culture*, 13: 419–436.

Bryans, P. and Mavin, S. 2006. Visual images: a technique to surface conceptions of research and researchers. *Qualitative Research in Organizations and Management: An International Journal*, 1(2): 113–128.

Buchanan, D. A. 2001. The role of photography in organizational research: a reengineering case illustration. *Journal of Management Inquiry*, 10: 151–164.

Butler, C., Finnear, J., Doherty, A. M. and Hill, S. 2014. Exploring identity: a figurative character image-elicitation approach. *Qualitative Research in Organizations and Management: An International Journal*, 9(2): 151–168.

Butler-Kisber, L. and Poldma, T. 2010. The power of visual approaches to qualitative inquiry: the use of collage making and concept mapping in experiential research. *Journal of Research Practice*, 6(2): 1–16.

Cassell, C. M. and Symon, G. 2012. Introduction: the context of qualitative organizational research. In G. Symon and C. M. Cassell (eds.) *Qualitative Organizational Research: Core Methods and Current Challenges*. London: Sage, 12.

Cassell, C. M., Malik, F. and Radcliffe, L. S. 2016. Using photo-elicitation to understand experiences of work–life balance. In K. Townsend, R. Loudon and D. Lewin (eds.) *Handbook on Qualitative Research Methods in Human Resource Management*. Cheltenham, UK: Edward Elgar, 146–162.

Checkland, P. 1981. *Systems Thinking, Systems Practice*. New York: John Wiley and Sons.

Clarke, J. 2011. Revitalizing entrepreneurship: how visual symbols are used by entrepreneurs. *Journal of Management Studies*, 48(6): 1365–1390.

Collier, J. R. 1967. *Visual Anthropology: Photography as a Research Method*. London: Holt, Rinehart and Winston.

Cornelissen, J. P. and Clarke, J. S. 2010. Imagining and rationalizing opportunities: inductive reasoning, and the creation and justification of new ventures. *Academy of Management Review*, 35(4): 539–557.

Cummings, S. and Wilson, D. C. 2003. *Images of Strategy*. Oxford: Blackwell.

Czarniawska, B. 2010. Translation impossible? Accounting for a city project. *Accounting, Auditing and Accountability Journal*, 23(3): 420–437.

Davison, J. 2010. [In]visible [in]tangibles: visual portraits of the business elite. *Accounting, Organizations and Society*, 35(2): 165–183.

Davison, J., Mclean, C. and Warren, S. 2012. Exploring the visual in organizations and management. *Qualitative Research in Organizations and Management: An International Journal*, 7(1): 5–15.

Duberley, J., Johnson, P. and Cassell, C. M. 2012. Philosophies underpinning qualitative research. In G. Symon and C. M. Cassell (eds.) *Qualitative Organizational Research: Core Methods and Current Challenges*. London: Sage, 15–34.

Fullana, J., Palliosera, M. and Vilà, M. 2014. Advancing towards inclusive social research: visual methods as opportunities for people with severe mental illness to participate in research. *International Journal of Social Research Methodology*, 17(6): 723–738.

Garcia, B., Welford, J. and Smith, B. 2015. Using a smartphone app in qualitative research: the good, the bad and the ugly. *Qualitative Research*. Published online before print 3 August 2015, doi: 10.1177/1468794115593335.

Griffin, M., Harding, N. and Learmonth, M. 2016. Whistle while you work? Disney animation, organizational readiness and gendered subjugation. *Organization Studies*. Published online before print 26 September 2016, doi.org/10.1177/0170840616663245.

*Guardian, The* 2015. www.theguardian.com/world/2015/sep/02/shocking-image-of-drowned-syrian-boy-shows-tragic-plight-of-refugees (accessed March 31, 2015).

Guell, C. and Ogilvie, D. 2015. Picturing commuting: photovoice and seeking well-being in everyday travel. *Qualitative Research*, 15(2): 201–218.

Gylfe, P., Franck, H., LeBaron, C. and Mantere, S. 2016. Video methods in strategy research: focusing on embodied cognition. *Strategic Management Journal*, 37(1): 133–148.

Hardy, C. and Phillips, N. 1999. No joking matter: discursive struggle in the Canadian refugee system. *Organization Studies*, 20(1): 1–24.

Harper, D. 2002. Talking about pictures: a case for photo-elicitation. *Visual Studies*, 17(1): 13–26.

Hassard, J. S. 2009. Researching work through ethnographic documentaries. In D. A. Buchanan and A. Bryman (eds.) *The Sage Handbook of Organizational Research Methods*. London: Sage, 270–282.

Hassard, J. S. and Buchanan, D. A. 2009. From *Modern Times* to *Syriana*: Feature films as research data. In D. A. Buchanan and A. Bryman (eds.) *The Sage Handbook of Organizational Research Methods*. London: Sage, 620–635.

Hinthorne, L. L. 2014. Using digital and instant film photography for research documentation: a research note. *Qualitative Research*, 14(4): 508–519.

Hurdley, R. 2007. Focal points: framing material culture and visual data. *Qualitative Research*, 7(3): 355–374.

Jarrett, M. and Liu, F. 2016. "Zooming with": a participatory approach to the use of video ethnography in organizational studies. *Organizational Research Methods*. Published online before print 11 July 2016, doi: 10.1177/1094428116656238.

Jarzabkowski, P., Burke, G. and Spee, P. 2015. Constructing spaces for strategic work: a multimodal perspective. *British Journal of Management*, 26: S26–S47.

Jick, T. D. 1979. Mixing qualitative and quantitative methods: triangulation in action. *Administrative Science Quarterly*, 24(4): 602–611.

Kaplan, S. 2011. Strategy and PowerPoint: an inquiry into the epistemic culture and machinery of strategy making. *Organization Science*, 22(2): 320–346.

King, N. 2012. Doing template analysis. In G. Symon and C. M. Cassell (eds.) *Qualitative Organizational Research: Core Methods and Current Challenges*. London: Sage, 426–450.

Knoblauch, H. 2012. Introduction to the special issue of *Qualitative Research*: video-analysis and videography. *Qualitative Research*, 12(3): 251–254.

Krippendorf, K. H. 1980. *Content Analysis: An Introduction to Its Methodology*. London: Sage.

Llewellyn, N. 2014. "He probably thought we were students": age norms and the exercise of visual judgement in service work. *Organization Studies*, 36(2): 153–173.

Llewellyn, N. and Hindmarch, J. 2010. *Organization, Interaction and Practice: Studies of Real Time Work and Organizing*. Cambridge: Cambridge University Press.

Luff, P. and Heath, C. 2012. Some "technical challenges" of video analysis: social actions, objects, material realities and the problems of perspective. *Qualitative Research*, 12(3): 255–279.

Mazzetti, A. and Blenkinsopp, J. 2012. Evaluating a visual timeline methodology for appraisal and coping research. *Journal of Occupational and Organizational Psychology*, 85(4): 649–665.

Meyer, A. D. 1991. Visual data in organizational research. *Organization Science*, 2(2): 218–236.

Meyer, R. E., Höllerer, M. A., Jancsary, D. and van Leeuwen, T. 2013. The visual dimension of organizing, organization, and organization research: core ideas, current developments and promising avenues. *Academy of Management Annals*, 7(1): 489–555.

Murthy, D. 2008. Digital ethnography: an examination of the use of new technologies for social research. *Sociology*, 42(5): 837–855.

Norris, J. 2008. Collage. In L. M. Given (ed.) *The Sage Encyclopedia of Qualitative Research Methods*. London: Sage, 94–97.

*Organizational Research Methods*. 2017. Special issue on Video-based methods, ed. P. Jarzabkowski, C. Lebaron, K. Phillips and M. Pratt.

Parker, L. D. 2009. Photo-elicitation: an ethno-historical accounting and management research project. *Accounting, Auditability and Accountability Journal*, 22(7): 1111–1129.

Pink, S. 2001. More visualising, more methodologies: on video, reflexivity and qualitative research. *The Sociological Review*, 49(4): 586–599.

Plakoyiannaki, E. and Stavraki, G. Forthcoming, 2018. Collage visual data: pathways to visual analysis. In C. M. Cassell, A. L. Cunliffe and G. Grandey (eds.) *The Sage Handbook of Qualitative Business and Management Research Methods* (in press).

Pritchard, K. and Whiting, R. 2015. Taking stock: a visual analysis of gendered ageing. *Gender, Work and Organization*, 22(5): 510–528.

Pritchard, K. and Whiting, R. Forthcoming, 2018. Analysing web images. In C. M. Cassell, A. L. Cunliffe and G. Grandy (eds.) *The Sage Handbook of Qualitative Business and Management Research Methods* (in press).

*Qualitative Research in Organizations and Management*. 2012. Volume 7, issue 1, special issue on Exploring the visual in organization and management, ed. J. Davison, C. McLean and S. Warren.

Ray, J. L. and Smith, A. D. 2012. Using photographs to research organizations: evidence, considerations, and application in a field study. *Organizational Research Methods*, 15(2): 288–315.

Rose, G. 2012. *Visual Methodologies: An Introduction to Researching with the Visual*. London: Sage.

Samra-Fredericks, D. 2010. The interactional accomplishment of a strategic plan. In N. Llewellyn and J. Hindmarch (eds.) *Organization, Interaction and Practice: Studies of Real Time Work and Organizing*. Cambridge: Cambridge University Press, 198–217.

Sheridan, J., Chamberlain, K. and Dupuis, A. 2011. Timelining: visualizing experience. *Qualitative Research*, 11(5): 552–569.

Shortt, H. and Warren, S. 2012. Fringe benefits: valuing the visual in narratives of hairdressers' identities at work. *Visual Studies*, 27(1): 18–34.

Simpson, A., Slutskaya, N. and Simpson, R. 2014. The use of ethnography to explore meanings that refuse collectors attach to their work. *Qualitative Research in Organizations and Management: An International Journal*, 9(3): 183–200.

Slutskaya, N., Simpson, A. and Hughes, J. 2012. Lessons from photo-elicitation: encouraging working men to speak. *Qualitative Research in Organizations and Management: an international journal.*, 7(1): 16–33.

Stiles, D. 2004. Pictorial representation. In C. M. Cassell and G. Symon (eds.) *Essential Guide to Qualitative Methods in Organizational Research*. London: Sage, 127–139.

Strangleman, T. 2004. Ways of (not) seeing work: the visual as a blind spot in WES? *Work Employment & Society*, 18(1): 179–192.

Sunderland, P. L. and Denny, R. M. 2002. Performers and partners: consumer video documentaries in ethnographic research. In *Qualitative Ascending: Harnessing Its True Value*. Amsterdam: ESOMAR, 285–303.

Symon, G., Cassell, C. M. and Johnson, P. 2016. Evaluative practices in qualitative management research: a critical review. *International Journal of Management Reviews*. Published online before print 13 September 2016, doi: 10.1111/ijmr.12120.

Toraldo, M. L., Islam, G., and Mangia, G. 2016. Modes of knowing: video research and the problem of elusive knowledges. *Organizational Research Methods*. Published online before print 14 July 2016, doi: 10.1177/1094428116657394.

Vince, R. and Warren, S. 2012. Participatory visual methods. In G. Symon and C. M. Cassell (eds.) *Qualitative Organizational Research: Core Methods and Current Challenges*. London: Sage, 275–295.

Walsh, S. and Clegg, C. W. 2004. Soft systems analysis. In C. M. Cassell and G. Symon (eds.) *Essential Guide to Qualitative Methods in Organizational Research*. London: Sage, 334–348.

Warren, S. 2002. Show me how it feels to work here. *Ephemera: Critical Dialogues on Organisation*, 2(3): 224–245.

Warren, S. 2005. Photography and voice in critical qualitative management research. *Accounting, Auditing and Accountability Journal*, 18(6): 861–882.

Warren, S. 2006. Hot nesting? A visual exploration of personalised workspaces in a "hot-desk" office environment. In P. Case, S. Lilley and T. Owens (eds.) *The Speed of Organization*. Copenhagen: Copenhagen Business School Press, 119–146.

Warren, S. 2008. Empirical challenges in organisational aesthetic research: towards a sensual methodology. *Organisation Studies*, 29(4): 559–570.

Warren S. 2012. Having an eye for it: aesthetics, ethnography and the senses. *Journal of Organizational Ethnography*, 1(1): 107–118.

Whiting, R. and Pritchard, K. Forthcoming, 2018. Digital ethics. In C. M. Cassell, A. L. Cunliffe and G. Grandy (eds.) *The Sage Handbook of Qualitative Business and Management Research Methods* (in press).

Whiting, R., Symon, G., Roby, H. and Chamakiotis, P. 2016. What's behind the lens? A reflexive analysis of roles in participatory video analysis. *Organizational Research Methods*. Published online before print 29 September 2016, doi: 10.1177/1094428116669818.

Whittle, A. Forthcoming, 2018. Ethnomethodology. In C. M. Cassell, A. L. Cunliffe and G. Grandy (eds.) *The Sage Handbook of Qualitative Business and Management Research Methods* (in press).

Wiles, R., Coffey, A., Robinson, J. and Heath, S. 2012. Anonymisation and visual images: issues of respect, "voice" and protection. *International Journal of Social Research Methodology*, 15(1): 41–53.

Woodward, S. 2008. Digital photography and research relationships: capturing the fashion moment. *Sociology*, 42(5): 857–872.

Wright, C., Darko, N., Standen, P. and Patel, T. 2010. Visual research methods. *Sociology*, 44(3): 541–558.

Zuboff, S. 1988. *In the Age of the Smart Machine*. New York: Basic Books.

# 27

# BUILDING GROUNDED THEORY WITH SOCIAL MEDIA DATA

*Emmanuelle Vaast and Cathy Urquhart*

## Introduction

In the last few years, new generations of web applications have dramatically increased people's ability to interact with each other electronically, to generate content online, and to immerse themselves in alternative universes (boyd and Ellison 2008; Damer 2008; Messinger et al. 2009; O'Reilly 2007). Social media have become widespread, and have led to new social practices (Koebler et al. 2010), sociability patterns (Van Den Eede 2010), learning practices (Greenhow and Robelia 2009; Kim and Abbas 2010), leisure activities, as well as social and political mobilization (Byrne 2008; Wattal et al. 2010). Social media use has also permeated the business domain (Culnan et al. 2010), triggering new business models (Lyons 2008), customer-relationship tactics (Di Gangi et al. 2010; Gallaugher and Ransbotham 2010), and managerial practices (Kaganer and Vaast 2010; Leidner et al. 2010; Leonardi and Vaast forthcoming).

The potential for research based upon social media data is also huge. Studies in sociology, marketing, and information systems, in particular, have started to examine social media in some depth (e.g., Beer and Burrows 2007; Cooke and Buckley 2009). Yet, much of this research has been *descriptive*, i.e., it has presented empirically, in sometimes great detail, what these new environments are. There is a growing need and opportunity for researchers to move beyond describing and towards theorizing with social media-based data (Majchrzak 2009).

Theory corresponds to "a statement of concepts and their interrelationships that shows how and/or why a phenomenon occurs" (Corley and Gioia 2011). We are interested in theory building that explicitly considers relationships between concepts as opposed to detailed description. This may encompass causal relationships. We also consider how theory-building elements inherent in grounded theory methodology (such as theoretical sampling to expand the scope of a theory) may deserve to be used more or differently with social media-based data.

We focus on grounded theory building from social media data, and highlight the opportunities and challenges that qualitative researchers are likely to face in this pursuit. It seems urgent for researchers to develop ways of building theory for social media because many researchers have started embracing these environments as contexts for their research (e.g., Huang et al. 2015; Vaast et al. 2013) and many more have been thinking about doing so. Consequently, there has been a growing concern, among scholars (e.g., Kane and Fichman 2009; Kane et al. 2012; Majchrzak 2009; Te'eni 2009), that the *methodological* aspects of researching with social media data, and subsequent implications for theory building have not yet been sufficiently examined. This paper elaborates on these emerging discussions by examining grounded theory building with social media data. We examine new and possibly unexpected methodological dilemmas the researcher may face, and suggest ways to collect and analyze social media data to build theory. It is not our ambition to provide the last word on these important issues. This would be unrealistic, especially as social media and the intricately related social and technical conditions they generate are in flux, with a stream of new applications becoming available and adopted. Rather, we present documented arguments for taking grounded theory building seriously with social media data.

## Social Media Data: A New Frontier for Researchers

Social media, or "Internet-based applications that build on the ideological and technological foundations of Web 2.0, and that allow the creation and exchange of user-generated content" (Kaplan and Haenlein 2010), have generated unprecedented opportunities for the development of new theories in research, as well as unanticipated methodological challenges for researchers. Opportunities lie in the multiplicity and diversity of methodological approaches that researchers might adopt in these environments: e.g., experiments (Antheunis and Scouten 2010; Minocha et al. 2010), ethnography (Garcia et al. 2009; Kien 2008), "cyber-archeology" (Zimbra et al. 2010), or case studies (Vaast and Walsham 2013; Veer 2011). The methodological challenges of dealing with these new environments are, however, also varied, and range from the technical (how to do it?) (Bollier 2010; boyd and Ellison 2008), to the legal (how legally accountable is the researcher?) (Allen et al. 2006; Lehmberg et al. 2008), and the ethical (what are the right courses of action?) (Beer 2008; Stanton 2010). Social media environments vary substantially (see Table 27.1).

As a caveat, we note here that it is not our intention to claim that everything about social media is new, and that the challenges and opportunities they afford researchers are always unprecedented. There is a body of research on online communities (e.g., Kraut et al. 2012; Vaast and Levina 2015) and open source software development (e.g., Fleming and Waguespack 2007; O'Mahony and Ferraro 2007; Shaikh and Vaast forthcoming; Von Hippel and Von Krogh

*Table 27.1* Examples of Widespread Social Media Environments

| Social Media Applications and Environments | Examples | Examples of Publications |
| --- | --- | --- |
| Social networking sites | Facebook, Myspace | (Grasmuck et al. 2009) |
| Wikis | Wikipedia | (Niederer and van Dijck 2010) |
| Blogging and microblogging | Huffington Post Twitter | (Macias et al. 2009) (Vaast et al. 2013) (Ferguson et al. 2013) |
| Virtual worlds | Second Life | (Schultze and Orlikowski 2010) |
| Tagging, bookmarking, online reviews | Del.ic.ious, Yelp | (Orlikowski and Scott 2014; Scott and Orlikowski 2010) (Levina and Arriaga 2014) |
| Photo and video sharing sites | YouTube | (Lange 2008) |

2003) that has for some time illustrated some of these challenges and opportunities. Vaast and Walsham (2013), for instance, examined how grounded theorizing methods, in particular, might be adjusted in these computer-mediated and social environments. However, the fast growing and increasingly pervasive popularity of social media in many aspects of everyday life, and the highly dynamic character of social media applications (and of their waves of popularity) have made it especially appealing for researchers to try to build grounded theory from social media data. Table 27.2 presents recent publications that have tackled this issue.

One of the major issues confronting the social media researcher is the question of what might be a legitimate unit of analysis when a whole range of social media data might (and perhaps should) be studied. The social media researcher has to deal, for instance, with web pages, chat threads, emails, and many visual images (see Table 27.3).

First, a digital text, by definition, is held in a digital format. The digital format can be held in any number of file formats, which can sometimes cause issues around data management.

The second characteristic, we think, is a common one – many social media researchers will be studying a particular website, or type of websites, e.g., social networking sites, dating sites, gambling sites, and so on. The question then is what sort of context does the website or sites provide? Can we see the website as providing an overall frame for the study? Can we thus conceptualize the website as providing the natural boundaries for the case study? Or does the boundary lie beyond the website?

The third characteristic – co-produced by more than one person – produces various ethical issues for the researcher. For instance, is the discussion on a public forum deemed as being in the public domain and therefore, like, say, a text from a newspaper? If the forum is membership only, and discusses sensitive issues, should the people on that forum know that they are part of a research project? What are our responsibilities when we too, participate in these forums? Gaining permission to use, for instance, a stream of collaborative "chats" about a project within an organization is a different matter from considering what ethical concerns might operate in a web forum.

The fourth characteristic, the ephemeral nature of the text, also creates problems for the social media researcher. There needs to be a systematic way of capturing the texts so they are not lost. This can lead to the collection of large amounts of data, which in turn gives rise to two other problems – data management, and critically, deciding which texts might be worthy of analysis.

The fifth characteristic is that digital texts usually embed other texts through hyperlinks. A digital text is indeed usually not a "stand alone" text. One of the key features of the digital environment is the ability to link content to each other. Therefore, digital texts are embedded in one another, creating new conditions for data collection.

The sixth characteristic, contains images, is, we think, an important characteristic. In such overwhelming visual environments such as those often afforded by social media (e.g., Facebook profile or pages) not to consider analyzing visual images that we encounter in such an environment may not do justice to that environment and its dynamics.

The seventh characteristic, contains video, underlines the previous characteristic. For instance, we know that video interviews give researchers much information from non-verbal cues. So we would suggest that the social media researcher might also gain insights from such video sources and should actively consider where, when, and how they can be incorporated into the case study design.

The eighth characteristic, lack of context, is also one we think that social media researchers should pay particular attention to. Regardless of whether one is analyzing a digital text, or crunching some "big data," it is impossible to infer patterns without context. For instance, if a

Table 27.2 Examples of Grounded Theorizing with Social Media Data

| Source | Research Question | Data and Methods | Key Findings |
|---|---|---|---|
| Vaast et al. (2013) | How do new actor categories emerge through new media? | Grounded qualitative analyses of blog posts of a new actor category | Theorization of the emergence of a new actor category through new media as an ongoing process in which the category identity may remain fluid, rather than progress to an endpoint |
| Beck et al. (2014) | What affects knowledge exchanges in electronic networks of practice? | Dataset of enterprise software messages analyzed quantitatively combined with qualitative content coding of a subset of the dataset | Knowledge seekers' characteristics and relational factors drive knowledge exchanges in social media-enabled electronic networks of practices |
| Toubiana and Zietsma (forthcoming) | How do emotions influence organizations in situations of institutional complexity? | Qualitative analyses of actors' emotive reactions on social networking website to organizational action | When people's expectations of an organization's actions are violated it can trigger a process of emotional escalation |
| Gibbs et al. (2015) | How does the use of new technologies influence communications across geographical and hierarchical boundaries in organizations? | Mixed-methods grounded analyses of:<br>• Server log data of technology use (quantitative data)<br>• 14 semi-directed interviews of employees | New technologies promote cross-boundary communication, but with distinct patterns for hierarchical and regional boundaries |

*Table 27.3* Illustrative Characteristics of Digital Texts

| Characteristic | Example |
| --- | --- |
| Held in digital format | Emails, chat threads, photographs |
| Contained on a website | Web content |
| Co-produced by more than one person | Web forums, wikis |
| Ephemeral | Comments on a link, a news feed in Facebook |
| Embeds other discourses | Link within a web page, linking digital text to one another |
| Contains images | Avatar, web content, photographs |
| Contains videos | YouTube clips |
| Lack of context | Microblog posts (e.g. "tweets" of 140 characters or less) |
| Linguistic innovations | Emoticons, acronyms (e.g. "lol") |

stream of Skype chats gets recorded, it might also be good for the researcher to note some basic context (e.g., time of day, day of week). Deeper context can be grasped by examining who are the people involved in these chats and, perhaps, by interviewing them. Adding context can help researchers make sense qualitatively of the phenomena and processes they observe through social media data (see, e.g., Vaast et al. 2013).

Finally, the last characteristic is that of linguistic innovations and includes the growing reliance upon acronyms (e.g., "lol" for "laugh out loud," "FYI" for "for your information," or "IMHO" for "in my humble opinion") in digital texts, as well as the tendency for digital "texts" to blur the distinction between iconic representations and discourse (Wolf 2000). Increasingly in web-based forums as well as in microblog posts, for instance, emoticons have complemented traditional language-based content and contributed to new ways of expressing complex ideas and sentiments online (Bos et al. 2007). They have transformed written text, making it in some ways closer to oral language, such as when "lol" punctuates a digital text in a similar way that laughter punctuates an unmediated conversation (Spencer and Mandell 2007). Another similar linguistic innovation is the evolving use of hashtags on Twitter. From being simple tags on which a search can be performed, they also perform the function of a summarized and often humorous take on the tweet in question (Vaast et al., 2012).

Taken together, these characteristics of social media environments provide unexpected challenges for researchers, who then need to adjust their theory-building methods.

## Challenge 1 – Case Study Design

A key challenge is related to the possibility to collect large data sets, much larger than what many qualitative researchers would have considered just a few years ago. In this section, we consider how we might design a case study for a social media environment, given these large data sets. It is important to note here that we are defining a case study in broad terms, as we believe that a flexible definition of what a case is makes sense in social media studies.

> In the sociological and anthropological literature, a case is typically regarded as a specific and bounded (in time and place) instance of a phenomenon selected for study. The phenomenon of interest may be a person, process, event, group, organization, and so on.
>
> *(Schwandt 1997)*

In particular, we consider how we might select data of interest within such large data sets, how we might decide on a case study boundary, how we might handle the issue of context, and whether single or multiple-case studies are appropriate.

The availability of "big data" has arisen from two main conditions. The first one, obviously, and aforementioned, is related to the growth of social media, in particular in terms of available platforms and features as well as in terms of their increasing popularity that have contributed to new ways of communicating, working, etc. The second condition comes from increased computational abilities that have enabled companies to develop and populate huge databases as well as computer-mediated communications to become socially omnipresent and very cost-effective (Jacobs 2009).

From the possibility to collect huge data for research purposes, new challenges have arisen. In particular, how does the researcher select what might be significant data in a welter of logs, chats, emails, and other data? The temptation for the unwary researcher is to collect as much data as possible – and of course, it is possible to collect a great deal of data in a social media environment. For instance, if collecting data on a virtual open source project, possible archival sources would include, for instance: emails; bug tracking data, or software version control logs.

For illustrative purposes, let us consider a situation in which researchers decide that they actually do need to collect large volumes of data, say from social networking websites, blogs, or microblog archives. They are likely to rely upon an application programming interface (API) that will help them access these data. One such publicly available API is Topsy, an openly accessible and relatively user-friendly search engine for Twitter, currently the most popular microblogging platform. Through Topsy, anyone, including researchers, can use the API to access the entire archive of Twitter (Topsy labs 2010). There are huge opportunities, of course, for researchers in being able to collect so much data and to be selective in their data collection (e.g., researchers can search for key terms and specific times). One problem here is that search engines and APIs can actually influence the data collection process: relying upon search engines and APIs can lead to biased samples, with the "bias" not always or easily understood by the researchers (Bollier 2010; boyd and Crawford 2011). In effect, rather than purposeful theoretical sampling, the data collection can become the result of an uncontrolled and little understood process of opaque algorithm-led, data extraction. Therefore, researchers need to be aware of how these algorithms might influence their data set.

So how might we begin to select data for grounded theory building? First, we might consider the notion of "central" texts, and less central texts, and how those texts should be analyzed. There is always a "depth versus breadth" concern in any qualitative research design; the more deeply a text is analyzed, the fewer texts may be analyzed. One possible route here is to analyze some texts more deeply than others – hence the notion of having central texts to analyze. Less central texts can be used to provide corroboration or triangulation. Readers may say at this point that this is merely primary and secondary data. We would beg to differ, because in fact, if theoretical sampling is used, "data slices" could, and should, come from different sources – so we prefer the distinction between "central" and "less central." The logic of settling on a central text helps to provide an entryway for the researcher and to think about which data sources are important in the design.

We think that the idea of a digital text also has some reach when considering the unit of analysis of a study. Of course, the unit of analysis is always dependent upon the specific research questions of various projects. Digital texts force researchers to think about what the unit of analysis of their research is, and what this unit of analysis means to them. For instance, in a recent study by one of the authors on bankers and online forums (Vaast and Levina 2015), the unit of analysis was the post, but other units could have been selected (e.g., threads as a whole).

Once central texts, and less central texts, have been identified, we should then arrive at the *boundary* of the case study. One important consideration for social media researchers is whether their boundary is the social media boundary – do they study purely virtual environments? While it is entirely appropriate for ethnographers to study "virtual worlds" as ethnographic environments, we contend that to place the boundary within or on a social media environment is not always advisable. First, when we consider the permeability of the division between "real" and "virtual" worlds, it is perhaps unrealistic to simply study what goes on in a social media environment. For instance, friendships in Facebook have corresponding relationships in "real" life. There is often a reflexive relationship between the two. Second, one major challenge of studying social media environments, we contend, is that of *context*. How can we interpret a digital text if we are not aware of its context?

If we agree that context is important in a social media environment, whether when using digital texts or when using "big data" expressed as visualizations, how do we build a context for our case study design? If we consider what our central text might be, we can at the same time consider how context can be built in. For instance, if we are interested in how hotel operators respond to negative reviewers on Trip Advisor, we might opt to use their responses on the website as our central text for the case study (Orlikowski and Scott 2014). It might also be worth interviewing those owners about their response to follow up on issues that come up from the analysis or simply to find out about other factors that were in operation at the time for that owner. Similarly, if we collect a stream of posts about the development of a software product, it would be sensible to relate this to field notes about what was happening in the project at the time. Even if the researcher focuses exclusively on the virtual environment, the same argument for context still applies. For instance, let us imagine that researchers are investigating microblogging (e.g., activity on Twitter) in various contexts and situations (e.g., Heverin 2011; Jansen et al. 2009; Vaast et al. 2012). Researchers in this situation are likely to select single microblogging posts (i.e., the "tweets") as their unit of analysis. At the same time, though, a tweet is very short (140 characters or less): making sense of a tweet in and of itself is difficult – tweets are to be understood within an ensemble (cf. the notion of "ambient awareness," see boyd et al. 2010; Marwick and boyd 2010). For researchers, the implication is that it is sometimes difficult, but important, to access the context of digital text data. Following our previous example, when studying microblogging, researchers could consider what was trending in Twitter at the time; they could consider the surrounding tweets, and the sequence of tweets and retweets (boyd et al. 2010; Lotan et al. 2011; Namaan et al. 2011).

While thus far in this chapter, the plethora of data available to the social media researcher can be seen as carrying some disadvantages, there is one respect in which it can be seen as a distinct advantage; many digital texts lend themselves to *theoretical sampling* for theory building. The beauty of this solution is clear, as the developing theory determines which data "slice" is examined next. In a social media environment, the ability to sample "data slices" is extremely flexible. It will probably not require consent (although terms of usage for social media applications change and need to be checked regularly), or another phase of a study for "member checking" as in a traditional case study.

Theoretical sampling can proceed in two ways. The first is exemplified in Eisenhardt (1989) where successive case studies are chosen on the basis of similarity or difference with the previous case and within case patterns. The second is a more systematic view from Glaser and Strauss (1967) where group differences are not only minimized or maximized, but sampling also unfolds with concept development. For instance, if the analysis of digital texts reveals many instances of a concept (e.g., self-presentation through Facebook status messages), one could choose to go on and sample more of that concept by interviewing individuals. Similarly, one could choose to sample further on a concept that has only occurred in a particular group of people, or is unusual (e.g., use of a Facebook status to communicate with only a few people in a very personal way). Glaser and Strauss suggest that sampling along diverse concepts quickly develops the theory and delimits the scope of the theory. Sampling using not only "different" and "similar" cases, but also looking for guidance in terms of concept development, means that we develop a much better, more grounded theory, with better scope.

Again, such flexible theoretical sampling of digital texts could be seen as a double-edged sword. When digital texts contain links to other digital texts that have some conceptual relevance, where should the researcher set the boundary for their case study? An obvious pitfall is that researchers might soon find themselves overwhelmed by potentially relevant data. At the very extreme, link-by-link, the whole Internet could become their research setting, making theory building all but impossible and meaningless. There is thus an increased need to set boundaries for the cases under investigation.

## Challenge 2 – Data Analysis

Generally, when analyzing textual data, there are two main options: either the researcher can code the text at a detailed level, or they can apply a thematic framework of some kind. This of course still applies in the social media environment, but there are many more texts that can potentially be analyzed. So, distinguishing between these two options is important because they have different analytical "loads"; if analyzing a text in detail, there will be less chance to analyze many texts. This of course does not mean that, in practice, the researcher should not employ multiple methods of analysis – but that the time needed to apply different methods should be considered. In short, there may be a "depth versus breadth" issue. As stated earlier, we suggest that social media researchers opt for some "central" texts that can be analyzed in depth, since there is no substitute for such in-depth analysis in qualitative research (with one important proviso – that this analysis is subsequently theoretically integrated).

When coding at a detailed level, there are three options for coding. First, bottom-up coding, where codes are suggested by the data. Grounded theory method is a very good example of this approach, and can yield rich results because of a close tie with the data. Grounded theory method also gives a systematic way to theoretically sample different digital texts, as discussed previously. Second, codes can be suggested by the literature and constructs used in instruments – this is "top-down" coding. Third, codes can be applied which are a mixture of codes suggested by the data *and* the literature. Overall, the coding approach gives the researcher assurance that what they have in their data really is in their data, because coding confers a more systematic approach to analysis. It also helps qualitative researchers defend themselves from charges of being selective about what they analyze.

Thematic frameworks are also frequently used to analyze qualitative data, and there are many possibilities available. For instance, there are many frameworks from discourse analysis and critical discourse analysis (e.g., Fairclough 1992) that could be applied to digital texts. Thematic frameworks or models built from relevant literatures, for instance a "sensitizing framework" as suggested by Klein and Myers (1999) is also a frequent strategy used by researchers. An alternative is to build a thematic framework from the data, as suggested in Braun and Clarke (2006).

We would also urge social media researchers to seriously consider how they might analyze *visual* digital texts they encounter, and the role that such analyses can play in extending and enriching the emerging theory. There are various ways of analyzing such visuals. First, the text can be coded as if it was any other type of digital text. Given that most qualitative data analysis packages do have the capability to both store such visuals and code them, there seems to be no obstacle to this type of analysis except a lack of familiarity, and a possible fear that this type of analysis might not be published. We could also view images as not neutral, but as constructed texts (Banks 2007). This makes sense particularly with social media, where people manage how they appear online, and there are websites, for instance, devoted to "photobombs" where the subject of the photograph is sometimes accidently, sometimes deliberately upstaged by another element in the photograph. We can take a Foucauldian view of the image – who is doing the looking, whom does society empower to look at and be looked at, and what knowledge does this produce? Of course, visual analysis is not new, it has a long pedigree in cultural studies, for instance. One useful perspective comes from Ball and Smith (1992) who point out that it is important to distinguish between manifest and latent content for analytical purposes. For instance, an old photograph may contain a man with a mutton chop beard (manifest content) but the latent content concerns the social meaning of that beard at the time the image was produced in Banks (2007). This brings us back to a key element which needs to be considered by the social media researcher when analyzing – context. This is why we would recommend that the issue of context be considered early in the case study design.

## Challenge 3 – Engaging in Mixed Methods

Social media environments also constitute unprecedented research settings, because they generate a wealth of digital text data that, technically at least, researchers may collect exhaustively and with little to no interference on the sociotechnical dynamics at play. This new situation has generated tremendous opportunities but also challenges for researchers (Bollier 2010; boyd and Crawford 2011; Lazowska 2008; Manovich 2011). Some of these challenges are legal, as detailed in Allen et al.'s (2006) seminal essay on regulatory implications of automatic electronic data collection. Other key challenges are of an ethical nature, and deal with, for instance, the blurring of the distinction between what is private and what is public, or questions regarding whether electronic data are public or private (Buchanan 2010; Buchanan and Ess 2008; Hudson and Bruckman 2004; Schultze and Mason 2011; Sveningsson 2004). Aware of these critical issues, in this essay, we focus on another important, and so far less discussed, challenging implication of "big data" for theory building, the need to engage in mixed methods.

In this regard, Anderson (2008) provocatively called for a drastic change in the scientific method, given the rise of electronic data becoming publicly available to many. He predicted that "the end of theory" was being brought about by the "data deluge" of the Internet, search engines, and social media. Intrigued by this provocative thesis, we, however, believe that the scientific community can still contribute to society not only by discovering and explaining correlations, but also by theorizing causations, and multiple-order effects between concepts. Others have discussed how electronic data might transform both the process of developing new theories and the resulting theories. John Seely Brown, for instance, as reported in Bollier (2010), addressed how newly available data can help researchers discover "generators" for new theories if researchers are able to make sense of what in their data, corresponds to "outliers" and what reveals meaningful patterns:

> How can you invent the "theory behind the noise" in order to de-convolve it in order to find the pattern that you weren't supposed to find? The more data there is, the better my chances of finding the "generators" for a new theory.

We argue that for researchers to be able to discover the "generators" for a new theory, they need more than powerful computational abilities, although they obviously do need such resources to be able to sift through huge volumes of data. To do so, researchers interested in theory building, and not just in descriptive analyses or in testing existing theories with electronic data, would do well to engage in mixed methods analyses.

The huge volume of data that researchers can collect in social media environments creates data processing, reduction, and management challenges. Obviously, such a volume of data can be impressive, but is also utterly meaningless per se. Collecting huge volumes of data, per se, does not guarantee a theoretical contribution for the research. If anything, big data might make building theory more difficult, because theorizing patterns and outliers becomes especially challenging in a wealth of decontextualized data. Researchers might not always feel well equipped to handle these data sets. Researchers who are usually engaged in qualitative research might find themselves intimidated by the volume of data, and might not know how to "attack" it to develop, for instance, a grounded theory of their phenomenon of focal interest. Getting deeply into a corpus of semi-directed interviews of reasonable duration is already formidable enough; how to make sense of years of archives from online discussion forums, for instance? For qualitative researchers dealing with such new contexts and new data, then, being able to delve into data from a more quantitative angle, thanks to descriptive visualization techniques, can be helpful.

Quantitative researchers are not immune to the challenges of big data for theory building either. A major issue for quantitative researchers is that, when huge volumes of data have been collected, the significance level loses some of its meaning, and putting too much weight on it for theory justification purposes, as opposed to the power of the analyses, might weaken the resulting theory (Bollier 2010; boyd and Crawford 2011). To build theories of these new environments, quantitative researchers therefore cannot rely singlehandedly on well-established statistical indicators, and need to be able to give meaning to their data. Adoption of more qualitative approaches to theory building may assist with achieving this sensemaking.

Therefore, handling digital text data for theory-building purposes might force researchers out of their typical (qualitative/quantitative) comfort zone, and lead them to embrace methodological creativity. Qualitative researchers might try to deal with larger data sets with descriptive quantitative methods, and quantitative researchers might delve into the meaning of their data, rather than focus mostly on the significance level of their statistical procedures. Obviously, calls for triangulation for better theory building are far from new (see, in organization research, Jick 1979; Shah and Corley 2006; Van Maanen 1979). Triangulation, in the sense of combination of different methods, especially involving qualitative and quantitative aspects, is particularly critical for theory building of social media contexts. For one, it can help researchers deal with and sift through a huge volume of data, relying upon multiple techniques, to identify patterns to be theorized. Moreover, mixed methods offer researchers the ability to develop complementary perspectives on the same phenomenon and to discern previously hidden connections among concepts.

On a practical note, many researchers are more familiar with qualitative or quantitative research, although many of us would also not consider ourselves exclusive proponents of a single method over other ones. Engaging in multi-method theory building research projects can help us reach beyond what we have usually become more familiar with methodologically. This, obviously, makes such research demanding, because it is not enough to develop "qualitative" or "quantitative" research, and researchers have to develop research projects that combine various methodological "ideal types." We therefore hope that the opportunities and challenges of developing mixed methods for theory-building purposes will lead researchers to reach out and develop collaborations across the traditional methodological divides. Researchers at ease with the latest computational methods can summarize vast amounts of data and develop impressive, yet descriptive, visualizations (Lazowska 2008). Other researchers, more attuned to discovering theories, could work with them in order to make sense of empirical patterns and soundly make the "creative leap" (Langley 1999) that is necessarily involved in any theory-building effort. Such mixed-methods research projects would still be challenging to develop, because there are still currently fewer established criteria to evaluate mixed methods than for more traditional methods. We would like to see researchers involved in mixed-methods projects be more explicit about their methodological choices, and engage in conversations about those choices.

## Conclusion

The purpose of this chapter was to reflect on grounded theory building with social media data and to articulate its unprecedented challenges and opportunities for researchers. Theory building remains an enduring challenge for many researchers in disciplines that deal with "applied" environments. The rise of social media data has ushered in major changes in both organizing and research. It is a much more collaborative era that allows for people to state their opinions, and for their opinions to be gathered, via crowdsourcing. This gives the researcher an increased opportunity to study varying viewpoints, and gain corroboration of particular viewpoints. Visuals, images, and videos have also become essential in social media and researchers could – and probably should – also deal with these new forms of data. The advent of "big data" cannot be understated as a development either; there is a huge potential to collect a large amount of data, but with a corresponding need to make sense of that data. The role of context in social media should in this regard be acknowledged, as it is required to make sense of either a large data set or a "slice" of data. We recommend then, that, when embarking on research in social media environments, there be an active consideration of how to account for context under investigation. Finally, the availability of large data sets has generated a critical need for researchers to go beyond their familiar methodological choices and to embrace mixed methods. Engaging in mixed methods could trigger productive collaborations among researchers and help generate thought-provoking conceptualizations.

This paper ambitioned to open a dialogue among researchers interested in grounded theorizing with social media-based data. We look forward to engaging with our colleagues, and to further elaborating on these ideas about possible methodological approaches.

## References

Allen, G. N., Burk, D. L., and Davis, G. 2006. "Academic data collection in electronic environments: defining acceptable use of Internet resources," *MIS Quarterly* (30:3) September, pp. 500–510.

Anderson, C. 2008. "The end of theory: the data deluge makes the scientific method obsolete," *Wired*, June 23, 2008.

Antheunis, M., and Scouten, A. P. 2010. "The effects of other-generated and system-generated cues on adolescents' perceived attractiveness on social network sites," *Journal of Computer-Mediated Communication* (16), pp. 391–406.

Ball, M., and Smith, G. 1992. *Analysing Visual Data*, London: Sage.

Banks, M. 2007. *Using Visual Data in Qualitative Research*, London: Sage.

Beck, R., Pahlke, I., and Seebach, C. 2014. "Knowledge exchange and symbolic action in social media-enabled electronic networks of practice: a multilevel perspective on knowledge seekers and contributors," *Management Information Systems Quarterly* (38:4), pp. 1245–1270.

Beer, D. 2008. "Researching a confessional society," *International Journal of Market Research* (50:5), pp. 619–629.

Beer, D., and Burrows, R. 2007. "Sociology and, of, and in Web 2.0: some initial considerations," *Sociological Research Online* (12:5) 17.

Bollier, D. 2010. *The Promise and Peril of Big Data*, Washington, DC: Aspen Institute.

Bos, D., Bos, A. E. R., and von Grumbkow, J. 2007. "Emoticons and social interaction on the Internet: the importance of social context," *Computers in Human Behavior* (23:1), pp. 842–849.

boyd, d., and Crawford, K. 2011. "Six provocations for big data," A Decade in Internet Time: Symposium on the Dynamics of the Internet and Society, Oxford, UK, 2011.

boyd, d. m., and Ellison, N. B. 2008. "Social network sites: definition, history, and scholarship," *Journal of Computer-Mediated Communication* (13), pp. 210–230.

boyd, d., Golder, S., and Lotan, G. 2010. "Tweet, tweet, retweet: conversational aspects of retweeting on Twitter," 43rd Hawaii International Conference on System Sciences, Hawaii, 2010.

Braun, V., and Clarke, V. 2006. "Using thematic analysis in psychology," *Qualitative Research in Psychology* (3), pp. 77–101.

Buchanan, E. A. 2010. "Internet research ethics: past, present, and future," in *The Handbook of Internet Studies*, R. Burnett, M. Consalvo and C. Ess (eds.), Malden, MA: Blackwell, pp. 83–108.

Buchanan, E. A., and Ess, C. 2008. "Internet research ethics: the field and its critical issues," in *The Handbook of Information and Computer Ethics*, K. E. Himma and H. T. Tavani (eds.), New York: Wiley, pp. 273–292.

Byrne, D. N. 2008. "Public discourse, community concerns, and civic engagement: exploring black social networking traditions on Blackplanet.com," *Journal of Computer-Mediated Communication* (13), pp. 319–340.

Cooke, M., and Buckley, N. 2009. "Web 2.0, social networks and the future of market research," *International Journal of Market Research* (50:2), pp. 267–292.

Corley, K. G., and Gioia, D. A. 2011. "Building theory about theory building: what constitutes a theoretical contribution?," *Academy of Management Review* (36:1), pp. 12–32.

Culnan, M. J., McHugh, P. J., and Zubillaga, J. I. 2010. "How large U.S. companies can use Twitter and other social media to gain business value," *MIS Quarterly Executive* (9:4) December, pp. 243–259.

Damer, B. 2008. "Meeting in the ether: a brief history of virtual worlds as a medium for user-created events," *Journal of Virtual Worlds Research* (1:1) July, pp. 1–17.

Di Gangi, P. M., Wasko, M. M., and Hooker, R. E. 2010. "Getting customers' ideas to work for you: learning from Dell how to succeed with online user innovation communities," *MIS Quarterly Executive* (9:4) December, pp. 213–228.

Eisenhardt, K. M. 1989. "Building theories from case study research," *Academy of Management Review* (14:4), pp. 532–550.

Fairclough, N. 1992 "Discourse and text: linguistic and intertextual analysis within discourse analysis," *Discourse Society* (3:2), pp. 193–217.

Ferguson, J., Soekijad, M., Huysman, M., and Vaast, E. 2013. "A vision for development? Blogging in ICT4D," *Information Systems Journal* (23:4) July, pp. 307–328.

Fleming, L., and Waguespack, D. M. 2007. "Brokerage, boundary spanning, and leadership in open innovation communities," *Organization Science* (18:2) March–April, pp. 165–180.

Gallaugher, J., and Ransbotham, S. 2010. "Social media and customer dialog management at Starbucks," *MIS Quarterly Executive* (9:4) December, pp. 197–212.

Garcia, A. C., Standlee, A. I., Bechkoff, J., and Cui, Y. 2009. "Ethnographic approaches to the Internet and computer-mediated communication," *Journal of Contemporary Ethnography* (38:1), pp. 52–84.

Gibbs, J. L., Eisenberg, J., Rozaidi, N. A., and Gryaznova, A. 2015. "The 'megapozitiv' role of enterprise social media in enabling cross-boundary communication in a distributed Russian organization," *American Behavioral Scientist* (59:1), pp. 75–102.

Glaser, B., and Strauss, A. 1967. "Grounded theory: the discovery of grounded theory," *Sociology The Journal Of The British Sociological Association* (12), pp. 27–49.

Grasmuck, S., Martin, J., and Zhao, S. 2009. "Ethno-racial identity displays on Facebook," *Journal of computer-mediated communication* (15), pp. 158–188.

Greenhow, C., and Robelia, B. 2009. "Old communication, new literacies: social network sites as social learning resources," *Journal of Computer-Mediated Communication* (14), pp. 1130–1161.

Heverin, T. 2011. "Use of microblogging for collective sense-making during violent crises: a study of three campus shootings," *Journal of the American Society for Information Science and Technology* (63:1), pp. 34–47.

Huang, J., Baptista, J., and Newell, S. 2015. "Communicational ambidexterity as a new capability to manage social media communication within organizations," *Journal of Strategic Information Systems* (24:2), pp. 49–64.

Hudson, J. M., and Bruckman, A. 2004. "'Go away': participant objections to being studied and the ethics of chatroom research," *The Information Society* (20), pp. 127–139.

Jacobs, A. 2009. "The pathologies of big data," *Communications of the ACM* (52:8) August, pp. 36–44.

Jansen, B. J., Zhang, M., Sobel, K., and Chowdury, A. 2009. "Twitter power: tweets as electronic word of mouth," *Journal of the American Society for Information Science & Technology* (60:11), pp. 2169–2188.

Jick, T. D. 1979. "Mixing qualitative and quantitative methods: triangulation in action," *Administrative Science Quarterly* (24:4), pp. 602–611.

Kaganer, E. A., and Vaast, E. 2010. "Responding to the (almost) unknown: social representations and corporate policies of social media," International Conference of Information Systems, St. Louis, MI, 2010.

Kane, G. C., and Fichman, R. G. 2009. "The shoemaker's children: using wikis for information systems teaching, research and publication," *MIS Quarterly* (33:1) March, pp. 1–17.

Kane, G. C., Levina, N., Pikorski, M. J., Ransbotham, S., Griffith, T., Majchrzak, A., Borgatti, S., Faraj, S., and Jarvenpaa, S. L. 2012. "Researching the informal economy: opportunities and challenges of social media research," in *Academy of Management Conference*, Boston, MA.

Kaplan, A. M., and Haenlein, M. 2010. "Users of the world, unite! The challenges and opportunities of social media," *Business Horizons* (53) January–February, pp. 59–68.

Kien, G. 2008. "Technography = Technology + ethnography, an introduction," *Qualitative Inquiry* (14:7) October, pp. 1101–1109.

Kim, Y.-M., and Abbas, J. 2010. "Adoption of library 2.0 functionalities by academic libraries and users: a knowledge management perspective," *The Journal of Academic Librarianship* (36:3), pp. 211–218.

Klein, H. K., and Myers, M. D. 1999. "A set of principles for conducting and evaluating interpretive field studies in information systems," *MIS Quarterly*, pp. 67–93.

Koebler, F., Riedl, C., Vetter, C., Leimeister, J. M., and Krcmar, H. 2010. "Social connectedness on Facebook: an explorative study on status message usage," Proceedings of the Sixteenth Americas Conference on Information Systems, Lima, Peru, August 12–15, 2010.

Kraut, R. E., Resnick, P., Kiesler, S., Burke, M., Chen, Y., Kittur, N., Konstan, J., Ren, Y., and Riedl, J. 2012. *Building Successful Online Communities: Evidence-based Social Design*, Cambridge, MA: MIT Press.

Lange, P. G. 2008. "Publicly private and privately public: social networking on YouTube," *Journal of Computer-Mediated Communication* (13), pp. 361–380.

Langley, A. 1999. "Strategies for theorizing process data," *Academy of Management Review* (24:4) October, pp. 691–710.

Lazowska, E. 2008. "Envisioning the future of computing research," *Communications of the ACM* (51:8) August, pp. 28–30.

Lehmberg, T., Rehm, G., Witt, A., and Zimmerman, F. 2008. "Digital text collections, linguistic research data, and mashups: notes on the legal situation," *Library Trends* (57:1) Summer, pp. 52–71.

Leidner, D. E., Koch, H., and Gonzales, E. 2010. "Assimilating generation Y IT new hires into USAA's workforce: the role of an enterprise 2.0 system," *MIS Quarterly Executive* (9:4) December, pp. 163–176.

Leonardi, P. M., and Vaast, E. Forthcoming. "Social media and their affordances for organizing: a review and agenda for research," *Academy of Management Annals*.

Levina, N., and Arriaga, M. 2014. "Distinction and status production on user-generated content platforms: using Bourdieu's theory of cultural production to understand social dynamics in online fields," *Information Systems Research* (25:3), pp. 468–488.

Lotan, G., Graeff, E., Ananny, M., Gaffney, D., Pearce, I., and boyd, d. 2011. "The revolutions we tweeted: information flows during the 2011 Tunisian and Egyptian revolutions," *International Journal of Communication* (5), pp. 1375–1405.

Lyons, K. 2008. "Toward a theoretically-grounded framework for evaluating immersive business models and applications: analysis of ventures in Second Life," *Journal of Virtual Worlds Research* (1:1) July, pp. 1–19.

Macias, W., Hilyard, K., and Freimuth, V. 2009. "Blog functions as risk and crisis communication during Hurricane Katrina," *Journal of Computer-Mediated Communication* (15), pp. 1–31.

Majchrzak, A. 2009. "Comment: where is the theory in wikis?," *MIS Quarterly* (33:1) March, pp. 18–21.

Manovich, L. 2011. "Trending: the promises and challenges of big social data," in *Debates in the Digital Humanities*, M. K. Gold (ed.), Minneapolis, MN: University of Minnesota Press.

Marwick, A. E., and boyd, d. 2010. "I tweet honestly, I tweet passionately: Twitter users, context collapse, and the imagined audience," *New Media & Society* (13:1), pp. 114–133.

Messinger, P. R., Stroulia, E., Lyons, K., Bone, M., Niu, R. H., Smirnov, K., and Perelgut, S. 2009. "Virtual worlds – past, present, and future: new directions in social computing," *Decision Support Systems* (47), pp. 203–228.

Minocha, S., Tran, M. Q., and Reeves, A. J. 2010. "Conducting empirical research in virtual worlds: experiences from two projects in Second Life," *Journal of Virtual Worlds Research* (3:1), pp. 1–21.

Namaan, M., Becker, H., and Gravano, L. 2011. "Hip and trendy: characterizing emerging trends on Twitter," *Journal of the American Society for Information Science & Technology* (62:5) May, pp. 902–918.

Niederer, S., and van Dijck, J. 2010. "Wisdom of the crowd or technicity of content? Wikipedia as a sociotechnical system," *New Media & Society* (12:8), pp. 1368–1387.

O'Mahony, S., and Ferraro, F. 2007. "The emergence of governance in an open source community," *Academy of Management Journal* (50:5), pp. 1079–1106.

O'Reilly, T. 2007. "What is web 2.0: design patterns and business models for the next generation of software," *Communications & Strategies* (1) First quarter, p. 17.

Orlikowski, W. J., and Scott, S. V. 2014. "What happens when evaluation goes online? Exploring apparatuses of valuation in the travel sector," *Organization Science* (25:3) May–June, pp. 868–891.

Schultze, U., and Mason, R. O. 2011. "Ethics of online research: inquiry in a fishbowl," in *Academy of Management Conference*, Boston, MA.

Schultze, U., and Orlikowski, W. J. 2010. "Research commentary – virtual worlds: a performative perspective on globally distributed, immersive work," *Information Systems Research* (21:4) December, pp. 810–821.

Schwandt, T. 1997. *Qualitative Inquiry*, Sage: London.

Scott, S. V., and Orlikowski, W. J. 2010. "Reconfiguring relations of accountability: the consequences of social media for the travel sector," Annual Meeting of the Academy of Management, Best paper proceedings, Montreal, Canada, 2010.

Shah, S. K., and Corley, K. G. 2006. "Building better theory by bridging the quantitative–qualitative divide," *Journal of Management Studies* (43:8), pp. 1821–1835.

Shaikh, M., and Vaast, E. Forthcoming. "Folding and unfolding: balancing openness and transparency in open source communities," *Information Systems Research*.

Spencer, R. J., and Mandell, D. L. 2007. "Emotional expression online: emoticons punctuate website text messages," *Journal of Language and Social Psychology* (26:3), pp. 299–307.

Stanton, J. M. 2010. "Virtual worlds, the IRB and a user's bill of rights," *Journal of Virtual Worlds Research* (3:1) November, pp. 3–15.

Sveningsson, M. 2004. "Ethics in Internet ethnography," in *Readings in Virtual Ethics: Issues and Controversies*, E. A. Buchanan (ed.), Hershey, PA: Idea Group, pp. 45–61.

Te'eni, D. 2009. "Comment: the wiki way in a hurry – the ICIS anecdote," *MIS Quarterly* (33:1), pp. 20–22.

Topsy labs. 2010. "Using influence to tune signal to noise on the social web."

Toubiana, M., and Zietsma, C. Forthcoming. "The message is on the wall? Emotions, social media and the dynamics of institutional complexity," *Academy of Management Journal*.

Vaast, E., and Levina, N. 2015. "Speaking as one, but not speaking up: dealing with new moral taint in an occupational online community," *Information and Organization* (25:2), pp. 73–98.

Vaast, E., and Walsham, G. 2013. "Grounded theorizing for electronically-mediated social contexts," *European Journal of Information Systems* (22:1), pp. 9–25.

Vaast, E., Davidson, E. J., and Mattson, T. 2013. "Talking about technology: the emergence of new actors with new media," *MIS Quarterly* (37:4) December, pp. 1069–1092.

Vaast, E., Negoita, B., and Safadi, H. 2012. "Symbolic action through microblogging during and after a crisis: tweeting the oil spill," in *Academy of Management Conference, OCIS Division*, Boston, MA.

Van Den Eede, Y. 2010. "'Conversation of mankind' or 'idle talk'? A pragmatist approach to social networking sites," *Ethics and Information Technology* (12), pp. 195–206.

Van Maanen, J. 1979. "Reclaiming qualitative methods for organizational research: a preface," *Administrative Science Quarterly* (24:4) December, pp. 520–526.

Veer, E. 2011. "Staring: how Facebook facilitates the breaking of social norms," *Research in Consumer Behavior* (13), pp. 185–198.

Von Hippel, E., and Von Krogh, G. 2003. "Open source software and the 'private-collective' innovation model: issues for organization science," *Organization Science* (14:2) March–April, pp. 209–223.

Wattal, S., Schuff, D., Mandviwalla, M., and Williams, C. B. 2010. "Web 2.0 and politics: the 2008 U.S. Presidential election and an e-politics research agenda," *MIS Quarterly* (34:4) December, pp. 669–688.

Wolf, A. 2000. "Emotional expression online: gender differences in emoticon use," *Cyberpsychology & Behavior* (3:5), p. 827.

Zimbra, D., Abbasi, A., and Chen, A. 2010. "A cyber-archaeology approach to social movement research: framework and case study," *Journal of Computer-Mediated Communication* (16), pp. 48–70.

# 28

# NETWORK MODELS OF ORGANIZATIONAL ROUTINES

## Tracing Associations between Actions

*Brian T. Pentland and Peng Liu*

Over the last several years, organizational researchers have been paying more attention to *practice* (Schatzki 2006; Whittington 2006; Feldman and Orlikoswki 2011), to *process* (Tsoukas and Chia 2002; Czarniawska 2008; Langley et al. 2013), and to *organizational routines* (Feldman and Pentland 2003; Parmigiani and Howard-Grenville 2011; Feldman et al. 2016). While *practice*, *process* and *routine* have diverse intellectual ancestry, they have a strong family resemblance. This resemblance can be attributed to at least one common trait: they are all concerned with action and patterns of action (Howard-Grenville and Rerup 2016; Feldman 2016). Organizational routines have long been seen as patterns of action (e.g., Cohen et al. 1996), but the recent "practice turn" (Parmigiani and Howard-Grenville 2011) helps us see routines as a member of a bigger family (Feldman 2016).

In this chapter, we focus on methods for tracing patterns of actions within organizational routines. Organizational routines have been defined as "repetitive, recognizable patterns of interdependent action carried out by multiple actors" (Feldman and Pentland 2003, p. 95). When actors carry out the actions, routines are enacted in practice. When fieldworkers describe routines using narrative descriptions, it is difficult to capture and represent the patterns of action in a valid and reliable way. Narrative is a natural way to describe the sequence of events in a routine or any kind of organizational process (Pentland 1999). Empirical research shows that a single routine can generate thousands of possible performances (Pentland et al. 2011); many of these performances are minor variations on a smaller set of typical performances. There may be a handful of typical patterns, but there could be a large number of variations and combinations of those patterns. Those variations are difficult or impossible to capture in a single narrative description of the routine.

To address this challenge, Pentland and Feldman (2007) proposed the narrative network as a simple way to represent the "pattern in variety" (Cohen 2007) that is typical of organizational routines. The narrative network provides a way to express the entire set of possible performances in a compact, convenient way. One performance of a routine can be described in a single narrative, but the overall pattern of performances cannot. It requires a richer description of the kind provided by a narrative network.

The network representation is also helpful for basic empirical operations such as comparing routines (Ragin and Becker 1992; Pentland et al. 2010), studying "technology in use"

(Orlikowski et al. 1995; Goh et al. 2011), detecting change in routines (Pentland et al. 2011), visualizing variability in routines (Hayes et al. 2011), discovering the relationship between variations and change (Pentland et al. 2012), and estimating the complexity of routines (Hærem et al. 2015). While some of these operations involve quantitative methods, they are based on the essentially qualitative problem of describing the narrative network in the first place.

Here, we outline two closely related methods for constructing a narrative network that describes a routine. One method can be considered a structured, ethnographic interview (Spradley 2016): one informant explains the routine. We will refer to this as the "top-down" method, in the sense that it relies on having an informant with an overview of the whole routine. The other method is based on collecting narrative fragments that describe specific performances of the routine, or parts of performances. We will refer to this as the "bottom-up" method. The performances can be drawn from a wide range of sources, including interviews, observation, or archival data.

Both methods rely on the idea that each performance of a routine can be conceptualized as a narrative: a sequence of actions or events that has a beginning, middle, and end. However, as mentioned, a single routine may generate a variety of different stories that a single narrative description cannot include. Further, as a practical matter, it is often difficult to collect entire performances, from beginning to end. Usually, we collect fragments. The two methods described here offer ways to solve these problems by tracing the associations between the actions to create an overall picture of the routine.

We begin by providing some background about narrative networks. As used here, this idea follows from Abbott's (1992) concept of narrative positivism. In particular, it assumes that it is possible to identify stable categories of events from narrative data. Then, we present the two methods and discuss some of their strengths and weaknesses.

## Describing Routines as Narrative Networks

The narrative network draws on concepts from actor network theory (Latour 2005), which gives artifacts the same status as human actors. In particular, the narrative network treats both actors and artifacts as equivalent attributes of an action or event. However, the narrative network perspective is different from actor network theory because the focus is on actions rather than actors or actants. In narrative networks, we are tracing relations between actions, rather than tracing relations between actants, as described by Latour (2005). Like other forms of networks, the narrative network is an inherently relational approach (Emirbayer 1997). Rather than treating organizational routines as static things, the narrative network perspective regards routines as dynamic and unfolding relations (Feldman 2016; Feldman et al. 2016).

A narrative network is based on the sequential relationship between pairs of actions or events within a process, practice, or routine (Pentland and Feldman 2007).[1] Technically, a narrative network is a directed graph where the nodes represent categories of actions or events. The nodes can be defined in terms of one or more attributes: actor, actions, artifact, or other salient properties of the narrative. The edges of the graph represent sequential relationships between the events. Narrative networks are unimodal (one kind of node – events) and unidimensional (one kind of edge – sequence). In the following sections, we break this down into the two parts of any graph: vertices (nodes) and edges (ties).

## *Identifying Nodes: From Occurrences to Events*

Following Abbott (1990), and the sociological literature on the analysis of events (Griffin 1993), we distinguish between occurrences and events. Occurrences are instantaneous observations (raw data), but events are the nodes (vertices) in the network that represent the organizational routine. The translation from occurrences to events is the essential first step in theorizing about sequential data (Abbott 1990; Langley 1999). In variance theory, we observe indicators, but we theorize about constructs; in process theory, we observe occurrences, but we theorize about events.

In effect, occurrences are indicators of events. For example, if you stumbled into a hotel ballroom and observed people in formal attire using a knife to cut a cake, you might think: this looks like a wedding reception! Cutting the cake is an occurrence; the wedding reception is a category of event. Events have duration (e.g., a honeymoon) and they can be marked by a wide variety of occurrences (see Figure 28.1). Historical sociologists have applied this framework to problems such as the formation of nation states (Tilly and Ardant 1975), the careers of musicians (Abbott and Hrycak 1990), and many others. Without distinguishing between (concrete) occurrences and (abstract) events, there would be no way to generalize about these phenomena.

The translation between occurrences and events is nothing more (or less) than coding of qualitative data into categories (Corsaro and Heise 1990; Corbin and Strauss 2014). Nodes in a narrative network represent *categories of events*, not particular events. In this respect, narrative networks are not like social networks, where particular nodes usually represent particular individuals. In a narrative network describing North American marriage rituals, the node for "wedding reception" would represent the category of wedding receptions, not just the particular one at that hotel ballroom. Stated differently, when there are multiple instances of an event in the data, they are represented by a single node in the network. Mapping instances into categories is the key idea that this method borrows from Abbott (1992).

### *Events Can Have Multiple Attributes*

When telling a story, it would be very unusual to include only the actions – we also include the actors, the location, the time, and other salient features. In defining the narrative network, Pentland and Feldman (2007) draw on the idea of a "functional event" (Hendricks 1972), which is a key event that moves the narrative forward. Functional events include the actor and the action, but the researcher can choose to use more or less in describing events. As mentioned above, each node in the network corresponds to a category of events, and each category is defined by a unique combination of attributes.

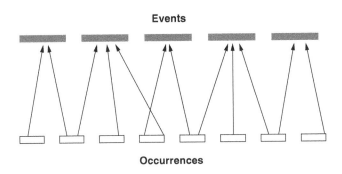

**Events**

**Occurrences**

*Figure 28.1*   Occurrences Are Indicators of Events

## *Identifying Edges: Tracing Relations between Events*

After one has defined the events, the next step is to identify relationships between the events. Abbott (1992) refers to this as "colligation": the logical relationship of events. The ethnographic method known as event structure analysis (ESA) focuses deeply on the relationships between events (Heise 1989, Corsaro and Heise 1990, Griffin 2007). The "structure" in ESA is conceptualized as narrative structure (Griffin 1993) and many kinds of relationships are possible (necessary, sufficient, sequence, part-of, kind-of, contributes-to, and more).

Here, we focus on one kind of relation: sequence. A narrative network summarizes the sequential relationships between the event categories. The edges in the network can be detected by following the stories in the data. Each time a story progresses from one event to the next, it indicates a relation between those events and an edge in the network. It is important to note that finding edges does not require complete narratives. One can use parts of stories that cover different parts of a routine.

## *The Grammatical Analogy*

A narrative network can also be thought of as a simple grammar for a routine (Pentland and Rueter 1994). Building on the linguistic metaphor, a narrative network embodies the paradigmatic and syntagmatic dimensions of a routine (de Saussure 1916/1996), as shown in Table 28.1. In a language (or a routine), the paradigmatic dimension includes the set of possible words (or events). It defines the lexicon or vocabulary for the routine. The syntagmatic dimension describes the sequential relationship between the elements in the lexicon. In linguistic terms, it defines how the words can be combined to make sentences. There are many ways to specify syntax, but the network model is the simplest because it considers only adjacent pairs of events. Higher order effects (i.e., the influence of prior, non-adjacent events) are not included in the basic model.

In the sections that follow, we present two methods for constructing a narrative network. For both methods, we will use the example of academic hiring, since it will be familiar to many readers. Conceptually, both methods involve the same basic steps necessary to define any network: (1) identifying the nodes and (2) identifying the edges.

## Constructing a Narrative Network: Top-Down

The first method is an interview protocol where a knowledgeable informant is asked to generalize about a focal routine. Thus, the data can be interpreted as an ostensive aspect of the routine from the point of view of that informant (Feldman and Pentland 2003). This method was used by Liu (2013). The interview protocol is included in Appendix A in English. It is also available upon request from the authors in Chinese.

*Table 28.1* Grammatical Analogy

| Nodes | Events | Paradigmatic | Lexicon |
|-------|--------|--------------|---------|
| Edges | Sequence | Syntagmatic | Syntax |

## *Bounding the Routine*

An essential first step is to define the boundary of the routine. Different people may define different boundaries, depending on their point of view (Pentland and Feldman 2005). In the case of academic hiring, one can imagine different choices for start and finish. Does the routine start when the department begins to recognize the need to hire (e.g., when someone leaves)? Or does it begin when the position is approved, or the search committee is formed? Likewise, the hiring process might seem to end when a candidate accepts or declines an offer. However, there are always additional steps (legal and institutional requirements) to complete the contract and bring the newcomer on board. And if the search fails, it may begin again.

The aim here is to find a clear boundary that makes sense to both informants and researchers. When we collect data to compare narrative networks, it is important to make sure that the boundary is consistent across different networks. For example, if we were comparing the academic hiring routine at public versus private institutions, we would need to define it in a consistent way.

In the interview, we start by asking the informant to identify a repetitive pattern of action that is part of his or her work. We ask the informant to describe the start and finish, since these are what provide the boundary of the routine.

## *General Description*

Once we have identified the routine, we ask them to provide a general description of its purpose, frequency, duration, location, and importance. This is like a "grand tour" (Spradley 2016), where the informant explains the whole routine in general terms. In this stage, we do not need to worry about the details, since those will be filled in later. For example, the specific sequence of steps might not be clear, and alternative possibilities might not be mentioned. The general description is like the "zoomed out" view of the routine. To get the patterns of actions, we need to "zoom in" to specify each step.

## *Define the Nodes (Lexicon)*

Given the description of the routine, we break it down into steps. In other words, we enlist the help of the informant in coding the description of the routine into categories. This has the advantage of helping the informant to remember additional steps that might have been left out. In this part of the protocol, we try to establish the categories and contrasts that define each step (Spradley 2016). This is important because the steps in the routine will become the nodes in the network. These steps are usually activities. They can be described in as much detail as the informant feels is necessary.

We start by specifying the first step and the last step which are the clear boundary of the routine. Using graph theory language, we specify the source and sink of the narrative network. Then we ask the questions of "what happens next" to fill the gap between the first step and the last step.

Next, for each step, it may be useful and necessary to add in some attributes, as events can have multiple attributes like the actants, the location, the time, and other salient features. In the interview, we may also be interested in the actants. If so, then we ask informants to specify the actants performing the step and the actants influenced by the step. For example, in "The search committee identifies candidates," the action is *identify*, and the actants are *the search committee* and *candidates*. It is important to emphasize that there are no predetermined rules for establishing these categories. The researcher should exercise his or her judgment about how much detail is necessary for the research question.

### *Defining the Edges (Syntax)*

Once the steps of the routine have been established, we begin to identify the sequence of steps: what happens first, what happens next and what happens last. This is the syntagmatic dimension of the routine. These sequential relationships will become the edges in the network.

In a typical routine, it is common to have alternative actions or branches. The alternative actions cannot happen at the same time, and only one alternative action or one branch can happen in each story. In the interview, we ask "Is that always what happens, or are there alternatives or exceptions?" The idea is to list all possible alternative actions over many different stories. For example the dean can either approve or reject the list recommended by the search committee.

### *Frequency of Variations and Exceptions*

We expect that any routine will have variations and exceptions. From the previous phase of the interview, we already know the positions of alternative actions or branches. Now, in the last phase of the interview protocol, we revisit these positions and focus on how often different alternatives or actions happen. So we ask the informant to estimate the frequency of each alternative or exception. This captures the variations that may be present in the routine, from their point of view. Figure 28.2 shows a narrative network for the same routine constructed with the "bottom-up" method described in the next section The result of this protocol is a narrative network that describes the routine (see Figure 28.2).

### Constructing a Narrative Network: Bottom-Up

The second method starts from narrative fragments that describe actual performances, or typical performances, of the routine. These fragments can come from any source (interview, observation, or archival). Depending on the source of the data, the resulting network could be interpreted as a reflection of the ostensive or performative aspects of the routine (Feldman and Pentland 2003). For example, if the data describe typified, abstract performances, then it would be best to interpret the resulting network as an ostensive aspect of the routine. If the data describe actual performances, then the resulting network would reflect the performative aspect of the routine. The general outline of the process is similar to the top-down interview protocol, but there are some important differences.

In this section, we will continue with the hiring example, but we will work "bottom-up," from actual performances of the hiring routine at a Midwestern public university. One search was successful, the other failed. The data for each case comes from the formal report to the university human resources department. Formal reports portray a selective point of view, of course, but they are adequate for our purposes here.

### *Bounding the Routine*

Conceptually, this is the same as we face in the top-down approach, but it is not necessary to have a routine that can be described by a single informant. Using archival records, it may be possible to cover a routine from start to finish, even if the people performing the routine are not aware of what each other is doing.

For example, in the hiring routine, the university requires a formal report for each academic position that is posted. The formal reports cover a larger scope of the process than was covered

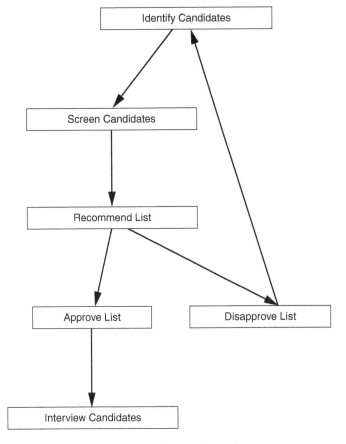

*Figure 28.2* Academic Hiring Routine Using Top Down Approach

in the top-down method, but it is still somewhat selective, and the boundaries defined in the archival record may not correspond to the needs of the research question.

## *Collect Narrative Fragments*

There are many possibilities for this step, including interview, observation (Goh et al. 2011), or archival data (Pentland et al. 2010). If collecting data from interviews, the focus would be on collecting descriptions of actual performances, rather than the top-down approach described above. With any of these methods, there are a number of unavoidable challenges, each of which threatens the completeness of the picture in a different way.

### *Covering the Whole Routine*

Since we no longer have the benefit of a single informant who understands the whole routine, from start to finish, the researcher needs to collect data that reaches to the boundaries. The risk here is that part of the routine might be missing entirely.

## Detecting Variations

Routines can have a large number of variations (Pentland et al. 2011). As a result, a small sample is unlikely to detect all of them. This may not be important to the research question, but it is a basic consideration. The risk here is that the routine might seem less varied than it actually is.

## Censoring

Data collected, especially from archival sources, will tend to reflect a particular point of view. Some actions will be highlighted, while others will be hidden. The risk here is that key steps in the routine may be omitted, which will also tend to decrease the apparent variety.

## Narrative Coherence

It is important that the event data are collected such that the raw occurrences are clearly related to the same coherent thread of activity (Abbott 1990). In other words, the data need to relate to the same story. The risk here is that sequential patterns in the data could be spurious or excessively noisy.

In practice, we expect that there will be trade-offs among these issues and probably no ideal answer. Researchers will need to adjust their data collection according to their needs. Here, for purposes of illustration, we used formal reports. These reports do a good job of covering the whole routine, from start to finish, but they are subject to a substantial amount of censoring (e.g., the entire process of campus visits for five individuals is compressed into a single, brief paragraph). Worse yet, we only have two of them, so we may be missing a lot of variations. As the technology of text mining and textual analysis improves (Weijters and Ribeiro 2011; Aggarwal and Zhai 2012), it will become possible to collect sequential data from a large number of different sources.

## Code Narrative Fragments

This is a familiar, basic step in qualitative research. We will not dwell on it here, since qualitative coding is a well-understood issue, and many resources are available (e.g., Corbin and Strauss 2014). However, there are a few distinctive issues that deserve attention.

In coding data for a narrative network, the main focus here is the verbs, as verbs represent actions or events. These will tend to anchor the main functional events (the nodes) in the network. After the actions have been identified, the actants associated with actions and any other relevant attributes can be identified, as well.

Table 28.2 shows the coded data for one performance of the hiring routine (completely anonymized). Each row is an occurrence in the hiring process. These occurrences will be aggregated into events in the network. We have included a column for each of the attributes that we are using to describe the occurrences. Notice that the column for "Who" can be used to represent a specific individual (such as dean or department chair), or it can be used to represent a role (such as the HR department). The level of abstraction in forming the codes depends on the research question, among other things.

In coding a given set of fragments, the researcher has two main degrees of freedom to consider. First, what attributes will be included in the coding scheme? These correspond to the columns in Table 28.2. Is it possible (or necessary) to use who, what, when, where, and why (Burke 1969)? Are there other attributes that are needed to describe this particular context? Second, within each attribute, how fine-grained does the description need to be? For example,

*Table 28.2* Data Coded from the Report of the Recruiting Committee

| Seq | Who | Action | What | Where |
|---|---|---|---|---|
| 1 | DeptChair | Forms | Committee | Department |
| 2 | Admin | Creates | Account | Email |
| 3 | Admin | Creates | Account | JobsDatabase |
| 4 | Committee | Writes | PositionDescription | Department |
| 5 | Dean | Approves | PositionDescription | College |
| 6 | HR | Approves | PositionDescription | University |
| 7 | Admin | Posts | PositionDescription | JobsDatabase |
| 8 | Admin | Posts | PositionDescription | HigherEdJobs |
| 9 | Candidate | Submits | Applications | JobsDatabase |
| 10 | Admin | Sends | Acknowledgment | Email |
| 11 | Admin | Monitors | Applications | JobsDatabase |
| 12 | CommitteeChair | Meets | AssociateDean | College |
| 13 | Admin | Posts | PositionDescription | PhDProject |
| 14 | Committee | Interviews | Candidates | Conference |
| 15 | Admin | Closes | Applications | JobsDatabase |
| 16 | Committee | Reviews | Applications | Department |
| 17 | Committee | Recommends | ApplicantPool | Department |
| 18 | DeptChair | Approves | ApplicantPool | Department |
| 19 | HR | Approves | ApplicantPool | University |
| 20 | Admin | Invites | Candidates | Department |
| 21 | Candidate | Visits | Campus | Department |
| 22 | Faculty | Interviewss | Candidates | Department |
| 23 | Faculty | Ranks | Candidates | Department |
| 24 | DeptChair | Offers | Job | Department |
| 25 | Candidate | Accepts | Job | Department |

"who" can be specific individuals, or it can be generic roles. "When" could describe specific days, or seasons, or work-shifts. The choice of attributes, and the granularity within each attribute is the qualitative foundation upon which everything else rests. Given a set of coded data, as in Table 28.2, the rest of the procedure is basically mechanical. In other words, the qualitative coding that defines the data directly defines the network. The narrative network can be thought of as a simple visualization of the coded data.

## *Define the Nodes (Lexicon)*

Nodes are defined by combinations of codes. It can be difficult to keep track of them all, but the principle is easy: create one node in the network for each unique combination of attributes. For example, "DeptChair Offers Job" is one node; "Candidate Accepts Job" is another. If the coding process seems to be creating too many distinct nodes (or too few), the researcher may consider removing (or adding) attributes, or recoding data within an attribute.

## *Define the Edges (Syntax)*

As suggested above, edges are created by tracing between events. Once the data are coded and combined to define nodes, tracing between nodes is straightforward. Within each narrative fragment in the data, one simply counts the transitions from one node to the next. The fragments can be rather long, as in Table 28.2, or as short as two events.

Because we are just counting steps along the paths in the observed performances, this method automatically identifies alternative paths. Rather than asking the informant to describe the relative frequency of each path, it becomes a function of the data in the sample. If accurate, quantitative estimates are needed, a large sample may be required.

## Define the Network

Given a set of coded data, as shown in Table 28.2, the narrative network can be constructed by hand, if so desired. For a small set of data, this is feasible. For a larger set of data, it could become somewhat tedious and error prone. Fortunately, since constructing the network is a mechanistic algorithm, we can use an automated procedure called ThreadNet (Pentland et al. 2015). The software reads in a spreadsheet (or .csv file) formatted like Table 28.2 and creates a narrative network. The graphs presented in Figure 28.2 were created with this tool, which can be downloaded from http://routines.broad.msu.edu.

## Applications of Narrative Networks

Because they provide a convenient way to summarize patterns of action, we anticipate that narrative networks could have many applications in organizational research on practice, process, and routines. In this section, we mention a few examples.

### Improved Description of Action Patterns

This methodology allows us to describe key features of a routine in more detail. For example, which paths through a routine, practice, or process are most common? What are the "ruts in the road"? By answering those questions, we create an improved and more complete description of the enactment of a routine, which serves the foundation for building a better theory on routine dynamics.

### Visualization of Action Patterns

The narrative network also provides a visual representation of an organizational routine. Unlike a formal flow chart, which may be based on an idealized version of the routine, a narrative network can reveal actual practices, especially when it is constructed from a "bottom-up" point of view. Like any methodology for process mining (van der Aalst 2012), it can also be used to reveal differences between normative practices and actual practices.

### Comparison of Action Patterns

Better description facilitates more accurate comparison of routines. Comparison is a basic operation in any empirical science. By using a network representation, we have a well developed set of tools for comparison. This idea is described in more detail in Pentland et al. (2010). We can also use narrative networks to compare aggregate properties of routines, such as their complexity (Hærem, Pentland and Miller 2015). This approach treats the routine as the unit of analysis (Pentland and Feldman 2005).

## *Building Better Process Theory*

Abbott (1990) noted that in most variance research, however, antecedents are linked to consequences without observing or measuring the underneath mechanisms or intervening processes connecting the antecedents and consequences. By representing action patterns explicitly, the narrative network provides researchers with a useful tool to fill in the missing processes or events, and to build a better process theory. For example, having a clearer picture of the patterns of action may facilitate the analysis of the factors that influence the formation, structure, and dynamics of routines.

## *Understanding Stability and Change*

The fundamental challenge is that routines are not things (Feldman et al. 2016). They are traces of interdependent activity that unfold over time and space. While routines can be remarkably durable, their apparent stability must be regarded as an on-going accomplishment. The patterns of action within a routine are stable for now, not forever. Routines are more likely to appear stable when viewed for a short period of time, or from a distance (Feldman et al. 2016). Once we begin to look more closely, we often find that variations and change are natural parts of routines. The narrative network provides a tool for carrying out this kind of investigation in a systematic way.

## Comparison of Methods

Either of these methods – top-down or bottom-up – will provide a visual map that describes an organizational routine. Either approach can potentially aid in research on the application areas mentioned above. However, they do offer somewhat different results, and they serve somewhat different purposes.

## *Ostensive versus Performative Aspects of a Routine*

As described by Feldman and Pentland (2003), the ostensive aspects of a routine refer to abstract patterns, from the point of view of particular people. The interview method produces an indicator of an ostensive aspect of the routine, as seen from the perspective of one informant. If you want to compare how different people perceive a routine, the interview method would be best. This method is also quite fast and does not require any software.

On the other hand, the performative aspect of a routine refers to the specific patterns of action involved in carrying out the routine. If you want to analyze the performative aspect of a routine (or set of routines), the bottom-up method is necessary. It is possible to construct the network by tracing through the data by hand. However, with a larger data set, an automated tool like ThreadNet is useful.

## *Etic versus Emic: Whose Perspective Is Being Represented?*

Because each of these approaches entails qualitative coding, it is important to realize that from a methodological perspective, either of these aspects (ostensive or performative) can be rendered from an *etic* or an *emic* perspective (Guba and Lincoln 1994). An emic perspective reflects the knowledge and vocabulary of the cultural insider. When working closely with an informant, it is easier to get a culturally informed (emic) perspective on the data. While the interview protocol imposes sequential structure on the data, it allows the informant to express their own view of what is meaningful about the boundaries of the routine and each event within those boundaries. In contrast, an etic perspective is generally considered to be an outsider's view, and it is often a theory-based view. When working with archival sources, a theoretically informed (etic) perspective may be more likely, especially in the absence of a cultural "insider" to assist with interpretation.

## *Granularity of Description*

A closely related issue concerns the granularity of the description. Particularly when adopting an etic perspective, actions can be divided into more detailed sub-actions (Abell 1987). In a narrative network, it is also possible to have more detailed actions. In this case, the network will be larger and the structure of the network may be different. Just like the two examples in our paper, the two narrative networks are very different: the network from the bottom-up approach is more detailed.

Generally, the bottom-up approach generates a more detailed network than the top-down approach. However, it is also possible to have a detailed network about the ostensive aspect of a routine and a brief network about a specific performance of a routine. The choice of granularity level depends on the research question; and as long as it makes sense to the informants and researchers, any granularity level should work.

## *Tools for Comparing Routines*

One of the primary reasons for constructing a narrative network of a routine is to compare with other routines, or to compare the routine to itself over time, longitudinally. Each of these methods has strengths and weaknesses for these purposes.

The top-down approach collects an abstract description of a routine, and it is a convenient way to study some aggregate understanding of a routine such as significance, purpose, frequency, and duration. The top-down method also provides quantitative descriptors, such as the number of steps, the number of branches and the number of people and digital tools involved. Such metrics may be associated with subjective measures of the routine: satisfaction, productivity, and capabilities. The approach would fit well within a research design where one wants to understand the antecedents or consequences of the pattern of action within the routine (Abbott 1990).

To study the change of routine, it is better to use the bottom-up approach, as it collects much more detailed data on the narrative or narrative fragments. Details usually include variety in the actual performance which is a prerequisite for change. In a longitudinal research setting, the bottom-up approach could reveal changes in the structure of a routine over time. These might include the formation of new pathways, the dissolution of existing pathways, or changes in the relative frequency of existing pathways.

## *Differences between Top-Down and Bottom-Up in Our Examples*

In addition to these general considerations, there are some interesting comparisons between our top-down and bottom-up examples.

*Boundaries Are Different*

There is a different start and stop to the process. We could have adjusted and harmonized the graphs easily enough, but showing two different perspectives on what is supposedly the same routine highlights the importance of researcher judgment in forming the boundaries. For the most part, they are not "given" in either of these methods. They must be constructed. The advantage of the top-down method is that we construct the boundaries in collaboration with a knowledgeable informant.

*Detail Is Different*

The actions, actors, and other details can be different in the two examples. A step from the top-down perspective may include several steps in the bottom-up perspective, or vice versa. For example, the step "interview candidate" in Figure 28.2 corresponds to step 14 in Table 28.2. Also, "recommend list" corresponds with step 17, and "approve list" corresponds with steps 18 and 19. Steps "Identify candidates" and "Screen candidates" summarize multiple steps from step 9 to step 13 in Table 28.2. It is also possible that a step in the top-down approach doesn't relate to any steps in the bottom-up approach. The step "Disapprove list" doesn't have any corresponding steps in Table 28.2, as the bottom-up approach used in Table 28.2 only includes two instances of hiring routines. When there are more instances, "disapprove" action may also show up in Table 28.2.

From these differences, we can begin to see that edges and branches may have different interpretations depending on how the data are collected and analyzed. In addition to the perennial issue of an insider vs. outsider perspective, the top-down view is more abstract and possibly more normative. It represents an informant's view of what *should* happen. In contrast, the bottom-up view represents a sample of data that shows what *actually did* happen.

## Narrative Networks Describe Dynamic Processes, Not Static Things

It may be tempting to treat narrative networks as descriptions of static objects, but it is important to remember that routines belong to the same family of phenomena as process and practice (Feldman et al. 2016). The processual nature of narrative networks becomes particularly clear when we consider the practical foundations of the methodology described here.

First, because routines have internal dynamics, they may be changing over time (Feldman et al. 2016). At best, any particular set of observations reflects a snapshot, so the same is true for networks that are constructed based on those observations. Observable action patterns are stable for now.

Second, different actors are likely to have different points of view. As a result, there may be multiple sets of narratives that describe any particular practice, process, or routine. From different points of view, different subsets of action may be visible. This raises the possibility of using narrative networks to compare alternative points of view, but it also reminds us that any particular network reflects a particular point of view.

There is good reason to expect that any particular point of view will be selective, at best. We typically think of participant observation as a rich, comprehensive source of data, but even participant observation is limited in time and space. If you are observing one part of a routine, you are probably missing the other parts. As a result, field notes generally contain fragments of routines, not whole routines. For the same reason, it may be difficult to find an informant with an overview of a routine, from start to finish. In some situations, archival records can solve the problem of going start to finish, but they are constructed from a pre-determined point of view that is always selective, and may not be well suited to the research question.

Finally, it is important to remember that the nodes in the network represent *categories* of action, not specific instances of particular actions. If we treat each instance of an action as uniquely indexed in time and space, then each narrative is unique, and there is no possibility of constructing a network. For example, "drive to work" can be regarded as a different action each day it happens. To construct the network, we need to assign all of the unique instances of "drive to work" to a general category. As mentioned above, this categorization involves a judgment call that is typical of all qualitative research. By treating "driving to work" as a category, we can locate it in a network of related categories, but the actual driving is different every day. In other words, the narrative network does not provide an escape from the paradox of Ecclesiastes and Heraclitus (Pentland et al. 2011).

Taken together, these methodological issues should reinforce the point that describing an action pattern using a narrative network does not somehow transform that action pattern into a static object.

## Conclusion

One of the key contributions of the "practice turn" in the study of organizational routines (Parmigiani and Howard-Grenville 2011, Feldman 2016) has been the emphasis on fieldwork – taking a closer look at the phenomena (Feldman et al. 2016). Rather than talking about routines "vaguely, in the plural" we are talking about them "concretely, in the singular" (Pentland and Rueter 1994, p. 484). Methodologically, the narrative network is one of the best tools we have for carrying out this vision. Constructing the network is a fundamentally qualitative research problem, based on coding narratives into events. The material presented here offers two alternative approaches for applying this tool in empirical research.

## Appendix A

### *Interview Protocol for Narrative Networks*

In this interview, we are trying to get an accurate description of one particular routine. A routine is a *repetitive, recognizable pattern of actions* that you do in your work. The interview should take less than an hour.

*[Insert additional material concerning informed consent and confidentiality here.]*

We will start by identifying a repetitive pattern of action you do as part of your work. It needs to have a definite start and finish. Ideally, it should involve more than one person (the other person might be a customer or a supervisor).

Once we have decided on the process to talk about, we will:

1  Get a general description of the process.
2  Break the process down into steps.
3  Identify the sequence of steps.
4  Estimate the frequency of alternatives or exceptions.

## Part 1: Get a General Description of the Process

Q1. Let's start by getting a brief description of the organization.
How would you describe this organization (not the name, but what it does)?
Q2. Now let's identify a particular process to talk about.
Can you tell me some things that you do in your work?
Q3. Which of those things do you do most often?
Q4. OK, let's focus on (name of the process) _____
Q4a. What is the purpose or goal of the process?
Q4b. Can you give me a broad overview of this process, from start to finish?
Q5. How often is the process done? _____
Q6. I'd like to know how long it takes to complete, from start to finish.
Q6a. From start to finish, what's the shortest/fastest? _____
Q6b. From start to finish, what's the longest/slowest? _____
Q6c. From start to finish, what's the typical time? _____
Q7. How important is this process to the organization?
Q8. Is there a lot at stake in how well this process works?
Q9. In this location, how many people are involved? Can you list the different jobs (or roles)? For example, in a restaurant, there might be a hostess, waiter, busboy, cook, cashier …)
Q10. For each of those jobs or roles, how many different individuals would you say are involved in doing this routine in your organization? For example, 2 hostesses, 12 waiters …
Q11. In how many different locations is this process performed?

## Part 2: Break the Process Down into Steps

Now I'd like to break this process down into steps. There may be quite a few steps, so we may need to go slowly. I appreciate your patience.

Q12. First, let's pin down the start and the finish
Q12a. What happens FIRST? How do you know the process has started?
Q12b. What happens LAST? How do you know it has ended?
Q13. Now talk me through it again, but let's go a little slower so I can write down each step. As we go, try to think of "what happens next." Once we've got the list, we'll go through it again and I'll ask if that *always* happens next, or if there are special cases, alternatives, or exceptions.

## Part 3: Identify the Sequence of Steps

Now let's go through it again and focus on sequence. And if I leave out any steps, we can add those in.

Q14. Starting with the first action, what happens next? Is that always what happens, or are there alternatives or exceptions? If there is an alternative, let's not worry about how often it happens. Right now I want to know if it's possible for the sequence to go another way or not.

### Part 4: Estimate the Frequency of Alternatives or Exceptions

Q15. Now let's go through this one last time and focus on how *often* different alternatives happen. For each place where there is an alternative or exception, I'm going to ask you to estimate how often that happens. Try to make your best guess. [Prompt with: 90–10? 80–20? 60–40? 50–50?]

ALL DONE. THANK YOU!

## Note

1 While the terms "action" and "event" are not perfect synonyms, we will use them interchangeably here.

## References

Abell, P. (1987) *The Syntax of Social Life: The Theory and Method of Comparative Narratives.* New York: Oxford University Press.

Abbott, A. (1990) "A primer on sequence methods," *Organization Science,* 1:375–392.

Abbott, A. (1992) "From causes to events: Notes on narrative positivism," *Sociological Methods and Research,* 20:428–455.

Abbott, A. and Hrycak, A. (1990) "Measuring resemblance in sequence data: An optimal matching analysis of musicians' careers," *American Journal of Sociology,* 96:144–185.

Aggarwal, C. C. and Zhai, C. (2012) *Mining Text Data.* New York: Springer.

Burke, K. (1969) *A Grammar of Motives.* Berkeley, CA: University of California Press.

Cohen, M. D. (2007) "Reading Dewey: Reflections on the study of routine," *Organization Studies,* 28:773–786.

Cohen, M. D., Burkhart, R., Dosi, G., Egidi, M., Marengo, L., Warglien, M., and Winter, S. (1996) "Routines and other recurring action patterns of organizations: Contemporary research issues," *Industrial and Corporate Change,* 5:653–698.

Corbin, J. and Strauss, A. (2014) *Basics of Qualitative Research: Techniques and Procedures for Developing Grounded Theory.* Thousand Oaks, CA: Sage.

Corsaro, W. A. and Heise, D. (1990) "Event structure models from ethnographic data," *Sociological Methodology,* 20:1–57.

Czarniawska, B. (2008) "Organizing: How to study it and how to write about it," *Qualitative Research in Organizations and Management: An International Journal,* 3(1):4–20.

de Saussure, F. (1916/1996) *Cours de linguistique générale.* Paris: Payot.

Emirbayer, M. (1997) "Manifesto for a relational sociology," *American Journal of Sociology,* 103:281–317.

Feldman, M. S. (2016) "Routines as process: Past, present and future," in J. Howard-Grenville, C. Rerup, A. Langley, and H. Tsoukas (eds.) *Organizational Routines: How They Are Created, Maintained, and Changed.* Perspectives on Process Organization Studies Series. Oxford: Oxford University Press, 23–46.

Feldman, M. S. and Orlikowski, W. J. (2011) "Theorizing practice and practicing theory," *Organization Science,* 22(5):1240–1253.

Feldman, M. S. and Pentland, B. T. (2003) "Reconceptualizing organizational routines as a source of flexibility and change," *Administrative Science Quarterly,* 48:94–118.

Feldman, M. S., Pentland, B. T., D'Adderio, L., and Lazaric, N. (2016) "Beyond routines as things: Introduction to the special issue on routine dynamics," *Organization Science,* 27(3):505–513.

Goh, J. M., Gao, G., and Agarwal, R. (2011) "Evolving work routines: The adaptive routinization of technology in healthcare," *Information Systems Research,* 22:565–585.

Griffin, L. J. (1993) "Narrative, event-structure analysis, and causal interpretation in historical sociology," *American Journal of Sociology,* 98:1094–1133.

Griffin, L. J. (2007) "Historical sociology, narrative and event-structure analysis: Fifteen years later," *Sociologica,* 1:1–17.

Guba, E. G. and Lincoln, Y. S. (1994) "Competing paradigms in qualitative research," in N. K. Denzin and Y. S. Lincoln (eds.) *Handbook of Qualitative Research.* Thousand Oaks, CA: Sage, 105–117.

Hærem, T., Pentland, B. T., and Miller, K. (2015) "Task complexity: Extending a core concept," *Academy of Management Review*, 40:1–15.

Hayes, G. R., Lee, C. P., and Dourish, P. (2011) "Organizational routines, innovation, and flexibility: The application of narrative networks to dynamic workflow," *International Journal of Medical Informatics*, 80:e161–177.

Heise, D. R. (1989) "Modeling event structures," *Journal of Mathematical Sociology*, 14:139–69.

Hendricks, W. O. (1972) "The structural study of narration: Sample analyses," *Poetics* 3:100–123. Reprinted in 1973, *Essays on Semiolinguistics and Verbal Art*. The Hague: Mouton, 152–174.

Howard-Grenville, J. A. and Rerup, C. (2016) "A process perspective on organizational routines," in A. Langley and H. Tsoukas (eds.) *The Sage Handbook of Process Organization Studies*. Thousand Oaks, CA: Sage, 323–337.

Langley, A. (1999) "Strategies for theorizing from process data," *Academy of Management Review*, 24:691–710.

Langley, A., Smallman, C., Tsoukas, H., and Van de Ven, A. H. (2013) "Process studies of change in organization and management: Unveiling temporality, activity, and flow," *Academy of Management Journal*, 56(1):1–13.

Latour, B. (2005) *Reassembling the Social: An Introduction to Actor-Network Theory*. Oxford: Oxford University Press.

Liu, P. (2013) *Evolutionary Dynamics of Digitized Organizational Routines*. PhD Dissertation, Michigan State University.

Orlikowski, W. J., Yates, J., Okamura, K., and Fujimoto, M. (1995) "Shaping electronic communication: The metastructuring of technology in the context of use," *Organization Science*, 6:423–444.

Parmigiani, A. and Howard-Grenville, J. (2011) "Routines revisited: Exploring the capabilities and practice perspectives," *Academy of Management Annals*, 5:413–453.

Pentland, B. T. (1999) "Building process theory with narrative: From description to explanation," *Academy of Management Review*, 24:711–724.

Pentland, B. T. and Feldman, M. S. (2005) "Organizational routines as a unit of analysis," *Industrial and Corporate Change*, 14:793–815.

Pentland, B. T. and Feldman, M. S. (2007) "Narrative networks: Patterns of technology and organization," *Organization Science*, 18:781–795.

Pentland, B. T. and Rueter, H. H. (1994) "Organizational routines as grammars of action," *Administrative Science Quarterly*, 39:484–510.

Pentland, B. T., Feldman, M. S., Becker, M., and Liu, P. (2012) "Dynamics of organizational routines: A generative model," *Journal of Management Studies*, 49(8):1484–1508.

Pentland, B. T., Hærem, T., and Hillison, D. (2010) "Comparing organizational routines as recurrent patterns of action," *Organization Studies*, 31:917–940.

Pentland, B. T., Hærem, T., and Hillison, D. (2011) "The (n)ever-changing world: Stability and change in organizational routines," *Organization Science*, 22:1369–1383.

Pentland, B. T., Recker, J., and Wyner, G. (2015) "A thermometer for interdependence: Exploring patterns of interdependence using networks of affordances," *Thirty Sixth International Conference on Information Systems*. Ft. Worth, TX.

Ragin, C. C. and Becker, H. S. (1992) *What Is a Case? Exploring the Foundations of Social Inquiry*. Cambridge: Cambridge University Press.

Schatzki, T. R. (2006) "On organizations as they happen," *Organization Studies*, 27(12):1863–1873.

Spradley, J. P. (2016) *The Ethnographic Interview*. Long Grove, IL: Waveland Press.

Tilly, C. and Ardant, G. (1975) *The Formation of National States in Western Europe*. Princeton, NJ: Princeton University Press.

Tsoukas, H. and Chia, R. (2002) "On organizational becoming: Rethinking organizational change," *Organization Science*, 13:567–582.

van der Aalst, W. (2012) "Process mining: Overview and opportunities," *ACM Transactions on Management Information Systems (TMIS)*, 3(2):7.

Weijters, A. J. M. M. and Ribeiro, J. T. S. (2011) "Flexible heuristics miner (FHM)," in *IEEE Symposium on Computational Intelligence and Data Mining (CIDM)*.

Whittington, R. (2006) "Completing the practice turn in strategy research," *Organization Studies*, 27(5):613–634.

# 29

# REWRITING THE PUBLISHING NARRATIVE FOR GROUNDED THEORY BUILDING

*Deborah Dougherty*

Our journal editors and peer reviewers do not do an adequate job of evaluating and shaping qualitative research that is submitted for possible publication. And since many of us have served as editors, most of us review for journals and conferences, and all of us choose to present our work in a particular way, we all participate in this inadequate enactment of publishing. We provide incomplete advice to authors and make injudicious judgments about publishing submitted manuscripts for many reasons. On the reviewing/editing side, sometimes editors and reviewers lack deep knowledge of qualitative methods, or of the problem the paper seeks to unravel. Some act like cultists and impose "the one best way," usually the way they use, to carry out a style of research, frame the analysis, or define concepts. On the authoring side, sometimes people submit bad research. Authors may present descriptive case studies or ethnographies of particular contexts with no effort to develop a more fundamental understanding of behavior that would help resolve a serious problem. And sometimes authors ignore the vast literature that already exists on similar topics and so do not advance what we already know.

This chapter focuses on one reason for inadequate evaluations of grounded theory building that editors/reviewers and authors jointly construct. The reason: we shoehorn studies into a "confirmation" narrative that is based on a strange enactment of the scientific method, one that assumes a linear, sequential execution of well-established steps that confirms predefined knowledge (Schon 1983; Sandberg and Tsoukas 2011). A narrative is a rich account of situations that portray the people, places, and artifacts involved in a structured manner with a beginning, middle, and ending. Through the use of a plot, the narrative offers a particular point of view on a situation (Garud et al. 2011). The plot of the confirmation narrative is the logic of deduction, where scholars deduce hypotheses that predict specific outcomes about some behaviors from established theory. The beginning of the confirmation narrative consists of claims of testing established theory, the middle details the data gathering, measuring, and reductive statistical analyses used to test the hypotheses, and the ending presents confirmatory findings.

We impose this confirmation narrative on submitted papers for two reasons. One is that the confirmation narrative embodies tidy criteria for evaluating the study. Editors and reviewers can assess the logic of how hypotheses are properly deduced from given theory, evaluate the type and quantity of data and measures for testing those hypotheses, and decide if the work involves adequate validity and reliability. The second reason is that we do not have an alternate narrative for grounded theory building.

I propose that we create and employ another narrative for publishing, the discovery narrative. Rather than simply exhort editors and scholars to include qualitative research, or create another outlet for qualitative research, we instead should create and then use a discovery narrative for developing and evaluating manuscripts for publication based on the alternate criteria for judging quality of the research. I do not suggest that we eliminate confirmation research, but rather add another narrative, and reduce the prevalence of confirmation studies in our journals from 95 percent to, say, 80 or even 75 percent. I am not aware of any journal statement of purpose that forbids the discovery narrative, but some editors and reviewers do. We can expand our narratives for quality research if we choose to do so.

When grounded theory building research is shoehorned into the confirmation narrative and is assessed through that particular lens, the research has an unclear rationale, fuzzy methods, and vague findings. To make sense of a study that does not follow the "proper" plot, reviewers ask what is the contribution to theory? The authors answer that they fill a gap in existing theory (Alvesson and Sandberg 2011). But since grounded theory building cannot fill gaps well, reviewers become suspicious of the methods, and impose the "Gioia" method for analyzing qualitative data (a currently fashionable template for "rigor," one of a long line of potentially simplistic recipes). In response, authors transpose their results into an outline of primary, secondary, and tertiary words rather than insights. In the hands of all but masters of this recipe, the study becomes a trite summary that merely describes people behaving as people. The end result: the study is rejected because we rightly do not publish trite summaries as research articles.

I develop a publishing narrative based on discovery, not confirmation, that encompasses the processes and objectives of grounded theory building, and suggests more appropriate criteria for conducting, writing up, and evaluating research for publication. This discovery narrative also fits science, but relies on the plot of abductive, not deductive, reasoning (Dunne and Dougherty 2016; Dougherty 2016). Many who participate in science (e.g., Mayr 2000; Grinnell 2009) or study scientists at work (Knorr Cetina 1999; Pavitt 1999; Nightingale 2004) show that scientists working at the frontiers of knowledge do not follow the linear, sequential, purely objective confirmation approach. When knowledge is incomplete and fragmented, scientists cannot predict outcomes because theories are not formulated well enough to provide explicit hypotheses (Nightingale 2004). If the premises from which specific hypotheses are drawn are themselves incomplete, deduction cannot be logical (Arthur 2014). Rather, scientists use a discovery style of research that seeks to understand, not to confirm, because experiments will typically fail. They tinker, create patterns to learn from, and iteratively generate better explanations that accumulate locally generated insights. Organization scholars can still be real scientists even when they cannot clearly confirm if they use the discovery narrative. Confirmation plays an important role, but confirming existing theory is not the only activity of real science.

## Rewriting the Publishing Narrative: New Story Lines for Contribution Claims, Rigorous Methods, and Findings

This section contrasts the confirmation narrative with the discovery narrative by the story lines of each narrative that are outlined in Table 29.1. The basic plot of each narrative is deductive versus abductive logic. Deduction presumes that the theory is complete and affords the deduction of well-reasoned hypotheses. However, as noted above, when there is no complete theory, deduction is illogical. Abduction, first articulated by Charles Peirce and other pragmatist philosophers, is the deliberate reasoning that leads to scientific discoveries (Nesher 2001). According to Peirce, abduction is the best answer we have to problems of discovery, since abduction alone among the forms of reasoning originates possible explanations and introduces new ideas.

*Table 29.1* Current and Proposed Publishing Narrative

|  | *(Current) Confirmation Narrative* | *(Proposed) Discovery Narrative* |
|---|---|---|
| *Narrative Story Lines* | | |
| Plot | Deductive logic | Abductive logic |
| Contribution claim | *Filling Gaps in Established Theory*<br>• Use simplified reality to confirm theory | *Resolving Grand Challenges*<br>• Use theory to understand complex reality |
| Methods | *Executing Prescribed Recipe*<br>• Linear: direct line from theory to hypothesis about single elements holding all else constant; problem and elements already given<br>• Rigor: objectivity, de-contextualization, abstraction of parts | *Cycling through Abductive Reasoning*<br>• Nonlinear: cycling through formulating, evaluating, and reframing hypotheses; need to define problem and its core elements, interdependencies, and how they go together<br>• Rigor: subjectivity, contextualization, keeping the whole |
| Presentation of findings | *Talking about Tables*<br>• Simple report of measured results<br>• Claiming confirmation of theory | *Explaining Learning Events*<br>• Simple report of learning events, with elaborate explication of how they capture problem and resolution<br>• Claiming revelations for problem and resolution, and for theory development |

Locke et al. (2008:907) quote Peirce to explain: "[d]eduction proves that something *must* be; induction shows that something *actually is* operative; abduction merely suggests that something *may be*" (emphasis in original). Weick (2005) describes the abductive reasoning as "clues giving rise to speculations, conjectures, and assessments of plausibility rather than a search among known rules to see which ones might best fit the facts." Simon (1977) also discusses discovering laws in raw data based on pattern recognition and abduction of hypotheses that may regulate observed patterns. I develop a methodical way to use abduction in the next three subsections.

Three contrasting story elements are: (1) defining the contribution as a gap-filling addition or extension of theory versus as resolving grand challenges; (2) gathering and analyzing data linearly by abstraction and reduction versus abductively cycling around formulating, evaluating, and reframing hypotheses that make sense of the problem; and (3) presenting the findings as talking about analytic tables versus as developing and explaining learning events in the journey of understanding. I deliberately exaggerate the limits of the confirmation narrative to highlight room for improvements.

## The Contribution Claim: Filling Gaps vs. Resolving Grand Challenges

The contribution claim begins the publishing narrative by determining the problem to be addressed, the questions asked, and how existing literature will be used. Many studies are rejected for not making a clear and substantial contribution. But contribution to what?

In the confirmation narrative, the contribution is advancing theory rather than addressing actual, complex problems that organizations and managers face. This contribution typically becomes filling gaps in existing theory, as demonstrated by Alvesson and Sandberg's (2011) analysis of the claims by many studies that are published in organization and management journals.

Exemplifying the gap filling objective, some teach students to focus on finding mediators and moderators within an established theoretical model of what X causes what Y. By making this contribution claim, the confirmation narrative focuses on theory, and uses data about practical challenges to explain the theory. Gap filling is an alluring way to begin the story of one's complex research because it provides a clear, simple rationale.

But grounded theory building cannot fill gaps in existing theory very well, so claiming this kind of contribution makes it seem that the research has no contribution. Many suggest alternate kinds of contributions. Nicolai and Seidl (2010) recommend that academics aim at enriching practitioners' understandings of the decision situations they face, and help them set their problems – that is, help figure out the decision to be made, the ends to be achieved, and the means which may be chosen (Schon 1983). Astley and Zammuto (1992) recommend that academics enhance problem-solving skills by developing complicated understandings, or the ability to understand organizational events from several perspectives. According to March (1999), academic ideas can open up new ways of seeing, and create new vantage points for managers. Jarzabkowski et al. (2010) argue that bridging theory and practice does not depend on better theories, but on better understandings of how theory is used in practice, and how practitioners draw on knowledge to think as they act. Sandberg and Tsoukas (2011) argue that the simple rationality that I find in the confirmation narrative underestimates the meaningful totality in which practitioners are immersed, and the contextualized interactions among things, people, actions, and options.

But how exactly can academics help practitioners understand and deal with complex problems in a way that also captures the meaningful totality in which practitioners are immersed? I propose that we focus some research on grand challenges (Ferraro et al. 2015). Grand challenges encompass many of society's most pressing problems that remain unresolved because they are complex and emergent and entail many unknown interactions. People cannot forecast the consequences of their actions and instead must experiment and learn, and build on multiple criteria of worth (Ferraro et al. 2015). Grand challenges include the co-evolution of sciences and technologies in domains such as health, education, or climate management, sustainable development, overcoming poverty in various settings, managing innovation that takes more than a decade to emerge, or enabling collaboration among disparate agents over long time periods. Management and organization scholars are uniquely positioned to inform important practical, strategic, and policy problems, because all grand challenges involve managing and organizing. Our theories can provide rich conceptual understandings to define key features and interdependencies. In addition, many organizations tackle grand challenges, so figuring out how to do so more effectively meets the definition of practical as discussed by Van de Ven (2007), Corley and Gioia (2011), and Kilduff (2006).

Using our theories to explain how to grapple with a real world problem is one heck of a contribution. Rather than use the situation to test the theory, researchers would use theories to understand the situation. Grounded theory building researchers select theoretical perspectives that they think fruitfully frame the grand challenge they study, and use the theories to identify the things of the situation that should be studied empirically. The study would begin with formulating an explanation by using existing theory to suggest what the critical elements might be and how those elements interact to produce the phenomenon being studied. Over the course of the study and analysis, researchers construct a coherent story about how important organizational and managerial features of the situation might work together to help resolve the situation. This process is problem setting, defined by Schon (1983) as the process of selecting what the researcher will treat as the "things" of the situation, set the boundaries of their attention to it, and impose a coherence on it which allows them to say what is wrong and the directions in which the problem situation needs to be changed. The researcher figures out which of the many possible features of a problem might play a role, how these features work together to generate the problem, and what the underlying mechanisms of this holistic pattern might be.

Examples of grand challenges in organizing might include how can people jump-start the co-evolution of sciences and technologies when many are in the era of ferment stage (e.g., very emergent with limited functionality)? A researcher could situate this question in a particular domain such as alternate energy systems or sustainable agriculture, which defines some of the particular "things" of this situation. Then the researcher draws on her extensive background knowledge of organizing to postulate possible organizing factors from theory that may also be things of the situation, such as learning under ambiguity, power and politics, networks of relations that provide access to particular resources, and so on. Or the researcher might begin with a particular topical or theoretical focus, such as what would it take for entrepreneurs to play a major role in jump-starting the emergence of a sustainable agricultural infrastructure in Western Africa?

Unfortunately, since the theoretical understandings emerge from the study, how to present them – in the beginning? At the end? – is a problem. Either option does not conform to the confirmation narrative which (presumably, and we all know of violations) begins with the theory and hypotheses already clearly laid out. I address different options for presenting the final theory that the study develops in the discussion section.

## Methods: Data Gathering and Analysis by Executing Prescribed Methods vs. Cycling Iteratively through Abductive Reasoning

As outlined in Table 29.1, the methods section lays out the process used to study the problem and the criteria for defining rigor. Confirmation narrative methods proceed linearly in a straight line from data to measures to expected outcomes. Grinnell (2009:4), a practicing microbiologist, summarizes the "scientific method" narrative:

> According to the linear model, the path from hypothesis to discovery follows a direct line guided by objectivity and logic. Facts about the world are there waiting to be observed and collected. The scientific method is used to make discoveries. Researchers are dispassionate and objective.

The problem is already given or "set," and the researcher focuses in on one or a few elements by abstracting them out of the complex interactions, and de-contextualizing the study to eliminate unnecessary noise. Rigor in the confirmation narrative comes from following prescribed steps and measurement techniques that are based on abstraction and de-contextualization. Since the facts are there, the narrative details the specifics for observing and collecting facts to test the hypothesis, but does not incorporate anything else that may also be relevant but unexpected. Objectivity emphasizes generalization, which becomes a process of abstracting factors from their context and decontextualizing the work by plucking out control factors for the analysis. The use of secondary data also assures objectivity and rigor.

Unfortunately, grounded theory-building methods are so far removed from the simple linear techniques of confirmation that uninformed reviewers cannot figure them out. In my experience, the confirmatory rigor is transferred to grounded theory building by imposing recipes. Editors have required that I demonstrate how I followed the Gioia method of analysis to prove the rigor of my study, even though I did not use this method. Gioia does not assume that his method is a one-size-fits-all approach to qualitative analysis either, so I can only conclude that editors and peer reviewers in organization studies do not know how to judge rigor except by recipe. In my own reviewing, I see that when researchers apply this recipe after the fact or implement it poorly, the analysis and findings sections read like a simple, linear, one-step-at-a-time recipe. A recipe ignores the intuition, the leaps of faith, and the passion for knowing that drive research and researchers (Knorr Cetina 1999; Grinnell 2009). When we fail to report on our leaps and our "Aha!"s we fail to present the findings as fully as we can, and should.

Grinnell (2009) goes on to say that this confirmation narrative is a "mythical account" of the everyday practice of science, because the path to discovery is convoluted and ambiguous. Grounded theory building iterates among problem defining and resolving and back again. Data are collected through continual iteration between questions, literature, hypotheses, and findings, as facts of the situation are enabled to emerge. The methods section in the discovery narrative explains the co-evolution of learning from theory to situations and back again that the researchers engaged in, and how the knowledge thus developed contributes to the resolution of the problem as well as to the theories we use.

Rigor in grounded theory building is based on how well the researchers overcome potential biases inherent in discovery, and how they fully report insights. Bias in grounded theory building arises from failing to grapple with the inherent subjectivity of the study, decontextualizing, and ignoring the whole. First, grounded theory building studies cannot claim objectivity, because the topic of the study concerns the subjectivity of participants in the situation. The analysis involves sifting through subjective data using researcher passion and intuition. Researchers deal with subjectivity intersubjectively by iterating with the perceptions of colleagues and engaging in discourse (Grinnell 2009). Second, bias in grounded theory building also comes from de-contextualization, because the things that define the situation cannot be known ahead of time and must be discovered. Beginning the study with abstraction biases problem definition, while failing to draw on unanticipated details biases the study from novel possibilities (Weick 2005). Third, grounded theory building is biased if the researcher fails to keep the whole in mind or fails to attend to the central unknowns, which are the interdependencies among elements of the whole.

Grounded theory building does follow a clear logic that can be articulated in the methods section so that the rigor can be assessed. First, as already explained, defining the problem is in itself an essential part of working on it and resolving it. One aspect of this logic is ongoing iteration. The process cycles back on itself as researchers work as reflective practitioners (Schon 1983) and continually make judgments about the likelihood of different explanations for why findings do not behave in the predicted way. Researchers iterate from the questions asked and the literature used to hypotheses about the situation to findings and back. Researchers collect data based on the reflexive process of theoretical sampling – that is, based on the theory of the problem that is emerging in the iterative process of research. Data collecting is entwined with data analyzing and problem formulating. Good qualitative research builds on lots of data that are varied in their nature and in the events they depict, because all these data are collected as the research emerges and examines failed expectations, surprises, and new hypotheses. The methods section addresses how and why all these data are collected and analyzed.

To capture these alternate logics of reasoning, some organization scholars propose abduction as the logic of reasoning that enables the discovery style of research (Grandori 2010; Van de Ven 2007). Dunne and Dougherty (2016) propose a way to use abductive reasoning based on Magnani's definition (2001:18): abduction "is the process of reasoning in which explanatory hypotheses are formed and evaluated." In a grounded theory study of how scientists deal with the complexities of drug discovery, they detail three processes for abductive reasoning: formulating hypotheses about a perplexing problem that try to explain the underlying difficulties; evaluating these hypotheses by using them to learn more and experiment to uncover new possibilities and examine assumptions; and reframing these hypotheses by reflexive deliberation that iterates among expertise and experimental settings to accumulate learning so far and reformulate the hypothesis. Other scholars develop similar processes, and each one may fit better with particular kinds of problems (e.g., Grandori 2010; Ferraro et al. 2015; Ansell 2011).

Here I outline the approach that is detailed more fully in Dunne and Dougherty (2016) and Dougherty (2016). The story line for methods in the discovery narrative would briefly outline the major cycles of hypothesizing, evaluating, and reframing, and detail how the evaluating generated new and sometimes surprising ideas and how these led to reframing. The grounded theory building study first formulates a hypothesis that sets a perplexing organizing problem from the materials of the problematic situation which are puzzling, troubling, and uncertain, and includes organization theories that the researcher thinks will reveal important insights. Questions are not given by perplexing situations, so skillful researchers use questioning to get into a problem.

Dunne and Dougherty (2016) find that good hypotheses are configurations of interdependencies among the things of the problem the researchers focus on. Researchers hypothesize relevant features for their problem, and more importantly, how these features interact and depend on each other. Focusing on interdependencies highlights the major source of uncertainty in complex systems, where failures often arise because of unexpected interactions. The hypothesis reflects how these features might mutually generate the outcomes of interest. Theories are clues to possible features and interdependencies. According to Weick (2005), clues point to a world in which they are meaningful, and so give rise to speculations, conjectures, and assessments of plausibility. Weick (2005) also emphasizes imagination, which "conceives a whole design almost at once, which it then fills out and gives body to by particular association.... The mind thinks simultaneously of specific parts and of their one organizing principle" (Engel 1981:82–83).

The next process is evaluating imagined configurations of interdependencies among features, to further contextualize and situate the possible configuration. The goal is learning, so researchers go beyond does the configuration work or not, and consider how and why it works and/or why it does not work. Researchers evaluate the imagined configuration by elaborating and narrowing around the interdependencies (Dunne and Dougherty 2016). Researchers empirically inquire into the actual effects of their hypothesized configuration to assess the nature of the mechanisms that govern the interdependencies. Researchers surface new and deeper insights about how, in the case of drugs for example, a chemical compound might behave in the body against the disease. Evaluating burrows into the mechanisms to explore how and why the configuration might work, what else may be going on, and what are the limits and contingencies. Tests of confirmation are part of the process of evaluating but they are not the primary form of evaluation, and they do not stand alone. Researchers seek to generate alternatives with more potential as they evaluate the hypothesis (Grandori 2010), and open up around the configuration, not close in on a single element. Looking at the configuration in action assesses the nature of the mechanisms that animate the possibilities.

The third abductive reasoning process is reframing the hypothesized configuration by iteratively integrating across disciplines and experimental situations to accumulate and synthesize information. By reframing, researchers holistically assess what they know so far and what they have learned. Different people see different aspects of the problem and how to resolve it. Iteratively integrating helps to overcome competency traps, push ideas, cross check possibilities, and generate a joint representation. Researchers are not simply searching, they are actively configuring. They drop some alternatives, develop new performance parameters, and adopt new consequences that seem more promising based on their collective learning. Reframing cycles back with a new hypothesis about a configuration of interdependencies to be evaluated again.

Together, these three abductive reasoning processes enable the study of grand challenges, because they build on available information despite the noise, they generate new meaning and new categories of knowledge, they keep the whole in mind, and they attend to the central unknowns in complex systems – the interdependencies. Cycling through abductive learning routines addresses research biases such as ignoring elements that may be important, overlooking situated contingencies, and failing to take the whole into account. The methods section recounts the main cycles of hypothesis formulation, evaluation, and reframing, and the unanticipated elements and interactions that the analysis revealed and then wove into the study. The findings section illustrates the cycling.

Three brief examples illustrate these methods. Strauss and Corbin (1998) use a study of adolescents' use of drugs to illustrate grounded theory building. The study interviewed many teenagers of various backgrounds. The analysis evaluated several different theories about why and how teenagers use drugs and the consequences, among them as a form of rebellion against adult society, serious addiction, peer pressure, and a way to take advantage of others. Each one fits only a portion of the data, and the authors illustrate the process of iterating among these various possible explanations to explore what they capture and fail to capture. The analysis ends up with a very simple explanation: teenagers use drugs as a rite of passage, with minimal consequences to their health and well-being (although a small minority do become addicted). Weick's (1993) analysis of the Mann Gultch disaster, where most of the firefighters who "jumped" into the fire died in the fire, iterated among theories of structure and of meaning with the data. The study ends up with the insight that structural frames and processes of meaning making mutually constitute social order. His discussion details how the two social processes together generate resilience, what happens when one is missing, and how people can deal with situations in which one of the two is missing.

Our study of innovation in pharmaceuticals and how the scientists learned (Dunne and Dougherty 2016) began with theories of complexity and differences between science and applied science, or technology. Neither set of ideas captured what we saw in the data, which included a deliberate learning process that all the scientists used in varying degrees but that managers tried to prevent, clues and searching for clues, and many interactions among disciplines over time. Two different colleagues who listened to early presentations told us we seemed to be talking about abduction, which we had not known about before. We then iterated with the literature and the data again, and discovered that we could map our findings onto a theory of abductive reasoning. We detailed three basic social mechanisms of abductive reasoning, and Dougherty (2016) developed the idea that these social mechanisms are abductive learning routines, based on Feldman and Pentland's (2003) theory. Many other examples exist in our published literature, even though the article may not describe cycling through ways to figure out what is going on, or explicitly say they are using abductive reasoning.

## Presenting Findings as Talking about Tables vs. Explaining Learning Events

The third story line of the publication narrative involves the findings and how to present them. The confirmation narrative presents the findings as "table talk," a simple report of what the statistical analyses show about the hypotheses. In research presentations at department seminars I have attended, scholars rarely get to their findings since most of the discussion focuses on the logic of the hypotheses and the methods. I assume from the tendency on the part of my confirmation colleagues to ignore findings that the findings do not matter much – it is all about the deductive logic itself, not what that logic generates. The discussion section then would simply recount the claims for contribution by filling a gap or applying existing theory to yet another empirical situation. The practical implications are discussed in one or two paragraphs that summarize what managers ought to do based on the results, not how they can actually do so.

Grounded theory building does not fit this confirmation findings story line at all, since the findings section is the largest and most important section of the paper, not something to be skipped over. Attempting to apply the confirmation findings story line results in very descriptive and surfacy ideas, not in a deep and succinct theoretical understanding that helps to represent the real complexities and how to deal with them. The surfacy results occur because the confirmation emphasis on table talk transfers to qualitative findings. Qualitative tables are also expected to demonstrate that the findings are true and correct, not to summarize the data for the reader. Some use what I call Miles and Huberman tables to "prove" that the findings are correct, even though Miles and Huberman tables are intended to show variability in the data and how the researcher connects data pieces into a pattern.

The findings from grounded theory building studies are theories. Theories are sets of well-developed concepts related through statements of relationships that together constitute an integrated framework that can explain or predict phenomena (Strauss and Corbin 1998). But the theory developed by a grounded theory study and reported in a single paper is not some "grand theory" that replaces what we know about, for example, institutions or social structure or motivation. Grounded theories are more substantive, and provide a succinct, clear explication of the grand challenge that was studied, what the analysis reveals for how practitioners can understand their situations more richly, and what the analysis reveals about deepening the theories. Rather than reinvent theories of institutions, motivations, strategy, communications, knowledge, or innovation (to mention just a few), grounded theory building integrates different theoretical views to capture the core dynamics of the problem being studied. The process of integrating may reveal that a particular theory is limited and needs rethinking, but the main story is the new understanding.

Studies of complex issues like grand challenges cannot find a final solution, since the problems themselves continually emerge. Societies will never finally solve education, health, or management since these challenges evolve and shift over time. But we can develop intermediary resolutions that work in particular settings, and can help generate new insights about how to incorporate additional variations in other settings. Like drug discovery scientists, we do arrive at learning events (Dougherty et al. 2013). We can publish learning events. Learning events are endogenous occurrences that emerge when researchers learn enough about the configuration of interdependencies they are working on to indicate the next thrust of their work on the problem. These learning events are moments of closure in the development that capture emerging understandings of the whole configuration of interdependencies well enough to enable researchers to explain what they think they know so far and identify plausible next thrusts in the research. Learning events are intermediary models or rough drafts of the emerging understanding that can be reported in published research.

I recommend that the findings section in the discovery narrative begins with a succinct (10–15 words) explanation of the learning events that capture what is really going on – a specific theory that explains the specific underlying mechanism(s) that animates the problem and leads to possible resolutions. This explanation encompasses relevant existing understandings, but integrates them and applies them to this grand challenge as this particular study approaches it. The succinct theory is the main learning event that the research arrived at to explain where to go next in the journey of understanding. Then the findings develop why the particular things of this situation are most relevant, how those things interrelate, and what are the core dynamics. All together, the findings explicate the practical realities and represent them in a new light, one that captures how particular organization theories operate in this complex situation to frame what is going on.

A few examples from my own work illustrate these ideas. In a study of how people working on new products understand user needs, given that those needs are new, I found that people in different departments understood users, needs, and product functions very differently (Dougherty 1992). They did not conflict and they did not each have partial views. Rather, they knew different things and knew things differently. The core theory: departments are like different thought worlds (from institutional theory defined by Mary Douglas), and each possesses essential if unique knowledge for the new product. The findings section presented this simple, clear theory, and then explicated the differences in departmental understandings by identifying core dimensions of difference, how these mattered for product innovation, and how in some cases people were able to integrate their unique understandings into a successful new product. In a study of the conflicts between managers and discovery scientists working on new drug therapies, my colleagues identified *time* as the core driver of conflict between the two groups, while I was initially expecting to find some sort of ideological clash (Dougherty et al. 2013). Specifically, we found that managers paced work according to clocks and calendars, while scientists paced work according to learning events that they anticipated but could not predict when, in clock time, the events would occur. Again, we finally arrived at a simple, succinct theory about conflicting temporal structures to explain the problem. The findings section elaborated the theory by explicating the divergent milestones and ways to gauge progress that the temporal structures implicated. In both examples, the findings build on and integrate existing theories into a coherent framework for the problem situation.

However, when I review qualitative work, I often see half-baked studies that have no real theory, only a list of "things" of the situation that make no sense by themselves. It seems that we cannot figure out when we are done enough to publish results, since we are studying inherently complex problems that cannot be resolved once and for all because they are broad, diffuse, and emergent. The findings should develop the theory that is revealed by explicating the learning events that the research arrived at and why these learning events are good understandings that enable science and scientists to proceed with ongoing study of this kind of grand challenge. This theory is a learning event in the journey of studying, for example, how different disciplines understand their work and can collaborate, or how managers can deal with innovations that take more than a decade to unfold.

## A Discovery Narrative for Tackling Grand Challenges Based on Abductive Reasoning

The contribution of a grounded theory building study is a rich understanding of a complex problem – one that identifies the core elements of this problem and how they interact to generate the challenges and their possible resolutions over time. The grounded theory building study applies some of the theories we have to address key challenges people face in managing and organizing for addressing grand challenges. In applying those theories, researchers also show how good the theories are, and develop them further by discovering new dynamics. Complex grand challenges cannot begin with a clear problem definition because the problem itself is not understood, so real science gets to a good problem definition, one that captures the problem rather than abstracting it away, but in a way that enables us to develop some resolutions.

Publications based on abductive reasoning would report the cycles of learning that a research project has developed so far that have led to one or more learning events developed in the journey of figuring out the grand challenge, what the researchers have learned and how, and what this learning means to the theories used and the practical challenges studied. Some studies would explain how theories are used in certain practices, and reflect on ways to improve both theory and practice. Studies accumulate and synthesize theories into richer, fuller understandings, or they reframe theories to take into account new kinds of technologies and/or social practices. Research based on abductive reasoning leverages the existing literature throughout all three story lines, and incorporates a richer use of this knowledge. Many studies would corroborate other analyses of configurations, but add new elements or reframe certain kinds of interdependencies. Some studies might encompass more variation, show that certain configurations do not work in particular settings, or move ideas into a new dimension of study. And some studies would discover novel possibilities. Our knowledge of complex realities is full of gaps, so simply claiming that a gap exists does not contribute to and does not leverage what we already know. Abductive reasoning provides a way to synthesize theories to address grand challenges.

In the introduction, I noted that we cling to the confirmation narrative in part because it provides tidy, easy-to-use criteria for evaluating submitted work. To break out of this box, I outline some criteria for publishing discovery narratives that use abductive reasoning:

1   Does the contribution go beyond how the empirical situation adds to theory, to also explain how the theory(ies) adds to our understanding of the problem being addressed? How and why does the study enable researchers and practitioners to deal with this grand challenge now that was not understood well enough to take useful action before? And how well did the study deepen or refine these theories to explain what we now know that we did not know before about them?

2   Does the study address interdependencies among several elements in the situation that generate particular outcomes or events? Do the researchers demonstrate empirically how and why these interdependencies are critical and what they have learned about them?

3   Does the study develop the findings as clues to understanding a complex challenge rather than as stand-alone answers or solutions? How do the clues lead us out of perplexity, what are their implications for ongoing study of this complex problem and how well reasoned are they?

4   How and how well do the learning events reported in the study allow us to proceed more fruitfully in understanding this kind of situation? Is the justification for finding a learning event adequate, reasonable, and richly articulated?

5   Does the study report the important surprises, failed predictions, and perplexing findings that the research surfaces, and make reasonable sense about their implications? Complex challenges should have surprises and failed predictions. How did the research proceed to delve into these findings to learn more about the theory and the phenomenon?

6   Did the study examine how and why the reframed understandings of the complex challenge actually help practitioners, based on empirical analyses of their challenges?

If we recognize that all published research is a step in the process of the co-evolution of knowledge among theories and practical situations, then contributions involve the creation of new insights from the co-evolving streams of thinking and acting. But several problems in editing and reviewing are more barriers to developing a new narrative – in addition to the ideology of deductive reasoning being the only true science.

One big barrier concerns what is a contribution? Our default is filling gaps in existing theories because we cannot agree on what constitutes real applied problems, and we perhaps do not know if we are really informing managers. I emphasize grand challenges even though these would vary by field. Each area in management research may have its own grand challenges too. I used the example from innovation about the co-evolution of emergent sciences and technologies. In strategy a grand challenge is how to strategize when opportunities may emerge over long periods of time, or why managers stick to the short term even when they know better.

A second barrier to developing new publication narratives is that abductive reasoning is not based on absolute truth, and so is inherently incomplete. Incompleteness makes it very difficult to assess scientific claims. Deductive logic does not work with complex problems like the grand challenges, which is why Peirce and others argue that abduction, not deduction, is the logic of scientific discovery. So how can we live with inherently incomplete findings? I have proposed using learning events, or intermediary learnings that define where we are in the labyrinth of ambiguity (using Denrell et al.'s (2004) metaphor) and where we might go next, all based on the combination of theories with findings.

A third barrier concerns how to present the study. The confirmation narrative begins with a clear summary of relevant theory and the hypotheses deduced from them. But discovery research does not begin with a clear problem. When tackling complex problems like grand challenges, no existing theory captures what is really going on because our understanding of these challenges is partial, fragmented, and emergent. Researchers "navigate through the labyrinth" of this grand challenge (Denrell et al. 2004; Dunne and Dougherty 2016). Some writers (e.g., Weick) masterfully describe navigating through the labyrinth, but most of us cannot do so well and most readers expect to see a linear story. We have several options. One is to report in the introduction the final outcome of problem setting and solving that the scholar arrives at after cycling through ongoing theoretical sampling and theory building. The rest of the paper would detail how this particular theoretical understanding was developed, how well it fits the data, and why this framing constitutes a good learning event in the larger scientific journey of understanding this grand challenge. Another option is to describe the grand challenge in general with some organization theory in the beginning, and briefly describe the unknowns that require additional study. The rest of the paper would develop how and why the sharper, perhaps reframed understandings capture the challenges.

A final barrier is that different scholars define abduction differently, and we tend to get bogged down in squabbling over definitions. I recommend that we can apply different views of abduction empirically, and squabble over the different studies in order to develop the research skills of abductive reasoning. To do so, we can draw on the idea that abductive reasoning reflects several principles of pragmatism, a wide ranging philosophy that encompasses logic, epistemology, aesthetics, political theory, psychology, and other topics (Ansell 2011). According to Farjoun et al. (2015), pragmatism (the Greek word "pragma" means action) reconstructs philosophy as an analytic perspective to help humans find their place in a hectic, complex, and often dangerous world. One principle is that pragmatism is a problem-oriented perspective that places a greater value on the open-ended process of refining knowledge than on specifying limitless principles of what is right, or just, or efficient (Farjoun et al. 2015). For pragmatists, problems are never defined neatly, and defining the problem is itself an essential part of its possible resolution (Ferraro et al. 2015:369). However, working on problems is also concrete because the process pins disputes about knowledge or values down to particulars (Ansell 2011).

A second principle of pragmatism is that meaning is linked to action; there are no dualities. Action is socially constructed and also leads to the discovery of meaning – or enactment as described by Weick (1979). Action builds on what Dewey calls habit, or learned behavior that is similar to skill (Cohen 2007). Habits shape feelings and beliefs, and abduction enables individuals to draw on surprises to conceive of larger and often unexpected possibilities. A third principle is that pragmatism is based on a rich view of human behavior. People are social, complex, creative, willing to experiment, and can reflect on their own actions and review their habits. Classical pragmatists portray human beings as situated actors, and as such as creatively responsive beings. Creative activity, or the improvisational responses of human beings to the concrete situations in which they are implicated, is the most basic form of human action according to Joas (1996).

In conclusion, applying our theories to help explain how people can grapple effectively with grand challenges is a heck of a contribution and merits publication in our journals. The discovery narrative provides organization and management scholars with the opportunity to put our extensive theoretical understandings to good use. In so doing, we can advance what we already know by incorporating the contingencies and multiplicities in actual organizational settings into our theories.

# References

Alvesson, M. and Sandberg, J. (2011) "Generating research questions through problematization," *Academy of Management Review*, 36(2):247–271.

Ansell, C. (2011) *Pragmatist Democracy: Evolutionary Learning as Public Philosophy*, Oxford: Oxford University Press.

Arthur, B. (2014) *Complexity and the Economy*, Oxford: Oxford University Press.

Astley, W. G. and Zammuto, R. (1992) "Organization science, managers, and language games," *Organization Science*, 3:443–460.

Cohen, M. (2007) "Reading Dewey: Reflections on the study of routine," *Organization Studies*, 28:773–781.

Corley, K. and Gioia, D. (2011) "Building theory about theory building: What constitutes a theoretical contribution?," *Academy of Management Review*, 36(1):12–32.

Denrell, J., Fang, C., and Levinthal, D. (2004) "From T-mazes to labyrinths: Learning from model-based feedback," *Management Science*, 50:1366–1378.

Dougherty, D. (1992) "Interpretive barriers to successful product innovation in large firms," *Organization Science*, 3:179–202.

Dougherty, D. (2016) *Taking Advantage of Emergence: Productively Innovating in Complex Innovation Systems*, Oxford: Oxford University Press.

Dougherty, D., Bertels, H., Chung, K., and Kraemer, J. (2013) "Whose time is it? Clock-time pacing and event-time pacing in complex innovations," *Management and Organization Review*, 9:223–264.

Dunne, D. and Dougherty, D. (2016) "Abductive reasoning: How innovators navigate in the labyrinth of complex product innovation," *Organization Studies*, 37:131–159.

Engel, J. (1981) *The Creative Imagination: Enlightenment to Romanticism*, Cambridge, MA: Harvard University Press.

Farjoun, M., Ansell, C., and Boin, A. (2015) "Pragmatism in organization studies: Meeting the challenges of a dynamic and complex world," *Organization Science*, 26(6):1787–1804.

Feldman, M. and Pentland, B. (2003) "Reconceptualizing organizational routines as a source of flexibility and change," *Administrative Science Quarterly*, 48:94–118.

Ferraro, F., Etzion, D., and Gehman, J. (2015) "Tackling grand challenges pragmatically: Robust action revisited," *Organization Studies*, 36:363–390.

Garud, R., Bartel, C., and Dunbar, R. (2011) "Dealing with unusual experiences: A narrative perspective on organizational learning," *Organization Science*, 3(22):587–601.

Grandori, A. (2010) "A rational heuristic model of economic decision making," *Rationality and Society*, 22(4):477–504.

Grinnell, F. (2009) *The Everyday Practice of Science*, New York: Oxford University Press.

Jarzabkowski, P., Mohrman, S., and Scherer, A. (2010) "Organization studies as applied science: The generation and use of academic knowledge about organizations," *Organization Studies*, 31:1189–1208.

Joas, H. (1996) *The Creativity of Action*, trans Jeremy Gaines and Paul Keast, Cambridge, MA: Harvard University Press.

Kilduff, M. (2006) "Editor's comments: Publishing theory," *Academy of Management Review*, 31:252–255.

Knorr Cetina, K. (1999). *Epistemic Cultures: How the Sciences Make Knowledge*, Cambridge, MA: Harvard University Press.

Locke, K., Golden-Biddle, K., and Feldman, M. (2008) "Making doubt generative: Rethinking the role of doubt in the research process," *Organization Science*, 19:907–918.

Magnani, L. (2001) *Abduction, Reason, and Science: Processes of Discovery and Explanation*, New York: Kluwer Academic/Plenum Publishers.

March, J. (1999) *The Pursuit of Organizational Intelligence*, Malden, MA: Blackwell.

Mayr, E. (2000) "Biology in the twenty-first century," *BioScience*, 50:895.

Nesher, D. (2001) "Peircian epistemology of learning and the function of abduction as the logic of discovery," *Transactions of the Charles S. Peirce Society*, 1(37):23–57.

Nicolai, A. and Seidl, D. (2010) "That's relevant! Different forms of practical relevance in management science," *Organization Studies*, 10:1257–1286.

Nightingale, P. (2004) "Technological capabilities, invisible infrastructure and the un-social construction of predictability: The overlooked fixed costs of useful research," *Research Policy*, 33(9):1259–1284.

Pavitt, K. (1999) *Technology, Management and Systems of Innovation*, Cheltenham, UK: Edward Elgar.

Sandberg, J. and Tsoukas, H. (2011) "Grasping the logic of practice: Theorizing through practical rationality," *Academy of Management Review*, 36(2):338–360.

Schon, D. A. (1983) *The Reflective Practitioner: How Professionals Think in Action*, New York: Basic Books.

Simon, H. (1977) *Models of Discovery and Other Topics in the Methods of Science*, Dordrecht: D. Reidel.

Strauss, A. and Corbin, J. (1998) *Basics of Qualitative Research*, 2nd edn, Thousand Oaks, CA: Sage.

Van de Ven, A. (2007) *Engaged Scholarship: A Guide for Organizational and Social Research*. New York: Oxford University Press.

Weick, K. (1979) *The Social Psychology of Organizing*, 2nd edn. Reading, MA: Addison-Wesley.

Weick, K. (1993) "The collapse of sensemaking in organizations: The Mann Gulch disaster," *Administrative Science Quarterly*, 38:628–652.

Weick, K. (2005) "Organizing and failures of imagination," *International Public Management Journal*, 8:425–438.

# 30

# THE LONG, HARD ROAD TO LEGITIMACY FOR QUALITATIVE RESEARCH

## A Personal–Professional Journey

*Dennis A. (Denny) Gioia*

I was trained as an engineer. For much of my early professional life I thought like an engineer, talked like an engineer and walked like an engineer. As part of my engineering training, I initially took a job with Boeing Aerospace at Cape Kennedy – assigned to the Ground Support Team for the Apollo 11, 12 and 13 missions to the moon. I was a member of a group responsible for the operation of the service arms that attached the Launcher Umbilical Tower to the Saturn V launch vehicle and the Apollo command and service modules. It was an engineers' world and an engineers' paradise! The place was populated mainly by like-minded, like-talking and like-acting engineers. Everyone (and I do mean *everyone*) was super-competent in their jobs. I was surrounded by nothing but bright people, which was both impressive and intimidating.

Of course all the systems that mattered were physical systems – engineering systems that obeyed physical science laws. If you needed to know the explosive bolt detonation strength (to separate the service arms from the Saturn at launch), it was no problem. A simple calculation would tell you that. You want to know the thrust required for trans-lunar injection (to escape earth orbit)? A little more difficult perhaps, but still calculable in a straightforward manner, because celestial mechanics laws were essentially inviolable. There was no problem we couldn't or wouldn't solve, either with a slide rule, a calculator or a computer – or engineering experience (e.g., electrical engineer John Aaron quickly counseling *not* to abort the Apollo 12 launch after lightning struck the Apollo/Saturn vehicle, dropping out all electrical systems – because he had seen the unusual failure mode in an earlier test. The quick decision under duress earned him the moniker, "a steely-eyed missile man" – the ultimate compliment).

The human and organizational systems required to support this heady enterprise were similarly impressive, but they were not the subject of any discussion I can remember. Perhaps because everybody on the launch team was *so* dedicated to the success of the mission that nobody seemed to care about organizational behavior, design or process. Didn't matter. We had a mission to accomplish together – and what a grand mission it was in terms of scientific, engineering, national and even international importance. The organizational systems worked well-enough, and those that didn't were subject to easy work-arounds, because "Can Do" and "Will

Do" attitudes were pervasive. Problem? No problem. We can solve it. Our job is to put this bird in the air and send these astronauts on their way into space so they can walk on the moon. All in all, a memorable experience working with people in an engineering-driven enterprise.

Wind the clock forward just a bit. My Boeing experience had taught me lots of things, but one of those things was that I was never going to be in the elite league of engineers. Too many scary-smart people who could think about engineering systems in ways I could never hope to replicate. So, I made a big decision and signed up for Florida State's MBA program. The combination of an engineering degree with an MBA got me a job with Ford Motor Company in 1972 at a time of recession when there were no jobs available to any graduates, *except* perhaps people with the odd combination of engineering/MBA. I ended up on the fast-track at Ford and soon had another big decision: choose a path toward, either (a) engineering/engineering management or (b) corporate management. Given my history with brilliant engineers, I chose (b).

Now, the reason that choice is significant is that it put me in positions where I could see how the *whole* organization worked. I ended up at a rather young age (26) as Ford's corporate recall coordinator – a job that required both an understanding of vehicle engineering and a good dose of organizational savvy (see Gioia, 1992). If I was accustomed to working with engineers and engineering systems at Boeing, that experience should have transferred easily to Ford, which is essentially a vehicle engineering company, right? Wrong. If Boeing at Cape Kennedy might best be described as an engineering system, Ford in Dearborn was better described as a *social* system. Nothing seemed to work as it was designed on the roadmap (the org chart). You had to know the back alleys. The organization chart might be of some help in learning who reported to whom, but that knowledge really didn't help to get work done. You had to know or figure out how things *really* worked if you wanted to accomplish anything.

I learned this lesson pretty quickly as Ford's recall coordinator. I was a lowly "Grade 8" (in a hierarchical system where Henry Ford II, the Chairman of the Board, was a Grade 25 or some such). Yet, if I picked up the phone and identified myself as the recall coordinator, Grade 16s would jump to respond to my requests. Hey, hey! Power at a young age! I also learned that stuff got done much more effectively on an informal basis and by ignoring the putative "rules." Frankly, I got pretty good at getting stuff done. So good in fact, that I was on my way to the top because I had gotten so good at the game. Trouble was, I was getting sucked into the game, *Tron* or *Matrix* style. And to become a master of the game, I had to become an even more integral part of the game.

That's when I realized that I was being unwittingly coopted. I also realized that I was much more fascinated by understanding the way the organization really worked, and therefore became more interested in studying the game than playing the game, so I went back to school for a doctorate in organizational behavior and theory. (I often tell people that if I had stayed at Ford, two things would now characterize my life: (1) I'd be retired; (2) I'd be rich. I am neither. Nor am I regretful).

## Formal Education and Informal Revelation

Early in my doctoral program, I was of course reading a lot of organizational literature. Yet, that literature seemed so removed from what I had experienced at Ford that I wondered if the authors were even describing the kinds of phenomena with which I had become so familiar. Part of the problem was that the articles were written in a language that I have since come to call "academese," rather than English. Oh, they were in English, of course, but such stilted, formal, arcane English that I wondered if we were sharing a communication medium appropriate to understanding my past experience. Maybe. But it didn't capture that experience in memorable or vivid terms that explained very much.

A bigger problem, however, was that the theory and research essentially treated organizations and the people within them as if they operated like machines. The basic assumption seemed to be that organizational/social systems could and should be treated as analogs of engineering/physical systems. Well, OK, that was familiar enough to me, so I went along for the ride to see what it could teach me. I thought I was most interested in small-group/team behavior, so I minored in social and organizational psychology, a field that was almost entirely built around lab studies, using 19-year-old undergraduate students with no organizational experience to run tightly controlled experiments manipulating independent variables and assessing effects on dependent variables. These experiments were so tightly controlled that they stripped away all semblance of organizational reality. Just as bothersome, the write-ups of the studies were simply torture, with stilted language describing stilted settings. Doing social "science" seemed to require that we adopt the assumptions and conventions used in the physical sciences if we in organization studies wanted to be seen as a "legitimate" field of scientific study. The key phrase here is "be seen as." Oh my. So image was at the root of all these stripped-down causal models (see Gioia et al., 2014, for a latter-day discourse on image in organizational life). We were a field desperately seeking legitimacy (see Clegg et al., 2007) and in some sense we seemed to be selling our souls to do it.

All this stuff was weighing on me when, by some stroke of good fortune, I landed at Penn State in 1979, where I soon began to think seriously about the grand notions of ontology, epistemology and methodology. (Now, let's first acknowledge that if I'm not a fan of academese, I probably shouldn't be throwing around big words like these, but the concepts are critical, even if they do have weird, multisyllabic labels.) Ontology has to do with our assumptions about the nature of the beast(s) we're studying; epistemology has to with how we know about those beasts; and methodology has to do with the techniques we use to study the beasts. Well, it should be apparent that the whole business starts with ontological assumptions. What then is the essential nature of organizing, organization and organizations?

In this light, I realized that conceiving of an organization mainly as a machine or mechanical system is a woefully impoverished way of appreciating a marvelously complicated accomplishment (even if the legitimate aim is to be seen as a legitimate scientific enterprise). An organization is a machine only in a very limited sense, however. That's why my experience at Ford was such a jolt. Organization and accomplishment at Ford had much more to do with understanding Ford as a *culture*, a *political system*, a *theater*, etc. Well. What to do about all these troubling recognitions – especially when I started to look at the literatures on organizations as cultures, political arenas and theaters, and discovered that most of the foundational work in those domains was *qualitative* – not the quantitative research that had so dominated my earlier training and education? Hmmm. A conundrum.

## The Essence of the Legitimacy Issue for Qualitative Research

Qualitative research actually has quite a long history. And I daresay that qual research is particularly acknowledged because of its revelatory potential (Lincoln and Guba, 1985; Charmaz, 2014). Yet, I might also venture that much of its revelatory ability is often treated by the mainstream readers as too "impressionistic" – of making insightful observations without having compelling data to support the insights. In other words, qual research is too often assumed to make strong assertions without adequate demonstration of the evidence for those assertions. For that reason, qual research also has a long history of living with the criticism that it engages in some revealing theorizing based on evidence that would otherwise not satisfy traditional criteria.

(Of course, Lincoln and Guba (1985), long ago took critics to task for imposing inappropriate criteria on qual research – criteria that were developed on the basis of functionalist ontologies, epistemologies and methodologies – and instead suggested that a different, more appropriate set should be used.)

As I have noted before (Gioia et al., 2013), many reviewers of qualitative research actually have an overriding concern with epistemology (even if they don't label it as an epistemological concern) – i.e., in getting a satisfactory answer to the core question: "How do you know what you are claiming?" (or probably more accurately, "How do *I* know that you know what you are claiming?"). The all-too-frequent answer to that question leads to a conclusion that the researcher has not supplied adequate evidence to justify his or her claims. And that kind of conclusion had led to the associated conclusion that the legitimacy of the work was tied to the presentation of evidence.

It is this very concern that set me on a path 30 years ago to create an approach that would provide an evidentiary basis for qualitatively based findings and conclusions. Reviewers for all our elite journals had become (and, to some significant extent, still are) accustomed to seeing deductive thinking, quantitatively based data displays, statistical methodologies and tests, and clear relationships between hypotheses, data presentations, results (not "findings") and conclusions. Reviewers often unwittingly adopt a stance of hard-science skepticism toward evidence. Qualitative (and especially interpretive) research, however, is not typically engaged in the pursuit of accuracy and the "right" answer, as a first principle. We are more often pursuing a *plausible, defensible explanation of the how and/or whys of a phenomenon* (Gioia et al., 2013). Nonetheless, the demand for the presentation of evidence is an entirely reasonable one. One of my early protégés, who was complaining vehemently about a reviewer's demand for more evidence, once took the stance that, "I was there! I know what I saw! So if they don't believe me, to hell with them!" Well, that sort of attitude is never going to fly, nor should it. So, what to do?

## Thinking Differently about Studying Organizing, Organization and Organizations

Let's start here. To me the single most important recognition for the conduct of organizational theory and research is that the organizational world is essentially a socially constructed world (Berger and Luckmann, 1966; Schutz, 1967; Weick, 1969/1979). Pause on that statement for a moment.… Consider what a strange statement it is for a person trained to have a profound appreciation for the nature of the physical world and the ways that engineering systems almost invariably obey physical *laws*. To study a social world defined by social construction implies that we turn our attention more to the ways in which organization members intersubjectively construct an understanding of their experience. My goodness. Think about the implications here. This is a world where people make stuff up and come to consensually agree on the made-up stuff as the "reality" with which they will deal. That's a tough (but necessary) proposition for a STEM person (Science, Technology, Engineering and Mathematics) to accept. There are no "laws" in this world; there are only rough approximations we call "principles." In this world we focus less on frequency counts and/or positions on some scale (as is common in quantitative approaches) and instead focus on the structures and processes of cognitive, emotional and behavioral interactive dynamics.

Such an approach is predicated not only on the recognition that much of the organizational world is socially constructed, but that the people doing the constructing are what I term "knowledgeable agents" – another fancy bit of academese that simply means that the people who inform on their experience know quite well what they are trying to accomplish and, just as important, can explain to us what they are trying to do, how they are trying to do it, and perhaps most important, why they are trying to do it. Treating informants as knowledgeable agents allows *them* to give an account of *their* experience in *their* terms. I'm near-fanatical about not imposing existing concepts and constructs on the informants' descriptions. That would simply be presumptuous, and I want to try to avoid pre-assumption. The upshot here is that I make a bend-over-backwards effort to give voice to informants in the earliest stages of research and to give prominence to that voice in the write-up. That means that my (and many others') reporting is often full of quotes from informants. Properly done, many of the quotes in text are "power quotes" (Pratt, 2008), but those quotes should be representative examples of a pattern of similar quotes that can be documented and presented in appendices or ancillary data tables.

In my way of thinking, these fundamental recognitions noted above imply that we need to account for a "first-order" level of understanding (i.e., one that is adequate at the level of meaning for the informants themselves). If it doesn't meet this criterion, then we really haven't captured the experience of the organization members. *But*, describing experience purely in lay terms is not necessarily theoretically informative, so we also need to account for a "second-order" level of understanding (i.e., one that is adequate at the level of meaning of descriptive or explanatory *theory* about the experience of the informants). (See Gioia et al. (2013) for a deeper and richer discussion of the underlying assumptions and techniques used to enact a research approach that meets these two key criteria. See Corley and Gioia (2011) for a deeper and richer discussion of theory and theory building.)

Truth is, it took me much of the 1980s to undergo a self-induced, if nonetheless wrenching "paradigm shift" in adopting an *interpretive*, rather than functionalist or positivist approach (see Burrell and Morgan, 1979). In brief, adopting an interpretive approach not only typically involves qualitative data, but more importantly, is intended to adequately represent the interpretations of the people experiencing a phenomenon. When I eventually surrendered my engineering mantle (and its attendant assumptions that the organizational-science world was a replicant of the physical-science world) and put on the mantle of the interpretive approach, it … just … felt … right. Finally, I had a way of doing research that not only could capture my own organizational experience, but could lend itself to writing about the research in terms that were both readable and revelatory.

Nonetheless, deciding to go the qualitative/interpretive route ran me into the buzz-saw of the then norms in the field. *That's* when I really discovered that our field was set up to accept mainly quantitative, functionalist research. The gatekeepers, you see, had themselves drunk the Kool-Aid, and acted *as if* the social and organizational world could be treated and studied by the readily available or adaptable techniques of the physical sciences. Like a converted smoker who rails against smoking, I began to rail against the assumption that we could act as if organization science were some rough analog of physical science. No! It's not! Come to your senses! We're being duped! And we're duping ourselves by playing along with inappropriate assumptions about the nature of our beasts. Of course, I now had a mountain to climb. Qualitative research was very much in the minority. And research that was both qualitative *and* interpretive had been relegated to a distant corner of the universe where only the crazies (like me) hang out. Legitimacy for this heretical set of assumptions? Not a prayer. Research based on assumptions like these had barely been granted a small voice in the obscure wilderness.

## The First Steps on the Empirical Journey

My first slap-in-the-face experience with the ontological/epistemological/methodological assumptions and quantitatively oriented norms of the field was the attempt to publish my first major interpretive work – the paper that eventually became the Gioia and Chittipeddi (1991) article in *Strategic Management Journal* (*SMJ*), which actually started life as a qualitative research project in 1983, yet wasn't ready for submission until late 1988 (perhaps another reason for why we see fewer qualitative research articles – the average time for inception to publication for one of my studies is over five years – *and* the research projects generally generate just one article. Yowser. Try to make tenure with that sort of approach).

The backstory on the *SMJ* paper is informative in appreciating the long, hard road to legitimacy for qualitative research. First, because it was a paper about the initiation of strategic change in a university, we decided to send it to *SMJ*. You need to understand *SMJ*'s orientation in those days. They had published few case studies (an "N of one" was not considered legitimate research, you see), and to my knowledge, they had never published an interpretive study. What you also need to understand is that most research of the era was not just quantitative work, it was *theory-testing* work – i.e., authors would describe the state of existing theory up front, formulate a set of derivative hypotheses, test them, and then articulate an incremental adjustment to the prior theory. That's the way normal science is done – contributions to science build incrementally on the works of others. The important point here, though, is that the theory is invariably presented *first*. Interpretive research projects, however, are typically *theory-generation* projects – i.e., the theory is grounded in and emerges from the reported data, which means that the theory is most appropriately presented *last*. That turned out to be a big issue.

The initial submission followed the classic interpretive presentational strategy. Now, if it was bad enough that *SMJ*'s reviewers weren't accustomed to reading a case study, it was worse that they weren't accustomed to seeing a manuscript that was structured "backwards." Still, the *story* we told about the difficulties of initiating strategic change was pretty damn engaging. I suspect that the reviewers found themselves in something of a quandary. The manuscript didn't look "normal"; it didn't contain "data" in the usual sense; it certainly did not have any numbers in it, yet it was a really informative narrative and it clearly produced some rather profound insights about sensemaking and sensegiving processes during strategic change initiation. Hmmm. If I am a traditional reviewer, what do I recommend to the editor when confronted with this strange creature?

It was clear from the reviews that the reviewers were flummoxed about this mysterious paper. My own projective reconstruction of the process went something like this:

> We can't accept it, because it's too strange; we probably shouldn't reject it because the authors clearly seem to know what they're doing (we had articulated the interpretive research tradition well), and we'd look like dummies if we recommend rejecting it; let's instead stall and ask to see a revision

– *but*, this backwards presentation of theory has got to go. The strongest counsel we got was to *Put the theory up front, please*. Nonetheless, we saw ourselves as purists, so we sent a much-improved revision back, with the theory still at the end. A non-starter. On the second round, they liked the insights even more, but the placement of the grounded theory was, if anything, even more bothersome to them. So, despite positive comments about the content, the structure of the paper became a "condition of acceptance" issue – present the theory in the normal way (up front) *or else*.

This little episode not only spoke volumes about the field's receptivity to qualitative research, it also reminded me of a rather telling episode of the old TV series *M★A★S★H* – a series about a Mobile Army Surgical Hospital, ostensibly set in the Korean Conflict, wherein civilian doctors located close to the front lines treat wounded soldiers (see Gioia, 2004). In this episode, a sergeant brings his buddy, who has a head injury, to the MASH unit, and demands that the doctors take care of him first. The doctors perform triage and determine that the soldier has a concussion that is not life-threatening, so they then carefully explain the principles of triage to the sergeant, noting that other soldiers with more serious injuries should be prioritized first. The sergeant, who is carrying an automatic weapon, then nods appreciatively, says that he completely understands the principles the doctors have just so clearly explained to him, but then turns the weapon on the doctors and demands that they nonetheless take care of his buddy first.

That's the way we felt. The reviewers had listened to our careful explanation of why we had structured the paper the way we did, nodded appreciatively that our explanation made eminent sense, but then used the power of the reviewers' position to force us to write the paper the way they saw as normal. There is a kind of happy ending to this little story, however, in that it enabled me to devise a technique that allowed me to articulate the (grounded) theory first (thus satisfying the basic cognitive tendency for people to understand better if they have an advance framework), while carefully explaining that the theoretical framework actually emerged from the study that follows. A lesson in turning lemons into lemonade.

## The Qualitative Conundrum

In subsequent years, as I got deeper and deeper into the interpretive perspective and qualitative research, I became an incorrigible traitor to my training. Oh, I appreciated my early training as an engineer even more, because it gave me a marvelous platform for understanding how most people (and reviewers) in our field continued to think – and especially how they judged qualitative research, even if some of them might technically not be qualified to review it. Knowing how the other side thinks confers a decent advantage if you're trying to convince a skeptical audience. Still, I became an avid reader of qualitative research in the 1990s.

I had learned fairly early on that there was a solid social scientific tradition for employing qualitative data to develop inductive "grounded theories" (Glaser and Strauss, 1967; Lincoln and Guba, 1985). Such theories provide rich theoretical descriptions of the content, processes and especially the contexts within which organizational phenomena transpire. Yet, as noted above, I also learned that many traditional scholars did not perceive that inductive research adhered to the kind of "rigorous" standards usually associated with scientific advancement (see Bryman, 1988; Campbell, 1975; Campbell and Stanley, 1963; Popper, 1959/2002 for good summaries of traditional standards). My own reading of qualitative work was that the traditional critiques actually had a good point. Much of this literature was wonderfully readable and often quite insightful, but it also came across as overly impressionistic and the reported evidence for the claims was, shall we say, a bit thin. I also concluded that too many qualitative narratives gave authors "a license to be brilliant" in telling an engaging story and then making a leap to some revelatory assertion on the basis of evidence that either could lead to a head-scratching question, "How did you arrive there?" or could plausibly be interpreted in other ways.

I also concluded that the credibility and legitimacy of qual research stemmed not only from the (qualitative) methodologies used, but also from the woefully inadequate explanation of those methodologies. Here's an example of what I mean. I went to Europe quite a lot in the 1990s as an evangelist for interpretive research. Now, in one sense, that amounts to preaching to the choir, because interpretivism has European roots and the case study was most often the preferred research approach. The curious thing, however, was that many universities in Europe wanted to adopt the American research model and to learn to publish in the elite American journals (which were seen as having higher standards and thus greater legitimacy). They still wanted to publish case studies, however, but they were just having a hard time doing it because they were running headlong into reviewers for these journals who used realist assumptions in judging research. I had given a well-attended talk entitled "Qualitative Rigor," organized by Gerry Johnson at Cranfield in 1994, so I became the guy with a reputation for appreciating European idealism but was also facile with American pragmatism (i.e., the pragmatics of publishing qualitative studies in predominantly quantitative journals).

I read a lot of my fellow qual scholars' work, and my general conclusion was that many of the (case) studies I read had the following form for the method section. First, it was short – often less than one page and not infrequently only one paragraph. Second, its prototypical form read like this: "I got entry into an important organization; I got permission to job-shadow the CEO for several weeks or to participate in a crucial decision-making group's meetings; here's what I found." Third, the findings section was an overview of the impressions derived from the observations made during the time in the organization, some of which were non-obvious and insightful, but also pretty mysterious as to their origins. Is there any doubt that this sort of reporting format led to concerns about the legitimacy of the work by reviewers? There was little "systematicity" to the work (if I can coin a term in my own dialect of academese). For these reasons, I would concentrate my critical comments on their method sections.

When I then showed my colleagues the methodology section to one of my papers (and I was floating the early versions of what became the Gioia et al. (1994) and Gioia and Thomas (1996), manuscripts at the time), people were astonished. Those methodology sections were *long*! They laid out philosophy-of-science assumptions, explained data sources and data-gathering procedures, data analysis techniques, first- and second-order analyses, the construction of the data structure(s), etc., etc. (i.e., much of what we see in many good qual research papers today). In other words, what this attention to the method section showed was not only that there was a systematic way of thinking about: (1) the design of the research project, (2) the specific research question (and there *always* is a specific research question guiding the study – I don't do fishing expeditions, which was another knock on qual research), (3) the data and their analyses, and (4) the presentation of the findings. Germane to all this was the presence of a "data structure," showing how first-order codes relate to second-order themes and dimensions. My little mantra is, "You got no data structure; you got nothin'." The data structure, its associated tables and/or appendices, and the grounded theory figure (which graphically transforms the data structure into a dynamic process model) are the heart of any study using the approach I have been developing and honing since the late 1980s.

All this elaborate research infrastructure was aimed not only at developing a "rigorous" mode of *presentation* (which is what too many people incorrectly assume is the primary purpose when they read one of these studies), but more importantly, developing a mode of thinking through the entire process of qual research from inception to conclusion – all while trying to maintain the imaginative/revelatory tradition of qualitative, inductive research in contributing to theoretical advancement in the organizational sciences.

## Qualitative Rigor

As noted, a key concern, was to devise a way of showing that the data gathering, data analysis and data presentation are all done systematically. Doing and presenting qualitative research more systematically was an avenue toward achieving what I had earlier termed "qualitative rigor" in showing how data generate theoretical insights. But, in my mind doing and presenting things systematically had to meet several other criteria: it not only had to allow for the voices of the knowledgeable people reporting on their experience, but also it had to allow for researcher imagination and creativity. Furthermore, it had to tell a good story (just because I like good stories).

The upshot of all these considerations, as noted above, is the use of both a "first-order" data and analysis (employing informant-centered terms) and a "second-order" analysis (employing researcher-centered concepts, themes and dimensions – see van Maanen (1979), for the inspiration for the first- and second-order labeling). The reporting of both informant and researcher voices allows both a qualitatively rigorous demonstration of data-to-theory connections (now seemingly the new *de rigueur* demand by reviewers) and the production of creative insight. Over the succeeding 25+ years, I have worked to refine and enhance this systematic approach and it seems to have caught on as at least one way to help reviewers and readers perceive the kind of qualitative rigor associated with "legitimate" approaches to research. There are of course other researchers who have developed their own approaches to qualitative presentation. I doubt that you'll hear many of them talking in terms of legitimacy, but in my mind, that sort of pursuit is at the heart of many of our endeavors.

## Legitimacy and Transferability

One of the obscure presumptions of interpretive work is that because the social and organizational world is socially constructed, findings are necessarily idiosyncratic (because they are processes devised and developed by unique individuals acting within unique contexts) and therefore do not lend themselves to being "generalized." I find that stance to be just silly. If there is no benefit that applies beyond a given setting, why would we do research in the first place (especially if the primary purpose of research is to inform theory)? Deriving concepts, and especially principles that are transferable to other settings (Lincoln and Guba, 1985), is the name of the game. Our findings simply must address a larger audience than qualitative acolytes. So many processes and concepts are similar, even to the point of being structurally equivalent (Morgeson and Hofmann, 1999) that they are of course transferable across domains.

My argument here is also a strong counter to the tired, old argument that one cannot generalize from small samples (and to many researchers a case study still counts as a sample of one). Is it even possible to generalize from a case study? It is an absurd question. Of course it is. One can transfer findings from a case – *if* the focal case generates concepts or principles that are relevant to some other domain. Furthermore, one of the great intents of research is to generalize to *theory* (Bansal and Corley, 2011). My stance on this point comes also from being a case teacher. Case teachers like me choose their teaching cases by first finding a specific case that demonstrates a more general principle. For that reason, I often talk in terms of "portable principles" – i.e., principles that are portable from one setting to another. That idea applies to the transferability of emergent concepts from a well-done qualitative study. That hallmark also forms a basis for legitimacy.

## A Methodology That's Taken on a Life of Its Own

In my longstanding quest to develop a qualitative approach that mitigates many readers' concerns about the credibility of qualitative data and its analyses, many other scholars now seem to have adopted it in some form. Is that a good thing? Yes, in the sense that we now at least have some consensus that qual researchers need to show the basis for their assertions and that there is at least some consensus over the key issue that we can no longer simply report impressions. No, in the sense that having a field settled on some standard approach (even if it's mine) runs the risk of undermining the great tradition of qualitative research for rich variety.

The funny thing is that I once tried to treat this methodological approach as my little secret – to be used only by myself and my protégés. Indeed, my early goal was to refine the approach with some new methodological feature with each new study. I was able to pull that off for many years (see the progressive iterations beginning with Gioia and Chittipeddi, 1991, then Gioia et al., 1994; Gioia and Thomas, 1996; Corley and Gioia, 2004; Nag et al., 2007; Gioia et al., 2010; Clark et al., 2010). Thereafter, I stopped honing and simply executed (e.g., Nag and Gioia, 2012; Patvardhan et al., 2015). In 2011 Dave Ketchen tried to talk me into writing up the methodology for consideration for an *Organizational Research Methods* special issue on concept development. I told him that I really didn't want to go public with a methodology that I considered proprietary. His colorful response was, "You're an idiot! A lot of people already know about it. Why don't you write it up so people understand the philosophy behind it and the steps to execute it properly?" I seem to invite slaps in the face. That one resulted in the Gioia, Corley and Hamilton. (2013) article wherein I came clean about everything.

I really have only two big concerns about others applying this general approach to their work. The first is that, although I'm a huge fan of giving voice to my informants (and thus for presenting their first-order understandings as integral to the research), the first-order/second-order terminology is becoming very prevalent. Royston Greenwood even cornered me one time and asked rather pointedly, "Well, is this it? Are we all going to talk mainly in terms of first- and second-order findings in our research reporting now?" I take his point, and would argue against myself now (not unusual, by the way, as I have long been my own paradox). I'm a fan of variety. Different research questions and different orientations should rely on different conceptualizations of data and different methodological approaches. Forcing data into the first-order/second-order scheme is not always the way to go, just because that's become common now. Different phenomenological needs augur for different approaches (see Bansal and Corley, 2011). I would still argue, however, that compelling data do need to be prominent in qualitative studies.

The second concern is that organizational researchers seem to be treating the methodology as some sort of template, cookbook or formula that tries to reproduce the precise format of some data structure from other studies. Some methodology sections now seem to adopt not only the format but almost verbatim procedural descriptions from other published works. This kind of trend gives me the willies. I meant the approach to be a "methodology," rather than a "method." To me, it is a guide to thinking systematically about not just the presentation of data, but the conceptualization of the whole study. I see it as an orientation toward qualitative, inductive research that encourages innovation, rather than as a "cookbook" for presenting qualitative research. When the approach acts as a template, it limits its innovative potential. Worse, it also undermines one of its main intents: demonstrating data-to-theory connections with qualitative rigor. Really, that's all you need to design, develop and deliver research that even skeptics can see as legitimate.

## Conclusion

So, what's happened in the interim since my memorable wrestling matches in the early 1990s and where are we now? My own retrospective is that we went through quite a period of change in the quality of qual research in the 1990s and early 2000s. In general, the quality across many of our empirical journals during this period was uneven, even if the quantity of qual research went up, thus giving it more prominence as a viable approach to doing organizational research. Still, it is interesting to me that a disproportionate share of "best paper" awards went to qual studies, even then (e.g., Gersick, 1989; Isabella, 1990; Dutton and Dukerich, 1991) – which to me is prima facie evidence that good qualitative research is more relevant and revelatory than its quant counterpart. A little investigatory legwork shows that over the past 25 years, nearly half of the best-paper awards in *AMJ* and *ASQ* have gone to qual studies, when qual papers made up less than 15 percent of the published works in those journals. What does that say?

For the last decade, as both a reviewer and an author, it is clear to me that the standards for qual research have only ramped up. Work that might have been published ten years ago gets shot down now, often on grounds of marginal or inadequately explained methodology. It remains difficult to publish qual research, but for very different reasons. Now, it is not so much a matter of trying to breach the barriers because the work is deemed to be unusual or impressionistic or idiosyncratic, but because reviewers have raised the bar on two key dimensions: (1) They are becoming ever more consistent about demanding better explanations for how data analysis was done and (2) they are becoming ever more insistent that data-to-theory connections be demonstrated, not just asserted. I might also note that two of our top journals, *AMJ* and *ASQ* now have associate editors devoted almost solely to handling qual research. It's getting tougher for yours truly, too. I'm having as hard a time publishing my work as I ever did, but now for all the right reasons.

In the end I still think what matters is quality, of whatever stripe. Qual research still retains the advantage of harboring more potential for surprising findings and theoretically interesting innovations, all couched within a form with greater storytelling potential. And all of us still love a good story, well told. That's where the rich opportunity for revelation comes from in discovering new concepts rather than just affirming existing concepts. And that's why I think qualitative research is now not only good, but will only get better.

# References

Bansal, P. and Corley, K. (2011) "The coming of age for qualitative research: Embracing the diversity of qualitative methods," *Academy of Management Journal*, 54(2): 233–237.

Berger, P. L. and Luckmann, T. (1966) *The Social Construction of Reality: A Treatise in the Sociology of Knowledge*. Garden City, NY: Doubleday.

Bryman, A. (1988) *Quantity and Quality in Social Research*. New York: Unwin Hyman.

Burrell, G. and Morgan, G. (1979) *Sociological Paradigms and Organizational Analysis*. Portsmouth, NH: Heinemann.

Campbell, D. T. (1975) "'Degrees of freedom' and the case study," *Comparative Political Studies*, 8(2): 178–193.

Campbell, D. T. and Stanley, J. C. (1963) *Experimental and Quasi-Experimental Design for Research*. Chicago, IL: Rand McNally.

Charmaz, K. (2014) *Constructing Grounded Theory*. Los Angeles, CA: Sage.

Clark, S. M., Gioia, D. A., Ketchen, D. and Thomas, J. B. (2010) "Transitional identity as a facilitator of organizational identity change during a merger," *Administrative Science Quarterly*, 55: 397–438.

Clegg, S. R., Rhodes, C. and Kornberger, M. (2007) "Desperately seeking legitimacy: Organizational identity and emerging industries," *Organization Studies*, 28: 495.

Corley, K. G. and Gioia, D. A. (2004) "Identity ambiguity and change in the wake of a corporate spin-off," *Administrative Science Quarterly*, 49: 173–208.

Corley, K. G. and Gioia, D. A. (2011) "Building theory about theory building: What constitutes a theoretical contribution?," *Academy of Management Review*, 36: 12–32.

Dutton, J. E. and Dukerich, J. M. (1991) "Keeping an eye on the mirror: Image and identity in organizational adaptation," *Academy of Management Journal*, 34: 517–554.

Gersick, C. J. (1989) "Marking time: Predictable transitions in task groups," *Academy of Management Journal*, 32: 274–309.

Gioia, D. A. (1992) "Pinto fires and personal ethics: A script analysis of missed opportunities," *Journal of Business Ethics*, 11: 379–389.

Gioia, D. A. (2004) "A renaissance self: Prompting personal and professional revitalization," in Frost, P. J. and Stablein, R. E. (eds.) *Renewing Research Practice: Scholars' Journeys* (pp. 97–114) Stanford, CA: Stanford University Press.

Gioia, D. A. and Chittipeddi, K. (1991) "Sensemaking and sensegiving in strategic change initiation," *Strategic Management Journal*, 12: 433–448.

Gioia, D. A. and Thomas, J. B. (1996) "Identity, image and issue interpretation: Sensemaking in academic administration," *Administrative Science Quarterly*, 41: 370–403.

Gioia, D. A., Thomas, J. B., Clark, S. M., and Chittipeddi, K. (1994) "Symbolism and strategic change in academia: Dynamics of sensemaking and influence," *Organization Science*, 5: 363–383.

Gioia, D. A., Price, K. P., Hamilton, A. L. and Thomas, J. B. (2010) "Forging an identity: An insider–outsider study of processes involved in organizational identity formation," *Administrative Science Quarterly*, 55: 1–46.

Gioia, D. A., Corley, K. G. and Hamilton, A. L. (2013) "Seeking qualitative rigor in inductive research: Notes on the Gioia methodology," *Organizational Research Methods*, 16(1): 15–131.

Gioia, D. A., Hamilton, A. L. and Patvardhan, S. (2014) "Image is everything," *Research in Organizational Behavior*, 34: 129–154.

Glaser, B. G. and Strauss, A. (1967) *The Discovery of Grounded Theory: Strategies for Qualitative Research*. Chicago, IL: Aldine.

Isabella, L. (1990) "Evolving interpretations as a change unfolds: How managers construe key organizational events," *Academy of Management Journal*, 33: 7–41.

Lincoln, Y. S. and Guba, E. G. (1985) *Naturalistic Inquiry*. Beverly Hills, CA: Sage.

Morgeson, F. P. and Hofmann, D. A. (1999) "The structure and function of collective constructs: Implications for multilevel research and theory development," *Academy of Management Review*, 24(2): 249.

Nag, R. and Gioia, D. A. (2012) "From common to uncommon knowledge: Foundations of firm-specific use of knowledge as a resource," *Academy of Management Journal*, 55: 421–457.

Nag, R., Corley, K. G. and Gioia, D. A. (2007) "The intersection of organizational identity, knowledge, and practice: Attempting strategic change via knowledge grafting," *Academy of Management Journal*, 50: 821–847.

Patvardhan, S., Gioia, D. A. and Hamilton, A. (2015) "Weathering a metalevel identity crisis: Forging a coherent collective identity for an emerging field," *Academy of Management Journal*, 58: 405–435.

Popper, K. (1959/2002) *The Logic of Scientific Discovery*. London: Routledge.

Pratt, M. G. (2008) "Fitting oval pegs into round holes: Tensions in evaluating and publishing qualitative research in top-tier North American journals," *Organizational Research Methods*, 11(3): 481–509.

Schutz, A. (1967) *The Phenomenology of the Social World*. Evanston, IL: Northwestern University Press.

Van Maanen, J. (1979) "The fact of fiction in organizational ethnography," *Administrative Science Quarterly*, 24: 539–550.

Weick, K. E. (1969/1979) *The Social Psychology of Organizing*. New York: Addison-Wesley.

# 31

# BLIND ALLEYS AND UNTOLD STORIES IN QUALITATIVE RESEARCH

*Ann Langley*

## Introduction

In my own career as author, editor and reviewer of qualitative research, I have often been confronted with studies that despite considerable investment, respectable amounts of qualitative data and careful analytical effort somehow just don't work. That is to say they do not seem to have what it takes to get published in top journals, and even if they do make it into publication somewhere some time, they are never likely to have much of an impact. These experiences are painful, and there might be much to be learned from them. We all, of course, naturally learn from our own experiences, and yet it is sometimes hard to share that learning widely with others (a) precisely because things that do not work also do not usually get into print, and (b) because wasted time and energy is generally not a source of pride. Methodology texts provide a lot of advice about how to do good qualitative research. And our journals are full of exemplary papers (often massaged repeatedly by multiple rounds of review) that have managed to find the sweet spot where rich qualitative data and insightful theorizing come together. This reflection is about the rest: the studies that got stuck down blind alleys, or whose stories could not be told for one reason or another.

Most of what I have to say here comes not from published articles and books, but from undocumented experiential sources. This includes on the one hand, some of my own studies started but never published (or not in the best outlets), and on the other hand, articles reviewed or edited that were, for one reason or another, rejected (though I cannot know what happened to them since then). One source for the latter is an experience as co-guest editor of the Special Research Forum on Process Studies of Change in Organization and Management in *Academy of Management Journal* published in 2013 (Langley et al., 2013), but some of my own pieces have met with a similar fate, and I include reflections on those as well. To illustrate my points, I introduce subsections of the chapter with quotations from reviews I have seen or received in the course of my career. These are paraphrased and anonymized but retain the flavor of the original comments. They hopefully resonate with readers and make the issues I am raising a little more vivid.

To begin these reflections, I note that pragmatically speaking, research involves three components: data (i.e., empirical materials collected from a specific context), theory (conceptual ideas about the nature of the world) and a process for coupling the two (which is where analytic methods come in) (Langley et al., 2003). Qualitative research involves data that are usually expressed in the form of words rather than numbers, and there is a tendency to see qualitative research as essentially "inductive" with data as a starting point and theory as an endpoint. Here, the coupling process is mainly data driven rather than theory driven. This unidirectional view has been contested with some suggesting that qualitative research may play a role in theory elaboration (Lee et al., 1999; Burawoy, 1998) or even in theory testing (Bitektine, 2007; Johnston et al., 1999). We will return later to more sophisticated ways of positioning qualitative research within the data-theory coupling space.

In the meantime, these three components of research: data, theory and the coupling process provide a neat way to structure my reflections on blind alleys and untold stories in qualitative research. I now consider these components in turn under three headings: "difficult data", (input) "contestable coupling" (process) and "stale stories" (theoretical output). I do not attempt to be exhaustive but will merely draw attention to some of the more common issues observed in my own experience, reflect on the causes of these difficulties and, where I think I can do this, offer potential solutions.

## Difficult Data

Qualitative data are purportedly rich and deep. In the form of interviews, they can give access to people's lived experiences, and in the form of observation, they can capture the micro-level behaviors and language of individuals in interaction, both very hard to obtain from other sources. Many obvious things can, however, go wrong with this portrait. We have all seen the one-line answer interview transcript where the interviewer is talking more than the interviewee. And we have all seen field notes that were obviously written up several days after the events observed, or where it seems as if the observer got bored. The amount of skill, attention, discipline and empathy that qualitative researchers need to do a good job of listening, seeing and capturing richness and depth is often underestimated. But let us assume that these basic qualitative research skills have been reasonably well mastered. What else can go wrong? Here are some places where I have myself tripped up, and where I have often seen others do so too. Beware!

### *Voluminous Unsaturated Data*

> I appreciate the effort that is involved with collecting over 80 interviews across many different organizations, but while you have clearly collected a lot of data, I'm not sure that you have the right kind of data for what you are trying to do.

A fairly common occurrence in my experience as an editor and reviewer of qualitative research is when a researcher has collected a huge volume of interviews about an organizational level issue across a large number of organizations, with perhaps one or two interviews in each organization. When I see this, my heart sinks. Clearly a huge amount of effort went into the research, but the design is flawed. I sympathize! Early in my career, I collected interviews and questionnaires on strategic planning processes in 33 hospitals from 59 participants (generally but not always two people in each organization). I had aimed to get one doctor and one administrator for each site and to collect documents where I could, thinking that this degree of triangulation would provide comparative data on the different sites that might enable me to derive some predictions about when strategic planning might be successful in these contexts. As a new qualitative researcher with a quantitative background, I think I was somehow seduced by the idea that a larger sample of cases would produce better research, and missed the crucial importance of empirical saturation for each case (Glaser and Strauss, 1967/2009). Part of the seduction also lies in the relative ease of access for doing this kind of data collection. It may be easier to get 59 interviews across 33 organizations than to obtain in-depth access to fewer. Ten carefully selected interviews from each of six carefully selected organizations would have been so much better (Eisenhardt, 1989), but rather more of a challenge to negotiate. Mistake!

So let us say that you did collect this kind of data. What can you do? One approach might be to consider shifting the unit of analysis downward towards the individual. Interviews can be a valuable source of narratives – stories people tell about their experiences (Mantere, 2008; Dameron and Torset, 2014). Seen this way, we no longer need to know whether a story is "true," and the focus moves from the organizational level to the person and their sensemaking processes around the phenomenon at the focus of the study. Of course, such a shift can only be made if the data are suitable: they ideally need to be full of specific stories and personal experiences and reflections (I never did this, but perhaps there was a place for a paper on professionals' individual understandings and reactions to organizational tools such as strategic planning).

An alternative is to do the reverse, to raise the level of analysis upwards. This is what happened to my data on strategic planning in the hospital sector. The body of interviews, documents and other materials became a single case (that of strategic planning) that was compared with another body of data on total quality management (the second case) in the same set of organizations. We used these data to develop an interesting comparative analysis of the "corruption of managerial techniques by organizations" (Lozeau et al., 2002), a study I am now quite proud of, but whose origins were not so propitious.

## *Mixed Methods Chimera*

> The paper does not present either a compelling weight of qualitative evidence or a
> statistical test through quantitative methods to establish causality.

As a teacher of qualitative research, I often encounter students who yearn after the best of both worlds. Yes – they tell me, they are interested in qualitative research, but their advisors favor quantitative methods and that seems to be the only way to get published. Their solution is "mixed methods." Now, I can see the potential value of the mixed methods thesis that has a qualitative study and a quantitative study in it that might address similar issues in different ways. There are also some truly admirable mixed methods papers published in some of the top journals, where the different methods are clearly rigorously done and fully complementary to one another (Edmondson, 1999; Elsbach, 1994; Salvato, 2009). These are jewels: shiny, beautiful, fascinating and rare! And not given to all. The effort required to be a strong performer on both sides of the divide is often quite seriously underestimated. In my own experience, it is something I have sometimes aimed to do, but not, so far, very successfully.

Mixed methods are attractive because of the complementary strengths of qualitative and quantitative data in terms of breadth, depth and comparability (Kaplan, 2015), but they have disadvantages too. Unless both parts are well executed, they can result not in the best of both worlds but the worst. Superficial interview data cannot, for example, be complemented by weak quantitative surveys where all variables come from the same source, as I have sometimes seen even in a few published papers. When doing mixed methods, as much effort needs to be invested in both sides of the study as would be invested in each if only one method was used. There is no economy of scale. Moreover, the challenges of reporting both qualitative and quantitative data together at the same level of rigor in the same journal length article are significant (Kaplan, 2015).

The result of this is that although I have been involved in collecting quantitative survey data along with qualitative data in several large studies of organizational change, mainly with a concern about having some broader assessments from a wider sample to accompany fine-grained qualitative analysis, I have almost never published them. When it comes to preparing material for publication, the need for detailed, subtle and rigorous qualitative data analysis and the process-oriented perspective that I have taken has squeezed out interest in these scales, which would in any case be merely descriptive, and narrowly time-bound. Numbers are not easily combined with qualitative process descriptions, and in the context of journal-length articles may even sometimes appear to diminish them in the eyes of readers because they can signal muddled ontological perspectives (Pratt, 2009). So hats off to those who can mix methods successfully. But beware of chasing two rabbits and catching neither.

## Contestable Coupling

In qualitative studies, data and theory have to be coupled together and shown to be so. The challenge is that data are specific and detailed, while theory is abstract and general. The trick is to show the flow from one to the other in such a way as to be convincing but at the same time move towards a level of abstraction that is theoretically insightful – grounded in the data, but not so bound by it as to seem to be an elaborated description. Gioia et al. (2013) have provided tools that are useful to illustrate the passage of abstraction from data to theoretical constructs via a diagram that they label the "data structure" and this has become very popular in published work. But as they note, the data structure is not enough: the theoretical constructs have to be placed in motion and linked together. Eisenhardt (1989) has offered tools for one form of linking captured in correlations across multiple cases. All these tools can be useful depending on the purpose and style of the research (Langley and Abdallah, 2011).

However, not all forms of theorizing are as easily captured this way. These tools tend to emphasize factors rather than processes (Cornelissen, 2016), limiting the range of conceptualizations possible. Moreover, they are tools for *displaying* linkages between data and theory, not for generating them in the first place. The creative process is fed and inspired by systematic analytical effort, but cannot be reduced to it. In strong and interesting qualitative research, there is always a piece of the coupling process that cannot be quite pinned down: this is the "conceptual leap" (Klag and Langley, 2013). Conceptual leaps are necessary, but not, however, sufficient either. I discuss some of the things that can go wrong here.

### *Loose Coupling*

I often encountered a certain difficulty in linking the empirical evidence with the proposed theoretical model. In other words, you provide a rich narration of events but often I cannot clearly see how those events fit the model you portrayed.

One of the key values of qualitative research is its potential to inspire discovery and conceptual insight. My own experience, however, is that these insights usually come not when I am working with detailed codes and bits of data – though this is always necessary to start the process, but some time after that when I have detached myself from the data and may be trying to communicate my study to a colleague, or (quite likely) preparing a PowerPoint presentation for a conference. Suddenly, I can see what all those data might mean and can draw an elegant diagram that sums it all up. This is a fantastic feeling … but rather dangerous. Various not so satisfactory things can happen at this point. First, it is easy to get enamored of the insights and connect them back to the data only selectively, blinded by the brilliance of the ideas to any disconfirming evidence (a premature closure problem). Or it may turn out that the insights, though potentially plausible and theoretically interesting, do in fact extend beyond the data that you have or could conceivably ever acquire (an extrapolation problem).

Premature closure is obviously something that all qualitative researchers need to guard against. Locke et al. (2008) suggest that researchers need to foster doubt to generate richer understandings that reach beyond initial ideas. They also suggest that exchanging with others in a community of scholars is a useful way to create the conditions necessary for doubt to be sustained and become generative. I agree and can recall many challenging conversations with students and colleagues that enabled them or me to complicate our thinking. At the same time, I have also seen doubt become paralytic when students or colleagues become excessively auto-critical of any potential insight they might have, returning obsessively to the data, sometimes drowning in their codes. The obverse of premature closure is perhaps "death by data asphyxia-tion" (Pettigrew, 1990). When this happens, I usually suggest that it is time to present at a conference. Having to create that PowerPoint is likely to get the creative juices flowing. A little loose coupling can be at least temporarily helpful, but then of course, it must be back again to the data. Nevertheless, the sparks that come from stepping outside it do play an important role, never to be underestimated, though risky.

But what if the generated insights and ideas still seem interesting and plausible but actually extend beyond the data. In other words, the ideas are *inspired* by data, but not exactly *grounded* in it in the sense of being tied up neatly with a bow (or a "data structure"). Yet you still think they are valuable. Could such a thing ever be possible or legitimate? I can remember being very frustrated as a doctoral student because of a sense that some of my work suggested useful ideas that I could not "prove" in the technical sense. I could use my data to *illustrate* the idea, but not to sew it up tightly in a way that reviewers demanded. Well, perhaps that is what "theory" papers are for. I remember being very struck by Sutton's (1997) *Organization Science* essay on "closet qualitative research" in which he argued that many theory papers are actually based on snippets of qualitative data or personal experience unpublishable in themselves, but that are then written up as conceptual pieces. Such articles resonate partly because they build on the nugget of insight and truth contained in the qualitative data even though the story is now wrapped up in references, and logical argument. I am reminded of this whenever I come across a paper to review with seemingly great ideas that are loosely coupled to data. One solution is to revisit the data and deepen the analysis, but this may smother the spark; the other (not so common or easy) may be to cut the data loose, and reframe the ideas theoretically.

## *Circular Coupling*

> The analysis is a form of labeling; here's something that happened, and this is what it would be called in our theoretical framework. This is not a "test" of the framework, but a "mapping" exercise.

One of the problems I have often seen and experienced myself in doing qualitative research is the issue of circularity. In the worst case, a researcher develops an initial conceptual framework for a research project (thesis supervisors usually expect students to have some initial conceptual ideas, even if the research is intended to be largely inductive), collects the data, and then proceeds to reproduce the framework they started with by placing data in the boxes of the framework. The result is entirely circular: a systematic but unsatisfying labeling exercise that does not add new knowledge or surprise. Although the framework might be adapted on the margins, there is no strong insight that reaches beyond it.

This kind of scenario seems perhaps most likely to occur when the researcher is trying to contribute to an already mature body of work. In that case, it is hard to proceed with a blank slate, so some of the analysis is almost bound to take the form of labeling with known categories. In most of the writing about qualitative research methods in management, there seems to be a strong assumption that "pure" grounded theorizing of one kind or another is the gold standard (Eisenhardt, 1989; Gioia et al., 2013; Locke et al., 2008). But much qualitative work is not really of this type, and it cannot be if researchers are to build on each other's work. It is also increasingly evident that qualitative research has inherent advantages for studying certain kinds of issues, notably those that involve a consideration of processes (Graebner et al., 2012) and it is not restricted in relevance to green field understudied phenomena. For example, studies of institutional complexity and of organizational routines are two fairly mature areas of study in organization theory, but ones where qualitative studies are still prevalent and well-represented as shown by recent special issues (Feldman et al., 2016; Suddaby et al., 2010; Vermeulen et al., 2016).

In cases like this, scholars inevitably draw at least in part on well-known concepts (e.g., institutional logics, ostensive and performative aspects of routines) and attempt to advance them in different directions. The challenge is to do so while creating a sense of movement and of novelty, i.e., clearly adding to prior knowledge. Similarly, for process studies in particular, certain types of theories (e.g., actor-network theory, structuration theory, conventionalist theory, complexity theory) have their own distinctive language repertoires that tend to structure data analysis. If those theories are relevant, then that language needs to be applied. And yet, a reader may well find that the labeling forces data into a preconceived framework and in the end simply reproduces it, yet one more time without adding anything new.

Even when new insight is indeed being developed in such studies, the writing process itself may render it difficult to make the balance between a priori theorizing and novel conceptual contribution transparent. I have continually struggled with how to present qualitative findings in such a way as to allow the reader to appreciate the richness of the empirical story, while at the same time having sufficient analytical cues to see how the empirical story connects to the theoretical story as the reading proceeds. A common and fairly effective device is actually to put the theoretical model upfront and use it to structure presentation of the empirics, while noting that the model actually emerged from the data (Bucher and Langley, 2016; Kaplan and Orlikowski, 2013). The danger here though is that this can again look like a circular labeling exercise. At the time of writing, I am working on an R&R on a paper whose first version had the upfront model structure, largely to help readability. The reviewers are asking us to turn the story around so that the model emerges at the end. Sometimes, quite clearly, it is the writing and not the analysis itself that makes data-theory coupling in qualitative research so challenging.

## Stale Stories

Now we come to the output of qualitative data analysis: the emerging theories or conceptual models themselves. The bar here is extremely high in the top level journals. For example, in *Academy Management Journal*, former editor Kevin Corley (in Bansal and Corley, 2011) noted that to be published, papers needed to offer a theoretical contribution that would "change, challenge, or fundamentally advance our understanding of a phenomenon. In other words, the findings cause us to think about a phenomenon in a way that past research would not normally suggest." This is a tough standard, and actually, given the adage that there is nothing really new under the sun, perhaps somewhat unrealistic.

Nonetheless, the bane of qualitative research is reinventing the wheel. This is so easy to do. The typical scenario for a problematic journal paper is a study that investigates what seems to be a new phenomenon, but after the findings, the discussion suddenly refers to literature that was not brought up in the upfront section. Once the findings appear, it seems that other people have written about related things with similar insights. Unfortunately, far from reinforcing the theoretical story as one might think, this undermines it – it is not new (!), and if the author gets an opportunity to revise the paper, he or she will be told to bring that discussion-based literature upfront and begin the story from that base, undermining still further any originality that might have been constructed in the beginning (yes, I have been there too). This is a particularly challenging message to receive. Unfortunately, beautifully done qualitative research may never see the light of day because it simply appears to confirm what someone has already said. Stale or potentially problematic theoretical stories take various forms. Here are three.

## Anti-theorizing

Saying "things are messy" is not enough.

Whatever you study as a qualitative researcher, you are almost bound to discover that things are messier than you could ever have imagined. You thought that a decision process would follow certain well-defined stages? – think again! (Mintzberg et al., 1976; Nutt, 1984). You have funding to study and evaluate a change process in a large organization over a period of three years? You will be lucky if any impact at all is detectable by the time the funding runs out, but at the same time enormous amounts of energy and angst will have been invested in the process (Yu et al., 2005; Cloutier et al., 2016). You thought that strategy was an organized process with predictable phases and outcomes? Not so! (MacKay and Chia, 2013). Things are messy. The problem is that we know that. It used to be that finding out that things are non-linear and messy (or that they do not follow the received views from the normative or descriptive literature) could be a significant contribution to theoretical understanding that might come from qualitative research. No longer is this enough. This forces scholars to dig deeper into the messiness and to find the patterns and theoretical mechanisms that produce the disorder, or that at least disturb and punctuate expected linearity.

For example, Jean-Louis Denis, Lise Lamothe and I (Denis et al., 2001) conducted a study of the dynamics of leadership and strategic change in pluralistic settings. We found that across all the settings we examined, the process was messy. Change always proceeded by stops and starts – it seemed as if as soon as it got going, there would be setbacks, and the leadership team had to start all over again, though from a different position. That insight was not enough, however. We had to dig into the theoretical mechanisms that could explain this. Eventually, we developed a model that showed how change evolved through the progressive coupling and uncoupling of linkages within the leadership group itself, between the leadership group and its internal stakeholders, and between the leadership group and external constituencies. We also theorized about the boundary conditions that would make this story more or less likely. Messiness needs to be pulled apart, analyzed and understood to make a contribution.

## Pattern Theorizing

The author divides the chronology into phases and claims to have found a temporal pattern. But the patterns are empirical regularities rather than fully theorized phenomena.

Another common problem in many qualitative studies is to mistake empirical regularity for theory. For example, if it seems that there is a common sequence of stages in a particular phenomenon across a series of cases, this is a wonderful finding that offers a lot of potential for developing insight. Yet, something is missing until the reasons behind that pattern have been understood. A case I find particularly revealing of this challenge is Connie Gersick's (1988) in-depth qualitative study of how teams working to a deadline organize their tasks over time. She found in a series of eight teams that right in the middle of their task timeline, they changed the way they worked on the problem. She also replicated this finding in an experimental study in the laboratory (Gersick, 1989). The problem was, as she explains in a reflexive piece on her research (Gersick, 1992), that she did not initially have a strong enough theoretical explanation for this empirical regularity. This became an issue in her first attempts at publication. It was only when she saw the parallels with punctuated equilibrium theory and other similar theories that described punctuated processes in the natural sciences that the theoretical logic underlying her findings became increasingly plausible, interesting and transparent (Gersick, 1991).

In my own research, I have almost never found linear phase models to be particularly appealing to express theoretical insights, perhaps because the processes I study generally have the "messy" quality I mentioned above. However, what has been immensely useful is the notion of phases (or time periods) as units of analysis within which theoretical mechanisms play out. Dividing timelines into temporal brackets (carefully chosen so that their boundaries correspond to discontinuities in activity) does more than offer a descriptive overlay to data. It also offers a basis to show the replication of temporally arranged theoretical process mechanisms from one period to another. Doing this has been highly generative, at least for me, in thinking through and analyzing the underlying theoretical processes that explain evolution over time (Bucher and Langley, 2016; Denis et al., 2011; Denis et al., 2001; Stensaker and Langley, 2010; Langley, 1999). Another recent example of published research using a temporal bracketing strategy is Howard-Grenville et al.'s (2013) study of the resurrection of a community identity (Tracktown USA) in Eugene, Oregon. Through the study of multiple attempts at identity resurrection, the authors revealed repeated interactive mechanisms of resource mobilization and authentication that enabled them to explain how, when and why these attempts succeeded or failed. I strongly recommend temporal bracketing as a possible path to reaching beyond pattern theorizing and finding a richer and more complex theoretical story.

## Patchwork Theorizing

> There are too many moving parts, a mash-up from different theoretical frameworks, with no strong integration.

Another trap that is easy to fall into with a qualitative study is to develop a tailored theoretical explanation for a particular phenomenon that includes everything but the kitchen sink, i.e., that draws on bits and pieces of different theoretical frameworks as they seem to fit. I have been guilty of this more than once. A tell-tale sign is that in the discussion section, a large number of references are brought in and discussed in very limited depth, and the discussion is not raised to an abstract level. A useful exercise is to try to write the discussion section without actually referring to the empirical case. When patchwork theorizing is involved, that is usually impossible because the bits and pieces of theory have been brought in precisely to explain the various elements of an idiosyncratic phenomenon. To my embarrassment when I look back on it, I once found it necessary to bring in agency theory, professional services literature, theories of radical change, role theory and theories of power dependence to explain mechanisms of integration of a new leader to an organization. Not surprisingly, the reviewers were unimpressed. The paper was fortunate to obtain a revise and resubmit decision. When we sent it back, we had slimmed down significantly the number and variety of theoretical references and turned the paper into something sharper and more focused (Denis et al., 2000). Specifically, our final theoretical model could be framed as an integration of two key theories of leader integration: "management control" and "socialization," where each theory appeared to be a better explanation for integration with respect to one of the two key stakeholder groups involved, and where their dynamic evolution and interaction over time added further explanatory elements.

While patchwork theorizing as described above is clearly a mistake, making a theoretical contribution that will be recognized as such nevertheless almost always involves some creative theoretical hybridization. Taking empirical data and telling a theoretical story that will resonate and yet be perceived as distinctively novel as required in the major journals (Bansal and Corley, 2011) cannot occur if we remain too deeply embedded in a very narrow theoretical stream. As Boxenbaum and Rouleau (2011) have suggested, since there is nothing fundamentally new under the sun, "new knowledge products" are generally constructed through metaphors and bricolage based on existing theoretical materials. This requires subtlety, coherence, and delicacy in weaving the pieces together and integrating them with empirical data as well: successful theorizing from qualitative data is actually more like lacework than patchwork.

Successful theorizing from qualitative data is also a moving target. What looked like a theoretical contribution in 2000 is not a theoretical contribution in 2010, and what was a theoretical contribution in 2010 may be stale by 2020. For the Special Research Forum on Process Studies of Change in Organizations and Management in *Academy of Management Journal* in 2013, the guest editors found that qualitative studies that revealed dialectical theoretical mechanisms, that showed multilevel interactions, or that focused on the processual dynamics of stability (i.e., what is required for organizations to reproduce themselves consistently) attracted the reviewers and were seen to offer novel theoretical contributions, as they introduced ways of thinking about phenomena that were unusual and insightful. I believe that perspectives like these still have potential. Moreover, I also think that practice-based perspectives have not yet reached their full potential. However, if pressures for novelty continue unabated, fresher forms of theorizing and storytelling may be needed in the future.

## Discussion and Conclusion

So far, this reflection may have appeared a little pessimistic. I have drawn attention to many things that can go wrong with qualitative research. I was inspired to do so by my perception that there is a huge body of qualitative research going on that never appears in print, at least to the degree that it deserves given the effort involved. I confess that I personally have data sets that have never been fully exploited. And seeing what I see as a reviewer and editor, I am certain that this is not an uncommon experience. Some of this might be inevitable. Not every research project is going to work out perfectly, even with the best of precautions. But there may be some ways to increase the chances of success. I suggest that understanding what does not work can help us to see what does or might. Here are some thoughts in that direction.

### *Deep Data*

The potential of the research begins with the *quality* of the data, not its sheer *volume*. Data sets need to be deep and rich, not shallow and superficial. In addition, I am increasingly persuaded that capturing naturally occurring interactions (e.g., through ethnography, detailed observation or potentially in the context of email exchanges) rather than (or usually in addition to) simply interviewing large numbers of people offers potential for much stronger forms of understanding. If audio or video-recording can be used in these efforts, so much the better but this may not always be necessary when field notes are rich, disciplined and systematic. Interactive and observational data are not always easy to handle – we are more used to seeing qualitative papers stuffed with interview quotes, but some scholars are finding ways to make them come alive (Jarzabkowski et al., 2014; Kaplan, 2011; Nicolini, 2011), and when they do, they seem to bring us so much closer to the life and work of people in organizations. Although access may be harder to obtain, the potential payoff is worth it.

## Credible but Creative Coupling

As Malvina Klag and I noted (Klag and Langley, 2013), "conceptual leaping" – i.e., bridging data and theory to arrive at strong abductive insight – is a dialectic process imbued with tensions. We noted the need to navigate among and around four kinds of tensions "between deliberation and serendipity; between engagement [with data] and detachment [from it]; between knowing and not knowing; and between social connection and self-expression" (Klag and Langley, 2013: 161). The notion of "credible but creative coupling" expresses this ongoing tension that we all feel when attempting to make sense of qualitative data. We need to stay grounded in the data, and yet we need to rise above it. Without the first, our stories will not be believable, and without the second, they will not be valuable. Weick (1989) called theorizing "disciplined imagination." In discussing grounded theory, Locke (2007) referred to the need to combine "rational control" with "irrational free play." The problems of loose or circular coupling occur when the balance between the dialectic tensions has slipped. There are no perfect recipes for ensuring that the coupling will be just right. However, the chances are stronger for effective coupling if time is devoted to both working with data and separating from it. I would add that while in my discussion of data, I insisted on the need for depth of coverage, one of my own mistakes in analyzing data has often been to try to include too much. Sometimes narrowing down the focus to certain key and striking elements in the data may lead to more productive and interesting theorizing.

## Stirring Stories

Since theory building is a creative process that refuses to be contained, it is hard to say what exactly might enable qualitative researchers to turn stale stories into stirring ones. Anti-theorizing, pattern theorizing and patchwork theorizing are clearly insufficient. That said, they and other kinds of unsuccessful representations may be elements on the path to something more interesting, and so they should not be set aside, but built on. If what you see is not what the "received view" would suggest (anti-theorizing), then it would be important to try to articulate why that is occurring and turn the negative (what this is not) into the positive (what this is). If you have detected an empirical pattern that seems to recur and you have a hunch that there is something universal about it (pattern theorizing), try to think through why that is. One way of doing this is to imagine what would make the pattern *unlikely* to occur. By focusing on the boundary conditions, suddenly you may be able to see what it is that explains its existence. You might even see how you could collect additional data that would enable you to enrich the explanation. If you have constructed your theory from too many bits and pieces arbitrarily patched together (patchwork theorizing), try to think through which of the pieces are really and truly central. Then consider how those pieces may be more subtly and elegantly woven together to generate something more parsimonious, more appealing and probably more general as well.

In fact, in my experience, most qualitative studies submitted to journals are not quite there in terms of the theoretical stories they are telling. However, there is often potential to turn them around, as long as the data have the potential, and as long as the authors have the skills to re-engage with them credibly and creatively. I would add too that the potential for insightful theory is also enhanced when the data collected reach beyond the run-of-the-mill. For example, they cover processes and practices that have rarely been studied in depth. They may do things that we rarely see such as looking at processes over longer periods of time than usually seen, or in more fine-grained detail, or following people and things as they move across different settings. It is hard to tell stale stories when the phenomena studied have rarely been captured before.

One final thing I have learned that is worthy of mention in this discussion is that over and above the elements mentioned here, there is always an element of luck in publishing qualitative research. Much depends on getting the right mix of reviewers who can see the potential in your data, and will help you build on what you have. Much also depends on being able to thread a path through their comments that will raise the manuscript to a significantly higher level of quality while keeping all of the reviewers on board. Of course, there are also mistakes to be made in engaging with reviewers. One mistake is to simply go through the motions: i.e., to respond ploddingly to every comment but fail to inject an additional spark of insight or of rigor and conviction that has potential to wow the reviewers over and above the first version. The opposite mistake is to overdo it, i.e., transform the manuscript so significantly that it is essentially a new "first cut" that the existing reviewers may not even be competent to judge because the theoretical framing has shifted so radically. This is not likely to be a productive approach because such a paper will simply have all the defects of a new submission without the required maturation. I have nevertheless seen this mistake more than once (and made it myself).

In conclusion, though certainly not exhaustive, this reflection aimed to open up a window on some of the blind alleys and untold stories of qualitative research – common no doubt to the experience of many but often hidden from view. I think I have learned from my own experiences as a researcher, an author, a reviewer and an editor and wanted to share some of that learning in this chapter. However, I must confess that I am still not perfectly sure that I know how to make qualitative research work infallibly, because there are many unpredictable and creative elements to it that can never be entirely mastered once and for all. I do not have a recipe. Nevertheless, I hope that the thoughts in this chapter may resonate, and possibly serve as a basis for ongoing reflections about how to do rigorous, insightful and impactful qualitative research.

# References

Bansal P. and Corley K. (2011) "From the editors: The coming of age for qualitative research," *Academy of Management Journal* 54: 233–237.

Bitektine A. (2007) "Prospective case study design: Qualitative method for deductive theory testing," *Organizational Research Methods* 11: 160–180.

Boxenbaum E. and Rouleau L. (2011) "New knowledge products as bricolage: Metaphors and scripts in organizational theory," *Academy of Management Review* 36: 272–296.

Bucher S. and Langley A. (2016) "The interplay of reflective and experimental spaces in interrupting and reorienting routine dynamics," *Organization Science* 27: 594–613.

Burawoy M. (1998) "The extended case method," *Sociological Theory* 16: 4–33.

Cloutier C., Denis J.-L., Langley A. and Lamothe L. (2016) "Agency at the managerial interface: Public sector reform as institutional work," *Journal of Public Administration Research and Theory* 26: 259–276.

Cornelissen J. P. (2016) "Preserving theoretical divergence in management research: Why the explanatory potential of qualitative research should be harnessed rather than suppressed," *Journal of Management Studies* 10.1111/joms.12210 (published online).

Dameron S. and Torset C. (2014) "The discursive construction of strategists' subjectivities: Towards a paradox lens on strategy," *Journal of Management Studies* 51: 291–319.

Denis J.-L., Langley A. and Pineault M. (2000) "Becoming a leader in a complex organization," *Journal of Management Studies* 37: 1063–1100.

Denis J.-L., Lamothe L. and Langley A. (2001) "The dynamics of collective leadership and strategic change in pluralistic organizations," *Academy of Management Journal* 44: 809–837.

Denis J.-L., Dompierre G., Langley A. and Rouleau L. (2011) "Escalating indecision: Between reification and strategic ambiguity," *Organization Science* 22: 225–244.

Edmondson A. (1999) "Psychological safety and learning behavior in work teams," *Administrative Science Quarterly* 44: 350–383.

Eisenhardt K. M. (1989) "Building theories from case study research," *Academy of Management Review* 14: 532–550.

Elsbach K. D. (1994) "Managing organizational legitimacy in the California cattle industry: The construction and effectiveness of verbal accounts," *Administrative Science Quarterly* 39: 57–88.

Feldman M. S., Pentland B. T., D'Adderio L. and Lazaric N. (2016) "Beyond routines as things: Introduction to the special issue on routine dynamics," *Organization Science* 27: 505–513.

Gersick C. J. (1988) "Time and transition in work teams: Toward a new model of group development," *Academy of Management Journal* 31: 9–41.

Gersick C. J. (1989) "Marking time: Predictable transitions in task groups," *Academy of Management Journal* 32: 274–309.

Gersick C. J. (1991) "Revolutionary change theories: A multilevel exploration of the punctuated equilibrium paradigm," *Academy of Management Review* 16: 10–36.

Gersick C. J. (1992) "Time and transition in my work on teams: Looking back on a new model of group development," in: Frost P. and Stablein R. (eds) *Doing Exemplary Research*, Thousand Oaks, CA: Sage, 52–76.

Gioia D. A., Corley K. G. and Hamilton A. L. (2013) "Seeking qualitative rigor in inductive research notes on the Gioia methodology," *Organizational Research Methods* 16: 15–31.

Glaser B. G. and Strauss A. L. (1967/2009) *The Discovery of Grounded Theory: Strategies for Qualitative Research*, Piscataway, NJ: Transaction.

Graebner M. E., Martin J. A. and Roundy P. T. (2012) "Qualitative data: Cooking without a recipe," *Strategic Organization* 10: 276–284.

Howard-Grenville J., Metzger M. L. and Meyer A. D. (2013) "Rekindling the flame: Processes of identity resurrection," *Academy of Management Journal* 56: 113–136.

Jarzabkowski P., Bednarek R. and Lê J. K. (2014) "Producing persuasive findings: Demystifying ethnographic textwork in strategy and organization research," *Strategic Organization* 12: 274–287.

Johnston W. J., Leach M. P. and Liu A. H. (1999) "Theory testing using case studies in business-to-business research," *Industrial Marketing Management* 28: 201–213.

Kaplan S. (2011) "Strategy and PowerPoint: An inquiry into the epistemic culture and machinery of strategy making," *Organization Science* 22: 320–346.

Kaplan S. (2015) "Mixing quantitative and qualitative research," in: Elsbach K. D. and Kramer R. M. (eds) *Handbook of Qualitative Organizational Research: Innovative Pathways and Methods*, New York: Routledge, 423–433.

Kaplan S. and Orlikowski W. J. (2013) "Temporal work in strategy making," *Organization Science* 24: 965–995.

Klag M. and Langley A. (2013) "Approaching the conceptual leap in qualitative research," *International Journal of Management Reviews* 15: 149–166.

Langley A. (1999) "Strategies for theorizing from process data," *Academy of Management Review* 24: 691–710.

Langley A. and Abdallah C. (2011) "Templates and turns in qualitative studies of strategy and management," in: Bergh D. and Ketchen D. (eds) *Building Methodological Bridges*, Bingley, UK: Emerald, 201–236.

Langley A., Denis J.-L. and Lamothe L. (2003) "Process research in healthcare: Towards three-dimensional learning," *Policy & Politics* 31: 195–206.

Langley A., Smallman C., Tsoukas H. and Van de Ven A. H. (2013) "Process studies of change in organization and management: Unveiling temporality, activity, and flow," *Academy of Management Journal* 56: 1–13.

Lee T. W., Mitchell T. R. and Sablynski C. J. (1999) "Qualitative research in organizational and vocational psychology, 1979–1999," *Journal of Vocational Behavior* 55: 161–187.

Locke K. (2007) "Rational control and irrational free-play: Dual-thinking modes as necessary tension in grounded theorizing," in: Bryant A. and Charmaz K. (eds) *SAGE Handbook of Grounded Theory*, London: Sage, 565–579.

Locke K., Golden-Biddle K. and Feldman M. S. (2008) "Perspective-making doubt generative: Rethinking the role of doubt in the research process," *Organization Science* 19: 907–918.

Lozeau D., Langley A. and Denis J.-L. (2002) "The corruption of managerial techniques by organizations," *Human Relations* 55: 537–564.

MacKay R. B. and Chia R. (2013) "Choice, chance, and unintended consequences in strategic change: A process understanding of the rise and fall of Northco Automotive," *Academy of Management Journal* 56: 208–230.

Mantere S. (2008) "Role expectations and middle manager strategic agency," *Journal of Management Studies* 45: 294–316.

Mintzberg H., Raisinghani D. and Théorêt A. (1976) "The structure of 'unstructured' decision processes," *Administrative Science Quarterly* 21: 246–275.

Nicolini D. (2011) "Practice as the site of knowing: Insights from the field of telemedicine," *Organization Science* 22: 602–620.

Nutt P. C. (1984) "Types of organizational decision processes," *Administrative Science Quarterly* 29: 414–450.

Pettigrew A. M. (1990) "Longitudinal field research on change: Theory and practice," *Organization Science* 1: 267–292.

Pratt M. G. (2009) "From the editors: For the lack of a boilerplate: Tips on writing up (and reviewing) qualitative research," *Academy of Management Journal* 52: 856–862.

Salvato C. (2009) "Capabilities unveiled: The role of ordinary activities in the evolution of product development processes," *Organization Science* 20: 384–409.

Stensaker I. G. and Langley A. (2010) "Change management choices and trajectories in a multidivisional firm," *British Journal of Management* 21: 7–27.

Suddaby R., Elsbach K. D., Greenwood R., Meyer J. W. and Zilber T. B. (2010) "Organizations and their institutional environments: Bringing meaning, values, and culture back in: Introduction to the special research forum," *Academy of Management Journal* 53: 1234–1240.

Sutton R. I. (1997) "Crossroads: The virtues of closet qualitative research," *Organization Science* 8: 97–106.

Vermeulen P. A. M., Zietsma C., Greenwood R. and Langley A. (2016) "Strategic responses to institutional complexity," *Strategic Organization* 14: 277–286.

Weick K. E. (1989) "Theory construction as disciplined imagination," *Academy of Management Review* 14: 516–531.

Yu J., Engleman R. M. and Van de Ven A. H. (2005) "The integration journey: An attention-based view of the merger and acquisition integration process," *Organization Studies* 26: 1501–1528.

# INDEX

Page numbers in *italics* denote tables, those in **bold** denote figures.

This volume brings together an impressive group of qualitative scholars and thoughtful perspectives on how to do high quality research. The numerous examples from published and ongoing research provide a useful resource for organizational scholars and other social scientists. I am eager to use this volume in my research and teaching.

**Martha S. Feldman,** *University of California, Irvine, USA*

This extraordinary collection of writings on qualitative research methods is remarkable for both its quality and its breadth. Its papers appropriately encompass attention to rigor and to artistry in qualitative research. Setting the stage with the historical perspective – seminal research across fields from biology to psychiatry was qualitative in nature – the book goes on to provide sophisticated and practical insights into such topics as the use of single cases, the role of context, sources of inspiration, and navigating publication.

**Amy C. Edmondson,** *Harvard Business School, USA*

Mir and Jain have put together an exciting and informative text. The chapters cover a range of topics from valuable reflections on tried and tested methods to innovative approaches to drive forward the use of qualitative methods. I expect that this text will be a key resource for all levels of researchers interested in developing an informed use of qualitative research methods.

**Paula Jarzabkowski**, *University of London, UK*

This is a breath of fresh air, reflecting the spirit of our times, in which qualitative researchers are not so much required to defend the validity of their research as to keep reflecting on what they do in order to reconsider their premises, update their methods, and refine their understandings. Mir and Jain have put together a well thought out, multi-vocal collection of chapters, ranging from the philosophical underpinnings of qualitative research to methodologies, contexts of application, and personal reflections, which will be useful to all practitioners of qualitative research, new and seasoned alike.

**Haridimos Tsoukas**, *University of Warwick, UK and University of Cyprus, Cyprus*